PORTS OF
THE ANCIENT INDIAN OCEAN

Ports of
the Ancient Indian Ocean

edited by

MARIE-FRANÇOISE BOUSSAC
JEAN-FRANÇOIS SALLES
JEAN-BAPTISTE YON

PRIMUS
BOOKS

PRIMUS BOOKS
An imprint of Ratna Sagar P. Ltd.
Virat Bhavan
Mukherjee Nagar Commercial Complex
Delhi 110 009

Offices at CHENNAI LUCKNOW
AGRA AHMEDABAD BENGALURU COIMBATORE DEHRADUN GUWAHATI
HYDERABAD JAIPUR JALANDHAR KANPUR KOCHI KOLKATA MADURAI
MUMBAI PATNA RANCHI VARANASI

First published 2016

ISBN 978-93-84082-07-9

Published by Primus Books

Lasertypeset by Sai Graphic Design
Arakashan Road, Paharganj, New Delhi 110 055

Printed at Replika Press Pvt. Ltd., India

Contents

FRENCH ARCHIVES

Editors' Note

The Kolkata meeting stands as the result of a long-drawn cooperation between Indian and French archaeologists and historians, and has been made possible through a programme of the French National Agency for Research (ANR) within the larger topic of 'the genesis of knowledges'.

The National Agency for Research is an autonomous government body of the Ministry of Higher Education and Research launched for the development of French research in all disciplines including Humanities and Social Sciences, giving a new impetus to these disciplines. The agency recently opened its offers to bi- or multinational programmes, first to European countries and now to new ones sometimes overseas—India has signed an agreement in Social Sciences.

The National Agency for Research addresses any type of research teams, universities, research centres, etc., who are allowed to submit projects within the general areas of study defined every year. A very strict selection with international jurys singles out different projects among hundreds of submissions, and when selected the project is granted with an important budget for a period of two-three years.

The full title of our MEDIAN project is 'The Mediterranean societies and the Indian Ocean. Representations, cultural interactions and genesis of knowledges, from the period of the ancient Greek *periploi* to the Portuguese seafarers'. It associates the University of Reims in France as a leader of the project, the CNRS/University of Paris 1 Medieval team of research (UMR 8147), the Maison de l'Orient et de la Méditerranée in Lyon (CNRS/University Lyon 2) and the National Library (BNF). More than fifty researchers are members of the programme together with several doctoral or postdoctoral students sometimes enrolled as assistants. Four main themes have been defined:

- The textual heritage, i.e. geographical works (in Greek,[1] Latin, Arabic), logbooks when available, travellers books (in French, Italian, Portuguese, Turkish, etc.) and any kind of other written sources. A selection of these sources is being prepared for publication at the end of the programme (2013).
- The actual places known in the Indian Ocean through the period, i.e. ports and places of exchanges, trade networks, maritime routes, etc. The Kolkata colloquium stands as a major meeting of archaeologists and historians concerned with the topic.
- The evolution of the cartography of the indian Ocean from the Greek Ptolemy to the Portuguese maps of the sixteenth century.[2]
- Finally, a study of the way of transmissions of all these knowledges in a global perspective.

Kolkata was selected as the best seat for an international meeting on ancient harbours of the Indian Ocean: its existence, through different locations and under various political powers, had been maintained for millennia as a major crossing-place in the eastern Indian Ocean. It was also a suitable place where to associate our Indian colleagues to this international research, and to repay a visit to the ancient wisemen and seafarers of India.

The organization of the colloquium would not have been possible without the never-ending help of our friends and colleagues of the Centre for Archaeological Studies and Training, Eastern India/Kolkata, and we are happy to warmly thank them for their involvement. In Lyon, Dr Caroline Durand provided invaluable support for the organization of the conference. We also acknowledge with much pleasure the support of the Archaeological Survey of India (esp. his DG Gautam Sengupta), the Rabindranath Tagore Centre (ICCR) who hosted the meeting, the Indian Museum and the French General Consul Jean-Louis Rysto who welcomed the colloquium in their premises. And we should emphasize two major moments of the meeting, the beautiful inaugural address of Professor Barun De, and the visit and impressionable allocution of HE Mr Jérôme Bonnafont, then Ambassador of France to India.

Marie-Françoise Boussac
Jean-François Salles
Jean-Baptiste Yon

Notes

1. The MEDIAN seminar 'Autour du Periple de la Mer Érythrée' (Lyon, December 2010) is now available, *Topoi* Supplement 11 (Maison de l'Orient et de la Méditerranée, Lyon). An English version is being prepared by an Indian editor.
2. The National Library (BNF) is presenting an exhibition 'L'âge d'or des cartes marine. Quand l'Europe découvrait le monde' (22 October 2012–27 January 2013). A beautiful catalogue—same title—is available at Le Seuil/Bibliothèque Nationale de France Editions, Paris.

From the Red Sea to India,
through Arabia and the Persian Gulf

CHAPTER 1

The Egyptians on the Red Sea Shore during the Pharaonic Era

Pierre Tallet

It is a common assumption that ancient Egyptians who focused almost entirely on the Nile Valley, would not know a lot about far reaching sea travel. The recent discoveries of many embarking points along the Egyptian Red Sea coast shows that they had, in fact, sharp knowledge of these matters (Map 1.1). It is more than likely that since the earliest periods, Egyptian boats were able to reach the Gulf of Aden, the coasts of Ethiopia and Yemen. Since the beginning of the twenty-first century, the knowledge of seafaring expeditions through the Red Sea towards the Sinai or the distant land of Punt has indeed seen considerable progress due to fieldwork conducted at port sites like Mersa Gawasis near the modern town of Safaga, and Ayn Soukhna, on the northern part of the Suez Gulf. A third harbour site was eventually discovered in 2011, Wadi el-Jarf, to the south of the coastal town of Zafarana. This important series of embarking points demonstrates the interest shown in seafaring activities during the pharaonic period. This chapter attempts to provide a slight idea of the function of these port sites during antiquity.

Mersa Gawasis

In 1976, the Egyptian archaeologist Abd el-Moneim Sayed discovered the Pharaonic seaport of *S3ww* on the present-day site of Mersa Gawasis (Plate 1.1) (Sayed 1977, 1980, 1983). Here, a series of votive monuments, fashioned out of ships' anchors (Plate 1.2), some engraved with commemorative texts, revealed exceptional information: the inscriptions, dating to the reign of Sesostris I, gave details of an expedition launched during that period (*c.*1950 BC) from some point on the coast to the

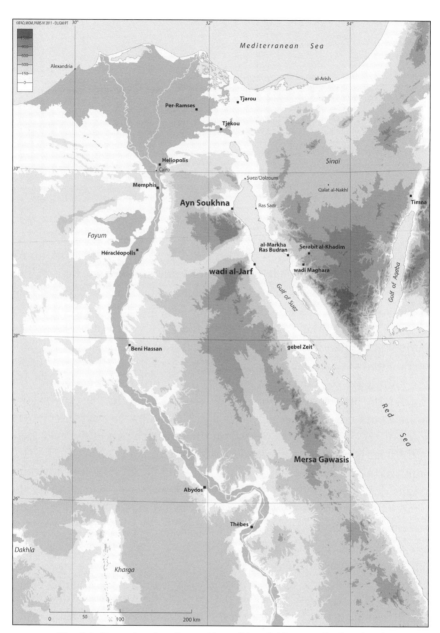

Map 1.1: Egypt showing the position of Ayn Sukhna, Wadi el-Jarf and
Mersa Gawasis (drawing D. Laisney).

Plate 1.1: General view of the site of Mersa Gawasis.

Plate. 1.2: Votive monument built with ship anchors.

mysterious Punt region, which most researchers nowadays locate on the southernmost coastline of the Red Sea. The Ankhu stela discovered on site provided an idea of how Egyptians in the Middle Kingdom operated: large vessels designed in the arsenals of Coptos, in the Nile Valley, were transported overland as 'ship kits' to the Red Sea coast—clearly designated in the documentation by the expression *Wȝḏ-wr*, the Great Green Expanse. These kits were then assembled there before the expeditions set off. The number of people manning the operations—about 3,500—is itself another indicator of the importance of such an activity for the Pharaonic State at the time. This discovery aroused considerable interest as soon as it was presented in the *Revue d'Égyptologie* (Sayed 1977) and was seen as evidence of a new dimension of Pharaonic civilization. Little known for their proficiency in maritime affairs, the ancient Egyptians nevertheless seemed to have been able seamen, capable of organizing long sea voyages. However, a small number of researchers (e.g. Nibbi 1981; Vandersleyen 1996) fiercely contested this interpretation of the data. One of the main stumbling blocks was the interpretation of the term *W3ḏ-wr* which is believed to not refer to the sea, but rather to the green stretches of the Nile Valley; the other debate concerned the location of Punt, often identified as being in central Africa, reached only by the Nile. The site's function as a port was regularly challenged, and the anchors of ships discovered there were considered to be votive monuments with no special link to maritime navigation.

Since 2001, the knowledge of Red Sea in the Pharaonic era has evolved considerably, thus reframing, to a large extent, the terms of the debate. When, in 2001, excavations were resumed at the Mersa Gawasis site, led by the joint team of the Naples Oriental Studies University and Boston University under the direction of Rodolfo Fattovich and Kathryn Bard, they produced a rich harvest of additional information about the use of the site, making it impossible henceforth to deny its function as a port (Bard, Fattovich 2007). Over the years, the mission has unearthed several additional anchors, some of which were not used for votive purposes. In addition, major parts of vessels were discovered in or around storage galleries dug into the rock face of a cliff on the site. A considerable number of commemorative stelae show that the site was used regularly over a period of at least 200 years covering the whole of the Twelfth Dynasty. These results provide evidence of the contacts between Egypt and the Bab el-Mandab region and have enabled researchers to conduct more specific studies of the conditions in which Egyptian ships navigated the Red Sea.

Ayn Soukhna

In 2001, excavations were also launched at the Ayn Soukhna site. Ayn Soukhna is located on the western bank of the Gulf of Suez, 120 km. east of the modern city of Cairo. The Arab name of the site is due to the presence of a hot water spring which emerges at the foot of the Gebel el Galāla el Bahariya overlooking the site and flows directly into the nearby sea (Map 1.2). The excavation and study of the archaeological remains, which were first brought to attention in 1999 (Abd el-Raziq 1999), have been conducted on a yearly basis since 2001 by a joint team from the Institut français d'archéologie orientale and the University of Paris-Sorbonne[1]

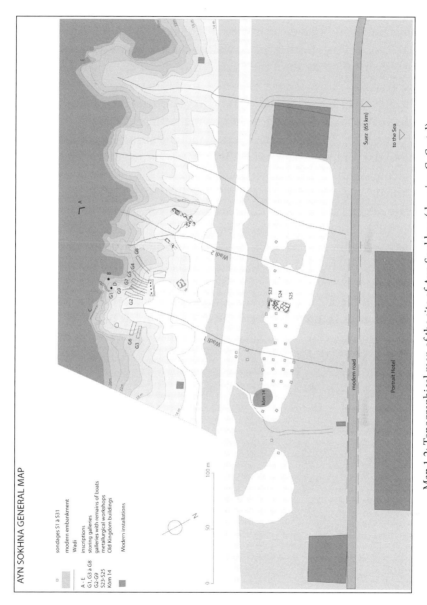

Map 1.2: Topographical map of the site of Ayn Soukhna (drawing G. Castel).

(Abd el-Raziq et al., 2002; Abd el-Raziq et al., 2011; Tallet 2006, 2009). It has been gradually established, during the course of these investigations, that the site was occupied extensively for over a millennium during the Pharaonic period, from the Old Kingdom to the New Kingdom. The latest findings clearly indicate the existence at the site of a port similar to that of Mersa/Wadi Gawasis further south, which seems to have been used mainly to cross over to the south of the Sinai Peninsula on the other side of the Gulf.

The site's most apparent feature, from the outset, has been an inscription-bearing rock wall dominating the area, where the archaeological vestiges are concentrated. In particular, it bears an important series of inscriptions dating to the Middle Kingdom (2000–1800 BC), which immediately point to the connection between Ayn Soukhna and the south Sinai zone that was mined by the Egyptians in the Pharaonic period (Plate 1.3). Actually, the texts refer to a 'Mining land', the common designation for that region in the Middle Kingdom, and mention turquoise, which is one of its most distinctive resources. They also record the names of some of the men in charge who left written testimonies of their stay in the Sinai mines themselves.[2]

The use of the site as a harbour has now been corroborated through the systematic investigation of a series of storage galleries dug into the foot

Plate 1.3: Rock inscriptions above the site.

Plate 1.4: Ayn Soukhna—storage galleries.

of the mountain that overlooks the site (Plate 1.4). The 2005 and 2007 field seasons successively uncovered two boats that had been carefully dismantled and stored in galleries G2 and G9 (Plate 1.5).[3] Unfortunately, there remains little more than burnt timber since the crafts were obviously subjected to deliberate destruction in antiquity—perhaps because setting fire to their boats might have been the surest way to curb the expeditionary drive of ancient Egyptians in those troubled times. Nonetheless, a detailed analysis of these remains, conducted by Patrice Pomey (CNRS, Centre Camille Jullian), yields valuable information. The boats were made of cedar wood and were specifically designed for seafaring expeditions, as evidenced by the mode of assembly that was chosen. They can be estimated to have been approximately 13-14 m. long, which makes for quite respectably-sized vessels. Radiocarbon dating, which was conducted on several samples of the timber, reveals that the last time the boats were stored away before being destroyed by fire probably occurred towards the end of the Middle Kingdom or during the Second Intermediate Period (c. 1700 BC), even though some of the thickest planks were found to pre-date that period by more than 500 years. It can be inferred from such discoveries that the site was used extensively throughout the Middle Kingdom period as a temporary harbour for expeditions to the mines in the south-west of the Sinai Peninsula.

Plate 1.5: Ayn Soukhna—remains of a ship.

The latest developments in the excavation, however, provide new insight into these findings. While it could be surmised that the site had also been used under similar conditions in previous periods of Egyptian history—at times when the site seems to have been densely occupied and when the storing gallery system was probably initially created—two official inscriptions now provide substantial evidence of prior occupation. These inscriptions were discovered in 2009 and 2010 in storage galleries G6 and G1, which had not been excavated until then because they were in a poor state of conservation.

The first text was found 3 m. into gallery G6, on the left hand side wall which had been smoothed over with plaster coating. The inscription was written in black ink on a surface which can be estimated to be around 65 cm. × 40 cm. in size. Unfortunately, only a small part of the document—a third perhaps?—had remained intact when it was discovered, the upper part of the wall having collapsed in antiquity. What remains seems to have been distributed between at least six columns separated by vertical lines, although the bottom of the composition, which displays horizontal annotations, may have followed a different organization. The writing and what can be observed of the 'layout' of the various elements are reminiscent of the meticulous grid-like framework of the Abusir papyri used to record the accounts of the royal mortuary temples towards the end of the Fifth Dynasty. A few other fragments of the text were found on flakes of plaster lying at the foot of the wall. These are significant as they disclose the name of the king who ordered the expedition, Djedkare-Isesi, the eighth and last-but-one sovereign of the Fifth Dynasty (c. 2400 BC), whose sealings had already been discovered at the site during previous field seasons.

Although it is impossible to reconstitute the whole document, its structure is quite clear: following the king's titulary—which begins with his Horus name—is a short narrative detailing the main aspects of the expedition, i.e. the means of transportation, the itinerary and the goods that were brought back. The last section was probably devoted to recording the different categories of staff. A noteworthy feature of the document is the recording of kbnt-boats, a 'Byblos' type of vessel that Egyptians seem to have used particularly for long seafaring expeditions.[4] To date, this is the most ancient mention of such boats in any Egyptian document. A similar find was made during the January-February 2010 field season, in the largest gallery, which had suffered more collapsing accidents than any of the other galleries over the years. A few metres into the gallery, the wall on the right-hand side was filled in with rocks and stones and then smoothed over with plaster under the Old Kingdom. On the prepared surface, yet another expedition-commemorating text was inscribed in black ink. The state of the document is excessively fragmented, the plaster coating having crumbled and gradually slipped to the foot of the wall. Most of the text has not been preserved but what has been bears the date of the seventh census of the reign of King Isesi (around year 14 of his reign), thus providing the date of a previously unknown expedition to the Sinai. The top line of the text also shows the name of an expedition leader, Sed-Hetepi, and furnishes one of the first distinct attestations of the imaged toponym used to refer to the Sinai Peninsula in Ancient Egypt, 'the Terraces of turquoise' (ḥtjw mfkꜣt).

Fortunately, the same official is also attested in other sources found in the Sinai itself, most notably in inscription IS 10, mentioning a 1,400-strong expedition, which was discovered in the Wadi Maghara.[5]

The discoveries made during the last two field seasons at the Ayn Soukhna site thus confirm the role of this settlement in the organization of seafaring expeditions on the Red Sea, as early as the Old Kingdom. They can be clearly connected with the material that was brought to light in the mining area itself, in the South Sinai, and especially with the Wadi Maghara which holds most of the carved Old Kingdom inscriptions found in the region.

Wadi el-Jarf

The discovery of the harbour of Wadi el-Jarf complements this general scheme.[6] The site is situated on the Egyptian coast, 90 km. south of Ayn Soukhna and 25 km. south of Zafarana. It is located at the mouth of Wadi Araba, a major corridor of communication between the Nile Valley and the Red Sea through which the expeditions passed (Map 1.3). Thanks to the narrow breadth of the Red Sea in this area, the western coast of the Sinai Peninsula lies at distance of only 50 km. from this point. In fact, Wadi el-Jarf lies exactly opposite the fortress of Ras Budran and the connection between these two is now beyond doubt.

Sir G. Wilkinson and J. Burton first reported the site in the early nineteenth century (Wilkinson 1832). It was rediscovered in 1954 by a group of French scholars, Fr. Bissey and R. Chabot-Morisseau, who carried out investigations that were prematurely stopped due to the Suez crisis. In 2008, the notes left by Bissey and Chabot-Morisseau (Lacaze, Camino 2008) and remote sensing work conducted on the Zafarana area with Google Earth satellite images helped to re-locate the site.

It consists of four groups of installations that are situated along the coast and at the foot of the mountains near the spring of St Paul's monastery. According to the pottery, all these installations date to the Fourth Dynasty, most likely the early part or the first half of it, with traces of occupation extending into the beginning of the Fifth Dynasty.

Five kilometres from the seashore lies a sizeable complex of 25 to 30 galleries (Map 1.3 and Plate 1.6). The excavations conducted at four galleries confirmed their use as storage facilities, as at Ayn Soukhna and Mersa Gawasis. They vary in length from 16 m. to 34 m. with an average width of 3 m. and a height of 2.5 m. All of them were carefully cut into the limestone bedrock following a pre-planned layout, which is reflected by their relative uniformity and synchrony. Long 'causeways' made of stone blocks of monumental size measuring more than 2 to 3 m. protected their accesses, and the entrances were closed by a system of 'portcullises' similar to those known from royal funerary installations of this time. Remains of an inscription have been found at the entrance of the largest gallery showing an official holding a staff, named as 'the Scribe of the Fayum, Idu'.

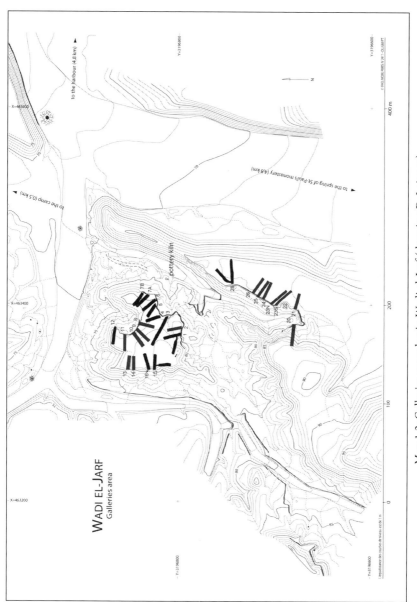

Map 1.3: Galleries complex in Wadi el-Jarf (drawing D. Laisney).

Plate 1.6: Photo of the galleries area.

The use of the galleries as storage facilities is underlined by the discovery of fragments of ropes, textiles, pieces of wooden boxes and hundreds of fragments of worked wood. Among the latter were several tenons of acacia and large pieces of wood, including the end of an oar, several fragments of Lebanese cedar beams, and a complete piece of floor timber, 2.75 m. wide (Plate 1.7). These finds clearly indicate the presence of boat elements on the site, probably stored as dismantled pieces in the galleries. Thousands of fragments of large globular storage jars have also been discovered *in situ* in several galleries. Those jars were used for water and food storage and their surfaces are frequently marked by large hieroglyphic inscriptions in red ink, corresponding to the names of teams of workmen, crews or even of the boats themselves. These jars were produced locally in very large quantities, as can be seen from the excavation of a first large pottery kiln at

Plate 1.7: Part of a ship, Wadi el-Jarf.

the site. Characterized by a very peculiar marl fabric, this local production has been found at all the various installations at Wadi el-Jarf. These jars have also been identified in small numbers in Fourth Dynasty contexts at Ayn Soukhna and in large quantities at the fortress of Ras Budran, where they have been incorrectly labelled as 'Sinaitic Ware'. The presence of this production on both sides of the Gulf of Suez confirms the close association of this fortified site with the Wadi al-Jarf installations.

At 500 m. north of the galleries area, three groups of camps and surveillance installations were noted. Situated on top of a long promontory, the most important one is characterized by a complex of rectangular constructions that are organized with cell-like rooms that served as dwelling places.

Another isolated construction, so far the largest pharaonic building ever discovered along the Red Sea coast, has been identified on the coastal plain between the galleries and the seashore facilities. It consists of a rectangular building 60 m. in length and 30 m. in width, divided into 13 elongated rooms, whose precise function is not known yet.

The last component of the site is situated directly on the coast. At 200 m. from the shore, an artificially created mound made of limestone blocks forms a reference point, a sort of visual landmark (*alamat*) measuring 10 m. in diameter and 6 m. in height and is surrounded by light camp installations. The main element of the coastal site is a long L-shaped mole

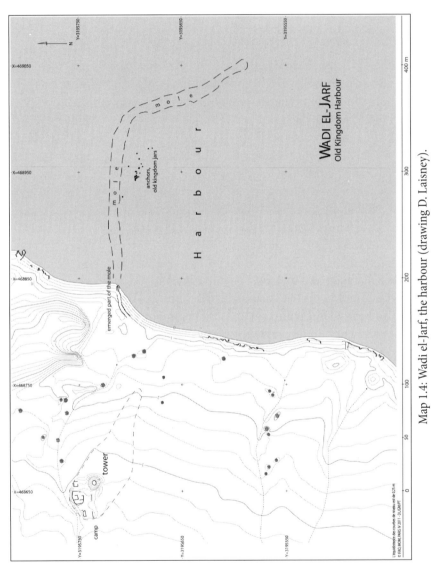

Map 1.4: Wadi el-Jarf, the harbour (drawing D. Laisney).

starting from the beach and extending east under water for over 160 m. (Map 1.4). It then runs in an irregular pattern towards the south-east for another 120 m. The constant winds and the force of the coastal north-south currents emphasize its role as a breakwater structure built to protect a vast zone of anchorage covering more than 3 ha.

The use of the site as harbour has been confirmed by the discovery of at least 21 limestone anchors and some complete storage jars of local production. The anchors, often found in pairs, measure 60 cm. to 80 cm. in height and 48 cm. to 62 cm. in width. They appear in triangular, rectangular and cylindrical shapes, all of them have a rounded top and a hole in the upper part without any vertical groove (Plate 1.8). It is possible that anchors have been permanently placed in the water for mooring boats in transit. This is however the first discovery of pharaonic anchors in their original context of use in Egypt and it constitutes the oldest and largest concentration of this type for the early Bronze Age. This group adds considerably to the number of ancient Egyptian anchors previously known (approx. 35 examples), mainly discovered in Mersa Gawasis, exclusively in contexts of secondary use and dating to the Middle Kingdom.

The recent discoveries at Wadi el-Jarf demonstrate once again the complex and extensive logistical organization of seafaring expeditions for

Plate 1.8: Anchor in the harbour.

the Old Kingdom. It emphasizes the determination, since the early Fourth Dynasty, to control the Red Sea coast and the access to the resources of the Sinai using a network of strategic installations on both sides of the Gulf of Suez. One can only wonder whether a port constructed on such a large scale was only used for crossing the sea to the Sinai or whether it would also have been used to reach the southern part of the Red Sea and the distant land of Punt.

Notes

1. The excavations are co-directed by Mahmoud Abd el-Raziq (Ismaelia University), Georges Castel (IFAO), and Pierre Tallet, on behalf of Paris-Sorbonne University.
2. Abd el-Raziq 1999; Abd el-Raziq et al. 2002.
3. Abd el-Raziq, Castel, Tallet 2004; Tallet 2006.
4. Tallet 2009.
5. Gardiner, Peet, Cerny 1952: n° 19, pl. IX; completed by E. Edel 1983: 158–63.
6. The Wadi el-Jarf excavations are co-directed by Pierre Tallet (University of Paris-Sorbonne) and El-Sayed Mahfouz (University of Assiut), with significant involvement of Grégory Marouard (Oriental Institute, University of Chicago) archaeologist, and Damien Laisney (Maison de l'Orient et de la Méditerranée, Lyon) who carried out the topographic recording of the site. The French Foreign Office, the CNRS, the IFAO and the generosity of the Aall Foundation support this research. A more detailed report on this first archaeological campaign is now published in *BIFAO* 112 (Tallet, Marouard, Laisney 2012).

References

Abd el-Raziq, M. (1999), 'New Inscriptions at El-Ein el-Sukhna', *Memnonia*, vol. 10, pp. 125–31.

Abd el-Raziq, M., Castel, G. and Tallet, P. (2006), 'Ayn Soukhna et la Mer Rouge', *Égypte, Afrique et Orient*, vol. 41, pp. 3–6.

Abd el-Raziq, M., Castel, G., Tallet, P., and Ghica, V. (2006), *Les inscriptions d'Ayn Soukhna (MIFAO 122)*. Cairo: Institut Français d'Archéologie Orientale.

Abd el-Raziq, M., Castel, G., Tallet, P. and Fluzin, Ph. (2011), *Ayn Soukhna II. Les ateliers métallurgiques du Moyen Empire*, Cairo: Institut Français d'Archéologie Orientale.

Bard, K.A., Fattovich, R. ed., (2007), *Harbour of the Pharaohs to the Land of Punt, Archaeological Investigations at Mersa/Wadi Gawasis, Egypt 2001–2005*. Napoli: Università degli Studi di Napoli 'L'Orientale' Dipartimento di studi e ricerche su l'Africa e paese Arabi Laboratorio di archeologia.

Edel, E. (1983), *Beiträge zu den ägyptischen Sinaiinschriften*, Nachrichten der Akademie der Wissenschaften in Göttingen I/6, 158–63. Göttingen: Vandenhoeck & Ruprecht.

Gardiner, A.H., Peet, T.E. and Cerny, J. (1952–5), *The Inscriptions of Sinai* I²-II. London: Egypt Exploration Fund.

Nibbi, A. (1981), 'Some Remarks on the Two Monuments from Mersa Gawasis', *Annales du Service des Antiquités de l'Égypte*, vol. 64, pp. 69–74.

Sayed, A.M. (1977), 'Discovery of the Site of the 12th Dynasty Port at Wadi Gawasis on the Red Sea Shore', *Revue d'Égyptologie*, vol. 29, pp. 140–78.

——— (1980), 'Observations on Recent Discoveries at Wadi Gawasis', *The Journal of Egyptian Archaeology*, vol. 66, pp. 154–7.

——— (1983), 'New Light on the Recently Discovered Port on the Red Sea Shore', *Chronique d'Égypte*, vol. 58, pp. 23–37.

Tallet, P. (2006), 'Six campagnes archéologiques sur le site d'Ayn Soukhna, golfe de Suez', *Bulletin de la Société Française d'Égyptologie*, vol. 165, pp. 10–31.

——— (2009) 'Les Égyptiens et le littoral de la mer Rouge à l'époque pharaonique', *Comptes-rendus de l'Académie des Inscriptions et Belles-Lettres*, pp. 687–719.

Tallet, P., Marouard, G., and Laisney, D. (2012), 'Un port de la IVᵉ dynastie au Wadi al-Jarf (mer Rouge)', *BIFAO* 112, pp. 399–446.

Vandersleyen, Cl. (1996), 'Les monuments de l'Ouadi Gaouasis et la possibilité d'aller au pays du Punt par la Mer Rouge', *Revue d'Égyptologie*, vol. 47, pp. 107–15.

CHAPTER 2

Ship-related Activities at the Pharaonic Harbour of Mersa Gawasis

Cheryl Ward and *Chiara Zazzaro*

Archaeological investigations since 2001 confirm the identification of the pharaonic anchorage of *Sww* with Mersa/Wadi Gawasis, about 25 km. south of Safaga, Egypt, and its use as a base camp to support sea voyages to the land of Punt primarily during the Middle Kingdom (Map 2.1).[1] Excavations directed by Kathryn Bard of the Boston University and Rodolfo Fattovich of the University of Naples 'L'Orientale' revealed evidence of maritime activities and the administrative structure that enabled voyages to and from the southern Red Sea to *Pwenet*, or Punt, the source of exotic animal and plant products, especially the aromatic incense critical to many religious practices.

At Gawasis, the ancient Egyptians excavated galleries[2] for work and shelter into a fossil coral reef on the edge of a lagoon and used them repeatedly over hundreds of years for expeditions like the one documented on a shrine built of anchors on a small peninsula at Gawasis, discovered by Abdel Monem el Sayed in the 1970s.[3] It describes an official expedition of the Twelfth Dynasty that began in the Nile Valley, traversed the Eastern Desert (approximately 150 km.) with over 3,000 men bringing supplies, trading goods, and ship 'kits' that subsequently were reassembled at the anchorage on the Red Sea coast.[4] The ships originally were constructed at royal shipyards in Koptos on the Nile, then disassembled for transport by men and donkeys.[5] Shipbuilders and other specialists were likely involved in the expeditions in order to reassemble the ships and equip them with rigging and anchors before the voyage to Punt.

After the voyage, which may have lasted four to five months, shipwrights evaluated the hulls and the condition of individual planks as

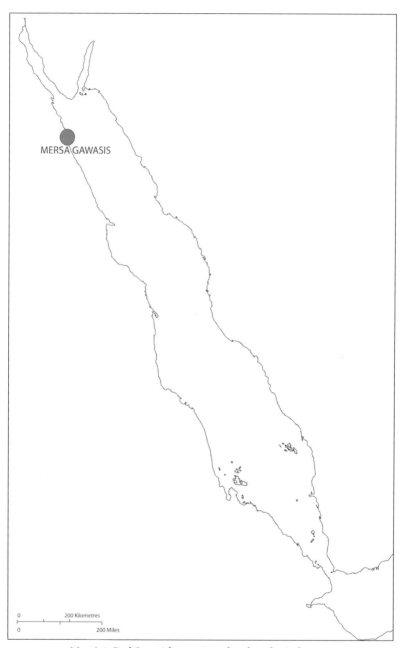

Map 2.1: Red Sea with mentioned archaeological sites.

they dismantled the ships at Gawasis. In addition to red marks painted on ship components that seem to mark damaged areas, barnacles, limpets and other marine encrustations scraped off wood surfaces, thousands of pieces of wood debris and dozens of reworked ship timbers are associated with the remains of improvised tools or serve as tools themselves, attesting to cleaning, disassembly, and modification of individual ship components.[6]

Since January 2005, documentation of approximately 100 identifiable ship and boat components has contributed new information about the size of ships and technologies adopted in ship construction by royal shipyards.[7] Despite technological similarities between Gawasis ship timbers and Dashur and Lisht riverine crafts,[8] seagoing ship timbers of the same date (primarily the Twelfth Dynasty of the Middle Kingdom) can be readily distinguished although we do not know which timbers may have belonged to the same ship or even the same king's reign. Many of the timbers were recycled as architectural supports or stabilization for walkways on site, and others were transformed from ship planks to deck planks, for example, and then embedded in floors and work areas during their lifespan. Nonetheless, significant information about the vessels and the work at the site may be extracted from what remains.

For example, estimating the size of ships for which only individual disassociated parts have been recovered is not a matter of matching plank sizes with the remains of other watercraft, but relies on comparing steering oar blades as they are well illustrated, proportionate in representations, and generally indicative of overall vessel size. Textual references to the size of contemporary seagoing ships are limited to the fanciful *Tale of the Shipwrecked Sailor*, a Middle Kingdom literary description of an expedition to the Red Sea in a ship 150 cubits long and 40 cubits wide (about 66 m. × 17 m.) with 150 sailors.[9] The exaggeration of other significant features of the story prompts most scholars to consider the ship size in the same way. The largest Egyptian vessel so far discovered is the royal ship of Khufu (*c.* 2600 BCE) at about 44 m. from prow ornament to stern.

To date, four steering oar blades are documented at Gawasis.[10] A pair of blades 2 m. long in the entrance to Cave 2 was one of the first recognized ship components, and a late Middle Kingdom deposit of steering gear outside Cave 6 incorporated a pair of blades, the longer 4.2 m. overall. Comparison of these complete steering oar blades with representations of both river and seagoing vessels of the pharaonic period suggests that they belonged, respectively, to ships about 20 m. and at least 30 m. in length.[11]

In addition to steering oar blades, the range of ship components at Gawasis includes beams, deck planks, hull planks, and auxiliary pieces from different vessels. The basic principles of hull construction reflect indigenous Egyptian practices shared between both river and seagoing watercraft. All major components of seagoing ships were made of cedar (*Cedrus libani*). In comparison to planks from riverboats, the Gawasis hull planks are more robust (14–22.5 cm. thick) and those from the lower hull (as indicated by the presence of shipworm on outer surfaces) are characterized by paired deep, unlocked, mortise-and-tenon fastenings about a cubit apart along plank edges. In contrast, much thinner planks, mostly of native Nile acacia, showing a previously unrecorded fastening system of small mortise-and-tenon joints associated with a lashing system, attest to the use of smaller boats as well.[12] As documented on some pharaonic riverboats, a few Gawasis boat and ship planks retain patches of a white substance similar to gypsum or plaster on the outer surface. Similar coatings are used by shipowners in the southern extremities of the Red Sea even in recent years to protect the wood from marine borers (shipworms) and erosion by wave activity.[13] The basic principles of hull construction reflect indigenous Egyptian practices shared between both river and seagoing watercraft.

Evaluation of archaeological finds suggests that the primary activity attested at Gawasis was the dismantling of ships and cleaning and reworking of ship planks. Data collected from different areas of the site contribute to explanations of the ship dismantling process and address the organization of ship-related activities there. Analysis of wood debris allows preliminary conclusions to be drawn about the techniques of ship dismantling, timber cleaning, and reworking of hull components. Some marine encrustations were removed from planks on the edge of the lagoon, and contents of sediment layers in the galleries show fine cleaning of timbers took place in some of galleries.

Despite an abundance of the reshaped wood components and the wood debitage associated with dismantling ships and removing eroded and degraded wood from ship timbers, almost no tools are present at the site. Stone scrapers, probably for removing marine encrustations, are the most common type, but we are forced to reconstruct the pharaonic tool kit from the marks left by tools on the wood surfaces with a single exception.

Ship timbers were reworked and reshaped using copper tools, including the broad axe, adzes, saws, and chisels, but the ancient Egyptians were careful to remove all such tools at the end of their expeditions. In one case, they left behind an adze handle (Plate 2.1) discovered in Cave 2, Room 2. The tool handle is not as well finished as contemporary adze handles recorded elsewhere in Egypt,[14] or three other tool handles from this site, but the shape and the characteristic inclination of the blade toward the handle are consistent with other adze handles from the Middle Kingdom. Made of opportunistic materials, it consists of two parts: a shaved

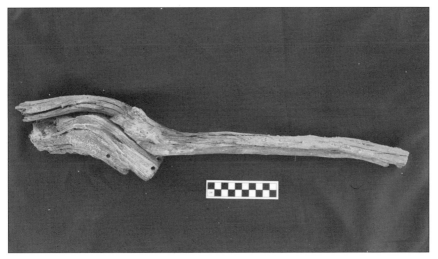

Plate 2.1: The adze.

mangrove branch (*Avicennia marina*) 55 cm. long and 3 cm. in diameter and a reworked fragment of a cedar-type ship plank heavily damaged by shipworm (19.5 cm. long and 9 cm. wide). Leather thongs or cordage in a groove originally bound the two parts together. The blade, which was not present, was attached to the cedar fragment at a point 5.5 cm. wide, suggesting that the adze blade measured roughly the same. This dimension corresponds to tool marks visible on many of the ship timbers recorded in the excavated contexts, and is a direct link to the workers and the work conditions at the site.

The most complete tool related to ship dismantling found at the site probably was abandoned. Tools seem to have been carried back to the Nile Valley after the expeditions. The adze found in Cave 2, Room 2 might have been left in the gallery because the handle was made of inferior material on the site. Further discoveries of tool elements could help to better understand the dismantling process, but the overwhelming impression we have from excavating the gallery floors and exterior areas is that all functional tools and materials were returned to the Nile with the workers. Only stone tool blades remain, and a broken tip from a single chisel blade stuck in a peg fragment on plank T34.

The lagoon and the anchorage

Recent geological investigations confirmed that a stable navigable lagoon fringed by mangrove thickets existed at Gawasis from the late Old Kingdom through the Middle Kingdom (Twelfth Dynasty) Map 2.2. A drop in sea

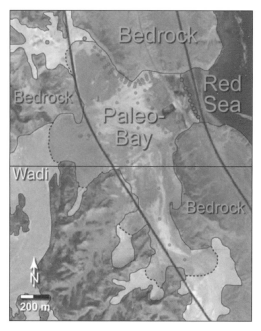

Map 2.2: Paleo-shorelines mapped using radiocarbon datas
and archaeological evidence (C.J. Hein).

level coincided with partial infilling of the lagoon and abandonment of
the harbour at the end of the Middle Kingdom, though the paleo-bay
did not entirely close until about 500 years ago.[15] The recovery of small
(21 cm. long) and large (86 cm. long) anchors, 1 m. to 2 m. below the
ground surface of the modern wadi off the south edge of the fossil coral
reef, illustrates the use of the lagoon by ships of different sizes. Excavations
there along the ancient shore produced more than 1,000 sherds from
large storage jars, possible evidence of intensive cargo transfer,[16] rubbish
disposal, or hardening the shore by using empty storage jars as illustrated
for the Roman period at Myos Hormos/Quseir al-Qadim just to the south
of Gawasis.[17]

West of the southern shore at the base of the terrace, archaeologists
recovered a large concentration of barnacles,[18] marine organisms that
attach themselves to wood surfaces of ship hulls at and below the waterline
and must be periodically removed (Plate 2.2). In this area, improvised
rough stone implements were found in association with barnacles but little
evidence of wood debris was present.[19] Here, planks probably received a
rough cleaning to remove the worst of the marine encrustations as they
came off the ship hulls during the dismantling process.

Plate 2.2: Barnacles found in the activity area at the base of the western terrace.

After removing marine incrustations, a job requiring a low level of skill and no carpentry, workers moved the planks to the lower galleries (Caves 2–6), at the top of the terrace slope. There, more skilled workers using sharp copper tools (broadaxe, adze, chisels of several sizes, saws) removed wood damaged by water action and marine borers, preparing the planks for reuse.[20]

Timbers at Gawasis were recycled in several ways. In some cases ship timbers were reused on site as access ramps outside entrances to Caves 3 and 4, as stabilization inside and outside Caves 2 and 3, as thresholds in Caves 1, 2, 3, 6, 7 and 8, as workbenches in Caves 2 and 3, and also as foundations for walkways inside Caves 2 and 3 (Figure 2.1). Timbers reused in these areas include hull planks from both ships and boats, and beams and deck planks from ships.

Work areas and ship timbers on the western terrace

Caves 2–6 were used for different purposes, during the same expeditions and also over a period of time. Stratigraphic layers mark different periods of use, and the contents of those layers give hints to the range of activities

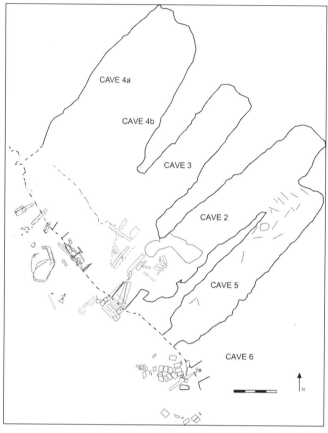

Fig. 2.1: Plan of the main group of galleries showing the location
of excavated ship timbers.

performed in the same place. Excavations revealed accumulations of wood debris from woodworking activities, and remains of equipment and storage containers employed during expeditions, including boxes, cordage, bags, ration bowls and food provisions, pottery fragments, including ostraca, were recovered from the western terrace.

A deep excavation conducted in the area outside Cave 3 revealed at least six different phases of human occupation accumulated above a level of sterile soil.[21] These phases seem to represent the result of clearing the galleries of materials accumulated by each expedition during the period of occupation. Inside the excavated galleries, despite the number of expeditions documented in texts and the six phases recorded outside the galleries, only two discrete phases of human occupation could be distinguished, although the galleries were reused many times.

In the area outside Caves 2, 3 and 4, at least three living floors marked by archaeological materials in coherent horizontal layers, as well as later stone windbreaks and hearths were investigated. The living floors of the two earlier phases are indicated by several large- and medium-sized ship planks, which seem to be related to the latest phase of use of these gallery entrances.

Outside the entrance to Cave 6, a deposit of ship timbers incorporated a complete plank, a pair of steering-oar blades that can be ascribed to the latest phase of occupation of the gallery, and a number of other timbers (Plate 2.3). The final occupation layer outside Cave 6 was characterized by scant archaeological material and represented a period of abandonment at the site during which windblown sand and leaves accumulated. This phase may date to the early New Kingdom, on the basis of an associated potsherd.[22]

The final phase overlies an earlier level characterized by artefacts including complete hull plank (T34), inscribed stelae, clay sealings, about 40 complete or fragmentary wooden boxes (two of which had painted inscriptions), ceramics, and about 50 shallow ration bowls (complete and fragmentary). Texts painted on the small wood boxes date this level to the reign of Amenemhat IV (*c*.1797–90 BC).[23] Plank T34 (3.29 m. long) almost certainly belongs to the timber deposit as its tip was in the gallery entrance, and its longitudinal axis was precisely aligned with those of the ship components below it.[24] These ship components lay beneath a heavy

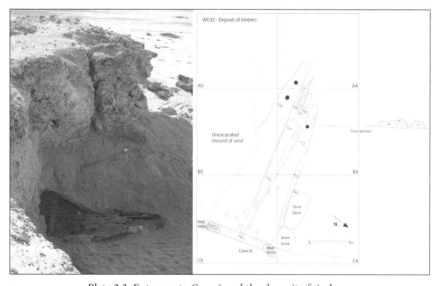

Plate 2.3: Entrance to Cave 6 and the deposit of timbers.

layer of salt concretion in association with mudbrick walls on either side of the entrance.[25]

Recognizable among these timbers were steering oar blades (T72 and T85) similar in form and wood type to blades T1 and T2 recovered from Cave 2,[26] but almost twice the size measuring ca. 3.25 m. and 4.20 m. in length. They are in a context of reuse, and lie parallel to one another at the bottom of the timber deposit. The parallel arrangement of all the other timbers suggests that they were placed there at the same time. Several of the timbers have a half-round cross section, but identification and detailed recording awaits removal of the salt encrustation that obscures them. Because most of the timbers described in this deposit remain obscured by heavy salt encrustation or *in situ*, it is not possible to provide a firm interpretation of its context. The alignment of the steering oars may indicate that they functioned as a ramp like smaller timbers outside Caves 3, 4 and 7.

Outside Cave 7, ship timbers reused as an entry, ramp and/or threshold were identified. This area also produced a large deposit of wood debris, clay sealings, wooden box pieces and multiple arrangements of hearths.[27] The results of excavations outside the galleries reveal the presence of different living floors and accumulations of materials employed during the expeditions, as well as different reuses of ship timbers. Wood debris found in excavation units outside the galleries is usually poorly preserved, compared to the debris found inside the galleries, reflecting the fact that the environment inside the galleries is more stable and the temperature and humidity are lower than outside. Deposits of wood debris usually incorporate box and ship component fragments often mixed with other organic materials, including mangrove leaves, charcoal, and branches. Sometimes the preservation of the wood is so poor that it can be hard to distinguish debris resulting from ship dismantling from fragments of broken boxes or other wooden objects.

Wood fragments identified as debris resulting from reworking ship timbers show evidence including tool marks and surface stripping, significant traces of gribble and shipworm, and traces of red paint. Wood debris deposited in the area outside Cave 2 is consistent with the deposit excavated outside Cave 7 and represents ship dismantling and hull cleaning activities that took place at the entrance of these galleries. This wood debris consisted of wood fragments removed from larger components using copper tools, as well as broken fastening elements, including tenons, dovetail tenons, and wood fragments with the remains of mortises visible (Plate 2.4).[28] Triangular-sectioned elements that can be interpreted as

Plate 2.4: Wood debris from outside the galleries (left) and
wood debris from Cave 2, Room 2 (right).

possible wedges or repair elements and spars with an oval section ca.
4.5 cm. in diameter, possibly oar loom fragments, were also present.

Apart from the entrance area outside Caves 4 and 5, which has not
been completely excavated, some of the caves show similar entrance
arrangements. Caves 2, 3, 6 and 7 have ship timbers employed as thresholds
to block the entrance of sand into the gallery and stone arrangements
along the sides of the entrance. Access to Caves 2 and 7 is characterized
by more than one short ship timber lying parallel to the ancient reef edge
and forming a sort of ramp. Cave 6 has an accumulation of ship timbers
perpendicular to the reef edge that may have had a similar function. The
position of the steering oar blades at the top of a pile of windblown sand in
the entrance corridor of Cave 2 does not seem to have the same purpose.
In this case, the blades might have been stored there at the end of the last
expedition or moved by someone during the abandonment of the gallery.
The results of excavations outside the galleries reveal the presence of
different living floors and accumulations of materials employed during the
expeditions, as well as different uses of recycled ship timbers.

The Galleries

In 2004–5, a complex of man-made galleries was discovered after removing
a deposit of ca. 3 m. of sand accumulated along the western edge of the fossil
coral terrace (Fig. 2.1).[29] The four galleries composing the main complex
(Caves 2–5) began as a large natural cavity, while four more galleries (Caves
1, 6, 7, 8) were excavated directly in the reef wall. The west terrace complex
includes six galleries from 19–22 m. in length, 4–5 m. wide and 1.5–2 m.
high. Their plan is rectangular and roughly south-west-north-east oriented

within a vaulted roof. Reused ship timbers and ship equipment are used as thresholds, as walking ramps, to arrange the living floor and to separate different galleries (Plate 2.5). The following discussion is focused on the best-studied galleries, Cave 2 and Cave 3.

Archaeological excavations conducted in Caves 2 and 3 revealed that the galleries were occupied at least twice during different maritime expeditions, followed by a phase of abandonment during which a deposit of windblown sand formed and portions of the cave subsequently collapsed. The galleries were used for different purposes: the entrances, naturally illuminated, were used for working activities including dismantling, cleaning and reworking of ship timbers, as attested by piles of wood debris. Evidence of food processing activities was also found, including grinding stones, barley, a rope bag for barley, bread moulds, shells (mostly *nerita*), fish bones, and some hearths. The galleries might also been used for the storage of ship

Plate 2.5: Entrances to Cave 2 and Cave 3

equipment as demonstrated by the discovery of coils of ship rigging stored in Cave 5.[30] Excavations were designed to collect more information about ship timbers and the use of space in the galleries as discussed below.

Cave 2

Cave 2 is 24 m. long and ca. 4–5 m. wide. Oriented south-west-north-east, this gallery consists of a large natural rock shelter that was extended by the ancient Egyptians. The entrance to Cave 2 was marked by a ramp made of five reused ship timbers (Fig. 2.1 and Plate 2.5). The ceiling is vaulted and plastered with mud. Its present maximum height is about 2 m. in the centre, but is as low as 1 m. near the walls. Three main sectors were identified: the Entrance Corridor; Room 1, and Room 2.[31]

Entrance: Six limestone blocks that can be identified as anchors, with coral and conglomerate stone, three ship planks and a deck plank, small blocks of stone, and mud-bricks reinforced the entrance walls. The wall elements were joined together with a mortar made of gypsum and mud plaster. When found, the cave entrance was filled with windblown sand, on top of which lay a pair of steering oar blades. Pottery dating to the seventeenth and early eighteenth Dynasties (*c.*1600–1400 BC) was found in strata associated with the steering oar blades.

Room 1: A 4 m. × 4 m. trench was excavated east of the entrance corridor. The roof of Room 1 is vaulted, with traces of burning and a deep fracture. In Room 1, five phases were distinguished. The most recent phases are represented by a deposit of small mammal bones (Phase 5) on the surface of rocks that have collapsed from the ceiling (Phase 4). The mound of collapsed rock sealed a large activity area for woodworking (Phase 3). Phase 2 consisted of similar evidence of activity and a possible living floor represented by five reused ship timbers and the remains of food, a basalt grinding stone with a chert nodule grinder lying on top of it, a few potsherds, a scoop for grain and a rope bag. The five ship timbers constitute the central passage in Room 1.

A wall on the western side of Room 1 separated Cave 2 from Cave 3. It was constructed with reused ship timber and stones and may be dated to Phase 1 like the arrangement of mud-bricks associated with a ship timber found parallel to the entrance and a concentration of pebbles, which possibly was a living floor, with sherds of small ceramic cups of the early Twelfth Dynasty.[32]

Room 2: Behind a large rock fall, Room 2 has an almost rectangular plan, ca. 17.5 × 4.5 m. in area. The walls are cut vertically and the ceiling is vaulted. The present height of the ceiling is about 2 m. in the middle of the gallery and 1 m. at the walls. The surface of Room 2 in Cave 2 is characterized by sand, concentrations of wood and rope fragments, and rock fall from the ceiling, a high concentration of wood debris and scattered fragments of rope along the centre of the trench and in the westernmost part, especially at a natural opening, probably due to wall collapse, which opens into Cave 5 where rope was stored. A compact sandy layer 10–20 cm. thick in a 4 m. × 2 m. trench (WG 64) contained approximately 47 litres of wood debris from cedar, acacia, and sycamore objects (Plate 2.4).

The wood debris is likely the result of dismantling, cleaning and modification of ship timbers. Only a few fragments retained adze marks and less than ten fragments displayed the red paint marks that we associate with cleaning activities, possibly because of the surface degradation. Wood debitage, fragmentary oars, gypsum remains and the adze handles, described earlier, attest to woodworking as the primary activity in this area, almost certainly ship dismantling and the subsequent modification of ship components. The debris is consistent with the size and types of wood debris excavated in the gallery Entrance.[33]

Barley seeds, insects and a few pottery fragments as well as hearths and concentrations of organic materials suggest that Room 2 was also a living area where food processing and/or food storage occurred and at least one hearth. A ca. 2-litre concentration of reeds and leaves was excavated along the north-western and northern limit of the trench, the deposit may be the remains of a pallet for sleeping or sitting. These finds are contemporary with the early Twelfth Dynasty occupation level previously identified in Phase 1, the gallery's Entrance Corridor.

Between Room 1 and Room 2: During the most recent field season, a trench (WG 71) was opened in the area obstructed by rock fall from the ceiling separating Room 1 from Room 2. This excavation revealed evidence of intensive work activities related to rope, timber cleaning and food processing. This trench was laid out to determine whether activities here were linked to those previously identified in Room 2. The surface layer includes rock fall from the ceiling, one or two probable oar loom fragments, wood debris, and jar sherds. The layer below it included scattered concentrations of organic materials, ship components, rope and wood debris. The south-west corner of the excavation area was characterized by a concentration (50 cm. × 40 cm.) of rope and wood debris lying on

Plate 2.6: Deposit of rope and wood debris lying on a compact stratum
of reeds in Cave 2.

a compact stratum of reeds that also included barley seeds, beetles, and
other small insects (Plate 2.6).

The wood debris is likely the result of dismantling, cleaning and
modification of ship timbers and is consistent with the size and types of
wood debris excavated in the gallery Entrance.[34] The discovery of a thick
layer of rope fragments, reeds (possibly from a mat), and seeds suggests
that the excavated level was a living area where rope-related activities, food
processing and/or food storage occurred. Wood fragments and parts of oar
looms also attest to woodworking activity.

Cave 3

The entrance to Cave 3 consisted of two walls constructed from a stone
anchor, ship planks, wood fragments, and stone blocks with mud plaster
similar to walls at the entrance to Cave 2. The walls reinforced the edge
of the coral terrace.[35] In Cave 3, trench WG 39 measured 22 m. × 4 m.
Gallery walls are cut vertically, and the vaulted ceiling was ca. 1.80–1.60 m.
Two occupation phases were identified in Cave 3. The latest phase is
characterized by a deposit of sand with several hearths, and wood debris
associated with shells, a few rope fragments and animal bones scattered on
the surface. The most significant activity recorded during this phase was
the use of ship timbers as fuel, probably by people not associated with a
pharaonic expedition.

The assemblage of timbers on the floor marks an earlier phase of occupation. Activities recorded during this phase include the reworking of ship timbers. A small, shallow concentration of seeds and insects was found close to the western gallery wall indicating that food process-related activities were also conducted inside the cave. Among finds that may be connected to ship-related activities was a deposit of a sort of white plaster (ca. 15 cm. in diameter) and a folded strip of copper. Traces of plaster have been found elsewhere on the wood surface of ship timbers discovered at the site.[36] Copper strip dimensions correspond to the remains of copper strips from ship components.

The entrance and central part of the cave is characterized on the surface by a large concentration of charcoal, concentrations of ash and very shallow hearths. Below the level of sand and ashes a large concentration of wood debris, timber fragments, rope and leather fragments of different sizes and configurations, and a few potsherds were found. An assemblage of 14 timbers was discovered below this deposit. The orthogonal disposition of six of these on a prepared floor suggests a deliberate arrangement (Plate 2.7). Pairs of timbers arranged parallel and perpendicular to gallery walls probably represent a seating and woodworking area. For example, the exposed surface of plank segment T64 is covered with tool marks seemingly unassociated with its original configuration or dismantling.

Plate 2.7: Ship timbers reused on the walking floor in Cave 3.

The debris in Cave 3 includes numerous pieces with significant traces of shipworm and gribble, attached barnacles, and evidence of tool marks and surface stripping. A small number of wood fragments bear traces of copper. A total of ca. 50 loose tenons varying in size, condition and features were recovered in Cave 3. More fastenings were recovered from the surface of Cave 3 than any similar area, and the fastenings include the largest dimensions recorded at the site. Dovetail tenons and free tenons are compatible with mortises in plank segment T64 (22.5 cm. thick) and in ship components from the deposit outside Cave 6.[37]

Excavations conducted in Cave 3 and at the entrance and Room 1 in Cave 2 suggest at least two main phases of human occupation mainly characterized by the evidence of woodworking activities, although the definition of a precise chronology is problematic due to the absence of a sufficient number of pottery samples.

The analysis of wood debris is a puzzle of information that needs to be related to full-sized ships and dismantling activities, as well as to the fact that the preservation of the wood debris is different in each excavation unit. Where the debris is badly preserved, it is difficult to understand whether it comes from a ship, a box or a branch of wood. For this reason, the methods of quantification and classification adopted so far are still experimental. Despite the preservation issue, it is clear that the debris found outside the galleries differ from the debris found inside the galleries, and that, for example, Cave 2 and Cave 3 were used at different times or for different sized ships. Further investigations to be conducted inside and outside the galleries will provide more detailed information.

Conclusion

Mersa Gawasis provides a rare opportunity to investigate phases of work and spatial organization of state-sponsored maritime activities in pharaonic Egypt. Excavated materials reflect a spatial diversification of work that may indicate differentiation of the carpenters' labour and skills. Within the same activity area, different phases of dismantling and modification of ship timbers can be distinguished, allowing us to work towards a reconstruction of the work process.

Notes

1. See Bard & Fattovich 2007 for a preliminary excavation report. Annual excavation season reports are published at http://www.archaeogate.org.

2. These galleries were originally thought to be caves, and are referred to as Cave 1, Cave 2, etc., in excavation publications, but they are man-made spaces for living and work.
3. Sayed 1977, 1978, 1980 and 1983.
4. Sayed 1999: 867–8. Other inscribed stelae and ostraca discovered more recently at the site attest to the existence of a number of expeditions throughout most of the Twelfth Dynasty, during the reigns of Senwosret I (*c*. 1956–11 BC), Senwosret II (*c*. 1877–70 BC), Senwosret III (*c*. 1870–31 BC), Amenemhat III (*c*. 1831–786 BC), and Amenemhat IV (*c*. 1786–77 BC) (Bard & Fattovich 2010: 36–8).
5. Large numbers of donkey mandibles and coprolites found in Gawasis excavations confirm the presence of donkeys, the standard cargo carrier of the early third millennium.
6. Ward and Zazzaro 2010.
7. Ward and Zazzaro 2010; Ward, Zazzaro and Abd el-Maguid 2010; Zazzaro 2009.
8. Ward 2000.
9. Foster 2002: 9–16.
10. Zazzaro 2009, Ward, Zazzaro and Abd el-Maguid 2010.
11. Ward, Zazzaro and Abd el-Maguid 2010: 389. Construction of the experimental ship *Min of the Desert* included replication of the smaller blades on a 5 m. loom; the steering system performed well on the 20-m.-long vessel (Ward 2009).
12. A tenon is a shaped slip of wood that joins two pieces of wood by fitting tightly into mortises cut into them. Ward and Zazzaro 2010: 41.
13. Plaster coatings are documented for the First Dynasty (*c*. 3050 BC) Abydos boats (Ward 2003), the Dashur boats of the 12th Dynasty ([Ward] Haldane 1984), and are attested since medieval times on traditional Arab ships in the Red Sea and in the Indian Ocean. Today, the mixture is made of pounded calcium carbonate (gypsum) and fish oil.
14. Killen 1994: 21 fig. 22, and 43 fig. 50.
15. Hein et al. 2011: 690.
16. Suggested by Fattovich in Bard and Fattovich et al. 2008 and in Bard and Fattovich et al. 2010.
17. Blue 2007: 271–2.
18. Childs and Perlingieri in Bard and Fattovich et al. 2007.
19. Lucarini in Bard and Fattovich et al. 2008.
20. It has been elsewhere pointed out by Ward (2004: 22–3) that ancient Egyptians seem to have recycled as much wood as possible, especially imported species such as cedar.
21. Manzo in Bard and Fattovich 2007: 57–8 and Bard and Fattovich et al. 2008.
22. Ward and Zazzaro 2010: 30–1.
23. Fattovich and Bard 2007: 47–8.
24. Ward 2009; Ward and Zazzaro 2010.
25. Bard and Fattovich et al. 2008.
26. Zazzaro 2009: 3–8.

27. Bard and Fattovich et al. 2008.
28. Calcagno and Zazzaro in Bard and Fattovich et al. 2008.
29. Bard and Fattovich 2007: 61.
30. Veldmeijer and Zazzaro 2008.
31. Room indicates a term of convenience. The entrance gallery was a single unit when originally manufactured, but rock fall divided the space into what we refer to as 'rooms'.
32. Bard and Fattovich 2007: 65.
33. Ward and Zazzaro 2010: 30–1.
34. Ibid.
35. Calcagno and Zazzaro in Bard and Fattovich 2007.
36. See note 13.
37. Ward, Zazzaro and Abd el-Maguid 2010.

References

Bard, K. and Fattovich, R. (2007), *Harbor of the Pharaohs to the Land of Punt. Archaeological Investigations at Mersa/Wadi Gawasis, Egypt, 2001–2005*, Napoli: Università degli Studi di Napoli 'L'Orientale' Dipartimento di studi e ricerche su l'Africa e paese Arabi Laboratorio di archeologia.

—— (2010), 'Recent Excavations at the Ancient Harbor of Saww, Mersa/Wadi Gawasis on the Red Sea', in *Offerings to the Discerning Eye. An Egyptological Medley in Honor of Jack A. Josephson*, Sue H. D'Auria, ed., Leiden-Boston: Brill, pp. 18–33.

Bard, K., et al. (2007), *Mersa/Wadi Gawasis 2006–2007 Report,* http://www.archeogate.com.

—— (2008), *Mersa/Wadi Gawasis Mission 2007–2008*, http://www.archaeogate.com.

—— (2010), *Mersa/Wadi Gawasis 2009–2010 Final Report*, http://www.archaeogate.com.

Blue, L. (2007), 'Locating the Harbour: Myos Hormos/Quseir al-Qadim: a Roman and Islamic Port on the Red Sea Coast of Egypt', *The International Journal of Nautical Archaeology*, vol. 36, no. 2, pp. 265–81.

Foster, J.L. (tr.) (2002), *Ancient Egyptian Literature. An Anthology*, Austin: University of Texas Press.

[Ward] Haldane, C. (1984), 'The Dashur boats', unpublished M.A. thesis, Texas A&M University.

Hein, C.J., FitzGerald, D.M., Milne, G.A., Bard, K.A. and Fattovich, R. (2011), 'Evolution of a Pharaonic harbor on the Red Sea: Implications for coastal response to changes in sea level and climate', *Geology*, vol. 39, no. 7, pp. 686–90.

Killen, G. (1994), *Ancient Egyptian Furniture*, Warminster: Aris and Phillips.

Sayed, A.M.H. (1977), 'Discovery of the site of the 12th Dynasty port at Wadi Gawasis on the Red Sea Shore', *Revue d'Égyptologie*, vol. 29, pp. 140–78.

—— (1978), 'The recently discovered port on the Red Sea shore', *Journal of Egyptian Archaeology*, vol. 64, pp. 69–71.

—— (1980), 'Observations on recent discoveries at Wadi Gawasis', *Journal of Egyptian Archaeology*, vol. 66, pp. 154–71.

—— (1983), 'New light on the recently discovered port on the Red Sea shore', *Chronique d'Égypte*, vol. 48, pp. 23–37.

—— (1999), 'Wadi Gasus', in *Encyclopedia of the Archaeology of Ancient Egypt*, ed. K.A. Bard, London: Routledge, pp. 867–8.

Veldmeijer, A. and Zazzaro, C. (2008), 'The Rope Cave at Mersa Gawasis', *Journal of American Research Centre in Egypt*, vol. 44, pp. 9–39.

Ward, C. (2000), *Sacred and Secular: Ancient Egyptian Ships and Boats*. Boston: Archaeological Institute of America (New Monographs Series, no. 5).

—— (2003), 'World's oldest planked boats: Abydos hull construction', in *Boats, ships and shipyards: proceedings of the Ninth International Symposium on Boat and Ship Archaeology*, C. Beltrame, ed., (Venice 2000), Oxford: Oxbow Books, pp. 19–23.

—— (2004) 'Boatbuilding in Ancient Egypt', in *Towards a Philosophy of Ancient Shipbuilding*, Hocker, F. & Ward, C., eds., College Station Texas: Texas A&M University Press, pp. 12–24.

——, 'Evidence for Ancient Egyptian Seafaring', in *Transfer and Exchange in Nautical Technology. Proceedings of the 11th International Symposium on Boat and Ship archaeology, Mainz 24-28 September 2006*, R. Bockius, ed., Mainz: Verlag des Römisch-Germanischen Zentralmuseums, pp. 9–16.

—— and Zazzaro, C. (2010), 'Evidence for Pharaonic Seagoing Ships at Mersa/Wadi Gawasis, Egypt', *The International Journal of Nautical Archaeology*, vol. 39, no. 1, pp. 27–43.

—— and Abd El-Maguid, M. (2010), 'Super-Sized Egyptian Ships', *The International Journal of Nautical Archaeology*, vol. 39, no. 2, pp. 387–9.

Zazzaro, C. (2009), 'Nautical evidence from the pharaonic site of Mersa/Wadi Gawasis: report on two parts of a steering oar/rudder blade', in *Transfer and Exchange in Nautical Technology. Proceedings of the 11th International Symposium on Boat and Ship archaeology, Mainz 24-28 September 2006*, ed. Bockius, R., Mainz: Verlag des Römisch-Germanischen Zentralmuseums, pp. 3–8.

—— (2010), 'Ship timbers and ship equipment in their archaeological context at Mersa Gawasis, Egypt', in *Recent Discoveries and Latest Research in Egyptology. Proceedings of the First Neapolitan Congress of Egyptology, Naples, 18–20 June 2008*, Raffaele, F., Nuzzolo M. and Incordino, I., eds., Wiesbaden: Harrassowitz Verlag, pp. 359–69.

CHAPTER 3

Living in the Egyptian Ports
Daily Life at Berenike and Myos Hormos

Roberta Tomber

The two most prominent Egyptian ports for Indian Ocean trade during the Roman period, Berenike and Myos Hormos (Map 3.1), are located in remote desert environs and were established specifically to facilitate this trade. This essay will investigate physical and social organization of the ports with reference to their environmental context. Drawing on the extensive archaeological evidence gathered since the 1990s, questions relating to port facilities, supply and demand, definition and role of their hinterland and catchment areas will be addressed in comparison with other Roman and Indo-Roman period port sites to assess to what degree their development was influenced by their physical setting. The long-term utilization of the Red Sea as a trade funnel, spanning the period between the third century BC and at least the early sixth century at Berenike, also allows diachronic changes in the region to be explored.[1]

Berenike and Myos Hormos (modern Quseir al-Qadim) are the two most important ports of the Early Roman period and are described by the writer of the mid-first century *Periplus Maris Erythraei*.[2] A third Egyptian port mentioned in the *Periplus*, Nechesia, is tentatively identified at modern Marsa Nakari. Although all three sites have been excavated, the most extensive evidence—both archaeological and textual—comes from Berenike and Myos Hormos and it is those sites that will be the focus here. From Berenike and Myos Hormos we see two very different site sequences. Berenike was established in the mid-third century by Ptolemy II, and there is archaeological evidence to at least the early sixth century AD; the archaeological sequence from Myos Hormos is much shorter, at

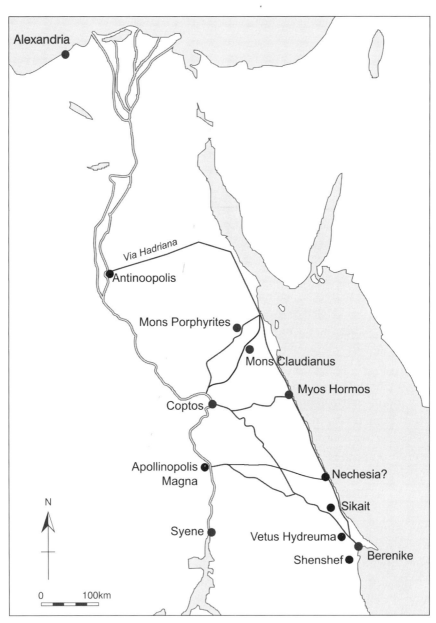

Map 3.1: Main Red Sea and Egyptian sites mentioned in the text (A. Simpson).

present beginning around the late first century BC through the mid-third century AD. It is probable that this site too had a Ptolemaic foundation, as indicated by both Strabo[3] and Pliny,[4] but problems of waterlogged deposits hindered excavation of its foundation. Both Myos Hormos and Berenike were established exclusively as trade ports: Berenike served the Ptolemaic trade with Africa and both for the more systematized trade throughout the Indian Ocean after the annexation of Egypt as a Roman province in 30 BC.

The transport of goods from the Red Sea involved a desert trek to the Nile and then transport onwards to Alexandria. On camel-back the desert trek is estimated at 6–7 days from Myos Hormos[5] and 11–12 days from Berenike.[6] Whitewright[7] has estimated the distance between the two ports by sea as extremely variable depending on the conditions, but up to 5.5 days. Much discussion has focused on the navigational problems of these ports, and the challenges in sailing against the Red Sea northerlies. However, their longevity attests to their overall efficiency and many factors other than wind regimes—including social relations—would have influenced initially their location and subsequently their sustainability.[8] While both ports are relatively inaccessible within Egypt, Map 3.2 clearly shows their strategic location within the Indian Ocean, fundamental to provisioning goods into the Roman world via Alexandria.

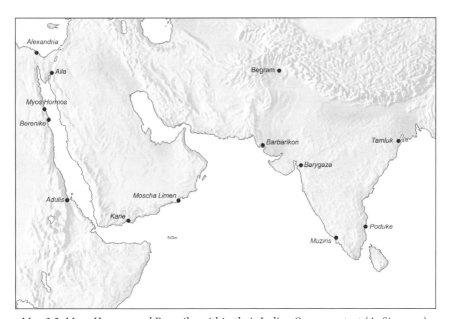

Map 3.2: Myos Hormos and Berenike within their Indian Ocean context (A. Simpson).

Physical Setting and Environment

Both sites are situated in a natural inlet or *mersa*. However, as will be discussed in further detail later, these coastlines are in some cases dramatically altered since Antiquity. Greater continuity exists with the overall environment, where changes in the climate influencing flora and fauna took place before the Greco-Roman period, between 2350 and 500 BC.[9] Today the region sees approximately 4–5 mm. of rainfall a year, with vegetation comprising especially the acacia tree, which was heavily exploited in Roman times, in particular for charcoal.[10]

Despite the hyper-aridity, through plant adaptation and excellent water management, the desert did support numerous types of sites and activities during Roman times. The Eastern Desert has some subsurface water that is stored in natural substrata, while another source is surface water from regular moisture and rain that can be quite heavy during November and December.[11] Wells, cisterns and wadi walls were amongst the manmade measures used to exploit and manage the available water resources.

Although not identified at the ports, elsewhere in the Eastern Desert wells are fairly common.[12] A particularly large example that would have supplied water to Berenike was found 8.5 km. south-west of the site at Wadi Kalalat;[13] the main source of water for Myos Hormos was at Bi'r an-Nakhil, located ca. 13 km. east of Myos Hormos as the crow flies.[14]

Other classes of evidence also inform on water management and the complex mechanisms involved. For example, during the 2009/2010 excavation at Berenike, an archive of ca. 240 *ostraca* detailing the supply of fresh water to the site, and the importance of the military involvement in this procedure,[15] were recovered from a first century AD dump. The detailed study of these texts should substantially increase our understanding of how water was controlled and distributed to the population.

Indirect evidence for water management comes from archaeobotanical studies. For Berenike, Cappers lists a number of crops that potentially may have been grown on site in small kitchen gardens—crops that include legumes (fava bean), herbs (dill, cumin, fennel, coriander), vegetables (beet, garlic) and some fruits, including watermelon and cucumber.[16] These same food plants have also been identified at Myos Hormos.[17] When exploited, these plants would have been grown on a small scale, with the bulk of food, including these same items, imported from the Nile Valley; nevertheless they provide some indication of water availability. Exploitation of desert plants was another source of local food.[18]

During the Late Roman period, the site at Sikait gives some indication of how this small-scale farming may have been conducted. Stone boxes interpreted as containers for wooden trellises that supported crops or other plants were excavated there. Situated in both the sun and shade, a variety of species may have been cultivated.[19]

The size of the ports attests to success in managing the limited water. Nevertheless, there still would have been environmental constraints on population size. Population estimates are necessarily imprecise but Late Roman Berenike has been estimated at 500–1000 inhabitants, fluctuating throughout the year; lack of an overall plan and information on domestic structures during the Ptolemaic and Early Roman periods means their size cannot be estimated, but the Early Roman may have been larger than the Late Roman.[20] Whitcomb suggested that occupation at Myos Hormos may have been seasonal.[21] Seasonality is difficult to identify and will be discussed later in the 'Hinterlands' section.

Harbour Installations

As the primacy of these sites was their function as ports, their harbour facilities are of special interest. At Myos Hormos, investigation of the natural harbour was a main focus of the 1999–2003 campaign conducted by the University of Southampton. Through the geomorphological study of these deposits, Lucy Blue was able to define the limit of the Roman and Islamic harbours and demonstrate the extensive siltation.[22] During the Roman period, a narrow channel led to a now silted lagoon which formed the harbour. On the north-east side of the lagoon an installation composed primarily of complete or near-complete Roman amphorae— mostly Egyptian 'Amphores égyptiennes 3'[23] and Italian wine amphorae especially from Campania—of the late first century BC/AD were identified. The full extent of this feature measured over 60 m. in length. Its function was twofold: to act as 'hard' to consolidate the intertidal, muddy zone and to form a jetty that facilitated the off-loading of goods. A sea-wall ran parallel at the back of the bay along the waterfront.

Harbour sites across the empire vary enormously and comprise the entire gambit from natural moorings to purpose-built installations, exemplified by the complexity and scale of those seen at Trajan's Imperial harbour at Portus. The Myos Hormos amphora quay is fairly low-level on such a sliding scale, but nevertheless is part of a widespread technology. The use of amphorae for harbour construction can be seen at other waterlogged sites, primarily clustered in southern France and northern Italy where they were sometimes encased in a wooden frame.[24] The feature from Myos Hormos provides the easternmost example of the technique and given the available resources, it is unlikely that it would have been reinforced with wood.

At Berenike two sea-walls dating to the late first century BC/AD have been excavated on the eastern side of the site.[25] One wall is composed of coral heads and ashlar blocks with wooden bollards, suggesting a landing area for small craft; the other of limestone blocks is a small segment of wall interpreted as a harbour wall. While geomagnetic survey has helped to locate potential areas of open water and anomalies perhaps indicative of harbour walls, the 2010/2011 season saw the first investigation of the harbour through coring undertaken by Anna Kortaba-Morley.[26] The results of this study will address questions regarding the evolution of the harbour and its siltation, which at present appears to have resulted in the gradual shift of the town east and southwards.[27] Another result of this study may be to locate harbour features in the area.

Living and Working

Town Planning and Architecture

Living spaces at the ports seem to vary somewhat between the Early (first-third centuries) and Late (fourth-sixth centuries) periods. At Myos Hormos where only the Early Roman is represented, mud-brick structures dominate. Excavations at Quseir al-Qadim by the University of Chicago between 1978 and 1982 concentrated on structures that they interpreted as domestic and public buildings. An area of dense mud-brick rooms were thought to function for domestic, industrial and commercial purposes.[28] Fewer structures were excavated by the University of Southampton but included one monumental building with dressed limestone base and mud-brick walls, originally stuccoed and painted at least in part. Within the building, a raised platform surrounded by terraces was suggestive of a North African temple, but the lack of votive objects argued against this; an alternative religious function would be as a synagogue, which is in keeping with the lack of objects and more generally the plan of the building.[29] While the precise function of the building cannot be stated definitively, it does seem to be a religious structure. Other features underscore the presence of communal activities but also reinforce the lack of site planning and monumentality. For example, ovens constructed from reused amphorae appear, by their scale and the presence of pounding tubs, to represent communal ovens rather than domestic ones.[30]

At Berenike, architecture is more widespread with numerous buildings, most of which date to the Late Roman period. During the late Ptolemaic/Early Roman period mud-brick and gypsum/anhydrite were used, with limestone boulders and cut stone more common during the Early Roman.

By at least the Late Roman period, coral-head (sometimes combined with other materials such as ashlars or wood and dubbed *opus Berenicum*) dominated,[31] although the sea-wall described earlier shows it was employed from the Early Roman period. Coral and cobble foundations with mud-brick walls, seen on one building at Myos Hormos, is a related but distinct technique dated to the Early Roman period.[32]

The Late Roman sequence at Berenike saw two-storey buildings with gypsum/anhydrite staircases that catered for lower floor shops and businesses with domestic residences upstairs,[33] very much in the Mediterranean style. Sidebotham[34] postulates that the Early Roman settlement may have been orthogonal, but is obscured by later building, with the first definitive evidence for a grid-plan in the Late Roman period. Clearly, throughout the sequence the exploited building materials were available locally, such as the gypsum/anhydrite blocks, reused teak (probably from ship planks) and coral.

Communal Life

Most communal structures at Berenike are religious in function. The best, or at least the longest known public building at Berenike was identified by Belzoni in 1818 as a Temple of Serapis,[35] a consistent feature of Greco-Roman sites in Egypt. The clearing and planning of this structure is now the focus of a study by Martin Hense, which will clarify its sequence and function for the first time.[36]

The largest religious building at Berenike is a basilica-style structure with annexes for food preparation and other domestic activities. The layout and the discovery of related artefacts (ceramic lamps, bronzes) with Christian motifs all support its identification as a church. A range of shrines used for mystery cults have also been identified including a substantial fifth century one, excavated in 2010 and 2011, dedicated to Isis. It contained numerous artefacts such as cowrie shells for augury and painted eggshell fragments (including one with a pentragram) that can be linked to Isis, who had a strong association with the opening of the sailing season.[37]

Religion would have played an equally important role at Myos Hormos and the one monumental building excavated by the British team has been tentatively identified as a Jewish synagogue (discussed earlier). In fact, religious structures are frequently identified at Indian Ocean sites. A building thought to be a synagogue, contemporary with the Late Roman period, has been excavated at Qana' on the southern Yemeni coast with associated bronze fragments from a menorah and an *ostracon* with Jewish references.[38]

Religion was always integrated into daily life, and throughout Egypt religious structures played a particularly visible role in town life. This may have been further emphasized here given the precarious nature of the voyage East, for merchants and sailors would have been eager for every protection they could gain. The *Synaxarion*, or list of the Coptic Saints, records that Berenike had its own bishop.[39] Apparently his seat or residence was in Coptos since he was subordinate to the Bishop of Coptos. A bishop was needed at Berenike so that merchants and mariners who travelled the Red Sea would be able to receive the sacraments before their voyage.

The number of religious structures compared with the lack of other public buildings underlines their significance. A forum, amphitheatre and bath, all of which are fundamental to any small Roman town, are absent. Of course, only a small portion of Berenike has been excavated, but to what extent we might expect to see a range of public buildings at these ports relates to both their population size and composition and their function. Population is notoriously difficult to estimate but Alston and Alston[40] have compiled statistics for towns in Roman Egypt which reflect a wide range of diversity according to the type of settlement, function and proximity to other centres, from 58,429 for the *metropolis* of Hermopolis Magna to 79 for the *kome* of Psenokaia. A Trajanic *ostracon* from Mons Claudianus shows 917 people present on one day,[41] not so very different from that estimated for Berenike.

Despite being faced with similar water issues, bathhouses are found at Mons Claudianus and Mons Porphyrites. Although this may be accounted for by military personnel, baths being an essential component of military life, nevertheless they appear to be absent from the ports, though there is some indirect evidence for bathing activities.[42] Equally the absence of *fora*, so important in the Roman world for international business transactions—as exemplified by the *Piazzale delle Corporazioni* at Ostia, Italy—has significance in terms of the social organization of these ports, reinforcing their lack of monumental harbour facilities and highlighting their function, in that they were not for merchant transactions, but only for transhipment to points beyond.

Local Production and Industry

At both sites most production is related to maintenance activities, which centred on boat repair. At Myos Hormos, bronze and iron working, interpreted as being for ship maintenance, was identified near the harbour.[43]

Similarly, at Berenike, bronze nails and tacks suitable for shipbuilding were used during the Ptolemaic period,[44] with large iron ones from the Roman.[45]

At Berenike, small-scale industry took place: working with mother-of-pearl and semi-precious stones during the Early Roman period; leather, wood, animal horn and turtle shell during the Late Roman. Sidebotham and Zych[46] draw attention to the trade of tortoise/turtle shell throughout the Red Sea and Indian Ocean as mentioned in the *Periplus Maris Erythraei* and suggest that the working of this material may have been for export. However, it is important to emphasize the small scale of these workings, which may also have found a market at Berenike. These craft industries lack the scale identified from other port sites where production for export is an important feature. For example, the trade site of Pattanam (Muziris) in south-west India was actively involved in the working of stone beads for export, as evidenced by large quantities of debitage.[47] Although the stone may have been imported from further afield in India, significantly Pattanam had an extremely rich hinterland that supplied items for export. Even elsewhere on the Red Sea, the port of Aila produced amphorae that were widely distributed throughout the Indian Ocean.[48]

Hinterland and Catchment Areas

The immediate hinterland of Myos Hormos and Berenike has important ramifications for the function of these ports. While the Eastern Desert as a whole is rich in natural resources that were heavily exploited during the Roman period, there is much regional variation. The northern part of the Eastern Desert was dense with mining activity and roads that facilitated these mines. At least until AD 132, the quarries and the ports were under the same administration, of the *praefectus Berenicis* (or *praefectus Montis Berenicidis* or *praefectus praesidiorum et montis Berenicidis*).[49]

Nevertheless, there is little evidence of the interaction of the two regions in material remains (the absence of Mons Claudianus granodiorite and the Imperial porphyry from Mons Porphyrites at Red Sea sites is notable). Certainly, decorative building stones are not mentioned in the *Periplus* as an export of Egypt. Coptos would have been the meeting point for these two areas. In this context, the presence of at least two complete Imperial Porphyry vessels in first century AD contexts at Begram, Afghanistan, alongside much Egyptian glass, alabaster and metal finds most likely travelled from the Red Sea ports.[50]

Mining activities closer to the ports, on the same road network and very much within the immediate Berenike hinterland, included the important emerald complex centred at Mons Smaragdus. Within this complex is Sikait, excavated as part of the Berenike project. While these emeralds are the most common gem found at Berenike, they may not have been for export to India as a higher quality emerald was available there, but instead for local consumption or for Africa.[51] Similarly, raw Red Sea red coral may have been for local use, rather than the better quality Mediterranean variety that was a prized export listed in the *Periplus* (*PME* 28, 39, 49, 56).[52]

Another site, 23 km. south-west of Berenike, is the hilltop settlement at Shenshef with its well-preserved architecture and fairly rich Late Roman assemblages suggestive of wealthy inhabitants. Located in a more fertile area than Berenike, with running water throughout the year,[53] Murray suggested it may have been an autumn retreat for the inhabitants from Berenike when the Red Sea would be particularly inhospitable.[54] Tempting though this interpretation is, at present there is no evidence to support seasonal occupation at Berenike. At Mons Claudianus it was possible to verify year-round working of the quarries through dated *ostraca* that were recovered for each month of the year apart from January,[55] but this level of written evidence does not yet exist for the ports.

According to Casson,[56] boats headed for as far south as Rhapta in Africa and for India departed around July. Those from Africa returned in November/December, while around February to April was the most opportune time for returning from India. Shorter journeys, African itineraries that only went as far as Adulis and those to South Arabia as far west as Kane, were much shorter and therefore their departure times more flexible. They could depart in September or earlier, and return from Africa by December; a similar departure date applied to the short South Arabian runs.

These estimates are approximations, and some leeway needs to be factored in when calculating fallow times at the ports. Certainly there were gaps of some months between the loading and unloading of ships, but some periods such as May-June, between the arrival and departure of boats to India, would have been busy. During these months, the population would have increased, with for instance more resident Indian sailors awaiting the return of their ships. That Indians were present on site we can infer from the quantity of Indian pottery found at Berenike and Myos Hormos but beyond the Red Sea only at Vetus Hydreuma, the first road station from Berenike to the Nile, and at Coptos, the Nile port.[57] Graffiti in Indian script, such as Tamil-Brahmi and Prakit-Brahmi, equally attest to the presence of Indians on site.[58] There may have been a slight decline in population between August and October, but even during the less active periods harbour maintenance and other maritime activities would have continued.

Depending on the routes employed, a further consideration for population composition and seasonality is the trade between the Red Sea and Palmyra. Again we know that Palmyrenes lived at Berenike, most forcibly demonstrated by a Palmyrene shrine and inscriptions.[59] They may have arrived by one of two main routes: through the Gulf and around South Arabia, or from the port of Antioch to Alexandria and then to the Red Sea. Although the former is generally favoured in the literature, the second has much to commend it, given the dominant quantities of LR Ampohora 1 with a potential source in the region of Antioch, found at Berenike. Should this be the case, a different, much more flexible, travel itinerary would apply than to Indian Ocean journeys and could mean that some sailings were taking place between the port of Antioch and Alexandria in summer/ autumn.[60]

Road systems that connected Myos Hormos and Berenike with elsewhere in the Eastern Desert are shown on Map 3.1 and included the Via Hadriana and routes from the Nile at Apollinopolis Magna and Coptos to the ports. The Via Hadriana is considered an administrative rather than commercial route,[61] while the Nile roads, particularly the one to Coptos, would have serviced the trade and were populated with way stations. Another route between Berenike and Syene is assumed but has not yet been located on the ground.[62]

It seems that the hinterland of Myos Hormos and Berenike offered little for subsistence or objects that were consumed on site. Instead, we must look at the catchment area, from which both ports were receiving goods. The variety and wealth of material indicates these comprised a range similar to that found in Alexandria, representing a pan-Mediterranean culture that would have arrived via Coptos. For whom was this material intended? Was this exotic range of glass and pottery, much of which can be identified in India, intended for the occupants of the ports or was it merely trade surplus? If surplus, was it legal or contraband?

A characteristic of ports throughout the Roman world is a high proportion of amphorae—the same applies to Eastern Desert sites where vast numbers were needed for provisioning. The composition of the amphora-quay at Myos Hormos, primarily Egyptian AE3 and Italian amphorae, is useful for examining consumption patterns at the port. Although common in Egypt, AE3 amphorae are found with varying frequency at Indian Ocean trade sites but in smaller numbers than Italian wine amphorae, the most common type in India. This pattern indicates that some of the same goods served for both on-site provisions and long-distance trade. Because of the high level of goods circulating in the region, there was a surplus enough to enable a high standard of living for the occupants, whether or not it was legal. In relation to non-Mediterranean imports from the East, Cappers similarly argues that the surplus in pepper enabled a good supply in the port.[63]

Conclusion

Despite their physical remoteness, Myos Hormos and Berenike were closely connected to the Mediterranean and Indian Ocean through people and objects. Alexandria might be seen as the true hinterland, or perhaps more accurately catchment area, of the ports. An overview identifies their port function as the sole justification for their existence on such a large scale and further defines them as transshipment centres rather than self-sufficient towns. This is reinforced by the tax system, for the 25 per cent tax on goods from the East was paid not at the ports—but most likely bonded at Coptos and paid in Alexandria.[64] The hyper-arid environment of the ports and their immediate hinterland is a determinant of their organization and development and contributes to the type of harbour facilities erected, and also the low level of industry in contrast to that seen at many other ports, Indian Ocean as well as Mediterranean. Nevertheless, many aspects of daily life including domestic architecture and the harbour facility itself are strongly Mediterranean and Roman in character, adapted to this specific environment.

Ancient Sources

Periplus Maris Erythraei (PME), see Casson 1989.
Pliny *NH* = Pliny the Elder, *Natural History* vol. 2, tr. H. Rackham 1961 (repr.), London.
Strabo *Geography Books 15–16* = Strabo, *Geography* vol. 7, tr. H.L. Jones 1995 (repr.), London.
Strabo *Geography Book 17* = Strabo, *Geography* vol. 8, trs. H.L. Jones 1967 (repr.), London.

Notes

1. My role in excavations at Myos Hormos and Berenike is as pottery specialist. I owe a debt to the other specialists from these projects and to the site directors for their invitation to work on the material from Myos Hormos (David Peacock and Lucy Blue) and Berenike (Steve Sidebotham, Willeke Wendrich

and Iwona Zych). Steve Sidebotham provided me with numerous images for the Kolkata presentation; Valerie Maxfield, Marijke van der Veen and Julian Whitewright kindly discussed aspects of the paper with me and Lucy Blue commented on an earlier draft. My warmest thanks go to all of them.

2. Casson 1989.
3. Strabo Geography 16.4.5.
4. Pliny NH 6.168.
5. Strabo Geography 17.1.45.
6. Pliny NH 6.104.
7. Whitewright 2007: 85–7.
8. Ibid.
9. Cappers 2006: 155.
10. Ibid., pp. 21, 155; Sidebotham et al. 2008: 25–6.
11. Sidebotham has discussed water in detail in Chapter 7 (pp. 87–124) of his 2011 book.
12. Maxfield 2001: 162.
13. Sidebotham et al. 2008: 311.
14. Peacock and Blue 2006: 177 and fig. 2.1.
15. Sidebotham and Zych 2010: 11, citing R.S. Bagnall and R. Ast pers. comm.
16. Cappers 2006: 158–62, table 6.3.
17. van der Veen 2011: 234, table 6.2.
18. Cappers 2006: 162.
19. Sidebotham et al. 2004: 14–5.
20. Sidebotham et al. 2008: 247; Sidebotham 2011: 68.
21. Whitcomb and Johnson 1982: 12.
22. Blue 2006, see especially fig. 4.13 for a reconstruction of the Roman waterfront.
23. Empereur and Picon 1998: 177, fig. 4.
24. Bernal et al. 2005, figs. 7 and 8.
25. Sidebotham 2011: 60–1.
26. Sidebotham and Zych 2011: 3.
27. Sidebotham 2002: 220–1
28. Sidebotham et al. 2008: 243–4.
29. Copeland 2006.
30. Thomas and Masser 2006: 132–3, fig. 7.20.
31. Sidebotham 2011: 57, 268.
32. Copeland 2006: 122.
33. Sidebotham et al. 2008, pl. 10.6 for a reconstruction.
34. Sidebotham 2011: 59.
35. Sidebotham et al. 2008: 135.
36. Sidebotham and Zych 2011: 14.
37. Sidebotham and Zych 2010: 15–17, 19; Sidebotham 2011: 266.
38. Salles and Sedov 2010: 87–122, esp. pp. 120–1; Bowerstock 2010: 396–6.
39. Fournet 2000: 208.
40. Alston and Alston 1997, table 1.
41. Cuvigny 2005: 334.

42. Sidebotham (2011: 81) mentions glass unguent bottles and hydraulic bricks from Berenike.
43. Peacock and Blue 2006: 176.
44. Sidebotham 2011: 205; see Hense 1998, fig. 9.2.
45. S. Sidebotham, pers. comm.
46. Sidebotham and Zych 2010: 13.
47. Cherian 2010.
48. Tomber 2004.
49. The role of this individual and more generally the organisation of the Eastern Desert are clearly outlined by Maxfield 2001, esp. pp. 147–50. She also cites an alternative viewpoint that continues the prefect of Berenike into the third century.
50. Mehendale 2011 (figs.103-4 for porphyry: p. 168–85; p. 197–209 for other potential objects); Whitehouse 1989.
51. Wendrich et al. 2003: 57–8.
52. Casson 1989: 42; Sidebotham 2011: 238–9.
53. Cappers 2006: 23.
54. Sidebotham (2011: 276), citing Murray (1926: 167).
55. Maxfield 2001: 157.
56. Casson 1989: 15, 285–91.
57. Tomber 2008: 74–5.
58. Tomber et al. 2011; Tomber (2008: 73–4) for a summary, citing Mahedevan 1996; Salomon 1991.
59. Sidebotham 2011: 64–6; 260; Sidebotham and Wendrich 1998: 93–4.
60. J. Whitewright, pers. comm.
61. Sidebotham et al. in preparation.
62. Sidebotham 2011: 3.
63. Cappers 2006: 165.
64. Rathbone 2000: 43.

References

Alston, R. and Alston, R.D. (1997), 'Urbanism and the urban community in Roman Egypt', *Journal of Egyptian Archaeology*, vol. 83, pp. 199–216.

Bernal, D., Sáez, A.M., Montero, R., Díaz, J.J., Sáez, A., Moreno, D. and Toboso, E. (2005), 'Instalaciones fluvio-marítimas de drenaje con ánforas romanas: a propósito del embarcadero Flavio del caño Sancti Petri (San Fernando, Cádiz)', *SPAL Revista de Prehistoria y Arqueologia*, vol. 14, pp. 179–230.

Blue, L. (2006), 'The sedimentary history of the harbour area', in *Myos Hormos— Quseir al-Qadim. Roman and Islamic Ports on the Red Sea. Survey and Excavations 1999-2003*, D. Peacock and L. Blue, eds., Oxford: Oxbow, pp. 43–61.

Bowersock, G.W. (2010), 'The new Greek inscription from South Yemen', in *Qāniʾ: le port antique du Hadramawt entre la Méditerranée, l'Afrique et l'Inde: fouilles russes 1972, 1985–89, 1991, 1993–94. Preliminary reports of the*

Russian Archaeological Mission to the Republic of Yemen, J.-F. Salles and A. Sedov, eds., Indicopleustoi 6. Turnhout: Brepols, pp. 393–6.

Cappers, R.T.J. (2006), *Roman Foodprints at Berenike. Archaeobotanical Evidence of Subsistence and Trade in the Eastern Desert of Egypt*, Cotsen Institute of Archaeology Monograph 55. Los Angeles: Cotsen Institute of Archaeology.

Casson, L. (1989), *The* Periplus Maris Erythraei. *Text with Introduction, Translation and Commentary*, Princeton: Princeton University Press.

Cherian, P.J. (2010), 'The tales that potsherds tell at Pattanam', *The Hindu*, 18 June 2010, http://www.thehindu.com/arts/history-and-culture/article472072, accessed on 21 August 2011.

Copeland, P. (2006), 'Trench 2B', *Myos Hormos – Quseir al-Qadim. Roman and Islamic Ports on the Red Sea. Survey and Excavations 1999–2003*, in D. Peacock and L. Blue, eds., Oxford: Oxbow, pp. 116–27.

Cuvigny, H. (2005), 'L'organigramme du personnel d'une carrière impériale d'après un ostracon du Mons Claudianus', *Chiron*, vol. 35, pp. 309–53.

Empereur, J.-Y. and Picon, M. (1998) 'Les ateliers d'amphores du Lac Mariout', in *Commerce et artisanat dans l'Alexandrie hellénistique et romaine*, J.-Y. Empereur, ed., Actes de la Table Ronde organisée par le CNRS, le Laboratoire de Céramologie de Lyon et l'EFA, Athènes, 10-12 Octobre 1988, *Bulletin de Correspondance Hellénique Suppl* 33. Athènes: École Française d'Athènes, pp. 75–91.

Fournet, J.-L. (2000), 'Coptos dans l'Antiquité tardive (fin IIIe–VIIe siècle)', in *Coptos. L'Égypte antique aux portes du désert. Lyon, musée des Beaux-Arts 3 février – 7 mai 2000*. Paris: Réunion des Musées Nationaux, pp. 196–215.

Hense, A.M. (1998), 'The metal finds', in *Berenike 1996. Report of the Excavations at Berenike (Egyptian Red Sea Coast) and the Survey of the Eastern Desert*, S.E. Sidebotham and W.Z. Wendrich, eds., Leiden: Centre of Non-Western Studies, pp. 199–220.

Mahadevan, I. (1996), 'Tamil-Brāhmi graffito', *Berenike 1995. Preliminary Report of the Excavations at Berenike (Egyptian Red Sea Coast) and the Survey of the Eastern Desert*, in S.E. Sidebotham and W.Z. Wendrich, eds., Leiden: Centre of Non-Western Studies, pp. 206–8.

Maxfield, V.A. (2001), 'Stone quarrying in the Eastern Desert, with particular reference to Mons Claudianus and Mons Porphyrites', in *Economies beyond Agriculture in the Roman World*, D.J. Mattingly and J. Salmon, eds., London: Routledge, pp. 143–70.

Mehendale, S. (2011), 'Begram catalogue', in *Afghanistan: Crossroads of the Ancient World*, F. Hiebert and P. Cambon, eds., London: British Museum Press, pp. 162–209.

Murray, G.W. (1926), 'Notes on the ruins of Hitân Shenshef, near Berenice', *Journal of Egyptian Archaeology*, vol. 12, pp. 166–7.

Peacock, D. and Blue L., eds., (2006), *Myos Hormos—Quseir al-Qadim. Roman and Islamic Ports on the Red Sea: Survey and Excavations 1999–2003*, Oxford: Oxbow.

Rathbone, D. (2000), 'The "Muziris" papyrus (SB XVIII 13167): financing Roman trade with India', in *Alexandrian Studies 2 in Honour of Mostafa el Abbadi, Bulletin de la Société Archéologique d'Alexandrie*, vol. 46, pp. 39–50.

Salomon, R. (1991) 'Epigraphic remains of Indian traders in Egypt', *Journal of the American Oriental Society*, vol. 3, no. 4, pp. 731–6.

Salles, J.-F. and Sedov, A.V., eds., (2010), *Qāni' : le port antique du Hadramawt entre la Méditerranée, l'Afrique et l'Inde : fouilles russes 1972, 1985-89, 1991, 1993-94. Preliminary reports of the Russian Archaeological Mission to the Republic of Yemen*, Indicopleustoi 6. Turnhout: Brepols.

Sidebotham, S.E. (2002), 'Late Roman Berenike', *Journal of the American Research Center in Egypt*, vol. 39, pp. 217–40.

——— (2011), *Berenike and the Ancient Maritime Spice Route*, Los Angeles: University of California Press.

Sidebotham, S.E. and Wendrich, W.Z. (1998), 'Berenike: archaeological fieldwork at a Ptolemaic-Roman port on the Red Sea coast of Egypt: 1994-1998', *Sahara*, vol. 10, pp. 85–96.

Sidebotham, S.E. and Zych, I (2010), 'Berenike: archaeological fieldwork at a Ptolemaic-Roman port on the Red Sea coast of Egypt 2008-2010', *Sahara*, vol. 21, pp. 7–26.

——— (2011), 'Berenike (Egypt)', *PCMA Newsletter 2011*http://www.pcma.uw.edu.pl/index.php?id=723&L=2, accessed on 10 July 2011.

Sidebotham, S.E., Nowens, H.M., Hense, A.M. and Harrell, J.A. (2004), 'Preliminary report on archaeological fieldwork at Sikait (Eastern Desert of Egypt), and environs: 2002-2003', *Sahara*, vol. 15, pp. 7–30.

Sidebotham, S.E., Hense, M. and Nowens, H.M. (2008), *The Red Land. The Illustrated Archaeology of Egypt's Eastern Desert*, Cairo: The American University in Cairo Press.

Sidebotham, S.E., Zitterkopf, R.E. and Tomber, R. (forthcoming), 'Survey of the Via Hadriana: final report'.

Thomas, R. and Masser, P. (2006), 'Trench 8', in *Myos Hormos—Quseir al-Qadim. Roman and Islamic Ports on the Red Sea. Survey and Excavations 1999–2003*, D. Peacock and L. Blue, eds., Oxford: Oxbow, pp. 127–40.

Tomber, R. (2004), 'Amphorae from the Red Sea and their contribution to the interpretation of late Roman trade beyond the Empire', in *Transport Amphorae and Trade in the Eastern Mediterranean. Acts of the International Colloquium at the Danish Institute at Athens, September 26–29, 2002*, J. Eiring and J. Lund, eds., Monographs of the Danish Institute at Athens 5. Aahrus: Aahrus University Press, pp. 393–402.

——— (2008), *Indo-Roman Trade: from Pots to Pepper*, London: Duckworth.

Tomber, R. with Graf, D. and Healey, J.F. and contributions by Römer-Strehl, C. and Majcherek, G. (2011), 'Pots with writing', in *Quseir al-Qadim 1999-2003. Vol 2. The Finds*, D. Peacock and L. Blue, eds., University of Southampton Series in Archaeology 6.2, BAR International Series Oxford: Archaeopress, pp. 5-10.

van der Veen, M. (2011), *Consumption, Trade and Innovation. Exploring the Botanical Remains from the Roman and Islamic Ports at Quseir al-Qadim,*

Egypt, Journal of African Archaeology Monograph Series vol. 6. Frankfurt a. M.: Africa Magna Verlag.

Wendrich, W.Z., Tomber, R., Sidebotham, S.E., Harrell, J.A., Cappers, R.T.S. and Bagnall, R.S. (2003), 'Berenike crossroads: the integration of information', *Journal of the Social and Economic History of the Orient*, vol. 46, no. 1, pp. 46–87.

Whitcomb, D.S. and Johnson, J.H. (1982), *Quseir al-Qadim 1980. Preliminary Report*, American Research Center in Egypt Report 7. Malibu: Undena Publications.

Whitehouse, D. (1989), 'Begram, the *Periplus* and Gandharan art', *Journal of Roman Archaeology*, vol. 2, pp. 93–100.

Whitewright, J. (2007), 'How fast is fast? Technology, trade and speed under sail in the Roman Red Sea', in *Natural Resources and Cultural Connections of the Red Sea. Proceedings of the Red Sea Project* 3, J.C.M. Starkey, P. Starkey and T. Wilkinson, eds., BAR International Series 1661, Oxford: Archaeopress, pp. 77–87.

CHAPTER 4

Al-Shihr, an Islamic Harbour of Yemen on the Indian Ocean (AD 780–2007)

Claire Hardy-Guilbert

A l-Shihr is located on the southern coast of the Arabian peninsula, in Yemen, 700 km. east of Aden and 60 km. east of Mukallâ, seat of the Hadramawt Governorate. Today, it remains an active fishing harbour (Map 4.1).

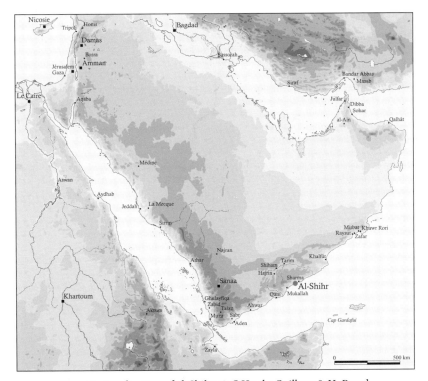

Map 4.1: Localization of al-Shihr. © C.Hardy-Guilbert & H. Renel.

Fig. 4.1: General plan of the city of al-Shihr with its districts. © N.Férault de Falandre & C.Hardy-Guilbert.

Located in the middle of a coastal plain, al-Shihr is crossed by the wadi Sam'ûn to the west and lined by the wadi Arâf and wadi Hard to the east, descending from the Hadramawt mountains. The history of the site begins in the pre-Islamic period, under the name al-As'â on a south Arabian inscription of AD 507.[1] It is referred to together with four other marketplaces, al-Mushaqqar/Hajar (al-Hasâ/Bahrayn), Suhâr (Oman), Aden and San'â' (Yemen) that are linked with pre-Islamic Mekka from the end of the sixth to the beginning of the seventh century AD.[2]

Today, the ancient city (120 ha.) preserves the remains of the Qu'aytî sultanate of the nineteenth century. The area comprises seven districts, called *hâfa*, surrounded by a city wall with nine of the original thirty-nine towers and two main gates: Bâb al-Aydarus, the northern gate, and Bâb al-Khor, the gate to the West. In 2002, it had *intra muros* 32 mosques that were still active and some large houses and monuments in ruins (Fig. 4.1). The al-Qariya Great Mosque is the Friday mosque; the al-Aydarus Mosque, Bâharun Mosque, Abû Baker Mosque, 'Abdullah Bel-Hadj Mosque, Bin 'Attiq Mosque, Shaykh S'ad Mosque and Isma'il Mosque are also important mosques in the city. Near the mosques, it is common to find a mausoleum covered with a *qubba*. The two biggest monuments in the heart of the city are Husn Bin 'Ayyâsh, the administrative fortress of the Qu'aytî sultanate built with stone, and Dâr Nâsir, the Qu'aytî palace, built with mud-brick, destroyed in 2008 (Plate 4.1). Several ruins of what were once large houses of merchants can be seen in the Bâ 'awin and Bâghrid areas even now.

Besides the abundant written documentation—more than 20 ancient Arabian writers[3] mentioned the city, as for example Ibn Hawqal in the

Plate 4.1: Dâr Nasir, the Qu'aytî palace (nineteenth century). © C.Hardy-Guilbert.

tenth century who named it *qasaba*, which means capital city, of Mahra province,[4] some graphic documents have to be quoted.

1. The map of the city under the Rasûlids (1229–1454) from *Irtifâ' al-dawla al-mu'ayaddiyya*, the anonymous manuscript of al-Malik al-Mu'ayyad Dâ'hûd bin Yûsuf al-Muzaffar,[5] the fourth sultan of the Rasûlid dynasty (1296–1321) who was earlier (1295) appointed *muqta'* of the harbour of al-Shihr. On this map is written, 'This is the representation of al-Shihr and its territories (*a'mâl*)', 'al-Shihr, its name is Las'â'. A circular city wall is drawn, with four gates located at the cardinal points, Bâb al-Sâhil, Gate of the Port, to the south, Bâb Hadramawt, to the north, Bâb Sam'ûn (name of the wâdî) to the west and Bâb Rayda to the east. Even if this map is a sketch, it proves that a wall surrounded the city as early as the thirteenth century.

The Hadramawt mountains and the main places Tarîm, Shibâm, al-Hajrayn and Qabr al-Nabî Hûd, the famous place of the pilgrimage to the tomb of the prophet Hûd, the most important prophet of Hadramawt, are also mentioned. The names of these cities written on this map indicate the importance of al-Shihr and the links between the coast and the hinterland of Hadramawt.

2. Many Portuguese maps use the name Xer, Xaer, Xaher, Xael for 'al-Shihr', such as the Miller Atlas dated 1519 where 'Xer' is written on the coast of 'Arabia Felix'.[6] Like Aden, al-Shihr was coveted by the Portuguese who unsuccessfully tried to take hold of it twice in 1522 and 1535.[7] They created six martyrs who have a grave still venerated in al-Shihr, in the Bâ'awîn quarter.

3. In 1835–9, the British Commandant S.B. Haines drew the anchorage of al-Shihr.[8] It was a modest agglomeration with a castle, the residence of the governor and two customhouses (old and new) to the seaward of the castle. However, this maritime map clearly shows the large high coral platform under the sea in front of it. Large boats had to stay 500 m. off. This was the case until 2005.

The Archaeological Results

Archaeological and architectural research was conducted on the site from 1996 to 2002 and in 2007.[9] The archaeological site, a tell of 1 ha. with 6 m. of archaeological levels (14°45'11"N, 49°36'19"E), is located in the oldest part, al-Qariya, 60 m. from the shoreline. We also dug in the wâdî Sam'ûn and to the east (Shihr-East), outside the Qu'aytî city wall searching for pre-Islamic remains. In the al-Qariya quarter, we opened 450 sq. m. and 7 deep soundings to the virgin soil.

Fifteen levels of occupation were identified which can be distributed into ten phases:

- The first occupation or phase one was only recovered inside the deep soundings, on a level of sand. It consists of clay ovens, deposits of ash, food, and common pottery, including Indian cooking pots, which date this first phase to the end of the eighth century.
- Phase two consists of three levels of beaten earth floors associated with imported ceramics from Iraq and Iran: a Samarran assemblage Sasanian-Islamic blue-green glazed jars, *eggshell* jugs, white glazed bowls and cobalt blue on white glazed bowls, lustre wares, which can be dated from the ninth to the first half of the tenth century (Plate 4.3).
- In phase three, large mud-brick buildings faced with stone blocks were erected to the south and east and were enlarged in a sub-phase. *Hatched sgraffiato* is associated with African pottery and white Chinese pottery, all dated to the eleventh century (Plate 4.2). This shows that the city was flourishing at this time. This period corresponds to the development of the nearby harbour of Sharma.[10]
- In phase four, the whole settlement was destroyed and filled in during the latter half of the twelfth century or the beginning of the thirteenth century.
- In phase five, an open air platform was built, on which huts were erected, as indicated by numerous post-holes. Many pits and ovens containing

Plate 4.2: Excavations in al-Qariyah, ancient quarter of al-Shihr: eastern sector, tenth-eleventh century buildings. © C.Hardy-Guilbert.

deposits of ash and fish bones were found. These structures were included inside a thick layer of ash, clearly visible throughout the tell. *Mustard ware* and *Late sgraffiato* associated with Longquan stoneware were found, dateable to the thirteenth-fourteenth century. It was the beginning of the Rasûlid sultanate.

These archaeological data testify to a radical change in the nature of the occupation and suggest an economic activity based on fishing during the latter half of the thirteenth to the first half of the fourteenth century.

- During phase six, at the beginning of the fifteenth century, the whole area was built over once more with mud-brick and stone houses. The floors were remade and continued to be in use until the sixteenth century. Other types of Tihamah ceramics (Haysi cups and dishes, blue Tihama bowls, monochrome green wares) replaced *Mustard ware,*[11] associated with blue and white Chinese porcelain.

- The sixteenth century was witness to phase seven, wherein a level of mud-brick houses was built with wall foundations of stone. A glass workshop with its hearth and crucibles belongs to this phase.

- In phase eight, a part of the site was left behind but mud-brick dwelling rooms were built in the southern area associated with Yemenite ceramics of the Ottoman period and Persian cups in fritware, imitating Chinese porcelain.

- At the end of eighteenth or in the nineteenth century, during phase nine, family stone houses stood atop the tell. They were already demolished when the site was discovered in 1995; a surface deposit, 1 m. thick, cut into by rubbish pits down to the level of phase eight, belongs to phase nine.

- In phase ten (twentieth century) a part of the site was covered with a platform for drying fish, made of a thick layer of mud and fish oil above a bed of pebbles. In 1995–6, a cold store of fish was built there.

In al-Shihr, the Islamic occupation, located 500 m. from the shoreline, covers twelve centuries (780–2000) and the dating of every phase of the ten levels is mainly achieved through the local and imported pottery.

The City's Main Resources

The main natural resources of the city and its market are well documented in the texts. They consist of:

- Fish which was exported as far as Basra as we learn from Al-Muqaddasî in his *Ahsan al-tâqâsim fi marifat al-aqâlîm* written about 985.[12] Marco

Polo in the thirteenth century AD describes the sea around al-Shihr as full of large fish. During excavations of the Phase 5 levels (AD 1250–1350), a great quantity of fish remains was recovered, some of them belonging to the order *Cetacea*. The biggest vertebra measured 0.21 m. in diameter. Other fish bones (worked vertebras), used as gaming pieces, were identified by J. Desse as coming from a shark 6 m. long. Ibn Hawqal and Marco Polo also mention the consumption of small fish—a kind of sardine—both by goats and camels and by humans. This remains true even today. Fishing in this area is an increasingly important activity. Since 1996, many cold stores have been built and export, mainly of tuna, reaches as far as Brittany in France.

- Incense, *lubân* in Arabic, is mentioned by twelve Arabian writers, from the eighth century, as a valuable product of al-Shihr.[13] The city is often referred to as 'Shihr of frankincense' in the *Kitâb 'ajâ'ib al-Hind* (c.AD 950).[14] Though incense itself was not recovered in the excavations, 60 clay incense-burners were found associated with almost all the levels and follow (after the 2007 typology) nine types. The earliest one is square, four-legged, decorated with rows of incised triangles whose origin and inspiration go back to the pre-Islamic south Arabian stone incense-burners of Shabwa, Raybûn and Timna.[15] Together, the textual and archaeological data suggest that al-Shihr replaced Qâni', the famous pre-Islamic frankincense emporium of Hadramawt which declined at the beginning of the seventh century.

- Amber and grey amber which was called '*anbar shihri*' is quoted by Sulaymân the merchant,[16] Abû Zayd al-Hasân,[17] 'Umâra al-Hakamî,[18] al-Mas'ûdî[19] et Yâkût al-Rûmî.[20] It was used as perfume and for medicinal purposes.

- Dates are quoted in the anonymous manuscript, *Nûr al-ma'ârif*, a Rasûlid account book (c.AD 1290–5), in the list of products of al-Shihr exported towards Aden, with their price: one dinar, two *qîrât* and two pennies for one *bâhar*, brokerage fees: one *qîrât*, galleys fees: two *qîrât* and three pennies.[21] Marco Polo mentioned the abundant palm trees in its area and the dates as food for the inhabitants of al-Shihr. Later, in the chronicle text of Shanbal (1468–1514), *Ta'rîkh Shanbal*, dates and palm trees in the country of al-Shihr were referred to several times.[22]

Besides, different goods were produced in the city and others were traded in its seaport, including spices, textiles, clothes, ceramics, glass, and silver. Fabrics and foodstuffs exported from al-Shihr are mentioned by the Rasûlid texts like *Nûr al-ma'ârif, Irtifâ' al-dawla al-mu'ayyadiyya*, and *Mulakhkhas al-fitan*.

Importance of al-Shihr as a Port in the
Indian Ocean attested by Imported Ceramics

From the Persian Gulf (from the harbours of Basra or Siraf) a Samarran assemblage (ninth century) reached al-Shihr: blue-green glazed Sasanian-Islamic jars with barbotine decoration (Plate 4.3: 1, 2) and unglazed *eggshell* jugs (Plate 4.3: 2, 3, 5) both made in Mesopotamia were recovered at al-Shihr. Similar pieces were found in Samarra, Susa, Siraf, and Basra. Several samples of a Yemeni *eggshell* type from Zabîd, in the western part of Yemen, were found in al-Shihr. It is a very fine brown ware, imitating the shape of the Mesopotamian type: a carinated jug with a knob handle. Monochrome white glazed bowls and white glazed bowls with cobalt blue decoration (Plate 4.3: 6, 7, 8, 10) and some (14 pieces) with metallic lustre from Iran (Siraf) or Iraq (Basra) (Plate 4.3: 12). *Hatched sgraffiato* bowls with floral or calligraphic motives were recovered, associated with African cooking pots found in the eleventh century levels.[23] This Islamic ceramic type circulated from southern Iran (Siraf, Qalât-I Jamshid, Tîz, Bushir)[24] as far as Kilwa, Gedi and Shanga (eastern Africa) or Lobu Tua near Barus (Malaysia).

Later (fourteenth-fifteenth centuries) came from Iran dishes and bowls in fritware that imitated the Chinese Blue and White porcelain and many unglazed jugs made in a thin clay (new *eggshell*) incised, combed, with floral, geometric or epigraphic patterns came from Iran; from Minab near Ormuz on the southern coast of Iran, moulded ceramics belonging to the fifteenth century (pilgrim flasks and jugs). Imported from Khunj in Iran some monochrome purple-grey and blue-green bowls or jugs (Khunj type), a glazed production of the sixteenth-seventeenth century, testify that the contacts with the Persian Gulf continued until that period.

From China, the earliest ceramic found is a Tang pottery bowl in very pale brown stoneware, decorated with a flower design painted on the interior in iron-brown and copper-green with a yellow or light grey glaze. It is fluted (4 external grooves) with an unglazed lower part on the outside and comes from the kilns of Changsha (in the Hunan province). This discovery is to be connected with the mention of al-Shihr as 'Shuego', as a port on a maritime road from Canton (Guangzhou), in the *Tang Shu*, the Official History of the Tang, written around the end of the eighth or in the beginning of the ninth century. The best comparison is a bowl with the same floral decoration excavated in the Belitung cargo, shipwrecked in the West Java Sea *c.*AD 826 (after the equivalent date inscribed on another Changsha bowl also found in the cargo).[25] Many bowls of green glazed stoneware (celadons) from the workshops of Longquan in the

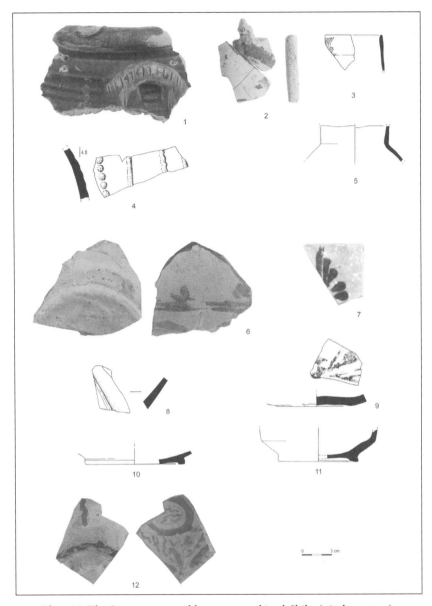

Plate 4.3: The Samarran assemblage excavated in al-Shihr (ninth century).
© C.Hardy-Guilbert.

1. SHR02 3016.1: the neck of a jar with handle under the rim in pale yellow ware (2.5Y 8/4); the interior and exterior covered by an alcaline blue-green glaze (Sasanian-Islamic type).

2. SHR97 2031.2: the neck and knob handle and handle of an *eggshell* jug in fine white ware (2.5Y 8/2) with a very pale brown slip (10YR 8/3).

3. SHR97 2031.1: the rim of an *eggshell* jug in fine white ware (5Y 8/1) with a combed decoration.

4. SHR96 1000: the fragment of wall of a jar in pale yellow ware (2.5Y 8/2) with pearls and curved lines (barbotine decoration) under alcaline turquoise glaze (Sasanian-Islamic type).
5. SHR96 1000.4: the neck and shoulder of an *eggshell* jug, in fine white ware (5Y 8/1).
6. SHR07 3042.2: the base of a bowl in fine pale yellow ware (2.5Y 8/4); the interior is painted in imitating koufic letters in cobalt blue on opaque white glaze.
7. SHR02 2999.2: the rim of a bowl in fine pale yellow ware (5Y 8/3) with a white glaze decorated with a cobalt blue palmette.
8. SHR00 2676.7: the fragment of a dish in white ware (2.5Y 8/2), the interior is ribbed under an opaque white glaze, imitating a porcelain dish.
9. SHR00 2654.1: the base of a dish in fine reddish yellow ware (7.5YR 6/6), the interior decorated with manganese ray lines on white glaze.
10. SHR00 2678.1: the base of a dish in fine very pale brown ware (10YR 8/3), under opaque white glaze.
11. SHR96 2000.Ω: a carinated jug in fine very pale brown ware (10YR 8/3), the interior and exterior is covered with a metallic grey glaze.
12. SHR07 3042.4: the base of a bowl in fine white ware (2.5Y 8/2), the interior and exterior decorated with an olive-green design painted in lustre on a white ground.

Zhejiang province were associated with the *Mustard ware* bowls during the fourteenth century. During this period too, bowls of Dehua in the Fujian province were imported. These include grayish stoneware covered with a white glaze decorated with moulded lotus leaves patterns on the exterior. These vessels were imported as crockery whereas the Far Eastern stoneware jars with a brown glaze contained goods such as perfume, according to the label written (in Chinese characters) on one of the jars.[26]

Ceramic exportations from China lasted until the nineteenth century. Another example of Blue and White porcelain of the Ming period is a dish with a very fine body and horizontal rim that can be compared to a dish of the Wanli period dated *c.*1600–19 from Anastacio Gonçalves Museum at Lisbon.[27] Both are painted with peach patterns in panels. In Hadramawt, the palaces of the Qu'aytî and Qahtânid sultans in Shibâm, Sai'un, and Tarîm were decorated with bowls in Blue and White Chinese porcelain dated to the eighteenth-nineteenth centuries, and which arrived in Yemen, landing at al-Shihr. The Far Eastern ware corpus is 3 per cent of the total excavated ceramics.

The proof of contact with eastern Africa via the Indian Ocean is attested by the presence of African pottery of Tana type also called of 'Swahili tradition' discovered in the eleventh century levels.[28] Parallels for this pottery are provided by similar items exhumed from key sites of the eastern Africa coast: Kilwa (Tanzania) excavated by Chittick, Gedi (Kenya) by Kirkman and Pradines, and Shanga (Kenya) by Horton.[29]

Contact between India and al-Shihr are testified by imported ceramics as early as the first Islamic occupation. It is an unglazed but polished ceramic with carinated shape and grooves on the lip, mainly cooking pots and lids. Three main types of Indian wares could be distinguished:

1. With a black core and the exterior decorated with a polished black slip (Plate 4.4: 7, 8),
2. In dark brown to reddish brown ware, with the exterior decorated with a polished reddish brown slip (Plate 4.4: 12, 1, 2, 3, 9, 11, 13), and
3. In reddish brown ware and black painted on a polished red slip (Plate 4.4: 5, 6).

Even if these importations continued until the seventeenth century, amounting to 8 per cent of the ceramic assemblage, we cannot say with precision from where they came and by which Indian workshops they were produced.[30]

It is the same case for the unique terracotta male figurine with a *scimitar* (*shamshîr*) on his knees, probably coming from India (Plate 4.5). In the Karnataka province, at Somanathapura, situated on the left bank of the Kauveri River, the Keshava Temple was built in AD 1268. The fourth frieze from the base of the façade depicts similar seated figures carved in stone. The carnelian workshops in Ratanpur and Khambhat (Cambay) are well known. Although the same mineral resources are present in central Yemen, they are difficult to exploit. The carnelian beads recovered in al-Shihr might come from Gujarat.

Another link with India include the glass bangles. A corpus of 500 fragments of bangles studied by S. Boulogne was recovered at al-Shihr.[31] Even if some workshops are known in Yemen, especially at Kawd am Sailah near Aden, some of the glass bangles could be from India, very famous for this handicraft product, perhaps from Kholâpur, from which there are parallels.[32]

These links are mentioned by several texts. *The Book of Wonders of India, al-Kitab 'aja'ib al-Hind*, gives the earliest reference to travels between our harbour and South Asia by mentioning a crossing that lasted 41 days from Kalah (that is to say the port of Keda in Burma) to 'Shihr of the Frankincense', in 929.[33] Later, a Rasûlid manuscript, *Nûr al-Ma'ârif*,[34] at the end of the thirteenth century, quotes that the Cholas transport by sea, silver in larger amounts from China to Zafâr and Shihr than to Aden.[35] At the same time, Marco Polo writes about Shihr: 'This city has a very good port, because, I tell you that for real, many boats and many merchants come there from India with many goods.' Finally in the seventeenth century, Sulaymân al-Mahrî, the pilot from al-Shihr, described a maritime road between al-Shihr and Diu in Gujarat.

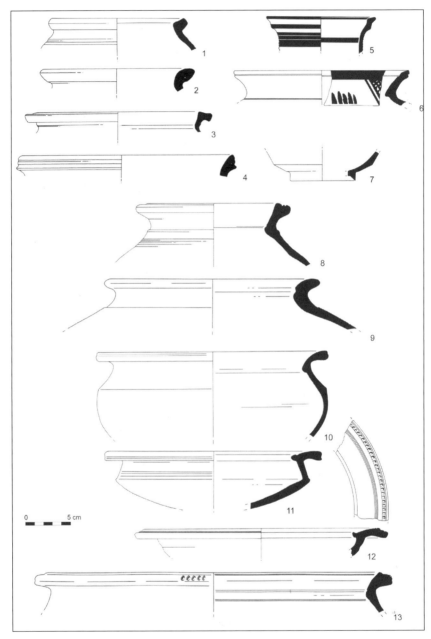

Plate 4.4: The Indian pottery excavated in al-Shihr (1-4: eighth-eleventh centuries; 5-12: twelfth-seventeenth centuries). © C. Hardy-Guilbert.

1. SHR00 2737.2: the neck of a jar with an everted rim, in reddish brown core (5YR 5/4), the interior and exterior covered with a polished pink slip (5YR 7/3).
2. SHR00 2738.3-4: the everted rim of a jar with a rolled lip in red core (2.5YR 4/6); the interior and exterior covered with a polished light red slip (2.5YR 4/6).

3. SHR00 2766.1: the neck of a cooking-pot with a horizontal lip, in light reddish brown core (10YR 6/4) and in dark reddish grey for the body (10YR 4/1); the interior and exterior covered with a polished yellowish red slip (5YR 4/6).

4. SHR00 2731.2: the everted rim of a cooking pot, in reddish brown core (5YR 5/3), the interior covered with a polished brown slip (10YR 5/3); the exterior with a polished dark greyish brown slip (10YR 4/2).

5. SHR96 2010: the neck of a jar in reddish-brown ware (5YR 5/3) with black painting on a red slip.

6. SHR99 2164: the neck of a cooking pot in very dark core (10YR 3/2) and a light red ware towards the surface (2.5YR 6/8), covered with red paint (10R 4/8) and with black painted lines on a reddish yellow slip (5YR 7/6).

7. SHR97 2123.4-5: the bottom of a careened cooking-pot in a very dark grey ware (2.5YR N3/), the interior and exterior covered with a polished black slip (2.5YR N2.5/).

8. SHR00 2777.1-2: the neck of a jar with a black core (2.5YR N2.5/) dark greyish towards the surface (10YR 4/2), the exterior covered with a polished black slip (7.5YR N2/).

9. SHR99 2459.7: the neck of a jar or cooking pot in light red ware (2.5YR 6/6).

10. SHR99 2459.5: a carinated cooking pot in red ware (2.5YR 4/6) covered with a polished reddish-brown slip (2.5YR 5/4).

11. SHR99 2459.6: a carinated cooking pot with a convex bottom, in red ware (2.5YR 4/6), covered with a light red slip (2.5YR 6/6).

12. SHR96 1000.45: a lid in dark brown ware (7.5YR 3/2) covered with a polished light red slip (2.5YR 6/6) and with a roulette decoration on the raised rim.

13. SHR99 2214.1: a large basin or cooking pot in reddish brown ware (5YR 5/3) covered with a red slip (2.5YR 4/6) and with a roulette decoration on the rim.

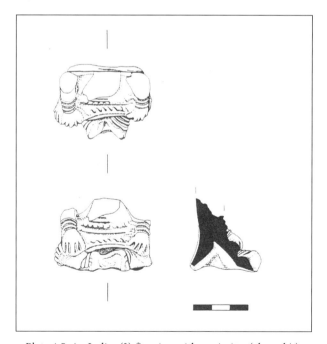

Plate 4.5: An Indian(?) figurine with a *scimitar* (*shamshîr*),
fifteenth century © S. Vatteoni.

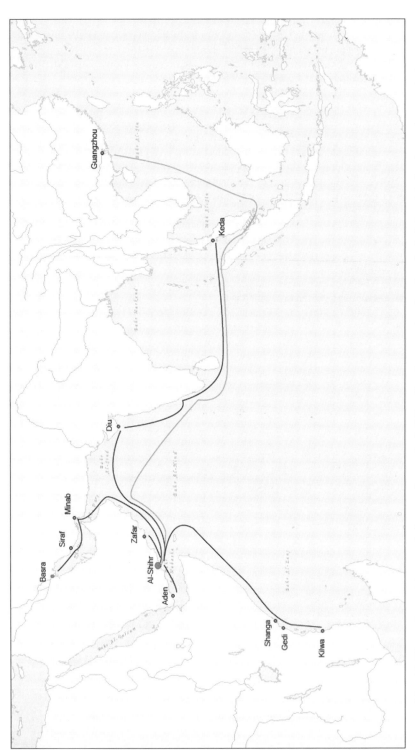

Map 4.2: The trade maritime roads from and towards al-Shihr after the textual and archaeological data (ninth–sixteenth centuries).
© C. Hardy-Guilbert & H. Renel.

Conclusion

Altogether textual and archaeological data provide evidence that al-Shihr was an international port connected with the Persian Gulf, South Asia and Far East as early as the middle of the ninth century. Along the southern Arabian coast, it was a permanent stopping point for transoceanic trade from this time to the nineteenth century, like Aden and Zafâr. In the Rasûlid period, it became a major centre for continental and intercontinental trade (Map 4.2).

Among the commodities, since the beginning, frankincense was the most significant. The decline of Qâniʾ, the pre-Islamic emporium at the beginning of the sixth century involved here the use and trade of the frankincense as an extension of one of the main customs in Arabia Felix.

Today, the history of al-Shihr continues: a 2007 Google map shows its urban evolution away from the old city, to the north, to the west where the Dufayqa village has been included. A new port has been built since 2005, just in front of the archaeological site. It provides very efficient protection and large boats henceforth can be moored inside the harbour. However, the location of the archaeological site is increasingly endangered, as economic development is often a threat to heritage.

Key to the Ceramic Description

The first number corresponds to the inventory number
SHR = Shihr; 96 = year 1996; 3016 = number of layer or artificial removal; Ω = unstratified.
The colour code for the body is that of the Munsell soil chart, ed. 1973.

Notes

1. Bâfaqîh, Robin 1979: 55–6, insc. Yanbûq 47/7.
2. Simon 1989: 56, 88–9, 166, n. 57.
3. These sources were published in Hardy-Guilbert 2005 and Hardy-Guilbert & Ducatez 2004.
4. Ibn Hawqal, *Kitâb sûrat al-ard* (Leyde) 1967: 38, and Ibn Hauqal, *Configuration de la terre* I (Kramers & Wiet) 1965, trad. pp. 36–7.
5. *Kitâb Irtifâʿ al-dawla al-muʾayaddiyya* (ed. Jâzim), 2008: 132, 395, in *fac simile*, p. 100 in the original manuscript (ms. Riyad, fº 100 rº) ; trad. Ducatez.
6. Pastoureau 1992: 54–5, fig.36, Bibliothèque Nationale, Rés. Ge. DD. 683, f. 3 vº.
7. Serjeant 1974: 52. The second time, in 1535, it was with ten ships led by Antonio de Saldanha. Already, in 1503, he was a member of the three commands appointed by King Dom Manuel (with Afonso de Albuquerque

and Francisco de Albuquerque), himself with an order to cruise off the mouth of the Red Sea against the ships of Mecca.

8. Map from the Surveys by Commander S.B. Haines, London, published in 1888 under the superintendancy of Captain W.J.L. Wharton.

9. Six seasons of excavations led by the author, have been carried out so far, with the participation of the following: K. Bâdhafari, I. Al-'Ameri, M. Bâharama, S. Mohammad 'Ali, A. Albary, A.K. Al-Bârakani, representatives of the Antiquities Department (GOAM) of Mukallâ and San'â'; D. Parent, D. Guimard, S. Dalle, topographers with AFAN; N. Férault de Falandre, architect DPLG, P. Philippe, draughtsman in architecture; S. Eliés and S. Vatteoni, draughtsmen; E. Alloin, S. Labroche, V. Monaco, conservators; A. d'Arcangues, archivist; P. Bâty, archaeologist with AFAN and INRAP; R. Alaoui, T. Creissen, N. Gilles, S. Gilotte, St. Guichou, A. Joyard, C. Juy, St. Le Maguer, A. Masson, H. Morel, G. Plisson, P. Siméon, D. Willems, students of archaeology at the Sorbonne, Paris IV and Paris I and the Universities of Nanterre, Aix-Marseille I; St. Boulogne, spécialist of glass, and G. Fusberti. This project is supported by the Centre National de la Recherche Scientifique (UMR 8167), the French Ministry of Foreign Affairs and by the General Organization of Antiquities, Manuscripts and Museums of Yemen (GOAM) under the direction of Dr Y. Abdallah and Dr A. Bâtaya, then Dr A.M. Bâwazir in San'â' and Dr 'Abd el 'Aziz ben 'Aqîl in Mukallâ. It is linked to CEFAS (Centre Français d'Archéologie et de Sciences Sociales in San'â').

10. Rougeulle 2004: 206–11.

11. See the synthesis about this fourteenth century Yemeni signature in Hardy-Guilbert 2005b.

12. Al-Muqaddasî, *Ahsan al-taqâsîm fî ma'rîfat al-aqâlîm* (Leyde) 1967: 84, and trad. 87.

13. Hardy-Guilbert and Le Maguer 2010: 47–51.

14. *Kitâb 'ajâ'ib al-Hind (Book of the Wonders of India)*: 129–30, history LXXXI; 147, history XCIII.

15. Hardy-Guilbert and Le Maguer 2010: 67.

16. Ferrand 1922: 22–3.

17. Ferrand 1922: 126.

18. *Kitâb al-Mufid fî akhbâr Zabîd*, Kay 1878: 6, and trad. 8.

19. *Murûdj al-dhahab*, Pellat 1965, I: 148, § 407.

20. *Mu'djâm al-buldân*, Wüstenfeld 1957: 327.

21. *Nûr al-ma'ârif*, Jazîm (ed.) 2003: 435, trad. Ducatez.

22. *Ta'rikh Shanbal*, Al-Habashî (ed.) 1994: 151, 226, 228, or Hardy-Guilbert & Ducatez 2004: 116, 121, 122: trad. Ducatez.

23. Hardy-Guilbert 2002, fig. 8.

24. Siraf: Whitehouse 1979: 58; Qalât-I Jamshid & Tîz: Stein 1937, pl. XXIV; Bushir: Williamson, see Rougeulle 1991, Fig. 19; Kilwa: Chittick 1974, colour plate between pp. 304–5 and pls.110d, 111e; Gedi: Kirkman 1954, Fig. 23 j, n; Pradines 2010, Figs. 154–64; Shanga: Horton 1996, Fig.206; Lobo Tua: Perret & Riyanto 2003: 183–8.

25. Krahl, Guy, Keith Wilson and Raby 2010: 57. This recent publication deals with the largest hoard of late Tang artefacts ever discovered at a single site— some 60 000 artefacts. The Belitung was an Arab dhow.
26. Hardy-Guilbert & Ducatez 2004, Fig. 21: 11.
27. Pinto de Matos 1996: 126–7, n° 54.
28. Hardy-Guilbert and Ducatez 2004, Fig. 20: 5–8.
29. Chittick 1974, Fig. 100 b, c, d, f, Fig. 101 d: f; Kirkman 1954, Figs. 11–9; Pradines 2010, Figs. 133, 135, 137; Horton 1996, Figs. 176, 186.
30. It is a major problem. Indian colleagues interested in archaeological sites of the same period did not show their excavated local ceramic (perhaps considering the local ceramic too common). However, we need available comparisons (origin and date of stratigraphical finds) for this type.
31. Boulogne & Hardy-Guilbert 2010: 135, Figs. 3–9.
32. Ibid.: 140–1.
33. *Kitâb 'ajâ'ib al-Hind,* Livre des merveilles de l'Inde: 129–30, history LXXXI.
34. *Nûr al-Ma'ârif,* Jazîm (ed), 2003: 496, Hardy-Guilbert & Ducatez 2004: 110, trad. Ducatez.
35. Moule and Pelliot 1938 (re'ed. 1991): 495.

References

Bâfaqîh, M. and Robin, C. (1979), 'Inscriptions inédites de Yanbûq', *Raydan,* vol. 2, pp. 15–76.
Boulogne, S. and Hardy-Guilbert, C. (2010), 'Glass bangles of al-Shihr, Hadramawt, a corpus of new data (14th-19th century) for the understanding of glass bangles manufacture in Yemen', *Proceedings of the Seminar for Arabian Studies,* vol. 40, pp. 135–48.
Chittick, N. (1974), *Kilwa, An Islamic trading city on the East African coast,* 2 vols. Nairobi: Memoir of the British Institute in Eastern Africa 5.
Ferrand, G. (1922), *Voyage du marchand arabe Sulayman en Inde et en Chine, rédigé en 851, suivi de remarques par Abû Zayd Hasan (vers 916),* Paris: Bossard.
Hardy-Guilbert, C. (2001), 'Archaeological research at al-Shihr, the Islamic port of Hadramawt, Yemen (1996-1999)', *Proceedings of the Seminar for Arabian Studies,* vol. 31, pp. 69–79.
——— (2002), 'Al-Shihr, un port d'Arabie face à l'Afrique', *Journal des Africanistes,* vol. 72, no. 2, pp. 39–53.
——— (2005a), 'The harbour of al-Shihr, Hadramawt, Yemen: sources and archaeological data on trade', *Proceedings of the Seminar for Arabian Studies,* vol. 35, pp. 71–85.
——— (2005b), 'La 'mustard ware' yéménite, un marqueur chronologique du XIVᵉ siècle', in *Chine-Méditerranée: Routes et Échanges de la céramique avant le XVIᵉ siècle, TAOCI 4* (Revue Annuelle de la Société Française d'Étude de la Céramique Orientale), pp. 117–25.

————, and G. Ducatez (2004), 'Al-Shihr, porte du Hadramawt sur l'océan Indien (Sources et Archéologie)', *Annales Islamologiques*, vol. 38, no. 1, pp. 95–157.

Hardy-Guilbert, C., and S. Le Maguer (2010), ''Chihr de l'encens' (Yémen)', *Arabian Archaeology and Epigraphy*, vol. 21, pp. 46–70.

Hardy-Guilbert, C., and A. Rougeulle (1995), 'Archaeological research into the Islamic period in Yemen. Preliminary notes on the French Expedition, 1993', *Proceedings of the Seminar for Arabian Studies*, vol. 25, pp. 29–44.

Hardy-Guilbert, C., and A. Rougeulle (1997a), 'Ports islamiques du Yémen. Prospections archéologiques sur les côtes yéménites (1993-1995)', *Archéologie Islamique*, vol. 7, pp. 147–96.

———— (1997b), 'Al-Shihr and the southern coast of Yemen: preliminary notes on the French archaeological expedition, 1995', *Proceedings of the Seminar for Arabian Studies*, vol. 27, pp. 129–40.

Horton, M. (1996), *Shanga, the archaeology of a Muslim trading community on the coast of East Africa* (Memoirs of the British Institute in Eastern Africa 14). London: British Institute in Eastern Africa.

Ibn Hawqal, *Kitâb sûrat al-ard,* in M.J. de Goeje, ed., Bibliotheca Geographorum Arabicorum. Leiden: Brill (1870; repr. 1967).

Kitâb 'ajâ'ib al-Hind, Livre des merveilles de l'Inde par le capitaine Bozorg fils de Chahriyâr de Râmhormoz. M. Schefer ed., French tr. L.M. Devic, Leyde: Brill (1883-6 repr. 1993).

Kitâb al-irtifâ, Le Livre des revenus, M. Jazîm (ed.), Sana'â': Centre Français d'Archéologie et de Sciences Sociales (2008).

Kirkman, J. (1954), *The Arab City of Gedi: Excavations at the Great Mosque, Architecture and Finds.* Oxford: Oxford University Press.

———— (1963), *Gedi, the Palace.* The Hague: Mouton and Co.

Krahl, R., Guy, J., Keith Wilson, K. and Raby, J. (2010), *Shipwrecked Tang treasures and monsoon winds.* Smithsonian Institute.

Al-Mas'ûdî, *al-Murûj al-dhahab,* Ch. Pellat, ed., Beirut (1965 and sq.).

Al-Muqaddasî, *Ahsan al-taqâsîm fî ma'rîfat al-aqâlîm,* in M.J. de Goeje, ed., Bibliotheca Geographorum Arabicorum, Leiden: Brill (1877; repr. 1967).

Nûr al-ma 'ârif fî nuzum wa-qawânîn wa-a 'râf al-Yaman fî al-'ahd al-muzaffarî al-wârif, Lumière de la connaissance. Règles, lois et coutumes du Yémen sous le règne du sultan rasoulide al-Muzaffar, M. Jazîm (ed.), Sana'â': Centre Français d'Archéologie et de Sciences Sociales (2003-5); 2 vols.

Pastoureau, M. (1992), *Voies océanes. Cartes marines et grandes découvertes.* Paris: Bibliothèque nationale.

Perret, D., and S. Riyanto (1998), 'Les poteries proche-orientales engobées à décor incisé et jaspé de Lobu Tua', in *Histoire de Barus, Le Site de Lobu Tua*, I. Études et Documents, C. Guillot, ed., *Cahiers d'Archipel*, vol. 30, pp. 169–88.

Pinto de Matos, M.A. (1996), *Chinese Export Porcelain from the museum of Anastacio Gonçalves, Lisbon*, London, Lisbon: Philip Wilson Publishers Ltd.

Pradines, S. (2010), *Gedi, Une cité portuaire swahilie, Islam médiéval en Afrique Orientale*, Le Caire: Institut Français d'Archéologie Orientale.

Rougeulle, A. (1991), *Les importations extrême-orientales trouvées sur les sites de la période abbasside: contribution à l'étude du commerce moyen-oriental au Moyen Age*. Ph.D. Université Paris IV-Sorbonne.

——— (2003), 'Excavations at Sharmah, Hadramawt: the 2001 and 2002 seasons', *Proceedings of the Seminar for Arabian Studies*, vol. 33, pp. 287–307.

——— (2004), 'Le Yémen entre Orient et Afrique: Sharma, un entrepôt du commerce médiéval sur la côte sud de l' Arabie', *Annales Islamologiques*, vol. 38, no. 1, pp. 201–53.

Serjeant, R.B. (1974), *The Portuguese off the South Arabian Coast, Hadrami Chronicles*, Beirut: Librairie du Liban.

Simon, R. (1989), *Meccan Trade and Islam: Problems of origin and structure*, Budapest: Akadémiai Kiadó.

Stein, A. (1937), *Archaeological reconnaissance in North-Western India and South Eastern Iran*, London : Macmillan & Co. Ltd.

'Umâra al-Hakamî, *Kitâb al-Mufid fî akhbâr Zabîd*, in *Yaman. Its Early Mediaeval History*, H.C. Kay, London, 1878.

Vallet, É. (2010), *L' Arabie marchande. État et commerce sous les sultans rasûlides du Yémen (626-858/1229-1454)*, Paris: Publications de la Sorbonne.

Whitehouse, D. (1979), 'Islamic glazed pottery in Iraq and the Persian Gulf: the ninth and tenth centuries', *Annali del Istituto Universitario Orientale di Napoli*, n.s., vol. 39, pp. 45–61.

Yâkût al-Rûmî, *Mu'djâm al-buldân* III, *Dictionnaire des Pays*, F. Wüstenfeld, ed., Beirut, 1957.

Zhao, B. (2004), 'L'importation de la céramique chinoise à Sharma (Hadramaout) au Yémen', *Annales Islamologiques*, vol. 38, no. 1, pp. 255–84.

CHAPTER 5

Indian Inscriptions from Cave Hoq at Socotra

Ingo Strauch

This essay deals with a corpus of texts, which were discovered about ten years ago in a cave on the island of Socotra, situated in the Indian Ocean between the coast of South Arabia and the Horn of Africa (Map 5.1). The island with ca. 45,000 inhabitants is today politically part of the Republic of Yemen. A majority of its population lives in the north where a large plain provides enough space for settlements and modest agriculture and easy access to the sea and its products. The granite core of the island is

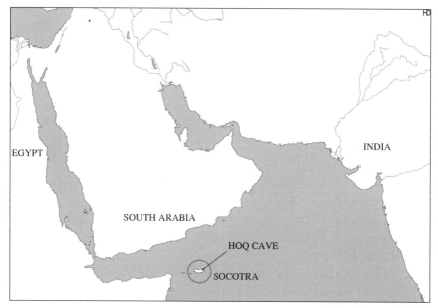

Map 5.1: Western Indian Ocean with Socotra and Hoq Cave
Courtesy: Hédi Dridi.

covered by thick layers of marine deposits like limestone, which is strongly karstified and caused the emergence of large cave systems all over the island (Cheung and DeVantier 2006: 23). In one of the numerous caves, which are part of this huge karst system, a group of Belgian speleologists discovered in 2000 numerous graffiti and drawings inscribed on the walls, stalactites, stalagmites and floors of the cave. The Belgian expedition was part of a larger enterprise called Socotra Karst Project, founded and run by Peter De Geest, at that time Ph.D. student at Vrije Universiteit Brussel. Thanks to him, Christian Robin and Hédi Dridi—then members of the French Archaeological Mission in Yemen—could visit the cave and prepare a documentation of these artefacts. They identified the textual remains and handed over the Indian materials—at that time only about 20 epigraphs— to my Russian colleague Mikhail Bukharin who invited me to work on them together with him. The results of this first study of the Indian texts were published in an article which came out in 2006 (Strauch and Bukharin 2004). The readings of the non-Indian epigraphs and presentation of the archaeological artefacts were published by the French colleagues in two fundamental articles in 2002 (Dridi 2002; Robin & Gorea 2002).

Some years later, the leader of the Belgian Socotra Karst Project, Peter De Geest, invited me to join his expedition in December 2005 and January 2006. During this visit, I had the opportunity to visit the cave myself and to prepare a new documentation,[1] which included much additional material and is the basis of the comprehensive catalogue of inscriptions and drawings published in the volume *Foreign Sailors on Socotra: The inscriptions and Drawings from the Cave Hoq* (= Strauch 2012). The present essay will shortly present the main results of the study of the Indian material (Strauch 2012: 254–365).

The Historical Background

As far as the palaeographical analysis allows, all Indian epigraphs can be bracketed between the second and early fifth centuries AD. It is well known that during this time Indians actively participated in the intercontinental trade contacts, which connected the Indian subcontinent with the West, not only with the Mediterranean, but also with the Arabian peninsula. An impressive number of literary and archaeological data bear witness of this period of global history.[2]

A major source on the Roman trade with the East, the anonymous *Periplus Maris Erythraei* (*PME*) written in the middle of the first century AD, gives a detailed account on the sea-route from the Red Sea up to the Indian subcontinent. This text also contains one of the earliest historical accounts on the island Socotra which is known to the author under the name *Dioskourides*. According to this account, the population of the island consisted of a mixture of Arabs, Indians and Greeks who settled there for the purposes of commerce. The island's products listed in the *PME* are tortoise and dragon-blood (*Dracaena cinnabari*), the resin of a tree which even today grows abundantly in the mountain areas of the island. According to the *Periplus*, Socotra was connected mainly by two routes with the Indo-Roman world: via Muza, i.e. the South Arabian harbour at the mouth of the Red Sea, and to the ports of western India, namely, Barygaza, the ancient Bharukaccha, and Limyrike which can be identified with the Malabar coast of south India (*PME* 30 + 31, Casson 1989: 67–9).

The data of the *Periplus* can be compared with both earlier and later Western sources which confirm the participation of Socotra in the Indo-Roman trade contacts and the role which Indian traders played in them. Among the earliest texts, which mention the presence of Indians in this part of the Indian Ocean, are the *Periplus* written in the middle of the second perhaps early first century BC by the Ptolemean officer Agatharchides of Cnidus (Burstein 1989: 169) and Diodorus' description of the mythical island Panchaea in his *Bibliotheca Historica* (5.41.4–5.42.4., Oldfather 1935).[3]

Despite this literary evidence, there are almost no clearly identifiable material traces of the presence of Indian traders on Socotra.[4] But the same can also be stated for other parts of the Indian Ocean networks. The sources for the presence of Indians mainly consist of ceramics and a few inscribed potsherds from the Red Sea ports Myos Hormos and Berenike (cf. Salomon 1991). As important as archaeological evidence might be—especially in the absence of literary reports—its testimony is a limited one. We hardly know anything about the people who took part from the Indian side in these trading activities. Where did they come from, what was their social and religious identity? Against this background, the newly discovered inscriptions from the Hoq Cave at Socotra gain an eminent importance. For the first time we dispose of a source which reflects the voice of one of the major agents in the Indo-Roman trade network—the Indian traders and sailors.

The Hoq Cave

The Hoq Cave opens at a height of about 350 m. above sea level facing the open sea to north-east (Plate 5.1). The cave is shaped as a rather narrow long corridor, about 2 km. long and up to 37 m. high. Without hesitation, it can be called a treasure house of speleology. All sorts of stalagmites

Plate 5.1: View from the cave's entrance towards the sea.

and stalactites from miniature size up to monumental compositions can be found along the way into the cave. It was confirmed by the Belgian specialists that Hoq is an outstanding example of cave architecture. Beside this natural beauty, it is also the relatively easy accessibility of the cave, which makes it an attractive place to visit. After a not too strenuous climb of about 2-3 hours, one reaches the entrance. The floor of the cave is flat and there are no subterranean lakes or rivers, which have to be crossed.

The first traces of the cave's ancient visitors are found only after about 1 km. walk. This spot onwards, the inscriptions are usually arranged in clusters along the path. Altogether, I could identify 18 different sites, where texts have been written on the surfaces of the walls, on the stalagmites and stalactites or on the floor (Plate 5.2). The texts were inscribed with the help of material, which was found in the vicinity of these places. Thus we have texts written with different types of mud from the floor and texts incised with the sharp ends of a broken stalagmite. One text is written with charcoal, which is taken from a torch. Remains of torches have been found at different places. Due to the complete darkness inside the cave, such torches were the only source of light for the premodern visitors. The difficult conditions under which these texts were written are also

Plate 5.2: Site 16 with inscriptions indicated.

responsible for their sometimes rather enigmatic character. Not all the signs are carefully inscribed, sometimes texts are written above each other.

Altogether, I could clearly identify 193 Indian epigraphs written by 117 different persons. Accordingly, some of the visitors left their texts more than one time. The most active of them was a certain Ravāhaka who inscribed his name in total 10 times at five different spots. Following his graffiti, it is thus even possible to reconstruct his route through the cave during his visit more than 1,500 years ago (Map 5.2).

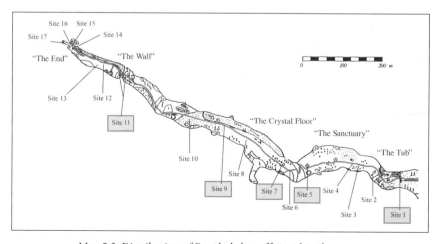

Map 5.2: Distribution of Ravāhaka's graffiti within the cave.

At some sites, the Indian texts are accompanied by South Arabian, Aksūmite, Greek and Bactrian texts. Of special interest is a wooden tablet bearing a Palmyrene inscription dated to AD 232 (Robin & Gorea 2002: 432–45; Gorea 2012).

The Corpus of Indian Inscriptions at Hoq Cave: Formal Features

With the exception of a single Kharoṣṭhī inscription, all Indian graffiti are written in the Brāhmī script, namely in a variety which can be attributed to the so-called Western Brāhmī of the Western Kṣatrapas which was in use in Gujarat and the adjacent regions from around the second century AD up to the fifth century AD.

Due to the occasionally enigmatic character of very short inscriptions and the homonymy of Sanskrit and Middle Indic in some cases, it is not always possible to provide a clear linguistic attribution of the texts. In the majority of cases, however, the language can be described as Sanskrit, sometimes intermingled with Middle Indian phonological features as it is typical for this kind of epigraphic texts. Only 21 inscriptions of the whole corpus (= ca. 11 per cent) are clearly written in Middle Indian.

According to their genre (see Table 5.1), the majority of inscriptions belongs to the type of personal inscriptions, i.e. graffiti containing the personal name of the scribe and occasionally some additional information (= Type A). This group corresponds to the category of 'Pilgrims' and travellers' records included in Salomon's 'Typological survey' on Indian epigraphy (Salomon 1998: 121f.). In most cases, these short texts contain only the name of a person, either in the genitive case or in the nominative. However, intermittently further elements are added, such as a verbal form like *prāpta* 'has arrived' or the name of the person's father, his title, profession or place of origin. These occasional additions make clear that the majority of people who left their names in the cave were participants of maritime expeditions from western India. Thus, these texts also bear witness of a considerable degree of literacy among the seafaring people of India.

Other types of inscriptions are only weakly attested. Thus, the corpus contains only seven texts, which can be ascribed a religious character (=Type B). Two of them are left by a person, who calls himself Rahavasu. His two short texts contain formulae for the worship of the Buddha. One of them (14:28) mentions the historical Buddha by his birth name—Gotama/ Skt. Gautama: *bhagavato gotamasa na[bha]katasa* 'For the Lord Gotama (Skt. Gautama), the *nabhakata*'. The term *nabhakata* is problematic. Since the text is written in Middle Indic language, the word should represent a Middle Indic lexeme. A possible Sanskrit equivalent is *nabhaḥkrānta*, a rather late term which according to some Sanskrit lexicographers— the oldest of them the twelfth century Jaina scholar Hemacandra from Gujarat—has to be regarded as synonym of *siṃha* 'lion'. There is no proof that Hemacandra's explanation goes back to a much older and possibly regionally distinct source. But if we consider this possibility, the term *nabhakata* < *nabhaḥkrānta* would refer to a well-known epithet of the Buddha, who is frequently called in literary sources *Śākyasiṃha* 'the lion of the Śākya (family)'. On a golden medallion from Tillya Tepe in Bactria we even find the legend: *siho vigadabhayo dharmacakraṃ pravatati* 'The fearless Lion turns the Wheel of the Teaching' (for excellent pictures see Sarianidi 1985: 188f.).

The second Buddhist inscription (11:43) uses another well known epithet and designates Buddha as *mahāmuni* 'Great Sage'. It runs in Middle Indian phonology: *bhagavato mahamuni[sa]* 'For the Lord "Great Sage"'.

The inscriptions subsumed under the last category—that is miscellaneous—probably belong to different types of texts. All of them are, however, rather enigmatic and their contents is not beyond doubt. The most interesting among them is a very short inscription (10:2) which consists of only three numerals: *100 50 4*. Due to the lack of any additional information and the unclear context, it is not possible to definitely fix the purpose of these numerals. But it is possible that they were meant to designate a date. According to the palaeographical evaluation, the script of this epigraph belongs to western India and can be dated to the second-

Table 5.1: Survey of the inscriptional genres represented at Hoq Cave

The Indian inscriptions of the cave Hoq	Texts		Scribes	
	Σ	%	Σ	%
TOTAL	193	100	117	100
A. Personal inscriptions	172	89	104	89
(1) Name only	90	52	55	53
(2) Name + patronym	34	20	21	20
(3) (Name) + (patronym) + provenance/profession/title	19	11	15	14
(4) Name (+ patronym) + (provenance/profession/title) + verbal form	33	19	21	20
B. Religious inscriptions	7	3.5	3	2.5
C. Miscellaneous inscriptions	3	1.5	3	2.5

Source: Strauch 2012: 279.

fourth century AD. The only candidate of the eras current in this region, which suits this dating, is the Śaka era commencing in AD 78. The number 154 would thus result in the year AD 232, a date which quite impressively matches the palaeographical evidence and the date of the Palmyrene tablet which was fixed by Maria Gorea to AD 257/58. If our interpretation of the Brāhmī numerals is correct, they would provide an important chronological argument for the entire Hoq corpus.

The Indian Inscriptions of Hoq: The Historical Information

Religious Affiliation

Our major source of information is, of course, the names themselves. In many cases, the religious and social status of a person or his family is expressed in his name. Thus, an onomastic analysis of the names of the Indian visitors of Hoq allows some cautious conclusions about the religious stratification of Indian sea traders in the first centuries AD (see Table 5.2). Due to the general sympathy early Buddhism showed towards

Table 5.2: Religious affiliation of personal names attested in Hoq (names of visitors are given in normal print, names of their fathers in italics)

Religious term	Indian names from Hoq
Buddhist	6 names (3 visitors)
Buddha	Buddhanandin, *Buddhamitra*
Dharma	*Dharma*
Saṃgha	Saṃghadāsa, Saṃghanandin, *Saṃgharaṅgin*
General	1 name (1 visitor)
Deva	Devila
Vaiṣṇava	7 names (5 visitors)
Viṣṇu	Viṣṇu, Viṣṇudatta, Viṣṇudhara, Viṣṇupati, *Viṣṇubhaṭṭi*, *Viṣṇula*, Viṣṇusena
Śaiva	8 names (6 visitors)
Śiva	*Śivaghoṣa*, Śivaba+pava, *Śivamitra*
Rudra	Rudradatta, Rudranandin, Rudrendra
	Iśaradasa (Skt. Īśvaradāsa), Īśvaraskanda
Other Hindu deities	9 names (8 visitors)
Skanda-Kumāra	Īśvaraskanda, Skanda, Skandabhūti, Skandamitra, Kumāraṣena, Bhaṭṭikumāra
Sūrya	Sūryasiṃha
Vedic deities	*Aryamabhūti*, Prajāpati

Source: Strauch 2012: 356–7.

trade and commerce it is not surprising to find Buddhist names, such as Buddhanandin, Buddhamitra or Saṃghanandin. Together with the devotional texts introduced earlier and some drawings of *stūpa*s inside the cave, there emerges a clear indication of the strong presence of Buddhists among the sea-trading population of India. Surprisingly, two of the visitors of Hoq call themselves *śramaṇa* 'Buddhist mendicant, monk' (11:32, 14:16). Whether this title referred to their actual religious status or to their former engagement in the Buddhist order, is not clear. Is it possible that Buddhist monks accompanied seafaring expeditions? It cannot be excluded, however, that *śramaṇa* is used here as a personal name. In this case, any speculations about Buddhist monastics on Socotra have to be abandoned.

Other religious groups, which can clearly be identified, are Vaiṣṇavas and Śaivas bearing typical names. In the case of Vaiṣṇava names, we find for example Viṣṇupati, Viṣṇudatta, or Viṣṇuṣena. The Śaivas are represented by names as Śivaghoṣa or Śivamitra. Many names refer to other Hindu deities like Sūrya and Skanda-Kumāra and even Vedic deities like Prajāpati and Aryaman. Śaiva visitors are probably also responsible for the drawings of tridents (*triśūla*) which are found at different sites in the cave (Plate 5.3).

Plate 5.3: Incised figure of a trident (*triśūla*), indicated by hand-drawing (16:18).

Social and Professional Background

Only few epigraphs mention the profession of the writers. It is no surprise that among them are terms referring to seafaring. Three scribes call themselves *nāvika* or *navika*:

Skandabhūti (scribe 31): *navik[o]* (6:1)
Viṣṇunena (scribe 55): *nāvika* (10:4), *n[ā]vika* (11:1)
Son of Humiyaka (scribe 93): *nāvika* (14:15)

In Sanskrit literature this term is often used in a rather generic way with the meaning 'mariner, sailor'. When found as a technical term or professional title, *nāvika* often bears a more limited connotation and designates one of the leading members of a ship crew, either the captain or the helmsman (Schlingloff 1976: 28; 1982: 54). Another term with a similar semantic range is *niryāmaka*, which is also found in an epigraph from Hoq. Viṣṇudhara, an inhabitant of the Indian harbour city Bharukaccha, uses the title *niryyāmaka* (11:12).

The nautical background of the scribes is also indicated by some drawings of ships which clearly represent the Indian type of seagoing vessels with multiple masts, highly curved sterns and two rudders (Plate 5.4). This ship type is found on the coins of the Sātavāhana ruler Gautamīputra Yajña Śrī

Plate 5.4: Mud drawing of a ship (6:13).

Sātakarni who ruled in the second century AD (see Schlingloff 1976: 21, figs. 4-7; 1982: 57, Abb. 4).

Another professional background is indicated by the use of the abbreviated title *vani* which probably goes back to Skt. *vanij* 'merchant'. The use of a similar abbreviation (*vani*) was common in the later period, as attested in the thirteenth century Sanskrit text *Lekhapaddhati* and in inscriptions of the same period (cf. Strauch 2002: 478). That it was known in a much earlier period can be shown on the basis of inscriptions along the Karakorum Highway (e.g. Oshibat 82:2, Bemmann & König 1994: 130).

Less clear is the exact meaning of the term *ārāmika* 'gardener' which is attested in two texts (7:4, 11:30).

An important historical and chronological argument is provided by two inscriptions, which refer to the title *kṣatrapa* (12:2, 15:5). As shown by Richard Salomon (1973), the use of this originally Iranian title is restricted to territories where the originally Iranian Śakas gained political power. It is attested in inscriptions from Gandhāra in the extreme north-west, in the Mathurā region and in Western India where a branch of the Śaka family established the Western Kṣatrapa dynasty. The period of its use can be determined as the time from the first century BC up to the early fifth century AD, when the rule of the Western Kṣatrapas came to an end. Based on the overall appearance of the script and the suggested geographical background of most of the Indian visitors of Hoq, it seems permissible to connect the *kṣatrapas* from Hoq with Western India, i.e. the domain of the Western Kṣatrapa dynasty. So far, the use of this title in this region was known either for the independent ruler or his heir-apparent. In light of the evidence from Hoq, it is now possible to introduce a functionally different type of *kṣatrapas* in Western India. It seems that the title was also used for subordinates to a sovereign ruler or even members of a noble family, i.e. noblemen. Such a type had already been observed in inscriptions from North-West India (Falk 2006: 400f.). It might be significant to note that the *kṣatrapas* from Hoq bear ordinary Indian names. One of them calls himself Bhaṭṭiṣena, son of Śivamitra (12:2). The name of the second *kṣatrapa* is not completely preserved, but begins with the element Śiva- (15:5). Accordingly, both persons obviously had a Śaiva background. This can be compared to the evidence from Western India, where the Śaiva names of some of the ruling *kṣatrapas* (e.g. Rudrasena, Rudradāman) indicate a rather advanced assimilation of this previously foreign group.

Table 5.3: Religious and official titles, professional designations

Religious titles	Official titles	Professional designations
śramaṇa	*kṣatrapa*	*nāvika* 'mariner, captain'
*'Buddhist mendicant'		*niryāmaka* 'mariner, captain'
		vaṇi 'merchant'
		ārāmika 'gardener'

Geographical Background

The palaeographical analysis of the corpus pointed to western India as the home of most of the Indian visitors. This evaluation is confirmed by the few instances where geographical designations are added to the writers' names. Five of the visitors point to Bharukaccha as their hometown:

Viṣṇudhara (scribe 67): *bhārukacchaka* (11:12)
Śūragaṃja (scribe 72): *bhārukacchaka-* (11:17), *bhāruka[cchaka]* (14:2), *bhārukacchaka* (16:19)
Siha, son of Viṣṇula (scribe 68): *[bhā]rukacchaka, bhārukaccha[k]a* (11:25)
Viṣṇuṣena (scribe 55): *bhārukacchaka* (11:11)
*Aruyaṇiputra (scribe 115): *bh[ā]rukacchaka* (17:1)

The harbour city Bharukaccha is well known in the *Periplus* and other Greek sources as one of the major harbours in western India (cf. Casson 1989: 199f.). It was one of the main trading centres during Sātavāhanas and Western Kṣatrapa rule and preserved this status up to the Muslim period (Jain 1990: 129f.). It is not surprising that sailors from Bharukaccha were part of the expeditions to Socotra. This evidence corresponds to all what we know about Bharukaccha's role in west Indian maritime trade.

Of particular interest is the second western Indian harbour mentioned at Hoq: Hastakavapra. A certain Saṃghadāsa, son of Jayasena, calls himself *hastakavapra[stav](y)[a]* (= Skt. *–vāstavya*) 'inhabitant of Hastakavapra' (2:23). Until recently, the Sanskrit name of this site was known only from rather late inscriptions of the Maitrakas of Valabhī, datable to the late fifth till eighth centuries AD (Gupta 1973: 73; 1977: 48). The Greek name of this place, however, is already attested as Ἀστακάπρα/ Ἀστακάμπρα in the *Periplus Maris Erythraei* (ch. 41, 43, tr. Casson 1989: 77, 200) and in Ptolemaios' *Geographia* (VII.1.60). Recent excavations showed that the site of Hastakavapra was occupied between the fourth century BC and the sixth century AD (Pramanik 2004: 136f.). Of special importance for the study of the Hoq corpus are the numerous inscribed sealings with personal names datable to the third-fourth century AD (Pramanik 2005: 108). The names on these seals published so far by Shubhra Pramanik show a number of structural parallels with those from Hoq and reflect the same Sanskritized language which is typical for the period of the Western Kṣatrapas. One of these seals mentions *hastakavappr[ā]dhikār(i)* 'the superintendent of Hastakavapra'. The seal thus confirms the authenticity of this geographical designation and corroborates the evidence of the Greek authors and the Hoq inscription about Hastakavapra's role in the maritime contacts of western India during the first centuries of our era (cf. Strauch 2012: 344-345).

There are few graffiti, which indicate a foreign origin of their writers. Two scribes add an ethnic designation to their name. One of them is Candrabhūtimukha who calls himself *yavana* (14:17). Although this term can designate persons of Greek origin, other ethnic affiliations—pointing more generally to a 'Western' origin—cannot be excluded. The presence of *yavanas* in western Indian during the Sātavāhana and Western Kṣatrapa periods is shown by numerous epigraphical sources (Ray 1988, 1995).

An Iranian background is indicated by the ethnonym *śaka* used by a visitor bearing the Indian (Sanskrit) name Ajitivarman (6:7). Like in the case of the title *kṣatrapa*, this ethnonym refers to the group of assimilated Iranians who lived in northern, north-western and western India in the centuries before and after the beginning of our era. Another Iranian group is represented by the short bilingual graffito of a person who calls himself Humiyaka (in Brāhmī script) and OMOIAGO (in Greek script) (16:8). According to N. Sims-Williams, both spellings represent the Bactrian name (H)umyag or (H)uməyag (Strauch 2012 Catalogue ad 16:8). It is not clear, from where this Bactrian originally hailed. Although most of the evidence from India points to the north-west (Gandhāra) as the area of Bactrian presence, it cannot be excluded that Bactrians were also present in western India, where the important sea ports certainly attracted a multitude of ethnicities from all over India. That (H)umyag/(H)uməyag used Brāhmī as his second script—and not Kharoṣṭhī, the script of the north-west—might also indicate his western Indian homeland.

At least one person, however, did clearly not belong to western India. He left his name Upali in the Kharoṣṭhī script, which was exclusively used in north-west India and in regions north from there. His text is found on one of the stalactites at the very end of the cave, at site 16 (16:13, Plates 5.5 and 5.6). Thus, this little text represents the westernmost evidence for the use of Kharoṣṭhī. It would be dangerous to conclude on the basis of this single epigraph that some of the expeditions to Socotra started from north-west India or one of the Indus harbours, which provided access to the sea. It is equally possible, that Upali originated from the Kharoṣṭhī writing area

Plate 5.5: Kharoṣṭhī inscription (16:13).

Plate 5.6: Kharoṣṭhī inscription, indicated by hand-drawing (16:13).

but used to live in western India from where he started for this journey. His graffito can also give a chronological indication. The Kharoṣṭhī script fell out of use in the end of the third, beginning of the fourth century AD (see Salomon 2008; Strauch 2011), which matches quite well with our suggestions about the date of the Brāhmī material from Hoq.

SUMMARY

The inscriptions preserved in the cave Hoq on the island Socotra bear witness of the activities of Indian sailors in the period following the description of the anonymous *Periplus Maris Erythraei* of the middle of the first century AD. According to the palaeographical evidence, the majority of Indian texts at Hoq can be dated to the period between the second and early fifth centuries AD. Both an earlier and a later dating are highly improbable, although cannot be definitely excluded. Thus one text (15:2) shows features, which point to the first century AD.

The Indians visited the cave together with persons from other regions bordering the Indian Ocean. Thus we find South Arabians, Ethiopians, Palmyrenes, Greeks and a Bactrian among those who left their graffiti inside the cave. The dating of these non-Indian records roughly corresponds to the Indian material, although there seems to be evidence for a slightly more expanded duration of South Arabian and Ethiopian presence inside the cave. According to Christian Robin, the earliest South Arabian texts can be dated to the third or second centuries BC, while three of the Ethiopian (Aksūmite) texts must be written between 500 and 575 AD (Robin 2012: 439–41).

It is difficult to accurately fix the frequency and the exact dimensions of the visits at the cave. But the manner in which the inscriptions are written at the various sites, and the recurrent overlapping of texts show that the cave was frequented over a certain period of time by different groups of visitors. The purpose of these visits is not completely clear. However, references to gods in the Palmyrene text and in one of the Greek graffiti (11:26) and the discovery of a considerable number of incense-burners (Dridi 2002, 2012) inside the cave might indicate that Hoq cave was considered the home of a deity and visited for religious purposes. Whether this was true for all visitors, must remain open for discussion. The Indian inscriptions show no references to any assumed local 'cave deity'. Instead, few of them refer to the Buddha or are accompanied by drawings of Indian auspicious or religious symbols (Strauch 2012: 361-65). While symbols like the 'filled vessel' (*pūrṇaghaṭa*) or the *nandyāvarta* hardly allow any conclusion about their specific religious meaning, drawings of *stūpa*s or the 'Wheel of the Law' (*dharmacakra*) clearly point to the Buddhist character of these symbols. However, the ritual or religious status of such inscriptions and drawings is far from being certain. If, for example, the *stūpa* drawings would have fulfilled any ritual function, we would expect to find traces of the circumambulation ritual (*pradakṣiṇa*) in the sand surrounding these drawings. Instead, the only visible footprint here originates from the artist who left these *stūpa* drawings. There are no signs of any subsequent ritual use.

The inscriptional and archaeological remains at Hoq show that India remained one of the main actors in the intercontinental trade networks of the Indian Ocean during the first centuries of our era up to the early fifth century AD. The evidence also narrates that the main line of trade with India during this period ran via its western harbours in present-day Gujarat.

Socotra was certainly not a hub in these trade networks, but rather at their edge. It can be suggested that this marginal position largely promoted the preservation of the artefacts at Hoq, which remained obviously untouched and unseen for nearly 1,500 years until the Belgian speleologists entered this part of the cave. The multitude of Indian texts in such a remote place can perhaps give us an idea about the immense sea-trading activities in the centuries after the beginning of our era. What we see, is definitely only the tip of an iceberg. According to its visible parts, it must have been a huge one.

Notes

1. My participation in the expedition and the printing of the book were possible thanks to the generous financial support granted by the Fritz Thyssen Stiftung. The book combines the research of several scholars on different aspects on the material from Hoq. It includes the comprehensive catalogue of inscriptions and drawings and special studies of the archaeological evidence and of the Indian, South Arabian and Ethiopian, Greek and Palmyrene texts. The numbers of the inscriptions cited in the present essay refer to the system used in the catalogue.

2. For a comprehensive survey on the relevant literary and archaeological sources see the excellent monograph *Indo-Roman Trade: From pots to pepper* by Roberta Tomber (2008).

3. Although there is no unanimous proof that these two works refer to the Socotra Island, they clearly point to Indians in the South Arabian sea and can thus be used as evidence for Indian activities in the western Indian Ocean in the pre-Christian period. The literary evidence on Socotra's ancient past is

impeccably subsumed by W.W. Müller (2001) and Zoltan Biedermann (2006). Another summary which focuses on the South Asian relations of Socotra is part of Strauch 2012 (366-406).

4. This picture is currently changing. During excavations at Kosh in the west of Socotra, Russian archaeologists discovered ceramic which they attributed to South Asian wares of the second-fifth century AD (Vinogradov 2012).

References

Bemmann, M., and D. König (1994), *Die Felsbildstation Oshibat* (Materialien zur Archäologie der Nordgebiete Pakistans, 1), Mainz: Verlag Philipp von Zabern.

Biedermann, Z. (2006), *Soqotra. Geschichte einer christlichen Insel im Indischen Ozean vom Altertum bis zur frühen Neuzeit* (Maritime Asia, 17), Wiesbaden: Harrassowitz.

Burstein, S. (1989), *Agatharchides of Cnidus. On the Erythraean Sea* (Works issued by The Haklyut Society, Second Series, 172), London: Hakluyt Society.

Casson, L. (1989), *The Periplus Maris Erythraei. Text with introduction, translation, and commentary*, Princeton: Princeton University Press.

Cheung, C., and L. DeVantier (2006), *Socotra: a natural history of the islands and their people* (Kay Van Damme, ed.), Hong Kong: Odyssey Books and Guides, Airphoto International Ltd.

Dridi, H. (2002), 'Indiens et Proche-Orientaux dans une grotte de Suquṭrā (Yemen)', *Journal Asiatique*, vol. 290, no. 2, pp. 565–610.

Falk, H. (2006), 'Three inscribed Buddhist monastic utensils from Gandhāra', *Zeitschrift der Deutschen Morgenländischen Gesellschaft*, vol. 156, pp. 393–412.

Gorea, M. (2012), 'The Palmyrene tablet "De Geest"', in *Foreign Sailors on Socotra,* I. Strauch, ed. The inscriptions and drawings from the cave Hoq (Vergleichende Studien zu Antike und Orient, 3), Bremen: Dr Ute Hempen Verlag, pp. 447–56.

Gupta, P. (1973), *Geography in ancient Indian inscriptions (up to 650 AD),* Delhi: D.K. Publishing House.

—— (1977), *Geographical names in ancient Indian inscriptions. A Companion volume to Geography in ancient Indian inscriptions (up to 650 AD)*, Delhi: Concept Pub. Co.

Jain, V.K. (1990), *Trade and traders in Western India (AD 1000–1300)*, Delhi: Munshiram Manoharlal.

Müller, W.W. (2001), 'Antike und mittelalterliche Quellen als Zeugnisse über Soqotra, eine einstmals christliche Insel', *Oriens Christianus*, vol. 85, pp. 139–61.

Oldfather, C.H. (ed. and tr.) (1939), *Diodorus of Sicily: in twelve volumes.* Volume III, *Books IV (continued)–VIII* (Loeb Classical Library, 340), Cambridge, MA, and London.

Pramanik, S. (2004), 'Hathab: An Early Historic Port on the Gulf of Khambhat', *Journal of Indian Ocean Archaeology*, vol. 1, pp. 133–40.

———(2005) 'Navigational Sealings of Early Historic Vanij (Merchants) of Hathab, Gujarat', *Journal of Indian Ocean Archaeology*, vol. 2, pp. 107–9.

Ray, H.P. (1988), 'Yavana Presence in Ancient India', *Journal of Economic and Social History of the Orient*, vol. 20, pp. 311–25.

——— (1995), 'The Yavanas in India', in *Athens, Aden, Arikamedu: Essays on the Interrelations Between India, Arabia, and the Eastern Mediterranean*, M.-F. Boussac & J.-F. Salles, eds., pp. 75–95, repr. Delhi 2005: Manohar.

Robin, C., and Gorea, M. (2002), 'Les vestiges antiques de la grotte de Hoq (Suqutra, Yémen)', *Comptes rendus de l'Académie des Inscriptions et Belles-Lettres*, pp. 409–45.

Salomon, R. (1974), 'The Kṣatrapas and Mahākṣatrapas of India', *Wiener Zeitschrift für die Kunde Südasiens*, vol. 18, pp. 5–25.

——— (1991), 'Epigraphic remains of Indian traders in Egypt', *Journal of the American Oriental Society*, vol. 111, pp. 731–6.

——— (1998), *Indian Epigraphy. A Guide to the Study of Inscriptions in Sanskrit, Prakrit, and the other Indo-Aryan Languages*. New Delhi: Oxford University Press.

——— (2008), 'Whatever happened to Kharoṣṭhī? The fate of a forgotten Indic script', in *The Disappearance of Writing Systems: Perspectives on Literacy and Communication*, J. Baines, J. Bennet, and St. Houston, eds., London: Equinox, pp. 139–55.

Sarianidi, V. (1985), *Bactrian Gold from the excavations of the Tillya-Tepe necropolis in Northern Afghanistan*, Leningrad: Aurora.

Schlingloff, D. (1976), 'Kalyāṇakārin's Adventures. The Identification of an Ajanta Painting', *Artibus Asiae*, vol. 38, pp. 5–28.

———(1982), 'Indische Seefahrt in römischer Zeit', in *Zur geschichtlichen Bedeutung der frühen Seefahrt* (Kolloquien zur Allgemeinen und Vergleichenden Archäologie 2), H. Müller-Karpe, ed., pp. 51–85. München: C.H. Beck.

Strauch, I. (2002), *Die Lekhapaddhati-Lekhapañcāśikā. Briefe und Urkunden im mittelalterlichen Gujarat. Text, Übersetzung, Kommentar, Glossar (Sanskrit Deutsch Englisch)* (Monographien zur Indischen Archäologie, Kunst und Philologie, 16), Berlin: Dietrich Reimer Verlag.

——— (2011), 'The Character of the Indian Kharoṣṭhī Script and the "Sanskrit Revolution": a Writing System between Identity and Assimilation', in *The Idea of Writing. Writing Across Borders*, ed. De Voogt, Alex & Joachim Quack, Leiden: E.J. Brill, pp. 131–68.

——— (ed.), 2012, *Foreign Sailors on Socotra. The inscriptions and drawings from the cave Hoq* (Vergleichende Studien zu Antike und Orient, 3). Bremen: Dr. Ute Hempen Verlag.

Strauch, I. and Bukharin, M. (2004), 'Indian inscriptions from the Cave Ḥoq on Suqutrā', *Annali dell' Istituto Universitario Orientale*, vol. 64, pp. 121–38.

Vinogradov, Yu.G. (2011), 'Важное археологическое открытие на острове Сокотра (Йемен)' 'An Important Archaeological Discovery on the Island Socotra (Yemen)]', *Vestnik drevneĭ istorii* (*Вестник древней истории*), no. 4, pp. 99-105.

CHAPTER 6

'Places of Call' in Madagascar and the Comoros Terminology and Types of Settlement

Claude Allibert

W hen scrutinizing the terms that signify 'port and places of call' in what the Arabs named *Komr* (i.e. the islands in the Mozambique channel 'below the Magellan clouds'),[1] we come across two linguistic connections: one with the Arabic language, the other with the Malagasy, without neglecting a Persian word.

The first clearly shows how important the influence of the Arab world was not only along the Swahili coast but also in Madagascar. We are going to explore what the fifteenth and sixteenth century authors gave us and will try to ascertain the location of those places of call. The second, clearly Malagasy, developed into a few words, typically Austronesian, whose meaning will have to be made precise because of the geographical and maritime implications they induce.

I will also point out the absence of other words which could imply the presence of other people coming to that section of the world. Does this then imply their actual absence and was there another reason that prevented them from using their own words, if they had any.

Historical Evidence of Arabic Terms
Knowledge of the Sixteenth Century

Besides the fact that archaeology points out the presence of Arab navigation from the ninth century onwards and very probably earlier, we have textual testimonies that pinpoint places of call. The major word is *bandar* which is systematically used by Ibn Māġid, Sulayman el-Mahri and Sidi Çelebi.[2]

Several authors[3] have tried to situate the different *bandar* given by the Arabs but they do not all agree about their position. Besides, the words given by the Arabs do not correspond to places known today, with a few exceptions such as Manakara[4] and Vohemar.[5]

All the coasts of Madagascar show places of call. This provides evidence that the area was mapped by the Arabs from much earlier than the sixteenth century. Unfortunately, we have no naval guidebooks even if a few 'routiers' were preserved by nineteenth century sailors, particularly Comorians.[6]

The location proposed by the scholars was chosen not only by taking into account present-day ports but also by considering the local geographical conditions particularly adapted to navigation such as bays, river mouths and estuaries, channels, etc. However, spotting precisely the ports located by the Arabs was not an easy task and except for a few of them, we remain in uncertainty, as can be seen in Map 6.1.

Strangely enough, with the exception of one or two cases (Richardson),[7] the word *bandar*[8] disappeared. The Malagasy terms are generally used now, going back to the very first settling of the island by the Austronesians.

Yet another word, *mokala* was preserved and appears in the north[9] and south[10] of Madagascar as well as on the Mozambique coast.[11] It is also found in the naming of the capital town and harbour of the Hadramawt (al-Mukalla) on the Gulf of Aden located 480 km. east of Aden and is the most important port in the Governorate of Hadramawt.[12] It is connected with the Antalaotse population, i.e. Arabo-Swahili-Malagasy admixture of traders who played the part of go-betweens in the region. Is the term *mokala*[13] a memory of the starting point of the migration or rather, which is more likely, the use of the word as simply meaning 'a port'?[14] Nevertheless, it is related to Arab navigation.

The Austronesian terms:
Further evidence of an earlier presence

When travelling around Madagascar, one comes across a few words that mean a place of landing. These words are:

- *serana*: a place where you can stop, 'many traces, many tracks, many lanes on the ground made by *laka* (outriggers)',[15]
- *tolia*: an ordinary landing place on the sand, already mentioned by Flacourt in the seventeenth century (under the spelling *italy*, which is the French understanding of 'i' (where) *tolia*,[16]
- *tafia* (or *tafiana*), or *antefia*: 'a strand of sand where you beach',[17] and
- *hoala*, or *ankoala*, on the western coast of Madagascar, and *ehoala* in the south-east of the island corresponding to a wide, open bay (cf. *kuala*

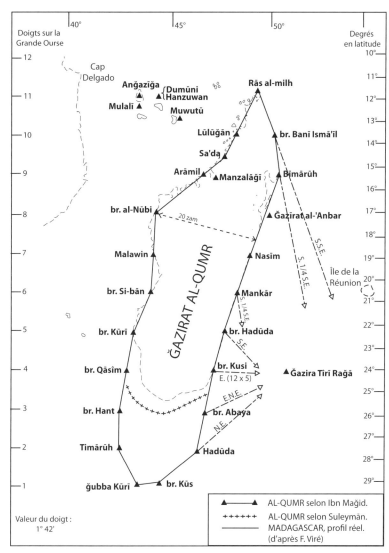

Map 6.1: Map of Madagascar.

(north-west coast of Borneo *ankuala*, *kuala* in Kuala Lumpur Malaysia) different from *lovoka*, 'a narrow-opened bay'.

All these words are characteristically Austronesian and are connected with geographical terms that are completely Malagasy, such as *ony*[18] 'river', or *pangalana*, an inland channel bordering the coast made by the junction of coastal lakes used to navigate more easily but which necessitates pushing the outriggers from one to the other.[19]

Another important word is found in three circumstances along the eastern coast, *harangazavaka*, which seems to have meant 'port of the Zavaga'.[20] Besides there is still another word with no connection to the Austronesian languages, *'lang'* which means a place of call, of connection. This is a Persian word.[21] It occurs in the European texts of the sixteenth and seventeenth centuries and is mainly found in the north-west of Madagascar. Strangely enough, in Piri Re'is, under the name *langani* (first edition,[22] 1521, with the Swahili locative ending *ni*) and *langasika* (second edition),[23] with the Malagasy possessive ending *isika*, meaning 'our'. This shows the presence of the two worlds (Swahili and Malagasy) for the same place, both using a Persian term, which might indicate a Shirazi influence.[24]

What did 'a place of call' mean?
Geographical settlements (establishments)
and social implications

We do not know much about the boats the proto-Malagasy used to reach the island. Borobudur boats may give us a hint, and the recent submarine excavation made at Cirebon (Java) may be a help, though no such boat is described in Western literature. In Madagascar, the only boats referring to large ones but not exceeding 10 m. in length are the *lakampiara*,[25] described at the beginning of the nineteenth century,[26] probably a simplified survival of their original boats[27] initially made of monoxyle twinned boats probably lashed together with the *fiara* fixed across. They may have beached whereas the Arab large *dhows* (*botry*[28] in Malagasy) but also the Cutch *kotia* still remembered in 1970 in Maore found a sheltered mooring. No doubt the Austronesian boats were larger than those double *laka* but had a similar aspect. They were more like a *catamaran*, which spared them a keel. It made crossing the bar easier with the tidal wave. Their places of call might be more like a beaching ground, as the word *serana* suggests, unless this word was simply used for smaller outriggers later.

As for the smaller *dhows* used locally, they sailed up the rivers to beach on the sandbanks where the moving mangroves did not grow. Guillain mentions that the Antalaotse on the western coast of Madagascar sailed up the rivers.

Could we then say that the Arabs and the Austronesians used the same places to land? In that case, shall we consider that the *bandar* and *tolia* were two words for the same thing? The Austronesian terminology sounds more adapted to beaching but we do know that the *dhows* (*botry* in Malagasy), and perhaps larger boats as *mtepe*[29] and *djahazy* also grounded. Today's Malagasy terminology seems more adapted to outriggers.

It is obvious that the situation of a 'place of call' is first determined by geographical elements: line of coast, rivers, winds, tides, reefs, etc. Madagascar is particularly characterized by two aspects, whether you take the western or eastern coast.

Concerning the eastern coast, Çelebi declares that ports like Bimaruh (Vohemar, north-east coast) are mostly dangerous because of coral reefs. Yet, one must keep in mind that this coast is low, the river mouths of which are perpetually silted up to such a point that most rivers cannot flow out and overflow the land to form marshes and ponds along the coast. That was the origin of the *Pangalana*. The first sailors probably tried to find ports along the rivers not filled up by sand, i.e. the only rivers protected by a reef. This can explain the use of the word *harana* (reef) to describe those ports.[30]

On the western coast of Madagascar and the Comoros, small islands near the coast were preferred by the Antalaotse.[31] Sheltered moorings were a protection against the inland Sakalava Malagasy. Small fortresses named *sada*[32] can be found also in the Comoros (Maore island) as in Madagascar. Some examples include: Dembeni (ninth-tenth century) in Maore was just above the river that opened on the lagoon facing the Bandele channel across the reef. Bagamoyo (tenth-twelfth century) was on the beach. In Madagascar, facing the Comoros was Mahilaka.[33] On the other coast, Vohemar (thirteenth-seventeenth century) was sheltered by a coral reef.

The Antalaotse, moving from the African coast to Madagascar (and the way back) played a part of go-betweens. Originally in part from Arab stock and mixed with African Swahilis and Malagasy,[34] they received the Arabs and Swahili in their ports and traded with the inland Malagasy, mainly the Sakalava dynasties. Gevrey[35] provides a brief vocabulary of those Antalaotse which shows the part played by Swahili, Arab and Malagasy languages but also European ones brought in by the White Sea traders. Their multicultural influences can be seen displayed in the jewellery for women (filigree earrings, nose-pins from India as well).

The Antalaotse sailed up the rivers to reach villages.[36] They had to pay customs taxes to the Sakalava chiefs according to the number of masts of their *dhows*.[37] They beached along the river shores as long as their boats were not too large and the river benefited from the tide, just as the local people did when returning from fishing as they still do today. Unless we consider larger ships from South-East Asia, for which we do not have strong evidence, everything depended on criteria such as the size of the boat, its water-drawing, its shape, *lakampiara* or *botry* or *djahazy*. There is no doubt that large *djahazy* had to moor and so did large Austronesian boats. The smaller *dhows* used to land goods beached just as they recently did in the Comoros. As for the *lakampiara*, much larger than the *laka*, they may be thought to have also beached like Austronesian sailing boats.

Besides being a satisfactory place of landing or beaching or mooring, it had to be a place with a specific trade opening onto the country. The concept of taxes, 'the paying of customs, taxes' is expressed in the translation of *serana* given by Richardson's dictionary.[38] We do not know much about what was obtained from the east coast except cattle, chlotitoschist (soapstone) vessels, mangrove poles, probably gums (copal, etc.) and mainly slaves taken to Jeddah and Yemen.[39] It is possible that some plants which were over-collected have since disappeared. Cattle was taken to the Arab countries. This trade was continued during European times as well. In the eighteenth-nineteenth centuries, Vohemar was the port from which cattle was taken to Mauritius. Therefore, on both sides of Madagascar, every port was prolonged by lanes going into the main land, some of them even joining two ports from the West coast to the east (from Mahilaka to Vohemar, for example). Slavery had always been one of the main activities. Slaves had to walk from the north-western coast to Vohemar when the boat they were supposed to be stocked in had already raised anchor, justifying the necessity of such inland roads linking the ports on both sides of the island.

It is also possible that Madagascar and the Comoros ports were used as storehouses for preserving goods (for example, ivory, rock crystal, slaves, cowries, etc.) from attacks that could have happened had they been on the African coast. For instance, the port of Langani[40] on the north-western coast of Madagascar, according to seventeenth century texts, received caravans coming from the Hova country (on the highlands) in March and April taking 'oxen and slaves'[41] down to the Antalaotse towns.

Conclusion

The different populations connected with Madagascar had their own terms to name ports. For example, the Swahili world used the Perso-Arab word *bandar*, Swahilized in *bandari*—indicating how much the Arab world played a part in the Swahili trading system. However, the toponyms mentioned in the Arab texts were given up on the Malagasy coasts which brings evidence that they were only used by their sailors without any further influence on the local people, with a few exceptions. Yet those ports played an important part as archaeology brings in the evidence (Vohemar, Dembeni, Manakara, and Mahilaka). The Malagasy people dropped those names and had their own (*tolia*, *tafia*, etc.) corresponding to their own way of beaching. Shall we say that it was simply a linguistic difference or does it imply a different mode of reaching the land? It might be so, inasmuch as the Malagasy terms convey more the notion of beaching than mooring, even if smaller boats (small *dhows* of the Swahili) also beach using the high tide to get near the coast and let herself strand when the tide goes down. The Malagasy words perhaps got coined when the former Austronesian boats arrived somewhat heedless of the coral bars and reefs thanks to their absence of keel.

The notion of port is always determined by the geographical characteristics of the place as well as the abilities and characteristics of the boat (keel or no keel, important water-drawing or surfing, etc.). That may be explained by the opposition between Arabo-Indian boats with keels and Austronesian sailing boats, no longer known but presenting characteristics like the *lakafiara*, with double outriggers and capable of beaching. The Malagasy words used for places of call are more connected with this notion of beaching, but it could be due to the modification of the size of those boats. Is it possible that the terms used specify a type of place of call characteristic of the migrants and the way they reached the land, i.e. beaching rather than mooring? It is impossible to have any certainty for now, without wrecks or texts.

An inland background was needed so that trade exchanges (slaves, rice, cattle) were possible. The need for fresh water, passages from inland to the coast and sometimes between two ports situated on opposite coasts (Mahilaka/Vohemar), the movement of herders pushing their cattle from one coast to the other according to the coming of foreign boats and the season must also be taken in account. However, material conditions such as the necessity of finding hands to load and unload boats, the need of animals and carts where there was not enough water for small *botry* (*dhows*) to transport goods from the anchored boat to the beach, as it is the case in Toliara today should also be kept in mind. Besides, such ports never lasted more than 300 years because of the changing geological conditions of the coast. Geological and climatic impacts will have to be studied and taken into account by archaeologists.

Another question arises: how to account for the absence of other words in other languages, mainly Indian and Bantu. Does it imply the absence of such people? As for the Indians, because they were mainly Gujarati,[42] they had the Arab word *bandar*. It was the Muslim Indians who have always been traders and the Arab word was used on the north-western coast of India[43] despite the important part played by the Gujarati world. As for the Bantu, Gueunier has shown that they had borrowed the Malagasy word in Madagascar.[44] There are two possibilities to account for this borrowing: either they were taken to Madagascar as slaves on Arab ships and had been taken inland in Africa. That could explain Idrisi's sentence: 'The Zendj have no boats to voyage at sea. Only the boats coming from Oman reach their coasts'[45] or they themselves used the Arab terminology for their own ships. Those who were on the coast of Madagascar, though continued to use their own Bantu language, used the Malagasy term and 'Bantuised' it.

On the east coast of Madagascar where the influence of the Arab world was permanent, one notices that the Arab terms were not preserved (with a few exceptions) and replaced by Austronesian terms, probably because the Austronesians had settled far earlier and their linguistic influence was deeply rooted in the country whereas the use of Arab terms gradually waned.

Notes
 1. Allibert 2001.
 2. See Ferrand 1986 (*Encyclopedia of Islam*[2] V, under Madagascar).
 3. Bittner & Tomaschek 1897 (see Tibbetts 1971, presenting Tomaschek's arguments); Ferrand 1923–5; Tibbetts 1971: 432–5; Khoury 1971; Grosset-Grange 1978; Viré and Hébert 1987; Jouannès 2001.
 4. Spelt Mankar (see the map). Grosset-Grange also proposed such a map that can be seen in Vérin (1984: 76).
 5. Also given by Piri Re'is in 1526 (Allibert 2011) under the name of the local sheik Bimar. Sometimes written Bimaruh.
 6. Gueunier, Hébert, Viré 1992.
 7. Richardson (1885: 80), presented *bandary* as provincial, on the Western coast.
 8. Even in the Swahili form *bandari* (Sacleux 1939: 91) 'rade, havre, port, ville maritime avec rade ou port. Ex: *bandari-*, *salama* ancien nom de Dar es-salam'.
 9. See Leguével de Lacombe (1840: 295) who mentions a '*monkale*, port des Antalaotse'.
10. See Ferrand (1905: 216). See also Rakotoarisoa (1993: 133–51) dating the site of Mokala back to the eleventh century. Besides, it must be remembered that the vowel 'u' is written 'o' in Malagasy, thus giving the same pronunciation.
11. See Hébert 1999: 11, note 2 who reminds us that the country of '*mongale*' was the name of a realm, one of the six realms that constituted what was named '*zanguebar*'. The port of '*mongalo*' was visited by Saulnier de Mondevit in 1785.
12. It is situated not far from Qane, the ancient principal Hadrami trading port between India and Africa.
13. The Malagasy spelling imposes the letter 'o' to express the sound 'u'.
14. See Vallet 2010: 116–17.
15. See Guillain (1845: 11). Dalmond 1842 gives *sirana* (probably *serana*) and *sirangha* ('gh' representing the velar 'n', in betsimisaraka. Richardson writes 'places where taxtes [*sic*] are levied' (see further on). The word is found in the Malagasy name *antseranana* (often mispronounced *antsiranana* 'where there is salt') that was substituted to the French Diego Suarez.

16. Webber 1855: 606. Dahl 1951: 331 'Maanjan *tudi* 's'asseoir' = merina *tody* 'arrivée au port' INC (t/uli) 'faire escale' et 's'asseoir' signifiant tous deux 's'arrêter, se reposer pour un moment à un endroit'. See also Molet 1957.

17. See Webber (1853: 606) and Vérin (1975: 405), 'the *tafia* (or landing-stages) were devoid of rocks' in Sakalava region and contemporary times. Vérin also notifies that 'the embarkation points along the river (*tafia*) varied according to the depositing of alluvium by the river and the growth of the mangroves' (1972: 168). *Antefia* (*ana*-place, *tafia*, in the north-west of the island, see the map of Wilde (1650, in Vérin 1975: 23) and Hacke (1680, in Vérin 1975: 131). Richardson (1885: 598) gives 'a landing place, a port' making a connection between the two meanings. Dalmond 1842: 63 gives *tafia*.

18. Which is a fundamental word inasmuch as it is the place of the first settling of the Austronesian population.

19. Also found in Malay, *pangkalan* or *pangkalar*. Manguin 1987 notices that the port to Mekka is named *panghalari Mekah* in Indonesian, probably because the sea route had to be abandoned to take the land track to reach the town.

20. Hébert (1993–4: 28–49). '*Harana*' meaning the coral reef (used as a protection from the heavy sea) and '*javaga*', the people from Java.

21. *Lang* means the stage posts for caravans (Beaujard 2007: 83).

22. See Allibert 1989.

23. See Allibert 2011.

24. See Allibert 2005.

25. Richardson 1885: 369 (*fiara* meaning 'a movable platform serving as deck', 'a built canoe with an outrigger' about 8–9 m. long with boards to raise the sides of the canoe). See also Webber 1853: 197 '*lakampiara* ou *lakafiara*, pirogue de plusieurs pièces comme celles des Sakalava'.

26. Thomlinson said he had seen in 1809 one of their outriggers. It was about 45 ft. long, 10–12 ft. wide. 'It had been made with skill and it was very much like the boats they used to catch whales. The different parts were assembled with wood pegs. . . . Each boat could have 15 to 35 men on board'. Quotation translated from the French in Gevrey 1870: 209–10. For the original text, see Salt 1814: 76.

27. See Madhi 1999: 145 presenting the likely evolution of Austronesian boats.

28. Probably the English word 'boat' adapted to the Malagasy language.

29. See Poumailloux 1999.

30. Hébert 1993–4: 43.

31. Antalaotra (Antalaotse on the western coast) from *alaotra*: the sea (malay, *laut*, *lautan*: ocean). Mixed population coming from beyond the seas.

32. Viré and Hébert 1987: 71.

33. Radimilahy 1998.

34. Fagereng 1971: 42 proposes the definition given by Grandidier A. et G.: 'Les Antalaotse ou "gens de mer" étaient originaires de Bassorah, dans le Golfe Persique, faisant donc partie d'une population mélangée de Perses (Iraniens) et d'Arabes, ces derniers ayant conquis le pays dans les siècles suivant la mort de Mahomet. . . . En quittant leur pays, ils avaient d'abord essayé de s'établir sur la côte orientale d'Afrique, avant de venir à Madagascar. Marins, voyageant

sur des boutres arabes, ils se sont établis sur des îles au large de la côte Nord-Ouest'. See also Allibert 1984.
35. Gevrey 1870.
36. Guillain 1845: 33.
37. Guillain 1845: 34.
38. Richardson 1885: 567.
39. See Allibert 1989.
40. First mentioned in Ibn Majid, 1460, and also named 'Lulangane' on the first European maps.
41. Mariano (in Grandidier 1904: 14).
42. Jain 1990: 125 rightly mentions that 'the traders and shippers who lived in Gujarat belonged to the region of the Persian gulf' which might explain the reason why the word *velakula* (Gujarati term) was not used in Madagascar.
43. Sacleux says that *bandar* is also used in Hindi.
44. Gueunier 2003: 218 (*oseranani*) and 200: '*oseranani*: mouillage (au) port (Maintirano). Emprunt au malgache *serana* (n vélaire) avec le suffixe locatif -ni du makhuwa'.
45. My own translation from Viré 1984: 20.

References

Allibert, C. (1984), *Mayotte, plaque tournante et microcosme de l'océan Indien occidental*, Paris: Ed Anthropos.
——— (1989), 'L'océan Indien occidental dans le kitab-i Bahrije de Piri Re'is (1521), [Transcription et traduction de Said Khorchid]', *Études Océan Indien*, vol. 10, pp. 9–52.
——— (2001), 'Le mot Komr dans l'océan Indien et l'incidence de son interprétation sur l'ancienneté du savoir que l'on a de la région', *Études Océan Indien*, vol. 31, pp. 13–33. Also in *Topoi* (2000), vol. 10, pp 319–34.
——— (2005), 'L'apport shirazi dans l'océan Indien occidental. Mythe ou réalité?', *Ya Mkobe* [Moroni (Comores)] vols. 12–13, pp. 133–41.
——— (2011), 'Le kitab-i bahriyye de Piri Re'is et l'océan Indien dans le contexte vohémarien. Analyse des versions de 1521 et 1526', *Études Océan Indien* 46-4–47 [*Vohemar, cité-état malgache*]: 197–220.
Beaujard, Ph. (2007), 'L'Afrique de l'Est, les Comores et Madagascar dans le système monde avant le XVIᵉ siècle', in *Madagascar et l'Afrique. Permanences et mutations de liens complexes*, D. Nativel and F.V. Rajaonah, eds., Paris: Karthala, pp. 29–102.
Bittner, M., and W. Tomaschek (1897), *Die Topographischen Capitel des Indischen Seespiegels Mohit mit einer Einleitung sowie mit 30 Tafeln von W. Tomaschek*. Wien: Verlag der k. k. Geographischen Gesellschaft in Wien.
Dahl, O. Ch. (1951), *Malgache et Maanjan. Une comparaison linguistique*. Oslo: Studies of the Egede Institute.
Dalmond, M. l'Abbé (1842), *Vocabulaire et grammaire pour les langues malgaches sakalave et betsimitsara*. Ile Bourbon: Imprimerie de Lahuppe, à Saint-Denis.

Fagereng, E. (1971), *Une famille de dynasties malgaches*. Oslo: Universitetsforlaget.

Ferrand, G. (1905), *Dictionnaire de la langue de Madagascar d'après l'édition de 1658 et l'Histoire de la grande Isle Madagascar de 1661 d'Étienne de Flacourt* (Publication de l'École des lettres d'Alger, Bulletin de correspondance africaine, XXXIII), Paris: Ernest Leroux Ed.

—— (1923–5), *Instructions nautiques et routiers arabes et portugais des xve et xvie siècles*. Tome 1: *Ibn Majid*. Tome 2: *Souleyman al Mahri et Ibn Majid, le pilote des mers de l'Inde, de la Chine et de l'Indonésie*. Paris: Geuthner.

—— (1986), (with additional material by Vérin) 'Madagascar', *The Encyclopaedia of Islam*^{2}, vol. 5. Leiden: Brill, pp. 943–8.

Gevrey, A. (1870), *Essai sur les Comores*, Pondichéry: A. Saligny, imprimeur du gouvernement.

Grandidier, A. et al. (1904), *Collection des ouvrages anciens concernant Madagascar*, tome 2, Paris: Comité de Madagascar.

Grosset-Grange, H. (1978), 'La côte africaine dans les routiers nautiques arabes au moment des grandes découvertes', *Azania*, vol. 13, pp. 1–35.

Gueunier, N.J. (2003), 'Documents sur la langue makhuwa à Madagascar et aux Comores (fin xixe – début xxe siècles) avec un lexique du makhuwa de Madagascar et des Comores', *Études Océan Indien*, nos. 35–6, pp. 149–223.

Gueunier, N.J., J.-C. Hébert, and F. Viré (1992), 'Les routes maritimes du canal de Mozambique d'après les routiers arabo-swahilis', *Taloha* [Antananarivo], vol. 11, pp. 77–120.

Guillain, M. (capt.) (1845), *Documents sur l'histoire, la géographie et le commerce de la partie occidentale de Madagascar*. Paris: Imprimerie Royale.

Hébert, J.-C. (1993–4), 'Les zavaga ou zabaga indonésiens (= vazaha), artisans et trafiquants du fer, commerçants ou pirates (?) à Madagascar et aux Comores, aux xiie- xiiie siècles', *Omaly sy Anio* [Antananarivo] no. 37–40, pp. 13–62.

—— (1993–9), 'Sur des ports esclavagistes de la côte Nord-Ouest de Madagascar dont le nom est devenu obsolète: Maringando ou Moringambo et Lulangani/Langany/Morumgany', *Études Océan Indien*, nos. 27–8, pp. 11–60.

Jain, V.K. (1990), *Trade and Traders in Western India* (AD 1000–1300), Delhi, Munshiram Manoharlal Publishers.

Jouannes C. (2001), 'La sufaliya d'ibn Majid, un poème du maître-pilote Shihab al-din Ahmad bin Majid', *Études Océan Indien*, vol. 31, pp. 35–114.

Khoury, S. (1971), 'La Hawiya, abrégé versifié des principes de nautique par Ahmad bin Magid', *Bulletin d'Études Orientales*, vol. 24, pp. 254–384.

Leguével de Lacombe, B.F. (1840), *Voyage à Madagascar et aux îles Comores* (2 vol.), Paris: Louis Desessart Ed.

Madhi Waruno (1999), 'The dispersal of Austronesian boat forms in the Indian Ocean', in *Archaeology and Language* III. *Artefacts, Languages and Texts*, R. Blench and M. Spriggs, eds., Routledge: London and New York, pp. 144–79.

Manguin, P.-Y. (1987), 'Études sumatranaises I. Palembang et Sriwijaya: anciennes hypothèses, recherches nouvelles', *Bulletin de l'École Française d'Extrême Orient*, vol. 76, pp. 336–99.

Molet, L. (1957), *Petit guide de toponymes malgaches*, Tananarive: Publications de l'Institut de Recherche Scientifique de Madagascar, Section des Sciences Humaines.

Poumailloux, P. (1999), 'Le 'mtepe', bateau cousu des Swahili, suivi d'un glossaire technique', in *Études Océan Indien*, nos. 27–8, pp. 227–328.

Radimilahy, Ch. (1998), *Mahilaka. An archaeological investigation of an early town in northwestern Madagascar* (Studies in African Archaeology 15), Uppsala: Department of Archaeological and Ancient History.

Rakotoarisoa, J.-A. (1993), 'Le site de Mokala dans la région dite Mozambique du sud-est de Madagascar', in *Données archéologiques sur l'origine des villes à Madagascar*. Antananarivo: Musée d'Art et d'Archéologie, pp. 133–51.

—— (1998), *Mille ans d'occupation humaine dans le Sud-est de Madagascar*, Paris: L'Harmattan.

Richardson Rev. J. (1885), *A new Malagasy-English dictionary*. Antananarivo: London Missionary Society (repr. 1967 Gregg Press).

Sacleux, C.S. Sp. (1939), *Dictionnaire swahili-français*. Paris: Institut d'Ethnologie.

Salt, H. (1814), *Voyage to Abyssinia and travels into the interior of that country (1809-10)*, London: Frank Cass & Co.

Tibbetts G.R. (1971), *Arab Navigation in the Indian Ocean before the coming of the Portuguese*, London: The Royal Asiatic Society of Great Britain and Ireland (see pp. 432–5 about Madagascar and the reappraisal of Tomaschek's identifications of Sidi Celebi's locations in *Die topographischen Capitel*).

Vallet, É. (2010), *L'Arabie marchande. État et commerce sous les sultans rasulides du Yémen (626-858/1229-1454)*, Paris: Publications de la Sorbonne (Bibliothèque historique des pays d'Islam 1).

Vérin, P. (1972), *Les échelles anciennes du commerce sur les côtes Nord de Madagascar* 2 vols.Thèse de doctorat présentée devant l'Université de Paris 1 (Service de reproduction des thèses, Université de Lille, 1975).

—— (1984), *The History of Civilisation in North Madagascar*, A.A. Balkema/ Rotterdam/Boston.

Viré, F. (1984), 'L'océan Indien d'après le géographe Abû Abd-Allah Muhammad ibn Idris al-Hammudî al-Hasani dit Al-Sarif al-Idrisi (493-560 н/1100-1166)', in *Études sur l'océan Indien*, Ottino, P., ed., St. Denis de la Réunion Collection des travaux de l'Université de la Réunion, pp. 13–45.

—— and J.-C. Hébert (1987), 'Madagascar, Comores et Mascareignes à travers la Hawiya d'Ibn Mâjid (866 H/1462)', *Omaly sy Anio* [Antananarivo] no. 25–6, pp. 55–80.

Webber, (Rév. Père) (1853), *Dictionnaire malgache-français rédigé selon l'ordre des racines par les missionnaires catholiques de Madagascar et adapté aux dialectes de toutes les provinces*. Ile Bourbon: Établissement malgache de Notre-Dame de la Ressource.

CHAPTER 7

The Port of Sumhuram
Recent Data and Fresh
Reflections on its History

Alessandra Avanzini

Several reports have been published since the University of Pisa began
its excavation at the site of Sumhuram in 1996 under the auspices of
the Italian Mission to Oman (IMTO).[1] From a perusal of a selection of
these papers, one gains a sense of how far our knowledge of this settlement
has increased and how the scholarly reconstruction of its history has
been revised over the years. We took as our starting point the results of
the American archeological expeditions to Sumhuram during the 1950s
and 1960s,[2] and for a certain period accepted the ostensibly clear and
indisputable, if perhaps overly Rome-centric, reconstruction of the history
of the port by the American team.

Sumhuram, which has been identified with the port of Moscha Limen
mentioned in *Periplus Maris Erythraei*, seems to have been active between
the first and third centuries AD. Its three hundred-year history coincided
with the most flourishing period of trade between Rome and India, which
followed the Roman conquest of Egypt. Sumhuram was founded by the
Hadramawt at the same time as the port of Qana' (the Kanê of the *Periplus*).

This long-distance sea trade primarily involved raw materials and
finished goods unobtainable around the Mediterranean. Commerce
between the Mediterranean and the Indian Ocean has traditionally been
considered as mainly consisting of luxury goods, with a particularly
prominent role played by aromates.[3] Incense produced by trees that at the
time still grew in large numbers further inland would have been brought
to Sumhuram and stored there until it could be loaded onto ships and

transported by sea to the port of Qana', from where it could be shipped to the Mediterranean and to Rome.

Moscha Limen seems to have had commercial ties almost exclusively with Qana', with which it was connected by a well-established sea route and upon which it was economically dependent. Moscha Limen was founded by the king of the Hadramawt as part of the expansion of its sea trade during the period of the Roman Empire.

When I began excavating Sumhuram I was more taken by the great beauty of the site, perched on the rim of the Indian Ocean (Plate 7.1), than by its history.

However, the archaeological work soon showed that the port had a much longer and more complex history than was previously thought. As we now know, the port of Sumhuram was founded at the end of the third century BC and abandoned during the fifth century AD. These dates in themselves suggest a completely different historical scenario from the one previously proposed.

The creation of the settlement coincided with the crucial, 'formative' phase in the development of sea trade across the Indian Ocean, occurring before the arrival of the Romans in Egypt, and long before the foundation of Qana'. Its slow decline followed the eclipse of the kingdom of Hadramawt, which was finally subdued by Himyar after many wars at the end of the third century AD.

The inscriptions that have been found in Sumhuram demonstrate that the Hadramawt maintained its hegemony over the town for a long period, governing through administrators sent from the capital. However, it has also emerged that the inhabitants of the city enjoyed a considerable degree of autonomy in commercial affairs and in the management of the port. This probably allowed the town to survive after the fall of the kingdom.

If I were asked today to choose two adjectives to describe the port of Sumhuram I would say that it was at one and the same time a completely *isolated* settlement and a remarkably *cosmopolitan* one.

Plate 7.1: General view of the storage area with the lagoon in the background.

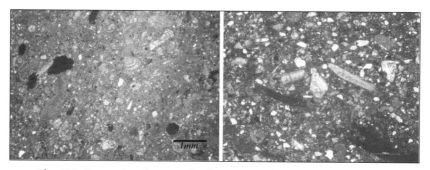

Plate 7.2: Comparison between the thin section of a mudbrick (on the left) and of a fragment of 'local' pottery.

Situated at a great distance from other urban centres, Sumhuram was inevitably characterized by a certain degree of 'regionalism', as reflected in the locally produced pottery and other objects found at the site. Indeed, we have established that Sumhuram had its own pottery manufacture. Archaeometrical analyses conducted on the clay in various samples have shown its composition to be identical to that of the mud-bricks used to build the town, which were made from the clay that could be found near the estuary of the wadi (Plate 7.2).[4] The work produced by local artists and artisans exhibit elements that were unique to Sumhuram; for example, beautiful incense burners have come to light whose form and iconography are quite distinct from those produced by the Hadrami artisans (Plate 7.3).

Plate 7.3: Incense burners from Sumhuram

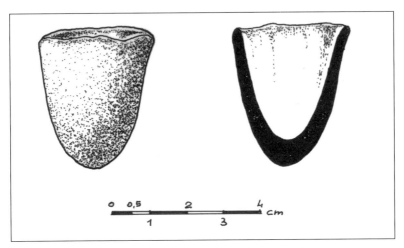

Plate 7.4: Complete conical crucible.

Sumhuram was not therefore only a port engaged in international trade, but also an urban centre with its own tradition of craftsmanship.

The American archaeological team has claimed that Sumhuram minted its own coins.[5] This fact, if confirmed, would be of great interest, as it would underline the town's autonomy from Hadrami rule. However, the data remain contradictory and we have not found evidence so far of grounds specifically dedicated to this activity, as was instead hypothesized by the American team. It seems therefore that coin production was restricted to the capital, with no minting allowed in peripheral regions.

Nevertheless, small crucibles with traces of metal residues corresponding to the alloys used in Hadrami coins have been discovered (Plate 7.4). Further, it is also known that Hadrami coins were minted in a variety of types.[6] Of particular interest to us is the series minted with a radiated male head, a winged caduceus, and the monogram of Sumhuram, a king with the same name as the city (Plate 7.5). Archaeometric analyses of coins bearing the name of the king have yielded interesting results. The alloy

Plate 7.5: Coinage of Sumhuram, series radiated head/winged caduceus, scale 1:1.

is composed almost exclusively of copper (98 per cent), while the copper content of other Hadrami coins is around 70-75 per cent. Therefore, the Sumhuram series appear to be atypical and we would suggest that they may have be minted locally using pure copper that had been imported by the inhabitants of Sumhuram via their extensive commercial ties, rather than a bronze alloy.[7]

The cosmopolitan dimension of Sumhuram is testified to by the extraordinary variety of imported pottery that has been found on the site. During its history, the port appears to have forged ties with nearly the entire known world. Much of the pottery originated, as would be expected, from different parts of the Hadramawt kingdom, and typical of the earliest occupied levels are the wavy rim or Bayhan bowls.

In this regard, I would like to discuss the hypothesis advanced by Alexia Pavan and Pasquino Pallecchi regarding the possible production of amphorae in Yemen.[8] Our excavations at Sumhuram have uncovered some shards of vessels, which, considering their size and the form of their handles, could have been amphorae. The most interesting aspect of these fragments is their fabric which petrological analyses have shown to consist in talcum with feldspar, pyrossens and traces of chlorite and micritic calcareous fragments (Plate 7.6). Based on the assumption that a vessel would usually have been produced within a reasonable distance of the site where the raw materials were available, the composition of this clay indicated a geological area characterized by outcrops of talcum schists and volcanic rock. One site that meets these geo-morphological conditions is located between

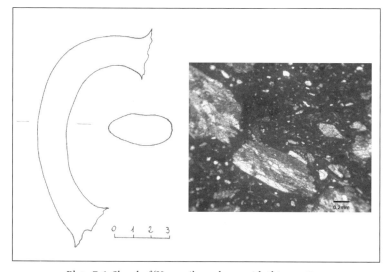

Plate 7.6: Shard of 'Yemeni' amphora with thin section.

the wadi Bayhan and the wadi al Jubah. Our identification of this site as the source of the clay for the pottery works of Sumhuram is supported by the fact that ceramics from both Hajar Bin Humeid and Hajar ar-Rayhani exhibit a similar talcum and chlorite content in their clay. Although this hypothesis leaves many questions unanswered, it is tempting to speculate that amphorae reflecting classical models were being produced in Yemen.

Sumhuram presents a rich assemblage of glazed pottery originating from the Gulf region and imported as early as the final centuries before the Christian Era, with the volume of this trade increasing over the following centuries (Plate 7.7). These finds confirm the suppositions put forward by J.-F. Salles essay.[9] The dearth of information in the *Periplus* regarding routes departing from points along the gulf's rim does not at all indicate that this area was marginal in long-distance sea trade. It merely reflects the fact that the author of *Periplus Maris Erythraei* was exclusively interested in the routes of the 'Greek' trading ships that he himself had taken and described.

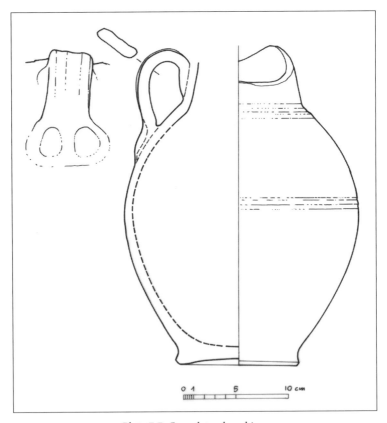

Plate 7.7: Complete glazed jug.

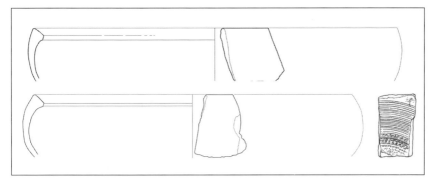

Plate 7.8: Shards of Rouletted Ware, scale 1:3.

Sumhuram's closest trading ties from the very beginning of her history were undoubtedly with India. The discovery of Indian pottery dating to the last centuries of the millennium is one of the most interesting pieces of data to emerge from recent excavations.[10] Perhaps the most exceptional is the discovery of shards of true Rouletted Ware (Plate 7.8), the only known evidence of this kind in the entire Arabian peninsula. Production of Rouletted Ware stopped in the first century BC. The fact that it has been found in the earliest layers of the settlement provides proof not only of the early founding date of Sumhuram, but also that the port quickly began to participate in the international trade between Arabia and India. This link is confirmed by the discovery of shards of paddle-impressed ware (Plate 7.9), one of the most typical forms of pottery produced in southern India and to be found nowhere else on the Arabian peninsula.

Plate 7.9: Shard of Paddle Impressed Ware.

If we study the map of their distribution, we discover that the simultaneous presence of these two types of pottery has been reported only in Arikamedu (and a few other urban centres in south India and Sri Lanka), in Sumhuram and in the Red Sea port of Berenike. Therefore, the once extremely hypothetical relationship between these three port towns, all of them founded in the third century BC, is now confirmed by the discovery of similar archaeological findings at all three sites.

A new scenario unfolded in the first century AD as the variety of forms and the quantity of pottery imported from India began to increase. Pottery dishes and storage containers imported from north India came into wide use, while lids and oil lamps similar to those produced in north-west India have also been found in large numbers. Archaeometric analysis of pottery samples from Sumhuram confirm the presence of rice-tempered cookware of the same type as that found in Berenike and produced in the region of Gujarat.

Therefore, it appears that during the course of its history two different sea routes connected Sumhuram with India. In the centuries before the Christian Era, ships followed a path that went to Sumhuram from Berenike and then crossed the open sea to south India. Later it seems that this route was supplanted in favour of trade links with northern India along the route described in the *Periplus.*

In Report 2 (2008), I sought to reconstruct the history of the port and the chronology of the Hadrami kings based on the inscriptions found there. I would now like to look at a reconsideration of the proposed date for the reign of the *mukarrib* of Hadramawt Yashhuril.

I have recently been re-evaluating the chronology of the kingdoms that ruled southern Arabia during the first millennium before the Christian Era, and now believe that some of my previous reconstructions must be revised. Up until just a few years ago, I accepted as entirely credible Robin's hypothesis that during the first millennium BC the title of *mukarrib* was never adopted simultaneously by more than one south Arabian ruler.[11] This provided a clear chronological grid for the history of south Arabia. However, recently I have concluded that this assumption is untenable and must be abandoned.[12] The consequences of this for our dating of the Hadrami kings cited in epigraphic texts from Sumhuram, and in particular King Yashhuril, are many.

I argued that the reign of Yashhuril should be dated to the second century BC, in opposition to Robin who placed his rule during the first century AD.[13] The early date of the founding of Sumhuram and the possible war between Qataban and the Hadramawt during the second century BC[14] led me to conclude that the kingdoms of the two Hadramawt *mukarribs*—

Sumhuram and Yashhuril—could be dated to the period between the end of the third and the beginning of the second centuries BC, i.e. before this war and prior to the reign of the Qatabanian *mukarrib* Shahr Yagul Yuhargib. I was not entirely satisfied with this hypothesis even as I was formulating it, but Robin's suggestion that the title of *mukarrib* could have been 'rotated' made it at least on a certain level credible. Though aware that such a date for the reign of Yashhuril was difficult to accept, I was unable to come up with a convincing alternative solution.

Yashhuril in fact is attested to not only in Sumhuram, but also in the inscription RES 2687 on the gate of the fortress of al-Bina'. The citation of Himyar in line 3 of the inscription—'when they fortified themselves in Himyar'—did not seem to be incompatible with my hypothesis of an earlier date for the king. It appears that Himyar was being used in this context simply as a geographical term, without implying the involvement of Himyar in a war against the Hadramawt. However, the geographic position of the fortress and the content of the text are not consistent with a dating of the second century BC for the king. The fortress was situated north of Qana' (Map 7.1) and its construction seems to have been connected with the building of the port; the inscription clearly states that the purpose of the fort was to protect the coastal area between the fortress and the sea. It seems therefore highly improbable that the fortress would have been built more than a century before Qana'.

One can imagine the kingdom seeking to reinforce its political position by gradually expanding from its capital towards the coast, building inland settlements before establishing ports to promote international trade. We know of the existence of a settlement—Hanun—located just inland from Sumhuram, where an inscription citing the *mukarrib* Sumhuram has been found, but the interval that separates the construction of the fortress from the founding of Qana' is clearly too long.

Once I set aside Robin's hypothesis that a Hadrami king with the title of *mukarrib* could not have ruled simultaneously with a Qatabanian *mukarrib*, the most credible date for the reign of Yashhuril became, in my opinion, the first century BC. It is interesting to note that recently Robin arrived at the same hypothetical date for the reign of Yashhuril.[15] Returning to a consideration of CSAI II, 14 = RES 4336, Robin proposed the first century BC as the date for this important inscription, drawing parallels between the war against the Hadramawt that it cites and the reference in RES 2687 to the need for the Hadramawt to build defensive fortifications in Himyar.

The inscription RES 4336 clarifies the political climate in southern Arabia during the second half of the first century BC. The expansion of commerce by sea made the region of Yemen's southern plateau politically

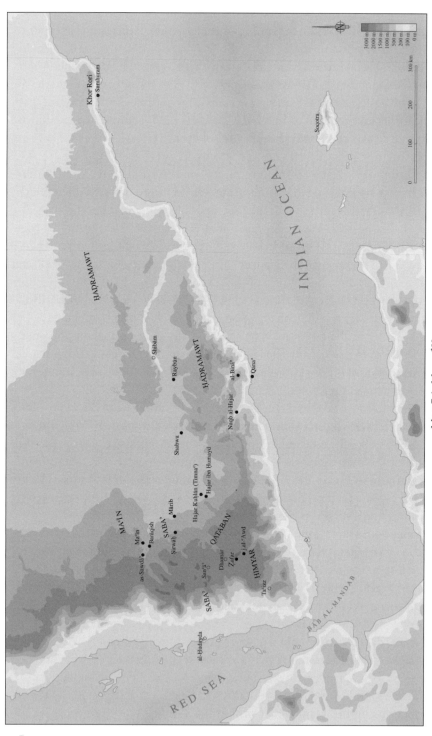

Map 7.1: Map of Yemen.

important for the international trade of the south Arabian kingdoms. Himyar was by now independent of Qataban and cut off any access to the sea by the Qatabanian kingdom. The Hadramawt took advantage of Qataban's weakness to reinforce its control of the coast, with the establishment of Qana' at the end of the first century BC.

Nevertheless some questions remain unanswered; in conducting its policy of economic expansion through sea trade, beginning in the third century BC, why did the Hadramawt build the port of Sumhuram so far to the east of its capital, and so much earlier than Qana'?

Perhaps our earlier discussion of the goods that were imported to Sumhuram could shed light on these points. From its very inception, Sumhuram was an international port but, as we have already reported, artefacts from India are much more abundant in the lower strata of the site. This provides one answer to the question as to why a site so far east of the capital was chosen for the port.

We can therefore conjecture that Sumhuram was established to facilitate Hadrami trade links with the East, in particular southern India. The demand for copper would have provided another reason for choosing a site so far east of the kingdom's borders. With just a small stretch of the imagination, we could find confirmation of this in the copper coins bearing the name of Sumhuram.

The types of amphorae imported provide another important piece of information. Regarding the huge corpus of amphorae in Sumhuram, Roberta Tomber—the archaeologist who is studying them—found very few specimens dating to the century before the Christian Era. The majority of amphorae from Sumhuram can be dated in the early centuries AD (Plate 7.10).

The contacts with the Mediterranean attested to by the amphorae and *terra sigillata* would have in large part developed later, arriving in Sumhuram through Qana'.

The intriguing reference in the *Periplus* to Aden, which fell into ruin before the first century AD, could turn out to be of great pertinence in this context. In the closing centuries before the Christian Era, the port of Aden, which was governed by Qataban, could have been an important link with Berenike and the Mediterranean, while Sumhuram would have turned eastward, conducting its trade primarily with India.

This long-distance trade was divided into segments, but widely separated ports were linked in an already well-established network of routes, as is confirmed by the unearthing of Rouletted Ware in Berenike. The variety of imported pottery found at Sumhuram testifies to the existence of a commercial network in which the ports of Berenike, Sumhuram and

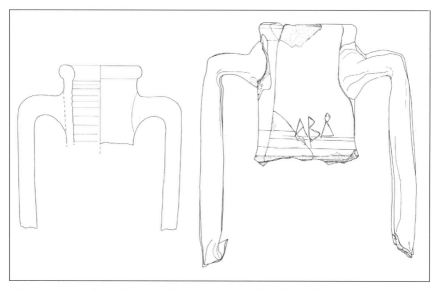

Fig. 13.11: Amphorae from Sumhuram, Koan (on the left) and Dressel 2-4, scale 1:3.

Arikamedu, which were founded in the third century BC, and probably the Qatabanian port of Aden as well, all played important roles.

The founding of Sumhuram can be linked to the trade between south India and the Gulf, with routes already crossing the open sea. The demand for goods from India and probably also copper from north Oman or the island of Masirah explains why this site, located so far east of the kingdom's frontier, was chosen and also justifies why it enjoyed such a degree of autonomy from Qana'. Sumhuram's links with the Mediterranean could have become closer after the founding of Qana', with the expansion of the Roman trade.

We find ourselves in agreement with the Greek historian Strabo that, with the arrival of the Romans in Egypt, commerce by sea underwent radical changes. Not only did the number of ships traversing the seas increase, but the number of routes across the Indian Ocean multiplied, with the expected development, of course, of preferential routes. Sumhuram and its inhabitants played a central role in this new expansion of trade during the Roman period, establishing ties with north India and multiplying their contacts with the Mediterranean through Qana'.

Notes

1. I will cite just a few of these studies: Avanzini (ed.) 2002, Avanzini, Sedov 2005, Avanzini (ed.) 2008, Avanzini (ed.) 2011.

2. Albright 1982, Cleveland 1960.
3. Among the most recently published studies, see Tomber 2008: 15–16, who also reviews the earlier bibliography.
4. Pallecchi, Pavan 2011.
5. Albright 1982: 32–3.
6. Sedov 1998.
7. Chiarantini, Benvenuti, 2013.
8. Pavan, Pallecchi 2009.
9. Salles 1993.
10. The pottery of Indian production dating to this period has been studied by A. Pavan and H. Schenk (Pavan, Schenk, 2012). A. Pavan is also preparing for publication her research on the typology of pottery discovered so far at the site of Sumhuram. The excavations conducted since 2011 have shed important light on the links between the strata in various areas of the city, making possible a chronological study of the typologies of pottery.
11. Robin 1996: 1151.
12. Avanzini 2010.
13. Robin 1994.
14. A victorious war of Qataban against the Hadramawt is quoted in the inscription CSAI I, 115 = Arbach-Sayun 1. The inscription could be dated to the second century BC.
15. Robin, Arbach, 2013.

References

Albright, F.P. (1982), *The American archaeological expedition in Dhofar, Oman (1952-1953)*, Washington, DC: The American Foundation for the Study of Man 6.

Avanzini, A. (2010), 'Reassessment of the chronology of the first millennium in South Arabia', *Aula Orientalis*, vol. 28, pp. 181–92.

—— ed., (2002), *Khor Rori, Report 1* (Arabia Antica 1), Pisa: Edizioni Plus, Pisa University Press.

—— ed., (2008), *A Port in Arabia between Rome and the Indian Ocean (3rd C. BC–5th C. AD), Khor Rori Report 2*. Rome: 'L'Erma' di Bretschneider.

—— ed (2011) *Along the aroma and spices routes, The harbour of Sumhuram, its territory and the trade between the Mediterranean, Arabia and India*. Pisa: MB Vision; Bandecchi e Vivaldi.

——, Sedov, A.V. (2005) 'The stratigraphy of Sumhuram: new evidences', *Proceedings of the Seminar for Arabian Studies*, vol. 35, pp. 11–17.

Chiarantini, C. and Benvenuti, M. (2013) 'The evolution of pre-Islamic south Arabian coinage: a metallurgical analysis of coins excavated in Sumhuram (Khor-Rovi, Sultanate of Oman)', *Archaeometry*, doi: 10.1111/arcm.12036.

Cleveland, R.L (1960) 'The 1960 American archaeological expedition to Dhofar', *Bulletin of American Schools of Oriental Research*, vol. 159, pp. 14–16.

Pavan, A. and Schenk, H. (2012), 'Crossing the Indian Ocean before the Periplus: pottery assemblages in comparison. The sites of Sumhuram (Oman) and Tissamaharama (Sri Lanka)', *Arabian Archaeology and Epigraphy*, vol. 23, pp. 191-202.

Pallecchi, P. and Pavan, A. (2009), 'Considerazioni su alcuni frammenti di anfore con impasto a base di talco rinvenute nell'antico porto di Sumhuram (Oman)', *Egitto e Vicino Oriente*, vol. 32, pp. 221–9.

—— (2011), 'Local raw materials used by craftsmen and in the development of the city of Sumhuram', in Avanzini 2011 (ed.).

Robin, Chr. J. (1994), 'Yashhuril Yuharish, fils de Abiyasa, mukarrib du Hadramawt', *Raydān*, vol. 6, pp. 101–11.

—— (1996), 'Sheba. Dans les inscriptions d'Arabie du Sud', in *Supplément au Dictionnaire de la Bible* 70, columns 1047–254, Paris: Letouzey & Ané.

Robin, Ch. J. and Arbach, M. (2013), 'Premières mentions de dhū-Raydān vers la fin du Ier s. av. e. Chr.', *Raydan*, vol. 8, pp. 79-93.

Tomber, R. (2008), *Indo-Roman trade. From pots to pepper,* London: Duckworth.

Salles, J.-F. (1993), 'The *Periplus of the Erythrean sea* and the Arab-Persian Gulf', *Topoi*, vol. 3, pp. 493–523.

Sedov, A.V. (1998), *Moneti drevnego Hadramauta*, Moscow: RosCentr.

CHAPTER 8

Ports of the Indian Ocean
The Port of Spasinu Charax

Jean-Baptiste Yon

Taking forward the discussion on ports of the Gulf by Jean-François Salles, this essay will focus on a specific part of the region, namely, the port of Spasinu Charax. The small kingdom of Characene (or Mesene) is well known in most of the evidence as a place where commercial transactions were conducted ('port of trade'), en route the Mediterranean and the Gulf, and further on to India. Curiously, a review of the literature shows that several ports are mentioned by ancient authors or by epigraphy with names like Apologos, Teredon, and Phorat, but their location, their mutual relations are unclear as is their relative chronology. One has to pay attention as well to the structure of this documentation as we know the first century by literary sources (Strabo, Pliny, Josephus, who gave mostly second-hand relations of the geography and history of the region, with the exception of *The Periplus of the Erythraean Sea*), the first half of the second century by Palmyrene epigraphy, and for the third century, until 250, some rare documents (*Acts of Thomas*, Manichean and gnostic texts, a few inscriptions). Later sources such as Ammianus seem to reflect much earlier documents, whereas Syriac and Arabic chronicles and documents reflect mostly ecclesiastical history. The most striking is the lack of archaeological evidence, as some of the sites have been surveyed but not actually excavated.[1] One can go as far as to say that almost no direct evidence is available: most of what we know comes from outside Mesene.

Our purpose here is first to shed some light on these ports from the end of the Hellenistic period to the first centuries of Sassanian rule in lower Mesopotamia, based on the available textual evidence. Second, this essay will focus on the meagre evidence for traders or travellers (most of them for religious purposes) using Mesene and its ports as a point of entry to the Gulf and further to India. Among them, Palmyrenes are the most obvious example, and the better known by a great variety of texts, but not the only one, and literary evidence such as the *Periplus of the Erythraean Sea* give details on the functioning of maritime trade routes between the Eastern Roman empire and its neighbours in the first century AD. This later text is a good example of the type of information one can find in the literature. We may cite extensively the few lines devoted to Charax (together with Ommana):

35. . . . there is a market-town designated by law, called Apologus, situated near Spasinu Charax and the River Euphrates. **36**. Sailing through the mouth of the Gulf, after a six-days' course there is another market-town of Persia called Ommana. To both of these market-towns large vessels are regularly sent from Barygaza, loaded with copper and sandalwood and timbers of teakwood and logs of blackwood and ebony. To Ommana frankincense is also brought from Cana, and from Ommana to Arabia boats sewed together after the fashion of the place; these are known as *madarata*. From each of these market-towns, there are exported to Barygaza and also to Arabia, many pearls, but inferior to those of India; purple, clothing after the fashion of the place, wine, a great quantity of dates, gold and slaves.[2]

The Many Harbours of Mesene/Characene

Mesene

Mesene or Characene was a small kingdom located between two branches of the lower Tigris in southern Mesopotamia but its extent has changed several times. The best definition would be to give it the limits of the territory irrigated by the combined waters of Tigris and Euphrates.[3] For most of the period, it was independent of the great empires which ruled Mesopotamia, that is the Seleucid Kingdom (from *c.* 140 BC), then the Parthian Arsacid empire, with its own local dynasty until the beginning of the second century AD.[4] The last king of local extraction, Attambelos, seems to have been Trajan' ally, during the latter Oriental expedition. The kingdom was destroyed by the Parthians, in AD 150–1, at the end of the reign of a member of the Arsacid dynasty, Meeradatès.[5] Clearly, this king, despite his family links, had sided with the Roman empire, which may explain why Palmyrene merchants were still firmly established in Spasinu Charax and Vologesias, helping their fellow traders who came there. After that period, Mesene was transformed into a province of the Arsacid, then Sassanid empire, and traffic was still going across Mesene, to India and Eastern Asia, but documentation is rather sparse. Caravans continued to come from Palmyra during the second part of the second century (and even later), with variations due to the political situation there. Manichean literature shows that ships to and from India were still sailing through the Gulf. In the third and fourth centuries, Meshan remained a centre for the import of spices, drugs, and gems from India as well as silk and cotton cloth and steel.

Spasinu Charax, the 'palissade of Hyspasinoès', from the name of the first king of Mesene, was described as an island, the island of Characene (between two branches of the Tigris). As Phorat and most likely Apologos, it was not directly on the coast, but on a river, near its mouth, a location that had many advantages, protecting it from maritime disturbances. By Pliny's time, we are told that Charax was *ca.* 193 km. from the coast.[6] But it is a question which cannot be resolved so easily, as we do not know exactly where the shore line was situated in the Roman period.[7] It is clear that the advance of the delta was very rapid, and that by the end of Hellenistic times the coast lay farther south than it is today. At the beginning of the Islamic period, the coast retreated appreciably, and marshes expanded widely. It is obviously an explanation for the variety of ports in the evidence.

Spasinu Charax and the ports of Mesene

It appears that the destination of the majority of Palmyrene caravans was Spasinu Charax, the capital city itself.[8] What remains to be seen is if it is only a name describing the whole country, or if trade was really taking place there. The latter would mean that Spasinu Charax was a port of trade, and that commerce from there towards India was in the hands of merchants from Mesene, from the Gulf, or maybe from India. However, other inscriptions from Palmyra clearly show that merchants from the oasis had established direct contacts with India (Scythia, i.e. north-west India) with Bahrain in the Gulf or were going at least to Phorat.[9] This last one, as Apologos, or other names have to be considered as well, and a short review of the evidence is significant.

Apologos

In the case of Apologos, described as 'a market-town designated by law', there is only one witness, namely, the *Periplus* (see the text cited earlier). The very existence of the city is problematic but may be corroborated by Ammianus Marcellinus writing in the fourth century (XXIII, 6, 23) who knew of an Apollonia: this name maybe a deformed version of Apologos. From a phonological point of view, the name Apologos may be a deformation of Ubullu (known from Akkadian cuneiform tablets) which became al-Ubulla in the Islamic period.[10] The latter can be localized on the right bank of the Shatt al-ʿArab opposite Forat at ʿAshshar, the modern port of al-Basra. Several other hypotheses have been proposed: for some, the form 'Apologos' (as in the mss. of the *Periplus of the Erythraean Sea* 35, see above), is a corruption of ἡ Ἀποδάκου, the 'City of Apodakès'.[11] In fact, we know (by coins) of a king of that name (*c.* 124–103 BC), the second king of Characene. In that case, identification with Ubullah is excluded. For others as David Graf, it may represent a corruption of the Greek name 'Vologesias' (an adaptation of an Iranian name, transcribed as *'lgšy'* in Palmyrene Aramaic) the Parthian emporium established by Vologesias I (AD 50–80) probably early in his reign after the revolt of Seleucia in AD 36–43.[12] Vologesias, which probably lay south of Babylon and Borsippa near al-Hira on the right bank of the Euphrates, was used by Palmyrene traders as a station on their way between Palmyra and Spasinu Charax.[13] Vologesias may very well have been for some time part of the kingdom of Mesene, and of the geographical region of the same name. Nevertheless, it was too far from the sea to be a real seaport. This identification is thus highly questionable.

Phorat

We reach firmer ground for Phorat. Its localization has been the subject of debate but Hansmann's proposition in the 1960s seems correct: situated by Pliny, 11 or 12 miles downstream from Charax, its site should be at Maghlub, 17.4 km. (10.8 miles) south-east of Djabal Khayabir.[14] Phorat appears as a port in the Manichean codex (discussed later), not as much in Palmyrene inscriptions which are not very informative on this particular point.[15] For Pliny reflecting on the current situation during the first century AD, it was a station of the Nabataean trade on the way to Charax, their final destination.[16] Such was not the case apparently for some of the Palmyrene traders as shown by inscriptions referring to travels by ships towards India (Scythia).[17] The *Kölner Mani Codex* is another source for the city at the time of the visit of Mani and his father—around 240—'to Pharat, the city near the island of the people of Maisan'.[18] As we will see, the codex goes into some detail about trade and traders in Phorat. In the same period or somewhat later, the bishop David of Basra is said to have left his office in Basrah to go to India.[19] The text may be not reliable *per se*, not only because the same description is given twice, but it may be used as another piece of evidence on links between Phorat (Perat-Maishan) and India,[20] a few years only after Mani.

Teredon

Another such station was Teredon. According to Strabo (II, 1, 26; XVI, 3, 2 and 4 = 765–6) and Ammianus Marcellinus (depending on Eratosthenes), it had a direct link to the sea.[21] Strabo, calling it an outlet of the Euphrates, used it as a point of measurement (μέχρι Τερηδόνος καὶ τῆς ἐκβολῆς τοῦ Εὐφράτου; 'as far as Teredon and the outlet of the Euphrates'), but he was referring to the time of Nearchus. Later Pliny described it as a mere village (*e Parthico autem regno navigantibus vicus Teredon*) and Ammianus did not give it particular importance. As in other cases, it has been proposed to identify it with other sites with similar (more or less) names. Thus, it could be Idikara, which may be a later name for the same city, but it is far from certain. One may note that Ptolemy in his *Geography* (V, 20, 5–6) gave coordinates successively for Terèdôn and for Idikara, the latter appearing a little earlier (V, 19, 4) with different coordinates. Eusebius, citing Abydenus, explained that Teredon had been founded by Nabouchodonosor to prevent the Arabs from storming the region.[22]

Likewise, Arrian, when describing in his *Indica* XLI, 6–8, the route taken by Alexander's the Great admiral, Nearchus, mentioned a village Diridotis[23] which is identified by some as another name for Teredon (see J.-Fr. Salles in this volume). It was probably situated near the mouth of the Euphrates facing the island of Bubiyan.

There are other likely candidates for ports in the same region. For instance, it may be argued that the *Acts of Thomas*, an apocryphal text of the second or third century, give evidence for another port which could be added to the list. The geography of these acts has been the subject of harsh debates and place names are difficult to put on a map. Such is the case with what appears to be a port where the merchant Ḥabbān and his slave Thomas put up at a town called Andrapolis in Greek and *sndrwk* in Syriac.[24] It is clear both from the Greek text and the Syriac that Thomas had not reached India yet. Only after his departure from Andrapolis '. . . news was heard of the Apostle (being) in the realm of India. . .' and only later does the text make reference to the time 'when Judas [Thomas] had entered into the realm of Indian with the merchant Ḥabbān.[25] The textual tradition is not unanimous and the name which could be interpreted as something like Sandaruk in Syriac appears as well as ΕΝΑΔΡΩΧ in some manuscripts.[26] It is often assumed that the journey of Thomas to India went through Mesopotamia. One commentator made the obvious connection between *sndrwk* and Hatra, which is called Hatra d-Sanatruq by some inscriptions.[27] It is nevertheless difficult to believe that Thomas' navigation took place on the Tigris (and Hatra is situated some 40 km. from the river), the apostle being on his way from Jerusalem to India. Likewise, the text makes clear that they were sailing on a ship (πλοῖον in Greek, 'lp' in Syriac). Evidence given by the 'Song of the pearl' is another argument for a journey by sea from southern Mesopotamia to India, but one should at least allow for a different solution: it is not so obvious that the shortest way from Palestine to India is through the Syrian steppe or the desert of Northern Arabia, and one should also consider the Red Sea Route, via Socotra, and to south India. If it is true, as proposed by Dihle,[28] that *Acts of Barthelemy* are more likely than Thomas' to have been at the origin of south Indian Christianity, evidence is poor. In the 'Song of the soul' of the *Acts of Thomas* (see below), the first part of the journey is bound for Egypt, a geographical term loaded with symbolism. The song is attributed explicitly in the Syriac version to Thomas himself when he was in the country of Indians (*b'tr' dhndwy'*). Fictionally at least, the relation to Egypt is confirmed by the narrator.[29] Thus, despite this symbolism, it can be argued that, as in other parts of the text, a reference to *realia* is made: commercial relations between Egypt, Mesopotamia, and the East were a reality. As we shall see, the same balance between those three regions is striking when it comes to Palmyrene trade, traditionally linked with Mesopotamia, but with strong Egyptian connections, at least from the third century onwards.

What must be underscored here is the role for trade of cities, which are not harbours themselves, but *emporia*, so not necessarily situated directly on the coast, and sometimes far from it. Vologesias is an example, Charax could be another.[30]

Mesene and trade

Mesene itself is often designated as the meeting place of the merchants from the East. Our best witness is the so-called 'Song of the soul' (or 'of the pearl') or 'Hymn of the Soul' of the *Acts of Thomas*. It is a highly symbolic description of the hero's expulsion from paradise and his return to his heavenly home. One prince declares 'I quitted the East and went down. . . . I passed through the borders of Maishan, the meeting place of the merchants of the East, and I reached the land of Babylonia' (l. 16-18; he then 'descended to Egypt'). On his return to the East, the prince's route was the same '(he) came to the great Maishan, to the haven of merchants which sits on the shore of the sea' (l.70–1).[31] Reference here is made to the kingdom, not directly to its ports, even if Spasinu Charax itself, without being a port, may have been an *emporion*. One century (or more) earlier, the conversion of some women of the entourage of King Izates of Adiabene, during his sojourn in Mesene, shows the variety of population concerned by trade in this area, although it gives no information on the ports. This Jewish merchant was, no doubt, another one of the people who came there to play a role between East and West.[32]

For a later period, several Palmyrene inscriptions make mention of Spasinu Charax, as if trade stopped there. Palmyrenes, merchants or others, seem to have had a special relation to Mesene and to its king. The best-known example of those men of influence is Iaraios, satrap in Bahrain/Thilouos (*IGLS* XVII 245) for the king of Mesene, the famous Meeradates (σατρά[π]ην Θιλουανων Μεεραδατου βασιλέως Σπασίνου Χάρακος). The same king was later vanquished by Vologeses the fourth, the Parthian king (*c.* AD 150). It is clear that the island was under Mesene domination and was part of the whole network of exchange controlled by this kingdom. The real function of Iaraios and its links with trade are not obvious but there are many examples of men of foreign extraction leading the administration for small sovereigns. Their independence from local societies was surely a great advantage for the king. Another Palmyrene of a well known caravan family may have been archont of Mesene: the interpretation depends on a restoration which is tempting but still remains very hypothetical.[33]

There is yet another example of a tradesman maybe of foreign origin who had a leading role. His name Ôg- could be restored as Ôgga, a well known name at Palmyra. Thus, he could be Palmyrene as well as anything else.[34] This very interesting text deserves full quotation as it is a unique example giving further insights on the way trade was really functioning and also because for once we can see social differentiation at work. Mani came with his father to Phorat in Mesene in AD 240 and met there a merchant named Ôg- (name unknown) who was a great influence on his fellow traders, 'in Pharat, Ôg[- -] by name, remarkable by his power and his influence on other men - - -. I watched as the merchants, who were preparing to ship up to Persia and India, sealed his goods, but stood still until he came on board.'[35]

Links with India

We know that Palmyrenes had real links with the sea. The first item of evidence is a famous relief of the third century (or end of second century) representing a boat[36] which could well have sailed from Mesene to India or in the Red Sea. In fact, the question of the routes used by Palmyrenes is not easily resolved. Two texts may be cited here, giving evidence of the return from Scythia (north-west India) of ships owned by Palmyrenes. They date to the mid-second century.[37] But as we have seen, by that time traffic was not flowing as well as before. There is no reason to think that those ships were not bound to Mesene (maybe Phorat) but documentation from a later period shows that other itineraries have to be considered as well. It is clear that Egypt was playing a major role for Palmyrene traders in the third century. Two of them were honoured at Coptos by Palmyrene wool merchants belonging to a company of maritime traders (*Palmyrene naukleroi of the Erythrean sea*).[38] One may think that those Palmyrenes had chosen to trade in Egypt, because the traditional route through Mesopotamia—now under the control of the Sassanids (as was the Gulf)—was closed to them. The importance of Egypt for Palmyra was an explanation of the strategy of Zenobia later in the century. However, that is another story.

Clearly, the Palmyrenes were developing other routes as is amply shown by recent discoveries of Palmyrene inscriptions at Qani and of South Arabian inscription in the Hadramawt which was obviously a meeting place for Indians, Chaldeans (most probably people from Mesene) and Palmyrenes. The most eloquent document is indeed the so-called Abgar inscription discovered in a grotto on the Socotra Island. I may refer here to Ingo Strauch's essay on the Indian inscriptions (in this volume). Evidence points plainly to a date around the middle of the third century.

Trade in Mesene is not further substantiated by documents after this period, at least by Western sources, and it is from the other side, from Persian and maybe Indian documents that something new may appear someday. Much new information is available and progress of archaeology on the western coast of India or in the Arabian peninsula will surely bring new material to supplement what we know now. As for Mesene itself, political conditions will have to change before something is done.

Abbreviations

IGLS: *Inscriptions grecques et latines de la Syrie*
SEG: *Supplementum Epigraphicum Graecum*

Notes

1. See Hansmann 1967 and 1984 for the available evidence.
2. W.H. Schoff, tr. & ed., *The Periplus of the Erythraean Sea: Travel and Trade in the Indian Ocean by a Merchant of the First Century* (London, Bombay & Calcutta 1912), slightly modified. **35**. ἐμπόριόν ἐστι νόμιμον, λεγόμενον ἡ Ἀπολόγου, κειμένη κατὰ Πασίνου Χάρακα καὶ ποταμὸν Εὐφράτην. **36**. Παραπλεύσαντι δὲ τοῦτο τὸ στόμα τοῦ κόλπου μετὰ δρόμους ἓξ ἕτερον ἐμπόριόν ἐστι τῆς

Περσίδος, τὰ λεγόμενα Ὄμανα. Ἐξαρτίζεται δὲ εἰς αὐτὴν συνήθως, ἀπὸ μὲν Βαρυγάζων εἰς ἀμφότερα ταῦτα τῆς Περσίδος ἐμπόρια πλοῖα μεγάλα χαλκοῦ καὶ ξύλων σανταλίνων καὶ δοκῶν καὶ κεράτων καὶ φαλάγγων σασαμίνων καὶ ἐβενίνων, εἰς δὲ τὰ Ὄμανα καὶ ἀπὸ Κανῆς λίβανος, καὶ ἀπ᾽ Ὀμάνων εἰς τὴν Ἀραβίαν ἐντόπια ῥαπτὰ πλοιάρια, τὰ λεγόμενα μαδάρα. Εἰσφέρεται δὲ ἀπὸ ἑκατέρων τῶν ἐμπορίων εἴς τε Βαρύγαζα καὶ εἰς Ἀραβίαν πινικόν, πολὺ μὲν, χεῖρον δὲ τοῦ Ἰνδικοῦ, καὶ πορφύρα καὶ ἱματισμὸς ἐντόπιος καὶ οἶνος καὶ φοῖνιξ πολὺς καὶ χρυσὸς καὶ σώματα.

3. Hansman 1967 and 1984.

4. On the political history of Characene, with ample evidence, see Schuol 2000.

5. Bernard 1990.

6. Pliny, *Natural History* VI 139-140: *iterumque infestatum Spaosines Sagdodonaci filius, rex finitimorum Arabum, quem Iuba satrapen Antiochi fuisse falso tradit, oppositis molibus restituit nomenque suum dedit, emunito situ iuxta in longitudinem VI p., in latitudinem paulo minus. prius fuit a litore stadiis X – maritimum etiam Vipsania porticus habet –, Iuba vero prodente L p. nunc abesse a litore CXX legati Arabum nostrique negotiatores, qui inde venere, adfirmant.* ('Pasines, the son of Saggonadacus, and king of the neighbouring Arabians, restored (Charax), and raised embankments for its protection, calling it after himself. It stood at first at a distance of ten stadia from the shore, and even had a harbour of its own. But according to Juba, it is fifty miles from the sea; and at the present day, the ambassadors from Arabia, and our own merchants who have visited the place, say that it stands at a distance of one hundred and twenty miles from the sea-shore.').

7. See Sanlaville 1989.

8. See the list in Gawlikowski 1994: 32–3.

9. The case of cities of lower Mesopotamia, Vologesias and perhaps Choumana (Ptolemy, *Geography* V, 20) is different.

10. See Kramers 2000: 765, *s.v.* al-Ubulla.

11. Habicht 1997: 130: 'Ein Emporion mit dem Namen ἡ Ἀποδάκου (ἡ Ἀπολόγου cod.) paßt dazu gut und wäre eine ausgezeichnete Entsprechung zu Spasinu Charax.'

12. Graf 1994: 146 (review of Casson 1989): '"Apologos", at the head of the Persian Gulf (*The Periplus of the Erythraean Sea* 35), may represent a corruption of Greek for "Vologesias", the Parthian emporium established by Vologesias I (AD 50–80) . . . . If this identification is correct, the *terminus a quo* for the *Periplus* is the Neronian era.'

13. On Vologesias, Chaumont 1974. For Vologesias and Palmyra, e.g. Gawlikowski 1994. See as well Graf 1994: 146: 'It appears as Vologesocerta in Pliny (*Natural History* VI 122) and Valashabad in Sassanian sources. In the Han Dynasty records of Kan Ying's expedition to the Persian Gulf in AD 97, the toponym *Yü-lo* probably represents Vologesias (s.v. the *Wei-lüeh* section at the end of chapter 30 in the San Kuo-chih). In Palmyrene Aramaic texts of AD 108–247 it is known as *'lgsy*'.

14. Hansman 1967.

15. *IGLS* XVII, 25: A caravan returning from Phorat and Vologesias; 246: a caravan returning from Charax and Vologesias, honours someone, who may be archon of Phorath in Mesene.

16. VI 145 *deinde est oppidum quod Characenorum regi paret in Pasitigris ripa, Forat nomine, in quod a Petra conveniunt, Characenque inde XII p. secundo aestu navigant* ('We next come to a city situated on the banks of the Pasitigris, Forat by name, and subject to the king of Charax: to this place people resort on their road from Petra, and sail thence to Charax, twelve miles distant, with the tide.').

17. *IGLS* XVII, 26, and 250: merchants back from Scythia.

18. *Kölner Mani-Codex* 140 εἰς Φαρὰτ᾽ τὴν [πό]λιν πλησίον τῆς [νήσ]ου τῶν Μαϊσα[νῶν].

19. His name appears in the so-called *Chronique de Séert* I [ed. by Mgr Scher, *Patrologia Orientalis* IV/3 (1908)] in two occasions. In the first one (p. 236, 'David, évêque de Bassorah (Al-Basrah), qui quitta son siège et partit pour l'Inde où il convertit une foule de personnes'), he is said to be contemporaneous with the pope Etienne [pope from 254 to 257]), and in the second (p. 292, 'David, évêque de Bassora, après avoir quitté son siège épiscopal, partit pour l'Inde. Il prêcha (la religion) aux habitants de ce pays et en convertit beaucoup'), with Athanasius of Alexandria (328–73). He is further attested by Bar Hebraeus, in his *Chronicon ecclesiasticum* (ed. & transl. J.B. Abbeloos and T. Lamy), Louvain, Peeters, 1872-1877, cols. 27-28, in connection with Papas first metropolites of Seleuceia-Ctesiphon, ['*Manum illi (i.e. Papas) imposuit David metropolita Maischanae, anno Graecorum quingentesimo septuagesimo septimo* (AD 265-266)']. This last text makes it quite probable that David was active in the second part of the third century. The confusion may arise from the fact that Mesene became seat of the metropolite only in 310, with Papas. Despite Bar Hebraeus, David was most likely only bishop of Phorat (as in the Chronicle of Seert), not metropolite (in the same sense, see fn.3 of Abbeloos and Lamy).

20. The name of the Archeparchy of Perat-Maishan was changed to Archeparchy of Basrah only in 1954.

21. Ammianus XXIII, 6, 11: *quibus angustiis permeatis cum latitudo patuerit nimis extensa, nauigatio ad usque urbem Teredona porrigitur, ubi post iacturas multiplices pelago miscetur Euphrates. 23. In omni autem Assyria multae sunt urbes. inter quas Apamia eminet Mesene cognominata et Teredon et Apollonia et Vologessia hisque similes multae.* (11. 'After one has passed through this narrow strait, a wide expanse of sea opens, which is favourable to navigation as far as the city of Teredon, where after many losses the Euphrates mingles with the deep.' 23. 'But in all Assyria there are many cities among which Apamia, formerly called Mesene, and Teredon, Apollonia and Vologessia, and many similar ones are conspicuous.').

22. *Preparatio evangelica* IX, 41, 8 ἀπετείχισε δὲ καὶ τῆς Ἐρυθρῆς Θαλάσσης τὴν ἐπίκλυσιν καὶ Τερηδόνα πόλιν ἔκτισε κατὰ τὰς Ἀράβων εἰσβολάς. Eusebius is using the works of Abydenus, historian, author of a *History of the Chaldeans and Assyrians*, maybe around 200 BC. See later Eusthatius (twelfth century

AD), in his *Commentary on Dionysius Periegetes* (976, 4-6) speaking of the Euphrates, which flows across Babylonia, εἰς τὴν Περσίδα θάλασσαν ἀπερεύγεται, παρὰ τὴν Τερηδόνα, πόλιν Περσικήν. Dionysios Periegetes is believed to have lived in the second century AD.

23. Arrian XLI, 6-8: καὶ ἦλθον σταδίους ἐνακοσίους, καὶ καθωρμίσθησαν ἐπὶ τοῦ στόματος τοῦ Εὐφράτου πρὸς κώμῃ τινὶ τῆς Βαβυλωνίης χώρης – ὄνομα δὲ αὐτῇ Διρίδωτις –, ἵνα λιβανωτόν τε ἀπὸ τῆς Γερραίης γῆς οἱ ἔμποροι ἀγινέουσι καὶ τὰ ἄλλα ὅσα θυμιήματα ἡ Ἀράβων γῆ φέρει. ἀπὸ δὲ τοῦ στόματος τοῦ Εὐφράτου ἔστε Βαβυλῶνα πλοῦν λέγει Νέαρχος σταδίους εἶναι ἐς τρισχιλίους καὶ τριακοσίους. ('They sailed nine hundred stades, and anchored in the mouth of the Euphrates near a village of Babylonia, called Diridotis; here the merchants gather together frankincense from the neighbouring country and all other sweet-smelling spices which Arabia produces. From the mouth of the Euphrates to Babylon Nearchus says it is a voyage of three thousand three hundred stades.').

24. *Acts of Thomas* 3–4 (p. *q'd* of Wright) *lsndrwk mḥwz'/ kd nḥtw dyn l'r'', w''lyn hww w 'zlyn lmdynt'.* εἰς Ἀνδράπολιν, πόλιν βασιλικήν. Ἐξελθόντες δὲ ἀπὸ τοῦ πλοίου εἰσῄεσαν εἰς τὴν πόλιν.

25. Translation W. Wright. *Acts of Thomas* 16–7 (p. *qpd–qph* of Wright) *'dm' d'štm' hw' ṭb' lšlyḥ' bhndw mdynt', w'zlw lwth w'tḥlḥw 'mh. wkd 'l yhwd' lhndw mdynt' 'm lbn tgr' 'zl lbn lšlmh dgwdnpr mlk' dhndw.* ὅτι ἐν ταῖς πόλεσιν τῆς Ἰνδίας κατήχθη καὶ ἐκεῖ διδάσκει. καὶ ἀπεῃθόντες κατεμίγησαν αὐτῷ. Ὅτε δὲ εἰσῆλθεν ὁ ἀπόστολος εἰς τὰς πόλεις τῆς Ἰνδίας μετὰ Ἀββάνη τοῦ ἐμπόρου…

26. Or ΕΝΑΔΟΧ, or ΕΔΡΟΝ.

27. See Huxley 1983: 73.

28. Dihle 1963: 61–4, citing Eusebius, *Ecclesiastical History* 5, 10.

29. See Poirier 1981: 265: 'la géographie de l'HP [*Hymne de la Perle*] n'a rien d'imaginaire ni de fantasiste.'

30. Gawlikowski 1994: 29: 'Later on, the merchants from Palmyra mostly go to and come from Spasinu Charax, capital city of the kingdom of Mesene, or a city called Vologesias.'

31. In the Greek version of the *Acts of Thomas*, l. 18–19 and 68–71: παρελθὼν δὲ καὶ τὰ τῶν Μοσάνων μεθόρια ἔνθα ἐστὶν τὸ καταγώγιον τῶν ἀνατολικῶν ἐμπόρων ἀφικόμην εἰς τὴν τῶν Βαβυλωνίων χώραν . . . καὶ καταλείψας ἐπ' ἀριστερὰ τὴν Βαβυλῶνα εἰς τὴν Μέσον ἀφικόμην τὴν μεγάλην οὖσαν παραλίαν (See Poirier 1981: 352–6).

32. Flavius Josephus, *Antiquities of the Jews* XX (34-35): καθ' ὃν χρόνον ὁ Ἰζάτης ἐν τῷ Σπασίνου χάρακι διέτριβεν Ἰουδαῖός τις ἔμπορος Ἀνανίας ὄνομα πρὸς τὰς γυναῖκας εἰσιὼν τοῦ βασιλέως ἐδίδασκεν αὐτὰς τὸν θεὸν σέβειν, ὡς Ἰουδαίοις πάτριον ἦν. ('Now, during the time Izates abode at Spasinu Charax, a certain Jewish merchant, whose name was Ananias, got among the women that belonged to the king, and taught them to worship God according to the Jewish religion').

33. *SEG* 20, 385 = *IGLS* XVII, 246.

34. *Kölner Mani-Codex* 144.

35. [. . . ἐ]ν Φαρὰτ᾽ Ὠγ [. . . τὸ ὄν]ομα, ἄν(θρωπ)ος ἐπί[σημος ἐ]πὶ τῆι αὐτοῦ [δυνάμει] κὰι ἐξουσίαι ων [. . .]. γ. ἀνδρῶν. [εἶδον δὲ] τοὺς ἐμπόρους [ὡς ἐπὶ τῶν] πλοίων εἰς Πέρ[σας καὶ ε]ἰς Ἰνδους πε[ριπλεύσο]ντες ἐσφρά[γισαν τὰ ὤνι]α αὐτοῦ οὐ[κ αἴροντες ἔ]ως ἀνῄει.
36. Colledge 1976, pl.103.
37. *IGLS* XVII, 26 and 250.
38. *SEG* 34, 1593: Ζαβδάλα Σαλμάνου καὶ Ἀνείνα Ἀδριανῶν Παλμυρηνῶν ναυκλήρων Ἐρυθραικῶν. [Ἀ]δριανοὶ Παλμυρηνοὶ ἐριέμποροι.

References

Bernard, P. (1990), 'Vicissitudes au gré de l'histoire d'une statue en bronze d'Héraclès', *Journal des savants*, pp. 3–67.

Chaumont, M.-L. (1974), 'Études d'histoire parthe III: les villes fondées par les Vologèse', *Syria*, vol. 51, pp. 75–89.

Colledge, M.A.R. (1976), *The Art of Palmyra*, London: Thames & Hudson.

Dihle, A. (1983), 'Neues zur Thomas-Tradition', *Jahrbuch für Antike und Christentum*, vol. 6, pp. 54–70.

Gawlikowski, M. (1994), 'Palmyra as a Trading Center', *Iraq*, vol. 56, pp. 27–33.

Graf, D.F. (1994), 'Book Review: Lionel Casson. *The Periplus Maris Erythraei*', *American Journal of Philology*, vol. 115, pp. 143–7.

Habicht, C. (1997), 'Zu Kapitel 35 des *Periplus des Roten Meeres*', *Zeitschrift für Papyrologie und Epigraphik*, vol. 115, pp. 128–30.

Hansmann, J. (1967), 'Charax and the Karkeh', *Iranica antiqua*, vol. 7, pp. 21–58.

———(1984), 'The Land of Meshan', *Iran*, vol. 22, pp. 161–6.

Huxley, G. (1983), 'Geography in the *Acts of Thomas*', *Greek, Roman and Byzantine Studies*, vol. 24, pp. 71–80.

Kramers, J.H. (2000), 'al-Ubulla', *Encyclopédie de l'Islam²* , vol. X, p. 765.

Poirier, P.-H. (1981), *L'hymne de la perle des actes de Thomas* (*Homo religiosus* 8). Louvain: Université de Louvain.

Sanlaville, P. (1989), 'Considérations sur l'évolution de la Basse Mésopotamie au cours des derniers millénaires', *Paléorient*, vol. 15, pp. 5–27.

Schuol, M. (2000), *Die Charakene. Ein mesopotamisches Königreich in hellenistisch-parthischer Zeit* (Oriens et Occidens 1), Stuttgart: Franz Steiner Verlag.

CHAPTER 9

Towards a Geography of the Harbours in the Persian Gulf in Antiquity (Sixth Century BC–Sixth Century AD)

Jean-François Salles

As far as we accept that, seen from India, what was Mesopotamia and its neighbours in Antiquity was referred to as Western Asia, the Persian Gulf is often mentioned in the Western sources from the third millennium BC onwards. Several texts and inscriptions mention the country and people of Dilmun, known as the major middlemen in trade between the Indus and the Tigris Valleys. Moreover, closer relations of different types (e.g. sealings, language, etc.) did probably exist between the two regions during the Harappan period. Considered since the mid-third millennium BC as a maritime nation, Dilmun was centred around the Bahrain islands and included the coastal area and hinterland of Eastern Arabia, Failaka island in Kuwait (*Agarum*) and southern Babylonia later called the *Sealand.* However, despite the fact that this large area should have offered many landing facilities to the seamen of the Gulf, not a single harbour is ever cited by any Mesopotamian sources of the third-second millennium BC, no toponym is ever mentioned.[1] Such a 'failure' of knowledge should undoubtedly raise the question: what was an ancient port during these early periods?

During the first half of the first millennium BC, Neo-Babylonian sources are more prolific about numerous places in the *Sealand*—some certainly maritime or fluvial, but almost all the cited toponyms remain without any reality. There is no way to suggest any tentative location when analysed through the present topography of the region, and no site could be found throughout the most southern Babylonia (*Sealand*) with archaeological remains of the period. Is it indeed necessary to evoke the frequent and crucial changes in the landscapes and topography of the area due to the fluvial and maritime variations (Sanlaville 1987, 1989).

In fact, we have to rely mainly on the Graeco-Roman sources to get some names, precise or more elusive, of ports/harbours in the Persian Gulf and southern Babylonia. Would that mean that Oriental people do not share the same concept and awareness(?) of such landing and trading places with the Mediterranean people—beyond the problem of local terms and their translation today? This, however, would go beyond the areas of this present essay.

The available evidence (texts, archaeology) (Map 9.1)

Herodotus in the fifth century BC tells us about the Gulf as a remote place, *ta eschata tès basileias* (the furthermost bounds of the [Persian] kingdom), where according to Ctesias, his informant, the Persian kings used to deport banished people, *anapastoi*; for instance, 'it is said that these banished people were living in islands' (III, 93; VII, 68, 80). The author does not

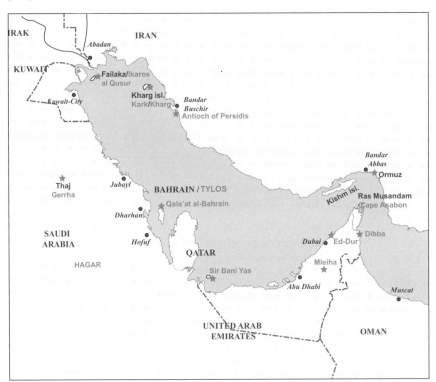

Map 9.1: Sketch map of the Persian Gulf © Maison de l'Orient et de la Méditerranée (Massoud Karim). *Black italics* : modern towns * Archaeological sites cited in the text and their ancient names, in blue the Christian sites.

give much more information about the region, apart from his description of the Persian armies, where he writes that the people of the Erythraean Sea were dressed and armed in the same way as the Medes (Persians), and that the neighbouring nation of the *Mycoi* (Oman peninsula) was dressed and armed as the Indians were. Such information probably confirms that the Persian Gulf was a kind of 'Achaemenid Lake'. It may also reflect a traditional and noticeable division inside the Gulf, its northern half being more turned towards the lands of Arabia, Persia and Mesopotamia, the Oman peninsula being largely turned towards India (Salles 1990). But we cannot find a single mention of any port or any trade in Herodotus.

A later reference to banished people in the Gulf can be found in Strabo (XVI, 3, 5–7) in his narrative of the navigation of Nearchus, the admiral of Alexander. Nearchus came accross a Persian, Mithropastès, a satrap banished by Dareios III, when he landed on the island of Ogyris near the mouth of the Gulf (actual Kishm?). Mithropastès became Nearchus informant for his navigation in the Persian Gulf (Salles 1992: 80), however, Strabo does not mention any port unless one interprets the mention of an island as the existence of a harbour *per se*(?). It should also be pointed out that the author does not mention any important harbour—a 'town', or a trading place—along the Iranian coast of the Gulf[2] which Nearchus sailed northwards: only small villages, watering places and other places of call are echoed. When the Greeks wrote their reports on Alexander's expeditions or re-wrote his history in the East (Arrian), they paid less attention to trade and commercial affairs than to the achievements of their heroes. Their narrative relates the daily hazards and adventures of the men without much consideration to the background of the regions they navigated. A new approach of trade, exchanges, and maritime facilities will appear in later sources, first century AD, Pliny and the *Periplus of the Erythraean Sea.*

However, one famous port is reported to have been active at the outlet of the Mesopotamian rivers since the sixth century BC: Teredon (Map 9.2). A tradition (unverified?) reported by Eusebius asserts that it had been founded by King Nebuchadnezzar 'to control the incursions of the Arabs' (Potts 1984: 87–91; Retsö 2004: 181). The toponym is mentioned by Hellenistic and later authors, Strabo, Pliny, Aelian, Dionysios of Alexandria, Ammianus Marcellinus.[3] Arrian calls it Diridotis and adds, quoting Nearchus: 'all the merchants gather together frankincense from the neighbouring country and all sweet-smelling spices which Arabia produces' (*Ind.*, XLI, 6–7). However, none of these authors agree on its description: for Strabo, Eusebius, and Ammianus Marcellinus it is a city, for Pliny a village. The location of the site is unknown as well and remains a matter of debate. Strabo mentions that the city is located at 'the outlet of

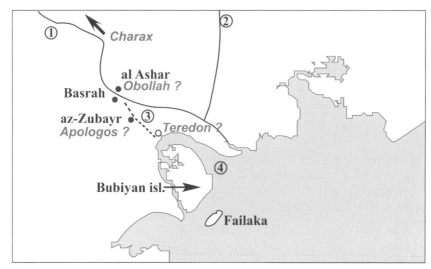

Map 9.2: A tentative reconstruction of the Euphrates mouth at the close of the era (J.F.S. and M.K.). 1 is the nowadays Shatt el-Arab; 2 the river Karun; 3 is the ancient channel of the Euphrates ca the end of the 1st mill. BC (Sanlaville 1989) and 4 its outlet in the Persian Gulf, now the Khor Abdallah (Kuwait)

the Euphrates' (II, 1, 25; XVI, 3, 2), and for Dionysions of Alexandria, 'the Euphrates flows into the Gulf near Teredon' (v. 984, Ch. Jacob ed.), both suggesting a location on the shores of the Gulf. This might be supported by another proposal: the name of the city might have been a Greek interpretation of an Aramaic name composed of *tr'*, the gate, and *dym'*, of the sea.[4] Pliny's description does not help very much, too: having stated that Teredon is located 'below [i.e. south of] the confluence of the Euphrates and the Tigris', he adds, 'those travelling by water from the Kingdom of Parthia come to the village of Teredon' (VI, xxxii, 145). Following these remarks, one way to reach Teredon in the south would be the rivers (Tigris or Karun), though part of their course flowed outside Parthia at the time of Pliny, the Characene/Mesene being largely independent. I would be inclined to read Pliny's words referring to a travel by sea from the East, from the eastern coastal areas of Parthia.

The short comment by Arrian (mentioned earlier) raises a couple of questions. First, who were the 'merchants' mentioned? Probably not Greek people as we have no information on any kind of Greek trade through the Gulf at the time of the author's sources, that is the historians of Alexander (mentioned earlier); most certainly Chaldaeans (? Teredon), Arabs (Gerrha and other unknown places) and Arabs from Bahrain (mentioned later), probably Persians as well? Second, '. . . frankincense from the neighbouring country': for sure there is no country that produces frankincense in the vicinity of Teredon, and if Arrian refers to an Arabian frankincense, its origin would have been located thousands of kilometres away to the South-West by sea[5] or through the desert, in Hadramawt and on the Yemeni plateaux. I have argued elsewhere that the Gerrhaean frankincense, for example, disclosed by Zeno's papyri (third century BC) was most likely imported by the Gerrhaeans from India, not from Arabia, then despatched to Syria, sailing up the Euphrates as cited by Strabo, or through a caravan desert route to Petra.[6] In a common assimilation pertinent across the ages, looking at Arab ships and seamen conveying frankincense, Nearchus would have ingenously concluded that it was Arabian frankincense. Third, the comment is similar for the 'sweet-smelling spices which Arabia produces', definitely not originating in Eastern Arabia, most probably coming from India.

I would thus assume that, in the late fourth century BC, Teredon used to be a port of entry of Indian products shipped on Arab vessels—a long tradition of Bahrain seamen, together now with the emerging Gerrha (third century BC, mentioned later), and maybe a couple of other Arab people (*Mycoi/Macae* of Oman?).

As it is brillantly analysed in this volume by Jean-Baptiste Yon, I will not discuss the Alexandria established by Alexander the Great at the head of the Persian Gulf (southern Babylonia), later rebuilt by Antiochus IV, which became Spasinu Charax in late Hellenistic-Roman/Parthian times, then Forat Maisan under the Sasanians. However, it should be emphasized that Spasinu Charax cannot be equated with the *emporion* Apologos of the *Periplus* which explicitly mentions a distance between the two cities: Apologos became the Arabic Ubolah/Obollah, near modern Basrah.

When dealing with the Persian Gulf, the Hellenistic authors do not provide us with much information about the ports of the Persian Gulf. Following a fourth-third century BC anonymous tradition (?), we hear of Gerrha and its trading activities through Agatharchides, Eratosthenes and Aristobulus cited by Strabo or Pliny, while Theophratus, basing his comments on Alexander's companions reports provides useful information about the landscape of Bahrain islands (Tylos in Greek).   However, the naturalist does not deal at all with the social or economic life of the archipel.[7] The island of Failaka is barely known, no port is mentioned, and even its military function is not really emphasized. Finally, the port of Oam(m)ana remains unnamed up the first century AD (the *Periplus*), although some archaeological data can be dated to the first century BC.

Gerrha was a place in Eastern Arabia (Map 9.3), although its precise location is still debated. Quoting Aristobulus, Strabo states that the Gerrhaeans would carry most of their merchandise on 'rafts' (*skediai*) up

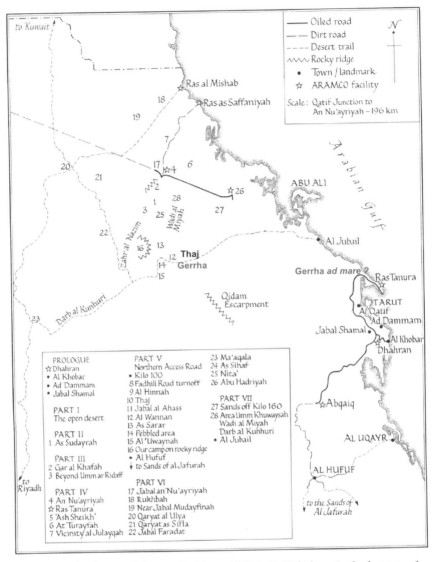

Map 9.3: Sketch map of Eastern Arabia, ca 1960, in E. Nicholson, *In the footsteps of the camel. A portrait of the Bedouins of Eastern Saudi Arabioa in mid-century,* Stacey International, London, 1983, p. 4. (Corr. M. Karim). The ancient (?)'desert trail' from Thaj to al-Jubail would suggest a location of Gerrha *ad mare* rather close to al-Jubail

to Babylonia, then to the North (Thapsacos) sailing up the Euphrates (XVI, 3, 3). Agatharchides writes that the Gerrhaeans conducted much trade in frankincense and other aromatics, and that they helped prosper both the Seleucids and the Ptolemies (*apud Geographici Graci Minores* [Muller 1861], 102). In the third century BC, the archives of Zeno, who worked for a high minister of Ptolemaic Egypt, provide evidence of Gerrhaean frankincense brought to Gaza, while describing a Moabite caravaneer (i.e. one living on the Jordanian plateau) who received Gerrhaean frankincense near Petra in Jordan (*Pap. Cairo Zen.*, I, 59009, see Durand 1997: 143–9). Therefore, Gerrha was not just a harbour for sure, but also a caravan nation crossing the deserts of Arabia.

But the location of the port remains an enigma. Strabo describes a Gerrha city (*polis*) located in a deep gulf of the sea, but two lines later states that the *polis* is about 200 stadia away from the sea. Pliny knows about the *sinus Gerraicus* (bay of Gerrha) and a large city, *oppidum*, but it is not clear whether this 'fortress' is located on the shores of the bay or elsewhere. Ptolemy repeats more or less the same information. The most common interpretation suggests that there were two places named Gerrha, one inland identified with the archaeological site of Thaj excavated by Dan T. Potts in the 80s; a large rampart encloses the city, what might be Pliny's *oppidum*. And another, Gerrha-*ad-mare*, somewhere along the coast of Arabia. However, several explorations and surveys—even before the pre-oil period and the recent strong urbanization of that area—were unable to find Gerrha, no traces of a coastal settelement/harbour were ever mentioned. In fact, what was a maritime harbour in Eastern Arabia in the third century BC?[8] The archaeology of Thaj/Gerrha indicates a slow decline during the first century-early second century AD, and the city seems to have been abandoned before the end of the second century. When he wrote his *Geography* (end of the first century BC), Strabo was one of the last to tell us about the trading activities of the Gerrhaeans, relying on earlier sources and not on his own time information. A few decades later, Pliny also seemed to be aware of the existence of Gerrha (VI, xxxii, 147) but nothing about the Gerrhaeans and their trade, probably from a first century BC source, Juba of Mauretania. Though his work is lost, Juba stated that the Gerrhaeans used to bring frankincense to the Parthians (Pliny XII, 40, 80).

Clearly, when seen from the West and the locations of the late Hellenistic and Roman authors, i.e. Alexandria, Athens, and Roma, the trade of frankincense was then centered in the Red Sea and along the caravans travelling south-north from Yemen/Hadramwt to Egypt and the Eastern Mediterranean (from the second/first century BC onwards). The Westerners, it seemed, continued to ignore most events in the Persian Gulf.

After years of debate it is now generally assumed, though not unanimously, that Om(m)ana of the *Periplus of the Erythraean Sea* should be identified with the site of ed-Dur in the emirate of Umm al Qawayn, about 40 km. north-east from Dubai (Map 9.1, Plates 9.1–2). The site is

Plate 9.1: Aerial photograph of ed-Dur site (1987), in E. Haerinck, *Excavations at ed-Dur*
(*Umm al-Qaiwain, United Emirates*). II *The Tombs*, The University of Ghent, Peeters,
Leuven 2001, pl. 4, M = Temple area; N = graves; L = the lagoon.

today separated from the open sea by a laguna which seems of recent
formation. Though the exact coastline of the first century AD cannot be
precisely reconstructed, there is no doubt that ed-Dur was a maritime
site. Archaeological remains reveal significant activity throughout the first
century AD—with some late Hellenistic antecedents, perhaps first century
BC(?). They show that the site was active during most of the second century
before a rapid decline and abandonment in the third century AD. Imported
items are numerous: a few Roman *Sigillata* poteries, the majority of the
ceramics coming from southern Babylonia or Iran, a controversial Indian
coarse black pottery,[9] and many other non-local objects. Reviewing part
of the monetary finds, E. Haerinck records 11 coins from Characene
(Charax/Apologos), 2 from South-Arabia, 4 from Parthia or Persia, 6 from
Nabatene of Palestine, 4 Roman and 5 Indian.[10]

Plate 9.2: Ed Dur, Tomb G 6130. Ibid., pl. 204.

The site has never been re-occupied since its abandonment,[11] so one would expect to find remains related to the maritime activity of a large 'market-town'(?) as designated in the *Periplus*. However, there is nothing of this kind. Indeed, the harbour constructions, if any, could have been buried under the sea, but the shallow laguna and the small offshore bar did not provide any built remains, just a small and ancient(?) cemetery. Archaeologists assume that the 'harbour' was nothing other than the beach. The site itself did not reveal much information. There are no dwellings or well-built houses, one can find a temple or sacred place, and the most interesting remains were large subterranean built tombs, probably family or clan burial-places, sometimes associated with camel burials. Remains of an enclosing wall frame a surface of about 10,000 sq. m., probably as a kind of defence in case of an attack(?)—or the limit of an important central area. But no traces of occupation were ever found outside the enclosing wall.

Such modest remains can hardly define an *emporion* as named in the *Periplus*, a port of trade. The common assumption is that ed-Dur was a true marketplace, but not a permanent location. In a recent paper,[12] M. Mouton emphasizes that the time taken to sail to and fro, the duration of time spent in the harbour, the system of winds and/or currents and other such factors would curtail constant activity all year along, and restrict the 'international markets' to a short, privileged time. A site like ed-Dur, and probably many others, thus became places of convergence for many groups concerned with international trade for a limited period, which in turn reduces the need for permanent buildings (local *barastis*, tents are enough). The market gathering was also a kind of fair, with social and religious undertakings and entertainments—see the temple—as well as visits and ceremonies to the clan or tribe burial-place, as is common in many Semitic populations.[13]

Such a reasonable hypothesis offers a new vision of the 'international trade' in the Persian Gulf, much more human and social beyond the tedious catalogue of vessels, merchandise, winds and currents. Here we find the actors of these exchanges, the attendants of these markets or fairs—the topic of the second part of this essay. However, the slow penetration of the Westerners (Greeks) in the Eryhtraean Sea from the third(?)/second century BC onwards and occasionally in the Persian Gulf did not arise as a hazard or as the result of individual exploits (e.g. Eudoxus of Cyzicus in the second century BC). D. Marcotte has shown that the Erythraean Sea has been seen from early on as an entity from the Nile to the western coast of India, first by the Achaemenids (exploration by Scylax of Caryanda) and Dareios conquests in northern India and reported so to the Greeks, as attested by several passages in Herodotus (Marcotte 2010). Such a vision was 'scientifically' developped by the geographer Agatharchides in the third century BC—the *mesambria*—, and it progressively turned into a political concern of the Ptolemies, e.g. with the creation of an epistrategy of the Thebaid and the Erythraean Sea in the late second century BC. The purpose was not conquest, but a large opening of the maritime *oikouménè* beyond the Mediterranean Sea, and the recognition of new populations. When the Romans had finally submitted Egypt, it became more an economic and financial matter,[14] but the earlier 'polity' of the Greeks had not disrupted the traditions and evolution of the riverine populations, which we will find as major actors of the exchanges in the Erythraean Sea.

Which actors in the Persian Gulf through the ages?

We have already met some of the actors in the Hellenistic/pre-Augustean period. First, the people of southern Babylonia, Chaldaeans and Arabs—and probably some Nabataean traders who used to travel along a north-eastern Arabian caravan route from southern Jordan/Syria to the head of the Gulf (via the Azraq oasis [accessible from Jordan and from southern Syria], the wadi Sirhan, the al-Jawf/Dumat al Gandal/Sakaka oases and then the head of the Gulf) (Map 9.4):[15] at least two or three harbours are referred to in the Hellenistic sources. I also mentioned the Gerrhaeans,

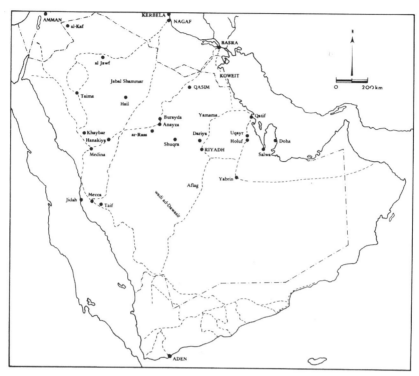

Map 9.4: Main Trans-arabian "routes", in D.T. Potts, 'Trans-arabian routes of the pre-Islamic period', p. 138, in *L'Arabie et ses mers bordières. I. Itinéraires et voisinages* (dir. J.-F. Salles), Maison de l'Orient, Lyon, 1988.

whether they were originally Arabs or Chaldaeans, who according to our sources were active from the third to the first century BC, but whose business is no longer documented during the first centuries AD: there was a Gerrha harbour, eventhough we cannot locate it. Strangely enough, the people of Tylos/Bahrain do not appear in the written sources, although archaeology lavishly demonstrates that they carried on their role of middlemen in the exchanges of the Persian Gulf: the coastal site of Qala'at al-Bahrain yielded important layers dated to the last centuries BC (Kervran et al. 2006). Finally, some Omani groups should have played some role, too; if ed Dur/ Om(m)ana come to be known from the first century AD only, Mleiha in its hinterland has been settled since the third century BC onwards. The settlement was not a remote and isolated one, and traces of external exchanges are rather numerous (Mouton 2009).[16]

Next to nothing is known about a maritime presence of Persians/Iranians in the Gulf during the last centuries BC. A Greek inscription dated to the early third century BC seems to be a letter by the Greek people from Antioch in Persidis to their compatriots at Magnesia on Meander in Asia

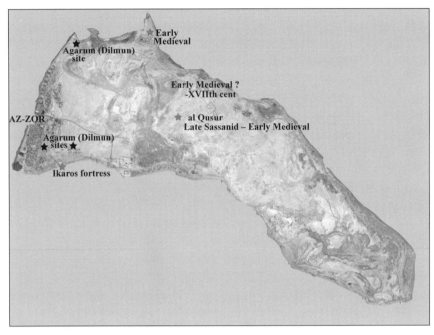

Plate 9.3: Archaeological sites on Failaka island, Kuwait.

Minor (reign of Seleucos I Nicator). This Antioch is usually identified as Bushire, but no archaeological remains of this period were ever retrieved

Plate 9.4: Ikaros (Failaka), the Hellenistic fortress (1989),
© Maison de l'Orient et de la Méditerranée.

in the excavations. And, the rest of the coast did not yield real traces of occupation during the same period.

Indeed, some Westerners—Greeks—were present in the Gulf. The island of Failaka off Kuwait has disclosed a Seleucid garrison at the site called Ikaros (Plates 9.3–4). Greek inscriptions, Greek coins and other related material were found in the fortress, alongwith some rather common pottery and daily life objects belonging to the local (?) population mentioned on one of the inscriptions. However, no contemporaneous site was ever found outside the fortress. A tomb inscription in Greek found in Bahrain honours a *kubernetès* (captain of a ship), probably son of a Phoenician merchant, and another Greek inscription is a dedication to King Hyspaosines and his wife (*c.*130 BC). One may conclude that part of the population in Tylos/ Bahrain could read and speak the Greek language. But which part was this? And how large was their number? Who were they? These remain unanswered questions, and the data should not be overestimated (Plate 9.5). During the Hellenistic period, written sources

Plate 9.5: The fortress and excavations at Qala'at al Bahrain, the main centre of the northern coast, in *Bahrain National Museum*, IMMEL Publishing, Bahrain, 1993, p. 100.

mention Antiochos III's expedition to Gerrha after his return from India (c.206/205 BC).[17] Nothing is really known of a supposed raid in the Gulf—or Indian expedition—by Antiochos IV c.165 BC. Two centuries later, Pliny relates a battle, probably naval and on land, which took place near what is now Abu Dhabi(?) under the reign of an Antiochos, maybe Antiochos IV—the admiral was known as Noumenius.

When reviewed carefully (both historical sources and archaeology), the Greek presence in the Gulf does not attest any commercial or trading concern (see also the silence about any harbour involved in exchanges) and most of the evidence point to a military policy only. The Seleucids were keen on keeping the maritime lane of the Gulf 'free' and 'safe', and many scholars support the idea of a Seleucid fleet in the Gulf up to the mid-second century BC. However, this was probably not for the immediate profit of the Seleucids (maybe through taxes, but no mention at all of any 'banking'), and the numerous and wealthy exchanges between India and Babylonia were continuously held by the local/riverine populations under the umbrella of the Seleucid sway.

The situation sounds slightly different in the Late Hellenistic/Roman period, first century BC onwards. On the one hand, when they deal with the Indian Ocean and Eastern countries, most classical authors still rely on the Alexander-time tradition, without new and first-hand information (see Philostratus, Arrian, Ammanius Marcellinus, etc.).[18] On the other hand, a new concern is emerging among Westerners (Greeks from Egypt, Romans, others?) which can be summarized by the words 'Rome-India trade'. This was already clear with Strabo in the late first century BC, it became more obvious with Pliny for whom one of his sources were *nostri negotiatores*, and the *Periplus of the Erythraean Sea* remains the best document for this new approach.[19] However, it would not mean that Westerners were present in the Gulf, either as residents or visiting seamen (maybe on some occasions?). The text of the *Periplus* almost totally ignores the region of the Persian Gulf to the exception of its two market-towns Apologos and Om(m)ana, providing no information at all on any other place (e.g. Gerrha and Bahrain are missing). When Pliny tells us about 'our merchants who visited the place' of Spasinu Charax, he forgets to mention whether they came by sea or by land. Also, there is growing consensus among modern scholars that the Roman items found in the archaeological sites of the Gulf were most probably loaded on vessels coming from Barygaza or Barbaricum in India (= marketplaces for the Romans),[20] not from Charax—with the possible exception of Kuwait and Eastern Arabia, where Nabataean or Nabataean-like pottery has been found as a result of caravan trade.

Before turning to later periods, one question has to answered: were there Indian people in the Gulf during the Hellenistic period? Nothing would lead us to answer yes or no; there is no textual evidence nor any archaeological remains,[21] which could attest that Indian ships were sailing and trading in the Persian Gulf.[22] More evidence turns up in the first century AD, both with the *Periplus* (dated *c.* 50 BC?) and with well identifed material data. The *Periplus* notes that large vessels were bound from Barygaza to Omana and Apologos, and there is no reason to deny that they were Indian ships. In terms of archaeology, some Indian pottery was dated to the first century AD at ed-Dur/Om(m)ana, and more Indian pottery from the second/third century AD is being recovered at Mleiha (UAE—personal communication by M. Mouton. See also Tomber 2008). Indian Red Polished wares reached Siraf (first[?]–third century AD, Tampoe 1989) and Bushire, or the Sea of Oman, Suhar for example (first[?]–fourth century AD, Kervran 1996). Among recent and numerous studies (e.g. the Indian pottery of Khor Rori, in Oman, Avanzini 2008), a particularly useful paper lists some ivory combs found in a collective tomb at Dibba (Emirate of Sharjah, coast of the Oman Sea, just below the ras Musandam). Two beautifully decorated combs (incised on the two sides) exhibit typical Indian scenes, and can be dated to the first century AD, like the rest of the material of the grave (Potts 2011). There can be no doubt that Indian vessels started to hang up at the harbours of the Persian Gulf in the first centuries AD.

True enough, there is no other text resembling the *Periplus* issued by Oriental people (West Asia, Iran, India, etc.) which could have helped expand our kowledge of the maritime history of the region, and we have to pick up scattered bits of information from the first to the sixth century AD and try to build a coherent assemblage. In order to maintain such a coherence, I will briefly mention the first Chinese embassy that visited the Gulf area in AD 97. Probably while sailing along the Persian coast of the Gulf, the Chinese reached what they depict as a semi-independent country called 'An Shi' (identified by modern scholars with Characene/Mesene, also called 'Tse San' in another source), they also mention a harbour An Ku on the Persian coast, identified with Bushire (Graf 1996, Inglebert 2008).[23]

Although it might not be directly connected to the Persian Gulf, recent excavations in Oman have revealed the specificity (history, epigraphy, archaeology) of a so far little known group of middlemen in the exchanges of the Indian Ocean, as well as a major port, the site of Khor Rori/ ancient Sumhuram. The latter makes clear the reality and role of the Hadrami people, involved in the trade of frankincense (Avanzini 2008), in close relationship with the Yemeni port of Qani' (Salles, Sedov 2010).

Oriental sources, i.e. no Graeco-Roman and in that case epigraphical, make known another actor of the exchanges, and probably a port. It consists of a series of graffiti discovered in a tomb on the island of Kharg, off Persia, more or less contemporary with the *Periplus*(?). Most of the inscriptions have been scratched and remain illegible, but at least two graffiti describe ships. The only legible text, unsigned, is in Aramaic language and might claim to be, according to the editors, a Jewish profession of faith (Steve 2003–inscription studied by É. Puech).[24] The antiquity of the island is characterized by its large monastery settled in the sixth century AD (or seventh/eighth? following other authors), and by rock-cut tombs richly decorated (facades), initially assigned to the Palmyrene style, now recognized as Nabataean-like cut-tombs.[25] Although no archaeological remains of a harbour were located, the island was probably a stage in the navigation from the Persian coast to the mouth of Euphrates.

It is well established that numerous Jewish families migrated to the East, especially to Babylonia, after the conflicts of the second/first century BC in Judea (Neusner 1969), and after the Jewish revolt and the destruction of Jerusalem in the first century AD. Syriac sources often refer to Jewish merchants in the Indian Ocean and in the Persian Gulf, some of them sailing down to India (*Seert Chronicle*).[26]

A text of the early third century AD, which narrates a story of the first century AD, the *Acts of Thomas* (the apostle), relates that a Jewish merchant from Jerusalem, named Hannan took Thomas on a voyage to India. They set sail from 'the country of the South', that is Maisan/Mesene at the mouth of the Euphrates, most probably from the harbour Forat Maisan[27] (Salles 2007). On their way, the travellers landed in a city called Andropolis (a hapax), which the Syriac version of the *Acts of Thomas* rendered as Sandaruk/Sanatruk, to be identified with Bahrain[28]—a first (?) written mention of a harbour in Bahrain. Jewish communities are also known in Eastern Arabia, designated sometimes as *Haggar* (present-day Dhahran/ Hofuf area). The area was also called *Hatta* (Syriac) in the letters which Manes/ Mani[29] used to send to his 'brothers' in religion settled in the region (Tardieu 1994). Tardieu argues that Mani had been recruiting his followers among the Baptist communities, composed of Jews who had embraced a 'simplified' Christianism, and concludes that Baptist communities were present in Eastern Arabia in the third century AD, maybe earlier. *Hatta* might be the *Atte* known by Ptolemy, a city along the coast of Eastern Arabia, a port? The presence of Jewish communities in the Persian Gulf and their attested role in the regional trade, together with numerous Christian communities also involved in maritime activities (discussed later) resulted sometimes in some controversial assertions:

Plate 9.6: The church at al Qusur (1989), © Maison de l'Orient et de la Méditerranée.
C is the choir, sc a side chapel, b is another chapel probably with a baptristry, N the
main nave. The plastered floor of the choir is scratched with noughts and crosses games,
evidence of the re-use of the building probably in the 8th/9th cent. ?(pottery)

'Jewish colonies in India paved the way for St Thomas' (Puthiakunnel 1970).

The political and economic situation in the Persian Gulf changed radically in the third century AD with the rise of the Sassanid Empire.

Plate 9.7: The church at al Qusur (1989), © Maison de l'Orient et de la Méditerranée.
The two rooms in front were probably part of the sacristy; the left one had been
transformed into a grinding area (8th/9th cent. ?).

Plate 9.8: The church at al Qusur (1989), © Maison de l'Orient et de la Méditerranée.
A plaster Christian cross of the decoration of the church.

Different causes were being brought into play: the severe crisis of the Roman Empire which opened new lanes of maritime traffic to the Persians,[30] and the development of numerous and lively Christian communities in the East, Syria and Persia (at least before Shapur's II persecutions in the fourth century AD). This has been quite beneficial to the region of the Persian Gulf, where local communities had been involved for a long time in maritime trade and moved early towards the new religions.[31]

Writers of Sassanid history recall that in the beginning of his reign (224–41), Ardashir I founded or re-founded several harbours—Rishahr on the Bushire peninsula, former Charax, former Forat of Maisan, Wahasht Ardashir on the Iranian coast, Batn Ardarshir on the Arab coast (Ritter 2009: 4–5; Malekandathil 2010: 2–5).[32] The most important ports of the Iranian coast were Rew Ardashir and Siraf, probably also Kharg Island as a stage at the mouth of the Euphrates/Tigris. However, one should not neglect the ports of the Arabian coast[33]—Bahrain where a large amount of Sassanid material was recovered—and the Oman peninsula (Kennet 2004).[34]

Viewed from India, Malekandathil carefully describes the activities of these communities, mainly Persian, but also Mesopotamian, where merchants and religious people were often the same. The *Seert Chronicle* mentions bishop David (bishop of Forat) who travelled to India for a commercial expedition *c.*AD 300. According to the same sources, a Nestorian catholicos, Ahai, was sent by King Yazdigird (*c.*AD 415?)

to investigate the piracy of the ships returning from India and Ceylon. A major event in the history of the Malabar church is the migration to Kerala of Thomas of Cana [Ur?] in the fourth century AD (Malekandathil suggests c.AD 315: 2) together with 72 families and a group of priests—it would correspond with the earliest persecutions in the Sassanid Empire. In the sixth century AD, Pahlavi inscriptions are engraved in churches in Ceylon and south-west India (Malekandathil: 5–6, quoting the works of G. Gropp). It is clear that the Persian Gulf, a now 'persianized' active and wealthy commercial route to India, Ceylon and further East (see Ritter 2009), was at the same time the main road of the Christianization of the southern East. Men, ideas, and faiths sailed together with the merchants.

The same echo comes from a couple of Western sources, Palladios (the story of the Theban lawyer), Philostorgius (the embassy of Theophilos the Indian), and Cosmas Indicopleustes, the latter going into much detail about the ports of Taprobane/Sri Lanka (e.g. Mantai) and the trading activities of the population (Weerakkody 1997). But that would be beyond the scope of this discussion.

Such a survey of the harbours known in the Persian Gulf over a dozen centuries will probably remain unsatisfactory considering that this specific maritime lane had been playing a crucial role in the exchanges between the East and the West from the third millennium BC at least until the present-day. For the periods concerned, one positive outcome should be emphasized: archaeology is providing an increasing amount of new data every year, and our knowledge is continuously growing and becoming clearer. When turning to the written sources, new discoveries may indeed occcur (see the Socotra inscriptions, in this volume), but the bulk of the data will remain the same, with the permanent vexing question of the most often one-sided vision of the authors, Classical or Oriental. The concept of globalization/mondialization is becoming *à la mode* in Ancient History, but many complex questions cannot be answered through such theoretical approaches and will remain pending for long. However, alongside the constant increase of archaeological knowledge, the historian should re-read and read again the same written sources in the expectation of new and stimulating understandings.

Notes

1. The only named port is Nippur, 'the (missing) quays of Nippur', a fluvial harbour upstream the Tigris. The bibliography on ancient Dilmun is enormous; I will refer only to a few stimulating works, Potts 1990 (vol. I). More recently, Potts 2009.

2. Bushire (infra) is not mentioned by Arrian—and no early layers have been ever found in the excavations of the site.

3. The city is also referred to by Alexander's bematists (they used to calculate the distances), who locate Teredon 3,000 stadia south of Babylon, at the mouth of the Euphrates. Pliny quotes the city which he says was regularly visited by the Parthians.

4. No archaeological data could help locating the site in this rather disturbed, changing and marshy area.

5. A direct navigation from Hadramawt or elsewhere on the Yemen coast up to the head of the Gulf/Teredon is almost impracticable, see Salles 1988. About the desert route from Petra to the head of the Gulf, recently Salles 2010.

6. Salles 2005: I will not develop here my arguments, see also Salles 1994. Bukharin 2007 denies the existence of an Indo-Gerrhaean frankincense and suggests a caravan route from the Hadramawt to Gerrha. Part of his arguments rely on the very controversial role of the people *Gabaioi/Gebbanitae* (*GB'N*), and archaeology did not reveal fourth or third century BC layers at Qaryat al-Fau which Bukharin considers as the major stage of the route.

7. No author refers to any port in Bahrain, although archaeology shows that maritime trade was still active during the Hellenistic period, Andersen 2007.

8. A complete description and analysis is available in Potts 1990 (vol. II), pp. 27–48 (Thaj), pp. 48–85 (Eastern Arabia), pp. 85–97 (Gerrha). See also Mouton 2009, for a critical evidence of archaeological data and their interpretation in the Gulf.

9. M. Mouton, currenly excavating in ed-Dur hinterland at Mleiha has confirmed this origin and acknowledges the presence of numerous different types of Indian pottery dated to the second-third century AD, personal communication.

10. Haerinck 1998. See also Mouton 2009: 198–9.

11. I saw it for the first time in 1977, almost untouched after a short Iraqi exploration.

12. Mouton 2009.

13. Although no archaeological or historical comparison could be established, one can find the same social-religious pattern in Nabataean (pre-Roman) Petra.

14. Even though the Romans undertook a couple of military campaigns in Arabia, e.g. Aelius Gallus, or Gaius Cesar.

15. Salles 2010. A theory suggests that the origin of the Nabataeans should be looked for in north-eastern Arabia, the ancient Haggar/Hasa (Graf 1990a, 1990b), or even further South-East to Oman (Schmid 2004). Some arguments sound solid (linguistics, onomastic), other ones are less reliable (ceramic comparisons), but there are no strong reasons which would lead to definitely reject the theory. Archaeology has provided few evidence of Nabataean pottery in Kuwait, in Bahrain and in Thaj, dated to the first century BC/ second century AD; earlier contacts are not attested archaeogically speaking. Pliny refers to a caravan route from Petra to Spasinou Charax.

16. Some stamped Greek amphorae reached the place in the second century BC.

17. It was generally assumed that Antiochos III had sailed straight from Antioch in Persidis (= Bushire) to Gerrha after his Indian expedition; actually, he first sailed back to Babylonia and then sent a 'special' expedition to Gerrha.

18. It sould be stressed that the discovery of the East by Alexander, especially India, and the whole tradition issued from these campaigns remained the leitmotive for most of the works concerned with India up to the Middle Ages.

19. See also Seneca the philosopher decrying the Indian luxuries (Letters to Lucilius).

20. Salles 1995; Tomber 2008; and Whitehouse 2010.

21. Although, for example, a large part of the 'common' pottery of these periods (third-first century BC) has never been studied in Bahrain.

22. One point would need more investigation, if more information were available. The treaty between Chandragupta and Seleucos I contained a clause for the delivery of many elephants to the Seleucid king, and the treaty was renewed by Antiochos III about a century later. The Seleucid armies had large groups of war elephants, as described by several authors. These animals needed special maintenance, most probably by numerous Indian specialists. Did these people came by sea or by land?

23. Since this essay was written, the author has become aware of more detailed Chinese sources which will be analysed in another essay.

24. Kharg island has never been referred to as a harbour until C. Niebuhr exploration of the region in the eighteenth century, and a brief control by the British presence in the nineteenth century.

25. What would open new perspectives on the role of the Nabataeans in the Gulf. . . .

26. A nice synagogue was cleared out at the site of Qani', in Yemen (Salles, Sedov 2010).

27. The place is recorded as the 'meeting place of all the merchants from the East' in the Syriac Hymn of the Pearl.

28. A king Sanatruk (a common name in Hatra) was reigning in Bahrain in the third century AD (Persian history), a metonymy being quite possible. Thomas met there a flute player, a Jewish girl.

29. The Iranian Manes/Mani developed the Manicheism religion in the east: he travelled himself to India c.240 AD, probably as a member of a commercial expedition.

30. Up to this period, the trade competition in the Indian Ocean was largely confined between the Romans (or Westerners) and the Parthians (the Mesene/Characene); the Ethiopians were just setting events in motion. The collapse of the two 'super-powers' created a completely new situation.

31. In the acts of a synod held in AD 410 at Rew Ardeshir, five bishoprics are listed in the province of Beth Qatrayeh—a region including Eastern Arabia and 'the Islands': two of them are well identified, Tarut in Eastern Arabia, and Muharraq in Bahrain. Mazun/Oman had its own Christian organization (Beaucamp, Robin 1983). Besides their role in the international trade and in the Christanization of India, the Christian communities of the Gulf did follow their coreligionists of the mainland especially through the development of an

early monachism: al-Qusur on Failaka (Plates 9.6–9.8), Kharg island, Sir Bani Yas in the UAE (Salles 2011).

32. Although recent and quite instructive, the two contributors still rely on the archaeological works by Whitehouse and Williamson (1993), despite new important data published now (discussed earlier).

33. The small island of 'Akkaz, off Kuwait, was not at all a kind of 'international harbour', but probably a stage of the Arabian coast to the mouth of the Euphrates. Remains of a small church and Sassanid archaeological material were uncovered here (Gachet 2011). The site of al Qusur on Failaka island was a true monastery complex, without any visible connections to maritime traffic (Bernard et al. 1991).

34. The revision of the chronologies of the main Christian sites of the Persian Gulf by Carter (2008) cannot be accepted.

Bibliography

Andersen, S.F. (2007), *The Tylos Period Burials in Bahrain*, vol. I: *The Glass and Pottery Vessels*, Culture and National Heritage, Kingdom of Bahrain, in association with Moesgaard Museum and Aarhus University: Aarhus University Press.

Avanzini, A., ed. (2008), *A Port in Arabia between Rome and the Indian Ocean (3rd cent. BC–5th cent. AD). Khor Rori Report 2*. Roma: « L'Erma » di Bretschneider.

Beaucamp, J. and Robin, C. (1983), 'L'évêché de Mashmahig dans l'archipel d'al-Bahrayn, v^e-ixe siècle', in *Dilmun. New studies in the archaeology and history of Bahrain*, ed. D.T. Potts, BBVO (Berliner Beiträge zum Vorderen Orient), Berlin: Dietrich Reimer Verlag, pp. 171–96.

Bernard, V., Callot, O. and Salles, J.-F. (1991), 'L'église d'al-Qousour, Failaka, État de Koweit', *Arabian Archaeology and Epigraphy*, vol. 2, pp. 145–81.

Bukharin, M.D. (2007), 'Der zentralarabische Zweig der Weihrauchstrasse', *Arabian Archaeology and Epigraphy*, vol. 18, pp. 80–5.

Carter, R.A. (2008), 'Christianity in the Gulf during the first centuries of Islam', *Arabian Archaeology and Epigraphy*, vol. 19, no. 1, pp. 71–108.

Chronique de Séert = Scher, A. (1911), *Histoire nestorienne inédite (Chronique de Séert)* II/1 ("*Patrologia Orientalis*" 7), Paris.

Durand, X. (1997), *Des Grecs en Palestine au IIIe s. av. J.-C. Le dossier syrien des archives de Zénon de Caunos (262-261),* Cahiers de la Revue Biblique 38, Paris.

Gachet-Bizollon, J., dir. (2011), *Le tell d'Akkaz au Koweït. Tell Akkaz in Kuwait*, TMO 57. Lyon: Maison de l'Orient et de la Méditerranée.

Graf, D.F. (1990a), 'The origin of the Nabataeans', *ARAM*, vol. 2, nos. 1–2 (*The Nabataeans*), pp. 45–75.

——— (1990b), 'Arabia during Achaemenid times', *Achaemenid History,* vol. IV *Centre and Periphery*, ed., H. Sancisi-Weerdenburg and A. Kuhrt. Leiden: The Netherlands Institute for the Near East, pp. 131–48.

—— (1996), 'The Roman East from the Chinese Perspective' (with the assistance of E.L. Dreyer), *Palmyra and the Silk Road, Annales Archéologiques Arabes Syriennes*, vol. 42, pp. 199–216.

Haerinck, E. (1998), 'International contacts in the southern Persian Gulf in the late 1st cent BC/1st cent AD: numismatic evidence from ed-Dur (Emirate of Umm al-Qaiwain, U.A.E)', *Iranica Antiqua*, vol. XXXIII, pp. 273–302.

Inglebert, H. (2008), 'Les relations entre le Daquin (l'empire romain) et le pays des Sères (l'empire chinois)', in Th. Piel, ed., *Figures et expressions du pouvoir dans l'Antiquité. Hommage à Jean-René Jannot*. Rennes: Presses Universitaire de Rennes, pp. 127–41.

Jacob, Ch. (1990), *La Description de la terre habitée de Denys d'Alexandrie, ou la leçon de géographie*, Paris: Albin Michel.

Kennet, D. (2004), *Sasanian and Islamic pottery from Ras al-Khaimah. Classification, chronology and analysis of trade in the Western Indian Ocean*, 'Society for Arabian Studies Mononographs' 1. BAR International Series 1248. Oxford: Archaeopress.

Kervran, M. (1996), 'Indian Ceramics in Southern Iran and in Eastern Arabia: Repertory, Classification and Chronology', in H.P. Ray and J.-F. Salles, eds., *Tradition and Archaeology: Early Maritime Contacts in the Indian Ocean*, Delhi: Manohar, pp. 37–58.

——, Herbert, F., Rougeulle, A. (2006), *Qal'at al-Bahrein. A trading and military outpost, 3rd millennium BC–17th century AD*, Indicopleustai, Turnhout: Brepols.

Malekandathil, Pius (2010), *Maritime India: Trade, Religion and Polity in the Indian Ocean*, Delhi: Primus Books.

Marcotte, D. (2010), 'La mer Érythrée et le Sud de l'œkoumène, thème politique dans l'ethnographie hellénistique', *Geographia Antiqua*, vol. XIX, pp. 39–46.

Mouton, M. (2009), 'The settlements patterns of north-eastern and south-eastern Arabia in late Antiquity', *Arabian Archaeology and Epigraphy,* vol. 20, pp. 185–207.

Neusner, J. (1969), *A History of the Jews in Babylonia*. I. *The Parthian Period*. Leiden: E.J. Brill.

The *Periplus Maris Erythraei*, ed. L. Casson, 1989, *Text with Introduction, Translation and Commentary*, Princeton: Princeton University Press.

Potts, D.T. (1984), 'Thaj and the location of Gerrha', *Proceedings of the Seminar for Arabian Studies*, pp. 87–91.

—— (1990), *The Arabian Gulf in Antiquity*, vol. I: *From Prehistory to the Fall of the Achaemenid Empire;* vol. II: *From Alexander the Great to the Coming of Islam*, Oxford: Clarendon Press.

—— (2009), 'The archaeology and history of the Persian Gulf', in *The Persian Gulf in History*, L.G. Potter, ed., Basingstoke: Palgrave Macmillan, pp. 27–56.

—— (2011), 'Indianesque Ivories in Southeastern Arabia', in *Un impaziente desidario di scorrere il mono*. Studi in onore di Antiono Invernizzi per il suo settantesimo compleanno, Monografie di Mesopotamia, vol. XIV. Firenze: Casa editrice Le Lettere, pp. 335–44.

Puthiakunnel, T. (1970), 'Jewish Colonies of India paved the way for St Thomas', in *The Malabar Church Symposium in honor of Rev. Placid J. Podipara C.M.I.*, J. Vellian, Orientalia Christiana Analecta 186. Roma: Pontificium Institutum Orientalium Studiorum, pp. 187–91.

Ray, H.P. (1994), *The Winds of Change. Buddhism and the Maritime Links of Early South Asia*, Delhi: Oxford University Press.

———, ed. (1999), *Archaeology of Seafaring: The Indian Ocean in the Ancient Period*, Delhi: Pragati Publications.

Retsö, J. (2003), *The Arabs in Antiquity: Their History from the Assyrians to the Ummayads*, London-New York: Routledge-Curzon.

Ritter, N.C. (2009), 'Vom Euphrat zum Mekong. Maritime Kontakte zwischen Vorder-und Südostasien in vorislamischer Zeit', *Mitteilungen der Deutschen Orient-Gesellschaft zu Berlin*, vol. 141, pp. 143–71.

Salles, J.-F. (1988), 'La circumnavigation de l'Arabie dans l'Antiquité classique', in *L'Arabie et ses mers bordières. I. Itinéraires et voisinages*, J.-F. Salles, ed., TMO 16. Lyon: Maison de l'Orient, pp. 75–102.

——— (1990) 'Les Achéménides dans le Golfe arabo-persique', in *Achaemenid History*, vol. IV: *Centre and Periphery*, H. Sancisi-Weerdenburg & A. Kuhrt, eds., Leiden: The Netherlands Institute for the Near East, pp. 111–30.

——— (1992), 'Découvertes du Golfe arabo-persique aux époques grecque et romaine', *Revue des Études Anciennes* (Colloque de la SOPHAU, Angers/Nantes, mai 1991), vol. 94, nos. 1–2, pp. 79–97.

——— (1994), 'Le golfe arabo-persique entre Séleucides et Maurya', *Topoi*, vol. 4, no. 2, pp. 597–610.

——— (1995), 'The *Periplus of the Erythraean Sea* and the Arab-Persian Gulf', in *Athens, Aden, Arikamedu. Essays on the interrelations between India, Arabia and the Eastern Mediterranean*, M.-F. Boussac and J.-F. Salles, eds., New Delhi: Manohar Publishers (reprint from *Topoi* 3/2, Lyon 1993, pp. 493-524), pp. 115–46.

——— (2005), 'La Péninsule Arabique dans l'organisation des échanges du royaume séleucide', *Le roi et l'économie. Autonomies locales et structures royales dans l'économie séleucide, Topoi*, in V. Chankowski and F. Duyrat, eds., Supp. 6, pp. 545–70.

——— (2007), 'Travelling to India without Alexander's Logbooks', in *Memory as History: The Legacy of Alexander in Asia*, H.P. Ray and D.T. Potts, eds., New Delhi: Aryan Books International, pp. 157–69.

——— (2010), 'De Pétra au Golfe, ou l'invention d'une route lagide', in *Eastern Arabia, and adjacent regions in the first millennium BC*, ed. A. Avanzini, [Proceedings of a conference held in Pisa, Italy, 12–13 May 2008], Rome: "L'Erma" di Bretschneider, pp. 57–68.

Salles, J.-F. and Sedov, A.V., eds. (2010), *Qani'. Le port antique du Hadramawt entre la Méditerranée, l'Afrique et l'Inde*, Indicopleustai 6, Turnhout: Brepols.

Sanlaville, P. (1989) 'Considérations sur l'évolution de la basse Mésopotamie au cours des derniers millénaires', *Paléorient*, vol. 15, no. 2, pp. 5–27.

Sanlaville, P., Dalongeville, R., Evin, J. and Paskoff, R. (1987), 'Modifications du tracé littoral sur la côte arabe du Golfe Persique en relation avec l'archéologie', *Déplacements des lignes de rivage en Méditerranée d'après les données de l'archéologie*, Paris: Éditions du CNRS, pp. 211–22.

Schmid, S.G. (2004), 'Les Nabatéens et leurs contacts avec la Mésopotamie et la région du Golfe Arabo-Persique', in *Le roi et l'économie. Autonomies locales et structures royales dans l'économie séleucide, Topoi,* V. Chankowski and F. Duyrat, eds., Supp. 6, pp. 463–84.

Steve, M.J. (2003), *L'île de Kharg. Une page de l'histoire du Golfe persique et du monachisme oriental,* Civilisations du Proche-Orient, Série 1, Archéologie et Environnement 1 (CPOA 1), Neuchâtel: Recherches et Publications.

Tampoe, M. (1989), *Maritime trade between China and the West: an archaeological study of the ceramics from Siraf,* BAR International Series 555. Oxford: Archaeopress.

Tardieu, M. (1994), 'L'Arabie du Nord-Est d'après les documents Manichéens', *Studia Iranica*, vol. 23, pp. 59–75.

Tomber, R. (2008), *Indo-Roman Trade: From Pots to Pepper*, London: Duckworth.

Weerakkody, D.P.M. (1997), *Taprobanê. Ancient Sri Lanka as known to Greeks and Romans*, Indicopleustai. Turnhout: Brepols.

Whitehouse, D. (2010), 'The *Periplus Maris Erythraei* and beyond (review of R. Tomber, *Indo-Roman Trade: From Pots to Pepper*)', *Journal of Roman Archaeology*, vol. 23, pp. 782–5.

ANCIENT PORTS AND
MARITIME CONTACTS OF INDIA

The Ports of the Western Coast of India according to Arabic Geographers (Eighth-Fifteenth Centuries AD): A Glimpse into the Geography

Jean-Charles Ducène

The aim of this essay is not to clarify or discuss the identification of the Indian ports attested in Arabic medieval geographic sources; it will examine whether these texts provide descriptions of these places and if topographic or urban elements can be found. In other words, how these ports have been viewed by the authors apparently interested in this question?

India and the Arabic Geographic Literature

We can notice that more historical writers know India by hearsay or by informant(s) than by personal experience, that is after travelling there. Among the few who had a real knowledge of life in India it is only possible to mention al-Mas'ūdī, who travelled to India in 915–916, al-Bīrūnī who lived in north India in the early eleventh century, and of course the most interesting author, Ibn Baṭṭūṭa, who stayed in India in the middle of the fourteenth century. Compilations make up the majority of our sources and can be divided into two groups—that division matching the chronology. Prior to the twelfth century, books dealing with trade relations between Arabs and Indians are written by curious compilers settled in the Arab world. This is true for the *Account of China and India* attributed to Sulaymān al-Tājir[1] and the *Book of the Wonders of India* formerly ascribed to Buzurg ibn Šahriyār and now attributed to Mūsā al-Awfī al-Sīrāfi.[2] After the twelfth century, compilers were encyclopaedists dealing with a vast material and tackling India in the geographic part of their encyclopaedias. We can put al-Idrīsī (twelfth century) apart because his account of India depends on his predecessors, Ibn Ḥurradāhbih (ninth century) and Ibn Ḥawqal (tenth century) but not only on them, inasmuch as we find original descriptions from contemporary informants who knew India.

Among these compilers, one is still unpublished. Muḥammad ibn Ibrāhīm al-Wāṭwāṭ (1235-1318)[3] was a bookseller in Cairo in the second half of the thirteenth century who wrote an encyclopaedia of natural sciences with a geographical part in which he listed Indian cities and ports. This work had been the main source for the Syrian compiler al-Dimašqī (d. 1327).[4] As he worked away from India, we might assume that he described a situation which was not entirely reflective of the actual India. On the contrary, we discover with pleasure that his list of Indian ports matches very well with that given by the *Nūr al-maʿārif* or *Light of Knowledges*, written in Yaman in 1290 and commented upon by Éric Vallet and Elizabeth Lambourn.[5] In fact, this literature must be seen as a complement to Indian epigraphy, and archaeological chronicles.

The chronology allows us to distinguish between authors before and after the thirteenth century. A glance at the tables (see appendix to this chapter) highlights the difference. From the ninth century to twelfth-thirteenth centuries, ports of Gujarat and northern Konkan alone find mention in our sources. The only exception is Kūlam (Quilon) in southern Malabar. But after the thirteenth century, ports along the Canara coast (in Karnataka) and those of Malabar prevail.

The general situation

The contours of the Indian subcontinent is not clearly defined by Arab geographers, and is rather represented as a long coast interrupted by bays, estuaries, peninsulas and ports. The general name for north India is the kingdom of Balharā.[6] According to Isṭaḥrī and Ibn Ḥawqal[7] (tenth century), the land of Balharā stretches from Kambāya to Saymūr, and al-Idrīsī (twelfth century) followed this description. On the western coast of India, we will focus on four regions, from north to south, Gujarat, Konkan, Canara and Malabar.[8] One notices that Arabic sources are first familiar with towns situated on this shore and only later with their hinterland. Al-Bīrūnī mentioned Kumkan for Konkan.[9] Concerning Gujarat, the Arabic form *Ǧazarāt*[10] is not attested before Ibn Saʿīd (thirteenth century) but the name of *bilād al-filfil* or 'land of pepper' for modern Malabar occurs for the first time in *The Book of the Wonders of India*.[11] Perhaps the first mention of Malabar by Arab geographers is by al-Idrīsī[12] under the form

Manībar, but in the thirteenth century, we find Malībar in Yāqūt[13] and Ibn Sa'īd.[14] Rašīd al-Dīn (d. *c.*1318) mapped out the whole coast from Gujarat to Kūlam, with Malabar and Konkan.[15] After Malabar, starts 'the country of al-Ṣuliyān which includes the big Ma'bar and the small Ma'bar',[16] that is Coromandel.

I will not deal with inland cities of India or those far away from the coast, as their development is linked to overseas trade.

We can divide this period into two parts, which reflects an evolution in circumstances.

Ninth-Thirteenth Century

Reading authors of the ninth century, we find a state of affairs that seems to have been established for a long time. According to Ibn Ḥurradāhbih,[17] 'Ūtkīn marked the beginning of India, from which he listed some places (harbours) along its Western coast, without mentioning that they were harbours. He only gave the name of the city without adding one of the Arabic words for harbour (*marsā* 'anchorage', *mīnā* 'haven', and *furḍa* 'trading place'). When the author refers to 'sailors' as informants, one understands that they were ports. In his list were cities that remain the main ports in our sources until the twelfth century:

- 'Ūtkin (written Ūbkīn): described by al-Idrīsī as 'an island' (*ğazīra*), it may be identified with Oykman/Okha, on the northern coast of Kathiawar, at the entrance of the Gulf of Kutch.[18]
- Mayd or Mīd: this term does not refer to a city but a tribal group and sea pirates who inhabited the coastal regions of Sind and Kathiawar.[19] As a port, this name may designate a place along the coasts of Kathiawar and Kutch. Maqbul Ahmad suggested the port of Mandvi.
- Kūlī: Kodinar,[20] north-west of Diu.
- Kanbāya: Cambay, the most important port of Gujarat before the rise of Diu.
- Barūṣ: Broach[21] on the Narmada River, ancient Indian Bharugaccha, known by the Greeks as Barygaza.
- Sandan: Sanjan, Sanjan Bandar on the banks of the Varoli Creek.
- Mulay for Kūlam Malay: Quilon[22] in Kerala.

Kūlam Malay, due to its position on the nautical road east of the Indian Ocean, is an important and necessary stop that is already mentioned in the *Aḫbār al-Ṣīn wa-l-Hind* (*An Account of China and India*) in the middle of the ninth century. At that time, Kūlam Malay was described as 'a military post . . . where taxes are collected from the Chinese boats' and 'It has sweet water wells.'[23]

In the middle of the tenth century, Ibn Ḥawqal added two Konkan ports: Sopara and Ṣaymūr in northern Konkan.

- Sopara was known in Antiquity and situated in a creek south of Mumbai.[24]
- Ṣaymūr was the principal port of the Rastrakutan kingdom during this period. It is modern Chaul,[25] 60 km. south of Mumbai.

The importance of these harbours is confirmed by al-Masʿūdī who mentioned them. He was also the first to write a description of Cambay: 'Cambay is situated on an estuary which is as wide as the Nile or like the Tigris and Euphrates. On the bank of the estuary one sees towns, villas, cultivation, gardens, palms, coconut-trees, peacocks, parrots, and other Indian birds. The city is at a distance of two days or less distant from the mouth of the estuary.'[26]

The same author mentioned the gulf (ḫalīǧ) of Ṣindābūra[27] and Tāna.

- Ṣindābūra is modern Chandore, mediaeval Candrapura, 80 km. south of Goa.
- Tāna is modern Thana,[28] situated on the western shore of the Salsette or Thana Creek.

As we can see, as early as the end of the tenth century, the main ports attested in Arabic sources are listed, and their importance is confirmed by the fact that they are mentioned in the *Book of the Wonders of India*,[29] written at that time. Unfortunately, since this book is a compilation of a series of accounts given by sailors, there is no description of these harbours or anchorages. The name is enough to designate the place where events happen. Unfortunately, al-Bīrūnī gave scarce details since his list of Indian ports included 17 places. We notice the mention of Somnath,[30] on the southern coast of Gujarat, mainly known by Arabic sources because it was attacked by Maḥmūd of Ghazna. However al-Bīrūnī wrote: 'The reason why in particular Somanath has become so famous is that it was a harbour (furḍa) for seafaring people, and a station (manzil) for those who went to and fro between Sufāla in the country of the Zanj and China.'[31] Later Abū l-Fidāʾ specified that 'it is situated on a headland which projects into the sea so that many ships bound for Aden touch it, because it is not in a gulf. It lies on the mouth of a river that comes down from the big mountains lying in the North-East,'[32] maybe the Harna River. Al-Idrīsī confirms this situation when he wrote 'it is a beautiful-looking town. Here boats set sail and unload. To it are brought all kinds of commodities and merchandise from everywhere, and from there they are exported in every direction. It is also situated on an estuary which boats enter and cast their anchors in. Water is in abundance in it'.[33]

Sūbāra is described by him as 'a civilized and populated town, which has a large number of residents. It has all kinds of commerce and ways of livelihood. It is one of the ports of the Indian Sea, and there are fishing grounds and diving beds of pearls'.[34] For Sandān, he wrote: 'it is a populated town and its residents are people full of dexterity and nobility. They are wealthy merchants accustomed to travelling. It is a big size town, and has a large traffic of travellers visiting it and leaving it'.[35] Tana is 'a magnificent town situated on the bank of a large estuary, into which boats and vessels enter and where goods are unloaded'.[36] Later, Abū l-Fidā specified that Tana is an island. It is the Salsette Island, delimited by Vasai Creek and Salsette or Thana Creek.

And finally, according to al-Idrīsī's account, Ṣaymūr 'is a spacious and beautiful town, with magnificent buildings and exquisite surroundings'.[37]

The same author gave the first Arabic description of Broach: 'it is a very large, magnificent and beautiful town, with fine buildings constructed of bricks and plaster. Its inhabitants have high ambitions, copious resources, solid wealth, and recognized trade. . . . It is a port for those who arrive from China, as well as for those who come from Sind'.[38]

Authors of the tenth century quoted only Kūlam on the Malabar Coast, but al-Idrīsī gave a partial description of the shore south of Canara. The first port of Manībar seems to be Fandarayna (today Pantalayini Kollam, north Quilandi/Koyilandi).[39] 'It is situated on an estuary of a river flowing down from the direction of Manībār. Boats of the merchants of the Indian islands, as well as those of Sind, cast their anchors here. Its inhabitants have an abundance of wealth, busy markets, and commercial centres and profits'.[40] After that the author continues with Jurbāttan (Srikandapuram, East of Taliparamha or more probably Cannanor),[41] also situated on a small estuary. The two last ports are difficult to identify with certainty: Ṣinğī may be identical with Šinklī, identified with Cranganore; and Kl.Ksār, according to Maqbul Ahmad,[42] might be Cahlacory, north-east of Cranganore.

Ibn Saʿīd completes the map by adding details about Sūmanāt. The town was famous for its idol, which is sheltered in a huge white building, visible from afar by ships.[43] Still in Gujarat but nearer to Sind, Ibn Saʿīd describes the port of Qaṣā for the first time, saying that it is visited by boats coming from Adan and is a place of call (*mandaḥ*). The Arabic word refers specifically to a place where a boat can be drawn ashore. And Ibn

Saʿīd adds that sailors could easily unload their goods there and sail back. Where is Qaṣā? Yāqūt[44] only indicated that the town was in India, but in the *Nūr al-maʿārif*[45] the name Qaṣṣ was used as regional name, for a locality. Following a suggestion by Elizabeth Lambourn it is possible to identify this city with Bhadreśwar, a small port on the coast of Kachh. Southernmost, in Malabar, Ṣaymūr is situated in a gulf in which one enters from the south. Between Fāknur and Manǧarūr (Mangalore), there is two days sailing but the journey is dangerous because of reefs and shelf.[46]

Twelfth–Fifteenth Century

We can put together al-Waṭwāṭ and al-Dimašqī, because the first is the source of the second regarding the geography. Although al-Waṭwāṭ gave only a list of ports, without any description, his list is interesting as many place names occur for the first time.[47]

- Dabū: Dabhoi,[48] East of Baroda.
- Kanbāya: Cambay, 'which is situated in a bay of two days length and one can reach it by the tide'.
- Land of Kank (for Kanawǧ or Qinnawǧ),[49] also called land of al-Kanūnāt(?), from which the capital-city (*al-qaṣba*) is Lalanūtī(?).
- Barkalī: 'it lies on the shore of a bay in which enter the ships', not identified.

Al-Dimašqī adds here:

- Fawful, where there is a pearl fishery, not identified.
- Ḥawrnal, not identified.
- Nawsārī (written Bawsārī): according to Ibn Māǧid,[50] north of Daman, today in Surat district.
- Ḏūn or Ḏūq according to al-Dimašqī, not identified.
- Akātī: Agashi, North of Dharavi island.[51]
- Sāhī: Vasai.[52]
- Tāna: 'it is also called Tānas, where there is a cathedral-mosque (*masǧid ǧāmiʿ*) for the Muslims.'
- Mahāyim: Mahim.[53]

After that one enters the 'Land of Tulwān',[54] in which are situated in particular:

- Sindābūr: or Ṣindābūra, modern Chandore.

- Hanawr: Honovar

By continuing southward one reaches the 'Land of Munībār'

- Fākanur: 'it lies on the shore of a bay in which enter the ships.'
- Manğarūr: 'Mangalore, that lies on the shore of a bay.'
- Harqali: Kasargord.[55]
- Hīlī: the port was near the Ra's Hīlī, a mount and promontory jutting into the sea. It should be the medieval port identified with the village of Mātāyī, north of the mouth of the Talipatamha River. Moreover, a mosque foundation inscription in Mātāyī/Mandayi is dated 518/1124.[56]
- Ğurbattan: Cannanore.[57]
- Dih-battan: Valarpattanam.
- Buddfattan: Darmapattanam.
- Fandarayna: Pantalayini.
- Sinklī: Crannagore, 'whose people are mainly Jews.'
- Kūlam: the last town of Malabar.

This list compiled at the end of the thirteenth century mentions ports that are found in Muslim sources for two centuries. Abū l-Fidā' and Ibn Baṭṭūṭa give more details.

I have already quoted the details given by Abū l-Fidā' about some ports, to which can be added two remarks of this author about Cambay and Kūlam. First, according to a traveller, he reported that Cambay 'is on a gulf the length of which is three day's journey. . . . Its buildings are of brick and there is also with marble; but there are only a few gardens in it.'[58] For Kūlam, he wrote that 'some travellers have related to me that it is situated on a sea gulf in a plain and its soil is sandy. There are many gardens and the long-wood grows there: this is a tree like that of pomegranate and its leave resemble that of vinegrapes. There is a quarter for the Muslims and a mosque.'

As for Ibn Baṭṭūṭa, who was in India around 1342, he was impressed by the architecture, mosques, trading places and at times by the palaces too. His attention also focused on the means of access to the cities. For example, Qūqa was 'a large town with important bazaars.'[59] He anchored four miles from the shore because of the low tide, and was transferred to shore in a small boat. The city had a mosque. He noted also the topographical situation of these ports. For example, he indicated that Sindābūr was an island in an estuary, where were located 36 villages. 'It is surrounded by a gulf, the waters of which are sweet and agreable at low tide but salty and bitter at high tide. In the centre of the island are two cities, an ancient one built by the infidels, and one built by the Muslims when they first captured the island.'[60] This is Candrapura (modern Chandore).[61] Ibn Baṭṭūṭa specifies that his boat did not anchor at this island but at another one, closer to the land, maybe Andjidiv Island. His next stop, Hinnawr, 'is on a large inlet navigable for ships', but this bay is very stormy during four months of the year. When he entered Malabar he described the towns situated on inlets: Abū Sarūr (Barcelore), Fākanūr (Bacanor) and Mangarūr: 'a large town on the inlet called al-Dumb, which is the largest inlet in the land of Malabar.' He continued his description in the same way going through Hīlī, Ǧurfattan, Dah Fattan and Budd Fattan. In Hīlī, Dah Fattan and Budd Fattan, he noted the size and the beauty of the mosques. After that he made a stop in Calicut and Kulam that 'is one of the finest towns in the Malabar lands. It has fine bazaars. . . . This is a colony of Muslim merchants, the cathedral mosque is a magnificent building, constructed by the merchant *khwāja* Muhazzab.'[62]

Before Ibn Maǧīd in the fifteenth century, we do not have more detailed description of the west coast. Qalqašandī compiled al-Idrīsī, Ibn Sa'īd and Abū l-Fidā.

Conclusion

First, it seems that the authors had no real interest in a topographical description of Indian ports. At worst, authors give only a name; at best, they describe the Muslim institutions (mosque, zawiya). However, these descriptions are vague, sketchy and stereotyped.

Features that have impressed our authors are the geographical locations of the ports on the coast. They note if they are located on an island, in a bay or in an estuary. They also notice the deep penetration of the tide into the land. It is interesting to note that no Arabic word is used to designate a port or an anchorage (*furḍa, mīnā', mīnā*); we understand that a town is a port because the authors note its location 'in a bay'. They often use the Persian word *ḥawr*, 'inlet, bay'. Of course, there is no a hierarchy between these harbours. Ibn Baṭṭūṭa only indicates that one is bigger than the other. As for the nature of the harbour, only the context allows us to deduce whether it is an anchorage, a commercial warehouse or a big market.

Finally, our gleanings are poor, but the best result is that the period of the emergence of Malabar in our sources agrees with its medieval growth. In fact, the names that occur in the source compiled in the thirteenth and fourteenth centuries match the harbours known by Arab fiscal documents of the same period. Strikingly, the Indian place names quoted in the Yemenite *Nūr al-ma'ārif* (*Light of Knowledge*), a collection of registers of the end of the thirteenth century, are mentioned substantially in the same order by an Egyptian encyclopaedist at the same time.

Notes

1. Maqbul 1989.
2. Abū 'Imrān 2006.
3. Al-Waṭwāṭ 1990, I: 342–4.
4. Mehren 1866: 172–4.
5. Lambourn 2008: 84–90; Vallet 2010: 564–77.
6. Maqbul 1991.
7. Ibn Ḥawqal 1939: 320.
8. Yule, 1967, IV: 72–9.
9. Sachau 1992, I: 203.
10. Ibn Sa'īd 1970: 120.
11. Abū 'Imrān 2006: 123; Freeman-Grenville 1981: 55.
12. Idrīsī 1982, p. 186; Maqbul 1989: 58 and 93.
13. Yāqūt 1990, V: 227.
14. Ibn Sa'īd 1970: 120.
15. Yule 1870: 340–56; Jahn 1980: 35–6. His text is partly borrowed from al-Bīrūnī.
16. Nainar 1942: 169.
17. Maqbul 1989: 4–5. 'Ūtkin is identified with Oykman/Okha, on the northern coast of Kathiawar.
18. Idrīsī 1982: 980; Maqbul 1960: 119–21.
19. Maqbul 1989: 21; Wink 1990: 164–6.
20. Maqbul 1960: 89–90.
21. Bhattacharyya 1999: 94; Lambourn 2008: 87.
22. Bosworth 1986.
23. Maqbul 1989: 38.
24. Arunachalam 2002: 342–6.
25. Maqbul 1960: 101–2.
26. Al-Mas'ūdī 1962, I: 102
27. Al-Mas'ūdī 1962, I: 85; Bhattacharyya 1999: 105; Chakravarti 2000: 39 and 43.
28. Chakravarti 1991: 166; Bāmaḥrama 2004: 149.
29. For a geographic commentary, see Van der Lith and Devic 1883: 225–30.
30. Bosworth 1998.
31. Sachau 1992, II: 104; Chakravarti 1991: 34–64.
32. Abu l-Fida 1840: 357; Zaki 1981: 72–3.
33. Maqbul 1960: 55.
34. Ibid.
35. Maqbul 1960: 56.
36. Maqbul 1960: 63.
37. Maqbul 1960: 56.

38. Maqbul 1960: 58.
39. Nainar 1942: 34-5.
40. Maqbul 1960: 63.
41. Nainar 1942: 40–1; Bosworth 1978.
42. Maqbul 1960: 157.
43. Ibn Saʿīd 1957: 38; Ibn Saʿīd 1970: 105.
44. Yāqūt 1990, IV: 416.
45. Lambourn 2008: 84; Vallet 2010: 573–5.
46. Ibn Saʿīd 1957: 38; Ibn Saʿīd 1970: 106.
47. al-Waṭwāṭ 1990, I: 342–4; Mehren 1866: 172–4.
48. Lambourn 2008: 86.
49. Maqbul 1960: 100-1. The locality is situated on the west bank of the Kālinadī.
50. Tibbetts 1981: 452; Bhattacharyya 1999: 233.
51. Tibbetts 1981: 453.
52. Lambourn 2008: 89.
53. Bāmaḥrama 2004: 149.
54. It is the Tuluva coast, Tibbetts 1991: 450.
55. Lambourn 2008: 87–8.
56. Bouchon 1975: 4–18; Lambourn 2008: 87.
57. Bosworth 1978.
58. Abū l-Fidāʾ 1840: 118.
59. Ibn Baṭṭūṭa 1994: 800.
60. Ibn Baṭṭūṭa 1994: 805.
61. Nambirajam and Gaur 1997: 117.
62. Ibn Baṭṭūṭa 1994: 816.

Bibliography

Abū l-Fidāʾ, *Taqwīm al-buldān*, ed. Reinaud, J.T. and Baron Mac Guckin de Slane (1840), *Géographie d'Aboulféda*, Texte arabe publié d'après les manuscrits de Paris et de Leyde aux frais de la Société Asiatique. Paris: Imprimerie royale.

Abū ʿImrān Mūsā ibn Rabāḥ al-Awsī al-Sīrāfī, *Al-ṣaḥīḥ min aḥbār al-baḥr wa-ʿağāʾibihā*, ed. Al-Hādī, Y. (2006), Damas: Dār Iqrāʾ li-l-tibāʿa wa-l-našr wa-l-tawzīʿ

Arunachalam, B. (2002), 'Use of Imagery in Reconstruction of the Past: A Case Study of Sopara', *Indian Cartographer* 2002, pp. 342–6.

Bāmaḥrama al-Ḥimyarī (2004), *Al-nisba ilā al-mawāḍiʿ wa-l-buldān*. Abū Ẓabī: Markaz al-waṯāʾiq wa-l-buḥūṯ.

Bhattacharyya, N.N. (1999), *The Geographical Dictionary*, New Delhi: Munshiram Manoharlal.

Bosworth, C.E. (1978), 'Kannanūr', in *Encyclopédie de l'Islam*, vol. IV, Leiden: E.J. Brill, pp. 570–1.

—— (1986), 'Kulām', in *Encyclopédie de l'Islam*, vol. V, Leiden: E.J. Brill, p. 361.

—— (1998), 'Sūmanāt', in *Encyclopédie de l'Islam*, vol. IX, Leiden: E.J. Brill, pp. 904–5.

Bouchon, G. (1975), *Mamale de Cananor. Un adversaire de l'Inde portugaise.* Genève-Paris: Droz-Minard-Champion.

Chakravarti, R. (1991), 'Horse Trade and Piracy at Tana (Thana, Maharashtra, India): Gleanings from Marco Polo', *Journal of the Economic and Social History of the Orient* (hereafter *JESHO*), vol. 34, no. 3, pp. 159–82.

Chakravarti, R. (2000), 'Nakhudas and nauvittakas: ship-owning Merchants in the West Coast of India (AD 1000-1500)', *JESHO,* vol. 43, no. 1, pp. 34–64.

Freeman-Grenville, G.S.P. (1981), *The Book of the Wonders of India*, London: East-West Publications.

Ibn Baṭṭūṭa, *Travels*, ed. Gibb, H.A.R. (1994), *The Travels of Ibn Battuta: AD 1325-1354*, vol. 4, London: The Hakluyt Society.

Ibn Ḥawqal, *K. ṣūrat al-arḍ*, J.H. Kramers, ed. (1939), *Opus geographicum auctore Ibn Ḥaukal secundum textum et imagines codicis Constantinopolitani conservati in Bibliotheca Antiqui Palatii n°3346 cui titulus est Liber Imaginis Terrae, edidit collato textu primae editionis aliisque fontibus adhibitis J.H. Kramers* (Bibliotheca Geographorum Arabicorum, II, 2). Leiden: E.J. Brill.

Ibn Saʿīd, *K. basṭ al-arḍ*, Vernet Ginès, J., ed (1958) *Libro de la extension de la tierra en longitud y latitud*, Tétouan: Instituto Muley el-Hasan.

Ibn Saʿīd al-Maġribī (1970), *Kitāb al-ǧuġrāfiyā*, I. Al-ʿArabī, ed., Beirut: Manšūrāt al-maktab at-tiǧārī liʾṭ-ṭibāā waʾn-našr waʾt-tauzī.

Al-Idrīsī (1982–4), *Nuzhat al-muštāq fī iḥtirāq al-āfāq. Opus geograficum.* Roma-Napoli: Istituto universitario orientale di Napoli.

Jahn, K. (1980), *Die Indiengeschichte des Rašid al-Dīn*, Wien: Verlag der Österreichischen Akademie der Wissenschaften.

Lambourn, E. (2008), 'India from Aden: khuṭba and Muslim Urban Networks in Late Thirteenth century India', in *Secondary Cities and Urban Networking in the Indian Ocean Realm, c.1000–1800*, ed. K. Hall, Lanham, MD: Lexington Books, pp. 55–97.

Maqbul, A. (1960), *India and the neighbouring territories in the Kitāb nuzhat al-mushtāq fiʾ khtirāq al-ʾāfāq of al-Sharīf al-Idrīsī*, Leiden: Brill (Uitgaven van de Stichting de Goeje 20).

—— (1989), *Arabic Classical Account of India*, Shimla: Indian Institute of Advanced Study.

—— (1991), 'Balharā', in *Encyclopédie de l'Islam*, vol. I, Leiden: E.J. Brill, p. 1022.

Al-Masʿūdī (1962), *Les Prairies d'or*, Ch. Pellat, tr., Paris: Société asiatique.

Mehren, F. (1866), *Cosmographie de Chems-ed-Din Abou Abdallad Mohammed ed-Dimichqui*, Saint-Pétersbourg: Académie impériale des sciences.

Nainar, M.H. (1942), *Arab Geographers' Knowledge of Southern India*, Madras: Madras University, Islamic series, no. 6.

Nambirajan, M., and Gaur, A.S. (1997), 'River ports and other archeological sites on the river banks of Goa', in *An integrated approach to marine archaeology: Fourth Indian Conference on Marine Archaeology of Indian Ocean Countries held at Andhra University, Visakhapatanam on 20–21 September 1994*, ed. S.R. Rao, Goa: National Institute of Oceanography, pp. 115–19.

Sachau, E. (1992), *Alberuni's India*, London: Kegan Paul, Trench, Trubner & Co; Reed (1910), Delhi: Munshiram Manoharlal.

Tibbetts, G.R. (1981), *Arab Navigation in the Indian Ocean before the coming of the Portuguese*, London: Royal Asiatic Society of Great Britain and Ireland.

Vallet, É. (2010), *L'Arabie marchande. État et commerce sous les sultans rasûlides du Yémen (626-858/1229-1454)*. Paris: Publications de la Sorbonne.

Van der Lith, P.A. and Devic, M. (1883-1886), *Livre des merveilles de l'Inde*. Leiden: E.J. Brill.

Jamāl al-Dīn al-Waṭwāṭ (1990), *Manāhij al-fikar wa-mabāhij al-'bar. Encyclopaedia of Four Natural Sciences*, Frankfurt-am-Main: Institute for the History of Arabic-Islamic Science Series C, Facsimile editions 49.

Wink, A. (1990), *Al-Hind: The Making of the Indo-Islamic World*, Leiden: E.J. Brill.

Yāqūt, [Šihāb al-Dīn] Abū 'Abd Allāh, *Mu'ǧam al-buldān* (7 vols.), Farīd 'Abd al-'Azīz Al-Ǧundī, ed. (1990), Beirut: Dār al-kutub al-'ilmiyyāt.

Yule, H. (1870), 'An Endeavour to Elucidate Rachiduddin's Geographical Notice of India', *Journal of the Royal Asiatic Society of Great Britain and Ireland*, vol. 4, no. 2, pp. 340–56.

Yule, H. (1916), 'The Medieval ports of Malabar', in *Cathay and the way thither*, H. Yule, vol. IV, London: The Haklyut Society; Millwood, NY (1967): Kraus reprint, pp. 72–9.

Zaki, M. (1981), *Arab Accounts of India during the Fourteenth Century*, Delhi: Idarah-i Adabiyāt-i Delli.

APPENDICES

The ports of the west coast of India according to Arabic geographers

I. Ninth-Thirteenth Centuries

Modern localities	Ibn Ḥurradāḏbih (ninth century)	Al-Istaḥrī Ibn Ḥawqal (ninth century)	Al-Masʿūdī (d. c. 956).	Al-Bīrūnī (d. c. 1050)	Al-Idrīsī (d. c. 1160)	Yāqūt (d. 1229)
Bhadreśwar						Qaṣṣa
Oykman/Okha	Awtkīn/Ūtkīn				Ūtkīn	
Kathiāwāṛ(?) Mandvi(?)	Mayd				Mayd	
Jaki Bandar				Lūhārani		
Not identified				Bakka		
Kachh-Mandvi				Kachh		
Baroda(?)				Bārūy		
Somnath				Sūmanāt		
Kodinar	Kūlī				Kūlī	
Cambay	Kanbāyā	Kanbāya	Kanbāya	Kanbāya	Kanbāya	
Ahmadabad				Asāwal	Asāwal	
Broach	Barūṣ			Bihrūǧ	Barūǧ	Ḥūr Barwaṣ
Sanjān	Sandān	Sandān	Sindān	Sandān	Sandān	
Sopara		Sūbāra	Sufāra	Sūfāra	Sūbāra	
Thana			Tāna	Tāna	Tāna	Tāna
Chaul		Ṣaymūr	Ṣaymūr	Ṣaymūr/ Ǧimūr	Ṣaymūr	Ṣaymūr
Candrapura/ Chandor			Ṣindābūra		Sindābūr	
Not identified					D.h.s.l	
Bakkanore					Fāknūr	
Mangalore					Manǧarūr	
Pantalayini					Fanda-rayna	
Srikandapura/ Cananor					Ǧurfāttan	
Cranganore Shingli	(Šinklī)				Ṣinǧī	
Cahlacory					Kl.ksār	
Kulam-Malay (Quilon)	Mulay				Mulay	Kawlam
Vallabha				Balabah		

II. Thirteenth-Fifteenth Centuries

Modern localities	Ibn Saʿīd (d. 1286)	Al-Waṭwāṭ (d. AD 1318)	Al-Dimašqī (d. 1327)	Abū l-Fidāʾ (d. 1331)	Ibn Baṭṭūṭa (d. 1369)	Qalqašandī (d. 1418)
Bhadreśwar	Al-Qaṣā		Qaṣṣ Bazāna Rakla			
Somnath	Sūmanāt	Sūmanāt		Ṣūmanāt		
Broach		Barūğ/ Barwaṣ	Barwaṣ			
Dabhoi		Al-Dabū				
Cambay	Kanbāya	Kanbāya	Kambāya	Kambāya	Kanbaya	Kanbāya
In front of Cambay					Kāwā	
Gandhar					Qandahār	
Bhatkal (South of Honawar)?		Barqalī	Barqalī			
Piram Island					Bayram	
Goga					Qūqa	
Nawsari		Nawsārī	Nawsārī			
Not identified		Dūn	Dūq			
Agashi		Akātī	Akānṯī			
Sopara		Sutāra	Sūbārah	Sufāra		
Vasai		Wasāhī	Sāhī			
Thana	Tāna	Tāna	Tāna	Tāna		Tāna
Mahim/Mahem		Mahāyim				
Sanjān				Sandan		Sandan
Not identified		Dabūna	Dabūh			
Not identified		Qarnāla	Qartālih			
Not identified		S.b.kīs	Sakbīs			
Chador		Sandābūr	Sindābūr		Sindābūr	
Honavar		Hannawr	Hannawr	Hannawr	Hinawr	Hinawr
Barcelore				Basarūr	Abū Sarūr	Basasūr
Bakkanore	Fāknur	Fākanūr	Fākanūr		Fākanūr	
Chaul	Ṣaymūr	Ṣaymūr	Ṣaymūr			
Mangalore	Manǧarūr	Manǧarūr	Manǧarūr	Manǧarūr	Manǧarūr	Manǧarūr
Kasargord		Harqalī	Harqaliya			
Raʾs Hili		Hīlī	Hīlī	Hīlī	Hīlī	
Srikandapuram/ Cannanore		Ğurbattan	Ğurfattān		Ğurfattan	
Valarpattanam		Dih-battan	Dih-Fattān		Dih-Fattan	
Darmapattanam		Buddfattan	Buddfattān		Buddfattan	
Pantalayini		Fandarayna	Fandarayna		Fandaraynā	Fandarayna
Chaliyam				Šāliyāt	Šāliyāt	Šāliyāt
Kozhikode					Calicut	
Shinglī		Sinklī	Šinklī	Šinklī		Šinkalī
Kulam/Qailon	Kawlam	Kawlam	Kawlam	Kawlam	Kawlam	Kawlam

CHAPTER 11

Ports of Western India in Latin Cartographic Sources, *c.*1200–1500
Toponymy, Localization and Evolutions

Emmanuelle Vagnon

The Map Department of the Bibliothèque nationale de France, as a partner of the 'Median' programme, considered the publication of a historical 'atlas' of ancient maps of the Indian Ocean, demonstrating the evolution of knowledge and cultural exchanges between two maritime areas, the Mediterranean and the Indian Ocean.[1] As a result of a primary investigation, this essay addresses the interest of Europeans for the western shores of India, the knowledge that was thus produced, and how the region was represented in European cartography of the Medieval and Renaissance periods. An atlas would contribute to a cultural study of the transmission of geographical information between East and West, with a close historical analysis of the purpose and context of each map.

At first sight, producing an anthology of old cartographic documents is not quite a new idea. On the contrary, it is closely linked with the history of map collections, such as the French Département des Cartes et Plans, founded in the early nineteenth century by Edmond Jomard.[2] At that time, when the History of Cartography intended to become a part of the historical sciences, specialists of ancient maps assumed the development of cartography was a consequence of the 'Great Discoveries' and the extension of Western knowledge to new lands. Therefore, the development of geography and cartography was presented as a linear/continuous progress from ignorance to knowledge, and from medieval primitivism to modern civilization. Ancient maps were collected in huge books called *Monumenta Cartographica*, and those collections are of course still very useful.[3]

Recently, the History of Cartography has undergone significant changes, especially since the 1990s, in terms of means of investigation, methods of finding information, ways of understanding and commenting on old maps.[4] Nowadays, new technology allows for a better access to rare and fragile documents through digital reproduction.[5] Some of the most famous old maps, mainly from the Middle Ages, have been recently published in scholarly editions, like other manuscripts, with a philological and critical approach.[6] Today, luckily, the 'positivist', 'progressist', and often 'nationalist' approach in which those documents were commented upon during the nineteenth and twentieth centuries is generally considered to be outdated, and we find less anachronistic judgements about the so-called 'accuracy' or 'truth' of the maps. Historians of maps underline the reasons why some representations existed at a particular moment in time, they focus on the sources and processes that lead to the visible results and emphasize the consequences (the reception) of geographical information and cartographic images. Everyone is now expected to be aware that a map (even today) is not the 'true' image of 'reality', but a shaping, an interpretation of a reality, following different readings and codes.[7] Moreover, as we will see, the study of place-names can also help archaeological investigations.

Thus, an anthology of ancient maps of the Indian Ocean should be built according to a new perspective:

- considering a maritime space without a nationalistic and 'land-oriented' point of view as a space of very ancient interactions between different lands and cultures;
- considering Western maps not only as the result of the western discovery of the world, but as the result of mixed sources coming from Antiquity and the Middle Ages, through the meeting of people and cultures;
- and finally, observing the 'errors' and 'inaccuracies' of the maps as traces of complex evolutions, resulting from the access to sources, their interpretation, and the transmission of information.

Having said that, I shall in this essay comment on some outstanding maps following a traditional chronological approach.

Medieval Nautical Charts

Starting with medieval maps, I will focus on the rise of portolan charts. Concerning the numerous, often schematic circular maps, Western medieval *mappaemundi*, I will roughly say that most of them, prior to the thirteenth century, give very little information about India. Whatever the content, it is largely taken from ancient sources such as Pliny, Solinus, and the medieval tradition of the History of Alexander the Great. Those *mappaemundi* are seldom very detailed and mostly deal with the historical and ethnological geography of the margins of the world, showing the 'marvels of the East'—which, incidentally, did not completely disappear during the Renaissance.[8] However, some recent studies have pointed out a real concern for accurate physical features and place-names of Eastern countries, especially during the time of the Crusades. For example, at the end of the twelfth century, a text describing coastlines from the Yorkshire (England) to the Mediterranean, called *De Viis Maris* is extended up to the Indian Ocean and the western shores of India; it mentions scattered information about cities of India, after thirty days of navigation from Arabia.[9] The text deals with the description of maritime sailing from port to port and gives information on the conditions of navigation. It is therefore what we call a 'portolan', a guide with basic nautical data in common use after the thirteenth century. Most historians agree that those 'portolan texts' are closely related to 'portolan maps', that is to say medieval nautical charts, which progressively incorporate Eastern knowledge about the Indian Ocean.[10]

From the end of the thirteenth and mostly during the fourteenth century, many Western travellers went to India: Marco Polo of course, but also Oderic de Pordenone, Jordan Catala de Severac and John of Marignolli.[11] Their reports, together with other oral sources that we can only suppose, were progressively used as sources for maps.[12] The *mappamundi* by Pietro Vesconte is an example of Western medieval representation of the Indian Ocean around 1320–30, with an addition of nautical information partly based on portolan charts, and connections with the Ptolemy's *Geography* through Arabic sources (probably al Idrisi).[13] According to this medieval knowledge, Asia was divided into three 'Indias', which included a part of eastern Africa; but for the first time, the Red Sea and the Persian Gulf are properly positioned. Nevertheless, the toponymy of the Indian Ocean remains very poor, and the Indian peninsula is not accurately represented. A century after Marco Polo's travels, an outstanding example of Western knowledge about India emerged: the famous *Catalan Atlas*, *c.*1375, kept in the French Royal Library since the end of the fourteenth century (*c.*1380)[14] (Plate 11.1). It is the first Western portolan chart that shows India with a triangular shape. A close study of the place-names along the western coast reveals an impressive accuracy. Most of them come from Marco Polo, as well as the majority of the other Asian names in the atlas. But some other place-names are completely new.

In order to show how ancient maps can be used for archaeological investigations, I would like to make reference to Monik Kervran's study about some place-names in the Sind and Indus Delta[15] (Plate 11.2). She

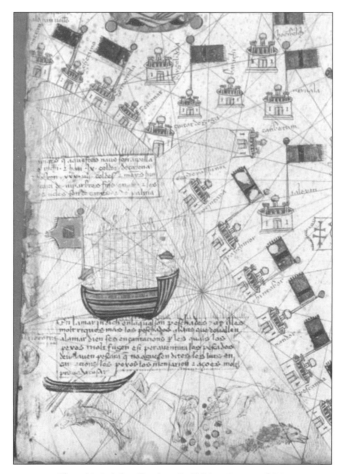

Plate 11.1: Atlas Catalan, BnF, Mss, Espagnol 30.

had pointed out in Arabic sources some brief allusions to a place called 'Damrila'. From an archaeological point of view, evidence of different building foundations strengthen the distinction to be made between the past 'Damrila' and the better-known 'Daybul'.[16] When looking for mentions of this place in ancient maps, Kervran came across a place-name 'Damonela' in the *Catalan Atlas*. It is usually interpreted as a Catalan form for Daybul, called 'Diul' or 'Diulsind', in later sources. But Kervran was the only scholar to make the link with the foundation of another city distinct from Daybul, called 'Damrila' in Islamic sources, where a mosque was founded around 1221–3 by Sultan Jalal al-din and later destroyed or abandoned. She later uncovered archaeological evidence (including ruins and a beautiful Kufic inscription) of a great mosque on a site called Jam Jaskar Goth, nowadays covered by sand and water most of the time. Obviously, the continual

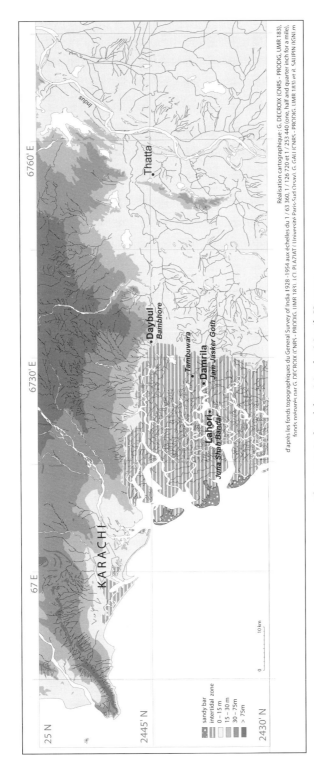

Plate 11.2: Indus delta. Map by Monik Kervran.

changing of the Indus Delta due to flooding and shifting of the river stream and sand banks, would explain the disappearance of the town. According to Monik Kervran's study, the *Catalan Atlas* is a rare but crucial example of the transmission of information on the Indus Delta from Arab sources into the Mediterranean world, even though the mechanism of transfer remains unknown.

After discussions with Monik Kervran, I have found two other Western documents mentioning 'Damonela' in the fourteenth century. The first one is the so-called *Medici Atlas*, kept nowadays in the Biblioteca Laurenziana of Florence, Italy.[17] The earliest possible date is 1351, according to a calendar placed at the beginning of the atlas, but some palaeographic evidence suggests that it should be dated to the end of the fourteenth century;[18] thus, the *Medici Atlas* would be contemporary with the *Catalan Atlas*. The list of place-names along the western shore of India is exactly the same as in the *Catalan Atlas*, in the same order and same locations, but with an Italian spelling. The only issue arises from doubts about the authenticity of the *Medici Atlas*.

In fact, the controversial nature of the *Medici Atlas* was already discussed during the nineteenth and twentieth centuries. Like other portolan atlases of the fourteenth century, the *Medici Atlas* is composed of several sheets of vellum, showing the usual parts of the Mediterranean and Atlantic Ocean, and a cosmographical calendar at the beginning. More oddly, it also includes a planisphere showing Africa with a quite accurate shape, long before the discovery of the Cape of Good Hope by Bartolomeu Dias in 1488. Historians of cartography are aware of the fact that the shape of Africa and the possibility to navigate around the South of the African continent was known in Eastern and Western countries long before the Portuguese discoveries. But this map is notably unusual for its time and, moreover, shows traces of corrections of the initial map, with an obvious change of the main colour of the painting (corrections which, by the way, are very roughly made). If we look closely, the place-names along the western coast of India are not part of the new painting, and probably belong to the original map. What can we deduce from this? First, whether it is a forgery or not, there is a very strong link between the *Catalan Atlas* and the *Medici Atlas*, and we can assume that both rely on the same source about the existence of a port called 'Damonela' near the mouth of the Indus. Second, the translation of the place-names into vernacular spelling can be observed on other maps of the fourteenth century (Dulcert/Dalorto),[19] and the change of painting does not seem to concern the place-names of India. Finally, if the *Medici Atlas* is a real forgery, it could have been made for nationalist reasons to reinforce for example the role of Italians in the discovery of Africa and Asia, by Italianizing the place-names.

The other document mentioning this place is the *Libro del conoscimiento*.[20] In the nineteenth century, it was first considered as the narrative of a real journey made in the fourteenth century by a Franciscan friar around the Mediterranean and in the Near-East. It appears today more likely to represent an imaginary trip based on the reading of a portolan chart or a portolan-based *mappamundi*, showing the entire world and decorated with coats of arms. The date of the *Libro* can be situated between 1376 and 1402.[21] But the presence of the place-name 'Damonela' creates a strong link with the Parisian *Catalan Atlas*, and we can imagine that both the *Medici Atlas* and the *Libro* rely on the same sources, coming from Muslim or Jewish merchants navigating the Indian Ocean and travelling to the West, where their knowledge could be collected in workshops such as that of Mallorca, which produced the *Catalan Atlas*. One wonders if this 'Damonela' was copied in other maps today lost; I could not find any other reference. The fact is that this tradition of place-names in the Indus Delta appears to have been greatly modified during the fifteenth century, as some of the toponyms were lost, whereas some new names appeared, following other sources and creating another cartographical tradition.

Fra Mauro's *mappaemundi* and the Golden Age of Ptolemy's Geography

At the beginning of the fifteenth century, the Latin translation of Ptolemy's Geography gave to Western geographers some Asian toponyms that were different from the medieval tradition.[22] But at the same time, it gave an archaic and inaccurate representation of a closed Indian Ocean. During the Renaissance, mapmakers had to choose between contradictory information concerning the Indian Ocean and India, and they tried to make a compilation of that information. The question was, what information would be relevant and on what grounds? Naturally, the history of cartography during the Renaissance never follows a simple progress from ignorance to knowledge, but rather sinuous paths from one state of knowledge to another state. In other words, maps are not the representation of a static state of knowledge at a given period, but a 'work in progress', showing a stratification of sources, points of view, and graphic solutions for different, often conflicting hypotheses.

This is obvious for the shape of India, the rivers Indus and Ganges, and the coastal place-names on Fra Mauro's world map, made about 1459 in Venice.[23] Whereas the number of place-names in the Indian Ocean increases, the main rivers of India are positioned very awkwardly. For instance, the Indus is placed in the eastern part of India, far from Gujarat and relatively close to the river Ganges, and there is some confusion with the place-names of the Ganges.[24] Nevertheless the Fra Mauro map is certainly the most complete and ingenious map of the period. The author, a Camaldolese Friar of Venice was commissioned by the Portuguese king to make a copy of this magnificent *mappamundi* based on the maximum information available at his time: names from Antiquity, medieval travel books by Marco Polo, Jordan of Catala and Nicolo de'Conti, numerous Arab sources, and Portuguese discoveries along the coast of Africa. He was helped by the cartographer Andrea Bianco, who was skilled in nautical charts. Many comments written on the Fra Mauro map criticize the sources, showing for example that Ptolemy was wrong to present the Indian Ocean as closed.[25] Obviously, for the shape of India, Mauro had to make some difficult choices. But his representation of the Indus and the Ganges is surprising, taking into account that both the *Catalan Atlas* and Ptolemy gave a better design. In Classical geography, the Indus and Ganges formed the borders of India '*intra Gangem*'. Here the cartographer followed the medieval tradition of the three 'Indias', displayed from West to East, and decided to give more surface to the regions of 'India prima', situated on the West of the Indus. The result is that a large part of what we call today the Indian peninsula appears as a narrow territory between two eastern rivers. From a comparison with Andrea Bianco's map one deduces that Fra Mauro, for this part of the map, probably made the wrong choice between several possibilities. For example, when he drew some parallel rivers going straight to the eastern part of the oecumene (according to older *mappaemundi* rather than to Ptolemy), or when he had to position on those rivers new place-names according to textual sources. However, other *mappaemundi* of mid fifteenth century based on both Ptolemy and Nicolo de'Conti are better shaped, though give fewer interesting place-names than Fra Mauro—for example the Genovese eye-shaped *mappamundi* of Florence and the Catalan-Estense map of Modena.[26]

The difficulty of interpreting Ptolemy's geography of India can be observed later in Henricus Martellus' world map. This German cartographer worked in Florence and specialized in several types of maps.[27] We know his 'aggiornamento' of Ptolemy's world map, made in 1489 and extant in his *Insularium Illustratum*[28] and in a separate map now at Yale University.[29] He claimed to have used for the shape of Africa the most recent information from Portuguese geographers (for example, Africa is 'breaking the border' of the map to show the circumnavigation of Bartolomeu Dias).[30] But it is easy to notice that the eastern shore of Africa, the Indian Ocean and India are still like that in Ptolemy, far less accurate than in the *Catalan Atlas*. Except for the copies of Ptolemy and the maps of Henricus Martellus, there is a time-gap of 40 years without any novelty between the impressive *mappaemundi* of the mid-fifteenth century and the maps showing the Portuguese discoveries in the Indian Ocean at the beginning of the sixteenth century.

The 'Great Discoveries': New Place-Names and Great Misunderstandings

After Bartolomeu Dias' and Vasco da Gama's travels, much new information came to Western Europe through written reports and maps. The new data were introduced in worldwide portolan charts linked to Portuguese patterns, using Portuguese toponyms and even showing the *padrões*, stone pillars that indicated the coastal places visited by the Portuguese navigators. Unfortunately, most Portuguese maps of the period were lost during the earthquake of Lisbon, but some very large and decorated documents came down to us: for example the Cantino map of 1502, and the map by Nicolao Caverio Genovese, of 1504–1506, now kept in the Bibliothèque nationale de France, an Italian copy closely related to the Cantino map[31] (Plate 11.3).

We immediately observe major changes in the toponymy of India: names are more numerous, and spellings different when compared with the *Catalan Atlas*, some of them coming from Portuguese sources and others from Ptolemy. The major task of the cartographers and of those interested in geography at that time was to make the link between ancient, medieval, Arab and Portuguese place-names. But how were choices made? Usually, a new Western name was given to 'virgin' coastal places, often along the African littoral: on maps of Africa at that time, places are frequently named after the saint of the day (as in South America). But in Asia, Portuguese navigators encountered already 'civilized' and urbanized lands and were eager to identify them correctly, according to local uses and former sources.[32] The 'standardization' of those place-names or, in other words, the finding of a common denomination valid for all Western cartography, could take a long time. First, the locations of cities and ports in the Indus Delta often shifted considerably, as Kervran noticed. Second, the place-name of a site could change as well: from the ancient Barbarica or Pattala to Daybul and Banbhore, or Damonela/Damrila, then Lahori Bandar or Bandel, then Diulsynd (Diul of the Sind) or simply Diul, a name derived from Daybul, as a generic name for the ports of the Sind in the sixteenth century (not to be confused with the Daybul of south India nor Diu in Gujarat), while nowadays Thatta and Karachi are the main cities of the

Plate 11.3: Nicolao Caverio, BnF, CPL, Ge SH ARCH-1.

Indus Delta. It is easy to understand how difficult it was for cartographers who had never been there, to situate those different place-names on a general map of the region.

I would like to conclude this essay by raising the issue of copying and compilation of geographical information, and how it is reflected in the genealogy of maps. We have to bear in mind that new maps were usually compilations and seldom based on entirely fresh information. This is most obvious in printed maps, two of which I would like to discuss here.

The modern map of India by Waldseemüller and his collegues (Plate 11.4) was made for a new corrected edition of Ptolemy's Geography published in Strasbourg in 1513. The authors were a team of geographers and humanists working at Saint-Dié in the Duchy of Lorraine, now a part of France. At the beginning of the book, they explain how they tried to correct and improve the original geography with new geographical information. Thus, the ancient maps are presented as historical ones, and the 'modern' maps as an 'aggiornamento' or 'updates'. If we look closely at the modern India map, we see that it is essentially a printed and simplified copy of the manuscript map of Nicolaus Caverio (including the design, but also the commentaries).

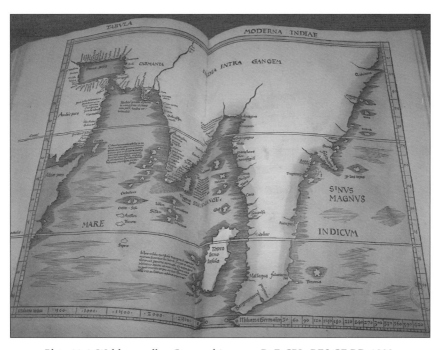

Plate 11.4: Waldseemuller, Geographiæ opus, BnF, CPL, RES GE DD-1009, pl 41: Tabula Moderna Indiae.

My second example is a map made by the Venetian Giacomo Gastaldi in 1561.[33] It is beautifully printed and apparently more complete than the nautical charts, for the inland too is covered. Information comes from classical sources, Portuguese and medieval travellers, as shown by a caption at the top of the map: the caption deals with the desert of Lop Nor, directly taken from Marco Polo's book. A table at the right shows the equivalence between antique and modern place-names. It would be interesting to study how those equivalences were made and if they are now considered as accurate. Moreover, the historian Piero Falchetta advances the hypothesis that some of the place-names of the Indus River on a map by Gastaldi came from the Fra Mauro world map, which could be seen in Venice.[34] Some information also came from Portuguese maps, such as a map by the Portuguese Reinel for the Persian Gulf at the beginning of the sixteenth century.[35]

The genealogy of that knowledge is very difficult to reconstitute, and would need a separate study. But we can underline here one particular inaccuracy, which is present in many maps of the sixteenth century, for example in the Miller Atlas (Plate 11.5): the Indus River (which was more or less correctly positioned in Ptolemy and Medieval nautical charts) is located east and south of Gujarat, about 500 km. too far from the real delta. There is most probably some confusion between the river of Cambay and the Indus Delta. As a result, the place name of Daybul/Diul of the Sind (Diulcinde in the Atlas Miller) is situated north-west, near the mouth of another river (named on some maps 'R. de Diulsinde'). But why would such an error be reproduced precisely when new geographical information was available in the West? Two answers are possible. First, this description of the mouth of the Indus near Cambay can be related to Nicolo de' Conti's report from the fifteenth century, and more precisely to the version translated and printed in *Delli navigationi et viaggi* by Giovanni Battista Ramusio from 1557–65[36]—note that this edition was illustrated by Gastaldi's maps. Thus, the error could be interpreted as derived from the compilation of old sources and old maps unrelated to fresh information in the sixteenth century.

And yet, we have to take into account some important geological changes that occurred during the past centuries. For example, the archaeologist Elizabeth Lambourn has found traces of a navigable connection between the river of Cambay and the Little Rann of Kutch, which 'for six months of the year turned Saurashtra into an island. This phenomenon ceased only as a consequence of a violent earthquake that shook western India in 1819 and raised the Saurashtran peninsula, thus terminating the annual flooding'. To support her hypothesis, Lambourn mentions several maps from the

Plate 11.5: Atlas Miller, BnF, CPL GE DD-683 (3 RES), ff. 3.

seventeenth century, representing Saurashtra as an island off Gujarat.[37] In this case again, ancient maps (and in this case, printed maps) may be taken as historical sources, demonstrating the close link between central Gujarat and the Indian Ocean, and explaining the use of stone and marble transported by boats as building materials in a region where only brick should be available. This being said, the fact that 'Kutch actually belongs geologically to the Indus delta' is not enough to prove that there was a mouth of the Indus in the Gulf of Kutch at the end of the Middle Ages, and even less so that the Gulf of Cambay had a connection with the Indus. This question certainly needs further investigation in cooperation with archaeo-geologists.[38] Nevertheless, the existence of a navigable connection between the Indus, ports of the Sind and the Gulf of Cambay is suggested in several maps, and a correct and prudent analysis of ancient maps must balance errors and traces of older traditions, as compilers always had to make a choice between several hypotheses. If we consider both manuscript nautical charts and printed maps of the beginning of the 1550–60s, we can observe how the uncertainty about the location of the Indus Delta, and the hypothesis of a navigable connection between the gulfs were interpreted in different ways. First, we notice that early, very simplified, printed maps of India, such as that of Sebastien Münster, or a Gastaldi map edited in 1548, place the Indus River east from Gujarat, like in the Miller Atlas.[39] But in the map printed for Ramusio's *Navigationi* in 1557–65, showing the Indian Ocean with the south at the top of the page, and decorated with fish-monsters and vessels,[40] the cartographer situated Gujarat as an island with the cities of Patan and Diu, off the coast, between Cambaia and Diul (Diulsind). And in a third, more elaborated version from 1561,[41] (Plate 11.6) the whole region, from Diul to Surat, is located inside the Indus Delta, separated into several navigable mouths, with Gujarat as a true island between Cambaia and the Sind. There are contemporary place-names (Goga, Mangalor, Diu, Baroche, Cambaia, Surat, and even Ahmedabad), but the cartographer also situated the ancient name of Pattala in the delta, and never mentions Kutch. This map is the source of Abraham Ortelius' map of 1570 and was largely diffused,[42] even when more accurate manuscript maps became available. For example, the Portuguese maps of the 1560s, closely related to fresh information, such as a map of Diogo Homem, 1561, or Lázaro Luís (from Goa), 1563,[43] make a clear distinction between the Indus (north-west) with the place-name Diulcynde, the Gulf of Kutch (*cacha),* Gujarat and the Gulf of Cambay (south-east). There is no visible connection between the gulfs, and neither Gujarat nor Kutch is represented as an island. But such information was not easily transmitted to printed cartography, even as late as the beginning of the seventeenth century.[44]

As we have seen, the Renaissance is not quite the age of the rise of scientific cartography that historians once believed it to be. We also need to underline the fact that the translation of Ptolemy's Geography cannot be considered to have constituted an 'epistemological revolution' as drastic as is often claimed. The Renaissance was an age of compilation and interpretation of often contradictory information, leading to many different maps depicting an expanding world. The real novelty of this age is the *amount* of new information available and its varied origins, taken from translated classical sources, medieval travel books, new explorations and, recent Arab/Persian/Indian sources. Access to data was further facilitated through the development of the printing industry. More information sometimes means more opportunities to get things wrong, either by making incorrect choices or by repeating previous mistakes. In this sense, compiling information in the sixteenth century was much more difficult

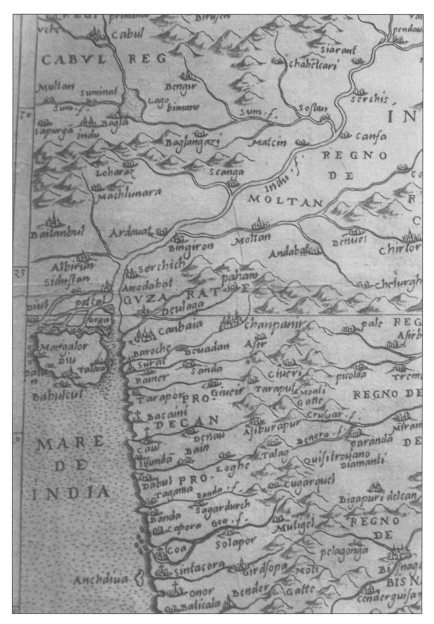

Plate 11.6: Giacomo Gastaldi, *Il designo della terza parte dell'Asia . . .*, Giacomo di Gastaldi. . .; Fabius Licinius excudebat, Venetia 1561, BnF, CPL, GE CC-1380 (68 RES).

than before. Place-names for example came from very different periods and places. The maps made during the Renaissance put together those data without clearly separating ancient and modern knowledge. It seems that a book documenting the early cartography of the Indian Ocean, presenting maps and other sources and analysing them with the help of archaeological and linguistic tools, would help us to better understand the stratification of sources.

Notes

1. http://median.hypotheses.org; see also the virtual exhibition of the BnF: http://expositions.bnf.fr/marine/
2. Jomard 1842.
3. Kamal 1926–51, Cortesaõ 1960. Most useful is the Atlas of printed maps collected by Susan Gole, see Gole 1980.
4. See the numerous volumes of the ongoing international *History of Cartogaphy*, published in Chicago: Harley and Woodward, ed., 1987–2007.
5. Many public libraries now have good websites with high-resolution images of maps, and several possibilities of zooming in, e.g. the Bibliothèque nationale de France http://gallica.bnf.fr and the National Maritime Museum (London) http://collections.nmm.ac.uk/.
6. Westrem 2001; Falchetta 2006; *Historical Atlas of the Persian Gulf* 2006.
7. About the epistemology of ancient cartography, see Jacob 1992.
8. Woodward 2007; Hoogvliet 2007.
9. Gautier Dalché 2005: 216 and 280. '*completis itaque XXX diebus et totidem noctibus quibus currunt ad velum, inveniunt civitates Indie, scilicet Baroch et Kortosten, Fivesim et Narroan et alias plures civitates. Si quis vult in Averam pergere, inveniet ibi insulas unde . . . species quamplures*'. This information comes probably from Arab sources, such as al-Zuhri, twelfth century, Arabic version, edited by Hadj-Sadok 1968: 281–5, and Bramon 1989: 41–7. According to al-Zuhri, the island of Nahrawan is 'the closest to Iraq'. It can be identified with Nahrwâla/Anhalwâra/Patan, capital of the medieval kingdom of the Gujarat (fourteenth-fifteenth centuries), well known by former Arab merchants in the twelfth century, as well as Kanbâya/Cambay (Kortosten?). The 'island of al-Burûj' (Bharuch, Broach) is said to be the seventh island of India, and the closest to Yemen. See *Encyclopédie de l'Islam*, I: 522. Patan is not close to the sea, but is a fluvial emporium. Averam could be an island near Aden, or Aden itself.
10. The undated Carte Pisane of the Bibliothèque nationale de France in Paris, which was until recently considered the earliest portolan chart preserved in the world, is dated by specialists to the end of the thirteenth century or the beginning of the fourteenth century. However, this map is limited to the coasts of the Mediterranean Sea and part of the Atlantic Ocean. Paris, BnF, Cartes et Plans, Ge B 1118 Rés. Pujades 2007: 40–1, 72. Pujades 2013. The earliest dated and signed portolan atlas is the one by Pietro Vesconte, 1311.
11. Jordan Catala de Severac, ed. Gadrat 2005; Jean de Marignolli, ed. Gadrat 2009.
12. The so-called 'maps of Marco Polo', described by Leo Bagrow in 1948 are now considered by most historians as a nineteenth century forgery. Bagrow 1948; Olshin 2007.

13. The *mappamundi* was used in association with portolan charts in the crusading project of Marino Sanudo (1321) and in the Chronicle of Paulin de Venise (here Paris, ms latin 4939, f. 9, dated 1329).

14. Fac-simile Atlas Catalan 1975, Atlas catalan 2005. The Catalan atlas is mentioned in the inventory of the French King's library dated November 1380 (BnF, ms. français 2700, f. 11v., n°201). Another atlas was ordered by the prince of Aragon to Abraham Cresques in 1381 to be offered to the young king Charles VI of France (1380–93). See Hamy 1891.

15. Kervran 1996; Kervran 2010.

16. According to M. Kervran, Daybul could be the ancient Barbarikè; the ruins are situated on the archeological site of Banbhore. The city was destroyed in the thirteenth century, but the name was used generically on maps until the seventeenth century to designate a port in the Sind.

17. Florence, Biblioteca Medicea Laurenziana, *Gaddi 9*, fol. 2v-3. According to Pullé 1905 (t. 2: 106) (and after him all other historians), Damonela should be interpreted as Daibal/Daibul et Diul, ignoring Damrila.

18. See Cavallo 1992, vol. I: 170–1, cat. I.25.

19. Pujades 2007: 491.

20. *El libro del conoscimiento*, ed. Marino 1999: 72: 'demonela'. *Libro del conosçimiento de todos los rregnos et tierras et señorios que son por el mundo, et de las señales et armas que han*, ed. Facsimilé del manuscrito Z (Múnich, Bayerische Staatsbibliothek, Cod. hisp. 15), ed. M. Lacarra, A. Montaner 1999: 173: 'demouel'.

21. *El libro del conoscimiento*, ed. Marino 1999: xxxvii, 24. There is some confusion concerning Nancy Marino's dating of this work after 1378 in relation with a reference to the presence of the pope in Avignon 'donde mora la corte de Roma et el Papa et los cardenales'. Avignon was 'city of the pope' since 1309. After 1378, during the Great Schism, there was a pope in Avignon and another in Rome.

22. Gautier Dalché 2009.

23. For an edition of the map and its content, see Falchetta 2006; for the explanation of the intellectual context, see Cattaneo 2011.

24. Falchetta 2006: 82–7.

25. Falchetta 2006, n°53, n°148.

26. Cavallo 1992, vol. I: 492–7.

27. Böninger, 2006, chapitre VII, ‚Arrigho di Federigho *Martello*; Bürgerknecht, Übersetzer und Kartograph': 313–54.

28. See the well known map conserved in London, British Library, Add. 15760.

29. Almagià 1940: 288–311; Vietor 1963.

30. Besse 2003: 140–3.

31. BnF, CPL, Ge SH ARCH-1.

32. Some place-names of the Sind are related to Portuguese navigations, like 'Rio dos Pilotos', on the Sind coast, for example on a map by Lázaro Luís, 1563 (*Historical Atlas of the Persian Gulf*: 140–1).

33. *Il designo della terza parte dell'Asia...*, Giacomo di Gastaldi...; Fabius Licinius excudebat, Venetia 1561, BnF, CPL, GE CC-1380 (68 RES).

34. Cosgrove 1992: 71–5; Falchetta 2000: 46; Falchetta 2006: 87–8.
35. Cortesao 1960; *Historical Atlas of the Persian Gulf* 2006: 86–97 and 132–3.
36. Nicolo de'Conti (1414–39): 'Naviando in questo modo insieme con la compagnia, arrivo in spatio d'un mese alla molto nobil città detta Cambaia, la qual e posta fra terra sopra il secondo ramo, donde sbocca in mare il fium Indo' (I was able to see the edition of 1606: Ramusio 1606, v. 1: 338. Galstaldi's map of India is at the beginning of the same first volume).
37. Many thanks to Elizabeth for this reference. Lambourn 2006, fig.7. She uses an atlas of ancient printed maps collected and edited by Susan Gole (see Gole 1980).
38. Lambourn 2006: 9.
39. Sebastian Munster, *India Extrema XXIIII Nova Tabula,* from the 1540 edition of Ptolemy, Basel. Gole 1980, n°6; Jacobo Gastaldi, *Calecut Nuova Tabula,* in Bascarini's edition of 1548, and 1564; Gole 1980, n°8.
40. Jacobo Gastaldi, Seconda Tavola, in Ramusio, *Delli Navigatione,* Venice, 1557-1565. Gole 1980, n°9.
41. Giacomo Gastaldi, *Il designo della terza parte dell'Asia. . .*, Giacomo di Gastaldi . . . ; Fabius Licinius excudebat, Venetia 1561, BnF, CPL, GE CC-1380 (68 RES).
42. Mercator *Atlas, India Orientalis,* Amsterdam, 1612, reproduced in Phillimore 1945, plate 3.
43. *Historical Atlas of the Persian Gulf*: 130–1 and 140–1.
44. Other examples in Kervran 1996: 69–75.

Bibliography

Almagià, R. (1940), 'I mappamondi di Enrico Martello e alcuni concetti geografici di Cristoforo Colombo', *La Bibliofilia*, vol. 42, pp. 288–311.

Atlas catalan, ed. Llompart Moragues, G., Pujades, R., Samso, J. (2005), *El mon i els dies : l'atles català, 1375*, Barcelona: Enciclopèdia Catalana.

Atlas Catalan, El atlas catalán de Cresques Abraham (1975), Primera edición con su traducción al castellano en el sexto centenario de su realización 1375-1975, Barcelona: Diafora.

Bagrow, L. (1948), 'The maps from the home archives of the descendants of a friend of Marco Polo', *Imago Mundi*, vol. 5, pp. 3–13.

Besse, J.-M. (2003), *Les grandeurs de la Terre. Aspects du savoir géographique à la Renaissance*, Lyon: ENS Éditions.

Böninger, L. (2006), *Die Deutsche Einwanderung nach Florenz im Spätmittelalter*, Leiden-Boston-Tokyo: Brill Academic Publishers.

Cattaneo, A. (2011), *Fra Mauro's Mappamundi and Fifteenth-Century Venice*, Turnhout: Brepols Publishers.

Cavallo, G., ed. (1992), *Cristoforo Colombo e l'apertura degli spazi: mostra storica-cartografica, Genova, Palazzo Ducale*, [1992], Roma: Istituto Poligrafico e Zecca dello Stato.

Chekin, L.S. (2006), *Northern Eurasia in Medieval cartography. Inventory, Text, Translation, and Commentary*, Turnhout: Brepols Publishers.

Cortesaõ, A. (1960), *Portugaliae Monumenta Cartographica,* Lisbonne: Comissao Executiva das Comemoracoes do Quinto Centenario da Morte do Infante D. Henrique.

Cosgrove, D. (1992), 'Mapping new worlds: Culture and Cartography in Sixteenth century Venice', *Imago Mundi*, vol. 44, pp. 71–5.

El libro del conoscimiento de todos los reinos, ed., tr., and study by Nancy F. Marino (1999), Tempe (Arizona): Mrts Publishers.

Falchetta, P. (2000), 'Carte Veneziane dell'Asia da Fra Paolino a Giacomo Gastaldi', in *Sciamani e dervisci dalle steppe del Prete Gianni*, G. Curatola, ed., Venezia: Multigraf, pp. 39–51.

——— (2006), *Fra Mauro's Map of the World. With a Commentary and Translations of the Inscriptions,* Turnhout: Brepols Publishers.

Gadrat, C. (2005), *Une image de l'Orient au xive siècle : les "Mirabilia descripta" de Jordan Catala de Sévérac*; édition, traduction et commentaire, Paris: Coll. Mémoires et documents de l'École des Chartes.

——— (2009), *Jean de Marignolli. Au Jardin d'Eden,* édition, traduction et commentaire, Toulouse: Anacharsis Publishers.

Gautier Dalché, P. (2005), *Du Yorkshire à l'Inde. Une géographie urbaine et maritime de la fin du xiie siècle (Roger de Howden?)*, Genève: Librairie Droz (Hautes études médiévales et modernes 89).

——— (2009), *La* Géographie *de Ptolémée en Occident (ive-xvie siècle),* Turnhout: Brepols Publishers.

Gole, S. (1980), *A Series of early printed maps of India in facsimile, collected by Susan Gole*, New-Delhi: Jayaprints Publishers.

Hamy, E.T. (1891), 'Cresques le Jeheu. Note sur un géographe juif catalan de la fin du xive s.', *Bulletin de géographie historique et descriptive*, Paris, pp. 218–22.

Harley, J.B. and Woodward, D., ed. (1987–2007), *The History of Cartography.* Chicago: University of Chicago Press.

Historical Atlas of the Persian Gulf (sixteenth to eighteenth centuries), ed. Biedermann, Z. (2006), Turnhout: Brepols Publishers.

Hofmann, C., Richard, H., Vagnon, E., ed. (2012), *L' Âge d'or des cartes marines. Quand l'Europe découvrait le monde*, Paris: BnF-Seuil Publishers.

Hoogvliet, M. (2007), *Pictura et scriptura. Textes, images et herméneutique des mapae mundi (xiie-xvie siècles),* Turnhout: Brepols Publishers.

Jacob, C. (1992), *L'Empire des Cartes. Approche théorique de la cartographie à travers l'histoire*, Paris: Albin Michel.

Jomard, E. (1842–62), *Les Monuments de la géographie. Recueil d'anciennes cartes européennes et orientales, accompagnées de sphères terrestres et célestes, de mappemondes et tables cosmographiques, d'astrolabes et autres instruments d'observation, depuis les temps les plus reculés jusqu'à l'époque d'Ortelius et de Gérard Mercator*, Paris: Duprat et al.

Kamal, Y. (1926–51), *Monumenta cartographica Africae et Aegypti,* Cairo: s.n. (Frankfurt am Main, 1987, Institut für Geschichte der Arabisch-Islamischen Wissenschaften an der Johann Wolfgang Goethe-Universität).

Kervran, M. (1996), 'Le port multiple des bouches de l'Indus: Barbarikè, Dēb, Daybul, Lahori Bandar, Diul Sinde', *Res Orientales*, vol. 8, pp. 45–92.

—— (2010), 'Damrila, un site perdu et peut-être retrouvé du delta de l'Indus', *La Lettre d'APIM*, electronic edition, octobre 2010 (http://median.hypotheses.org/files/2010/10/apim_lettre.pdf).

Lambourn, E. (2006), 'Brick, timber and stone: building materials and the construction of Islamic architectural history in Gujarat', *Muqarnas, An Annual on the Visual Culture of the Islamic World*, vol. 23, pp. 191–217.

Libro del conosçimiento de todos los rregnos et tierras et señorios que son por el mundo, et de las señales et armas que han, ed. Facsimilé del manuscrito Z (Múnich, Bayerische Staatsbibliothek, Cod. hisp. 15), éd. Lacarra, M., Montaner, A. (1999), Zaragoza: Institución Femando el Católico (CSIC).

Nicolo de'Conti (1414–39), éd. Ramusio, v. 2, p. 790.

Olshin, B.B. (2007), 'The mystery of the Marco Polo maps. An introduction to a privately held collection of cartographic materials relating to the Polo family', *Terrae Incognitae*, vol. 39, pp. 1–23.

Phillimore, R.H. (1945), *Historical records of the Survey of India. Volume I. 18th century*. Dehra Dun: The Offices of the Survey of India.

Pujades, R. (2007), *Les cartes portolanes: la representació medieval d'una mar solcada*. Barcelona: Lunwerg Editores S.A.

—— (2013), 'The Pisana Chart. Really a primitive portolan chart made in the 13th century?', *Cartes marines: d'une technique à une culture. Cartes et Géomatique*, vol. 216, pp. 17–32.

Pullé, F.L. (1901–5), *La cartografia antica dell'India* (Studi italiani di filologia indo-iranica, Anno iv, vol. 4 [Text and Atlas]) Firenze: Tipografia G. Carnesecchi e Figli.

Ramusio, Giovanni Battista (1550–88), *Delle Navigationi et Viaggi, raccolte da M. Giovanni Battista Ramusio in tre volumi* (repr. Venetia, 1606), Venetia: Giunti.

Vietor, A.O. (1963), 'A Pre-Columbian map of the world, circa 1489', *Imago Mundi*, vol. 17, pp. 95–6.

Westrem, S. (2001), *The Hereford Map*, Terrarum Orbis 1. Turnhout: Brepols Publishers.

CHAPTER 12

Ancient Technology of Jetties and Anchorage System along the Saurashtra Coast, India

A.S. Gaur and *Sundaresh*

Introduction

The Gujarat coast has been a focal point for maritime activities since the Harappan times. It is punctuated with several creeks and tidal rivers, which provide sheltered harbours. A few coastal sites, namely, Lothal (Rao 1979), Ghogha (Gaur 2010), Padri (Shinde 1992), Hathab (Pramanik 2004), Somnath (Sankalia 1974), Porbandar (Gaur and Sundaresh 2006), Dwarka (Ansari and Mate 1966; Rao 1990; Gaur et al. 2008), Bet Dwarka (Gaur et al. 2005) and Nageshwar (Hegde et al. 1990) have been excavated extensively and the remains of maritime activities have been documented. The time bracket for these sites varies from the early Harappan phase to the medieval period. Archaeological records from Gulf countries indicate that during the Harappan period, traders from the Saurashtra coast plied their boats as far as Oman, United Arab Emirates, and Bahrain. During the historical period, fourth century BC to third century AD, Romans traded extensively along the Saurashtra coast, as evidenced by a large amount of data recorded from this region. In the medieval period, the Saurashtra coast accounted for the most number of ports as numerous stone anchors of medieval period indicating anchoring points have been found at several places.

*I thank K.H. Vora, for providing facilities during the study and thanks also due to the members of the Marine Archaeology Centre for the help rendered during the fieldwork. S.B. Chitari prepared line drawings.

Literary Background of Ports

An ancient Sanskrit text *Arthasastra* (Kangle 1963) of Kautilya, mentions a *Navadhyaksha* (Superintendent of Shipping), who was in charge of seafaring ships and strictly enforced the rules framed for the management of ports. He was empowered to kill pirates and punish those who did not follow the rules. The shipowner had to pay taxes before leaving the port, for example. Further, the anonymous author of the *Periplus of the Erythraean Sea*, dating to the first century CE (Schoff 1912) mentioned a chain of ports along the Indian coast. The ancient texts, including Indian (such as Tamil Sangam literature, Persian literature) and foreign sources (Ptolemy's *Geography*, Arrian's *Indica*, etc.), have also made ample references to the existence of harbours and ports along the Indian coast during the historical and the medieval periods. Further, *pattana* is a Sanskrit term for the word port that has been used in various ancient texts. The ports appear as two types: *Samudrapattana*, i.e. port on the coast of a sea and *Jalapattana*, i.e. port on the bank of a navigable river (Roy 1994).

Ancient Ports in Archaeology

In an archaeological context, structures associated with ports and jetties have been discovered along the Mediterranean coast, including at Carthage and Thapsus on the Tunisian coast (Muckelroy 1977), Caesarea on Israel coast (Raban 1992), etc. Excavations carried out on the bank of the river Euphrates, at Ur revealed a massive brick structure, identified as a harbour (Woolley 1974), the oldest remnant of any port structure in the world. Similarly, archaeological studies of the oldest known civilization of the Indian subcontinent, the Indus Civilization, indicate the existence of port structures at Lothal (Rao 1979), and Kuntasi (Dhavalikar et al. 1996). Further, underwater explorations along the Indian coast, since the late 1990s, have yielded significant data on ancient ports, jetties, and anchoring points. In the last case we refer to places where vessels are known to have moored, i.e. were anchored offshore. An important artefact for identifying a port and anchoring point is the anchor itself. Usually, these are lost, having parted from the parent boat through a break in the cable or other accident such as being abandoned due to the sudden onset of storms or being caught on the seabed. These lost anchors are amply found all along the Indian coast.

This essay thus deals with some elements of the underwater archaeology of ports, jetties and anchoring points along the Indian coast, with specific focus on the Saurashtra coast as an example of the nature of this resource.

The important antiquities mentioned include underwater and onshore timber and stone structures and stone anchors recovered during the maritime archaeological explorations. A comparative study has also been made with modern traditional jetties found along the Indian coast.

Marine Archaeological Investigations along the Saurashtra Coast

With the exception of the Okhamandal region, the major marine archaeological explorations on the Saurashtra coast have been carried out in the first decade of the twenty-first century. Important sites include Dwarka, Bet Dwarka, Miyani, Visawada, Kindar Kheda, Porbandar, Mithivirdi, Kodinar, and in the Gulf of Khambat/Cambay (Map 12.1). Numerous stone anchors were found from these sites. A brief description of each site is given below.

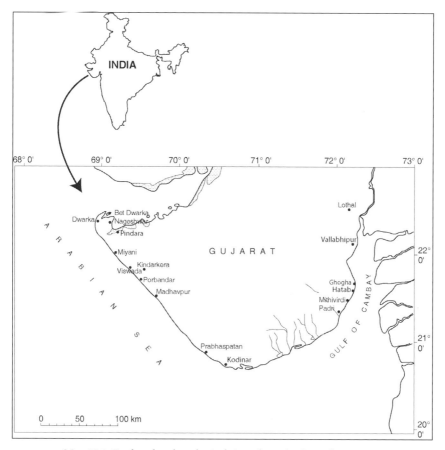

Map 12.1: Explored archaeological sites along the Saurashtra coast.

Dwarka

In 1983, maritime archaeological investigations were initiated at Dwarka, and continued for almost two decades. The extensive diving operations have been undertaken in depths ranging from intertidal zones to water 25 m. deep, 1 km. off Dwarka. The nearshore underwater topography consists of beach rock formations, covered with dense vegetation. Thick sand deposits, in the small channels, are occasionally noticed. Topography beyond 10 m. water depth is sandy with rock boulders and sparse vegetation. A number of artefacts were discovered during offshore explorations in water 3 m. and 16 m. deep.

Several stone structures were noticed off Dwarka, of various shapes and sizes. A few semicircular structures joined with a hard mortar are partially intact. Structures with 2–3 courses have been noticed at least at ten locations. The semicircular structures were constructed by using L-shaped blocks with provision for dowels. Besides semicircular structures, numerous rectangular structures have been noticed here. They are scattered over a vast area and do not follow any regular plan. However, at a few places, 2–3 courses of blocks appear to be the remains of fallen structures. These blocks are found close to the semicircular structures, which indicate that they might have been parts of a larger structure.

Earlier, underwater structures, particularly semicircular ones, were described as the remains of bastions of a fort wall similar to the one at Harappa and dating to the historical and the medieval periods (Rao 1990). However, the absence of any other artefact, like pottery, suggests that this may not have been a habitation site (Gaur et al. 2004). Therefore, it may be suggested that the remains noticed off Dwarka could be parts of a jetty. The circular and semicircular structures are presumably the bases of pillars and the rectangular dressed blocks portions of the superstructure of a jetty that extended from shore to 300 m. offshore. Sankalia (1966) has mentioned that, 'Sayajirao Gaekwad of Baroda had built a dock along the Gomati creek and a landing place on the opposite side, with huge stone pillars to facilitate tying the ship'. It is quite likely that the remains lying on the shore and offshore regions are of the same dock. The presence of stone anchors lying along these structures also supports this hypothesis.

The discovery of 125 stone anchors of different shapes and sizes was another important feature of the Dwarka investigations. The anchors were noted between the intertidal zone and 16 m. water depth, with the greatest concentration in 6–8 m. of water. Broadly, these anchors have been divided into three groups: composite, Indo-Arabian, and ring stone anchors. Composite anchors are often chiselled out of a thin limestone block and

Plate 12.1: Composite type stone anchor from Dwarka.

are triangular in shape (Plate 12.1). They include an upper circular hole known as a rope hole and two rectangular lower holes referred to as fluke holes. These anchors range from 16 to 496 kg. and were probably used by local fishermen for short voyages. Indo-Arabian anchors were cut from a long stone block and are characterized by a tapering upper end, pierced with a circular hole and a wider lower end containing two rectangular holes on either face of the block. These anchors are larger than the composite anchors, ranging from 82 to 668 kg., and were used by large vessels undertaking extended voyages such as the Arabian dhow. Similar anchors have been reported from several port sites of India, Sri Lanka, the Arabian coast, and the east African coast. Twenty-four ring stone anchors were also found in the Dwarka waters; they are of various sizes and weigh between 20kg. and 245 kg. Similar ring stone anchors have been reported from Oman waters (Vosmer 1999).

Bet Dwarka

The Island of Bet Dwarka is situated about 30 km. north of Dwarka, at the entrance of the Gulf of Kachchh. It is famous for its temple dedicated to Lord Krishna. The Island is a narrow, crooked strip of sand and rock about 13 km. long. The area is referred to as the Gulf of Barake in the Greek sea guide *Periplus Maris Erythraei* (Schoff 1912), although Ptolemy mentioned Barake as an island in the Gulf of Kanthi, which has been identified as the Gulf of Kachchh (McCrindle 1885).

In the seventeenth century BC, the late Harappans established settlements on the north-west part of the island (Gaur and Sundaresh 2003). They used rich fish and shellfish resources available around the island, as evidenced by a large fishhook and several shell artefacts recovered from the site (Gaur and Sundaresh 2004; Gaur et al. 2005). The scanty habitation deposit suggests that the site was abandoned after a couple of centuries. The south-east coast of the island was inhabited during the eighth century BC. A vast expansion followed and reached its zenith during the historical and medieval periods. Bet Dwarka continued to be an important centre of maritime activity until the emergence of the Okha port in the Okhamandal area in the mid twentieth century.

The large quantity of amphorae sherds that were discovered includes examples whose morphology is very similar to Roman amphora types of the fourth-fifth century AD (Plate 12.2). These ceramic wares were used to export wine and olive oil originating in the Roman Empire. As olive oil was in less demand in India and the sherds exhibit a resin coating, it is possible that the majority of the Indian finds represent wine amphorae (Gaur et al. 2006).

Numerous stone anchors representing composite and Indo-Arabian types have been found in 6 to 8 m. of water, close to the present jetty of

Plate 12.2: Roman amphora from Bet Dwarka waters.

Bet Dwarka. The majority of the composite anchors were cut from locally available limestone blocks. Their circular upper hole is often broken whereas the lower two rectangular holes tend to be found in preserved states. The anchors are very similar to those reported from Dwarka and other places in Saurashtra. The Indo-Arabian anchors are predominantly made of a hard rock such as basalt, although some examples are made of hard stone. The stone anchors have been dated to the historical and medieval periods. In addition to the stone anchors, the expeditions also uncovered two 70 kg. lead anchors in the vicinity of the amphorae. They are circular in shape with an axial hole and are very similar to ring stone anchors recovered from Dwarka and other places in Saurashtra.

Pindara

The ancient temple site of Pindara is situated on the northern Saurashtra coast in the Gulf of Kachchh. A huge temple complex (10 m. × 10 m.) is exposed during low tide at Pindara, about 300 m. from the high water line (Gaur and Sundaresh 2007). A floor area of dressed limestone blocks (Plate 12.3) is well preserved, although the upper works have been destroyed and the stone blocks have been washed or taken away. It appears that the temple was dedicated to Lord Shiva, as a *yoni* is present in the sanctum (*garbhagriha*). The architectural feature of the submerged complex corresponds more or less with the existing temple on the shore of Pindara. The submerged temple must have been contemporary to other

Plate 12.3: Remains of an ancient temple exposed during low tide off Pindara.

surviving temples in the Pindara group of temples that date to the seventh through tenth centuries AD. The archaeological evidence indicates that the shoreline has changed significantly during the last 1,000 years on the Saurashtra coast.

Miyani

The ancient site of Miyani is situated between Dwarka on the east and Porbandar on the west. It is famous for ancient temples dating back to the tenth century AD (Sampura 1968: 87). On the coast of Miyani, there stands atop a high hill, a temple dedicated to a goddess locally known as *Harshad Mata*. A vast creek known as Meda Creek runs a few kilometres into the hinterland area, which has been used as a sheltered harbour for the country craft, particularly fishing vessels. Underwater explorations have been undertaken about 1 km. offshore of *Harshad Mata* temple. The seabed comprises sandy channels and rocky outcrops, but sparse vegetation growth. At several places, small gravels were also noticed. The sand comprises a clay-like element which makes visibility very poor. Twelve artefacts were discovered from here.

Visawada

Visawada, also known as Mul Dwarka, is situated about 40 km. west of Porbandar and approximately 20 km. east of Miyani. A Hindu pilgrimage centre and a temple dedicated to Lord Krishna, are situated in the middle of the town. Kindari Creek runs a long distance, at least up to Kindar Kheda (a Harappan town); perhaps the name 'Kindari' is derived from this particular ancient town. On the western side of the coast is a high cliff, while the eastern coast is a sandy beach.

Explorations have been undertaken off Kindari Creek about 500 m. from coastline. Seabed topography consists of sandy channels and rocky outcrops, small boulders and dense growth of vegetation were observed. Water depth varies between 8 and 5 m.; however, archaeological findings were concentrated between 5 m. and 6 m. water depths. In all, 14 stone anchors have been found, belonging to the three varieties known as composite, Indo-Arabian and ring stone types.

Somnath

The Prabhasa-Somnath coast reveals a vivid manifestation of marine eolian and fluvial processes that have resulted in numerous important geomorphic land forms, as the near shore zone is characterized by the

Plate 12.4: Ring stone anchor in Somnath waters.

formation of recent alluvium deposits, sand bars, mud flats and mangrove swamps. The coastal zone is covered with beaches and littoral sand, oyster beds and sand dunes.

The explored area in Somnath waters is 400 m. south-west of the Somnath temple. The study area comprised rocky outcrops and sandy patches. During the first phase of exploration (1991), six ring stone anchors were found, eight during the second (1992); and in 1999–2002 yielded 21 ring stone anchors. A large number of ring stones (Plate 12.4) have been recorded off Somnath on the Saurashtra coast. The water depth varies between 7 m. and 15 m. Ring stones were noticed in less than 8 m. of water depth and the growth of seaweeds was also observed. Ring stones located deeper display a layer of greyish marine growth.

Kodinar (Mul Dwarka)

A small coastal village, Mul Dwarka near Kodinar in the district of Junagad is one of the claimants of the original Dwarka of the *Mahabharata*. Because of its proximity to Junagadh hills on the north and the sea on the south, the town has been associated with Dwarka (Sankalia 1966: 7). An ancient temple dated after the tenth century AD (Sampura 1968: 113) is situated on raised land close to the sea. A circular structure, called Diva Dandi lighthouse (Plate 12.5) about 4 m. high, constructed with dressed limestone blocks, was noticed. If this structure has served as a lighthouse in the past, it may be the earliest remains of a lighthouse on the Saurashtra coast.

Plate 12.5: Medieval period lighthouse at Muldwarka (Kodinar) on
the Mid-Saurashtra coast.

Explorations in intertidal zones yielded a composite stone anchor, which
lies exposed during low tide. Made of sedimentary rock, it has an upper
circular hole and two square lower holes. Its upper portion is semicircular
and edges are sharp. Its thickness gradually increases from 12 cm. (at the
upper end) to 20 cm. (at the lower end). The anchor is similar to those
reported from Dwarka (Gaur et al. 2008: 23–57) and Bet Dwarka (Gaur
et al. 2005: 113–29) and dated between the historical and the medieval
periods.

The underwater investigations in and around Mul Dwarka (Kodinar)
have been crucial for an understanding of the archaeology of this region.
Now that data for underwater explorations from all three Dwarkas on
the Saurashtra coast are available, one of their most obvious common
characteristics observed is the presence of similar types of stone anchors.
Another common aspect of these sites is the presence of Harappan and
late Harappan settlements within close proximity: for example, Nageshwar
and Bet Dwarka near Okhamandal Dwarka, Kindar Kheda near Mul
Dwarka (Visawada) and Kanjetar and Kaj near Mul Dwarka (Kodinar).
All three Dwarkas have ancient temples dated to the tenth–twelfth century
AD. Nonetheless, these sites were busy ancient ports and perhaps temples
served as worship places and coastal marker points for navigators before
they embarked on a voyage.

Mithi Virdi

The small village of Mithi Virdi is situated about 30 km. south-east of Talaja, a *taluka*, headquarter. It lies on a raised plateau close to the seashore. A small seasonal river merges with the sea on the western side of the village. An archaeological site is located about 1 km. west of the village in an agriculture field. The reddish soil mixed with small quartz gravel, signifies the flow of the river channel from this area.

Five stone anchors lie in an agricultural land about 1 km. north of the seashore. Three anchors (one of which is broken) lie together at a distance of 10 m., oriented in an east-west direction. A fourth anchor is partially buried north of the other three and oriented in a similar direction. The anchors are all similar in shape and size. They have rectangular cross-sections and trapezoidal longitudinal sections. They are sharp-edged and display clear chisel marks. They have been cut from conglomeratic sedimentary grit rock, which is dark brown in colour, with bits of gravel also present. The anchors have only two rectangular lower holes, with no upper circular hole.

Ghogha

The town of Gogha is located on the mid-western coast of the Gulf of Khambhat in Bhavnagar district of Gujarat. A famous Gujarati proverb *'Lankani lari ane Ghoghono var'* ('Bride of Lanka and groom of Ghogha') speaks of direct overseas relations between Gogha and Sri Lanka in the past (Chaukasi 1989: 634). The presence of ancient Jaina temples at Gogha dating back to the tenth-eleventh centuries suggests that it was also a religious centre. The earliest Arabic inscription from Gogha dates to AD 1170 (Oza 1885: 2). During the British period, ships up to 1,500 tonnes were loaded here (Habib 1982: 23).

The exploration at Gogha was undertaken during low tide and findings were recorded with still photography and drawing. A large number of stone anchors were discovered at a distance of 100–200 m. from the high water line. The majority of the anchors belong to the Indo-Arab type (Plate 12.6) and about 40 per cent are fragmented. Interestingly, the fresh surface of broken parts suggests that fragmentation of the anchors took place during the manufacturing stage and not during the anchoring processes. A composite anchor made of limestone is another noteworthy find from the site. The presence of a few unfinished anchors at Gogha and Hathab, which lie submerged in 5–7 m. water during high tide, indicates that big boats were anchored at this point during high tide. The author of the *Periplus*

Plate 12.6: Indo-Arab type stone anchor from Ghogha.

of the Erythraean Sea also mentions that during low tide boats rest on the seabed.

Exploration in this intertidal zone has also yielded several sherds of glazed ware (Plate 12.7) in the vicinity of stone anchors. One jar is glazed inside and on its upper part outside, whereas the other sherds are glazed only on the inside. There are three main types of glazed ware (green, blue and brown), quite similar to the Islamic glazed ware found in various parts of

Plate 12.7: Medieval period Glazed ware from the intertidal zone of Ghogha.

Plate 12.8: Medieval period Chinese type stone anchor found off Hathab.

India (Mohammad 1985: 105). The medieval glazed ware from Hastinapur (Lal 1954–5: 5–151) was found with coins of Balban (AD 1206–87). The sherds recovered from Ghogha are similar to those reported from another medieval period site at Lashkarshah in Khambhat, which have been dated to the fourteenth–sixteenth centuries (Bhan 2006: 90–5). Thus, the glazed sherds from Ghogha may also be dated to the late medieval period.

Hathab

Hathab is an early historical site, referred to as Astacampra in the *Periplus of the Erythraean Sea* (Schoff 1912: 40). It is located about 1 km. in the hinterland. On shore excavation has yielded rich antiquities of the historical period, indicative of maritime contact with the West. Explorations in this intertidal zone have yielded two anchors similar to those of the Indo-Arab type and one anchor with a wide groove across the middle of the anchor (Plate 12.8). This is very similar to those reported from Japan and Chinese waters.

Gopnath

Gopnath serves as the entry point to the Gulf of Khambhat. The coast is marked with high cliffs, rocky and sandy beaches. Located close to the gulf, the tidal range is very high and a large area gets exposed during low tide. Innumerable broken sculptures can be noticed in the intertidal zone area.

Plate 12.9: An Indo-Arab type anchor exposed during the lowest low tide off Gopnath.

An Indo-Arab type of stone anchor, 2.2 m. long, has been reported at the lowest water line and is exposed during the low tide of new moon days. Made of hard basaltic rock (Plate 12.9), it has two square lower holes and a circular upper hole. It lies about 2 km. offshore from high water line.

Vallabhipur

Vallabhi has been described as one of most famous universities of ancient India; it is situated on a seasonal stream merging on the western bank of the Gulf of Khambhat. Its topographical location suggests that the river must have been a tidal creek in the past. This ancient site is located on the bank of the Vallabhi River. Until a few decades ago, boats would come up to the site from sea. Now, however, because of heavy silting, this is no more the case.

During onshore explorations around Vallabhi, two anchors were reported near the present bus stand and were then shifted to the Taluka office. They are channel marker buoys, made of iron. No information is available in the Taluka office about their uses and period. However, observation and comparative studies suggest that these artefacts are British period buoys for channel indicators. The discovery at Vallabhipur indicates that during the British period, ships/boats used to come up to Vallabhipur. Later, because of silt deposits in the river, the present shoreline is about 4 km. away from Vallabhipur. Thus, it may be argued that rapid shoreline change must have affected the function of the historical and medieval period ports around the Gulf of Khambhat.

Conclusion

Ports play a dominant role in facilitating sea trade and there were several ports all along the Indian coast since antiquity. Prerequisites for the selection of any port site includes a sheltered place, particularly protection from high winds and rough seas, sufficient water depth to sail a vessel and a suitable anchoring point. Besides the structural part of the port, it is also important to keep in mind that products from the hinterland are brought to the port and are taken from the port to the hinterland. Most ancient ports were situated on riverbanks and along the backwaters. A few Harappan sites, including Kuntasi (Dhavalikar et al. 1996), Amra, Lakhawavel and Vasai (Rao 1991) on the northern Saurashtra coast are located on the banks of tidal rivers where tidal variation is as high as 5 m. This has helped mariners reach the site during high tide.

Archaeological findings indicate the existence of several ports, jetties, and anchoring points along the west coast of India from the protohistoric period (Ray 2003). The discovery of many stone structures and anchors at Dwarka suggests that it was a busy port during the historical and the medieval times (Gaur et al. 2004), when large limestone blocks were used for its construction. Whereas, a later period jetty at Rupen Bandar was made of stone blocks as well as of wooden logs. As a form of comparison, similar jetty remains have been reported from Australia, dating back to the late nineteenth century CE. There are also comparative instances, especially in north-west Australia where the tidal range is often in excess of 10 m. There, in the nineteenth century, at places where there are no jetties, even very large sailing ships were run aground at high tide. As the tide receded leaving bare sand beneath the ship, passengers and cargo were moved to and fro, with the help of large carts drawn by bullocks (McCarthy 2002). This is a direct reflection of the practices referred to earlier. Though there are no remains of an ancient jetty at Bet Dwarka, the presence of stone anchors in intertidal zones indicate that high tide was effectively used to beach the boats. Conversely, the north-west coast of India has jetties in creeks, which are made of limestone blocks while southern side traditional wooden jetties continued to be in use.

The tidal variation and seabed topography played a significant role in construction of jetties. As stated earlier, the higher tidal variation in Gujarat has been used by navigators to anchor boats in intertidal zones, whereby loading/unloading of boats becomes easier. This has been confirmed with the discovery of stone anchors from intertidal zone areas of Dwarka, Bet Dwarka and Armada. The stone anchors are indicators of ancient anchoring points and underwater findings have indicated that the preferred anchoring points on the Saurashtra coast fall between 5 m. and 7 m. water depth.

References

Ansari, Z.D. and M.S. Mate (1966), *Excavations at Dwarka*, Pune: Deccan College Postgraduate and Research Institute.

Bhan, K.K. (2006), 'Towards an Understanding of Medieval Glazed Pottery Manufacture from Lakshkarshah, Khambhat, Gujarat', *Man and Environment*, vol. XXXI, no. 2, pp. 90–5.

Chaukasi, U.M. (1989), *Gazetteer of Bhavnagar District* (in Gujarati), Ahmedabad: Government of Gujarat.

Dhavalikar, M.K., M.R. Raval and Y.M. Chitalwala (1996), *Kuntasi: A Harappan emporium on West Coast*, Pune: Deccan College Post-Graduate Research Institute.

Gaur, A.S. (2010), 'Gogha: An Indo-Arab trading Post in the Gulf of Khambhat (Cambay)', *International Journal of Nautical Archaeology*, vol. 39, no. 1, pp. 146–55.

Gaur, A.S. and Sundaresh (2003), 'Onshore excavation at Bet Dwarka Island, in the Gulf of Kachchh, Gujarat', *Man and Environment*, vol. XXVIII, no. 1, pp. 57–66.

——— (2004), 'A late Bronze Age Copper Fish-hook from Bet Dwarka, Gujarat: An evidence on the Advance fishing Technology', *Current Science*, vol. 86, no. 4, pp. 512–14.

——— (2006), 'Excavation at Bokhira (Porbandar) on the Southwestern coast of Saurashtra', *Man and Environment*, vol. XXXI, no. 1, pp. 33–9.

——— (2007), 'Evidence of Shoreline changes in the Gulf of Kachchh, based on the submerged temple complex at Pindara', *Current Science*, vol. 92, no. 6, pp. 733–5.

Gaur, A.S., Sundaresh and K.H. Vora (2005), *Archaeology of Bet Dwarka Island: An Excavation Report.* New Delhi: Aryan Books International.

——— (2008) *Underwater Archaeology of Dwarka and Somnath (1997-2002)*, New Delhi: Aryan Books International.

Gaur, A.S., Sundaresh and P. Vardhan (2005), 'Ancient shell Industry at Bet Dwarka', *Current Science*, vol. 89, no. 6, pp. 941–6.

Gaur, A.S., Sundaresh and Sila Tripati (2004), 'Dwarka: an ancient harbour', *Current Science*, vol. 86, no. 9, pp. 1256–60.

——— (2006), 'Evidence for Indo-Roman trade from Bet Dwarka waters, West Coast of India', *International Journal of Nautical Archaeology*, vol. 35, no. 1, pp. 117–27.

Habib, I. (1982), *An Atlas of the Mughal Empire*, Delhi: Oxford University Press.

Hegde, K.T.M., K.K. Bhan, V.H. Sonawane, K. Krishnana, and D.R. Shah (1990), *Excavation at Nageswar Gujarat: A Harappan Shell working site on the Gulf of Kutch*, Vadodara: M.S. University of Baroda.

Kangle, R.P. (1963), *The Kautilya Arthasastra, Part II, An English Translation with Critical and Explanatory Notes,* Bombay: University of Bombay (later edition, 1972).

Lal, B.B. (1954–5), 'Excavations at Hastinapura and Other Explorations in Upper Ganga and Sutlej Basins', *Ancient India*, vols. 10–11, pp. 5–151.

McCarthy, M. (2002), 'Archaeology of the jetty', *Bulletin of Australasian Institute for Maritime Archaeology*, vol. 26, pp. 7–18.

McCrindle, J.W. (1885), *Ancient India as described by Ptolemy* (Reprinted in 1985), New Delhi: Today & Tomorrow's Printers and Publishers.

Mohammed, K.K. (1985), 'Glazed ware in India', *Puratattva*, vol. 15, pp. 105–10.

Muckelroy, K. (1977), *Maritime Archaeology*, Cambridge: Cambridge University Press, UK.

Oza, V.G. (1885), *Old research collection of Bhavnagar*, Bhavnagar.

Pramanik, S. (2004), 'Hathab: An Early Historic Port on the Gulf of Khambhat', *Journal of Indian Ocean Archaeology*, vol. 1, pp. 133–40.

Raban, A. (1992), 'Sabastos: the royal harbour at Caesarea Maritima: a short-lived giant', *International Journal of Nautical Archaeology*, vol. 21, pp. 111–24.

Rao, S.R. (1979), *Lothal: A Harappan Port Town,* Memoir of Archaeological Survey of India, 78, New Delhi: Archaeological Survey of India.

—— (1990), 'Excavation of the legendary city of Dvaraka in the Arabian Sea', *Journal of Marine Archaeology*, vol. 1, pp. 59–98.

—— (1991), *Dawn and Devolution of the Indus Civilization*, New Delhi: Aditya Prakashan.

Ray, H.P. (2003), *The Archaeology of seafaring in ancient South Asia*, Cambridge: Cambridge University Press, UK.

Roy, U.N. (1994), 'Dronimukha and Lothal', in *The Role of Universities and Research Institutes in Marine Archaeology,* Rao, S.R., ed., Goa: National Institute of Oceanography, pp. 33–6.

Sampura, K.F. (1968), *The structural temples of Gujarat*, Ahmedabad: Gujarat University.

Sankalia, H.D. (1966), 'Dwarka in Literature and Archaeology', *Excavations at Dwarka* (Ansari and Mate), Pune: Deccan College Postgraduate and Research Institute.

—— (1974), *Prehistory and Protohistory of India and Pakistan*, Bombay.

Schoff, W.H. (1912), *The Periplus of the Erythraean Sea: Travel and Trade in the Indian Ocean by a Merchant of the 1st century*, New York (repr. 1974), New Delhi: Oriental Books Reprint Corporation.

Shinde, V. (1992) 'Padri and the Indus Civilization', *South Asian Studies*, vol. 8, pp. 55–66.

Vosmer, T. (1999), 'Maritime Archaeology, Ethnography and History in the Indian Ocean: An Emerging Partnership', in *Archaeology of Seafaring: The Indian Ocean in the Ancient Period*, H.P. Ray, ed., Delhi: Pragati Publication, pp. 291–312.

Woolley, L. (1974), *Ur Excavations VI: Buildings of the Third Dynasty*, London: British Museum.

CHAPTER 13

Bharuch Fort during the pre-Sultanate Period

Sara Keller

Amongst various types of human settlements, ports play a specific role: they are the nodal points where land and sea meet. This intrinsic connecting function gives them an identity which drastically differentiates them from other towns and settlements. As border places founded at the edge of the land, they stand as gates for goods and persons going to and coming from land and overseas, and fulfil trading, fishing, and/or cultural, religious, military purposes. However the 'land-sea gateway' identity of the port is not a homogeneous phenomenon, and its characteristics are affected by location conditions and port functions. While some sea towns are clearly oriented towards the ocean—as for places dedicated to transshipment, shipbuilding, water-food supply—other ports are rather looking inland—cities on trade routes, markets places for local and overseas goods, etc.

While the development of specialized settlements was usually rather limited (for instance, for the Gujarati coast, the medium size port of Mandvi is known for its shipyards, or Ghogha as a transshipment place), few ports were supported by a strong hinterland economy, and they quickly developed into major economic places for the trade of local and overseas goods. They automatically combined several political, economical and social responsibilities linked with their trade activities and overseas connections. And they eventually became vital elements of the local economy, famous places in the context of global trade, and attractive goals for prospective invaders and rulers.

The long coastline unwinding between Sindh and Maharashtra, which is known as a consistent and dynamic region for trade and overseas activities since the Harappan period, is dotted with countless coastal settlements with various functions and different eco-political impacts. Each time period was also characterized by the economical rule of one particular port city: Bharuch was the first major ancient and medieval port of the region, followed by Khambhat, Surat, and Bombay for the latest period.

Bharuch (or Broach)[1] is mainly known through ancient and early medieval written sources, whether local or foreign, which praise its economic activities and socio-cultural and urban qualities from the late antiquity till the Solanki period (tenth century).[2] 'Barúh [Bharuch] is a large handsome town, well-built of bricks and plaster. The inhabitants are rich and engaged in trade, and they freely enter upon speculations and distant expeditions. It is a port for vessels coming from China, as it is also for those of Sind.'[3] No socio-economic study of this period ignores the role played by Bharuch;[4] however, the city lacks a systematic archaeological and historical study that is able to draw a complete picture of the port and its evolution. My archaeological approach (connected with written sources and references) is a first attempt to open the discussion on historical remains and their interpretation concerning the history and identity of Bharuch as a city and as the major port of medieval north India.

Some historical and architectural works have been the starting point for this study: the chapter on Bharuch, especially its Jumā Masjid, in the 'Muhammadan Architecture' by Burgess (1896: 20–2); the paragraph on 'Broach' from the revised edition of *Gazetteer of India, Broach District* revised and published in 1961 (1961: 731–46), and a monograph published in Gujarati by G.H. Desai in 1914. We should also salute the compiling effort of Adhya Saxena in her paper on Bharuch history (2001: 227–38).

Bharuch Fort Wall

One would be surprised to state that the pre-Mughal architectural remains of Bharuch are mainly of defensive character: its most important historical structure is the monumental city wall surrounding the ancient core of the town on the south-west and south-east sides. To the south-east, the wall overhangs the large Narmada River over a length of 1,300 m. The city had developed on the right (northern) bank of the Narmada, one of the largest rivers in India, and approximately 40 km. away from the delta where the river meets the Gulf of Khambhat (Plate 13.1). The walled city stands next to the Bhrigu Rishi Sthan, dedicated to the saint who, according to tradition, founded the city (Plate 13.2).[5] The imposing fortification, alternating gates, towers and walls, is preserved on the river side, while its northern part was sacrificed to the urban growth and infrastructural changes towards hinterland.

Plate 13.1: Location of Bharuch (left: Bharuch near the Narmada delta; right: walled city of Bharuch on the Narmada).
Courtesy: The author, from satellite image from Google Earth (www.earth.google.com)

Plate 13.2: Ancient marble relief conserved at the Bhrigu Rishi site.
Courtesy: The author.

The Jumā Masjid built during the fourteenth century, after Alauddin Khilji's raids (AD 1297, Plate 13.3), stands as the other monumental pre-Mughal structure of the city, while other major constructions are later additions[6] (the big *hāvelis* and merchant houses dominating the city landscape, especially the southern urban elevation, belong to Mughal and colonial periods, see *Gazetteer* 1961: 740–5). It is particularly astonishing that neither traces of the successive ruler palaces, nor port infrastructures are identifiable. In the absence of excavations and archaeological researches which alone could answer questions concerning the urban structure and life, the study of the architectural remains, especially the city walls, should give us some research inputs.

The importance of the fortification, in length, width, material, and number of towers, speaks of the defensive character of the city, and the obvious concern of the rulers to achieve an appropriate protection: the question remains about the object of concern. Was the defence meant to protect the country from overseas invasions? Or was it supposed to protect the city itself and its much coveted trading activity? Were the fortifications defending the city, its warehouses, its rulers, its ships, from foreign armadas, from land invaders? Or was the city wall simply a symbol of a strong local power, and to define a 'city' area where the local fiscal system had be to respected?

Plate 13.3: View on the prayer hall of the Jumā Masjid of Bharuch.
Courtesy: The author.

Plate 13.4: The city wall on the bank of the Narmada River (western gate on the south-east wall). *Courtesy:* The author.

Let us have a closer look at the wall itself (Plate 13.4). The construction is a complex structure with two distinct parts: the base and up to approximately 3–4 m. high (from present ground level) a stone construction made of large cut sandstones of irregular height and width (varying 1.5–5.0 m. high), and of various colour shades.[7] The earliest masonry benefited from a very meticulous stone cutting work, as one can see at some places protected from the weather. However, sandstone is a fragile material and thick lime mortar joints show multiple repairs of the wall structure. The wall itself is plain and does not present any deliberate decoration—except for the carved *spolia* visible at multiple places (Plate 13.5). A frieze, with irregular motives—apparently from reused stones, adorns the west gate of the south-east fort wall (Plate 13.4). The stones are free from any coating or lime washes (*chunam*) traces.

The lowest part of the wall is pierced at regular intervals with water outlets which allow waste water to be discharged from the city into the river. The height of the city level beyond the wall, on the hill, protects it from any flooding by the waters of the Narmada River. The outlet is of a quite good size (approximately 50 cm. × 50 cm.), which could easily allow the passage of a man, but there is no trace of any metal screen protecting the opening from potential intrusion.

Plate 13.5: *Spolia* used in the lower part of the fort construction. *Courtesy:* The author.

The upper part of the fortification (including gates and towers) is made out of flat bricks and lime mortar. It is topped with large crenellations with typical features of Mughal defensive constructions (high crenels with a Persian arch form on the top).[8] The bricks were covered with a lime-based coating, most of it still existing. The fort wall clearly gave the illusion of being a complete massive stone construction, as only the stone basis was seen.

Archaeological observations of the fortification show that it is a two-phase construction. The first clearly identifiable construction is the lower stone wall built with cut stones and *spolia*. It is a typical construction from the Sultanate period (see Keller 2009: 194 and following). An epigraphic source confirms this archaeological conclusion, as an Arabic-Devanagari inscription originally found at Makki gate presents the fort wall as a work of Sultan Bahadur Shah. The same is confirmed by the *Mirāt-i Sikandarī* which says that the new city wall was completed, after five years of work, in 1533 (*Mirāt-i Sikandarī* in Bayley 1866: 339). 'A ditch was also ordered to be dug round the fort for the protection of the town. The ditch was supplied with water from the Narmada and also from the tanks Fatā Talāv and Ratan Talāv. An Arabic and a Nāgrī *līpī* inscription dated 944 AH (1533 AD) relating to these repairs is lying in the Custom House mosque.'[9] (*Gazetteers* 1961: 741).

The second phase—the brick Mughal crenel—should be related with the fort reconstruction ordered by Aurangzeb in the late seventeenth century. The chronicles mention that the Mughal Sultan ordered the destruction of the fort in 1660 to punish the people. But the same emperor gave the order for its reconstruction 25 years later, to protect the city from the Maratha assaults (*Gazetteers* 1961: 741).

According to 'tradition', the earliest fortress was built by the Rajput king Siddha Jaisinghji of Anhilwara (1094–143) in the early twelfth century (*Gazetteers* 1961: 741).[10] We know from the chronicles of Alau'd-din Khilji's raids on Bharuch in 1297: the original fortification was possibly damaged at this occasion, and little remains from this structure.

The successive orders to rebuild and repair the fortification wall show a clear commitment to strengthen the defensive equipment of the city. However a detailed observation of the wall tends to demonstrate that the massive structure is primarily a dissuasive construction that lacks real defensive artefacts. The extremely long south elevation of the wall, which gives an impressive city look to the vessels coming from the gulf, is accentuated by the numerous towers (one tower every 600–800 m.), and the large stone basement of the wall. It undoubtedly used to make (and one should add, still does) a strong visual impact (Plate 13.6).

However, the openings do not suggest actual military efficiency. I have already mentioned the large water drainage facilities without metal screens. It is also to be noticed that the gates on the river side, though small in number (only four), are built in strict alignment to the fort wall. We know from many other local fort constructions (the nearest being Dhaboi),[11] that city gates were usually built, since the Rajput time, in angular plans to facilitate its defence.

The Sultanate fortification wall was built within the context of encounters with the Portuguese, and the measures taken by the Sultans of Gujarat were

Plate 13.6: 'Baroche on the Banks of the Nerbudda in Guzerat', Engraving by James Forbes (22.3 cm. × 29.1 cm.), from the *Oriental Memoirs* by James Forbes, vol. 2, 1813. *Courtesy:* British Library (Ref. 455.c.8)

to protect the sea towns and the land against any Portuguese attacks.[12] In this context, it can be understood that the main attention was given to the possibility of controlling the movement of vessels into the mouth of the river. This gives a strong dissuasive appearance to the fort city and makes it resistant to long fire points artillery and siege engines. According to the *Zafarul Walah*, the Portuguese 'anchored near the fort' (see *Zafarul Walah* in Lokhandwala 1970: 240). There, cannons were kept 'at the turret' (if we want to take this sentence literally, it would probably refer to the south-west tower, as the word is a singular), and it was enough to force the Portuguese to turn back their boats when they attempted to attack Bharuch in 1547.[13] This account is very appreciative of Bharuch, its population and Sultan Muhammad III, while the efficiency of the defensive capacity of the Sultanate fort system is repeatedly questioned by accounts of plunders. According to other narrations, like the one by the historian Diogo de Couto, Bharuch city was plundered several times during the sixteenth century (*Gazetteers* 1961: 746). In 1547, the Portuguese could enter the city, 'in the dead of night' and 'fell upon the unarmed and defenceless population which being awakened from sleep was in the utmost confusion and terror. After a merciless slaughter, the invader ordered the houses to be sacked and set on fire, so that those who escaped the sword were consumed in the conflagration, and in a few hours "the nobility and the people, the gardens and the houses, were reduced to ashes"' (Account of Diogo de Couto reported by Commissariat 1938: 450–1).

The event, and the defencelessness of the people of Bharuch are explained, in this account, by the absence of the garrison which was out with the nobleman Imad-ul-Mulk at the Sultan's court.

Thus the fortification should not be restricted to a defensive function. The wall was above all an earthwork intended to hold and reinforce the hill on which Bharuch city developed: it was crucial to protect the hillock against water and soil movements, which were generated by the meeting between the river and tides, and constantly tended to reshape the river banks. Due to this strong earthen work, the buildings erected on the hill behind the fort walls were also protected against any water rising that could flood streets.

The city wall also clearly delineates the city area, and is in that way an essential fiscal tool for controlling the movement of goods and payments of taxes. Unfortunately no architectural traces allow us to identify warehouses, city palace and duty offices. However, it is very likely, that the large south-west *buruj* (tower) played a vital role in the trade and fiscal system (Plate 13.7). The tower is built near the mouth of the Narmada (that is where the vessels entered the river from the Indian Ocean through the Gulf of Khambhat), and was obviously not limited to a simple function of observation and defence. It is distinctly separated from the rectangular fortification plan, and overlooks the south-west corner of the fort wall. Its surface is particularly wide (approximately twice that of other towers),

Plate 13.7: The south city wall towards the Narmada River, the rich *hāvelis* beyond the wall, and, on the left: the large south west *buruj*. *Courtesy:* The author.

which could be explained by the fact that the tower housed the duty offices in addition to cannons and garrison. We shall note that this area of the city is still named '*Furza*', which means 'custom house' (Hasan 1993 : 712). The merchandise unloaded from the vessels might have been brought into the city through the western gate, which allowed the officers of the tower to control the flow of wares and merchants.

While waiting for a historical study based on merchant accounts and the trading system of medieval Bharuch, we can rely on the detailed work of M.N. Pearson on brokers and trade in the nearby port of Khambhat. Pearson argues that, unlike the more state supported system operating at Calicut or Diu, the trade system of Khambhat was mainly in the hands of local merchant brokers: 'In Cambay these foreign traders were usually received . . . by local Gujaratis who specialized in this brokering or intermediary role' (Pearson 1988: 469).

The broker would receive the travelling merchant, take care of his merchandise, pay custom duties for him, and bring the regulated goods into the house borrowed by the merchant for his stay. In this system, the role of warehouses would be restricted to the storage of local goods, if not completely taken over by the private storing capacity of merchant houses. Considering that Bharuch had a similar broker tradition, the absence of warehouses could be explained by the fact that the goods were not stored at a state controlled place. In areas where merchandise was stored in state warehouses, these buildings were carefully built and controlled, and their remains and defensive arrangement are still standing (see the study by Picard 1996: 45–66).

The entrepreneurship of locals and the empowerment of merchant communities could also explain the complete absence of any significant palace remains, whether on the site or in local memory. The merchant controlled system would not have shown the necessity, nor given the space, for a powerful ruler or governor. A local political figure or a representative of the local ruler was of course present, and the late history of Bharuch occasionally mentions the local governor and *nawwab*. However, the building intended for his residence and functions probably was of non lasting material (brick and timber) as other merchant houses; the latest version of these constructions are still visible on the river front and elsewhere in the city (Plate 13.7), and see the descriptions of the Begum Badi, the Lallubhai Haveli, etc., in *Gazetteer* 1961: 740–5.

It is also surprising that no structure directly related to maritime activity is visible. We know from various written sources (chronicles and travellers accounts), that vessels would anchor at some distance from the city (Lokhandwala 1970: 240). Smaller ships would carry goods to shore where they were unloaded and directed toward the city. The shore therefore played a major role, not only for trade (broker and terms of residence were discussed, business made,[14] goods despatched), but also for ship work (vessels were drawn ashore for repairs, and new ships were constructed, Plate 13.8).[15]

Major size vessels (probably those which were more than 1,000 tonnes) would anchor outside the Narmada delta, in the Gulf of Khambhat, and goods were carried out with the help of medium size ships to the shore of Bhadbhut and Bharuch. The silting up of the Bharuch site was long believed to be a major reason for the decline of its port on behalf of the neighbouring towns of Khambhat and Surat. The Narmada River gradually receded till approximately a kilometre away from the city wall (as it is now), which definitely affected the anchoring habits, the port system, and probably the volume of traded goods. However, the written sources, foreigners accounts in first person, testify of the continuous activity of Bharuch port during the Sultanate and Mughal periods (but with some major breaks, especially after the encounters with Turkish rulers, Saxena 2001: 229). 'The Portuguese, . . . in 1546, except for its streets, "so narrow that two horsemen could not pass through them at the same time, admired the city, with its castlelike Lisbon, its magnificent and lofty houses with their costly lattices; the famous ivory and blackwood workshops; and its townsmen well skilled in mechanics, chiefly weavers, who made the finest cloth in the world'. (*Gazetteers* 1961: 746)

Plate 13.8: Ship in construction on the shore of Mandvi port (Kutchh, India).
Courtesy: The author.

The mercantile communities of Bharuch and its extremely rich and productive hinterland (especially metal and stone work in the early medieval period, and cotton cloth in a later one)[16] played a major role not only in the development, but also in the survival of port activity.

City Plan

An archaeological analysis of the fortification also gives precious informations concerning urban development. As already mentioned, the north site of the fortress has disappeared due to expansion of the city. However, plotting the housing patterns provides good enough indications and allows us to trace the original layout of the entire wall, at least on the west side.

The fortress has a very regular shape, forming a long rectangle of approximately 400 m. by 1.3 km., with its longer side along the river shore (Fig. 13.1). Towers are not spaced identical along the whole construction. While the first seven towers, on the south, are built at just 60 m. from each other, the others are less frequent, as they are spaced at 80 m. The wall with the seven closely built towers forms a construction of approximately 400 m., that is the same length as the south-west wall.

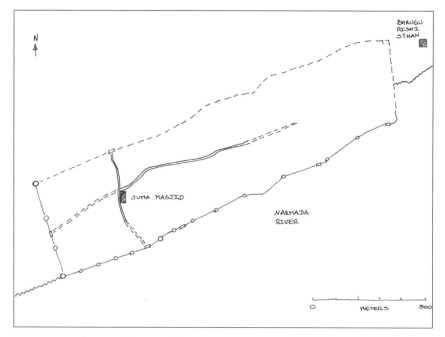

Fig. 13.1: Architectural remains from the ancient times to the Sultanate (Bhrigu Rishi site, Jumā Masjid and city walls and gates). *Courtesy:* The author.

From this observation we assume that this south square area is the ancient core of the city. It is also the highest hill point of the site. This first square city could be the early medieval town fortified by the king Sidh Singh during the early twelfth century, while the long rectangle fortification erected by Bahadur Shah 400 years later would have included the city extension on the north side.

Another major monument of Bharuch is its Jumā Masjid, built at the top of the city. According to Persian chronicles, the mosque was built by Sultan Alauddin Khaliji in 1297, after his conquest of the city and region. Therefore, the Bharuch mosque is not just a prayer place built by a local Arab merchant settling in the city for trade purpose, as one notices at Bhadreshwar or Junagadh. It is the earliest known example of a mosque built by a foreign ruler of Turko-Persian origin.

In the square area and the ancient core of the walled city, the Jumā Masjid occupies the very central place, and the highest point on the hill.

The street running along the *qibla* wall goes so far as an important crossroad on the north-west side of the building. A straight line parallel to the south-west wall of the city, and using the path of this street would reach, on the south the first gate of the fort. Therefore this street probably was the main north-south axis of the city since the construction of the Friday mosque, in the early fourteenth century. Another street, crossing the previous one on the north side of the mosque, forms what could probably be an old perpendicular axis in the centre of the city (Fig. 13.2).

Let us recapitulate the different urban phases which can be traced from this preliminary archaeological-topographical study. The twelfth and thirteenth century town is a square fort of 400 m. side, built directly on the river bank, on a hard hillock. After Alauddin Khaliji's invasion a Friday mosque was built in the city (during the fourteenth century) which was, at that point, still an active port and marketplace for overseas trade. The growth of the city showed the necessity of increasing the fortified area, which explains why the fort wall construction conducted by Bahadur Shah resulted in the building of a large rectangle city more than thee times the size of the original one.

Housing and colonies largely continued to be located outside the city wall, as attested by late accounts like the one written by Thévenot, who described the town developing at the foot of the hill, and where a market for locally woven cotton cloths and bleaching activities were found.

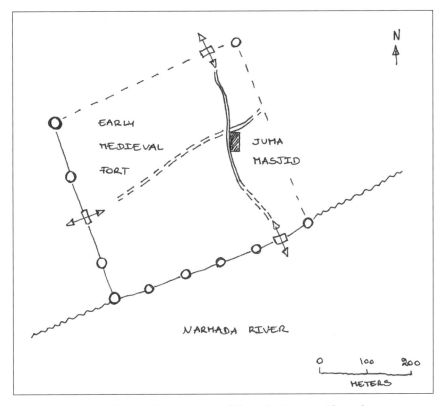

Fig. 13.2: The pre-Sultanate city of Bharuch. *Courtesy:* The author.

Conclusion

From an archaeological observation of the ancient, early medieval and pre-Mughal structures of Bharuch, notably its fortification, one can arrive at a better understanding of the trading identity of the city. Before being a defensive milestone on the Indian coastline, a transshipment place or any other sea related settlement, Bharuch was a converging point for goods of the rich Indian hinterland, the local productions and the overseas goods. Strong merchant communities developed a probable broker base system, while rulers were eager to keep a well organized fiscal system. The late fortification work done by Sultan Bahadur Shah integrates the ancient city core plus the later urban development along the river shore. The construction of the new city wall has to be understood as an urban development measure of the Sultanate period, and a decision taken in the context of encounters with the Portuguese, like other city wall constructions on the sea coast during the same period (Surat was fortified in 1539, also

Mangrol, Ghogha). These new city walls play mainly a dissuasive role and have a strong influence on the urbanism of the port cities of Gujarat.

This brief architectural look at Bharuch introduced a research discussion that would need joint archaeological and historical work to complete an urban and eco-political sketch of the maritime and trade city of Bharuch. Archaeological digging would give precious information concerning the urban development, and a study of written sources, especially foreign accounts, would surely help to answer some of the socio-economic and political questions.

It would be particularly relevant to introduce the debate on the political status of the city, and, for this matter, the role of monasteries,[17] later on the importance of Mahajans and mercantile communities.

Notes

1. Also named 'Bharukachchha' (in Sanskrit geography), 'Barugaza' (in Greek sources), 'Barakacheva' by the Chinese traveller Hsuan Tsang (seventh century), 'Barus' in the early Arabic texts. See Burgess 1896: 20; Watters 1996; Dar 2001: 44.
2. See the references in *Periplus* (Schoff 1912: 14–49).
3. Account of Al Idrisi in Elliot 1867–77, vol. 1, pt. I, chap. VIII. See also the account of Masudi, Biruni, Yaqut and Dimashqi (see Dar 2001: 50; Jain 1990: 129–30).
4. See Chaudhuri 1985; Commissariat 1938; Gupta 1994; Hourani 1995; Mehta 2009; Pearson 2003.
5. The Bhrigu Rishi site does not have any historical architectural remains, but still bears several ancient sculptures and 17 old *lingās* (Gazetteer 1961: 740).
6. However, Bharuch has several minor architectural remains of pre-Mughal era: the Idgāh in Vejalpur, dated 1326 by a stone inscription (Gazetteer 1961: 741, Commissariat 1938: 67); the mausoleum of Imad ul-Mulk (1560) on the hillock of Bābā Rayhan (tenth century, see Commissariat 1938: 468; Gazetteer 1961: 741–2; and Dar 2001: 50); and the mosque in Kot Parsiwad which awaits a study for its dating (constructed 1609, but with older pillar basis, see Gazetteer 1961: 743; and Commissariat 1938: 47); a mausoleum (built 1563) in Ali suburb (Gazetteer 1961: 742). Several Hindu sculptures, like those of the Bhrigu Rishi site, or the Somnath Temple, are the only remains of the Sultanate era.
7. The colour of the sandstone is due to the variety of granular components and linking matrix, even when stones come from the same quarry. We know that Dhangadhra, a major local quarry for sandstone, produces stones with pinkish, yellowish and greenish shades.
8. The bricks are of the standard brick size used in Gujarat during the Mughal period; they are joined with thick layers of lime mortar containing crushed brick material (see Keller 2009: 205).

9. Or the mosque near Furza. For the translation of the inscription: see Commissariat 1938, I: 336–7.
10. Dar mentions several raids perpetuated on Bharuch by Arab rulers in the early medieval period. These encounters might have been the reason for the construction of the ancient fortification (Dar 2001: 44).
11. The fort wall and city gates of Dabhoi were built by Siddhraj Jaisinh in the early twelfth century.
12. 'In AD 1507, The Sultan [Mahmud Bgda] led an expedition against the Portuguese, who, having become powerful on the western coast of India, had of late usurped the dominion of the sea, and attacked the Gujarat possessions of Mahim and Bombay', Dosabhai 1986: 92.
13. 'The residents fought with them . . . and drove back to their boats. . . . He [the Sultan] personally fought and smashed them with the sword. They [the Portuguese] fled to Div', Zafarul Walah in Lokhandwala 1970: 240.
14. See Thévenot's account in Lach and Kley 1994: 802: 'The town on the side and foot of the hill is surrounded by stone walls flanked by regularly spaced large round towers. The chief market at the foot of the hill sells the locally woven *baftas*, or cotton cloths, that exported to all the Indies.'
15. Vessels might have been drawn ashore at Bhadbhut, as they could not be grounded near Bharuch fort (as mentioned in the Zafar ul Wālih, see Lokhandwala 1970). Fewer references are given to the ship building industry at Bharuch, but we can suppose, from a mention on an armada gathered by Mahmud III, that ships were built there at least during the Sultanate time (Gazetteers 1991: 22).
16. See Mendelslo's account in Lach and Kley 1994: 669: 'The majority of its inhabitants are weavers who produce *baftas*, textiles "finer than any made [elsewhere] in the province of Gujarat"'.
17. See the account of the Chinese traveller Hsuan Tsang about 640 (Watters 1996).

References

Bayley, E.C. (1866), *The history of India as told by its own historians, The local Muhammadan Dynasties: By the late Sir Edward Clive Bayley, K.C.S.I. Partially based on a translation by the late Professor John Dowson [of the 'Mirát-i-Sikandarí' of Sikandar ibn Muhammad]. Published under the patronage of H.M.'s secretary of state for India. Forming a sequel to Sir H. M. Elliot's History of the Muhammadan empire of India*, London: W.H. Allen and Co., publishers to the India Office.

Burgess, J. (1896), *On the Muhammadan Architecture of Bharoch, Cambay, Dholka, Champanir, and Mahmudabad in Gujarat*, London: W. Griggs and Sons.

Chaudhuri, K.N. (1985), *Trade and Civilisation in the Indian Ocean: An Economic History from the Rise of Islam to 1750*, New York: Cambridge University Press.

Chakravarti, R. (2000), 'Nakhudas and Nauvittakas: Shipowning merchants in the West coast of India (*c.* AD 1000-1500)', *Journal of the Economic and Social History of the Orient (JESHO)*, vol. 43, no. 1, pp. 34–64.

Commissariat, M.S. (1938), *A history of Gujarat, Including a Survey of Its Chief Architectural Monuments and Inscriptions*, London: Longmans, Green and Co.

Dar, M.I. (2001), 'Early Muslim settlements in Gujarat', in *Cultural and literary activities in Gujarat*, M. Bombaywala, New Delhi: Hazrat Pir Muhammad Shah Library and Research Centre, pp. 44–51.

Desai, G.H. (1914), *Bharuch Sheherno Itihaas*, Bharuch.

Desai, Z.A.H. (1961), 'Arabic Inscription of the Rajput period from Gujarat', in *Epigraphia Indica: Arabic and Persian Supplement*, pp. 1–24.

——— (1982) *Persian and Arabic epigraphy of Gujarat, their historical significance*, Baroda: Department of History, Faculty of Arts, Maharaja Sayajirao University of Baroda (Department of History series no. 8).

Dosabhai, E. (1986), *A history of Gujarat, From the earliest period to the present time*, New Delhi: Asian Educational Services, (repr., 1894).

Elliot, H.M. (1867–77), *The History of India, as Told by Its Own Historians: The Muhammadan Period*, London: Trübner.

Gazetteer 1961 = *Gazetteer of India*, Broach District, Ahmedabad (revised 1961).

Gazetteer 1991 = *Gujarat State Gazetteer*, Part II, Gandhinagar (1991).

Gupta, A.D. (1994), *Merchants of Maritime India, 1500-1800*, Norfolk: Variorum, Ashgate Publishing (Variorum Collected Studies Series; CS 441).

Hasan, F. (1993), 'The Mughal Fiscal System in Surat and the English East India Company', *Modern Asian Studies*, vol. 27, no. 4, pp. 711–18.

Hourani, G.F. (1995), *Arab seafaring in the Indian Ocean in ancient and early medieval times*, Princeton: Princeton University Press, New Jersey.

Keller, S. (2009), 'Les monuments islamiques de la cité d'Ahmedabad (Inde, XVe-XVIIIe s.): étude archéologique', Ph.D. thesis in publication process, microfilms available in all French Universities.

Lach, D.F. and Kley, E.J. van (1994), *Asia in the making of Europe: A century of advance*, Book 2, Chicago: The University of Chicago Press.

Lokhandwala, M.F. (translation) (1970), *Zafar ul Wālih bi Muzaffar wa Ālihi, An Arabic History of Gujarat by Abdullāh Muhammad Al-Makki Al-Āsafi Al-Ulughkhāni Hāji ad-Dabir*, vol. I, Maharaja Sayajirao University of Baroda, Oriental Institute, Baroda.

Mehta, M. (2009), *History Of International Trade And Custom Duty In Gujarat*, Ahmedabad: Darshak Itihas Nidhi.

Pearson, M.N. (1988), 'Brokers in Western Indian Port Cities, Their Role in Servicing Foreign Merchants', *Modern Asian Studies*, vol. 22, no. 3, pp. 455–72.

——— (2003), *The Indian Ocean*, London and New York: Routledge.

Picard, C. (1996), 'Fortification et fonctions portuaires sur le littoral atlantique musulman', *Archéologie Islamique*, vol. 6, pp. 45–66.

Saxena, A. (2001), 'Urban growth in south Gujarat: A case study of Bharuch from fourteenth to mid-eighteenth century', in *Proceedings of the Indian History Congress, 62nd Session, Bhopal*, pp. 227–38, Kolkata (2002).

Schoff, W.H. (1912), *The Periplus of the Erythraean Sea*, London: Longmans, Green and Co.

Watters, T. (1996), *On Yuan Chwang's Travels in India 629-645* AD. London: Royal Asiatic Society (1904), repr., Hesperides Press.

Wink, A. (1990), *Al-Hind: The making of the Indo-Islamic world, vol I: Early medieval India and the expansion of Islam*, Leiden: E.J. Brill.

CHAPTER 14

The Archaeological Project of Bassein's Portuguese Settlement
A New Appraisal

Dejanirah Couto

I n retracing the history of the port of Bassein under Portuguese rule (1534-1739), this essay aims to draw attention to the need of launching archaeological work in one of the most important possessions of the *Estado da Índia*, which played a key role in the economic life of the western Indian Ocean in the sixteenth and seventeenth centuries, and was a no less significant issue in the political games between the colonial and Maratha powers in the eighteenth century. Admittedly, some urban centres and coastal fortifications of the Indian Ocean have already been excavated[1] and the results of archaeological campaigns published. Yet cities and ports which have experienced a long period of Portuguese rule in the Indian Ocean have never been excavated,[2] which was not without effect on the historiographical production. In fact, publications, both in Portugal and elsewhere, are largely based on textual or sometimes epigraphic data: the archaeology of the Portuguese or Luso-Asian possessions has not yet emerged.

A glance at a map of India—which assesses the geographical location of Bassein—helps to understand why the Portuguese had such a strong interest in it. Belonging to the modern state of Maharashtra, the urban centre, currently a 'ghost town', is located on the west coast of the Indian subcontinent, on the Konkan coast, specifically on one of 25 islands of the Mumbai archipelago, between Bassein/Vasai and Khanderi, about 70 km. north of Mumbai.

Unlike other ports of Gujarat, Bassein, founded on the north shore of the Ulhoa (or Bahayandar), a river with deep water on a peninsula south of the island of Vasai, enjoyed excellent conditions for defence. The island was separated from the mainland along a north-south axis by a channel linking the Ulhoa River to the Vaitarna, north. The Ulhoa bathes a large area of saline lands and swamps flooded at high tide and during the monsoon. The port town of Bassein and its basin were thus limited to the south-west by the sea, to the south-east by the Ulhoa River,[3] and to the north-east by a river (formed by an arm of the Ulhoa to which the Portuguese gave the name of *esteiro*) that protected its north/north-west front. Due to deposits of the river and sand carried by tides, the creek experienced a gradual silting, causing, as in many other coastal landscapes in the Indian Ocean, the decline of the port.

Marshlands still surround the ruins of the city and fortress in the north-east but alluvial fields have replaced the site of the former branch of the Ulhoa; they offer a landscape of diverse cultures, however, marked by the ubiquitous rice fields.

The history of the area is complex and the etymology of the name 'Bassein' controversial. The port, commonly known under the name of Vasai (from the Sanskrit word meaning 'home' or from *varsa,* meaning flock)[4] remained unrecognized for an extended period. References we have, as well as some archaeological remains, mention the port of Kalyan, which is now far from the coast and the port of Supara,[5] further east, on the shore of one of the bends of the Ulhoa. Kalyan and Supara are mentioned in the inscriptions of the Kanheri caves occupied by Buddhist monks from the first century AD.[6]

Kalyan remained a dynamic port in contact with the Mediterranean during the Gupta period under the reigns of Samudra Gupta (335–75) and Chandra Gupta II (375–415). Cosmas Indicopleustes (sixth century) mentions the port of Kalyan in connection with the trade of wood and fabrics. It was prosperous during the reign of the Chalukya rulers (who disappeared in the eighth century to be replaced by the Rashtrakutas) whose power was the result of trade relations with the ports of the Arabian Sea and especially the Persian Gulf. This period, during which many trading communities, Jains, Buddhists and Muslims, settled in the region, also consecrated Gujarat as an economic power.[7] Port Thana, further south, near a branch of the Ulhas River that separated the Salcete island from the mainland also experienced a boom. Its privileged position allowed it to develop trade links with the hinterland, including Malwa.

Thus, it is possible to deduce how in this region of Gujarat, the emergence of new ports was closely linked to the silting of certain waterways. Of course, the technological changes in shipbuilding, shifts in the patterns of maritime trade and impact of coastal piracy played their part, but the geographical conditions have no doubt played a decisive role in the decline of Supara and Kalyan. During the medieval period, it is Thana[8] which is noted as the major port of the region. Deep-watered, it also enjoyed a fertile agricultural hinterland and exported leather goods, cotton and metals.[9]

As there were no archaeological excavations, dating when people settled at Bassein is uncertain, but the region was incorporated in the Sultanate of Delhi in the second decade of the fourteenth century, after the annexations by Muhammad bin Tughluq and the creation of Daulatabad, the ancient capital of the Yadava dynasty.[10] In the fourteenth century, new political powers, such as the Bahmani Sultanate of Deccan born on the ruins of the Sultanate of Delhi, upset the balance of the region. The Bahmanids were supplanted in their turn by the Nizam Châhi of Ahmadnagar, who claimed ownership of the island of Salcete, Mumbai and Chaul.[11]

Regardless, the *Livro* of Duarte Barbosa, the most important European treatise on commercial geography of the Indian Ocean in the early sixteenth century, already mentions the port of Bassein.[12] Compared to Kalyan, Thana's advantage of its geographical position has quickly been taken into account by Muslim merchants: located just south of Supara, near the coast, it was deported further west. Merchants who settled there consolidated their position by marrying low-caste women from the coastal cities, belonging to families of fishermen and artisans working in shipbuilding. These social dynamics favoured the Muslim groups related to maritime trade. Their commercial dynamism has made famous the Sultanate of Gujarat in all the ports of the Indian Ocean as far as the East Indies.[13]

The hinterland of Bassein was rich with dense forest areas, producing high quality wood, including teak, prized in shipbuilding.[14] Sites built boats for coastal navigation but also offshore, which probably influenced the further development of the port.[15] Cultivated areas produced opium, areca nut, betel leaf,[16] rice,[17] wheat, anil (indigo plant) and sugarcane.[18] Bassein also exported salt, fish, cotton (which was redistributed by the Portuguese as far as the Bay of Bengal under the name of *panos de Cambaia*) and horses, although it could not compete with Chaul, Dabhol, Goa or Bhatkal, true hubs of a trade that made the fortune of cities in Oman and the Persian Gulf.[19]

In the early sixteenth century, and more specifically after the founding of the *Estado da Índia* in 1505, the Portuguese renewed their interest towards Gujarat, especially the port of Diu, whose ships swarmed across the Indian Ocean. Very quickly, their goal was to dismantle and replace the Gujarati networks in maritime trade.[20] This marketing strategy was based on political reasons: because of its relations with Qânsûh al-Ghûrî, the Mamluk Sultan of Cairo, enemy of the Portuguese Crown, the Gujarati Sultanate was an opponent of the Portuguese.[21]

However, despite their efforts (as evidenced by a succession of maritime expeditions, culminating with the one commanded by the governor of the *Estado da Índia* Nuno da Cunha in 1531)[22] the Portuguese could not lay hold of Diu. Therefore, turning to another tactic they began weakening the Sultan of Gujarat by a war of attrition (while breaking no diplomatic contacts with him). This strategy eventually paid off: in 1513, the Portuguese managed to open a factory in Diu, and left as its director Fernão Martins Evangelho. However, it was closed in 1521 due to pressure by Gujaratis.[23] Regardless, the idea to build a fort there, as part of a more ambitious goal, that of building (from 1519) forts at Chaul, in the Maldives, in Sumatra and the Moluccas continued to make its way.[24]

Like other ports of the Konkan Coast, economically linked to Diu, Bassein was also looted and destroyed by the Portuguese. Out of the eleven Portuguese expeditions launched in the region in the first half of the sixteenth century, seven were directed against Bassein.[25] Moreover, some of the pages of the *Décadas* written by the chronicler Diogo do Couto provide particularly objective descriptions of the ferocity of the Portuguese.[26]

Forwarded to the Viceroy D. Francisco de Almeida when he attacked Dabul in 1509, information about the prosperity of Bassein and its strategic importance explains the Viceroy's intention to attack the port.[27] Under the mandate of the Governor Nuno da Cunha (1529–38)[28] the Portuguese wanted to avoid at all costs Bassein being transformed into a 'second Diu'.[29]

As already mentioned, the port was destroyed by Heitor da Silveira in 1529, in the wake of the attack against Surat and Reynel.[30] On 20 January 1533, the city and port facilities, which had been rebuilt in the meantime, were destroyed again by Nuno da Cunha, who razed the fortifications. However, the Portuguese failed to settle despite the importance of the military assets carried out. If they managed to settle in Bassein in 1534 and built the fortress at Diu in 1536 it was through diplomatic negotiations, which led to the first concession of Bassein—the first jurisdiction in the *Estado da Índia* to have a considerable area (about 2000 sq. km)[31]—by Sultan Qutb-ud-Din Bahadur of Gujarat (1526–37), son of Shams-ud-Din Muzaffar Châh II on 23 December 1534.[32] Circumstances are well known: caught between the Portuguese who regularly besieged his ports, the progress of the Mughals and his own military campaigns against the Rajput states (Malwa and Chitor) Bahadur resigned himself to give Bassein to Nuno da Cunha as a means of defusing conflict with the Portuguese, removing them away from Diu and saving time concerning Humayun.[33]

The first phase of the Portuguese presence in Bassein was disrupted by the volte-face of Bahadur, who annulled several provisions of the concession agreement on freedom of maritime trade, which had been validated during the signing of the Treaty of 25 October 1535, treaty allowing the Portuguese to settle in Diu.[34] Deciding to contest the supremacy of the latter, the Portuguese had first demanded that merchant ships pay fees at Bassein; Bahadur (who had accepted this clause in the first place) in turn demanded that rights were paid again at Diu, in accordance with the customs of maritime trade in the Indian Ocean. But Bahadur Châh was assassinated in 1537 under unclear circumstances, where we discern—if we believe the Lusitanian and Indo-Persian chroniclers—the hands of the Portuguese.[35]

Between 1538 and 1540, the Gujaratis maintained military pressure on Bassein as testified by incursions headed by Malik Ilias (*Melique Acem*) and by Burhân-ul-Mulk (*Bramaluco*), former governor of the territory and his nephew Nasir Malik-ud-Din (*Melique Naçaruto*).[36]

However, despite such instability, the Portuguese were able to complete an administrative reorganization of the territory along the lines of traditional agrarian system. Lands were distributed according to the *prazos* system, a hybrid form of territorial organization inspired by the *iqtas*, the feudal system existing in Muslim India. Insofar as all Muslim recipients did not abandon their plots, it was only very gradually that *fidalgos* Portuguese (and some Brahmins of Goa) received land under the new system. Over time, the system evolved: the recipients, who were required to reside first *intra muros*, were allowed to stay three months in their villages, which allowed them to better explore the land that had been allocated.[37] The territory was first divided into administrative units—14 in total—called *praganas* (when they incorporated settlements of some importance with the lands around them, usually suburban lands called *pacarias*) and *caçabés* (when they embodied predominantly rural regions).[38] What was this territory in geographical terms? A discontinuous space with a 75-km. long coastline stretching between islands and peninsulas, 30 km. wide, flatter in the south mountainous when going north, dotted with about 350 villages.[39] With the territories incorporated in 1556, the surface slightly increased: it reached 2,100 sq. km. and 115 km. in length, although the width of the rectangle has not changed substantially.

In a few decades, Bassein became the seat of a powerful landed aristocracy formed by a few large families, to the point of deserving the epithet 'D. Baçaim' and 'Northern Capital' and competing from this viewpoint with Goa, political and administrative capital of the *Estado da Índia*.[40] The urban tissue, where beautiful private homes were reported by travellers of the seventeenth century, was structured around public buildings (the *Misericórdia* was founded in 1540)[41] and several churches, showing which mission the Crown of Portugal wanted to assign its new territory, enclosed in a region dominated by a Muslim power. The missionaries were agents of this policy and they often played a more important role, particularly the Franciscans and Jesuits, than the agents of the king. Indeed, members of these orders have even managed Bassein, and their action was crucial in the expansion of the territory to rural areas, especially in *caçabés* of Bassein and Agaçaim, as well as the island of Salcete.[42]

The results of the arrival of the first monks at Bassein were the construction of places of worship, like the chapel of Nossa Senhora da Vida (1535). We do not know exactly when work started at the church of S. José (initiated in 1547 and continued in the decade of 1550?), but it certainly existed in 1554.[43] Led by Frei António do Porto, the Franciscans settled there from 1546,[44] first in a College of modest size they shared with the Jesuits. A little later the work of the church and convent S.António began in 1547 and 1552 respectively[45] (Plate 14.1).

The visit of St. Francis Xavier in March 1548 (followed a few months later by the installation of pe Melchior Gonçalves) prefigured the establishment of the Jesuits, who began converting people in 1548–9.[46] However, the college and the church of the Society (called Sagrado Nome de Jesus in 1568) were probably built between 1549 and 1636, the primitive structures

Plate 14.1: Franciscans Cloister. *Courtesy:* The author, in Couto 1994: 265.

of the college years probably dating from 1552 to 1555. Around 1564, it was the turn of the Dominicans to establish themselves in the north-east of the main square of the city, bounded by the municipality (*Câmara*), the Misericórdia Hospital and the church of the same name, and later (this is an assumption) the residence of the Northern General. As has been noted, the architectural complex of the Dominicans was the only one to be built 'far from defensive structures', i.e. the primitive citadel.[47]

Indeed, the context for conversions was not very favourable and there were few of them until 1565.[48] The 1534 treaty stipulated some amount of religious freedom (part of the income of Bassein was assigned to the maintenance of mosques), but the Portuguese power intentionally kept a 'carrot and stick' policy according to the political and religious orientations advocated by the Crown (and sometimes governors).

Actually, as the century progressed, similar to concurrent events at Goa (where the inquisitorial court with jurisdiction in all the territories of the *Estado da Índia* was founded in 1560), the climate of the Counter-Reformation was felt also at Bassein: mosques and Hindu temples were razed in 1549. On 2 August 1549, Governor Jorge Cabral issued an *alvará* prohibiting their rebuilding, finalizing the hardening process of the religious policy. Finally, after some rather violent actions—as the coating of the temples ponds steps with fresh cow blood[49]—they were banned in 1566, as well as public demonstrations of Hindu cults and practices.[50]

In this context, Franciscans and Jesuits assumed enormous economic power, competing with each other for donations of land, buildings, and revenue taken from the villages of Bassein. For example, that of the income from Mandapeshvar (*Manapacer*) on the island of Salcete, granted to the Franciscans, while the Jesuits received land and houses to finance the construction of their college.[51] In addition, the Society also received donations from land recipients (*foreiros*); for instance, Inês Aguiar sold them the revenues of several villages in the island of Salcete (1560) amounting to 600 *pardaus*, as did Isabel Francisca (1567). The island of Salcete thus counted among the areas of the Bassein territory where Jesuit Estates have increased substantially.[52] One also appreciates how much weight Bassein had in the economy of the Society of Jesus—to serve its expansionist policy in Asia—if one knows, for example, that around 1621, the Mission to Japan was funded with the revenues from the Condoti village on the island of Salcete, with those of Sargi, Mori, Curlem (between 1560 and 1590), to which were added the revenues from the villages of Mulgão, Poinser and those of the *caçabé* Caranja (between 1590 and 1621). The economic weight of Bassein within the Society, helps to understand, at least in part, the visit of Alexander Valignano in 1576.[53]

Dominicans, and Augustinians as well were not as fond of land as the Jesuits, and to a lesser extent, the Franciscans (Plate 14.2). However, the Augustinians tried to compete with the Jesuits, as soon as opportunity arose, which was the case at the time of D. Frei Aleixo de Meneses, the Archbishop of Goa and governor of the *Estado da Índia* which belonged to the Congregation.[54] But the Crown watched, eager to control privileges and property held by religious orders.

In any case this allows us to better understand why different congregations built their churches in Bassein. Besides the great college, convent and church of the Jesuits,[55] the Dominicans erected in their turn S.Gonçalo (1564) and the Augustinians Nossa Senhora da Anunciada (1596). Therefore Bassein in 1674 had six churches (including four belonging to convents) two colleges and four convents.[56] This frenzy of constructing religious buildings spread elsewhere throughout the territory, which was dotted with a large number of churches: in 1615 there were 52 buildings of Christian worship, most of which—located along the coast—belonged to the Franciscans, followed closely by the Jesuits.[57] Such an effort of evangelization, however, did not hide, as indicated, the growing difficulties for getting new conversions. Given by some authors, the number of converts in 1613 (20,000) seems excessive to say the least.[58]

Plate 14.2: Church of S. António (Franciscans).
Courtesy: José Manuel Fernandes, in Couto 1994: 264.

Shipbuilding, facilitated by the quality of the different types of local wood, greatly contributed to the growth of the urban centre and several sources of the sixteenth century praise it, among them the famous naturalist doctor Garcia da Orta[59] or the intendant of finances Simão Botelho.[60]

The tradition of shipbuilding in teak and exporting this material had been maintained in the village of Agashi, in the northern territory of Bassein. According to the chronicler Gaspar Correia, in the first half of the sixteenth century this wood species was 'transported to Mecca', that is the ports of the Red Sea (Jeddah and Aden), where it was adjudicated by the Ottomans for the construction of their ships.[61] In 1540, the Portuguese of Bassein launched an expedition against Agashi to seize a vessel of large tonnage which had just been built. The confiscated ship was assigned to the travels of the *Carreira da Índia* to Portugal.[62] In 1555 a fire in the shipyards (Ribeira) in Goa[63] led the authorities of the *Estado da Índia* to seek assistance from Bassein.[64] Portuguese law prohibited wood cutting without prior approval and the obtention of a royal licence.[65] Having this privilege, masters of Bassein sometimes supplemented their fees by selling teak wood to several individuals; complaints also indicate fraudulent transactions.

Shipbuilding grew in the late sixteenth century, with the creation of the North Fleet (*Armada do Norte*) to prevent the raids of Indian pirates, but also to protect ports and convoys of merchant ships sailing to (or from) Saudi ports. These boats at the beginning had a modest tonnage and Asian type, as the Portuguese did not hesitate to 'orientalize' their fleets in order to make their war navy more powerful in the Indian Ocean.[66] Bassein thus had a 'master of galleys and galleasses' (*mestre das galés e galeaças*), and in 1564, a man in charge of the shipyards (*mestre da Ribeira*) who coordinated the activity of caulkers.[67]

In the early seventeenth century, the French Pyrard de Laval boasted the quality of shipbuilding in Bassein and compared it to Biscay.[68] Around 1663, Father Manuel Godinho stressed the importance of its shipyards, where, he said, 'are built all the *galliots* of the rowing fleets the king has in the seas of India; galleons, *pataches* and very beautiful and strong galliots are also built'.[69]

The Portuguese first urban centre developed around the dock. This area was also where the Gujarati city grew. It stretched from the pier to the interior in an east-west direction, parallel to the river Ulhoa in an extension which was estimated at 400 m.[70] Artisans and traders held their stalls there, and the toponymy of the Portuguese city has also kept the memory of trades (goldsmiths, shoemakers) traditionally exercised in this sector.[71]

It is worth quoting that the religious complexes (churches and monasteries) were built much farther, outside this axis, with the exception of the church of S. José, built around the dock and the factory that it served. Indeed, in 1534, after Bassein was conceded to the Portuguese, a small customs house was built in this area near the mouth of the *esteiro*. To this *Mandovi* was added in 1535, a little further south, a factory (*feitoria*), a building prolonged by a long canopy that opened onto a large esplanade slightly elevated, surrounded by a palisade; warehouses allocated to the storage of bundles of goods were subsequently added. It is around the factory that were built—thanks to existing quarries inland—the homes of the first hundred men,[72] and later, the church of S. José, a building with a rectangular nave, rather long with axial façade built on narthex, like the church of Nossa Senhora do Rosário in Goa (1543).[73] Within the perimeter of the pier was later built the imposing *Porta do Mar* 'Sea Gate'.

It is somewhere in this area that once stood a Muslim fortress. It should be remembered that Bassein was attacked by Heitor da Silveira in 1529 (during the incursion against Surat and Reynel) that the city was burned, and the gardens and plantations of sugarcane were destroyed. Portuguese sources that relate the episode only mention a fence for protecting the pier, with 60 pieces of artillery protected by moats.[74] As da Silveira did not linger on the scene, the inhabitants fortified Bassein after his departure, probably between 1529 and 1532 or 1533; the command was given to Malik Tughan (*Melique Tocão*), Captain of Bahadur Châh of Gujarat and son of Malik Ayaz, one of the Governors of Diu.[75]

When Nuno da Cunha in his turn attacked Bassein in 1533, he found a Muslim fortification along the *esteiro* near the dock, in the area where the factory (*feitoria*) would be built later. Well furnished with artillery, the fort had a square plan, two floors, with corner towers surmounted by turrets. The walls were broad and masoned. Iron cannons of large calibre (about thirty) were arranged in good order on the ground floor. The upper floor housed the containers (*panelas*) for powder and wicks. In the centre of the fortress, one could observe a half-buried building, whose interior was lined with wooden planks to preserve from moisture. There were stored wood tanks filled with powder. The surroundings of the fortress on the banks of the *esteiro* were equipped with small turrets formed with baskets filled with earth.[76] The defensive device was completed by a masoned bastion placed further toward the interior of the *esteiro* but at the waterfront, also provided, according to the same system (two floors), of artillery; a catapult (*trabuco*) was placed between the bastion and the fort. Waters licked the walls of the two fortifications at high tide. Low tide uncovered sharpened stakes buried in the sand, designed to prevent landings.[77] Finally, a number of artificial canals filled with water (*cavas*) made the crossing of the wetlands near the fortress even more uncertain. The limits of this extension were defended by many wooden fences equipped with artillery. A little further, on a small hill, was a mosque with its well and its stone basin carved. The fortress was visible from this elevation.[78]

According to the testimony of two Portuguese sources (Gaspar Correia and Fernão Lopes de Castanheda), Nuno da Cunha blew up the Gujarati fortress to its foundations.[79] However, the account, albeit later, of António Bocarro deserves our attention. The author of *Livro das Plantas das Fortalezas, Cidades e Povoações do Estado da Índia Oriental* visited Bassein in 1634 and left a fairly complete description of the city. He reported the existence of a fortified wall (*serca*) near the original Portuguese fort, also known as the 'citadel', built in 1536. According to him, '. . . the city of Bassein has buildings where the captain lives, adjoining the church of Mercy, which incorporate an old brick enclosure, where it seems that Muslims, to whom it belonged, took refuge, and a round stone bastion that is on the pillory, a small building that has not been restored and is in ruins.'[80] The identification of the 'residence of the Captain' (which we know would have been located close to the wall of the Gujarati fortification) has not been formally established, as the identification of some buildings is quite uncertain—incidentally an additional reason to explore Bassein.

In any event, most authors consider that the residence of the Captain, situated, as it was customary, inside the Portuguese fortress, is still visible in the sketch drawn by Gaspar Correia on its north-east corner.[81] This residence, which would have two floors, rises slightly beyond the line of walls and extends about 80 metres.[82] However, in later illustrations, but essentially of the same time (seventeenth century) such as the one by Pedro Barreto de Resende annexed to the report of António Bocarro, *Livro das Plantas de todas as Fortalezas, Cidades e Povoações do Estado da Índia Oriental* (Goa, 1635)[83] or by António Mariz Carneiro in its *Descripção da Fortaleza de Sofala, e das mais da Índia, com uma Relaçam das Religiões todas, que há no mesmo Estado*, these constructions are no longer represented there. However, some buildings reported in these illustrations south-east inside the citadel, were identified as the early prison of the sixteenth century (*tronco*). As for the manuscript No. 1471 of the Ducal Palace of Vila Viçosa, (Portugal) edited by Luís da Silveira, it does no longer show buildings at the north-east corner, but at the north-west corner inside the fort[84] (Plate 14.3).

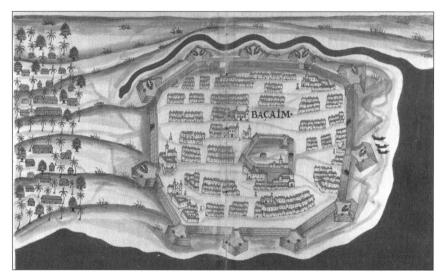

Plate 14.3: Pedro Barreto de Resende in *Livro das Plantas de todas as Fortalezas (1634–1635)* of António Bocarro, Biblioteca Pública de Évora, Ms. CXV/2-1.

According to Bocarro, the Captain lived 'next to the Church of Mercy' (*igreja da Misericórdia*). We know that it was adjacent to the Misericórdia Hospital, built around 1540 near the north-west corner of the walls of the citadel. Finally, a report of the *Archaeological Survey of India* in 1907 reported the existence of two quite distinct layers of masonry visible on some walls of the fort; the lower, judging by its quality would be 'Indian'. Thus, the cylindrical bastion that divides the two walls of the north face, and a part of these walls adjoining the embedded *igreja de Nossa Senhora da Vida* would be of pre-Portuguese origin.[85]

These converging data suggest that the primitive Portuguese fortress was therefore more or less built on the site of the Gujarati fortifications, which would not have been completely destroyed by the Governor Nuno da Cunha. This assumption is quite likely considering how little material resources the Portuguese had in 1536 to build their own fortifications.

The threat of an attack by Malik Tughan gave a boost to the construction plan of the Portuguese fort. The ceremony of setting the foundation stone took place on 26 March 1536 in the presence of the governor; a mass was said in honour of S. Sebastião (to whom the fortress was dedicated) in memory of the day when Nuno da Cunha attacked Bassein (20 January 1533). Gold coins were placed under the foundation stone while *fidalgos* dug the foundations trenches.[86] An inscription *in loco*, sealed in the south-western wall of the fort testifies to the event indicating that the citadel was built in 1536 by Captain Garcia de Sá under the orders of Governor

Nuno da Cunha.[87] In 1537, much of the walls had already been built. In 1538 it lacked only slots (*ameias*); but Captain Garcia de Sá, brother in law of Nuno da Cunha,[88] a victim of intrigues, was arrested and sent to Portugal. His property was confiscated. His successors, António da Silveira and João de Mendonça finished the citadel in three months. In 1539 it was practically over[89] (Plate 14.4).

The geo-political context explains why the work was performed so fast. Fearing an Ottoman intervention in the Indian Ocean—which eventually came to pass with the expedition led by Hadım Süleyman Pacha against Diu in 1538[90]—the Portuguese were committed to hastily strengthening the major Indian ports they administered. To this threat was added another, far more palpable: the troops of Malik Ilias (*Meliqueacem*) launched a series of attacks on Bassein in February 1539. Wooden palisades were erected and ditches dug in the streets, but the Portuguese population—about 300 men—had to take refuge near the Portuguese citadel.[91]

The sketch already mentioned, drawn by Gaspar Correia, gives a hint of what it looked like, and its ruins are still visible in the centre of Bassein. An irregular polygonal structure punctuated by two round bastions at its north-west and south-west corners; a third bastion of the same type divided the north curtain into two portions; a rectangular redoubt—with a wall on which was the inscription of the foundation of the citadel—included the

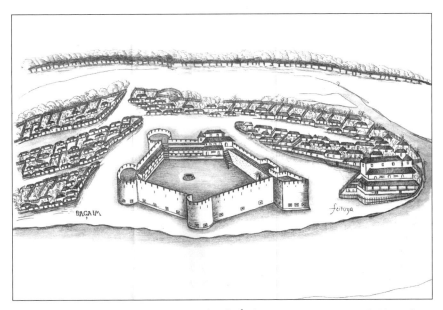

Plate 14.4: From Gaspar Correia, *Lendas da Índia*, Arquivos Nacionais da Torre do Tombo, Lisbon.

main entrance to the south-east (from which the staircase lead up the wall) and an angle (north-east) without bastion (which was probably, as we have indicated, the area of the residence of the captain). Contiguous to the north wall can be seen today overgrown ruins of the church of Nossa Senhora da Vida,[92] which had a direct access from the nave to the citadel. The church overlooked the site of the pillory, where were the city hall (*câmara*) and the charitable institution of *Misericórdia* with its church.

As the fort was somewhat unable to face the rapid Gujarati attacks, and it was necessary to cope with the increase of the Christian population (with consequences on the development of urban area),[93] the growing of the town,[94] and the Crown decided to build much larger fortifications around the S.Sebastião fort.[95] The construction of the new rampart was initiated in 1552 or 1554,[96] and the work was continued until the Maratha conquest of 1739.[97] This imposing defensive structure, providing compromise in a time of transition between tradition and new formalism in military engineering[98] was designed by the Milanese Giovanni Battista Cairati, military engineer in the service of the Portuguese Crown, Chief-Architect (*arquitecto-mor*) of the *Estado da Índia* since 1583, who also designed, among others, the fortifications of Daman (1590) and Fort Jesus in Mombasa (1593).[99] The structure is formed by an enclosure whose walls are on average 9-10 m. high (twice the citadel S. Sebastião) dotted with ten polygonal bastions.[100]

Although these new structures underwent repairs and modifications at later periods (some made by the Marathas in the strongholds of *Elefante* and *S. João*), strategic concerns are patent in the ways walls were fortified and bastions strengthened: the front line along the Ulhoa River between that of *S. Sebastião* (probably the first to be built),[101] and that of the *Madre de Deus*, including bastions of *S.Paulo*, *S. Pedro*, *Elefante* (later of *S. Francisco Xavier* when he became the saint patron of Bassein instead of *S. Sebastião*) and *S. João*, could be defended by the Portuguese squadron (twenty boats fitted with artillery) which monitored the river and the coast washed by the Arabian Sea. The walls are one face and the walkway narrow.

On the other hand, the northern bastions—those of *Reis Magos*, *Santiago*, *S.Gonçalo* to that of the *Madre de Deus*—in front of the *esteiro* and marshy areas which could be swept by artillery from a distance were powerfully fortified with interior buttresses but without double curtain and without obscuring the buttresses. The area most exposed to enemy attacks, and therefore more vulnerable, was located at the west, inland (where the Marathas gave the final assault against Bassein in 1739). Hence, the wall between the bastions of *Reis Magos*, *Nossa Senhora dos Remédios*, *Cavaleiro* (in which is located the 'Land Gate', *Porta da Terra*) and *S. Sebastião* was

Plate 14.5: Walls. *Courtesy:* José Manuel Fernandes, in Couto 1996: 115.

reinforced with a double facing and filled with mortar of at least four metres wide[102] (Plate 14.5).

In the seventeenth century, António de Mariz Carneiro (following António Bocarro, who visited Bassein in 1634) states that the bastions were 'three fathoms, or three fathoms and a half high, while the edges were three to five cubits thick'.[103]

According to several testimonies, the construction of bastions, typical of 'geometricism Mannerist', to maximize crossings fire and defend the corners of the structure,[104] lasted until 1582. The ultimate goal was to push the fortified line to the natural boundaries (the river, the *esteiro* and the sea), enclosing the urban areas that had developed to the north and west. This allowed putting in the protected area major religious buildings that were built later on the periphery of the urban centre.[105]

The rampart was pierced by two main gates, already mentioned: that 'of the Sea' (integrated into the bastion of *S. João*), near the wharf, described in 1726 as 'lying on the beach on the shore of an arm of the river', by the bishop of the Cathedral of Goa, Henrique Bravo de Morais in his *Notícias do Arcebispado* de Goa,[106] and, opposite, that of the 'Earth' or the 'Land' (*da Terra* or *do Campo*) incorporated into the stronghold of *Cavaleiros* in the vicinity of the Franciscan convent.

Like the one that gives access to the interior of the citadel, these doors are double, following the classic 'angled' or 'siphon' types, also implemented in the fortress of Chaul (Fort Revdanda).[107] Some elements of their classic

Plate 14.6: Entrance of 'Gate of the Land' (Porta da Terra). *Courtesy:* Dejanirah Couto, in Couto 1994: 260.

design, such as columns, pilasters, niches and 'Roman' low reliefs at the inner and outer ridges are the result of later restorations (Plates 14.6–7).

Plate 14.7: Detail of 'Gate of Land' entrance. *Courtesy:* Walter Rossa, in Rossa 2010: 165.

The development of shipbuilding and the increase of the surface of the yards (*Ribeira*) determined the opening of several passages (*postigos*) mainly in the southern part of the enclosure overlooking the river: among them the gate of S. *Pedro* (1599) is near the church of S. José; two other ones are near the Hospital for the Poor (*Hospital dos pobres*) (located between the bastion of the *Elefante*, or of S. *Francisco Xavier*, and of S. *Pedro*) and in the vicinity of the Jesuits buildings. The only one we can date (by epigraphy) is S. *Pedro*'s gate: a plaque fixed on the wall says that the works were carried out in September 1599 during the tenure of Captain Francisco de Noronha. The upper part of the inscription bears the papal arms.[108] Another passage, more inconspicuous, gave access to the *esteiro*, east of the city, near the bastion of the *Madre de Deus*. Besides there was a quite sophisticated system of tunnels and secret passages, particularly in the area of the bastion of *Reis Magos*.[109]

Bassein made a strong impact on seventeenth and eighteenth century travellers, Portuguese as well as foreigners. While describing the buildings, many of them attempted to evaluate its surface. For example, according to Father Manuel Godinho (1663) its perimeter was 'thousand geometrical feet'.[110] According to ancient estimations the distance between north and south strongholds amounted to 532 m., and the horizontal axis in the east-west direction to 1064 m. The area within the walls would be 0.5 sq. km.[111] Today we know, thanks to more accurate readings, that the North-South axis (from the extremities of the S. *Pedro* and *Reis Magos* strongholds) measures 621.2 m. and its perpendicular counterpart (extremities of S. *Sebastião* and *Madre de Deus* strongholds), 1038.2 m. Taking into account the outside perimeter of about 3204.9 m., the area is 41 ha., although the overall perimeter without the outline of the bastions is 2,496 m., that is to say, a little more than 39 ha.[112]

On 17 May 1618, Bassein was hit by an earthquake of great proportions, followed by a tsunami (*maremoto*). Most of the buildings were destroyed or badly damaged and casualties were significant. However, reconstruction, carried out quickly enough, gave a new character to the urban tissue from an architectural point of view. Provided with buildings 8-10 m. high, churches with cornices from 12-15 m., and towers of 20-30 m., which rose above the ramparts (which were, as said earlier, 9-10 m. high) the impressive urban complex impressed travellers and could be seen from afar.

Grouped in the north-west of Fort *S. Sebastião* the *Câmara*, the new prison (1639), provided with an arched façade on the ground floor,[113] the *Misericórdia* with its church and hospital of the same name, as well as the pillory, surrounded the main square (*praça*) which served as a crossroads, and the starting point for the alignment of streets.[114] These, with a line drawn in the east-west direction, show a clear intention to rationalize urban space:[115] alternating with some perpendicular paths (*travessas*) they form a dense network. Three of them, in the east-west direction, were particularly important: the main artery of the city called, as in all Portuguese colonial cities from Brazil to Macao, 'Main Street' (*Rua Direita*) linked the main square (*praça*) with the Franciscan monastery situated at the extreme western edge of the city. To the east, the street of goldsmiths (*rua dos ourives*) articulated the Customs (*alfândega*) with the square, as did the S. Paulo street, which, further south, connected the shipyards area (*ribeira*) with the large buildings of the Jesuits; it was the same with its parallel, the shoemakers street (*rua dos sapateiros*).

North of the square, a long street, 'the street of married men' (*rua dos casados*)[116] ended nearby the *Porta da Terra*. It was a parallel to the 'street of the nobles' (*rua dos nobres*). Both crossed the residential district, with the great mansions of *fidalgos*, built in the beautiful stone of Bassein, equipped with deep balconies, arcades and large windows embellished with panes formed (in the fashion of Goa) by translucent sheets of oyster shells mounted on wooden frames (*carepas*). These main streets were paved, which seems unique among Portuguese cities in Asia. Three tanks, probably dating from the period of construction of walls, supplied water (from extramural sources located on the other side of the river), as well as two wells located, the first near the 'Gate of the Sea' (*Porta do Mar*) and the second West of the Customs.

It is not the scope of this essay to detail the history of Portuguese Bassein, including that of the seventeenth and eighteenth centuries,[117] until the Maratha victory, 16 May 1739, won by Chimnaji Apta, one of the best generals of Peshwa Bajirao I, nor beyond: it suffices to recall that Bassein, called Bîjâpûr, was at the heart of the Anglo-Maratha war. In 1774, the Portuguese, then under the government of Sabastiao de Carvalhoe Melo, the Marquess of Pombal (the builder of Lisbon after the great earthquake of 1755), armed a fleet in the hopes of regaining Bassein, but the British East India Company had taken the lead, and it was impossible to compete with the English. Bassein was recovered in 1780, but the Marathas took it over in 1782 (Treaty of Salbai)[118] and Elphinstone took it again only in 1818.

The granting of a sugar refinery (whose furnaces were installed inside the church and hospital of the *Misericordia*)[119] in 1852 to Major Littlewood accelerated the ruin of Bassein. The square was dug in the hope of finding enough water to feed the furnaces. What we see today is a collapsed basin, with muddy and stagnant waters, surrounded by dense vegetation. The factory went bankrupt, but outside of this initiative, the English have contributed much to the destruction of the city: they transformed it into a military depot (1818–30) and dynamited some buildings.[120] The site opened to the public in 1830, was then the victim of other lootings, for reasons related to treasure hunts or search for materials for domestic purposes. Due to these vicissitudes, some inscriptions (out of which are still preserved 100 dated to the sixteenth and seventeenth centuries), were lost. Three of them were important for dating some significant buildings and events related to city life. Unfortunately epigraphic readings leave much to be desired.[121]

In fact, the city was virtually deserted by the Portuguese after the Maratha conquest but had been weakened well before for various reasons, geopolitical as well as military and economic. The wars against the Nizam Shâh (1570-1) and the Sultanate of Ahmadnagar (1593-4 and 1613-15); the raids conducted by the troops of the small kingdom of Mahaved Kolis; the weakening of the network of defensive outposts (Manora, Asserim, among others) which is in the hinterland, protected the territory of Bassein;[122] the onslaught by Omanites, who burned and looted the city in 1661; and finally the successive Maratha attacks (the sardar Moro Pant besieged Bassein in 1674, and Shivaji in 1676 and 1690).[123] This decline culminated with the loss of the port of Kalyan in 1719-20, and got worse with the transfer of the island of Bombay to the British Crown in 1661 who gave it to the East India Company in 1665.[124]

Devastating epidemics (such as in 1719-20) also contributed greatly to its demographic decline. The figures given by some historians being certainly exaggerated, it seems reasonable to estimate its population, in the seventeenth century, as a little over a thousand people, distributed among families of Indo-Portuguese origin, Hindu population, foreigners and slaves. The tombstones unearthed with inscriptions recording distinguished Bassein families confirm this hypothesis.[125]

Despite the many vicissitudes that have marked its history (the last being the 1993 earthquake), which have been briefly mentioned, Bassein survived. Churches, though badly damaged, are still standing, as the citadel of S. Sebastião, walls and tanks. However, other threats are hanging over it. The first is probably the exploitation of offshore gas deposits, which feed the fertilizer industrial complex of the Mumbai megalopolis, the endless coming and going of trucks transporting this gas between Vasai and Mumbai have devastating effects on the foundations of these historic buildings, which will not long withstand exhaust and vibrations caused by the incessant passage of trucks. As such, the parking in front of the *Porta do Mar* is, to say the least, highly questionable.

Moreover, the geographical position of Bassein, at a short distance from Mumbai, will make it a suburb of the city in the near future, with consequences easy to imagine. Although under the auspices of the Archaeological Survey of India, interventions in terms of urban planning, aimed at promoting its attractiveness to tourists (especially since 2007) remain controversial. The opening of an east-west highway in the northern part inside the ramparts led to the destruction of parts of the walls, the construction of two buildings inhabited by customs officials along this way clashes with the coherence of the historical complex, as well as two small temples located in the city centre, and a third one that obstructs the drain of the *Porta da Terra*.[126]

It is vital that authorities urgently launch a campaign of excavations at the site, given the importance of the architectural heritage, essential to understand both the history of modern India and its relationship with colonial powers, as well as the urbanism of colonial cities in Asia and the political, economic and cultural interactions between Europe and Asia in the modern era.

The site has attracted since the nineteenth century some Indian, Portuguese and English scholars, including J. Gerson da Cunha,[127] Joaquim Heliodoro da Cunha Rivara, A. Bragança Pereira,[128] Amâncio Gracias,[129] James Campbell, and especially the engineer Brás A. Fernandes (1881-1951) who published a few guides and studies on Bassein.[130] In 1924, he also drew the first map of the ramparts and the city centre[131] and carried out the epigraphical study of the Bassein inscriptions in the book *Armas e Inscrições do Forte de Baçaim* (1957, re-edited in 1998).

Unfortunately, this ancient literature, sometimes taken uncritically by more recent studies,[132] continues to be a source of errors and has greatly complicated current research; for this reason some assertions are questionable in the absence of an archaeological intervention.

This intervention supported by the building of a local museum for the conservation and exhibition of materials excavated, would have a significant cultural and educational function; it could effectively contribute to regional revitalization focusing on the valorization of the historical and architectural Luso-Indian and Indian heritage.

Notes

1. See for instance the case of Bahrein, excavated under the direction of Monik Kervran: Kervran, Hiebert, Rougeulle 2005.
2. Except for Fort Jesus in Kenya: Kirkman 1974.
3. The riverine beach has become a village of fishermen of the Koli caste, called Vasai Koliwada. See Rossa 2010: 160 (an earlier version of this text was also published under the title 'Baçaim. Sete Alegações para uma Aproximação ao Espaço Físico': Rossa 1999a: 105–23, with a proposed restitution of the plan of Bassein, pp. 122–3).
4. See Teixeira 2010: 20. The etymology of the word has been studied by several Indian authors without any convincing result. See da Cunha 1993: 117 (first edition [1876]); David 1987: 91; De Barros 1995: 41.
5. Deloche 1980: 65, referring to an Asoka edict mentioning it as a dynamic harbour during the Mauryan empire. It is called Sûbâra by Al-Istahirî Ibn Hawqal, Sufâra by Al-Mas'ûdî, Sûfâra by Al-Bîrûnî, Subâra by Al-Idrîsî (see Jean-Charles Ducène in this volume).
6. As in Kondevati (Mahakali), Jogeshwari, Mandapeshwar and Magathan, this big monastic complex located in the island of Salsete is composed of numerous *viharas* cut in the rock. It is mentioned by the Portuguese chronicler Diogo do Couto and by the naturalist Garcia da Orta. The first speaks of 3.000 cells and of the water containment system; the other mentions only 300: do Couto [1788-] 1973-: *Década VII*, Liv.III, chap.X, pp. 238–9; da Orta [1891] 1987: 341. Teaeira 2010: 21.
7. About the political powers that controlled the region, see Teixeira 2010: 22–3.
8. 'Tana' according to Al-Mas'adi, Al-Bîrûnî and Al-Idrîsî: see Jean-Charles Ducène in this volume.
9. Da Cunha 1993 [1876]: 171–8. On Thana urbanism, its mosques and temples see Teixeira 2010: 25. Testimonies in Barbosa 1996: 229–30.
10. Teixeira 2010: 25.
11. Teixeira 2010: 26.
12. Barbosa 1996: 229–30.
13. See Bouchon 1999: 215–25; also her review of Michael N. Pearson, *Merchants and Rulers in Gujarat. The Response to the Portuguese in the Sixteenth Century*,

New Delhi: University of California Press, 1976: Bouchon 1980: 145–58; Wink 2002: 267–8 and for the case of Gujarat, pp. 269–75.

14. About the technical capacities of the boats built at Bassein see Barata 2003: 117–18. According to the governor D. João Castro, the gains from wood trade were an argument for the conquest of Bassein: Letter from D. João de Castro to the Infante D. Luís, [Goa, 30.X.1540], in *Obras Completas de D. João de Castro* III, 1968-1981: 26–30.

15. D'Silva 1997: 94.

16. Betel consumed, at least in the Indian west coast, partly came from the port of Vijayadurg North of Goa, and was sent to Gujarat: Loureiro 2005: 10.

17. The export of rice was particularly important: Teixeira 2010: 343–4.

18. Correia 1975, III, chap.VIII, p. 277.

19. Couto 1994: 259. About horses see Loureiro 2009: 139.

20. About these networks and their trade patterns in general, see Pearson 1976: 7–29; Mathew 1995: 187–95.

21. Aubin 2006: 465–79; Couto 1999: 181–200.

22. In addition to the expedition by Nuno da Cunha, it is worth mentioning that of Diogo Lopes de Sequeira in 1526, of Heitor da Silveira in 1529— also directed against Surat and Reynel—of Lopo Vaz de Sampaio first and António da Silveira later in 1530. See details in Teixeira 2010: 28–9; Couto 1995: 119.

23. Aubin 1971: 4 and Couto 1995: 118.

24. Costa 1991: 131. For the projects concerning Diu see also Subrahmanyam 1999: 54–7 (fn.56 to book V, I. 22).

25. Teixeira 2010: 29.

26. The paradigm is the destruction of the island of Beth, near Diu: Do Couto, 1973- [1788-]. I.Book VII, chap. III, pp. 358–60.

27. Couto 1995: 117 fn. 9.

28. Concerning Nuno da Cunha, see Carvalho 2005: 117–27; Garcia 1999: 123.

29. Teixeira 2010: 30.

30. de Castanheda 1979, II, Book VII, chap. XCVII, pp. 540-2.

31. It should be reminded that the Portuguese settled between 1534 and 1739 in the greater part of what is now the 'Greater Mumbai', except for the island of Mumbai ceded to the British in 1661-5 (on the issue see the last section of this essay).

32. Couto 1995 : 120–2; Couto 1994: 258–66; Couto 1996: 106–18. On the content of the treaty, see de Castanheda 1979, II, Book VIII, chap. C, pp. 734-5; the letter sent by Bahadur to Nuno da Cunha (29 September 1535), which accompanied the treaty has been edited by Alam and Subrahmanyam 2002: 256-7 [Arquivos Nacionais da Torre do Tombo (thereafter AN/TT), *Cartas Orientais,* 31 (*Rabi* II), 942 H /29 September 1535]. On the circumstances of the treaty see also Alam and Subrahmanyam 2002: 248–50.

33. Couto 1995: 119; Mathew 1985: 133–4 (following Portuguese chronicles); Alam & Subrahmanyam 2002: 245-7. On the campaigns of Bahadur, see as well *Medieval Gujarat* 1987; Chaube 1975; Nay 1965. On the conflict against

Silhadi, see Kolff 1990. Description of Humayun progress in Do Couto 1788 [1973], Liv. IX, chap. V, pp. 335–43.

34. Couto 1995: 121.

35. Events related by Do Couto 1788 [1973], Liv. I, chap. IX, p. 101 and by Gaspar Correia (in Almeida 1975: 781, chap. XCV). See as well Subrahmanyam 1998: 147 (exhibition catalogue): according to the chronogram of the Gujarati Wazîr Ikhtiyar Khan (943 н), the 'Sultan al-Bar, Shahîd al-Bahr, reigned during 11 years and 3 months before being murdered by the Portuguese.' The murder is also related by Mullah ʿAbd-ul-Qadir Badaʾuni in the first volume of his *Muntakhab-ut-Tawârîkh* (choice of chronicles) written around 1595, and by the Hadrami chronicler Ibn al-Fakih.

36. On the raids against Bassein at this time, Teixeira 1994: 78–82; on the attacks by Burhân-ul-Mulk, Couto 1993: 89–96. The raid of Burhân-ul-Mulk may correspond to an attempt by Mahmud II (1537–54), the successor of Bahadûr Shâh after the short reign of Mirza Muhammad Zaman, to recover the revenue of the villages of Bassein.

37. The first inventory of lands was done by Simão Botelho between 1546 and 1554. For more detail, see Teixeira 1994: 36–7.

38. *Pragana* or *parganá* may come from Marathe *parganâ*, 'district' (Dalgado 1919–21, II, p. 177). *Caçabé* or *cassabé* is from Arabic *qasba*; *pacaria* or *pacari* may come from Marathi *pakhâdî* denoting the suburban part of an urban area (Dalgado 1919–21, I, pp. 223–4, and II, p. 126). For the subdivisions in general, see the carefully prepared and detailed topography by Teixeira 1994: 38–52. Its districts included roughly Thana (with 3 fortresses) and the island of Salcete. The latter encompassed the islands of Mumbai, Bandra, Mazagan, Elefanta, Caraja and Mahim. In 1537, Agacim, Supara and Sanedivan, Vanguarana and the fortresses of Canguaça and Carnala were added. In 1542, other places in the island of Salcete were appended. Manora and Asserim were transferred in 1556. Couto 1995: 121.

39. In 1663, according to pe. Manuel Godinho, there were about 2,000 villages in the territory of Bassein, an exaggeration. The agricultural area spanned some 60 km. See Costa 1994: 109. On Godinho, Loureiro 1989: 3–27; Afonso 1990.

40. Teixeira 1994: 318–9; see Godinho 1974: 28.

41. Pinto 2003: 25; more generally on the institution, Sá 1997.

42. Teixeira 1994: 320.

43. D. João III gave orders in that sense to *Vigário-Geral* de Goa Miguel Vaz by a diploma dated to 5 March 1546: Couto 1994: 261. Contrary to our first thoughts on the matter (Couto 1994: 261–2, and 1996: 114) the church did not exist yet in 1546. See the letter of the assembly (*cabido*) of the Misericórdia of Bassein, renewing its request to the king for its construction on 30 October 1548 (in *Documentação para a História das Missões do Padroado Português do Oriente*, IV, p. 23). Following the visit to Bassein of archbishop D.Aleixo de Meneses in 1598, the church was restored in 1601. Description of the church in Rossa 2010: 167–8 and Rossa 1997: 61–2.

44. See da Trindade 1964: 100–1, fn. 1.

45. Couto 1994: 261; da Trindade 1964: 104, fn. 1.

46. According to Schurhammer 1992: 252–6, he travelled to Bassein driven by the need to address issues related to the mission of the Moluccas, the mission at Malacca, and the travel to China of his friend Diogo Pereira.

47. Rossa 2010: 161.

48. See the letter of Frei António do Porto to the king (Bassein, 7.IX.1548), in *Documentação*, IV, pp. 60-1.

49. See the letter of Padre Emanuel Teixeira to the brothers in Portugal and Europe [Baçaim, 1.XII.1561] in *Documenta Indica* 1958: 299 (doc.45): 'e *pera que ao lavatorio não tornacem mais os gentios, lhe emficionarão todos os degraos e luguares dele com o samgue e emtranhas de huma vaqua que ali matarão pera lhe comtaminar aquelle luguar.'*

50. *Documenta Indica* X, p. 45 (letter of Gomes Vaz to the General of the Society of Jesus [Goa, 14.XI.1576]).

51. On this point, see 'Tombo da Índia' (1554), edited in *Subsídios para a História da Índia Portuguesa* 1868: 27; Teixeira 1994: 322. On private donation and Jesuit economic interests in Bassein, see Borges 1995: 49–55.

52. Teixeira 1994: 323–4.

53. Teixeira 1994: 326. See table 2, p. 331: '*Rendas jesuítas no território de Baçaim em 1621 em pardaus de Baçaim'.*

54. Teixeira 1994: 325.

55. The church Nossa Senhora da Graça as well was built by the Jesuits. In the correspondence of Valignano, one can find precise information on the construction of the monastic complex. See *Sumarium Indicum* (*Documenta Indica*, XIII, p.1) [08.XII.1577]: '*Il collegio è bem situato vicino al mare et tiene una buona traccia, anchorché non sai finita di fabricare, perché non sonno fatti se non doi quarti, et il 3° com la sua clausura sta anchora per farsi, et dal altro tiene una chiesa molto commoda, grande et capace di una nave, di molto buona architettura, la quale già, sta del tutto finita. . . '.* For political aspects, see Alden 1996.

56. Couto 1994: 262. The church Nossa Senhora da Saúde was built by the Hospitallers of S. João de Deus apparently in 1685.

57. See the map of localization of the buildings in Teixeira 1994: 187, fig.31; Couto 1994: 262.

58. Teixeira 1994: 185.

59. Garcia da Orta praises the *faufel* (areca wood), which was exported to Ormuz. The best one came from Mumbai, but *faufel* was found on the whole territory of Bassein. It was exported as well to Deccan: da Orta 1987, I, p. 326 (col. 22).

60. See the letter of Simão Botelho to the king [Bassein, 24.XII.1548] (AN/TT, CC, I-81-125, edited in *Subsídios para a História*, pp. 4-18).

61. Mathew 1984: 11–20; D'Silva 1997: 94-7.

62. D'Silva 1997: 96.

63. On shipbuilding in Goa, de Carvalho 2008: 123-7.

64. See the letter of Francisco Barreto to the king (Bassein, 6.I.1557) (*Documentação*, VI, p. 26).

65. *Documentação*, VI, p. 95.

66. See Rodrigues 1995: 247-8.

67. Teixeira 1994: 365.

68. *Voyage de Pyrard de Laval aux Indes orientales (1601-1611)*, ed. Castro and Bouchon 1998: 588 and 757. The shipbuilding peak in Bassein occurred in the seventeenth century. Despite the high price of ships, demand was high. The dockyard of the two brothers Rui and Fernão Viegas had a staff of 340 men, Portugueses, Muslims and Hindus: Couto 1994: 265. On the period, see Teixeira 1994: 375–8.

69. Godinho 1974: 29–30. On the diverse types of ships, see Domingues 2004: 252–8 (galleons) and 274 (galliots).

70. Rossa 1997: 64

71. Schurhammer 1992: 253, fn. 203, for the name of some groups in Bassein (from Garcia da Orta 1563): Naitias, Curumbis (Khumbis: peasants), Malis (horticulturists), Parus (Prabhus: writers), Baneanes (Banyans: traders), Deres (Dhers: sweepers).

72. Correia 1975, III, chap. XV, p. 586 (figure of the factory, from the hand of Gaspar Correia, between pp. 688–9). Couto 1994: 262; 1995: 123–4. The factory was abandoned, then later used as a public granary.

73. On the building, beautiful witness of Catholic architecture in Asia, and an inspiration for Daman cathedral (end of 1603) and other churches in Gujarat (Nossa Senhora do Amparo in Thana, 1630) see Moreira 1995: 404 ; Rossa 2010: 160 and 167–8 (description of the church restored in 1601 by the vicar Pedro Galvão Pereira, according to an inscription on the portal, now missing).

74. De Castanheda 1979, II, liv. VII, chap. XCVII, pp. 541–2: the fortifications were not well known in 1529. Heitor da Silveira who had encountered the fleet of Ali Shâh, captain of Bassein, near Thana, had sent one of his men, Cristovão Correia, to assess the defences of the port, before attack. Detailed description of the battle in Correia 1975, III, chap.VIII, p. 277.

75. Malik Tughân, the son of Malik Ayâz, was the brother of Malik Ishaq, both governors of Diu. The *Mirât-I Sikandarî* of Sikandar Ibn Manjhu relates the conflict with his brother. In 1531, he rebelled at Thana after falling from grace. He was however in the service of Bahadur Châh in 1533 and in 1534–5, as captain of Diu garrison (do Couto 1788 [1973] II, p. 273).

76. De Castanheda 1979, II, liv. VIII, chap. LIC, p. 664; Correia 1975, III, chap. XXXVI, p. 465.

77. Correia 1975, III, chap. XXXVI, p. 465. Stakes buried in the sand, with the same purpose, can still be seen around the Portuguese fortress of Fort Jesus, in Mombasa, Kenya.

78. Correia 1975, III, chap. XXXVI, p. 465.

79. Correia 1975, III, chap. XXXVI, p. 474; Couto 1996: 109. According to Castanheda, the mining process took about eight days. Correia does not give information on the duration, but insists on the technics used.

80. Bocarro 1992: 109. '*Esta cidade de Baçaim tem dentro, pegado com a Igreja da Mizericordia, huas cazas onde vive o capitão, com hua serca de ladrilho velha, onde parece que os mouros, cuja foi, se agazalhavão, com hum baluarte*

redondo de pedra, que fica sobre [sic] *o pilourinho, couza pequena e que, por nao ser de momento, se não fas reparar do tempo, que a vay ja arruinando.'*

81. One has to emphasize that the chronicler Gaspar Correia was part of the expedition of Nuno da Cunha in December 1531. He was thus witness of the first Portuguese settlement in Bassein. On his biography see, de Carvalho 2009: 44–5. Fernão Lopes de Castanheda and Gaspar Correia were part of the expedition of the governor to Diu as well (February 1531).

82. Rossa 2010: 164.

83. *Arquivo Distrital* of Évora, Inv. Nr. CXV-2-1.

84. The prison (*cadeia*) of the seventeenth century was built, as the city hall (*câmara*) around 1639: Rossa 1997: 161.

85. Mendiratta, in Mattoso 2010: 165, does not give references for the Archaeological Survey of India report he mentions. See above the description of Bocarro, fn 80.

86. Correia 1975, III, chap. LXXVII, p.689.

87. See Fernandes 1957: 115–16.

88. Garcia de Sá arrived to India with governor Nuno da Cunha's fleet, which had left Portugal on 18 April 1528; do Couto 1973- (*Década Quarta da Ásia,* II, p.308, with fn.57 by Paulo Guinote to Liv.V, I, 46).

89. Correia 1975, III, chap. CVI, p.837; de Castanheda 1979, II Liv.VIII, chap. CXXXIX, pp.795-6; Couto 1996: 111.

90. Couto 1999: 181–200; 1998: 491–500; 2010: 77–96. The Ottoman threat was taken very seriously in 1546 (second siege of Diu) and in the 1550s (attack against Ormuz): see Couto 2011: 145–66 (and documents on pp. 166–75).

91. Those attacks, under the direction of Malik Nasir-ud-Din (*Melique Naçaruto*), continued in 1540, as mentioned in the instruction of the trial of the Ormuz judge (*ouvidor*) Jerónimo Rodrigues, who had been sent to Bassein at the end of 1540 (AN/TT, CCI, I, 74, 4 and CCI, 68, 70 [letter of Sebastião Garcês to the king, from Goa, on 3.II.1540]): Couto 1993: 89 with fn. 6–16. In 1546, rumour had it that Burhân-ul-Mulk (*Bramaluco*) intended to attack Bassein: Schurhammer 1992: 253 and 265.

92. And not the 'church of Mercy'(*igreja da Misericórdia),* on the other side of the square, as in Mendiratta, in Rossa 2010: 165. The description of Bocarro may lead to a confusion between *igreja da Misericordia* and *igreja Nossa Senhora da Vida.* See above.

93. D.João de Castro granted land revenues to the nobles who took part in the second siege of Diu in 1546: Couto 1995: 122; Thomaz 1985: 536.

94. On this, see Teixeira 1995: 337–65.

95. Letters to D.João in the years 1545–6 emphasized the need to improve the defence of Bassein: Couto 1996:111–12. Captain D. Jerónimo de Noronha had a fence and a trench built in 1546 while expecting Burhân-ul-Mulk to attack.

96. Rossa 2010 gives the date as 1554. A letter sent by D. Afonso de Noronha to D.João III [on 16 January 1551] shows that the defences of Bassein were deemed at the time very inadequate (AN/TT, CCII, 242, 44).

97. As in Mazagan (Marocco), the second wall of Bassein was built without a

previous outline: see Rossa 2010: 163 and 1997: 64–5. On the detail for the financial support to the construction by the Crown (and then by Jesuits), see Teixeira 1010: 125–30; Dias 2009: 82–6 makes mention of the letter of Filipe II of Spain (first of Portugal) to the viceroy D. Duarte de Menezes (1586) expressing concern because of the slow progress (p. 82).

98. Rossa 2010: 163.

99. Moreira 1994: 129.

100. Couto 1996: 114; Rossa 2010: 164 draws attention to the fact that the eleven bastions of the documentation (Bocarro) are actually ten, as the bastion *Cavaleiro* is an inside tower, defending to the East, the 'Gate of the Land' (*Porta da Terra*).

101. Couto 1996: 112.

102. Rossa 2010: 164

103. Carneiro 1990: 29. Dias 2009: 83 draws attention to the fact that the bastions had various dimensions: the bastion of *Nossa Senhora dos Remédios* was 3.5 fathoms high, that of *Reis Magos* 3 fathoms.

104. Couto 1996: 114. Compared to previous studies, the identification of bastions was modified according to the documentation. Such is the case for the bastion of *S. Paulo*, which was destroyed by the tide and then restored ('*perdido e quebrado do mar bater nele*').

105. Couto 1996: 112. The progress of the construction (first phase) is stressed by the correspondence of viceroy D. Francisco Coutinho addressed to royal secretary Pedro de Alcáçova Carneiro (AN/TT, CCI,105, 79, letter of 20.XII.1561), as edited by Wicki 1959: 36–89. D. Francisco relates the completion of the wall. The increase of the perimeter of about a hundred cubits was needed to incorporate a lake—in view of supplying the city with fish in case of a long siege. On the phasis of the construction and its progress during the seventeenth century, see Teixeira 2010: 126–32.

106. Couto 1994: 262.

107. On Chaul, Rossa 'Chaul [Revdanda Fort]', *Património*, pp. 92–3 and 96; Mittelwallner 1964.

108. Couto 1996: 112; Fernandes 1954: 88–9 and 22 (nr.120).

109. Rossa 2010: 165. According to the author, it is related to the relocation in this area (where ruins remain) of the second captain's residence. However, in the absence of excavations, it is impossible to determine whether this is indeed the second captain's residence. It does not seem logical that the captain would come to live in this very remote area, far from the city centre and the citadel of S. Sebastião (symbolically very important), even though this sector was adjacent to the vulnerable area (facing the fields). It is also doubtful that the building identified as the residence of the 'General of the North' (two floors with nine gates, arches on the second floor above a large balcony) slightly north of the citadel was the second residence of the captain as stated by other authors.

110. Pe Manuel Godinho, 1974: 27. Among the foreigners were John Fryer and Gemelli Carreri.

111. Couto 1996: 114.

112. Rossa 2010: 164.
113. The location of the 'Money House' has yet to be identified. It was built in 1611.
114. The fishmarket (*Bazar do peixe*) was in the same area, most probably with its own building (still not identified).
115. See da Silveira 1956: 319–28.
116. It took its name from the settlers who were at the basis of the demographic growth of the Portuguese Oriental Empire, established by Afonso de Albuquerque after the conquest of Goa in 1510. The *casados* were at the origin of the Luso-Asiatic society.
117. Generally see Ames 2008: 129–48.
118. In the Salbai treaty signed by Mahaji Sindhia, the Salcete Island was fully given to the EIC. Its possession was confirmed by the Bassein treaty (31 December 1802: Couto 1994: 266; Couto 1996: 116).
119. Fernandes 1954 relates that tombstones were destroyed and a tomb unsealed, with the remains of a man and a horse, separated by a sword. Such information may well be legendary.
120. Couto 1994: 266–7; Couto 1996: 118. In 1921, a report of the Archeological Survey of India (Western Circle) makes mention of this. Rossa 2010: 163.
121. The loss of eight tombstones was mentioned between 1876 and 1905. Among the three most important of them, one was close to the *Porta da Terra*, and two in the vicinity of the *Câmara*. Despite corrections by António Machado de Faria, in the volume edited by Brás A. Fernandes, readings are very inaccurate. Albuquerque 1995: 311–20 did not correct the readings and added some new mistakes. New readings and a proper scientific edition are needed.
122. On these two outposts conquered in 1556, Rodrigues 1995: 254–6.
123. Kulkarni 1985: 957–69.
124. On the context, see Couto 1952; Macedo n.d.: 158–93; Teixeira 2010: 193–202 and 218–25; on the transfer Keay 1991: 131; Santos 1996: 267–78; Dossal 2000: 403–18; Dossal 2000: 855–66; Gomes and Rossa 2000: 210–24; Nobre 2008.
125. According to J. Gerson da Cunha, in 1720, there were 60,000 inhabitants: among them 2,000 were Europeans and 58,000 christianized Hindus. P^e Manuel Godinho had an evaluation of 3,400 souls. Couto 1996: 117. Other sources have between 100 and 400 families, *c.* 1635, and 1,000 Christians, including 300 Europeans, *c.* 1662.
126. Rossa 2010: 164.
127. Da Cunha 1993.
128. Pereira 1935: 97–315.
129. Gracias 1905: 256–65.
130. Among them, 'Os Portugueses em Baçaim', *O Oriente Português* 7-9 (1934-5), pp. 97-315; 'The Last Days of Bassein', *The Indo-Portuguese Review* III (1924-5), pp. 56-9.
131. Brás A. Fernandes, '*Planta da Antiga Cidade e Fortaleza de Baçaim Fundada por Nuno da Cunha em 1536. Conquistada e destruida pelos Maratas em 1739*',

92 × 59 cm., scale 46 mm., Lisbon, Geographical Society, Inv. Nr. *Cartografia* 3-G-36. See the commentary by Rossa 1999: 140–1. The map has been edited in 'Antiquities of Chaul and Bassein', *The Mission Field,* Daman, 1925, pp. 511–32.

132. One example in David 1987: 89–103.

Appendix

The seminar held on 26-8 February 1987, at Girij, Vasai, on the initiative of the Heras Institute of Indian History and Culture, Mumbai, in collaboration with the Indian Council of Historical Research (ICHR), with the presence of the Governor of Maharashtra and researchers from Mumbai, Pune, Goa and Hyderabad, reflected a renewed interest in the historical site. The publication of a selection of papers (Heras Institute Magazine, vols. 45-6, September 1987) provided some insights, but also showed doubts about the reliability of some information. In 1994, the VII Seminar of Indo-Portuguese History, which was held in Goa, helped to systematize some of the information, promoting first thoughts on how to restore the monuments and save the site, which, despite having been listed in 1904, has continued to deteriorate. The necessity to start an archaeological intervention, initiative which does not contradict any restorations of monuments, already underway in 1994 (on the apse of the church of S. António) was then highlighted. Contacts were made on this occasion by the author of this article with INTACH and ICHR.

In 1997, following a proposal by Walter Rossa, the Committee for commemorating Portuguese Discoveries (CNCDP) commissioned Indian architects for a model of Bassein, under the direction of this architect. After some preliminary work *in situ*, the model was started in February 1998 and completed in April of the same year; it was eventually featured in the exhibition *Os Espaços de um Império* (1999)[1] (Plate 14.8).

In 2002, following the publication in Portugal of three articles specifically devoted to Bassein, attention was drawn to the importance of the architectural complex.[2] The Foundation for Science and Technology of Portugal (FCT, Portuguese Ministry of Higher Education and Research) has funded a three-year research project submitted by the *Centro de História de Além-Mar* of the New University of Lisbon, in partnership with the Oriente Foundation (Lisbon and

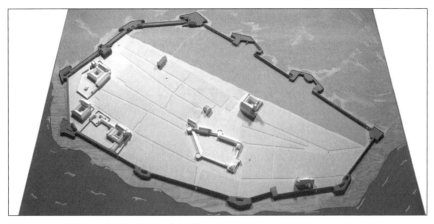

Plate 14.8: Model of Bassein, in Rossa 1999b: 140.

Macao) and the Centre for studies of architectural history at the University of Coimbra, entitled '*Baçaim antes dos Ingleses. A Marca Portuguesa no Território da Península de Bombaim*' (POCTI/HAR/47225/2002) ('Baçaim before the English: Portuguese footprint on the territory of the peninsula of Mumbai'). This project, led by the architect Walter Rossa, was at the origin of several studies reported in the bibliography of this essay. We shall mention, out of the importance of the documentation he collected and the strength of his study, the doctoral thesis submitted by the archaeologist André Teixeira in 2010, which focuses on economic and politico-administrative aspects of the management of the city and the territory.[3]

Beyond the restoration and consolidation of existing buildings, (based on the inventory of visible structures and on a diagnosis about their state of conservation), an excavation of the site might concern (schematically) five areas:

1. The port area, including the shipyards sector (*Ribeira*), the 'Sea Gate' (*Porta do Mar)*, the factory, the customs and the church of S. José.

2. The north and north-east sector inside the citadel of S. Sebastião, its northern bastion and the church of Nossa Senhora da Vida, in the hope of finding, perhaps, traces of the Muslim fortification.

3. The urban centre (*praça*) in the area of the *Misericórdia* and *Câmara* likely to provide more information about the city life, trade, movement of goods, aspects of material culture.

4. The interior of the Franciscan church, whose nave, lined with inscribed Portuguese tombstones, could provide anthropological data on aristocratic elements of the population of the city.

5. One of the dwellings (or more) of the *Rua des Casados* or *Rua des Nobres* would give information about habitat and home furnishings (Fig. 14.1 with legends, 267)

Notes

1. Scale: 1:1500, 18,6 × 151 × 222 cm.; drawing: João Pedro Paiva; direction: Manuel Luciano; executive director and coordinator: *The Bombay Collaborative* (David Cardoz, Rahul Mehrotra and Sandhya Savant); topography and drawing: G.G. Hukkerikar Surveyors and Engineers (Sageer Muckba, Ramola Naik, Kalpesh Solanki and Vandana Agrawal).

2. See Couto and the above-mentioned references.

3. Two studies are forthcoming: Rossa and Mendiratta (in press); Teixeira (in press).

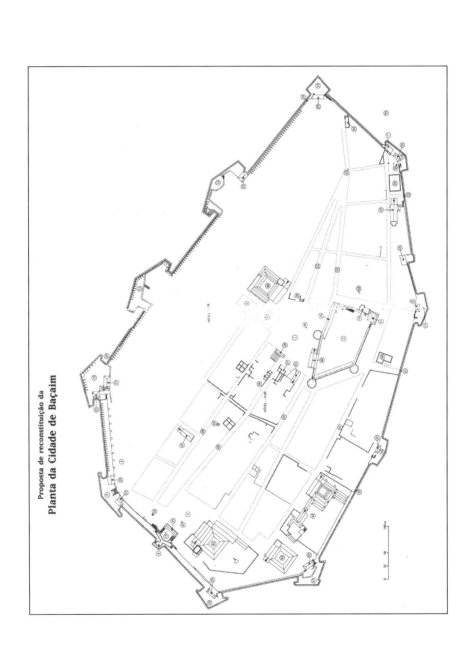

Proposta de reconstituição da
Planta da Cidade de Baçaim

1. Main square
2. Citadel of S. Sebastião
3. Courtyard of S. Francisco
4. Ball play
5. Market
6. Fish Bazar
7. Gate of the Sea (*Porta do Mar*)
8. Gate of the Land (*Porta da Terra* or do *Campo*)
9. Bastion of *Remédios*
10. Bastion of *Reis Magos*
11. Bastion of *Santiago*
12. Bastion of *S.Gonçalo*
13. Bastion of *Madre de Deus*
14. Bastion of *S. João*
15. Bastion of *Elefante*, later of S. Francisco Xavier
16. Bastion of *S. Pedro*
17. Bastion of *S. Paulo*
18. Bastion of *S. Sebastião*
19. Bastion *Cavaleiro*
20 and 21. Passages (*postigos*)
22. Passage of S. Pedro
23 and 24. Passages (*postigos*)
25. Casemates (or bunkers)
26. First residence of the Captain of Bassein
27. Second residence of the Captain of Bassein
28. Palace of the 'General of the North'
29. Town Hall (*Câmara*) and Prison (1639) (*Cadeia*)
30. Pillory
31. Former prison (*Tronco*)
32. Shell's fountain (*Fonte das Conchas*)
33. Well
34. Customs house
35. Factory and later Public Granery
36. Salt house (*Casa do Sal*)
37. Hospital of Misericórdia
38. Hospital for the Poor (*Hospital dos pobres*)
39. Church of S. José
40. Church of Nossa Senhora da Vida
41. Church of Misericórdia
42. Monastery of S. António (Franciscans)
43. Monastery of Nossa Senhora da Anunciada (Augustinians)
44. College of Sagrado Nome de Jesus (Jesuits)
45. Monastery of Nossa Senhora da Saúde (Hospitaller Order of S. João de Deus)
46. Church of S. Gonçalo (Dominicans)
47. Cross of Stone (*cruzeiro*)
48. Street of married man (*rua dos casados)*
49. Street of the nobles (*rua dos nobres*)
50. Main street (*Rua Direita*)
51. Street of S. Paulo (*rua de S. Paulo*)
52. Goldsmiths street (*rua dos ourives*)
53. Shoemakers Street (*rua dos sapateiros*)
54. Gate of the citadel (fort) of S. Sebastião
55. Shipyards (*Ribeira*)

Fig. 14.1: Plan of Bassein, in Rossa 1999a: 122–123.

References

Afonso, John Correia (1990), *Intrepid Itinerant. Manuel Godinho and his Journey from India to Portugal in 1663*, Mumbai: Oxford University Press.

Alam, Muzzafar & Subrahmanyam, Sanjay (2002), 'Letters from a Sinking Sultan', in *Aquém e Além da Taprobana.Estudos Luso-Orientais à Memória de Jean Aubin e Denys Lombard*, ed. Thomaz, Luís Filipe F.R., Lisbon: Centro de História de Além-Mar, pp. 239–69.

Albuquerque,Teresa (1995), 'Epigraphy of Bassein', *Mare Liberum*, vol. 9, pp. 311–20.

Alden, Dauril (1996), *The making of an Enterprise. The Society of Jesus in Portugal, Its Empire, and Beyond 1540–1750*, Stanford: Stanford University Press.

Ames, Glenn J. (2008), 'The Province of the North: Continuity and Change in an Age of Decline and Rebirth, *c.*1571-1680', in *Portuguese Colonial Cities in the Early Modern World*, ed. Brockey and Liam Matthew, Londres: Ashgate Publishers, pp. 129–48.

Aubin, Jean (1971), 'Albuquerque et les négociations de Cambaye', *Mare Luso-Indicum*, vol. I, no. 2, pp. 3–63.

―――― (2006), in Flores, Maria da Conceição, Thomaz, Luís Filipe, Aubin, Françoise, eds., *Le latin et l'astrolabe. Études inédites sur le règne de D. Manuel, 1495-1521,* vol. III. Paris: Centre culturel Calouste Gulbenkian.

Barata, José Alberto Leitão (2003), *Os Senhores da Navegação. O Domínio Português dos Mares da Ásia por Meados do Século XVI,* Cascais: Câmara Municipal de Cascais.

Barbosa, Duarte (1996), *O Livro de Duarte Barbosa (edição crítica e anotada)*, Maria Augusta Veiga e Sousa (éd.), I, Lisbon: Instituto de Investigação Científica Tropical.

Barros, Joseph de (1995), 'A Presença Portuguesa em Baçaim: sua Génese Geo-Histórica', *Mare Liberum*, vol. 9, pp. 41–7.

Bocarro, António (1992), *Livro das Plantas das Fortalezas, Cidades e Povoações do Estado da India Oriental, II.Transcrição,* Isabel CID (transcrip.), Lisbon: Imprensa Nacional-Casa da Moeda.

Borges, Charles J. (1995), 'Jesuit Economic Interests in the Portuguese Province of the North till the mid-18th century', *Mare Liberum*, vol. 9, pp. 49–58.

Bouchon, Geneviève (1980), 'Pour une histoire du Gujarat du xve au xviie siècle', *Mare Luso-Indicum*, vol. IV, pp. 145–58.

――――(1999), 'Quelques aspects de l'islamisation des régions maritimes de l'Inde à l'époque médiévale (xiie-xvie siècles)', in *Inde Découverte, Inde Retrouvée 1498-1630. Études d'histoire indo-portugaise.* Lisbon/Paris: Fundação Calouste Gulbenkian/Comissão Nacional para as Comemorações dos Descobrimentos Portugueses, pp. 215–25.

Carneiro, António de Mariz (1990), *Descrição da Fortaleza de Sofala e das mais da India* (rep. of the illuminated codes 149 of the National Library of Lisbon), Pedro DIAS (éd.), Lisbon: Fundação Oriente.

de Trinidade, Frei Paulo, Conquisto Espiritual do Oriede, Lopes, F. Fetix, ed. (1964), II Parte, Lisbon: Centrode Estudos Hist. ricos Ultramarinos.

de Carvalho, Andreia Martins (2005), 'The King's Agent in the East: the Choice of Nuno da Cunha, Governor of Portuguese India', in Gracias, Fátima da Silva, Pinto, Celsa, Borges, Charles, eds. *Indo-Portuguese History—Global Trends.* Panjim: s/ed., pp.117–27.

de Carvalho, Maria João Loução (2009), *Gaspar Correia e dois Perfis de Governador: Lopo Soares de Albergaria e Diogo Lopes e Sequeira: em busca de uma Causalidade,* MA Dissertation in History Lisbon: Universidade Aberta of Lisbon.

de Carvalho, Patrícia Catarina Sanches (2008), *Os Estaleiros na Índia Portuguesa (1595-1630),* MA Dissertation in History and Archaeology, Lisbon: Universidade Nova.

de Castanheda, Fernão Lopes (1979), *História do Descobrimento e Conquista da India pelos Portugueses,* Manuel Lopes de Almeida (éd.), 2 vols., Porto: Lello & Irmão.

Chaube, Jharkhande (1975), *History of the Gujarat Kingdom, 1458-1537,* New Delhi: Munshiram Manoharlal.

Correia, Gaspar *Lendas da India* (1975), de Almeida, M. Lopes, éd., III. Porto: Lello & Irmão.

Costa, João Paulo Oliveira e (1991), 'Do Sonho Manuelino ao Realismo Joanino. Novos Documentos sobre as Relações Luso-Chinesas na Terceira Década do Século XVI', *Studia,* vol. 50, pp. 121–55.

—— (1994), entry 'Baçaim', in *Dicionário de História dos Descobrimentos Portugueses,* ed. de Albuquerque, Luís, I. Lisbon: Caminho, p.109.

Couto, Adriano José Ernesto (1952), *A Cessão de Bombaim à Inglaterra,* BA dissertation, Lisbon: Faculdade de Letras, Universidade de Lisbon.

Couto, Dejanirah (1993), 'Jerónimo Rodrigues—ébauche d'une carrière orientale', (Série *From Biography to History: Essays in the Social History of Portuguese Asia 1500-1800*) *Mare Liberum,* vol. 6, pp. 89–96.

—— (1994), 'Baçaim, a Capital do Norte', *Oceanos,* vol. 19, no.20, pp. 258-66.

—— (1995), 'Em Torno da Concessão e da Fortaleza de Baçaim (1529-1546)', *Mare Liberum,* vol. 9, pp. 117–32.

—— (1996), 'A Fortaleza de Baçaim', *Oceanos,* vol. 28, pp. 105–18.

—— (1998), 'No Rasto de Hadım Suleimão Pacha: alguns aspectos do Comércio no Mar Vermelho', *A Carreira da India e a Rota dos Estreitos,* Angra do Heroísmo: Universidade Católica Portuguesa, pp. 483-508.

—— (1999), 'Les Ottomans et l'Inde portugaise', in *Vasco da Gama e a Índia: Conferência International/Vasco da Gama et l'Inde: conférence internationale/ Vasco da Gama and India: International Conference,* de Souza, Teotónio R. and Garcia, José Manuel, eds., I. Lisbon: Fundação Calouste Gulbenkian, pp. 181–200.

—— (2010), 'Le *Viaggio scritto per un comito veneziano* et la *descriptio peregrinationis Georgii Huzti*: quelques témoignages sur les équipages de l'expédition de Hadim Süleyman Pasa dans l'océan Indien (1538)', in Bernardini, Michele and Taddei, Alessandro, eds. *Études en l'honneur de Jean-Louis Bacqué Grammont, Eurasian Studies,* vol. VIII, pp. 77–96.

——— (2011), 'Portuguese-Ottoman Rivalry in the Persian Gulf in the Mid-Sixteenth Century: the Siege of Ormuz, 1552', in *Acta Iranica. Portugal, The Persian Gulf and Safavid Persia,* Mathee, Rudi and Flores, Jorge, eds., pp. 145–66 (and pp. 166–75: documents). Louvain: Peeters, 2011.

do Couto, Diogo (1973-), *Da Asia de Diogo do Couto. Dos feitos que os Portugueses fizeram na Conquista e Descubrimento das Terras e Mares do Oriente, (Décadas IV-XII),* Lisbon: Livraria Sam Carlos (from the edition Na Regia Officina Typografica, 1788-).

da Cunha, J. Gerson (1993), *Notes on the History and Antiquities of Chaul and Bassein.* New Delhi: Asian Educational Services (first edition, Bombay: Thacker Vining & Co., 1876).

Dalgado, Sebastião Rodolfo (1919-21), *Glossário Luso-Asiático,* 2 vols., Coimbra: Imprensa da Universidade.

David, M.D. (1987), 'Historic Bassein', *Indica,* vol. 24, no. 2, pp. 89–103.

Day, Upendra Nath (1965), *Medieval Malwa: A Political and Cultural History, 1401-1562,* New Delhi: Munshiram Manoharlal.

Dias, Pedro (2009), *Arte de Portugal no Mundo. India. Urbanização e Fortificação.* Lisbon: Público.

D'Silva, R.D. (1997), 'Ship-building in Portuguese Baçaim, 1534-1739', in *Shipbuilding and navigation in the Indian Ocean Region A.D. 1400-1800,* ed. K.S. Mathew, New Delhi: Munshiram Manoharlal, pp. 94–7.

Deloche, Jean (1980), *La Circulation en Inde avant la Révolution des Transports,* vol. II, *La Voie d'Eau,* Paris: École Française d'Extrême-Orient.

Documenta Indica, Wicki, José s. J., ed. (1958), vol.V, Roma: Monumenta Historica Societatis Iesu.

Documentação para a História das Missões do Padroado Português do Oriente, Índia, Rego, António da Silva, ed. (1992), vol. IV. Lisbon: Fundação Oriente, Comissão Nacional para as Comemorações dos Descobrimentos Portugueses.

Domingues, Francisco Contente (2004), *Os Navios do Mar Oceano. Teoria e Empiria na Arquitectura Naval Portuguesa dos Séculos XVI e XVII,* Lisbon: Centro de História da Universidade de Lisboa.

Dossal, Mariam (2000), 'Continuity and Change: the Portuguese Presence in British Bombay, *c.* 1660-1860', in *Vasco da Gama and the linking of Europe and Asia,* Disney, Anthony R. and Booth, Emily, eds., Delhi, Oxford: Oxford University Press, pp. 403–18.

——— (2001), 'From Bassein to Bombay: Territory, Colony and Property', in *Universo Urbanístico Português 1415-1822. Actas do Congresso Internacional,* Rossa, Walter, Araujo, Renata and Carita, Hélder, eds., Lisbon: Comissão Nacional para as Comemorações dos Descobrimentos Portugueses, pp. 855–66.

Ducène, Jean-Charles (2015), contribution 'The Ports of the Western Coast of India according to the Arabic Geographers', (in this volume).

Fernandes, Brás A. (1924-5), 'The Last Days of Bassein', *The Indo-Portuguese Review,* vol. III, pp. 56–9.

——— (1925), 'Planta da Antiga Cidade e Fortaleza de Baçaim Fundada por Nuno da Cunha em 1536. Conquistada e destruida pelos Maratas em 1739', 92x59 cm., scale 46 mm. Lisbon: Société de Géographie, n° Inv. Cartografia 3-G-36. (Map published in « Antiquities of Chaul and Bassein », The Mission Field, Daman [1925], pp. 511–32).

——— (1934-5), 'Os Portugueses em Baçaim', O Oriente Português, vols. 7-9, pp. 97‑315.

——— (1954; re-ed.1998), Armas e Inscrições do Forte de Baçaim, de Faria, António Machado, ed. Lisbon: Academia Portuguesa de História.

Garcia, José Manuel (1999), 'Os Governadores do Estado da India', Vasco da Gama e a India, I. Lisbon: Fondation Calouste Gulbenkian, pp. 121–3.

Godinho, Pe Manuel (1974), Relaçãodo Novo Caminho (que fez por Terra e Mar vindo) da India para Portugal (no Ano de 1663) ed. Guerreiro, A. Machado, Lisbon : Imprensa Nacional-Casa da Moeda.

Gomes, Paulo Varela and Rossa, Walter (2000), 'O primeiro território: Bombaim e os Portugueses', Oceanos, vol. 41, pp. 210–24.

Gracias, João Baptista Amâncio (1905), 'Antiguidades Portuguezas em Baçaim', O Oriente Português, vol. 2, pp. 256–65.

Keay, John (1991), The Honourable Company. A History of the English East India Company, New York: Macmillan Publishing Company.

Kervran, Monik, Hiebert, Frederik, Rougeulle, Axelle (2005), Qal'at al-Bahrein: a trading and Militay Outpost 3rd Millenium B.C.-17th Century A.D., Turnhout: Brepols.

Kirkman, James. S. (1974), Fort Jesus: a Portuguese Fortress on the East African Coast. Oxford: Oxford University Press.

Kolff, Dirk H.A. (1990), Naukar, Rajput, and Sepoy: the Ethnohistory of the Military Labour Market in Hindustan,1450-1850, Cambridge: Cambridge University Press.

Kulkarni, A.R. (1985), 'Shivaji and the Portuguese', in II Seminário Internacional de História Indo-Portuguesa.Actas, de Albuquerque, Luís and Guerreiro, Inácio, eds., Lisbon: Instituto de Investigação Científica Tropical, Centro de Estudos de História e Cartografia Antiga, pp. 957–69.

Loureiro, Rui Manuel (1989), 'Para uma Nova Leitura da "Relação do Novo Caminho" do Padre Manuel Godinho' (1989), Ler História, vol. 15, pp. 3–27.

——— (2005), 'A Verde Folha da Erva Ardente': o Consumo do Bétele nas Fontes Europeias Quinhentistas', in Mirabilia Asiatica. Produtos Raros no Comércio Marítimo/Produits rares dans le commerce maritime/Seltene Waren im Seehandel, Alves, Jorge M. dos Santos, Guillot, Claude, Ptak, Roderich, eds., vol. II. Wiesbaden: Harrassowitz Verlag, Fundação Oriente, pp.1–20.

——— (2009), 'Portuguese Involvement in Sixteenth Century Horse Trade through the Arabian Sea', in Pferde in Asien: Geschichte, Handel und Kultur. Horses in Asia: History, Trade and Culture, Fragner, Bert G., Kauz, Ralph, Ptak, Roderich, Schottenhammer, Angela, eds., Wien: Verlag der Österreichischen Akademie der Wissenschaftende , pp. 137–43.

Macedo, Jorge Borges (s/d), História Diplomática Portuguesa. Constantes e Linhas de Força. Estudo de Geopolítica. Lisbon: Instituto da Defesa Nacional.

Mathew, K.S. (1984), 'Portuguese Shipbuilding in India', *Quarterly Review of Historical Studies*,vol. 23, no. 4, pp. 11–20.

―――― (1985), *Portuguese and the Sultanate of Gujarat*, New Delhi: Mittal Publication.

―――― (1995), 'Maritime Trade of Gujarat and the Portuguese in the Sixteenth Century', *Mare Liberum*, vol. 9, pp. 187–95.

Medieval Gujarat. Its Political and Statistical History based on Mohammed Ali Khan's Mirat-i-Amadi transcribed in 1822 by Narsain Dass of the Kait Tribe at Ahmedabad (English transl. by James Bird) (1987). Delhi: Indian Bibliographies Bureau, Balaji Enterp.

Mendiratta, Sidh (2010), 'Forte de S. Sebastião', in *Ásia Oceania: Património de Origem Portuguesa no Mundo. Arquitectura e Urbanismo*, Mattoso, José, ed., pp. 165–6.

Mittelwallner, Grittli von (1964), *Chaul. Eine Unerforschte Stadt an der Westküste Indiens*. Berlin: Gruyter.

Moreira, Rafael (1994), 'Fortalezas do Renascimento', *A Arquitectura Militar na Expansão Portuguesa*, Lisbon: Comissão Nacional para as Comemorações dos Descobrimentos Portugueses, pp. 143–58.

―――― (1995), 'From Manueline to Renaissance in Portuguese India', *Mare Liberum*, vol. 9, pp. 401–7.

Obras completas de D. João de Castro, Cortesão, Armando and de Albuquerque, Luís, eds. (1968-81), vol. III, Coimbra: Academia Internacional da Cultura Portuguesa.

Nobre, Pedro (2008), *A Entrega de Bombaim ao Reino Unido (1661-1668)—um processo político-diplomático*, MA in History of the Universidade Nova of Lisbon.

da Orta, Garcia (1987), *Colóquios dos Simples e Drogas da Índia (reprodução em fac-símile da edição de 1891 dirigida e anotada pelo Conde de Ficalho)*, vol. II, Lisbon: Imprensa Nacional–Casa da Moeda.

Pearson, Michael N. (1976), *Merchants and Rulers in Gujarat. The Response to the Portuguese in the Sixteenth Century*, New Delhi: University of California Press.

Pereira, A.B. Bragança (1935), 'Os Portugueses em Baçaim', *O Oriente Português*, vols. 7-9, pp. 97–315.

Pinto, Carla Alferes (2003), 'A Misericórdia de Baçaim (1540-1739)', *Ler História*, vol. 44, pp. 25–43.

Rodrigues, Vítor Luís Gaspar (1995), 'A Organização Militar da "Província do Norte" durante o Século XVI e Princípios do XVII', *Mare Liberum*, vol. 9, pp. 247–65.

Rossa, Walter (1997), *Cidades Indo-Portuguesas. Indo-Portuguese Cities, Contribuições para o Estudo do Urbanismo Português no Hindustão Ocidental/A Contribution to the Study of Portuguese Urbanism in the Western Hindustan*, Lisbon: Comissão Nacional para as Comemorações dos Descobrimentos Portugueses, pp. 61–7.

—— (1999a), 'Baçaim. Sete Alegações para uma Aproximação ao Espaço Físico', *Os Espaços de um Império.Estudos,* pp. 105–23 (with a proposal for the restitution of the plan of Bassein, pp. 122–3), Lisbon: Comissão Nacional para as Comemorações dos Descobrimentos Portugueses.

—— (1999b), *Os Espaços de um Império, Catalogue,* Lisbon: Comissão Nacional para as Comemorações dos Descobrimentos Portugueses, pp.140–1.

—— (2010), 'Vasai Fort (Baçaim/Baçaím/Bassaim/Bassein (India)', in *Ásia Oceania: Património de Origem Portuguesa no Mundo. Arquitectura e Urbanismo,* Mattoso, José, éd., Lisbon: Fundação Calouste Gulbenkian, pp. 158–65.

—— (2010), 'Chaul [Revdanda Fort] (Índia)', in *Ásia Oceania: Património de Origem Portuguesa no Mundo. Arquitectura e Urbanismo,* Mattoso, José, ed., pp. 92–6.

—— and Mendiratta, Sidh (in press), 'Ghost Towns. Ruined and disappeared Portuguese Colonial Settlements in Coastal Maharashtra, India: New Research Results', communication at the *61st Annual Meeting of the Society of Architectural Historians* (Cincinnati, 23-7 April 2008) .

Sá, Isabel dos Guimarães (1997), *Quando o Rico se faz Pobre: Misericórdias, Caridade e Poder no Império Português 1500-1800,* Lisbon: Comissão Nacional para as Comemorações dos Descobrimentos Portugueses.

Santos, Esaú (1996), 'A Cedência de Bombaim aos Ingleses', *Mare Liberum,* vol. 9, pp. 267–90.

da Silveira, Luís (1956), 'A Cidade Ideal do Renascimento e as Cidades Portuguesas da India', *Garcia de Horta, Revista das Missões Geográficas e de Investigação do Ultramar* (numéro special), pp. 319–28.

Schurhammer, Georg S.J. (1992), *Francisco Javier. Su vida y su Tiempo, India, 1547-1549,* vol. III, Gobierno de Navarra, Compañia de Jesus, Arzopispado de Pamplona.

Subrahmanyam, Sanjay (1999), 'O interesse e os projectos da conquista de Diu', in Diogo do Couto, *Década Quarta da Ásia, Edição Crítica e Anotada,* Cruz, Maria Augusta Lima, éd., II, Lisbon: Comissão Nacional para as Comemorações dos Descobrimentos Portugueses, Fundação Oriente, Imprensa Nacional-Casa da Moeda, pp. 54–7.

—— (1998), 'A Crónica dos Reis de Bisnaga e a Crónica do Guzerate: dois Textos Indo-Portugueses do século XVI', in *Os Construtores do Oriente Português,* Flores, Jorge, éd., Porto: Commissão Nacional para a Comemoração dos Descobrimentos Portugueses (catalogue of the exhibition), p. 147.

Subsídios para a História da Índia Portuguesa, Felner, Rodrigo José de Lima, éd. (1868). Lisbon: Typographia da Academia Real das Sciencias.

Teixeira, André (2004), 'Os Primórdios da Presença Portuguesa em Baçaim— 1534-1554: notas sobre a situação financeira e político-militar do primeiro "território" do Estado da Índia', *D. João III e o Império. Actas do Congresso Internacional Comemorativo do Nascimento de D. João III* (2004), Lisbon: Centro de História de Além-Mar, Centro de Estudos os Povos e Culturas de Expressão Portuguesa, pp. 337–65.

Teixeira, André Pinto de Sousa Dias (2010), *Baçaim e o seu Território: Política e Economia, 1539-1665* (Ph.D Thesis), Lisbon: Centro de História de Além-Mar, Universidade Nova de Lisboa.

—— (in press), 'Baçaim, the city and its Hintherland', International Seminar on 'Cities in Medieval India', Delhi: Centre for Historical Studies/Jawaharlal Nehru University.

Thomaz, Luís Filipe F.R. (1985), 'Estrutura Política e Administrativa do Estado da India no Século XVI', *Actas do II Seminário de História Indo-Portuguesa,* Lisbon: Centro de Estudos de História e de Cartografia Antiga, pp. 515–40.

Voyage de Pyrard de Laval aux Indes orientales (1601-1611), de Castro, Xavier and Bouchon, Geneviève, eds. (1998), 2 vols., Paris: Éditions Chandeigne.

Wicki, Joseph (1959), 'Duas Cartas Oficiais de Vice-reis da India, escritas em 1561 e 1564', *Studia*, vol. 3, pp. 36–89.

Wink, André (2002), *Al-Hind: The Making of the Indo-Islamic World*, vol. II, Boston, Leiden: Brill.

CHAPTER 15

Mamallapuram, the Port City
New Revelations

Sathyabhama Badhreenath

The Pallavas who ruled over the northern portions of Tamil Nadu from the sixth to the ninth centuries CE had their capital city at Kanchipuram, well known at that time as an educational centre;[1] Mahabalipuram, also known as Mamallapuram was the port of their kingdom. Situated about 60 km. south of Chennai, Mamallapuram is a much sought-after tourist destination. The area from the present-day Kovalam village southwards to the Palar confluence looks like an ancient estuary which was successfully exploited by the Pallavas for their port city. Just 6 km. to the north of present-day Mamallapuram, at a place known as Saluvankuppam, is a well known cave temple of the Pallavas called Tiger's Cave. This Saluvankuppam, a decrepit coastal village on the east coast today might once have been a part of the large port city of Mamallapuram, which is generally considered to extend from Saluvankuppam in the north to Vayalur in the south with Mamallapuram as the central point (Map 15.1).

The first evidence to the port of Mamallapuram is found in the *Peria Tirumozhi* hymns of Tirumangai Alvar,[2] an eighth century Vaishnava Bhakti saint of Tamil Nadu. Alvar refers to the place as *Kadalmallai* (port of *Mallai*). Earlier evidence to a port in this region is given by *Periplus of the Erythraean Sea*, in the first century CE, while Ptolemy, in the second century CE, refers to a place, Malange, which is identified with Mamallapuram.

Most of the features of Mamallapuram which have survived up to the present-day are undoubtedly the architectural wonders of the Pallava period consisting of low reliefs, monolithic temples, rock cut caves and structural temples. Apart from these, some brick structures of unidentifiable nature have also been reported. However, very little of the port's activity has come to light.

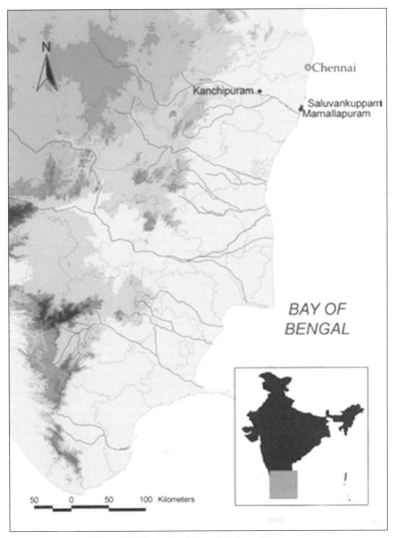

Map 15.1: Location Map of Saluvankuppam.

The Temple Site

The tsunami that ravaged the east coast of India in 2004 exposed an inscription of Krishna III at Saluvankuppam near Mamallapuram, which led to the excavation of a temple dedicated to Subrahmanya. The inscription of Kulottunga III[3] of the Chola dynasty inscribed on the rear side of the boulder, assumed a new implication with the recently discovered inscription of Rashtrakuta king, Krishna III[4] (Plate 15.1).

The temple dedicated to Subrahmanya had undergone numerous changes due to the constant threat of floods; the temple area also progressively

Plate 15.1: General View of the Site before Excavation.

expanded because of religious and ritual needs and finally because of the growth of the village. While these factors contributed to the expansion of the temple, they made the work of the present-day excavator an uphill task, as it is very difficult to identify the various stages of development without destroying the present ruined structure. Accordingly, only wherever possible and required, the structure was disturbed to understand the progressive development of the complex. Besides, the loose sandy soil ensured that stratigraphy occupied a backseat in the excavation. The different phases of structural activity have been defined sequentially, based on evidence within the framework of construction activity at the temple site.

This is the first time that a temple complex evolving from a rudimentary brick structure into a stone construction has been unearthed through excavations in Tamil Nadu.

Phases of Structural Activities

The excavation has exposed multiple occupational levels showing different phases of structural activities. The nature and evidence of the exposed structure reveal that the temple has experienced three phases of construction:

Phase I: Early Pallava period (pre-6th century CE)
Phase II: Sub-phase A Pallava period (c.sixth-eighth centuries CE)
          Sub-phase B Late Pallava period (c.eighth-tenth centuries CE)
Phase III: Chola period (c.tenth-thirteenth centuries CE)

Phase I

The earliest building activity within the temple complex was detected close to the rock boulder. Its shape and location gives it the appearance of a seated elephant keeping watch over the excavation site. Since the rear portion of the boulder evokes the hind part, the structure has been constructed north of it. The complex, as it should have been in its early stages, was a modest one and consisted only of a rectangular structure using bricks of size 40 cm. × 21 cm. × 7 cm. on average, which is characteristic of early structures. In this phase, brick with dressed laterite was used for the foundation. Above the laterite foundation (0.85 m. high), it is likely that only four courses of bricks were laid as excavation evidence revealed only one layer of lime plaster. The laterite foundation comprises a single layer of brick laid on a cushion of river sand. It was a very moderate structure, with a simple rectangular plan [(7.50 m. (east-west) × 8.0 m. (north-south)] and an entrance from the north.

The base of the structure was river sand, over which was laid a layer of bricks of different sizes, some of them reused. The core of the structure was filled with layers of fine sand and silt, chips of laterite and finally pure sand, over which the floor was probably laid. Four courses of dressed laterite blocks were laid as an inner and outer veneer. The intervening core was filled with fine river sand. The outer surface of the laterite wall—the top course and half of the second course—was plastered with lime, with the four courses of bricks above it. Clay was used to bind the lower courses of laterite, as also for the inner wall of the structure. Two pillar bases were placed perpendicular to the laterite wall on the north and in alignment with the centre of the structure. It can be surmised that the entrance to the structure faced north (Plate 15.2).

A redeeming feature was the discovery of a conical vase in the foundation level on the western side, just abutting the laterite. A Roman coin (identified as being of Arcadius, 395–400 CE, with two standing figures and a legend on the reverse) alongside terracotta lamps were found outside the structure on the west, in line with the upper most course of laterite. The find spot just outside the *garbhagriha* can probably help in dating the earliest structure to fifth century CE. A radiocarbon date of 405–564 CE[5] corroborates the other dates.

The use of both a layer of brick and laterite for the foundation is noteworthy, as the porosity of these prevents capillary action, especially in coastal areas.

The first phase of activity in this complex, as stated earlier, was very modest and did not exhibit any of the customary features usually associated

Plate 15.2: Close view of the *garbhagriha*

with a temple. The inner and outer veneer walls of laterite were plain and merely plastered above the foundation levels, in all likelihood more as a protective measure in saline conditions. There are no other indications to establish the nature of this structure. It can be surmised that it was possibly a temple, keeping in mind the inscriptions of the later period. The fact that the temple faces north does not give it pre *agamic* status, as temples dedicated to Subrahmanya, can be north-facing as per the *agamas*.[6]

Phase II

Events surrounding the temple reached its climax during this phase in both building and cultural activities. This level is found at a depth of about 1.90 m. This phase can be categorized into two sub–phases, viz., A and B, wherein some additions and alterations had been carried out to the already existing structure.

SUB-PHASE A

The level was probably raised to 2 m. by adding another ten courses of brick. The brick size remained the same, i.e. 40 cm. × 20 cm. × 7 cm. A *prakara* with a stone-pillared cloister *mandapa* was constructed, enclosing the *garbhagriha* and the large boulder. A *mukhamandapa* was added in the north with four pillars. To accommodate the pillars near the sanctum, the first laterite course was cut into on either side but the alignment of the entrance was not disturbed. Lateral entrances from the east and west were added, though the primary approach was still from the north. Sockets for pillars on the eastern side were possibly meant to support a small *mukhamandapa*.

Plate 15.3: Front view of the main temple.

On plan, at this stage the temple comprised a *garbhagriha,* and a *mukhamandapa* which was enclosed by a cloister *mandapa* and a *prakara* wall (Plate 15.3). All these structures seem to have been plastered with a fine coat of lime plaster, as indicated by patches of plaster. The rise in the level of the temple is directly proportional to the rise in the level of the *garbhagriha* (Plate 15.4). This has been observed with the additional levels in the core, comprising chips of laterite, a thin layer of sand mixed with brickbats, and a layer of sand mixed with clay and brickbats.

Plate 15.4: Inner view of the *garbhagriha.*

Plate 15.5: View of boulder from the south

The floor of the cloister *mandapa* was plastered with lime and its inner side lined with granite. Traces of plaster on the outer surface of the wall (observed east) mean that it was a later addition. The inner portion of the cloister was lined with granite pillars, which along with the *prakara* wall probably supported a tiled roof. The cloister *mandapa* on the southern side had been pierced with an entrance whose lower layer consisted of small boulders (Plate 15.5).

In front of the temple and aligned with the *garbhagriha* (north-south), is a stone spear (*vel*) similar to the one at Arvalem, Goa. As an attribute of Subrahmanya, i.e. (*ayudha*) it has been placed on a square platform constructed with broken bricks 3.40 m. north of the *mukhamandapa*. Shaped like the spear of Subrahmanya, the pillar is 1.60 m. high and fixed at the point where the *dhvajastambha* of the temple is generally located (Plate 15.6). It is made of granite, hexagonal in section and similar in profile to the pillars in the cloister *mandapa*. The uppermost portion of this unique piece is shaped like a spearhead 0.35 m. high and decorated with two rows of *padma*[7] and *urdhvapadma*,[8] respectively. Below is a flat band and a bulbous, curved portion which ends in a flat rectangular base. The entire pillar is a faceted hexagonal with narrow facets at the sides and a broad one at the centre. The lower most part is buried in the brick platform and not dressed. This type of stone spear has not been reported from any temple in Tamil Nadu.

Further north and still in the axis of the main temple is a brick *balipitha* with a *padabandha adhisthana*. It has mouldings like *jagati, tripattakumuda, kantha* and *pattika* and is plastered with lime. A granite stone base has been provided to this structure.[9]

Plate 15.6: View of the stone Vel (Spear).

In this phase, two ring wells with thirteen courses of terracotta rings near the ruined *mahamanadapa* and another adjacent to the *balipitha* were exposed. Fresh potable water trickled out from both wells.

The earliest inscriptions found at this temple and datable to the middle of the eight century of the Pallava period can be associated with this phase. Both refer to a donation of gold to celebrate the festival of *Kartigai* at the temple.

The earlier structure was meticulously modified with bricks of similar size and now exhibits all the features of a temple. The construction of a cloister round the boulder also seems to indicate its sanctity. Considering the rock's that appearance is similar to that of a seated elephant—one of the *vahanas* of Subrahmanya, the cloister *mandapa* might have been constructed around it. The lateral entrances, the *balipitha* and the stone spear might indicate that the temple had now started adhering to the *agamic* injunctions. The reference to a temple dedicated to Subrahmanya in the inscriptions recovered during the course of the excavation, has lent credence to its religious affiliation. The fact that donations were made for *Kartigai* festivities indicates that the temple dedicated to Subrahmanya might have already been in existence and had gained sufficient popularity.

SUB-PHASE B

This phase also records a spurt of structural activity. A general rise in the working level is noticed all around the temple. The cloister level was raised to 2.50 m. high. The lateral entrances, i.e. three steps in stone were added on either side of the main temple. A few broken pillars were converted into steps as seen on the western side. Besides, the front wall of the earlier rectangular structure (*garbhagriha*) was replastered. The cloister floor level was raised and carried a series of stone pillars at regular intervals of approx. 2 m. The pillars are hexagonal in shape and section with a flat centre. Only a few are extant while most of them are broken at the base level and are only about 30 cm. high.

The cloister *mandapa* floor was plastered with lime and was paved with granite on the sides facing the boulder. The floor has on its surface shallow depressions both on the granite and lime sections. The southern entrance to the cloister was closed by packing stone boulders and building a brick wall. Wherever the earlier cloister *mandapa* had collapsed, it was strengthened with stone elements.

On the northern side the *mukhamandapa* of the earlier phase gave way to a new *mukhamandapa* with four pillars about 6 m. from the *garbhagriha*. A proper offset has been provided at the two sides and has provisions for the erection of pilasters. Patches of plaster are also noticed here. Moulded bricks 40 cm. × 20 cm. × 7 cm. have been retrieved from this area. The northern cloister was pierced east and west to make access easier thanks to the lateral steps. The steps have been supported by four courses of brick. On either side of the *mukhamandapa*, two rectangular chambers were added. The chamber on the west has *adhisthana* mouldings, like *jagati* and *tripatta kumuda*, which have been finely plastered. No proper passageway has been provided to this structure. The chamber to the east has three slots, presumably for pillars. The binding medium is unbaked shell lime and the plastering is coarse. At a level lower than the other chamber, it gives easy access to the *mukhamandapa* by a step.

A rammed floor of earth and tiles was seen to the north, within its centre the spear has been placed on a brick platform. A raised platform using broken pillars and stone members has been laid as an entrance to the *ardhamandapa* of this phase.

Most of the inscriptions of the Pallava, Rashtrakuta and Chola periods are associated with this sub-phase, giving reasons to justify that the temple received the maximum patronage. The inscriptions convey information about donations endowed to the temple and are mainly centred on the gift of gold and land for the burning of perpetual lamps that would never go out.

The temple structure did not undergo radical changes in this phase, but some improvements were made, such as the provision of stone steps and the extension of the cloister on the northern side. The *garbhagriha* remained a simple brick structure. The southern entrance of the cloister *mandapa* was closed by filling it up with large boulder stones.

Plate 15.7: View of the Excavated site from the north-east.

Phase III

This last phase of temple activity heralded a new mode of construction as the temple was converted into a stone structure. The dressed stone used is extant on the western side only. This level of activity is found at a depth of 1.20 m. The earlier brick structure was modified both by strengthening the earlier brick activity and by raising the floor level of the temple (Plate 15.7).

The temple plan at this stage was conventional, comprising a *garbhagriha*, *ardhamandapa, mahamandapa* and *mukhamandapa*. The floor of the main temple was paved with stone as evidenced on the western side. The floor of the *garbhagriha* was plastered with lime after the core area had been raised systematically with clay and finally with sand and shell. The stone wall of the sanctum has a brick core (Plate 15.8).

To accommodate the *mahamandapa*, a stone wall running east–west and parallel to the wall of the *garbhagriha* was constructed, which abutted the *mukhamandapa* offsets of phase IIA. The intervening void was filled with brick bats, sand, small chunks of lime plaster, etc. In this cavity a number of potshards like bowls, pieces of grooved tiles, brickbats, stucco pieces, both painted and plain, were found (Plate 15.9). A thirteenth-century inscription was noticed here. The entry points of phase II were filled up with earth and brickbats. The inner stone veneer of the extant *mahamandapa* on the western side was supported at the bottom by broken pillars of the earlier phase. As seen with the extant wall of this stage, the construction pattern comprised plain dressed stone elements such as veneering and brickbats, and stone chips as filling for the core. Material such as pillars, terracotta tiles, and bricks were freely recycled to raise the *mukhamandapa* of the temple. Terracotta tiles were rammed on the eastern and western sides.

Plate 15.8: View of the temple complex.

Excavations exposed intact stone pillars arranged in north-south and west orientations on the western side, as also partially on the northern side. Numerous pillars were traced in the central filling, including inscribed ones of the Pallava rulers Kamphavarman, Nrpatunga, and Chola Rajaraja I; the last two were broken and placed on either side of the stone spear. All of them were found at the same level (1.60 m.). A Chola coin of Rajaraja was also found (Plate 15.10). The spear, which was given prime importance in phase II, was now buried up to its neck portion, though its position and orientation was undisturbed. Radiocarbon dates from this level read 1019–1161 CE, which corroborates the date of the inscriptions and coins.

Another object, the *balipitha*, lay buried beneath a semi-circular and rectangular stone slab which was laid over it, probably signifying the new

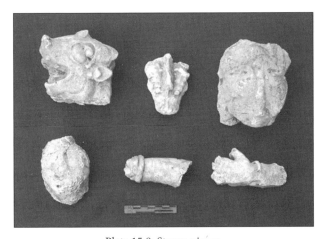

Plate 15.9: Stucco pieces.

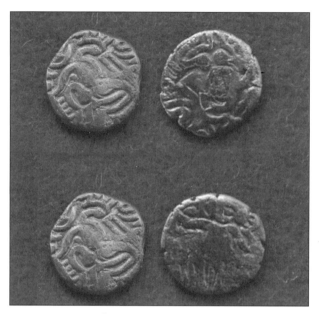

Plate 15.10: Copper coins.

balipitha. The total height of the *balipitha* is 1.25 m. A wall dressed in brick of very poor construction runs north-south for 10 m.

During this phase, the *prakara* wall and cloister *mandapa* were completely buried. The entrance and approach to the temple was restored to its original direction of north. The lateral entrances of phase II were blocked by the walls of the *mahamandapa* of this phase. Further, north of the *balipitha* is a ring well with thirteen courses. On the outer sides, i.e. on the eastern side from the accumulated black soil containing dumps, full bricks (40 cm. × 20 cm. × 8 cm. and 40 cm. × 19 cm. × 6 cm.), bricks with lime plaster, broken stucco figurines, broken terracotta pieces and roofing tiles, terracotta *nandi,* lamps, and votive Siva *linga* were retrieved.

The beginning of stone activity in the temple might be due to the lingering significance of the cult of Subrahmanya. Even during this phase of development, no image was found and no ritualistically aligned development is seen in the *garbhagriha.* A noteworthy feature of this temple is the remarkable modification carried out in the *garbhagriha,* which conceal earlier constructional processes.

A number of stray finds, like stone architectural elements along with inscribed stone pillars were found scattered amidst the sandy accumulation. Since all the architectural members have not been recovered and some look unfinished, it can be tentatively concluded that the temple was perhaps never completed.

As no sculpture has been found so far, one wonders what type of idol was worshipped. The *garbhagriha* too does not betray any religious characteristics. A palm portion of a right hand made of sandstone was found. This could perhaps be symmetrically fixed to a damaged sandstone sculpture found in front of the Atiranachanda cave at Saluvankuppam. Whether this sculpture could have been the presiding deity remains a topic for further research.

Notes

1. *Epigraphica Indica* III, p. 32.
2. Ramaswami 1989, vol. 1: 19-21.
3. *Annual Reports on Indian Epigraphy*, 1890, no. 57.
4. Velanjeri copperplates of Pallava (ninth regnal year, i.e. 884 CE) refers to the temple of Subrahmanya atop the hill at Tiruttani as already in existence when he made some donations to it. However, the earliest inscription in the Kandasami (Subrahmanya) Temple at Tirupporur is that of Pallava Narasimhavarman II.
5. Rajendran et al. 2006.
6. Gopinath Rao, 1998, vol. II: 487.
7. Inverted cyma recta moulding with lotus petal pattern.
8. Minor inverted cyma recta with lotus petal pattern.
9. Noticed in most of temples of the Rajasimha period, for example Shore Temple, Kailasanatha Temple, Kanchipuram.

References

Rajendran, C.P. et al. (2006), 'Evidence of Ancient sea surges at the Mamallapuram coast of India and implications for previous Indian Ocean Studies', *Current Science*, vol. 91, no. 9, pp. 1242–7.

Ramaswami, N.S. (1989), *2000 years of Mamallapuram*, vol. I (Text), New Delhi: Navrang.

Rao, T.A. Gopinath (1998), *Elements of Hindu Inconography*, vol. II, Delhi: Motilal Banarsidass.

CHAPTER 16

The Routes of Early Historic
Tamil Nadu, South India

V. Selvakumar

Theoretical Background

R outes or tracks, which are the means for movement, migration,
dispersal, communication, and connectivity, also facilitate passage of
people, ideas, and goods. For humans, they are the vital lifelines, without
which no culture can flourish. This essay will survey and explore the
communication (trade) routes of Tamil Nadu, south India, during the early
historic period, *c.*300 BCE to *c.*500 CE. In conventional archaeology, routes
do not often get due academic attention, since the focus is on the large 'sites'.
New archaeology of the 1960s and the influence of ideas from geography
have enabled a holistic understanding of the region and the interactions
between humans and their environment as part of the settlement system
studies (Renfrew and Bahn 1991). The settlement system and the landscape
archaeological approaches give due importance to the study of routes.

The loci of human activities on the space could be classified into specific
points, routes, smaller territories, and broader landscapes as practised
in ecological modelling (Gaucherel 2011). Routes, which are linear and
constitute complex networks and link the loci of human settlements and
resources and culturally important sites on the landscapes, form part of the
cultural and natural landscapes. They help a settlement/culture negotiate
and interact with the external world. Routes have specific points, where
cultural memories/beliefs, activities and events are represented through
material remains or symbolic vestiges. They are either created by humans
or associated with the tracks of natural agencies. Routes, which are
essential for a community to exploit natural resources, to interact with the
neighbouring communities culturally as well as commercially, and to fulfil

political, administrative, and religious needs, are the arteries of cultural systems. They are the carriers of cultural stimuli that can lead to social and cultural transformations.

The smaller routes or paths connect a settlement with the resources in the vicinity; the larger routes link the settlements, and the major routes connect the markets and political centres. The size and importance of a route depend upon the nature of the settlements, urban centres and trade activities.

The Study Area: Tamil Nadu

Tamil Nadu is located along the east coast, towards the southernmost part of the Indian peninsula, approximately south of Lat. 13° N (Map 16.1). This region, along with Kerala was known as Tamizhagam in the early historic period, which is enclosed by the Arabian Sea in the west, Indian Ocean in the south and Bay of Bengal in the east.

Geographically, Tamil Nadu has coastal plains and deltas, and sloping terrains with isolated hillocks in the east, and mountainous regions with the Western and Eastern Ghats in the west. The Western Ghats are a major wall-like landmark that separates Kerala from Tamil Nadu. This mountain blocks the south-west monsoon winds, and helps Kerala to get more rainfall than Tamil Nadu. As a result, the western hill boundary of

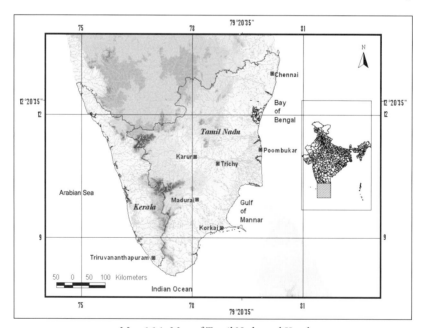

Map 16.1: Map of Tamil Nadu and Kerala

Tamil Nadu and Kerala is green, while a large part of Tamil Nadu is dry. This essay confines itself to the region of Tamil Nadu. The Palaar, Kaaviri, Vaigai, and Taamiraparani are the major rivers of this region, besides there are several small rivers. The Paalakkaad (Palghat), Aaralvaaymozhi and Aramboli Passes connect Tamil Nadu with Kerala; Dimbam Pass connects Coimbatore region with Mysore region; and a few passes connect Tamil Nadu with Andhra Pradesh and Karnataka.

Historical Background

Tamil Nadu was inhabited from about Mid-Pleistocene as revealed by the Lower Palaeolithic artefacts around Chennai (Allchin and Allchin 1982; Pappu 2001, Pappu et al. 2011). Mesolithic/microlithic sites occur throughout Tamil Nadu (Selvakumar 2002; Selvakumar et al. 2012), and the Neolithic culture, which began around c.3000 BCE in south India (Fuller et al. 2007), is represented mainly in the north-western part of Tamil Nadu (Ramachandran 1980).

In Tamil Nadu, settlements began to appear abundantly from the beginning of the Iron Age around 1000 BCE (Rajan et al. 2008), when the Megalithic tradition became popular (Leshnik 1974). The historical period begins around the third century BCE, with the references to the dynasties of the Tamil region, namely, the Cheras, Cholas and Pandyas in the Asokan inscriptions, the Sangam Tamil literature, datable from the first to the third centuries CE (Nilakanta Sastri 1972; Ramachandran 1980) and the Tamil-Brahmi inscriptions (Mahadevan 2003).

The early historic period, between 300 BCE and 500 CE, witnessed the efflorescence of culture and the rise of urban settlements and ports-cum-markets, along the coasts and the hinterland (Raman 1991). In the early historic period, *Ventar* level (chief), pre-state political formations are considered to have co-existed with other forms of social formations (Gurukkal 1989). Tamizhagam contributed greatly to the Indian Ocean trade and exchange network, and pepper and spices from this region went to the Roman Empire and West Asia (Tomber 2008, Selvakumar 2010). Roman coins, imported amphorae, glass and terra sigillata occur in the early historic settlements. The heterodox religions of Buddhism and Jainism came to Tamil country, and were supported by merchants, kings and chieftains, and a section of the society.

In the medieval times, polities such as the Pallavas, Cholas, Pandyas and Vijayanagara and Nayaks controlled this region, until the arrival of the Europeans in the sixteenth century, and contacts with China, South-East Asia and West Asia were very active.

Previous Research

Trade routes have not been focused upon sufficiently in the context of Tamil Nadu, both at macro- and micro-levels. In the Indian context, Nayanjot Lahiri has analysed the trade routes of ancient India (Lahiri 1992). Champakalakshmi (1996) has studied the economy and trade of the early historic and early medieval Tamil Nadu. Rajan (2001) discusses the context of the Early Historic trade patterns and suggests the possible routes that existed in Tamil Nadu. Thiyagarajan (2006, 2009) has researched the medieval routes of Tamil Nadu. Darsana (1997) has studied the megaliths of the Palar basin as markers of landscape and routes based on Tilley's (1994) phenomenological approach. These publications very briefly discuss the routes in general, there is no specific study available on the routes of the early historic period.

Sources

The sources for the routes of early historic Tamil Nadu consist of archaeological, epigraphical, textual, and ethnographical evidence. Direct archaeological evidence for the routes, i.e. the actual roads, is very little. Because of historical continuity, the ancient routes are still in use or often pass nearby modern highways. As a result of current use, developmental activities, and poor visibility, unlike the archaeological mounds, ancient routes are not archaeologically traceable. But indirectly, the location of settlements, Roman coin hoards and Tamil-Brahmi inscriptions suggests the existence of ancient routes. The routes of later periods also offer clues to the ancient routes. In a rare instance, a portion of a medieval route is preserved near Sundaikkamuttur, west of Coimbatore near the Palghat gap (Poongunran 2005; Pers. comm. 2011).

Epigraphs form an important source for studying the highways of the Medieval period, i.e. after the fifth century CE (Thiyagarajan 2006). The early historic inscriptions have their locational value, although they do not have direct references to routes.

Sangam Tamil literature, especially the texts of *aarruppatai* genre (Zvelebil 1974; Ramanujan 1996) have several references to the ancient routes. The ancient Tamil epic *Cilappathikaaram* (*Silapathikaram*) graphically describes the routes that existed in the early historic period.

Ethnographic data does help to reconstruct the routes, as many of the ancient routes are still in use. Often along the ancient routes, sacred sites and occasionally dilapidated *chattirams* (rest-houses) of later periods exist.

Tamil Literary Genre: *Aarruppatai* literature

In ancient Tamil country, bards or wandering poets sung in praise of the chiefs and received donations. *Aarruppatai* is a category of literature that guides a bard, who is in need of gifts or blessings for his survival, to the location of a patron, who could be a king or god. This literature describes the generosity of chieftains in offering gifts, and the routes to reach his palace. *Porunaraarruppatai*, *Perumpaanaarruppatai*, *Thirumurugaarrupatai* and *Cirupaanaarruppatai* are the important texts of this genre in Tamil, datable to the early historic period. *Thirumurugaarrupatai* guides the devotees to the abodes of the god Murga, and *Porunaraarruppatai* talks about the Chola king Karikaalan. The *Cirupaanaarruppatai* and *Perumpaanaarruppatai* are very useful to understand the ancient routes and the cultural scenario along the routes and at the settlements.

Perumpaanaarruppatai guides the poet from the port of Neerpeyarru, located on the east coast (identified with Mamallapuram) to the palace of Tondaiman Ilantiraiyan at Kanchipuram. It beautifully describes the scenes along the route and the lifestyles of various communities, such as the fishermen on the coast (*Neytal*), farmers (*Marutam*) and hunters of the dry (*Paalai*) region, and also at the port of Neerpeyarru and the town of Kanchipuram.

Similarly, *Cirupaanaarruppatai* guides the poet to the court of Nalliyakkodan, who was the chieftain at Kidangil. It mentions the settlements of Eyirpattinam, Velur, and Amur along the route to Kidangil, which is identified with Tindivanam.

Some of the details offered in the literature could be exaggerated, but a few of the narratives certainly reflect the reality, which could not be reconstructed through archaeological remains.

Early Historic Routes of Tamil Nadu

The Early Historic period had a vast network of main routes linking interior Tamil Nadu with other parts of India, and the coastal ports that connected to the Indian Ocean regions. A few of the important, main routes are discussed below, though there existed many other minor routes which are not discussed here in detail.

The river Kaaviri flows from the Mysore plateau in Karnataka to north-western and central parts of Tamil Nadu, and joins the Bay of Bengal near Kaaviripoompattinam. The central and lower parts of the Kaaviri basin witnessed the emergence of Iron Age settlements around 1000 BCE. The route between Kaaviripoompattinam and Uraiyoor (Uraiyur), respectively,

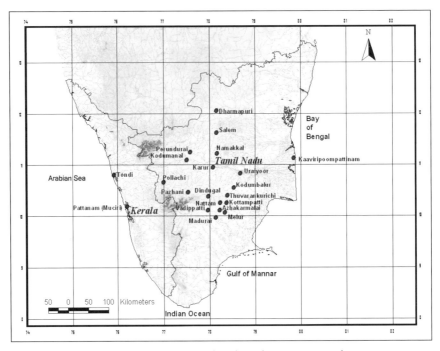

Map 16.2: Map of Central Tamil Nadu with Important Settlements
connected by Main routes.

the port and capital of the Cholas, who controlled the Kaaviri delta, was
an important highway that went along the banks of the river Kaaviri to
Karoor, the Chera capital and to Muciri and Tondi, the ports of Kerala
(Map 16.2).

Uraiyoor, a part of Tiruchirappalli, has evidence for the early historic
period (Raman 1988). Kaaviripoompattinam has important architectural
remains such as the wharf and a Buddhist *vihara* of this period
(Soundararajan 1994). Tamil literature mentions that sea incursions
destroyed the town—also substantiated by underwater explorations
conducted here (Sundaresh et al. 2004; Tripati et al. 2004).

This highway, which passed through the northern bank of the Kaaviri
to reach Uraiyoor, is described in *Cilapathikaaram*, a Tamil epic datable
to the fifth century CE. This epic presents the story of the hero Kovalan,
who belonged to a merchant family and his devoted wife Kannaki.
Kovalan along with his wife leaves Kaaviripoompattinam for Madurai
in search of a better livelihood. The route travelled by the couple from
the gates of the Kaaviripoompattinam enroute to Madurai is vividly
portrayed (*Cilapathikaaram*, Canto 10). After crossing the town gate, they
worshipped at the Vishnu temple and the Buddhist monastery and then

walked 'past a grove to the north of fertile Kaaviri, they trudged a mile and entered a bower' (*Cilappathikaaram*, Pillai 1989: 35). Here the distance to Madurai is mentioned as 5 × 6 = 30 *kaatham*. *Kaatham* is a traditional unit of linear measurement. The distance between Kaaviripoompattinam to Madurai via Uraiyoor is approximately 240 km. Thus, the distance of a *kaatham* could be around 8 km. (cf. Deloche 1994: 603). Could the monastery mentioned here be the Buddhist *vihara* (Soundararajan 1994) excavated at Pallavaneswaram? Potholes on the path, due to the digging of roots by food-gatherers, the rural scenes of farmers plucking weed and throwing them on the field boundaries, ponds in between the fields of rice and sugarcane, red-eyed buffaloes wallowing in soft-mud and the Brahmin settlements are described in detail. The couple reached Thiruvarangam (Sri Rangam), the river island in the Kaaviri near Thiruchirappalli and then crossed the river on a watercraft to reach Uraiyoor.

This route, which passed north of the Kaaviri, must have crossed through Mayilaaduturai, Aaduturai, Kumbakonam, Umaiyalpuram, Swamimalai, Thillaisthanam, Thirukkattuppally, Kovilady, Thiruvanikkaval and Thiruvarangam (Map 16.3). These sites or their vicinities have early historic and/or early medieval remains. Several settlements occur south of the Kaaviri; therefore, while the main trade route must have passed north of the Kaaviri, many ferry points (or *thurai*) existed along the Kaaviri for crossing.

Uraiyoor was a major junction of the Kaaviripoompattinam-Uraiyoor-Perur route, a southbound route towards Madurai and beyond, and the northbound route towards Karnataka. The route between Uraiyoor and Karoor, the Chera's inland capital, passed through the southern bank of the Kaaviri (Map 16.4). Karoor has been excavated and brick architecture,

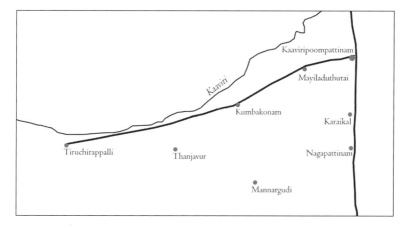

Map 16.3: Kaaviri Valley Highway—Kaaviripoompattinam-Uraiyoor

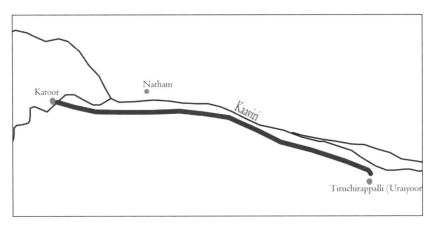

Map 16.4: Kaaviri Valley Highway—Uraiyoor-Karoor

Roman coins, and amphora have been found (Nagaswamy 1990). The early historic settlements of Thirukkampuliyur and Alagarai (Mahalingam 1970) and Aivarmalai with Tamil-Brahmi inscription (Mahadevan 2003) are located along this route.

The route from Karoor to Mysore and Karnataka connected western and northern India with Tamil Nadu (Map 16.5). It linked the early historic Tamil-Brahmi sites of Pugalur, Araccalur, and Erettimalai adjacent to the river Kaaviri; it deviated west from Perundurai, which has black-and-red pottery, and via Avanashi (*IAR* 1961–2), Gopichettipalayam, and Sathyamangalam, and perhaps crossed the Dhimbam Pass to Mysore.

Another route from Karoor crossed Naamakkal, via Salem and Dharmapuri, and went to Karnataka. It is attested by the milestones of a later-day highway Athiyamaan Peruvazhi (Athiyaman Highway) mentioned in the inscriptions of the thirteenth century CE (Deloche 1994). Mohanur (*IAR* 1961–2: 26) and Kulattuppalayam (Roman coin site) along this route yielded early historic archaeological evidence.

Karoor was the junction of major routes linking all cardinal directions. It was connected with Kerala across the Palakkad Gap through the sites of Kodumudi, Nathakkadaiyur, Kodumanal, Sulur, Vellalur, and Perur along the river Noyyal. This route reached the ports of Kerala, e.g. Muciri and Tondi (Map 16.6).

Kodumanal (Rajan 1994; Kelly 2009; Subbarayalu 2009) was an important settlement of craftsmen and traders with pottery inscriptions of Tamil-Brahmi, rouletted ware and evidence of ornament manufacturing. Peroor (Shetty 2003), Sooloor, which yielded Roman coins, and Vellaloor, which produced 650 Roman coins and jewellery, are the important settlements along this highway. This region has produced the maximum

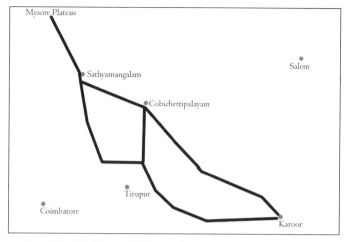

Map 16.5: The Kaaviri Valley Highway—Karoor to Mysore Plateau

amount of known Roman gold coins (Turner 1989), which suggests its commercial significance.

Kaarradumpaarai near Sundakkaamuttur (10°57′ 25″ N; 76° 55′ 29″ E) produced a Tamil-Vattezhuttu rock inscription of Rajakesari identified with Aditya I Chola (871–909 CE). This is the earliest and only highway inscription in Tamil Nadu.

Padiyoor near Gangeyam was a major source of beryl stones and crystalline formations that were used for ornament manufacturing (Rajan and Athiyaman 2004). An alternate route from Peroor, via Palladam, Kangeyam, Vellakovil to Karoor might have also existed. In Kerala, Muciri is identified with Pattanam located close to Paravur (Cherian et al. 2007).

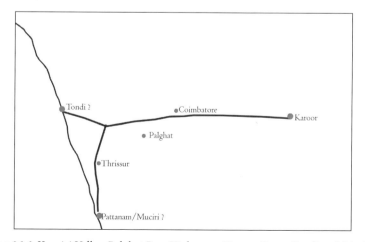

Map 16.6: Kaaviri Valley-Palghat Pass Highway—Karoor-Perur-Tondi and Muciri

Uraiyoor (Thiruchirappalli) was connected with Madurai, the capital of the Pandyas, who controlled the southern parts of both Tamil Nadu and Kerala (Map 16.7). A major commercial centre, Madurai is described in the Sangam text of *Maduraikaanchi*. Madurai has early historic evidence at Pazhangaanattam and Kovalanpottal. *Cilappathikaaram* beautifully portrays the nature of this route. When Kovalan enquires of a Brahmin about the way to reach Madurai, the Brahmin replies, 'after crossing the hills and rocks in the dry region, you come to a junction which looks like a trident' (Canto 11, line 64). Here the junction of three routes like a trident is mentioned around Kodumbalur. The middle route went via Thuvarankurichi, Nattam, and Azhakarmalai, where the presence of a Vishnu temple on the hill is mentioned. Another route crossed via Kottampatti, Meloor and east of the Anaimalai hill. The western route passed west of the Sirumalai hill via Vaadippatti.

Alagankulam, located near the mouth of the river Vaigai, was an early historic port-cum-market that had connections with the Roman trade (Shetty 2003) (Maps 16.8–16.9). This is one of the nearest ports to Madurai and it has evidence of amphora, terra sigillata, and Roman coins. An important route that connected Madurai and the site of Alagankulam passed close to the bank of the river Vaigai.

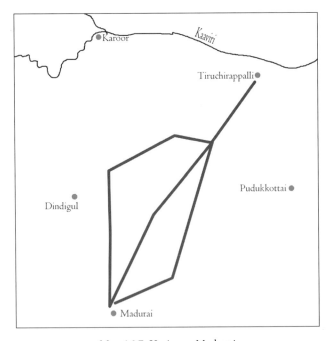

Map 16.7: Uraiyoor-Madurai

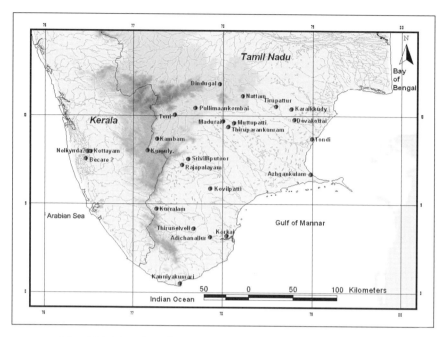

Map 16.8: Map of Southern Tamil Nadu with Important Settlements connected by Main Routes.

Muciri/Muziris on the Periyar River was the port of the Cheras, who controlled central Kerala and western parts of Tamil Nadu (Casson 1989). Pattanam in the Periyar delta, considered to be a part of Muciri, has produced evidence for Roman as well as other artefacts (Shajan et al. 2004, 2008; Cherian et al. 2007). Roman coin hoards have been found around the site.

The route from Madurai to Muciri (Map 16.10) crossed through the settlements/hillocks of Thiruparankunram, Muttupatti, Kongarpuli-yankulam, Mudalaikkulam, Vikkiramangalam and Amanamalai, all of which have rock shelters with Tamil-Brahmi inscriptions (Mahadevan 2003: 25) (Map 16.8). This route connected Pullimaankombai where a hero-stone with Tamil-Brahmi inscription was found (Rajan et al. 2006). An inscription at Muttupatti mentions the name of a merchant from Muciri, which suggests that traders used this route. From Teni, it crossed the Western Ghats near Bodinaayakkanoor, which yielded a hoard of Punch marked coins (Vanaja 1983). Through Adimaali, Kothamangalam, Perumbaavoor, and Aluvaa in Kerala, it must have reached the region of Muciri. From Kothamangalam, the waterway on the Periyar river would have also been used in addition to the land route.

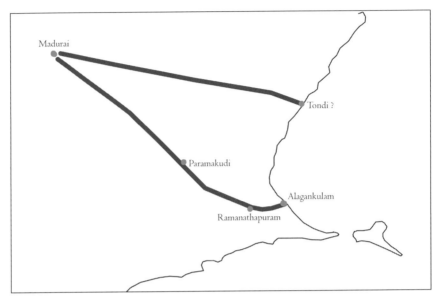

Map 16. 9: Vaigai Valley Route—Alagankulam-Madurai

Becare and Nelkynda were the ports/marts south of Muciri in Kerala mentioned in the *Periplus* (Casson 1989). Their exact identification is uncertain, but these towns are placed around the Kottayam-Alappuzha region, which was controlled by the Pandyas, due to its trade importance. Madurai was linked to these ports from Teni to Kambam-Kumuly. This area has Megalithic sites and Roman coin evidence (Maps 16.10–11).

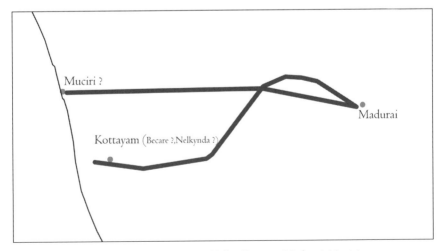

Map 16.10: Vaigai-Periyar Valley Route—Madurai-Muciri

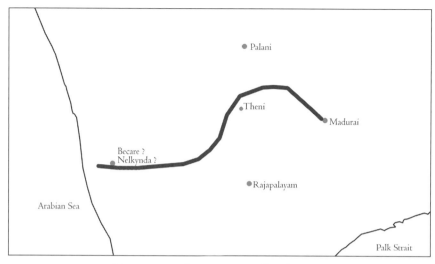

Map 16.11: Madurai-Becare-Nelkynda Route

A route connecting Madurai and Kerala via Pazhani existed in the south-western part of Tamil Nadu. It went through Nattam-Oddan-chattiram-Naykkarpatti-Kozhumam-Udumalaipet-Pollachi (Map 16.12). After Pollachi, it must have reached Palakkadu via Perur, and also directly to southern and central Kerala through Kollengode. Many Megalithic burial sites are found along this route. The famous Megalithic site of Porunthal lies close to it (Subramanian 2010). There are two routes to this region, one via Nattam east of the Sirumalai hill, and another via Vaadipatti west of the Sirumalai hill.

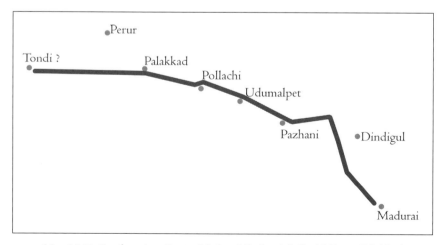

Map 16.12: Southwestern Route: Madurai-Pazhani-Pollachi-Perur-Palakkad

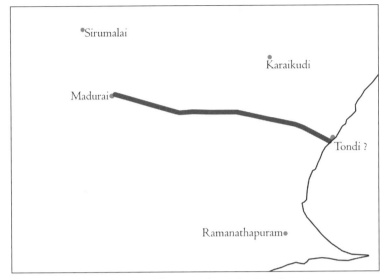

Map 16.13: Madurai-Tondi, on the East Coast.

A branch of this highway must have connected with Karoor and further north directly from Dindugal, which appears to be an important highway junction. Traders and Jainism from Karnataka and further north must have reached Tamil Nadu through this route.

The port of Tondi, on the east coast, was connected with Madurai via Tirupattur, Karaikkudy, and Devakottai (Map 16.13). This route linked the Madurai-Uraiyoor highway at Nattam. The sites of Sittannavasal, Mankulam, Keezhavalavu, and Mangudy lie along the route that connected Madurai with Pudukkottai region.

The Pandyan port of Korkai near the mouth of Tamiraparani was an important centre for pearl fishery and shell bangle industry. It was connected with Madurai perhaps via Aruppukkottai. Korkai has evidence for Roman amphora and rouletted ware (Nagaswamy and Majeed 1978). There was also a route linking Madurai with the Thirunelveli region and Kanniyakumari in the south via Kovilpatti (Map 16.14). There exist several Megalithic burial sites along these routes.

Korkai was obviously connected with the interior region of the Tamiraparani valley via Korkai-Adichanallur-Kurralam-the Western Ghats-Kerala along the river Tamiraparani (Map 16.15). This port must have exported the spices that came from the Western Ghats and Kerala. Adichanalloor and Kurralaam have yielded Megalithic burials and a rich variety of artefacts.

Apart from the routes that touched the coastal ports, and interior towns, there existed highways linking the interior regions along the foothills of the

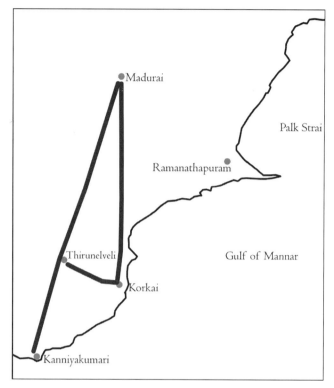

Map 16.14: Madurai-Korkai-Thirunelveli-Kanniyakumari.

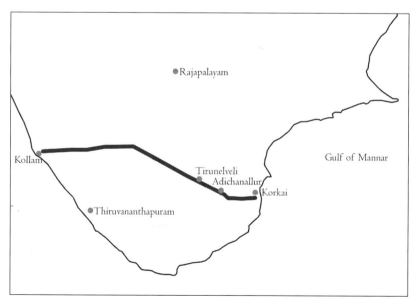

Map 16.15: Korkai-Adichanallur-the Western Ghats.

Western Ghats. Several megalithic settlements and the Roman coin hoard at Nattappatti near Rajapalayam Sri Villiputuur suggest this.

Coimbatore region was connected with the northern and south-eastern parts of Tamil Nadu (Maps 16.16–17). A route connected with the Palakkad gap via Peroor-Tiruchengodu-Rasipuram Aattur-Viruddhachalam-Vadaloor-Cuddalore. Another route led via Kallakurichi-Thirukkovaloor to Arikamedu, the port with Roman trade connections (Wheeler et al. 1946; Begley et al. 1996, 2004). Thirukkovaloor was the capital of the Malayaman kings. This route must have passed via Thiruvennainalloor, and Thiruppathirippuliyoor, which are sacred (*devaaram*) sites sung about by Saivaite saints.

Thirukkovilur was connected with Thiruvannamalai and Chengam, which has numerous hero-stones (Rajan 2000), via Harur-Uttangarai-Krishanagiri. This must have connected Tamil Nadu with the Kolaar region in Karnataka region, and further north.

This route is discussed in *Perumpaanaarruppatai*. It connected the port of Vasavasamudram north of the Palar and/or Mahabalipuram with Kaanchipuram, adjacent to the bank of the river Palar via Thirukkazhukunram, Chengalpattu (a Megalithic burial site), Thirumukkootal, which is a sacred site, Waalaajabaad and Kaanchipuram. From

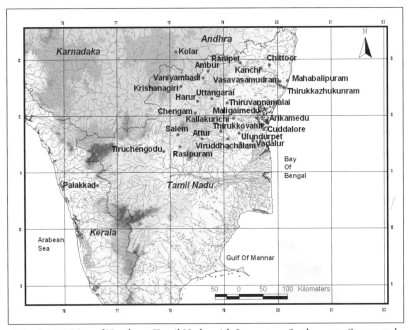

Map 16.16: Map of Northern Tamil Nadu with Important Settlements Connected by Main Routes.

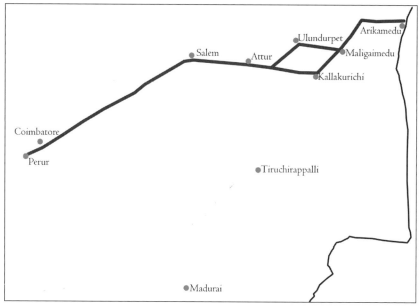

Map 16.17: Perur-Salem-Attur Pass-Kallakurichi-Ulundurpet-Maligaimedu-Arikamedu.

Kaanchipuram via Thirupputkuzhi, Raanipet, Kottanatham, it reached Chittoor in Andhra Pradesh following the river Ponnaiyar (Map 16.18). Another route perhaps went via Gudiyattam and the Peranaampattu Pass to Andhra. This route further proceeded to Ambur, Vaniyambadi to Krishnagiri, and connected with Kolar as well as the Andhra region.

The coastal ports of Tamil Nadu such as Mayilapur, Vasavasamudram, Arikamedu, Kudikkadu, Kaaviripoompattinam, Tondi, Alagankulam, Korkai, and Kumari were linked by a coastal sea-route. A coastal highway

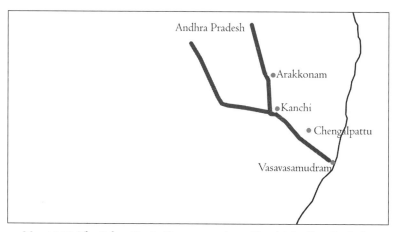

Map 16.18: The Palaar Route-Vasavasamudram-Kanchi-Andhra Pradesh.

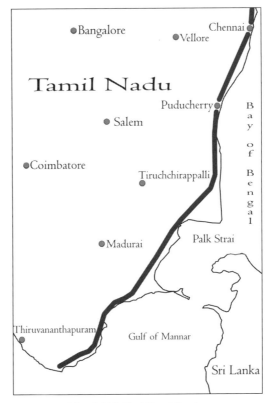

Map 16.19: East Coast Route.

over the land adjacent to the coast must have linked these ports. Perhaps the crossing of the river was facilitated by the ferry points at regular intervals. The Tamil Nadu State Highway 49 (the East Coast Highway) now passes through this section.

Natural and Cultural Features along the Routes

Apart from the cultural markers, natural hillocks and trees also served as landmarks on the land routes, a few of which are discussed below. Routes could be categorized, based on their size, into: (a) single tracks meant for the movement of a single person (Plate 16.1), (b) larger, main tracks meant for vehicle movement (Plate 16.2). In terms of volume of traffic, they could be classified into: (1) small tracks linking two villages, (2) medium-sized tracks linking two regions, (3) larger tracks linking major political regions or towns. The last category of routes could be classified as highways, known as *peruvazhi* (larger routes) in Tamil. Although the routes are often labelled 'trade routes', they were used for various purposes.

Plate 16.1: A single person's track, Porpanaikottai, Pudukottai District.

Plate 16.2: A cart track, near Pudukottai.

Natural Features

Rivers

'*Vazhi*' means path or passage and also 'to flow' in Tamil. '*Aaru*' means river (*Madras University Tamil Lexicon*, p. 259), and also path or ways of life (Subrahmanian 1966: 97) in Tamil. This is because the courses of rivers and streams also acted as paths for animals and humans (Plate 16.3).

Plate 16.3: A course of stream used as path by animals and humans near
Thiruppaththur.

In prehistoric times, humans moved along the course of the rivers and
streams, since walking on the plains with bushes and scrubs would be very
difficult. The dry passage without water is mentioned in the Sangam Tamil
text of *Ahanaanooru* (75: 8–9). Perhaps rivers and streams, in addition to
the tracks created by animals, gave prehistoric humans the idea of a path.
The prehistoric groups used the streams as their pathways and located
some of their camps close to waterways or streams. This is well attested by
the recent excavations at the Palaeolithic site of Pillayarpatti (Selvakumar
et al. 2012). Rivers in fact determined the location of the settlements in
Tamil Nadu, which is generally dry. This explains why many of the tracks
are within the course of the rivers and streams or just very nearby. River
mouths had additional importance, since they facilitated the location of the
port towns, and thus the coastal and riverine routes met at these localities.
Medieval inscriptions do mention such *peruvazhi* (e.g. Thirukkattalai Siva
temple inscription, *IPS* no. 38, p. 18, fig. 23), often while referring to land
boundaries. A Late Medieval Vijayanagara inscription in the same temple
mentions Rajarajan Peruvazhi (*IPS* no. 714, p. 492). This suggests that the
peruvazhi perhaps did not have a name in the early Chola period and in the
later Chola period the highway was named after the Chola king Rajarajan
(Plate 16.4).

Plate 16.4: Thirukkattalai inscription mentioning about Peruvazhi.

Hillocks

Hillocks and mountains serve as points of importance on the landscape (Plate 16.5), because of their visibility. The hills have water resources, rock shelters and in addition, as landmarks they guide travellers to a particular spot. Along the Madurai-Muciri route such hillocks, which also had Jain monasteries, exist.

Plate 16.5: An Isolated hillock near the dolmen site of Mallasandram, Dharmapuri District.

Passes (Churam)

Churam in Malayalam refers to the pass between hills and the tough curvilinear paths for climbing. *Churam* and *arunchuram* (*Ahanaanooru* 35, 53) are mentioned in the Tamil literature as difficult locations along the paths. In Tamil, *churam* refers to dry, desert tracts. The Tamil term for mountain pass is *Kanavaai*. Some of the modern villages near such passes have been named as Kanavaaipatti, in which 'patti' refers to a settlement.

Trees

Naturally grown as well as planted, trees formed an importance place for the resting of animals and contemporary hunter-gatherers choose such trees for camping. It is common to find such trees along the routes, and such spots bear the names of trees, below which sometimes Buddha or Ganesha images or hero-stones exist. Trees with good canopies are very important in the tropical region of India. The emperor Asoka too planted trees to facilitate the movement of people on the highways.

Cultural Features and Communities

Apart from the natural landscape features, cultural features and communities are intimately associated with routes.

Settlements

Settlements are the key targets of routes. Settlements of various kinds, such as small villages, towns, ferry points, pilgrim centres, markets, and ports are linked by routes.

Sacred Spots/Burials/Hero stones

Sacred sites are also common along the routes. The presence of Jain caves at Amanamalai, Muttupatti, and Vikiramangalam near Madurai suggests this. Many of the Saivaite Devaram sites of medieval Tamil Nadu are linked by routes, which were used by pilgrims. The Buddhist *vihara* and Siva temple at Pallavaneeswaram on the route to Kaaviripoompattinam are good examples for this.

In the early historic period, hero-stones were erected for the warriors who died for common cause. The Sangam texts mention that such hero-stones had names of people inscribed on them. They continued to survive in the Medieval period. Some of these hero-stones are located close to the highways. The *Ahananooru* poems mention that people would often try going close to hero-stones (*Ahananooru* 297: 6-10). Another poem mentions hero-stones that were damaged by the movement of the bullock carts of the traders. Such stones were erected on the highways to popularize the deeds of the warriors. The hero-stone of Pullimankombai is located close to the Madurai-Muciri route.

River Crossings/Ferry Points

In Tamil, river crossing points are called *turai*, the equivalent of *pattanam* in Prakrit. Many such settlements near the river mouths were called *munturai*. These points existed along the rivers and sometimes close to the routes and at times, when a river lay across a route. Thiruvarangam-Uraiyoor crossing was an important ferry point across the river Kaaviri. Such points had boats and boatmen associated with them, who help the travellers to cross the rivers (Plate 16.6).

Junctions (*Kavalai*)

Junctions are meeting points between two or more branches of roads. *Kavala* in Malayalam refers to the junction of two, three or more roads (Burrow and Emeneau 1984: 129, 1325; *Ahanaanooru* poem 53, Manikkanar 9: 286-287) mentions that the crossing such roads is risky. The term for a fork-like shape is *kavalai*; referring to a road similar to the shape of a 'Y'. A trident-like point (road junction) is mentioned in *Cilappathikaaram*. Such points on highways also served as diversions to settlements located off from the main routes.

Plate 16.6: A small watercraft (coracle) on the Kaveri, Bhavani Kuduturai
for crossing river.

Head-load Bearers

In rural Tamil Nadu, a major feature of the highways of the yesteryears was head-load bearers or *sumaithaangi* (Tamil) or *chumaduthangi/attaani* (Malayalam) (Plate 16.7). *Sumai* or *chumadu* means head-load and *taangi* means bearer or supporter. They are made of stone slabs with a horizontal slab supported by two vertical stones. They are erected in memory of women who passed away during pregnancy. These stones were used by travellers for rest during their journey. They could keep their head-loads on these stones, and continue their journey by shifting head-loads directly on their head without the help of a third person. Such monuments also occur in Kerala. Nowadays, many have been destroyed due to developmental activities. It is not clear when such monuments were introduced in Tamil Nadu, but some of them appear to be two or three hundred years old. Kerala has several villages with the name *attaani*.

Chattirams/Resthouses

Resthouses of the Modern period (post-sixteenth century), called *chattirams* (choultery) and *mandapams* (halls) occur along the ancient trade routes. Many such *chattirams* which were in use until the early twentieth century are found in dilapidated conditions. They point to the existence of old trade routes.

Plate 16.7: A *sumaitaangi* of 1979 near Pudukkottai.

Tanks and Wells

Sometimes tanks and wells were dug by people along the routes for the benefit of travellers and animals.

Milestones/Signposts

It is not clear if the milestones existed in the early historic period, but they did exist in the Medieval period. Milestones are called *Kaathakkal* as they denoted the distance between places in terms of an ancient measurement unit called *kaatham*, which is considered to be equal to 6.7 km., according to Manikkam and Kandasamy (1995: 83), while others place it around 8 km. (cf. Deloche 1994: 603). Several such milestones are found along the highways. Two milestones dateable to the thirteenth century are found in Dharmapuri district of Tamil Nadu. One milestone at Gengipatti near Maatlampatti has an inscription in Tamil (Plates 16.8–9), which reads:

Athiyamaan Peruvazhi Naavarthaa
valattukkukk k
aatam 27

'Athiyaman Highway, the distance to Naavarthavalam is 27 Kaatham'.

Another milestone referring to the same highway, found east of Dharmapuri, mentions that the distance is 29 *kaatham* to the same destination (Manikkam and Kandasamy 1995: 82–3). The stones have the

Plate 16.8: A Thirteenth-Century Milestone near Maatlampatti.

Plate 16.9: The Plate 16.8 as cup marks on the Thirteenth-Century Milestone near Maatlampatti.

distance written as numerals and also as symbols with large circles carved to mark the numeral ten and small circles to mark the numeral '1'. Perhaps this system was adopted to enable people, who were not literate, to understand the distance. Naavarthavalam is a place, which has not been identified; it must be in the northern side, as indicated by the direction of the location of these milestones.

In addition to the milestones, inscriptions as at Sundaikkmuttur (Plate 16.10) and merchant guild inscriptions are found in Tamil Nadu.

Vehicles of Transport

Bullock Carts

Bullock carts were used extensively for transport. Graffito of bullock cart occurs on the Megalithic pottery (Gurumurthy 2001). They are also depicted in the rock shelter at Edakkal in Kerala. Salt traders (*Umanars*) used such carts frequently, according to the literature. A seal impression of a chariot has been found at Arikamedu (Sidebotham 1996). The kings of the Sangam Age owned horse-drawn chariots. Animals were used for carrying loads.

Plate 16.10: Inscriptions on the Rajakesaripperuvazhi.
Courtesy: Tamil Nadu State Archaeology Department.

Donkeys/mules

Beasts of burden were also used for transporting goods. The Sangam poem *Pattinappalai* (186) mentions pepper bags carried by donkeys to the port of Kaveripoompattinam.

Water Crafts

Water crafts were used in the river crossings. *Odam* (boat) was a craft, and *Parisal* (coracle, Plate 16.6) was also perhaps used in the rivers for small scale transport.

Communities and People

Traders

Traders were a dominant group of this period; and they are considered to be responsible for the introduction of script in Tamil Nadu. The Sangam texts frequently describe how the hero and heroine are separated when the former goes in search for wealth. This implies that trade and associated movements were common activities of this period. The names of poets in Sangam literature and their names in Tamil-Brahmi inscriptions from the rock shelters suggest there was active movement of traders across the landscape.

Caattu

A group of merchants that travelled together is called *caattu* in Tamil. The traders were known as *caattuvan*. Such groups moved on bullock carts and camped along the routes. They had guards to protect them from robbers.

Highway Robbers

In the early historic period, the routes crossed the *Paalai* (dry) region, which was infested with highway robbers as attested by the Sangam poems. The robbers attacked the passerby and also the merchants.

Yavana Guards

The traders employed *Yavana* (Westerners/West Asians) guards to protect them from the highway robbers, as revealed from the Tamil literature (Singaravelu 1966).

Salt Traders

Umanars, salt traders, frequently moved on the highways. Their bullock carts were driven by women and they carried monkeys along with them. Their camps and ways of life are described in detail in the Tamil texts (Singaravelu 1966).

Monks and Pilgrims

The arrival of Jainism and Buddhism in Tamil Nadu did have an impact on the social formations, and the traders supported these religions actively. The Jain monks, because of the respect that they commanded in the society, indirectly offered protection to the travelling merchants, who had to face the highway robbers. The sacred centres also perhaps emerged around the shrine of Murugan on the hills. In *Cilapathikaaram*, the Brahmin from Maankaadu reports he was visiting the Vishnu shrine at Thiruvarangam, which reveals that people also travelled for religious purposes.

Discussions and Conclusions

The routes served as arteries linking the early historic settlements; the main routes connected the capitals, commercial centres and ports. The routes enabled the movement of commodities produced in the settlements, and people for social and cultural purposes. The boost in the Indian Ocean trade around the beginning of the Common Era contributed to the rise of urban centres and the active use of routes in this region. Human movement of this period was remarkable, as all kinds of groups were travelling. There are frequent references to the heroes travelling, leaving their wives at home, in search of wealth in the Sangam poems, which suggests the intense involvement of people in trade activities. The crossing/passing of the *churam* (pass) is always spoken of with dread in the literature. Adventurous people who were involved in trade by reaching the markets and urban centres of faraway regions could make a lot of wealth. This must have encouraged people to involve themselves in commercial activities.

Geographical features definitely contributed to the location of settlements and highways. Rivers and hills to some extent determined the location of the settlements and thus influenced the routes too. Some of the routes were probably the paths used from the prehistoric times by people for foraging and migration; the development of permanent settlements and urban centres converted them as main routes.

Historical continuity is seen in the use of ancient routes. Many of the ancient highways have medieval vestiges and sacred centres and even modern national or state highways nearby. Routes of the early historic period were named after the destination town or a particular geographic region. Only in the medieval period, the routes were named after the kings and their size, especially width, was demarcated and defined, as land used for cultivation was precious for cultivation and taxation purposes.

In the early historic period, there is little evidence for state intervention in the development of trade routes. In some areas, perhaps taxes were collected, and protection was also offered. In the medieval period, when the state formation was very active, the kings named the highways after their names, as known from the case of Rajakesaripperuvazhi. Here the chiefs established their authority over the landscape by naming the highways. This indirectly suggests that the interference of the political formation was comparatively limited in the early historic period.

Overall, travel to settlements, resource locations, urban centres, markets, manufacturing centres, the places of the chiefs and places of worship in search of economical, spiritual and social satisfaction was frequent and common. The wealth that moved on the routes tempted a few foraging groups to rob the traders. Travel and travellers (target for plunderers) became a means of survival, and on occasion a search for peace (pilgrimage). The routes contributed to the cultural dynamic and transformations of the region.

References

Allchin, B., and F.R. Allchin (1982), *The Rise of Civilization in India and Pakistan*, Cambridge: Cambridge University Press.

Begley, V., and R. D. De Puma, eds. (1991), *Rome and India: The Ancient Sea Trade*, Delhi: Oxford University Press.

Begley, V. et al. (1996), *The Ancient Port of Arikamedu: New Excavations and Researches 1989-92*, vol. 1, Pondicherry: École Française d'Extrême-Orient.

—— (2004), *The Ancient Port of Arikamedu: New Excavations and Researches 1989-92*, vol. 2, Pondicherry: École Française d'Extrême-Orient.

Burrow, T. and Emeneau, M.B. (1984), *A Dravidian Etymological Dictionary*, 2nd edn., Oxford: Clarendon Press.

Casson, L. (1989), *The Periplus Maris Erythraei* (Edited with an English translation), Princeton: Princeton University Press.

Champakalakshmi, R. (1996), *Trade, Ideology and Urbanization: South India 300 BCE to AD 1300*, New Delhi: Oxford University Press.

Cherian, P.J., V. Selvakumar and K.P. Shajan (2007), 'The Muziris Heritage Project: Excavations at Pattanam', *Journal of Indian Ocean Archaeology*, vol. 4, pp. 1-10.

Darsana, S. (1997), 'Protohistoric Investigations in the Upper Palar Basin, Tamil Nadu', Poona: Ph.D. Dissertation submitted to the University of Pune.

Deloche, J. (1994), 'Itinerary Measures and Milestones in Thirteenth century Tamil Country', in *Pandit N.R. Bhatt Felicitation Volume*, Filliozat, P.-S., Narang, Satya Pal, Panduranga, C. eds., Delhi: Motilal Banarsidass, pp. 597-604.

Fuller, D., N. Boivin and R. Korisettar (2007), 'Dating the Neolithic of South India: new radiometric evidence for key economic, social and ritual transformations', *Antiquity*, vol. 81, pp. 755-78.

Gaucherel, C. (2011), 'Introduction to tools for spatial analyses', paper presented at IGBP PAGES PHAROS Workshop on *Land-cover reconstructions in the monsoon affected Tropical world: Pollen modelling approach and data synthesis*, held from 27-9th January 2011. French Institute, Pondicherry, India.

Gurukkal, R. (1989), 'Forms of production and forces of change in ancient Tamil Society', *Studies in History*, vol. 5, no. 2, pp. 159-75.

Gurumurthy, S. (1999), *Deciphering the Indus Script*, Chennai: University of Madras.

IAR = *Indian Archaeology: A Review*, New Delhi: Archaeological Survey of India.

IPS = Inscriptions of Pudukkottai State.

Kanakasabhai Pillai, V. (1966), *The Tamils Eighteen Hundred Years Ago*, Tirunelveli: SISSW.

Kelly, Gwendolyn O. (2009), 'Craft Production and Technology during the Iron Age to Early Historic Transition at Kodumanal', *Tamil Nadu. Tamil Civilization* 23 (October-December), pp. 1-14.

Lahiri, Nayanjot (1992), *The archaeology of Indian trade routes up to c. 200 BC: resources use, resource access and lines of communication*, New Delhi: Oxford University Press.

Leshnik, L.S. (1974), *South Indian Megalithic Burials: The Pandukal Complex*, Wiesbaden: Franz Steiner Verlag.

Mahadevan, I. (2003), *Early Tamil Epigraphy: From the earliest times to the sixth century AD*, Harvard Oriental Series, 62. Cre-A: Chennai.

Mahalingam, T.V. (1970), *Report on the excavations in the Lower Kaveri Valley (Tirukkampuliyur and Alagarai), 1962-1964*, Madras: University of Madras.

Manikkam, R. and Kandasamy, A. (1995), 'Kaatha Thooram', *Avanam*, vol. 6, pp. 82–3.

Nagaswamy, R. (1990), *Roman Karur*, Chennai: Tamil Arts Academy.

—— (1991) 'Azhakankulam: An Indo-Roman Trading Port', in *Indian Archaeological Heritage, K.V. Soundara Rajan Felicitation Volume*, Margabandhu, C. et al., eds., New Delhi: Agam Kala Prakashan, pp. 247–54.

Nagaswamy, R. and A.A. Majeed (1978), *Vasavasamudram*, Madras: Tamil Nadu State Archaeology Department.

Narayanan, M.G.S. (1977), 'Cattle Raiders of the Sangam Age', *Proceedings of the Indian History Congress, 38th Session held at Utkal*, Utkal University, Bhubaneshwar, pp. 70–82.

Nilakanta Sastri, K.A. (1972), *Sangam Literature: Its Cults and Culture*, Madras: Swati Publications.

Pappu, S. (2001) *A Re-examination of the Palaeolithic Archaeological Record of Northern Tamil Nadu, South India*, Oxford: British Archaeological Reports.

Pappu, S., Gunnell, Y., Akhilesh, K., Braucher, R., Taieb, M., Demory, F., Thouveny, N. (2011), 'Early Pleistocene presence of Acheulian Hominins in south India', *Science*, vol. 331, pp. 1596–9.

Pillai, R.S. 1989, *Silapathikaram* (trans.), Tamil University, Tanjore.

Poongunran (2005), *Coimbatore Mavattakkalvettukal*, Chennai: Tamil Nadu State Archaeology Department.

Rajan, K. (1994), *Archaeology of Tamil Nadu (Kongu country)*, Noida: Book India Publication Company.

—— (2000), *Hero Stones of South India*, Thanjavur: Manoo Pathippakam.

—— (2001), 'Recent Advances in Early Historic Archaeology of Tamil Nadu', in *Kaaviri: Studies in Epigraphy, Archaeology and History*, Rajagopal, S., ed., Chennai: Panpaattu Veliyittakam, pp. 229–47.

Rajan, K. and N. Athiyaman (2004), 'Traditional Gem Cutting Technology of Tamil Nadu', *Indian Journal of History of Science*, vol. 39, no. 4, pp. 385–414.

Rajan, K., N. Athiyaman, M. Rajesh, and M. Saranya (2005), 'Excavations at Thandikudi, Tamil Nadu', *Man and Environment*, vol. 30, no. 2, pp. 49–65.

Rajan, K., V.P. Yatheeskumar, and S. Selvakumar (2006), 'Pulimankombai Sangakala Nadukarkal', *Aavanam*, vol. 17, pp. 1–5.

—— (2008) *Catalogue of Archaeological Sites in Tamil Nadu* (2 vols.), Thanjavur: Heritage India Trust.

Ramachandran, K.S. (1980), *Archaeology of South India: Tamil Nadu*, New Delhi: Sundeep Prakashan.

Raman, K.V., ed. (1988), *Excavations at Uraiyur-Thiruchirapalli 1965-69*, Madras: University of Madras.

Raman, K.V. (1991), 'Further evidence of Roman trade from coastal sites in Tamil Nadu', in *Rome and India: the Ancient Sea Trade*, Begley, V. and De Puma, R.D., eds., New Delhi: Oxford University Press, pp. 125–33.

Ramanujan, A.K. (1996), *Poems of Love and War (from the Eight Anthologies and Ten Long Poems of Classical Tamil)*, New Delhi: Oxford University Press.

Renfrew, C. and Bahn, P. (1991), *Archaeology: Theories, Methods and Practice*, London: Thames and Hudson.

Selvakumar, V. (2002), 'Hunter-gatherer Adaptations in the Upper Gundar Basin', *Asian Perspectives*, vol. 41, no. 1, pp. 71–102.

—— (2010) *Tamil Cultural Connections across the World*, Thanjavur: Tamil University

Selvakumar, V., Rajaguru, S.N. and Jhaldiyal, R. (2012), 'Palaeolithic occupation of southern Tamil Nadu, India: New evidence from south of the river Kaveri', *Quaternary International*, 269, pp. 74–86.

Shajan, K.P., R. Tomber, P.J. Cherian, V. Selvakumar (2008), 'The external connections of Early Historic Pattanam, India: the ceramic evidence', *Antiquity Online*, vol. 82, no. 315, March 2008 http://antiquity.ac.uk/Projgall/tomber/index.html.

Shajan, K.P., Tomber, R., Selvakumar, V., and Cherian, P.J. (2004), 'Locating the Ancient Port of Muziris: Fresh Findings from Pattanam', *Journal of Roman Archaeology*, vol. 17, pp. 312–20.

Sidebotham, S. (1996), 'The Chariot Seal Impression', in *The Ancient Port of Arikamedu: New Excavations and Researches 1989-92*, Begley, V. et al., vol. 1, Pondicherry: École Française d'Extrême Orient, pp. 389–90.

Singaravelu, S. (1966), *Social Life of the Tamils: Classical Period*, Kuala Lumpur: University of Malaya.

Soundararajan, K.V. (1994), *Kaveripattinam Excavations 1963-73: A Port City on the Tamil Nadu Coast*, Delhi: ASI Memoirs.

Subrahmanian, N. (1966), *Pre-Pallavan Tamil Index*, Madras: University of Madras.

Subramanian, T.S. (2010), 'Great Past in bright Colours', *Frontline*, vol. 27, no. 20, 25 September-08 October, 2010.

Subbarayalu, Y. (2009), 'Visaki kuviran', in *Early Historic Tamil Nadu c 300 BCE-300 CE*, Chennai: Kumaran Book House, pp. 95–122.

Sundaresh, Jayakumar, S., Gaur, A.S., Chandramohan, P., Jena, B.K. (2004), 'Submergence of Poompuhar—Study based on underwater explorations and coastal process', in *Third Indian National Conference on Harbour and Ocean Engineering* (INCOHE 2004), Mandal, S., SanilKumar, V., Jaya Kumar, S. eds. ,vol. 2, NIO,Goa. http://www.nio.org/index/option/com_eventdisplay/task/view/tid/4/sid/114/eid/92, pp. 820–32.

Thiyagarajan, L. (2006) 'Peruvazhikal', in *Tamizhakak Katalcaar Varalaru*, N. Athiyaman, N., and Jayakumar, P., eds., Thanjavur: Tamil University, pp. 115–26.

——(2009), *Cholar Kaala Vanigaperuvazhikal*, N. Sanajeevi Endowment Lecture, Thanjavur: Tamil University.

Tilley, C. (1994), *A Phenomenology of Landscape: Places, Paths and Monuments*, Oxford: Berg.

Tomber, R. (2008), *Indo-Roman trade: from Pots to Pepper*, London: Duckworth.

Tripati, Sila, A.S. Gaur and Sundaresh (2004), 'Marine Archaeology in India', *Man and Environment*, vol. XXIX, no. 1, pp. 28–41.

Turner, P.J. (1989), *Roman Coins from India*, London: Royal Numismatic Society.

Vanaja, R. (1983), *Indian Coinage*, New Delhi: National Museum.

Wheeler, R.E.M., Ghosh, A. and Krishna Deva (1946), 'Arikamedu: An Indo-Roman Trading Station on the East Coast of India', *Ancient India*, vol. 2, pp. 17–124.

Zvelebil, K. (1974), *Tamil Literature*, Weisbaden: Harrassowitz.

CHAPTER 17

Routes, Ports and Networks in Bengal: China Connection

Rila Mukherjee

Introducing the Subject

This essay revolves around two hypotheses. One, we discern very clearly in history a regional unit that I call the northern Bay of Bengal—which comprises within itself parts of four modern states: China, India, Bangladesh and Burma. At first sight, as Pearson notes, this seems a surprising claim for this unit encompasses the fringes of many early states in history, with a host of ethnicities, religions, languages, and practices. However, the beauty of this approach is that it enables us to abandon several conventional ways of looking at places: one, the state-centric analysis, two, the area studies categorization, three, the practice of not extending our analysis into the China seas while studying trade in the Indian Ocean and four, ignoring the long-standing distinction between uplands and lowlands. The regional unit approach shows that none of these four artificial differences are valid, at least in the case of the northern sector of the Bay of Bengal, until the seventeenth century, when this unit broke down, due to the maritime withdrawal of China, the shrinking of Burma and early colonial penetration.[1] The Qing concentration on Central Asia in the seventeenth century did not recreate the mobility of the Tang-Song-Yuan periods, nor

*This essay draws heavily on the work of Nicholas G. Rhodes. Rhodes attended some of the sessions of the conference 'The Ports of the Indian Ocean, From the Red Sea to the Gulf of Bengal' in Kolkata in February 2011. He passed away in July 2011 at London before he could see the publication of *Pelagic Passageways: The Northern Bay of Bengal Before Colonialism* in which one of his last pieces—much referred to here—is published.

did it generate the synergy visible earlier between land and sea routes in the eastern Indian Ocean.

Two, we must remember that historically there was not one delta but two in Bengal. The first in present Paschim Banga or West Bengal, India, centred on Kolkata and the second in Bangladesh, centred on Dhaka. Although there is, geologically speaking, only the one delta, known as the 'Bengal delta', the two parts showed very divergent traits in their histories. Not just in their location, but on a historical axis too, the two deltas underwent different experiences as they followed disparate trajectories, dictated in part by their geographies. This essay will accordingly refer to these two deltas as the western delta and the south-eastern delta. It was the south-eastern delta that had the most interactions with Burma and China, although the port of Tamralipta in the western delta, the recorded site of Chinese pilgrim-scholar crossings, has attracted more scholarly attention.

Spatial and Temporal Fluctuations in the Northern Bay of Bengal

This regional unit under study oscillates between unification and fragmentation, between centrality and marginality in the larger space of the Bay of Bengal. Within the relatively narrow and confined space of the northern Bay too, there is a certain amount of oscillation to be observed, particularly with respect to the lands to its north, as rivers change course, as fragmented deltas consolidate geologically, as coasts are therefore made and remade, as uplands come closer to, or move away from, rivers. Old routes fall into disuse; new routes emerge. Ports appear and disappear overnight. So too in its immediate maritime space—the foreland of the northern Bay of Bengal—is a certain amount of fluctuation to be seen, particularly in its commercial fortunes, as routes, ports and networks are frequently reconfigured.

This regional unit comprises within it various local units: local in terms of their preoccupation and perception, and in the rewriting of their history and politics. Simultaneously, these local units are also global units in that they form part of religious networks that transcend their geographical boundaries: Saivism, Vaisnavism, Jainism, Mahayana and Tantric Buddhism, Nestorian Christianity, Catholicism and Islam. Many local units also form part of economic, cultural, and social networks that go beyond their local confines: the overland silk and wool roads and the maritime silk route are three examples that come readily to mind. Therefore, the local histories form part of global history as well.

The Bengal littoral assumes great significance in this visualization. Certain local units from the littoral interact with the larger spatial unit of the Bay, whereby their history too forms a part of global history. It is necessary to establish the links between the points of origin and the final destinations of ships, caravans, peoples, commodities and ideas—a task that is not always easy. The attempt here is to articulate the continuities and discontinuities in the littoral and to move between them, to identify the alternation of sea and land routes at precise moments in history, to see beyond these alternations and to map the modifications, adjustments, adaptations, variations and shifts in Bengal-China relations.

Land and Fluvial Routes into the Bengal Deltas from the East

Any discussion on Bengal's place in the late ancient trading system must take into consideration its links with China through the overland routes. Variations of this route went from the south-eastern delta, through the Brahmaputra-Meghna waterway, through the present North-East of India, through the Shan states of upper Burma (present Myanmar) into Yunnan and China. This route, and its branches, comprised various fluvial, and not maritime, ports. Therefore, although the theme of the conference privileged the maritime route—'The Ports of the Indian Ocean, From the Red Sea to the Gulf of Bengal'—I suggest that we cannot understand Bengal's place in early trade solely by referring to maritime trading networks. Ports and port-cities along rivers, especially on the Brahmaputra and the Ayerawady (Irrawaddy) rivers and their tributaries, played a very significant role in fostering connectivities between Bengal and China, and these, as mentioned, spanned various regional and political units.

Economic and cultural flows to the Bengal coast came from the uplands, and nowhere were the uplands more significant than around the northern Bay of Bengal. All through history, until the colonial intrusion into the Bay in the seventeenth century, the northern Bay lands were noteworthy for Bengal's economic growth: precious stones including jade and rubies came from northern Burma, the Shan states and Yunnan, and silver, gold and other metals arrived from this area through the uplands and river routes. The Yunnan-Shan corridor, and Burma's silver mines, supplied Bengal with most of its metal needs throughout its history. Yunnan was the pivot around which both the Bengali and Chinese economy revolved in the ancient and medieval periods, because neither possessed significant silver resources in its domains.

Although seemingly marginal on the maritime map, particularly as far as the West to East maritime networks were concerned, unlike the Sindh and Gujarat coasts, which figured in all major sailing routes, the Bengal deltas possessed one singularity. Both were sourcing regions for maritime commodities in the trade of the Silk Route from *both* ends—western (Persian) and eastern (Chinese)—of the caravan routes. At the centre of this long route lay the vast expanse of Central Asia, with its trading towns of Chinese Turkestan, later called 'Grand Tartary', and its various mercantile peoples, such as the Sogdians. Down south lay Kamarupa (within present Assam in India) and the many principalities of the south-eastern Bengal delta—a significant area that connected Bengal to China. The Bengal deltas' link with Central Asia through Kamarupa was a *vertical* network linking the sea-lanes to the overland routes, which then connected up with the *horizontal* Silk Roads running from East to West. Thus, both maritime and fluvial ports featured in these linkages and upstream-downstream connectivities are crucial to the exchanges.

From the second century BC, once China discovered Bactria and the Chinese attempted to open trade with western India (Sindh), ambassadorial expeditions were sent from China overland through Central Asia.[2] This may be because the sea route from China to India was unknown at the time. Also, the aim was to find a safe overland passage to Central Asia. Tansen Sen writes:

> Strategic cooperation had, in fact, been considered as far back as the second century BCE. Zhang Qian, a Western Han (202 BCE-23 CE) envoy to Central Asia, in 126 BCE recommended the annexation of a vital route that linked south-western China to India. The aim was to establish a safe passage through India to Central Asia and form an alliance against the menacing Xiongnu tribe. The secret mission to secure the road failed, we are told in Chinese sources, due to the hostile tribes in the Sichuan area.[3]

Soon after, Schoff writes, 'overland caravan routes [from the Roman side], became exceedingly active between the first and third centuries of the Christian era through the discovery of the periodicity of the trade winds and the opening of active maritime traffic.'[4] These linked up with caravan routes running eastward. The Chinese noted shortly thereafter that the Huang-chih region, identified tentatively with Vanga or Gange, exported pearls and opaque glass while importing gold and silk.[5] Therefore, they must have come to know of the existence of a maritime route into Bengal, through such endeavours.

Maritime Routes

How far the Chinese experienced practically these western maritime routes in the early days is not certain, as they were gradually getting to know the sea only from the first century AD. The account of *Wei-lio* (written before AD 429) suggests that the Chinese first encountered the Indian Ocean from the Persian Gulf. They were told:

The sea [Indian Ocean] is vast and great; with favorable winds it is possible to cross within three months; but if you meet slow winds, it may also take you two years. It is for this reason that those who go to sea take on board a supply of three years' provisions. There is something in the sea which is apt to make a man home-sick, and several have thus lost their lives. When Kan-ying heard this, he stopped.[6]

Wang Gungwu writes that although trade with the Shan kingdoms was by land in the first century CE, there was a Shan mission that came by sea to China in AD 132. Two missions came by sea from T'ien-chu (India, place not precise) in AD 159 and 161.[7]

Schoff writes that there was a Shan mission sometime before AD 120 and that the Ta-ch'in or Ta-tsin (eastern Roman Empire) sent a mission in AD 166:

. . . the route [of a Shan mission recorded in Chinese annals in AD 120] is, however, clear; the embassy [from Ta-tsin] came by sea to the southwest of the Shan country, that is, the Gulf of Martaban, the shores immediately east of the modern Rangoon, and proceeded inland up one of the river valleys. The modern rail route leaving Rangoon follows the valley of the Sittaung river to Mandalay, thence up the Irawadi. At Bhamo, the head of navigation on that river, the overland route to Yun-Nan began crossing the parallel gorges of the other rivers by suspension bridges. The earlier route probably ascended the Salwin passing the Shan capital Theinni and crossing the other rivers a little lower down, both routes having as their destination Yun-nan-fu, Cheng-tu-fu, and finally Singan-fu. Another Chinese record informs us that in AD 166 the king of Ta-Tsin, 'An-tun,' who may of course be identified with Marcus Aurelius, 'sent an embassy with tribute from the frontier of Jih-Nan,' and that 'merchants of this country frequently visit Fu-Nan, Jih-Nan, and Kiao-Tsi,' but that 'few of the inhabitants of those southern frontier states ever went to Ta-Tsin.' . . . Another record dating from the fourth century gives us the route from the Chinese capital to its Tong-King seaport, and the routes down the other rivers as follows: 'southeast you come to Kiao-Tsi; there is also connection by water [in fact by both river and ocean routes] with the principalities of Yun-Nan and Yung-Chang [near Bhamo; that is, through Burma].' Chinese interest in distant lands is reflected in this same record. . . .[8]

Several routes in the eastern Indian Ocean seem to have existed. Wolters wrote:

. . . as late as the middle of the third century the Straits of Malacca were not normally used for the transport of cargo from India or Ceylon to China. The usual route would have been over the northern Peninsula and along the coast of Indo-China, the earliest axis of international trade through South-East Asia. On this axis, and probably as a result, the Mekong delta state of Fu-nan became a great empire. But by the fifth century the situation had changed. A number of South-East Asian states which cannot be, and have never been, identified as states on the well-documented Peninsula or elsewhere on the mainland were beginning to send embassies to China.[9]

A Plethora of Routes

These routes, combinations of land and riverine pathways and sea-lanes, were soon popular. But now, even more new routes came into being. The most important of the vertical routes radiated toward China through Tibet or through Burma-Yunnan from very early times.[10]

The first route passed through Bengal and Tibet into Central Asia. In very early times, this was an area of extremely limited circulation of coinage: with trade in horses, jade, silk, and bamboo.[11] Not much is known about it. By the third century AD, the Tsang-ko route through Szechuan, Yung-ch'ang and Tibet was the shortest route to India.[12] During the seventh century in the Tang period, the route through Tibet into India became very popular,[13] a variation thereof connecting to eastern India.

Pelliot wrote that the second route from China into eastern India through Yunnan and Burma, which also connected the Bengal delta and the Bay of Bengal with the Bay of Tongkin by way of the Red River, was more favoured as geographical knowledge advanced in Tang China.[14] I Tsing noted, in the seventh century, that one of the Gupta kings (possibly Srigupta at the end of the third century AD) had erected a 'Temple of the Cinas' to honour the visit of 20 Chinese pilgrim scholars using the land route from Yunnan and Burma to his kingdom.[15] This suggests that there was such a route, that it was maintained through royal patronage and that it was reasonably well frequented.

Yet another route was through Nepal; Chavannes mentioning however that this seems to have not been popular before the Tang.[16] But by the seventh century Anshuverma's Nepal formed part of a quadrangle controlling the Tang-Sassanian trade from the South Asian end; the other three were the Tibet of Songsten Gampo, the Kamarupa of Bhaskaravarma and the northern India of Harshavardhana.[17] Consequently, this route too now became popular.[18] We should keep in mind that both Kalyanavarma and Bhaskaravarma of Kamarupa were reputed to have the sea routes to China under their control between the fifth and seventh centuries AD. Although this may have been mere hyperbole, the claim certainly evidences reasonably strong Kamarupa-China links.

There was also a longer route. As mentioned earlier, the sea route into eastern India starting from the Bay of Tongkin, off the Vietnamese coast with its many ports, was popular. Many of the Chinese pilgrim-scholars who came through this route then moved on to north India and from there into Central Asia and usually returned from Central Asia to China by the land route. Sometimes they came to Central Asia first, then came down to India and returned to China by the land or sea routes. Moore writes that at the end of the eighth century a route was described from Yung-ch'ang to the Pyu capital, then going up the Chindwin and on to Manipur.[19] But it seems that by this time the direct route through Burma and Kamarupa became more popular as it was shorter.[20]

All these routes connected with roads leading to the interior of Bengal. Roadways were fairly well developed. Bhattacharyya writes that land grant documents of ancient and early medieval Bengal speak of an infrastructure which had developed out of link roads, that a network of communication existed in Bengal and that this connected with southern India, as seen from the Chola and eastern Chalukya invasions of Gaur and Kamarupa.[21]

By the seventh century therefore Bengal was, theoretically at least, accessed by the Chinese from all points. It was around the end of the seventh century that Central Asian and Chinese Buddhists came definitively to know of the south-eastern Bengal delta, of a place called Ganga Dwara, signifying, literally, the portal of the Ganga. This was the entry from the sea into Bengal, into the south-eastern deltaic area of Harikela and onward into the state of Kamarupa, which by way of the Karatoya and the Brahmaputra rivers linked deltaic Bengal with the land routes fanning left into Tibet and right into Yunnan.[22] But where was Ganga Dwara located?

Ports

Schoff suggests that Ganga Dwara may have been Suvarnagrama or Sonargram in present Bangladesh: 'The "golden route" of the Chinese was known in India as the Golden Coast, Suvarna Bhumi, and near one of the mouths of the Ganges was an important port of India named Suvarna Grama, the Golden Port, better known in the days of Arab trade as Sonargaon'.[23] But Suvarna Bhumi refers usually to Burma and sometimes Sumatra, so this identification may be suspect.

Bhattacharyya suggests Gange or Ganga Dwara may have lain in the Deganga region of North 24 Parganas in present Paschim Banga. B.N. Mukherjee indicates that Gange was probably located in the Chandraketugarh region, also in the western delta.[24] The location of this port is therefore uncertain.

The Central Asians and the Chinese knew of the Bengal deltas not just because Bengal was the seat of Buddhism but also because the Bengal ports functioned as subsidiary clearing houses of the larger India ports involved in the Roman trade. Moreover, the deltas connected with significant overland routes into Central Asia as noted and once there, the routes radiated both east and west, making it easy for people and commodities to travel.

The main port at this time in the western delta or Vanga was of course Tamralipta, which linked up through land routes with Bodhgaya in the interior. By this time, around 420–78 CE, Chinese ships were sailing directly to South Asia.[25] Both Fa-hien (in the early part of the fifth century AD, he returned to Shandong in AD 414) and I Tsing (end of the seventh century, AD 695) used this port, I Tsing returning to China from Tamralipta via Kedah. Hiuen Tsang is the only monk who arrived and returned via Central Asia in AD 645.

By the eighth and ninth centuries, at the time when the Tang-Sassanian trade was in decline and the circulation of coinage in Vanga was diminishing, the ports of Harikela in the south-eastern delta—Samandar on the Meghna and Chattagrama on the Karnaphuli—became more prominent. Saptagrama in the western delta appeared as the most important port from the tenth century onwards; ports, if any, in the western delta in the interim period between the eighth and tenth centuries cannot be located, because Tamralipta possibly silted up by the eighth century. This seems to suggest that Bengal-China links declined in the western delta. Ports in the south-eastern delta now carried on the links with China.

By the fourteenth century, when Ibn Battuta visited Harikela, Chattagrama had become the most important port in Bengal; he does not mention Samandar, perhaps because it was no longer operational. I will now attempt tracing routes and interactions from the second century BC to the fourteenth century, a period roughly comprising 1,600 years.

China-Bengal Interactions

Second Century BC to Third Century AD

During this time-span the Central Asian route was troublesome for most of the time for the Chinese, and overland contacts varied in intensity. For the Chinese, the Bengal ports were important, though the networks of the Bengal deltas with China would fluctuate over time, as we shall see. The conquest of Yunnan in the second century BC was advantageous to China for accessing both new routes and new commodities. While the Chinese attempted to find an alternative route to Central Asia through Yunnan and India at this time, Schoff writes that commodities were no less important:

From the hills of Yun-Nan came gold, silver, and precious stones, silk, and the fragrant cinnamon bark so greatly prized in Rome. The upper Yang-Tse in Chinese speech is still the 'river of the golden sands,' and a recent traveller refers to a neighbouring river valley as being called the 'silver shore'. The overland route from Yun-Nan to the upper

Irawadi was used by conquering Chinese troops in the 18th century and was by them called the 'gold and silver route'. The southern port of China mentioned in the record as south-east from Yun-Nan, that is, down the Song-Koi or Red River of Tong-King and named Kiao-Tsi, we may safely follow Richthofen in identifying as the Kattigara (or Katti-nagara, from some Prakrit-speaking pilot?) of Ptolemy and other Roman writers. This gave the Chinese Empire an outlet to the southern seas, the sailing course from which, being within the tropics, was steered by the southern cross and not the north star. The south seems to have been the cardinal direction with the Chinese. The magnetic needle having already been known to them for centuries, although apparently not put to practical uses for navigation, was also called the south-pointing chariot.[26]

In the second century BC it was Cheng K'ien possibly who gave the first account of Yunnan as the 'elephant riding country', akin to India, where too people rode and bred elephants.[27] From this time, once the Chinese moved to 'pacify' south-west China,[28] they encountered Yunnan and progressively discovered the Bengal coast, where they met with a rice-eating culture that was very close to their own. The importance of rice as monetary equivalent in second century BC Han China is seen by the fact that Han China awarded men thus: 'more than a hundred men received appointments as ministers to the feudal states, or as prefects, or [positions with salaries corresponding to] two thousand stones [of rice]. [Positions yielding incomes corresponding to] one thousand stones, or less, were given to a thousand men each'.[29]

Meanwhile, Burma too was getting known. Schoff continues:

Adjoining Yun-Nan in the water-sheds of these Burmese rivers was located the kingdom of the Shans, then an important tribal federation, and there is reason to believe that an active trade existed out of China through Yun-Nan with the Shans as intermediaries. A Chinese record dating from AD 120 informs us that 'the king of the country of Shan sent an embassy to the Chinese Emperor offering musicians and jugglers,' whose accomplishments suggest the juggling of India, and who said: 'We are men from the west of the sea. The west of the sea is the same as Ta-Tsin. In the south-west of the country of Shan one passes through to Ta-Tsin'.[30]

Moore notes:

The Han dynasty establishment of a prefecture at Yung-ch'ang in Yunnan in 69 AD prompted increased mention of these areas although reference to kingdoms precedes mention of the P'iao. The earliest note is in the work of two envoys, K'ang T'ai and Chu Ying, sent to the court of Funan in southern Cambodia, possibly around 240 AD. There they met an emissary from India who gave them information about a number of kingdoms to the west. Upon their return home, K'ang T'ai in particular included these stories in his report (Briggs 1951: 21). Only fragments of these texts survive, and only in versions copied into later works. One passage mentions a kingdom known as Chin-lin located on a large bay over 2000 li west of Funan. Another 2000 li west was the kingdom of Lin-yang, accessible only overland, not by water. The people of this kingdom were said to be Buddhist.[31]

Lin-yang has not been conclusively identified, but the locations suggested are Beikthano, Halin, and Thaton of the Pyu Empire in Burma, with all of whom the Bengal deltas had strong commercial connections.

By the third century AD, Chinese interests had begun to penetrate the Bengal littoral. The Southern Dynasty of the third century at Nanking claimed that they had appointed Tamralipta's 'king' and that the people of Tamralipta owed allegiance to the Southern Dynasty.[32] Tamralipta seems to have been the chief port of a kingdom called Tan-mei by the Chinese, whose ruler sent letters as vassal to the Chinese court.[33] We cannot determine the precise dates of the embassy sent by Tamralipta to the southern Wu at Nanking, but it was sometime in the third century AD.[34] Haraprasad Ray notes that:

... the period ... includes some of the most troubled times when China was divided into as many as fourteen small states, like Wei (AD 220–265), Shu (221–263), Wu (222–280), Western Jin (265–317), Eastern Jin (317–420), Song (Liu-song, 420–479), Qi (479–502), Liang (502–557), Chen (557–589), Northern Wei (386–535), Eastern Wei (534–550), Northern Qi (550–577), Western Wei (535–556) and Northern Zhou (557–581), followed by unification by the Sui (581–618), followed by the golden period of the Tang Dynasty (618–907). It is remarkable that Buddhism started flourishing in China during this period of political flux, even though it is supposed to have been first introduced under the Han emperor, Ming Di (AD 58–75).[35]

Wang Gungwu paints a picture of commercial decline under the Wu, particularly as regards the Central Asian trade. This meant that the overland Yunnan-Burma route into the Bay was threatened throughout the third century AD. So, the Nanhai or southern trade came to be developed through the maritime route in the third century.[36]

Third Century AD to the Seventh Century AD

The maritime route drew Bengal into larger commercial and diplomatic networks, a period that may be called the golden age of Bengal-China interactions. K'ang T'ai wrote, in the middle of the third century, of the visit of the Fu-nan envoy Su Wu to Bengal but also noted that Fu-nan had no direct trade with north India, referring to the path up the Ganga from Bengal. Rather, trade with Ta-ch'in or India was carried on through the Malay Peninsula, Sri Lanka, and south India.[37] This was the case because the maritime route through Sri Lanka and peninsular India was always privileged over the sea route into Bengal because from the earliest times, the Chinese aim was to reach the ports of the Persian Gulf and the Red Sea. K'ang T'ai's account also suggests that Bengal was not seen as part of India, quite correctly for the time under review, as there seems to have been no attempt made by Su Wu to travel up the Ganga into the Gangetic plains. Nor was Bengal seen as a gateway to the Ganga plains at the time, as was the case later.[38]

But the greatest trade network from the east, one from which both the Bengal deltas benefitted, was the Chinese silk trade into Sassanian Persia. This touched the western delta, evidenced from the number of gold coins then circulating in Samatata. We do not know whether this trade was conducted through a wholly overland route; the inclusion of Bengal as a node in this network suggests that a part of it may have been a maritime route, or a fluvial one, at least. Rhodes suggests that: 'The silk may have been imported from China via the sea route, up the Bay of Bengal to Samatata, and thence through Pataliputra in the kingdom of Harsha Vardhana, through Nepal and Tibet and further on to Bukhara and beyond to the Sassanian Empire of Iran.'[39]

This trade lasted only one century, the seventh century, and seems to have declined soon after, as we surmise from numismatic evidence.[40] Between the sixth and early seventh centuries, the various units in Bengal—Pundravardhana, Samatata, and Harikela—maintained separate currency zones. It seems that Samatata in the western delta had more access to gold through its role as an entrepot in the silk trade between Tang China and Sassanid Persia.[41] The political confusion attendant upon the deaths of rulers controlling this route, and the fall of the Sassanids between AD 644 and 651 created political uncertainties that had a negative bearing on the overland routes. This is corroborated by the declining coin standards of the Lichhavis of Nepal. As a result, the gold coins of Samatata declined in purity after AD 670 and by the early eighth century, gold coins from Samatata stopped circulating. We assume that the decline in the Tang-Sassanian silk trade was most likely due to political factors: the near simultaneous deaths of Harshavardhana of north India, Bhaskaravarma of Kamarupa, and Songsten Gampo of Tibet, all around AD 650, meant that the South Asian side controlling this transit trade collapsed. Soon after, land routes in Central Asia entered once again into a period of unrest.

Seventh Century AD to the Tenth Century AD

Sen mentions four Tang embassies to Middle India, despatched between 641 and 658, as especially noteworthy because at no other time, at least until the Ming dynasty (1368–1644), were Chinese embassies sent to any Indian kingdom so frequently and within such a short period.[42] Did the embassies mentioned by Sen use the maritime route? It is not clear. Since the seventh-eighth centuries saw turmoil in the Central Asian route from the Chinese end, it is unlikely that many used this route into Bengal. However, we should also remember that Hiuen Tsang arrived in India through Central Asia and also returned to China via Central Asia in AD 645.

The year AD 645 must have been some kind of watershed in Central Asia. We know that the Sassanid Empire collapsed in face of the Arab invasions in AD 644. That this created political disturbances along the Central Asian routes seems likely. Elisseeff, quoting the *Biographies of Eminent Monks*, tells us that before AD 644 some 710 monks used the Buddhist route and only 633 used this route between AD 645 and 988.[43]

The eight century was more turbulent. Hye Ch'o, the Korean monk who came to India by the southern sea route, and who then travelled in the region from c.AD 724 to 727 noted the various political units governed by the Arabs, the different Turkish tribes, the Tibetans and the Chinese. Hye Ch'o's account suggests that the 'pacification' achieved by China, as recorded by Cheng K'ien in the second century BC, was falling apart. The weakening Chinese control over Central Asia from the eighth century (by 763 China lost control over the Central Asian route), and the wars with Nan Zhao in the eighth and ninth centuries meant that the overland routes into Bengal were progressively threatened. Hye Ch'o wrote that Tang China and its Turkish allies were then confronting Arab military progress into Central Asia. Arab expansion in the region soon upset the delicate balance of power. In the significant battle of the Talas River in AD 751, Turkish groups, former allies of Tang China, joined the Arabs and upset Chinese control of Central Asia. Shortly after Hye Ch'o's visit, the Arabs became firmly ensconced in Central Asia. Henceforth Buddhism declined in Central Asia, and concomitant to its decline, the rising Islamic force in Central Asia attempted to block the traditional overland routes wherein Buddhist ideas, trade, travel, and diplomacy had flourished.[44]

Tansen Sen mentions armed conflicts along the Taklamakan and the Yunnan-Burma areas as one of the reasons for the decline of land routes and the rise of a maritime trade between China and India from the ninth century.[45]

Malekandathil writes of the ninth century trade impetus provided by Abbassid Persia and T'ang China:

This was a time when long distance trade circuits between Abbassid Persia (750–1258) and T'ang China (618–907) had incorporated several ports and regional economies of maritime India into their orbits . . . the Indian Ocean was subdivided into several interlocking circuits, each being controlled by a set of political and economic actors who resorted to different methods and devices to translate trade profits into political assets . . . the very shifting of the capital from Damascus to Baghdad was motivated by the desire of the Abbassids to appropriate a sizeable chunk of profit accruing from the trade in the Indian Ocean.[46]

But the Bengal coast lost out now. There are no recorded sailings from Tamralipta after the eighth century and we assume that the port must have declined from this time onwards, because the new maritime route bypassed the Bengal coast. Malabar, and not the Bengal coast, was the beneficiary of this new route and consequent networks, paving the way for the long Chinese interaction with the Malabar and Ma'abar coasts. Soon after, as Marco Polo noted, southern Chinese ships appeared with bullion to buy goods at the Malabar ports.[47]

This new reorientation of routes meant a further decline in the Bengal-China maritime trade. The gold coinage of Samatata was taken over by the silver coinage of Arakan and Harikela from the eighth century thus suggesting that Samatata now lost out as the preferred zone of maritime contact and that Harikela (the south-eastern delta) started expanding as an economic unit at that time. Until the tenth century at least, silver supplies from Burma and Yunnan continued to circulate in Bengal, in the form of the Harikela coins.[48]After this period there was a hiatus, leading us to speculate on what really happened to Bengal-China relations and trade and currency in general.

The Eleventh Century

The eleventh century presents a paradox: on the one hand, there was the 'trade revolution' in the southern Bay attendant upon the defeat of Srivijaya at the hands of the Cholas, and, on the other, no such discernible revolution in the northern Bay. Although the eleventh century trade revolution in the Indian Ocean facilitated emporia trade and more such ports appeared in South Asia and South-East Asia,[49] in South Asia these were mostly located on the Ma'abar coast and in Sri Lanka,[50] and not on the Bengal or Orissan coasts. We assume that there was no such 'trade revolution' in the northern Bay.

Linked with the absence of a 'trade revolution' in the northern Bay is the worrisome question of a lack of minted coinage. We see a movement away from minted coinage in the region at this time, not only in the Bengal deltas from the tenth century, but in large parts of South-East Asia as well, which had earlier been Bengal's trading partners. Political and economic destabilization must have been the reason for the disappearance of coins at centres such as Bagan, Sukhotai, and Angkor, in regions where coins had been used previously, as Gutman has suggested. Indeed, this whole region and Bengal had displayed an unusually stable monetary system for quite some time. Now, coins disappeared and fairly standardized lumps of silver and gold served for transactions.[51] Moreover, there was a metal shortage in China, leading the Songs to issue interdictions on metallic coin exports and to experiment with paper money instead. The crisis in metals was thus, evidently, widespread. In Bengal, rice became a prominent export commodity in lieu of silver.

How far the dynamics resulting from the eleventh century trade revolution in the Indian Ocean reinforced the changeover from silver to rice in the *kauri* network emanating from Bengal is yet to be looked at. Rhodes, while studying the demise of silver coins in Bengal's *kauri* network within a monetary and political decay in the region as a whole, concluded that Bengal possibly abandoned a metal currency between the ninth and the twelfth centuries, at the time when Nan Zhao's power waned and when Kamarupa struck the first copper coin.[52] Arab trade may also have taken large quantities of silver. There was thus a shortage of silver in circulation. This fact reinforces the link between Bengal and Yunnan for we know that much of the silver of Bengal came from Yunnan (Nan Zhao) and Burma.

Bagan, a new empire that rose in central Burma in the ninth-tenth centuries and whose core area had formed earlier the connective passage between Bengal and China, expanded considerably in the eleventh century and subsequently chanelled most of its own silver, much of which had been exported to Bengal earlier, into building massive pagodas and endowments.[53] So, not much silver was coming in from the east. It is likely that once the Muslims conquered Bengal in the thirteenth century they looked west and not east for their silver supplies. There were obviously various kinds of systemic instability at work here, not rectified until later centuries, but about which we know nothing.

Until the Fourteenth Century

The eleventh to the fourteenth centuries was also a significant time for India's north-east and the states it interacted with. Bagan fell to the Mongols in 1287. The Ahoms (emanating from the Shan area) had earlier defeated Kamarupa by around 1231. The decline and fall of Kamarupa resulted in a political flux, witnessing unprecedented state formation and state extinction to Bengal's north-east. The Hedamba kingdom or the Dimasa/ Cachar state took shape around AD 1086; the Khen dynasty began *c.* 1185, and the older Srihatta state decayed by the twelfth century into the Sinic Cachari state and partly into a Hindu polity. What remained of Srihatta then coalesced into an Islamic polity in the fourteenth century. The rise and demise of numerous states created political disorder to Bengal's north-east, the old corridor into China. How far the absence of any single large and stable, political unit in this region, such as Bagan or Kamarupa, hampered or fostered connectivities is yet to be investigated.[54] However, Kuroda suggests that the Mongols set in train a 'silver century' and once they acquired power in China as the Yuan dynasty they connected Eurasia through silver between the 1270s and 1360s, quoting the issuance of silver coins by Muslim rulers from the south-eastern delta as one of the examples.[55]

Bengal–China Networks

The foregoing passages show that a spatial and temporal mapping of visible networks between the two spaces is vital but unfortunately it is not possible to undertake it here. I will therefore mention instead some noticeable, and reasonably stable, networks between Bengal and China visible along both maritime and land routes at various points over time.

The Kauri Network as Defining the Regional Unit

There were enduring commercial networks emanating from China and South-East Asia that connected to the Bay of Bengal ports. The long history of *kauri* imports into Yunnan from the Maldives via Bengal and from the ports of Siam and Burma (probably by accessing *kauris* from Luzon and Maluku) and then transported into Yunnan by the overland route, as well as smaller amounts brought into the Chinese ports and then transported by river and land routes into Yunnan, show a long term cycle of trade relations between South Asia, Central Asia, South-East Asia and China. The *kauri* zone extended to Africa, parts of Arabia, Bengal, Orissa, Srihatta, Arakan, Pegu, Martaban, and Siam.[56] This network is as old as the horse network mentioned here, if not older.

The Horse Trade Network as Extension of a Regional Unit

The Kushanas or the Yueh-chih, from the north-west region of South Asia, carried on the horse trade in Central Asian horses. The trade was extended to Fu-nan by exports through the Bengal ports. The kingdom of the Great Yueh-chih or the Kushanas lay in Bactria, Afghanistan and

Gandhara, and later around Peshawar and Jalalabad, now in Pakistan.[57] B.N. Mukherjee tells us that in pre-Gupta Bengal, there existed such a large colony of people from north-west India that a new script, the Kharosti-Brahmi, evolved in Bengal and spread to Oc Eco in Fu-nan and U-Thong in Thailand by the third century CE.[58] Thus, from this time we can thus postulate a direct connection between Central Asia, through Khotan, Kabul, Gandhara (Qandahar) and the western Punjab, the upper valley of the Jhelum (the original Kashmir), and the Bengal ports.[59] This is known as the horse trade network.

The evidence cited shows that while the China-Persia silk network had a translocal node on the Bengal coast, the north-western horse trade to South and South-East Asia had a terminal point here when the track switched from a land to a maritime route. The recent discovery of a Kushana copper coin hoard at Paniparul, near Digha in West Bengal, bearing coins of Kanishka I and Huvishka, affirms this view.[60] Therefore, other than the Tang-Sassanid silk network over Central Asia in which the Bengal coast figured as a maritime node and which was the source of its wealth until the eighth century, as Rhodes tells us, there was also the horse trade with coastal Bengal as an important node until that time. The fact that the horse trade seems to have declined at around the same time that the Tang-Sassanid network faced a crisis indicates that the two networks were connected.

Chakravarti too suggests that the horse trade went through Bengal by the third century AD.[61] The western Bengal delta, through Tamralipta and Chandraketugarh, may have also supplied the Kaveri delta, Wang Gungwu's preferred choice of location for the horse trade on the eastern coast, with horses. Chakravarti adds that the Bengal coast played a crucial role in the horse economy of a far-flung area, with the rise of the early states and their insatiable demand for horses.[62]

Wang Gungwu however suggests that in the first century the horse trade was in the hands of south Indian merchants and shippers rather than those from Bengal, and that most commodities, once they reached the west coast of the Malay Peninsula, were put in ships belonging to south Indian merchants, as also perhaps those of Fu-nan, the proto Chams and the Malays.[63]

The kingdom of Hua'ng-chi, which the Han envoys visited around the fifth century AD, is thought to be located in south India[64] although Mukherjee suggested that it was in Vanga.[65] Bhattacharyya, following Petech (1950), suggests that Hua'ng-chi was Gange or Ganga.[66] The argument for Bengal as a transit point for the early horse trade hinges around the identification of Hua'ng-chi.

There was a Kushana port in the south-eastern delta as well, not yet identified, which played a significant part in the Central Asian-Bengal trade network. The recent find of a hoard of Kushana-type coins of *c.* third century CE indicates the existence of such a port. In such a case it would be the south-eastern delta of Bengal, rather than just the western delta, that was another terminus for the horse trade.

If the early horse trade passed through the deltas it is not known as to which particular merchant network, group or guild organized this trade at the Bengal end. But the trade in horses continued to prosper and by 1300 the horse network in Bengal embraced not only horses from Persia and Arabia, but as these were brought into India increasingly by the maritime route from AD 1000 into the west coast, Bengal searched for supplies closer home. Central Asia remained a priority zone for Bengal for sourcing horses and Central Asian regional networks such as the Tibetan and Yunnanese networks for hill ponies now developed further within Bengal.

The Glass Network

Yet another network along this route was the glass-manufacturing network, which by the early fifth century extended into China. The *PME* refers to three kinds of glass: coloured glass, glass vessels and unworked glass and it is obvious that by the first century AD trade was brisk in these items. Glass vessels were imported into the north-west of South Asia while peninsular South Asia received raw glass.[67] A lot of this went into the bead-making industry along the east coast, subsequently exported as far as China.[68]

The Chinese treated both coloured and opaque glass as semi-precious stones.[69] It is not clear whether this technology was introduced into China from Syria (Ta-ts'in) or north-west India (Ta-yueh-chi)[70] but we do know that Bengal became in subsequent centuries a leading manufacturer of glass and glass beads, as well as a leading exporter to South-East Asia and China of these items.

Underwriting Early Trade: Silk and the Silk Currency Zone Network

We have already referred to the Tang-Sassanian silk network that connected Bengal with China in the seventh century and which transcended several state forms in the region. Many states along the route adopted silk as money. Therefore, another network that we distinguish is the silk-as-currency zone: the state of Nan Zhao in Yunnan used silk as money in the ninth century, but this practice, also prevalent in Chinese Central Asia, was gradually displaced in Yunnan by *kauris* from the ninth century onwards, when Nan Zhao declined.[71] The *kauri* network flourished in Yunnan despite the presence of gold and silver in the region and continued into the nineteenth century, as Bin Yang writes.[72]

From the eighth century, Chinese silk routes through Central Asia were threatened and the fact that the *kauri* network could supersede the silk currency network is indicative of how political events could change networks. There are other lessons to be learnt: the displacement of the silk currency network demonstrates both that a stronger network could swallow others and that the economy of landlocked Yunnan was becoming increasingly integrated into that of the Indian Ocean.

The Buddhist Scholar–Pilgrim Network

This can also be termed the cotton-for-silk network. In addition to manuscripts, the Chinese took back with them Bengal cotton seeds, cotton yarn and cotton cloth, as these were highly prized in Tang and Song China. In return, they introduced Chinese silk into Bengal, and exchanged scientific ideas. For example, Buddhist monks from the Mahabodhi monastery in Bodh Gaya in Bihar taught a Chinese delegation how to make sugar in AD 643 and some of them, along with two sugar makers, accompanied the delegation back to China.[73] This was a technology-exchange link as well.

We know of at least three famous Chinese scholars—Fa-hien (early part of fifth century AD, he returned to Shandong in AD 414), I Tsing (end of the seventh century, AD 695), and Hiuen Tsang who visited Bengal. While Hiuen Tsang used the Central Asian route, returning to China in AD 645, the other two used the maritime route and the port of Tamralipta. But the fact that Srigupta erected a 'Temple of the Cinas' in Bengal suggests that many other scholar pilgrims than those we know of used the land routes. If further excavations support our hypothesis of numerous land routes from China into Bengal that we do not know of, our assumption of many more Buddhist scholars from China using a myriad of routes through the present north-east of India and north Paschim Banga, and perhaps through Nal Rajar Garh, discussed below, will be vindicated.

The Metal Network and Military Complex

The land routes between Bengal and China spanned the north-east of India. Excavations at the enigmatic Nal Rajar Garh or fort (Garh Mendabari), in Chilapati forest in Jalpaiguri district in present Paschim Banga show it to be a military outpost of the late Guptas in the north-east. The ruins are thought to display plans similar to Changa'an, the capital of the Suis and Tangs in China, suggesting the antiquity of the complex, as well as the cultural continuity between India and China. A sophisticated system of waterways, boat harbours, canals and culverts, as well as kiln-fired bricks used in construction, and numerous iron-smelting works in the complex suggest that it was not just a military outpost but a fortified township to ward off aggression from neighbouring China, Tibet and Nepal.[74] Further excavations suggest that this late Gupta site may have had continuous occupation, shrines dating from the Pala period have been found and Nal Rajar Garh may possibly have been a Khen fortification in the thirteenth century.[75] In that case the fort complex may have still acted as a frontier defence post against China.

Perhaps also late Gupta in origin, but certainly part of medieval Kamarupa, Bhitargarh seems also to have functioned both as defensive fort as well as a township, like Nal Rajar Garh, although Bhitargarh's defences seem less secure.[76] Dating from the sixth-seventh centuries, Bhitargarh certainly existed during the Pala period. 'Kambojas', i.e. a Mongoloid race from the Himalayan tablelands arrived at Bhitargarh in the tenth century; while the polity was Buddhist, black basalt images of Manasa and Hanuman have also been found, indicating existence of Hindu beliefs.[77] Bhitargarh's urban development was accelerated through trade and its strategic position as node on the trade routes between Sikkim, Nepal, Bhutan, Tibet, Assam, Koch Bihar, and the Middle and Lower Ganga valleys cannot be ignored.[78] Along with Nal Rajar Garh, Bhitargarh may also have been an important node in the metal network.

The discovery of smelting works in Nal Rajar Garh supports our hypothesis of nodes and clusters in the north-eastern corridor for the transmission of metals from south-west China and north Burma into Bengal, metals that were indispensable for the development of a regional coinage.[79] Further support comes from archaeological finds of numerous copper and bronze idols in the region, which also circulated in the northern Bay as Buddhist votive objects cast in late ancient Bengal.[80]

The excavation of not just Nal Rajar Garh in India but also of Bhitargarh now in Bangladesh, and the presence of numerous similar mud forts and fortified cities in the Tista-Karatoya belt, testify to the commercial significance of the region, as well as the region's role as transmitter of ideas and technology. Paradoxically, this zone of intense connectivity was also marked by fortifications signifying the defensive nature of the contact-zone. The fortifications are also suggestive of the strategic nature of the area.

Expanding Commerce:
The Eunuch Trade Network

In addition to the silk and *kauri* network, there also existed the eunuch trade network. The *turuskas* possibly started the trade in eunuchs from Bengal; and we know that Srihatta was an important sourcing area.[81] The site is significant because the very geographic situation of Srihatta enabled easy transport of this human cargo to the littoral by river as well as through mountain routes into Turkestan. Srihatta connected to the Bay of Bengal as well, by way of river routes. It is significant that the contours of two upland subregions, Harikela and Pundravardhana, the outermost boundaries of Srihatta, expanded up to the Bay in the eleventh century.

Most eunuchs were sent on to Persia and Rome; China was also a market. Eunuchs were valued as palace and *harem* guards. For some reason, Bengal seems to have had a quasi monopoly on this commodity but not much is known about this trade.

A Braided Network:
The Aloes Wood Trade

Yet another network that we discern is the aloes wood network. The fragrant aloes were found in Kamarupa and its environs and by way of the Meghna-Brahmaputra river system could be sent both East and West. Aloes wood was a commodity in great demand in both China and Persia, at Rome and later at the Abbassid court at Damascus.

We now see that there were many kinds of networks visible between Bengal and China: commodity networks (horses, silk, eunuchs, aloes), currency networks (*kauri* and silver), scientific networks (glass-making, sugar refining, metal smelting), human networks (pilgrims-scholars-monks) and defensive networks. Networks did not always occupy spatially different zones; indeed some networks could function within others. For example, the aloes network operated within the larger horse and silk networks that stretched between China and the West and may have been braided with the *kauri* network as well. Again, the silk-as-currency network operated independently of, but functionally complementarily to, the *kauri* network.

This account of networks suggests that the economies of the two deltas were more nuanced than earlier supposed; that both of them interacted with China through numerous fluvial, maritime and land routes and that the networks varied both spatially and temporally.

Other Networks

There were five more phases of Bengal–China interactions that we can glimpse, and at least five new networks; but all five fall beyond the scope of this essay. One was visible in the twelfth century when Mahayanist Song China and Mahayanist Pala Bengal interacted; a story that is well documented. A second was seen briefly in the thirteenth century when we discern a Tantric Bengal and Tantric Yuan China network.

Hall notes for this network:

. . . from the tenth century, three new centers of international Buddhism emerged. India's Bihar-Bengal region, with Tibet and Central Asian connections, was the initial center in the evolution of Tantric Buddhism, under the patronage of the Pala rulers of northeast India. . . . Meanwhile, China emerged as the new center of Buddhism's Mahayana sects. Significantly, each of these new Buddhist schools was centered in a strategically important region of the international trade. [82]

Mahayanist Buddhism predominated until at least the twelfth century (China, Champa, Vietnam, Korea, Japan), as also among the Palas of Bengal and Srivijaya, when Yuan patronage of Tantric Buddhism added another dimension to religious stimuli along the Bay.[83] Bengal as leading centre of Tantric Buddhism also interacted with the Yuan world, by way of land routes, less by sea.

The third Bengal–China network was the gunpowder network. Sun Laichen writes that both Chinese gunpowder and Chinese artillery and canons penetrated into the Avan and Ahom states in the fourteenth and fifteenth centuries. It is intriguing to speculate how far this new technology was disseminated within Bengal, if at all.[84]

The fourth Bengal–China network we observe was in the fifteenth century, when political, diplomatic and commercial networks between Ming China and Bengal through the maritime route were particularly noticeable. The fifth network comprised the many Portuguese and Ottoman smuggled pepper initiatives from Cochin around the middle of the sixteenth century; initiatives that used the Bengal ports to smuggle in pepper and send it along the overland routes through the north-east into China.[85]

Conclusion

The present Look East Policy of the Indian Government bases itself on the assumption that ties and connectivities can be recreated through investigations into the past. This essay shows that our investigations into old connectivities do not go back far enough. Most analysts only go as far back as the nineteenth century—a time when most of the ties mentioned here had been torn asunder and the space had been reconfigured.

It is obviously necessary to go beyond the immediate past. But how do we map past interactions, both geographically and historically? One way to do this would be by studying the various networks that spanned Bengal and China. This essay is intended as a modest step in that direction.

Tansen Sen has argued that Buddhist networking rather than commercial interests dominated the early phase of China-South Asia contacts (the Tang and Song periods), although Chinese motivations were usually threefold: military, commercial and religio-cultural. The first was to secure its borders with Indian help; the second was to tap the maritime route when the Central Asian land route became hazardous and the third was to acquire texts and scholars to give authenticity to Chinese Buddhism.[86] India was obviously very important to China. Within this relationship, Bengal played a significant role but we see here that China–Bengal interactions fluctuated in intensity over time. In commercial matters, if the overland route was disturbed then the Chinese strategy was to use the routes into the Bengal deltas, or make use of the maritime route to access the Bengal deltas directly. But once the maritime route from China to the West was established, and once the Chinese-built larger ships by accessing Arab seafaring technology, Chinese ships preferred to touch the peninsular ports instead, bypassing Bengal. Ports on the Ma'abar coast and Sri Lanka as well as the ports of the Persian Gulf and the Red Sea, rather than the Bengal or Orissan ports, were always a priority for the Chinese.

But Bengal and Orissa were seen as centres of Buddhism and so they remained important. But here too we see fluctuations. As far as religious matters were concerned, China seems to have evolved its own version of Mahayanist Buddhism by the tenth century, and had no further need to seek legitimacy from eastern India's Buddhist centres. This is observable in the dwindling number of scholar–pilgrims from China into India. The Yuan patronage of Tantric Buddhism may have led to a renewed interest in Bengal, but this interest seems to have permeated through the overland routes, once the *Pax Mongolica* ensured safety in the overland routes between China and Bengal, and they lie in an area about which we have very little information. The same can be said about the metal, gunpowder and pepper networks. Perhaps Portuguese and Turkish sources will offer us a clue about these last two networks.

In conclusion, just as Bengal-China interactions fluctuated over time, so too did the networks between the two regions. These networks were not just economic; embedded within them were political, military, technological, religious, tributary and diplomatic imperatives. The subsequent relations they generated determined to a large extent the function and operation of the routes and ports that linked the Bengal deltas to China in history. It is vital that we recover the histories that these relations produced.

Notes

1. Mukherjee, R. 2011: 'Introduction': 1–260. The notion of artificial distinctions in Bay studies derives from the comments of Professor M.N. Pearson at the launch of *Pelagic Passageways* at the international workshop 'Ports as Gateways' held at Hyderabad in July 2011. I quote from his text.
2. Hirth 1917: 98–9, 102–3.
3. Sen 2001: 4.
4. Schoff 1917: 240.
5. Mukherjee, B.N. 1996. See: 181.
6. Halsall July 1998. See also, Hirth 1885: 39; Hourani 1951: 16.
7. Wang 1998: 24.
8. Schoff 1917: 243.
9. Wolters 1960: 343.
10. Wade 2009a.
11. Pelliot 1904: 36, 103, 137–8.
12. Bhattacharyya 1998: 160.
13. Sen 2001: 24.
14. Pelliot 1904: 371 for Kia Tan's two routes from Yunnan-Burma into Kamrupa, Pundravardhana, Magadha.
15. Stargardt 1971: 41; Pelliot 1904: 150.
16. Chavannes 1903: 386–7.
17. Rhodes 2011: 266.
18. In the seventh century Harsha of Kanauj, Bhaskaravarma of Kamarupa, Anshuverma of Nepal and Songsten Gampo of Tibet seem to have often worked together politically, diplomatically and of course commercially with the Tangs. See Sen 2001: 8–10, 14–16.
19. Moore 2004: 10.
20. Bhattacharyya 1998: 160.
21. Bhattacharyya 1998.
22. Lévi 1904: 547–9; Lévi 1905: 273.
23. Schoff 1917: 244.
24. Bhattacharyya 1998: 161; Mukherjee, B.N. 1996: 181.
25. *Sung-shu*, ch. 97 in Hourani 1951: 48.
26. Schoff 1917: 244.
27. Hirth 1917: 98–9.
28. Kingsmill 1900.
29. Hirth 1917: 115.
30. Schoff 1917: 242–3.
31. Moore 2004: 6–7.

32. Bhattacharyya 1998: 163 and endnote 38.
33. Petech 1950: 53.
34. Petech 1950: 55.
35. Ray 2007. See: 509.
36. Wang 1998: 29–30.
37. Wang 1998: 33–4.
38. Sen 2006: 443–5.
39. Rhodes 2011: 266.
40. Rhodes 2011.
41. Rhodes 2011: 265.
42. Sen 2001: 2.
43. Elisseeff 2000. See: 5.
44. Han Sung Yang, Yun Hua Jan, Shotaro Ida and Laurence W. Preston 1984; 1985: 14–15, 21.
45. Sen 2003: 211, 213.
46. Malekandathil 2010: 63.
47. Latham 1958: 290.
48. Rhodes 2011: 273.
49. Kulke 1999: 17–35; Wade 2009b: 221–65.
50. See the papers in Noboru Karashima, ed., 2002; Abraham 1988; Pelliot 1904; Rockhill 1914; Rockhill 1915.
51. Gutman 1978. See: 9–10.
52. Rhodes 2006. See: 72–3.
53. Mukherjee 2012.
54. Mukherjee (forthcoming).
55. Kuroda 2009: 250, 253, 255–6.
56. Vogel, Hieronymus 1991. See: 232–6, 238–41.
57. Petech 1950: 60, 64, 73.
58. Mukherjee, B.N. 1996.
59. For the northwestern route into India, see Petech 1950: 69, 73.
60. Basu Majumdar, Rehan 2010: 149–53.
61. Chakravarti R. 2009: 145–59, see p. 151.
62. Chakravarti R. 2009: 152; Wang 1998b.
63. Wang 1998: 21. For the importance of the horse in nation-building and constructing an economy, see Kelekna 2009.
64. Wang 1998: 21 and endnotes 26 and 27, p. 27.
65. Mukherjee, B.N. 1996: 181.
66. 61. Bhattacharyya 2004: 6.
67. Parker 2008: 175.
68. *Chau ju-kua* (repr. 1965): 227–8.
69. Hirth, 1885: 233–4.
70. Hirth, 1885: 230–1, says that during the time of T'ai-wu of the Northern Wei (AD 424–52) glass-making was introduced by the yueh-chi traders, while the *Sung-shu* claims that this was introduced by the Ta-ts'in during the period of Emperor Wen-ti of the Sung (AD 424–54). Note that the two dates are similar

despite the contradiction in provenance of the technology. However, since this introduction, glass-making in China became very cheap.

71. Vogel 1991: 234.
72. Bin Yang 2008.
73. Sen 2001: 9–10.
74. Santra 2005: 29–36. In Bangla. Pareshchandra Dasgupta, appendix, in Santra 2005: 65–81.
75. Deshpande, ed., 1975: 46; Chakrabarti 2001: 62.
76. Jahan 2010:188, 197. I am indebted to Jean-Francois Salles for this reference, as also the paper.
77. Jahan 2010: 178, 187–8, 195.
78. Bhitargarh was possibly an important node in commercial and cultural networks between Bengal, the Middle Ganga Valley, the Middle Brahmaputra valley and the Trans-Himalayan Region. Being situated on the Talma, the main channel of the Karatoya, Bhitargarh could trade with Tibet by way of the Tista and also with Pundravardhana, which was situated by the Karatoya. Dhumgarh was the port-site and its paleochannel served as anchoring points. Bhitargarh probably connected ancient Magadha with Yunnan/Szechwan/ Tonkin via the Brahmaputra Valley, the Namkin range of East Tibet, the western side of the Mekong, Batang and the southern section of the eastern bank of the Mekong, according to Jahan 2010: 196.
79. Manda, Barnali, Prasanta K. Datta and Chattopadhyay 2010. See: 224–7.
80. Hall 2010: 6–7.
81. Blaeu 1663: 164.
82. Hall 2004. See: 217–18.
83. Hall 2004: 217–19.
84. Sun 2003a: 495–517; Sun 2003b.
85. Malekandathil 2010: 168–74.
86. Sen 2003: 15–54

Bibliography

Abraham, Meera (1988), *Two Medieval Merchant Guilds of South India*, New Delhi: Manohar.

Basu Majumdar, Susmita, Rehan Ahamad (2010), 'Kushana Copper Coin Hoard from Paniparul, West Bengal', *Pratna Samiksha: A Journal of Archaeology*, Kolkata: Centre for Archaeological Studies and Training, eastern India, pp. 149–53.

Bhattacharyya, A. (1998), 'Trade Routes of Ancient Bengal', in *History and Archaeology of Eastern India*, Asok Datta, ed., New Delhi: Books and Books, pp. 157–72.

——— (2004), 'Studies in Hydrography of Ancient and Mediaeval Bengal', *Selected Essays*, Kolkata: Centre for Archaeological Studies and Training, Eastern India.

Bin Yang (2008), *Between Winds and Clouds: The Making of Yunnan, Second Century BCE–Twentieth Century CE*, New York: Columbia University Press.

Blaeu J. (1663), *Le Grand Atlas, Cosmographie Blaviane*, 12 vols. Amsterdam: Theatrum Orbis Terrarum Ltd., (1968).

Chakrabarti, D.K. (2001), *Archaeological Geography of the Ganga Plain: the Middle and Lower Ganga*, New Delhi: Permanent Black.

Chakravarti, R. (2009), 'Equestrian Demand and Dealers: The Early Indian Scenario (up to c. 1300)', in *Horses in Asia: History, Trade and Culture*, B.G. Fragner, R. Kauz, R. Ptak and A. Schottenhammer, eds., Vienna: Verlag der Osterreichischen Akademie der Wissenschaft, pp.145–59.

Chau ju-kua: his work on the Chinese and Arab trade in the twelfth and thirteenth centuries: entitled Chu-fan-chi, translated from the Chinese and annotated by Hirth, F. and Rockhill, W.W. (1911). St. Petersburg, Taipei: Literature House (repr., 1965).

Chavannes, ed. (1903), 'Voyage de Song Yun dans l'Udyāna et le Gandhāra', *Bulletin de l'École Française d'Extrême Orient*, vol. 3, on. 1, pp. 379–441.

Deshpande, M.N., ed. (1975), *Indian Archaeology 1966–67: A Review*, New Delhi: Archaeological Survey of India, Government of India.

Elisseeff, V. (2000), 'Introduction: Approaches Old and New to the Silk Roads', in *The Silk Roads: Highways of Culture and Commerce*, V. Elisseeff, ed., New York: Berghahn Books; Paris: Unesco Publications, pp.1–26.

Gutman, P. (1978), 'The Ancient Coinage of Southeast Asia', *Journal of the Siam Society*, vol. 66, no. 1, pp. 8–21.

Hall, K.R. (2004), 'Local and International Trade and Traders in the Straits of Melaka Region: 600–1500', *Journal of the Economic and Social History of the Orient*, vol. 47, no. 2, pp. 213–60.

——— (2010), 'Indonesia's Evolving International Relationships In The Ninth To Early Eleventh Centuries: Evidence From Contemporary Shipwrecks And Epigraphy', *Indonesia*, vol. 90, pp. 1–31.

Halsall, P. (1998), East Asian History Sourcebook *Chinese Accounts of Rome, Byzantium and the Middle East*, c. 91 BCE–1643 CE, an East Asian History Sourcebook, available at http://depts.washington.edu/silkroad/texts/romchin1.html. accessed on 11 August 2010.

Han Sung Yang, Yun Hua Jan, Shotaro Ida and Preston, L.W. (tr., text and editing) (1984), *The Hye Ch'o Diary: Memoir of the Pilgrimage to the Five Regions of India*, Korea: Asian Humanities Press, Po Chin Chai Ltd. repr. 1985.

Hirth, F. (1885), *China and the Roman Orient: Research into their Ancient and Mediaeval Relations as represented in Old Chinese Records*, Leipzig, Munich, Shanghai and Hongkong: Kelly and Walsh.

——— (1917), 'The Story of Chang K'ién, China's Pioneer in Western Asia: Text and Translation of Chapter 123 of Ssï-Ma Ts'ién's Shï-Ki', *Journal of the American Oriental Society*, vol. 37, pp. 89–152.

Hourani, G.F. (1951), *Arab Seafaring in the Indian Ocean in Ancient and Early Medieval Times*, Princeton: Princeton University Press.

Jahan, Shahnaj Husne (2010), 'Archaeological Investigations at Bhitargarh in Panchagarh District', *Journal of Bengal Art*, vol. 15, pp. 173-200.

Karashima, Noboru, ed. (2002), *Ancient and Medieval Commercial Activities in the Indian Ocean: Testimony of Inscriptions and Ceramic Shards*. Report of the Taisho University Research Project 1997-2000. Tokyo: Taisho University.

Kelekna, P. (2009), 'The Politico-Economic Impact of the Horse on Old World Cultures', *Sino-Platonic Papers*, vol. 190 (June), available at www.sino-platonic.org, accessed on 11 August 11 2010.

Kingsmill, Tho. W. (1900), 'Han Wu Ti and the Aboriginal Tribes on the South-Western Frontier of China', *The China Review*, Shanghai: 24 November, 103–9, accessed on 17 January 2010 from http://sunzi.lib.hku.hk/hkjo/view/26/2600423.pdf.

Kulke, H. (1999), 'Rivalry and Competition in the Bay of Bengal and Its Bearing on Indian Ocean Studies', in *Commerce and Culture in the Bay of Bengal 1500-1800*, Prakash, Om and Lombard, D., eds., New Delhi: Manohar/ICHR, pp. 17–35.

Kuroda, Akinobu (2009), 'The Eurasian silver century 1276–1359: commensurability and multiplicity', *Journal of Global History*, vol. 4, pp. 245–69.

Latham, R., tr. and intr. (1958), *The Travels of Marco Polo*, London/New York: Penguin.

Lévi, S. (1904), 'Notes chinoises sur l'Inde: IV. Le pays de Kharostra et l'écriture kharostri', *Bulletin de l'École Française d'Extrême Orient*, vol. 4, no. 1, pp. 543–79.

Moore, E. (2004), 'Interpreting Pyu material culture: Royal chronologies and finger-marked bricks', *Myanmar Historical Research Journal*, vol. 13, pp. 1–57.

Mukherjee, B.N. (1996), 'Coastal and Overseas Trade in Pre-Gupta Vanga and Kalinga', Vinayatoshini (Benoytosh Centenary Volume), Chakravarti, S., ed., *Naihati: Benoytosh Centenary Committee*, Calcutta, pp. 181–92.

Mukherjee, Rila (2011), 'Introduction', *Pelagic Passageways: The Northern Bay of Bengal Before Colonialism*, Mukherjee, R., ed., Delhi: Primus Books, pp. 1–260.

——(2012), 'Silver Links! Bagan-Bengal and the Metal Corridors into Bengal: 9th to 13th Centuries', paper read at international conference 'Early Myanmar and Its Global Connections', Bagan, February.

—— (forthcoming), 'Between Land and Sea: The Integration of "Small" Polities into a Northern Bay of Bengal Economic System Between the 9th and 19th centuries', Nalanda Srivijaya Centre, ISEAS, Singapore.

Parker, G. (2008), *The Making of Roman India*, Cambridge: Cambridge University Press.

Pelliot, P. (1904), 'Deux itinéraires de Chine en Inde à la fin du VIIIe siècle', *Bulletin de l'École Française d'Extrême Orient*, vol. 4/1, pp. 131–413.

Petech, L. (1950), Northern India According to the Shui-Ching-Chu. Serie Orientale Roma II: Instituto Italiano Per il Medio ed Estremo Oriente.

Ray, Haraprasad (2007), 'Introductory Notes to a Course on Chinese Sources of India-China Relations', *China Report*, vol. 43, pp. 501-20.

Rhodes, N.G. (2006), 'Harikela Coins: An Attempt Towards a Chronology', *History Culture and Coinage of Samatata and Harikela*, vol. 1, Achargee, Jahar, ed. and comp., Agartala: Rajendra Kirtishala, pp. 55–77.

——— (2011), 'Trade in South-East Bengal in the First Millenium CE', *Pelagic Passageways: The Northern Bay of Bengal Before Colonialism*, Mukherjee, R., ed., Delhi: Primus Books, pp.263–75.

Rockhill, W.W. (1914), 'Notes on the Relations and Trade of China with the Eastern Archipelago and the Coast of the Indian Ocean during the Fourteenth Century", *T'oung Pao*, Second Series, vol. 15, no. 3, pp. 419–47.

——— (1915), 'Notes on the Relations and Trade of China with the Eastern Archipelago and the Coast of the Indian Ocean during the Fourteenth Century", *T'oung Pao*, Second Series, vol. 16, no. 4, pp. 435–67.

Santra, Tarapada (2005), *Jalpaiguri Jelar Purakirti*, Kolkata: West Bengal State Archaeology Department, pp. 29–36.

Schoff, W.H. (1917), 'Navigation to Far East under the Roman Empire', *Journal of the American Oriental Society*, vol. 37, pp. 240–9.

Sen, Tansen (2001), 'In Search of Longevity and Good Karma: Chinese Diplomatic Missions to Middle India in the Seventh Century', *Journal of World History*, vol. 12, no. 1, pp. 1–28.

——— (2003), *Buddhism, Diplomacy, and Trade: The Realignment of Sino-Indian Relations, 600-1400*, Asian Interactions and Comparisons, published with the Association for Asian Studies, University of Hawai'i Press, 2003.

——— (2006), 'The Formation of Chinese Maritime Networks to Southern Asia, 1200-1450', *Journal of the Economic and Social History of the Orient*, vol. 49, pp. 421–53.

Stargardt, J. (1971), 'Burmas' Economic and Diplomatic Relations with India and China from Early Medieval Sources', *Journal of the Economic and Social History of the Orient*, vol. 14, no. 1, pp. 38–62.

Sun, Laichen (2003a), 'Military Technology Transfers from Ming China and the Emergence of Northern Mainland South-East Asia (*c.* 1390–1527)', *Journal of Southeast Asian Studies*, vol. 34, no. 3, October 2003, pp. 495–517.

——— (2003b), 'Chinese Military Technology and Dai Viet *c.* 1390-1497', *Asia Research Institute Working Paper Series*. No. 11.

Vogel, H.U. with the assistance of Hieronymus, S. (1991), 'Cowry Trade and Its Role in the Economy of Yunnan, the Ninth to the Middle of the Seventeenth Century', in *Emporia, Commodities and Entrepreneurs in Asian Maritime Trade, c. 1400-1750*, R. Ptak, and D. Rothermund, eds., Stuttgart: Franz Steiner Verlag, pp. 231–62.

Wade, G. (2009a), 'The Polity of Yelang and the Origins of the Name "China"', *Sino-Platonic Papers*, nr. 188 (May) available at http://www.sino-platonic. org/complete/spp188_yelang_china.pdf, accessed on 15 October 2009.

——— (2009b), 'An Early Age of Commerce in South-East Asia, 900–1300 CE', *Journal of Southeast Asian Studies*, vol. 40, no. 2, June 2009, pp. 221–65.

Wang, Gungwu (1998), *The Nanhai Trade: The Early History of Chinese Trade in the South China Sea*, repr., Times Academic Press.

Wolters, O.W. (1960), 'The 'Po-ss' Pine Trees', *Bulletin of the School of Oriental and African Studies*, vol. 23, no. 2, pp. 323–50.

CHAPTER 18

'Describing a Lost Camel'—Clues for West Asian Mercantile Networks in South Asian Maritime Trade (Tenth-Twelfth Centuries AD)

Elizabeth Lambourn

As the literature on the economy of the medieval Indian Ocean grows in the wake of a booming interest in ocean spaces as categories of analysis and in transoceanic connections, scholars are increasingly brought face to face with the diversity and disparity of data sets across the area. Historians face a wide range of textual sources in innumerable languages as well as highly diverse regional historiographies which are almost never commensurate. Parallel to this is a growing body of archaeological data which poses its own problems of comparability and commensurality; widely variable archaeological formation processes across the region, and different archaeological traditions and historiographies make these data sets as complex to use as the first. Between the two lie several hugely important bodies of evidence including numismatic, sigillographic and more broadly epigraphic material which are sometimes incorporated into these larger disciplines, sometimes rejected, but rarely shared. Work upon the economy of the medieval Indian Ocean cannot afford to ignore the pluridisciplinary character of the sources but above all it cannot set aside the serious problems posed by their simultaneous use. Thinking in terms of densities of data rather than in terms of bounded and exclusive categories of primary source—for example as documentary vs. historical vs. geographical vs. epigraphic vs. numismatic vs. architectural vs. archaeological vs. archaeo-botanical and faunal—can certainly help to map areas rich in primary sources, as well as highlighting the large gaps that remain. However, the problem remains of how to marshall such a wide range of data sets at the level of individual sites or regions, and then of how to deploy them comparatively across the greater Indian Ocean area.

Successive generations of scholars have undoubtedly faced some or all of these problems more or less explicitly but for me the issue crystallized when I was invited in 2007 to participate in a collaborative project that aimed to write a 'histoire événementielle'—a 'history of events' or 'event history'—of the western Indian Ocean between 950 and 1150 CE.[1] The parameters of the project were set by the lifespan of the recently excavated maritime entrepôt of Sharma in the Yemen, and my role was to write an 'event history' of South Asian ports and trade networks over this period, linking them in to the lifespan of Sharma. While this Sharma-centric exercise is the object of a separate publication, my essay here offers me the opportunity to further discuss these problems and with a wider audience. This essay seeks to write a broader 'event history' of South Asia in the maritime trade of the western Indian Ocean over the tenth to twelfth centuries CE and in so doing to explore the problems that this exercise in a particular type of history and historical time poses for South Asian sources. As the western seaboard of India and Sri Lanka formed the main interfaces with West Asia, it is on these coastal regions, from Sind to southern Sri Lanka, that this discussion centres. In order to streamline the discussion, my focus is on the West Asian trade communities which feature so prominently in a number of these sources. I use them as a prism through which to explore the challenges of working with these pluridisciplinary data sets and the different timespans of history that they present. Taking its cue from the original brief to write a 'histoire événementielle', this essay explores more broadly how these sources also contribute to histories of 'conjonctures' and the *longue durée*. Due to the volume of the material involved, and the timing of its publication, this essay excludes from its discussion the so-called 'India Book' material from the Cairo Geniza which only became widely accessible in 2008.[2]

'Histoire événementielle' has been described as history at the scale of 'calendar time', time in terms of days, weeks and years, it might be described as the default setting of traditional historical narrative and as a genre it certainly goes back to European and Middle Eastern forms of history writing and ideas of history—the medieval European chronicle and the Islamic universal history are themselves 'histoires événementielles'. Unsurprisingly, the translation of this timescale to South Asian historical sources poses huge problems in a historiographic tradition where chronicles and universal histories were not commonly written. As any chapter in any one of the major historical surveys of medieval India shows, historians of medieval South Asia still struggle to establish the regnal dates of even major dynasties while the territorial boundaries of many polities remain uncertain (see for example Majumdar and Dasgupta 1981–2; Sharma and Srimali 1992–2008, or Wink 1991). The fact is that we often cannot say who held a particular port city along the South Asian seaboard in a particular year or even decade, let alone drill down to questions of trade and economy, and the possibility of a South Asian 'histoire événementielle' seems distant. Nevertheless, South Asian 'histoires événementielles' are neither impossible nor indeed undesirable; as I will discuss shortly, the Medieval period has been badly neglected in South Asian history writing but with resources and new approaches we will be able to refine our understanding of even these most basic questions and move closer to some sort of 'histoire événementielle' albeit on altogether South Asian terms (for example Ali 2000).

The precarious character of the South Asian 'événement' is an important reminder that even the 'events' of the chronicle or universal history are only ever a fiction, a constructed narrative, they remind us to 'mind the gap'. Part of this essay will concern itself with acknowledging and even highlighting the gaps in the South Asian data and the impossibility of knowing certain things. That said, as the *Annales* school discovered, the 'histoire événementielle' is as important as a concept to react against as it is as a concept to think with, seen as part of a tripartite layering of time, working alongside 'conjonctures'—phases of perhaps ten to fifty years—and finally the much better known 'longue durée', different types of primary source take on different roles within these different time scales. As I will explore here, in the absence of South Asian sources, Middle Eastern geographies can prove useful indicators of broad 'conjonctures' or phases of trade interaction across the western Indian Ocean during the period under consideration. It is also at the timescales of 'conjonctures' and the 'longue durée' that archaeological data promises to find its most natural place. Archaeology only rarely encounters event history, for example in the destruction of Pompei or other sudden dramatic events, but is much better at capturing long-term change in daily material culture and exchange. In spite of the fact that we face particular problems finding medieval strata in South Asian archaeology—and more specifically in Indian archaeology—it is here, at the level of the 'longue durée' and perhaps the 'conjuncture' that archaeology promises to make its most significant impacts.

The 'histoire événementielle' experiment in medieval South Asia also helps to foreground sources unique to the region and thus particular methodological problems distinct to South Asia. Although South Asia largely lacks what might be described as traditional dynastic histories, epigraphic materials and notably grants and legal documents inscribed on stone or copper sheets form the single most important category of written source for the medieval period. Many of these documents are grants made for the endowment of religious institutions, only a minority are directly connected with maritime trade, for example the taxation of ships, however some provide unexpectedly rich data. Individual grants contribute to event history, for instance giving detailed biographical portraits of significant individuals involved in the administration of international trade or changes to taxation or administration at particular port sites; in rarer cases sequences of grants contribute to the history of 'conjonctures', for example mapping regional shipping networks over a century. Yet as these exquisite micro-histories occur outside the chronicle or universal history format and are surrounded by so many gaps they pose huge problems of interpretation. The old problem of the relationship between micro- and macro-history is crystallized here in an extreme way, and it remains unclear whether they can be read only as individual case studies or can function as a basis for the construction of broader paradigms or generalizations.

Despite a recent surge in research and writing on trade and trade communities, I am still left with an eclectic collection of small insights and few satisfactory larger narratives.[3] A famous essay by Carlo Ginzburg, the father of micro-history, reflects on the deep history of observation and evidence in history writing. In it, Ginzburg relates a story of three brothers who met a man who had lost a camel:

> they describe it for him without hesitation: it is white, blinded in one eye, and carries two goat-skins on its back, one full of wine, the other of oil. Then they have seen it? No, they have not. So they are accused of stealing and brought to trial. For the brothers this is a moment of triumph: they demonstrate in a flash how, by means of myriad small clues, they could reconstruct the appearance of an animal on which they have never laid eyes. (Ginzburg 1992: 102)

In the following pages I am constantly reminded of Ginzburg's three brothers, describing a lost camel on the basis of the smallest tracks and traces. My problem is that sometimes I am not even sure which animal I am tracking and at the end, I still have no owner to confirm my final identification.

Sources for Medieval Maritime Trade in South Asia: A Survey

The historical sources of the various regions that surround the Indian Ocean bring us face to face with their many differences, and often their startling disparities. South Asia presents very different textual and material sources to those we expect to find in the Middle East and these differences are compounded by extremely varied historiographical and archaeological traditions and agendas. Bringing South Asia into the 'histoire événementielle' of the western Indian Ocean is no easy task. Interconnected regions do not necessarily present interconnected sources and they certainly rarely present commonly held and coherently developed agendas and methodologies. Throughout the centuries under study here, as indeed throughout its history, the Indian subcontinent presents a complex political geography, with numerous largely land-centred polities engaged in a variety of collaborative and occasionally hostile relations with myriad coastal states and port polities. Linking this political landscape to the wider patterns of change in the western Indian Ocean and, for example, the lifespan of entrepôts such as Sharma is no easy task. Yet without efforts at dialogue and integration, any larger history of the Indian Ocean at this period risks being built on easy and unproven assumptions and producing nothing more than coarse or even misguided generalizations.

I begin with a review of the textual and archaeological sources for the mediaeval period, and the historiographical trends which produced them. The following sections may seem to stray far from the stated remit of writing a 'histoire événementielle' of South Asia from the tenth to twelfth centuries. However, the discussion that follows will hopefully explain why archaeological data currently plays only a very minor part in our understanding of medieval maritime trade in South Asia, and is thus, almost entirely absent from the main discussion.

Texts and Material Sources of
South Asian Maritime Trade

South Asia at this period presents very different texts and archaeologies to those available for the Arabian Peninsula. Those mainstays of Islamic and Middle Eastern historical research, the dynastic history and the world history, simply do not exist for South Asia at this period. Texts, such as they are, consist predominantly of land grant documents, more rarely of documents concerning tax or commercial matters. Most often concerned with the donation of land to religious institutions, historical references and references to trade and West Asian diasporas are frequently incidental to the main subject of these grants. Furthermore, while grant documents are recognized as a key source for medieval history in South Asia,[4] many texts, though edited, remain untranslated and thus inaccessible to those unable to work in Sanskrit, or one of the other myriad Indic languages in which they are written such as Tamil, Malayalam, Telugu or Kannada.

Material data also differs markedly between the two regions under comparison. Decades of sustained archaeology along the entire Arabian coast and research into the related maritime spaces of the Red Sea and the Gulf has produced a relatively well-explored Arabian archaeological landscape and seascape into which new sites can now be set. For example, archaeological data, rather than textual sources, provided the foundation date for the site of Sharma in southern Yemen which appears to have developed as an international entrepôt *ex nihilo* around 980, suddenly ceasing activity around 1150 CE. Thanks to the length and depth of Arabian archaeology, the single site of Sharma and its material remains can be contextualized relatively accurately and easily, at least as regards connections with these adjacent areas. The dates of its activity can be set within the context of the rise and fall of other port sites in these regions, its architecture and the excavated remains of its daily life and trade can, for the most part, be contextualized in the material from other sites across these regions. Yet Sharma's trade was international and extended far beyond these regional networks: Chinese ceramics represent a significant percentage of the site's overall ceramic assemblage while even more significant finds of East African ceramics, some with clear links to the site of Ras Mkumbuu on Pemba Island (Horton, personal communication), offer clues to its networks along the African coast. Here with regards to Africa but particularly as regards China, a relatively strong tradition of archaeological investigation and ceramic study allows the identification and sourcing of these ceramics to specific regions, and sometimes even to precise sites of manufacture. South Asian ceramics are also present at Sharma in significant quantities and it is here that the disparities between South Asian archaeology and its peers around the Indian Ocean rim emerge.

Looking for the medieval in South Asia

It is fair to say that South Asian history and archaeology have only recently begun to pay due attention to the medieval period, and only more recently still have they begun to focus on medieval maritime trade and port sites. This is not the place for an extensive historiographical discussion of the particular trends and prejudices that explain this pattern, suffice it to say that South Asian history writing has traditionally disregarded the early mediaeval period onwards, as Ranabir Chakravarti usefully summed up the trend,

historians of Indian feudalism cited the relative silence about merchants and cities in the inscriptions as evidence of the marginalization of trade, in particular seaborne long distance trade during 500-1000 AD. The emphasis on epigraphic data led to a persistent neglect of other types of data. Ships, sailors, merchants and pilgrims frequenting the Indian Ocean in the post-500 AD period became almost invisible in this historiography (Chakravarti 1992: 307).

This trend hardly bodes well for the writing of an integrated history of trade in the western Indian Ocean.

The paucity of textual sources on South Asian maritime trade after 500 CE offers a unique opportunity for archaeological data to take the centre stage, however, the lesser regard for the medieval period had, until comparatively recently, also engendered a significant disregard for the archaeological investigation of mediaeval layers and particularly sites linked to medieval maritime trade.[5] Where maritime trade has been a focus of archaeology it has tended to centre on Harappan maritime connections[6] and on what is often termed the Early Historic period, a term which has in effect been equated with the period of Indo-Roman trade.[7] Although generally impossible to prove and document definitively, numerous anecdotes circulate of medieval archaeological layers being simply dug away to reach more significant, read 'older', archaeological levels. Even where medieval levels or sites have been excavated, medieval sherds are often optimistically classed as Early Historic or assigned to much later dates, some are simply not published in sufficient detail to be used by other researchers.[8] As Derek Kennet observes in his review of the many problems that surround the archaeology of Vakataka western India at this period, 'the absence of ceramic "type fossils" that can be used to identify late Early Historic and Early Medieval occupation is a major reason why occupation dating to these periods is almost never identified' (Kennet 2004: 14).[9]

The parallels between historical and archaeological trends in the study of the medieval period in India are unsurprisingly close, but still worth underlining. Just as the silence about trade in medieval texts had led historians to assume that there was no trade, so the failure to identify medieval ceramics in archaeological excavations often led to the conclusion that ceramics were not being produced in the medieval period and that sites had been abandoned. Both are self-fulfilling circular arguments. Paradoxically, it has often been archaeologists working in the Middle East, rather than their colleagues excavating in South Asia, who have appealed most strongly for the proper study and classification of medieval Indian ceramics in order to help them interpret the often substantial finds of Indian ceramics at sites in the Middle East (Kervran 1996, 2004; Sedov 1996).

Trends and Problems in the Medieval
Archaeology of South Asia

Fortunately, medieval archaeology in South Asia is beginning to change, and with it maritime archaeology. The 1970s saw the birth of coastal surveys, many of them incorporating medieval sites and/or material. The pioneer of these surveys appears to have been John Carswell who, following promising work in the Maldives (Carswell 1976–7), carried out an extensive coastal survey of South Asia in 1976 with backing from the Oriental Ceramic Society and the British Academy (Carswell 1977–8). This survey appears to have led directly to Carswell's later excavations at Mantai (from 1980 to 1984), one of the major trans-shipment ports on the Jaffna peninsula in Sri Lanka and which offered the chance of previously unparalleled evidence for medieval international trade via South Asia (Carswell and Prickett 1984, 1989; Prickett-Fernando 1990). It was also in the 1980s that Taisho University in Tokyo began research into trade in medieval south India under the project banner 'Medieval Commercial Activities in the Indian Ocean as Revealed from Inscriptions and Chinese Ceramic Sherds' (Karashima 2002, 2004). National initiatives in maritime archaeology also appear to have started around this time. In 1981, the National Institute of Oceanography in India began its project on 'Marine Archaeological Studies in the Indian Waters', and in 1987 the Archaeological Survey of India proposed the creation of an Underwater Archaeology Wing (Rao 1988), however, it was not until the early 1990s that formal centres appeared and policies were adopted. The Marine Archaeology Centre of the NIO was founded in 1990 and in the same year, the Sri Lankan Department of Archaeology resolved to promote maritime archaeology and began training staff.[10] Since then, coastal surveys and maritime archaeology have become substantially more common in India and Sri Lanka and this work is beginning to pinpoint productive sites for study, of which medieval layers and medieval sites form a natural part.[11] For the first time, this work is also documenting off-shore/underwater sites such as shipwrecks or stone anchor clusters which all offer opportunities for new data.[12]

Thanks to a number of archaeological projects in Pakistan, India and Sri Lanka over the last two decades we are now in a position where textual data on port sites and regions involved in maritime trade can sometimes be associated with archaeological evidence, however, the dialogue between the two is by no means evident. In spite of this recent surge of activity, medieval archaeology as a whole is in many ways still in its infancy in South Asia and within this, maritime archaeology still has far to go. In fact, the first monograph specifically dedicated to medieval archaeology in India, M.S. Mate's *Archaeology of Medieval India*, was published as recently as 2005 and does not actually deal with coastal sites or maritime trade (Mate 2005). The Archaeological Survey of India's Underwater Archaeology Wing, first proposed in 1987, only opened in 2001 and the first Sri Lankan underwater excavations began the same year. The challenges are enormous, across South Asia site conditions and excavation methodologies differ widely, making comparison between sites extremely labour intensive if not impossible.[13] Furthermore, medieval ceramic typologies are far from universally agreed and sherd reference collections are only beginning to be constituted.[14]

The problems still facing medieval archaeology in South Asia have recently been summarized by Shinu Abraham. In a view which corroborates Chakravarti's earlier assessment, she describes scholars as challenged by the idea of relying on archaeological data to derive models of socio-economic behaviour, in other words, the majority of scholars are still more comfortable with textual sources. Within the discipline of archaeology itself Abraham pinpoints 'an over-emphasis on data collection and site identification (rather than problem-oriented data analysis), as well as poor chronological control, and a lack of regional data management' (Abraham 2009: 14). While Abraham's comments are expressed in the context of a discussion of south Indian scholarship, they apply across South Asia. Clearly, it is time for the large sweeping surveys of the 1970s and 1980s, useful as they were, to develop into focused regional studies intent on establishing clear chronologies, and aimed at solving specific problems and questions. Fundamentally, Abraham is calling for future projects to reflect more deeply about how archaeology and material culture can inform us about trade and trade communities, and how to go about gathering the type of data that will usefully answer such questions.

More 'problem driven' excavation decisions, as Abraham calls them, have in fact been taking place. Kervran's work in Sind, begun in 1989, already understood and addressed the issues of regional data management and chronological control highlighted by Abraham. The French project carried out surface surveys across the entire south Indus Delta area, examining 26 sites in detail, at the same time focusing on the excavation of three sites, Sehwan Sharif, Ratto Kot and Lahori Bandar. Sehwan was selected precisely because the tell there promised to yield (and has in fact yielded) the first ever complete ceramic sequence for Sind extending from the fourth to third centuries BCE to the twelfth-eighteenth century CE. Once published, Sehwan promises to contribute decisively to the dating of other sites across the Indus Delta and elsewhere in western South Asia.[15] At the other end of the spectrum, the systematic survey of the Delta has contributed a regional picture of the development and movement of river channels and associated ports and settlements from the Harappan to the modern period. Meanwhile, at the opposite end of the western seaboard, excavations at the Keralan site of Pattanam, promise to apply these approaches to the site of Muziris, the key south Indian port involved in Indo-Roman trade, and its surrounding region (Shajan et al. 2004, 2008; Selvakumar 2005).

Problems with medieval ceramics in South Asia

A key problem facing medieval archaeology in South Asia centres around ceramic typologies and chronologies, still the core building blocks of much archaeological method. It would be inappropriate and also simply take too long to catalogue the many problems that currently exist in this area but one cannot avoid mentioning the lack of research and sometimes outright confusion that reigns here.

We have already mentioned that medieval archaeological layers in South Asia frequently 'disappear' during excavations, sometimes by being physically cleared away, but most often by being mis-assigned to either earlier (i.e. Early Historic) or later (i.e. Late Medieval/Pre-Modern) periods. Deep historiographical prejudices and assumptions about the medieval underlie this, but it is also worth asking whether a key part of the problem also hinges around the character of the medieval ceramic record in South Asia. To the best of my knowledge, there is currently no single agreed identification or description, let alone chronology, of the main types of South Asian ceramics in use in different parts of the subcontinent in the period after the fifth century. While a number of regional ceramics types have been identified across South Asia for the Early Historic period, notably Rouletted Ware (RW) and other fine grey wares from the Ganges Delta, and Red Polished Ware (RPW) from western India, the period after 500 CE is far less easy to categorise.[16] The period after 500 CE appears to be marked by the decline, or indeed the almost total disappearance, of such fine wares. Instead, the ceramic production of most regions appears to consist almost exclusively of a range of coarse to medium-coarse wares principally made up of storage and cooking vessels, with a small number of lamps, cups and other types. Where descriptions do exist it is largely because of the continuity of earlier types into the medieval period. Thus, Coarse Red-Slipped Wares (CRSW), recently identified as being manufactured in Kerala, Organic Black Ware from the Gujarat area and Coarse Ware and Paddle Impressed Ware storage jars from eastern India, show a remarkable continuity into the medieval period and sometimes even beyond. Unfortunately, this very continuity also makes these wares extremely imprecise chronological markers.

It is critical at this point to appreciate the very different status of ceramics in South Asia, as compared to the Middle and Far East. As Carla Sinopoli has helpfully underlined, ceramics and potters in South Asia had a low status and issues of ritual pollution linked to the porosity of earthenware meant that ceramics were largely restricted to use for storage and cooking. 'It is thus the case, she writes, historically as well as at present, that Hindus do not dine off of earthenware vessels, instead preferring more easily cleansed metal vessels or disposable banana leaves' (Sinopoli 1996). Earthenware ceramics were also manufactured for use in Hindu ritual (lamps, specific types of pots and so on), as well as for utilitarian purposes such as ring wells or roof tiles. Another South Asian particularity underlined in Sinopoli's article is that, 'in marked contrast to East and South-East Asia, large-scale industrial manufacture of ceramic vessels never developed in pre-modern Hindu India' (Sinopoli 1996). As Sinopoli explains, pottery production is organized at the level of the household workshop—relatively small-scale units composed of a nuclear or extended family with production activities typically taking place within the family residence. Particularly in the medieval period, we find ourselves looking at myriad local productions of generally low-end ceramics, often simply referred to as 'Coarse wares'. Sinopoli's work on the ceramic assemblage from the medieval Deccani capital of Vijayanagara (fourteenth–sixteenth centuries) in fact demonstrated that 'while ceramics were important in ritual activities and were used by elites, there were no locally produced ceramics that can be readily identified as elite wares *per se*' (Sinopoli 1996).[17] Ceramics in South Asia were a traditional and generally static form; they were not subject to the same paces or ranges of innovation and change as seen in Middle or Far Eastern ceramics. In the light of this, might we do best to regard the Fine Wares of the Early Historic period not as the norm, but rather as helpful anomalies in the history of South Asian ceramic production? As middle- to low-end ceramic types tend to show continuity of fabric and form rather than evolution, this poses obvious problems if they are to be used as part of stratigraphic analysis and dating, yet they cannot be ignored. Even at sites of international trade, local and regional ceramics will always be the main component of any South Asian ceramic assemblage. Without a basic skeleton built around the understanding of such local types, the chronology of many sites has to be anchored to numismatic evidence (itself fallible and by no means consistent) or tied to better-known ceramic chronologies such as those that exist for imported wares from the Middle and/or Far East (and here again, these are not without their problems). Carswell's emphasis on

Chinese sherds in his coastal survey of 1976 and Taisho University's later emphasis on the same area may reflect, in part, the basic lack of study of local ceramics and the long continuities of these types. More sophisticated description and analysis of these myriad medieval period Coarse Wares appears to be the solution to this impasse.

It would be unfair to give the impression that such problems are exclusive to South Asian medieval ceramics. Roberta Tomber's current re-classification of many so-called 'Indo-Roman' amphorae as Mesopotamian torpedo jars dateable to the Parthian to early Islamic periods indicates the extent to which even key West Asian ceramic types linked to the study of trade leave ample room for refinement or even outright revision (Tomber 2007).[18] Similar problems surround the typology and dating of Turquoise Glazed Wares (TGW) or Turquoise Glazed Pottery (TGP)—also known as glazed ware, alkaline glaze ware, TURQ or Sasano-Islamic—the large group of blue-green glazed wares, ranging from bowls to large storage jars, which were produced in or around the area of Basra from the Parthian through to the early Islamic period (Kennet 2004). Like Chinese glazed ceramics, Turquoise Glazed Wares are easy to spot in the field, and are often excitedly picked out at South and South-East Asian sites as signs of international trade with West Asia, but many problems still surround their use as a chronological marker. As Derek Kennet recently pointed out, the absence of any consistent study of TGW's fabric and glazes means that vessel form and/or decoration currently remain critical to the dating of excavated sherds (Kennet forthcoming).[19]

This discussion may appear to have strayed far from the stated remit of writing a 'histoire événementielle' of South Asia from the tenth to twelfth centuries. Yet it surely also points to the central place archaeological material could and should take in future studies. I can only hope that in ten or twenty years time we will be able to write a very different and more archaeologically grounded history of South Asia's medieval maritime trade.

West Asians in Sanjan and the Rastrakuta Domains: A Case Study of Three Tenth Century Sources

This analysis opens with what can only be described as an exceptional intersection of sources on West Asians in the domains of the Rastrakuta dynasty in western India. Middle Eastern geographical texts, a grant document and archaeological data from a known port site can be overlaid to provide one of the richest pictures anywhere in tenth-century South Asia of the presence and position of West Asian trade communities in the region's maritime trade. The unique opportunity to overlay and compare a variety of sources for a single South Asian site and at a defined period explains why this analysis is given such prominence within this paper. Sites such as Sanjan illustrate the potential for interweaving Indic and West Asian textual sources with archaeological data for a holistic study of medieval maritime trade, writing in parallel urban histories, histories of trade institutions and trade commodities, and cultural histories of these maritime worlds. The picture that emerges is nevertheless highly fragmentary and raises more questions than it answers, highlighting the comparative 'youth' of the medieval period in South Asian historical research.

378 AH/988 CE—Ibn Hawqal's Kitab surat al-ard and the 'conjonctures' of South Asian Maritime Trade

Contemporary Arabic geographies provide a more overtly trade-focused perspective on South Asia than indigenous sources and it seems both justified and helpful to begin looking at the subcontinent through this lens. Despite traditional reservations about certain of these texts, most obviously the tendency of so-called geographical works to repeat older information and conventions rather than transmitting up-to-date information on port sites, the Arabic sources usefully distil the complex political geographies of this vast area into the trading blocks and ports which were perceived to be most vital to West Asian trade at the period, thus offering an insight into its main 'conjonctures', if not its event history.

In a history with few dates, 988 CE, the year in which Ibn Hawqal completed his revised edition of the *Kitab surat al-ard*, provides a marker of sorts. His geography was completed before his death for a patently Iranian patron, Abu al-Sari Hasan Isbahani, and provides both useful Iranian and Gulf-centred starting points and displays an overt interest in economic conditions and trade connections. As Ibn Hawqal himself states, his book gathers 'everything that should be known about each region, which is to say the various sources of wealth, taxes, tithes, property taxes, distances of travel, exports and commodities' (Ibn Hawqal 2001, vol. I: 2).[20]

Ibn Hawqal's description of South Asia begins with Sind, technically part of the *dar al-islam*, and then under the semi-independent and Muslim Habbarid dynasty. Sind for Ibn Hawqal is the frontier of the Islamic world, 'the furthest point of the *dar al-islam*' along the northern edge, while the ocean beyond Oman represented its eastern limit (Ibn Hawqal 2001, vol. I: 41, 44). However, perhaps surprisingly, only a blunt picture emerges of the region's pivotal role in regional and Indian Ocean trade. The capital of al-Mansura is described as prosperous but there is little sense of Sind's ports as the main interface between the western Indian Ocean and the Indus River system (Ibn Hawqal 2001, vol. II: 313–14). Although excavations at al-Mansura and Banbhore yielded very rich material culture remains, these have never been comprehensively published, subsequent publications have tended to prioritize the built structures which were uncovered, notably the city walls, the mosques and their inscriptions (Khan 1960; Nabi Khan 1990) neglecting the evidence for trade. A Pakistani-Italian-French project recently initiated at the site of Banbhore (2011) promises to bring much-needed clarity to this situation but for the moment, some of the strongest evidence is slightly earlier and comes from Early Historic Sri Lanka where work by Osmund Bopearachchi has highlighted the richness of material connections between Sind and Sri Lanka (Bopearachchi 2002).

Fascinatingly though, Ibn Hawqal's description of Sind includes substantial parts of al-Hind—Qamuhul (Srimala/Bhinmal), Cambay, Sanjan and Saymur (Chaul), areas of western India which were in fact outside direct Muslim control—and devotes considerable attention to recording the distances and interconnections between these ports and cities. The majority of the locations discussed by Ibn Hawqal in fact belonged to the Rastrakutan kingdom, an enormous empire with multiple associated feudatories, which stretched across northern, central, and southern India, and constituted one of the main trade partners with the new Islamic Empire in West Asia.[21] Many elements of this part of Ibn Hawqal's account are clearly built on a descriptive backbone going back to the mid-ninth century and texts such as Ibn Khurdadhbih's *Kitab al-masalik wa al-mamalik*, where the *Ballahara* or Rastrakutan monarch is described as the great friend of the Arabs (Ibn Khurdadhbih 1889). It is a measure of the time-lag of these geographies that by the time Ibn Hawqal completed his revised text in 988 CE, the Rastrakuta dynasty had already ceased to exist. Its capital city was plundered by the ruler of Malwa in 972/73 CE and the dynasty is generally held to have ended by the early 980s (Sastri et al. 1981: 483). However, the inclusion of the Rastrakutas is surely testimony to the region's continued importance to the economies of both Sind and Buyid Iran irrespective of who precisely controlled them. The only Indian city to be mentioned by Ibn Hawqal and patently not part of the Rastrakuta territories is Qamuhul, believed to correspond to the great trade centre of Srimala or Bhinmala in the Jalor district of Rajasthan, and then under the control of one of the Gurjara rulers. The inclusion of this region suggests that it also welcomed West Asian traders and belonged to the network of land routes connecting Sind to western India in spite of the Jurz's earlier reputation for being the enemy of the Muslims.

The importance of trade between the Gulf and the Rastrakutan domains is also borne out by other types of sources and notably several voyages recorded in the collection of seafarers' tales and accounts commonly known as the *'Aja'ib al-hind*, or the *Book of the Wonders of India* in English (Buzurg 1981), a text we now know to have been compiled in Cairo sometime in the 960s or 970s CE by a scholar named Abu 'Imran Musa ibn Rabah al-Awsi al-Sirafi under the title *Al-Sahih min akhbar al-bihar wa-'aja'ibiha*.[22] Irrespective of this new attribution, the compilation includes several accounts of West Asian merchants who resided on the west coast at Tana-Subara or travelled to Sindan, Saymur, and Tana from Siraf or Oman (ibid.). Again, in a landscape with few dates, Buzurg's text often seeks to establish the veracity of its accounts by providing names and dates. Thus, we know that in AH 306/918 CE Ismailawayh ibn Ibrahim ibn Mardas sailed from Oman to the ports of western India in only eleven days. Ibn Hawqal's equal emphasis on overland and sea connections is also borne out by the *'Al-Sahih min akhbar al-bihar* record of a voyage from al-Mansura in Sind to the Rastrakutan capital of Manyakheda in the Deccan via the port of Cambay and which is most likely to have taken place by land (ibid.).

Underlying the intense contacts between West Asia and the Rastrakutan territories were formal treaties which allowed for the growth of free and peaceful trade relations. The existence of such treaties and their effects on trade in the Indian Ocean is documented most overtly in the Ibadi *fiqh* literature from Oman which discusses both truces and peace agreements with non-Muslim polities in the Indian Ocean (Wilkinson 1981). As J.C. Wilkinson makes clear, since India, East Africa and China 'formed part of the *dar al-harb*, with which the Muslims were constitutionally at war, trade could theoretically only be carried out by annually renewable agreements, presumably valid for each monsoon season' (ibid.: 278) and numerous examples of *fiqh* rulings demonstrate how, in Oman, such treaties determined the taxation of goods coming from these areas. A telling passage in *Al-Sahih min akhbar al-bihar* in fact refers to the *shurut* (agreements or provisions) then regulating relations between 'us' (the Arabs) and the rulers of Saymur (Buzurg 1981: 83).

In Ibn Hawqal's text the South Asian seaboard beyond the northern Konkan and ports such as Saymur (modern Chaul) fades away into a broader, ill-defined *bahr al-fars* the ends of which are marked by the frontiers of China at one end and Qulzum or Suez at the other (Ibn Hawqal 2001, vol. I: 11). Ibn Hawqal's focus on western India is a measure of his Iranian allegiances, the revised text was completed for a patently Iranian patron, and Gulf-centric perspective but also reflects the very reality of contacts between these areas. The intensity of these contacts is explained not only by the obvious proximity of the Gulf to western India but also by the fact that the sea in this region was 'open', that is to say navigable, all year round, in spite of the monsoon. Year-round navigation obviously conditioned the frequency and thus the very nature of contacts and trade between these areas; this contrasts with the much more seasonal character of contacts between the central and southern parts of India's western seaboard and the facing east coast of the Arabian Peninsula, as also the Gulf and Red Sea.

It is clear that significant Muslim mercantile groups settled or sojourned for long periods within the Rastrakuta domains. Ibn Hawqal's text describes the presence of mosques at major Rastrakutan ports and cities, as well as the existence of developed systems of autonomous administration and Islamic justice in these areas. Ibn Hawqal reports that in these regions 'Muslims live there and only a Muslim has authority over them, who the ruling Balhara puts in his place over them' (Ibn Hawqal 2001, vol. II: 313), adding elsewhere that 'there are *jami'* mosques and the Muslim institutions of law (*ahkam*) are practiced openly' (ibid.: 317). It is also apparent that in this environment West Asian merchants were marrying locally, leading to the emergence of a new class of Indian Muslim. Thus al-Mas'udi relates how at Saymur (Chaul) there existed a group of people known as *bayasira* (sing. *baysar*) who were those born in Hind to (male) Muslims (al-Mas'udi 1962–79, vol. I: 187). While Ibn Hawqal and authors such as al-Mas'udi focus on Muslim communities, other sources suggest that Muslims were only one of a number of West Asian faith groups involved in trade with the region, a situation that entirely befits the prominence of Zoroastrians, Jews and Christians from West Asia in the pre-Islamic trade with India. Thus, Abu Dulaf Mis'ar ibn Muhalhil's largely lost tenth century text, the *'Aja'ib al-buldan*, states that at Saymur 'there are Muslims, Christians, Jews and Fire worshippers. ... there are mosques, Christian churches, synagogues and fire temples' (Ferrand 1913, vol. 1: 223).

17/18 April 926: The Chinchani Copperplate Grant

As highlighted by Chakravarti and other historians, Rastrakuta grant documents and inscriptions as a genre generally give us little idea of the region's growing involvement in either regional trade networks or the international maritime trade glimpsed through West Asian sources. Yet one exceptional document offers an unprecedented portrait of a Rastrakuta port city and of a West Asian merchant who had entered the Rastrakuta administration.

Currently, the single most detailed piece of written evidence for the place of West Asian mercantile diasporas in the Rastrakutan kingdom and of the Rastrakuta kingdom in international maritime trade comes from a grant document relating to the port of Sanjan (Sindan in the Arabic sources). The so-called Chinchani copperplate grant was found just under 30 km. south of Sanjan, at the small coastal settlement of Chinchani, and concerns the endowment of land there to maintain two religious institutions at Sanjan during the reign of Rastrakuta Indra III (Sircar 1957–8a).[23] The endowment made provision for the maintenance of a monastery or temple (*mathika*) and the shrine of a goddess at Sanjan and was made in *Saka* 848, on the third day of the bright fortnight of the month of *Vaishakha*, equivalent to 17 or 18 April 926 CE. As was common practice at the period, the endowment was announced before an assembly of the main local players of Sanjan, headed by the governor (*nrpati*) of the *mandala*, Madhumati Sugatipa, son of Sahiyarahara (Shahriyar) of the *tajikanvaya* (Tajika or Arab) community who oversaw the endowment process on behalf of the Rastrakutan monarch. Madhumati is a common Sanskritization of the Arabic name Muhammad and indicates the Muslim faith of this individual but far more tantalizing are the clear indications of this individual's West Asian origins, given in the text.

Indic grant documents as a genre commonly include short biographical passages about prominent individuals involved in the legal processes being recorded, and it is here, in the Chinchani grants discussed here as well as in a small number of later documents, that some of the richest textual clues to West Asian trade communities can be found. As legal documents these sources are all precisely dated, they bring chronological markers into a historical landscape that is often more easily understood in terms of 'conjonctures' or the 'longue durée' at the same time challenging what we usually define as a historical event. Although described as a *tajika* or Arab, Muhammad's father was named Sahiyarahara, itself a Sanskritization of the Persian name Shahriyar which thus clearly suggests a Persianate background. Brief biographical details given in the grant indicate that Madhumati (Muhammad) had been appointed to this post during the earlier reign of Krishna II, thus before 915 CE, and had therefore been in post for over a decade by the time of this endowment. Perhaps just as significantly, we are told that he had been appointed after he had conquered all the kings of the harbours on behalf of his overlord and placed his own (Madhumati's) officials in them, a phrase which suggests that Madhumati had commanded ships in the service of the Rastrakutas, and also possessed a network of administrative collaborators, possibly also West Asians, who had risen with him. Indic documents often refer back to earlier endowments and thus we know that Madhumati had previously been involved in the establishment of 'a free ferry' and also a feeding house at the port. It is important to emphasize here that in order to function for over a decade within the Rastrakutan administrative system, our Muhammad or Madhumati must have been at the very least bilingual and bicultural, able to function competently within both Arabo-Persian and local Konkani milieus. Muhammad or Madhumati appears to have worked in close collaboration with his Indian minister Puvvaiya.

The legal character of such grant documents affords us a uniquely close view of Sanjan's administration and Madhumati's place in it. As always in a legal document, the members of the assembly are specifically listed and these included the *dhruvas* or superintendents of the collection of the royal share of crops, the *vishayik-adhikarikas* or officers of the various administrative offices together with the *Sri Samyana hamyamana-paura* or 'citizens of the *hamyamana* of Sri Samyana [Sanjan]' (Sircar 1957–8a: 48). The first two categories of witnesses in the assembly played major roles in the port's administration, collecting the royal share and administering the port. The nature of the *hamyamana* has been the subject of much debate since the nineteenth century, discussed alongside the variants *hanjamana*, and the term *anjuvannam* found in south India. An important recent publication by Yellava Subbarayalu surveying this earlier research has concluded that the term represents 'a trading body composed of West Asian seafaring merchants' which gathered both ethnic Arabs and Persians across faith groups (Subbarayalu 2012: 185). The exact make-up of any one of these *anjuman* assemblies clearly depended on the particular West Asian communities present at any one locality and inscriptions across South Asia from the mid-ninth to fifteenth century include Zoroastrians, Eastern Christians, Jews, and Muslims in various ethnic and linguistic combinations. Much about these *anjuman* assemblies remains unclear, we do not know how they were constituted or administered, nor how they mapped onto the purely faith constituted groupings which undoubtedly existed, as described by Ibn Hawqal for the Muslim community. Madhumati Sugatipa's relationship to this assembly is also unknown and we can only speculate as to whether these local assemblies formed part of a larger network or a more formal trade association similar to a medieval European guild. It is, however, clear that Sanjan's *anjuman* assembly continued to play an important part in local government after the fall of the Rastrakutas, since a grant dated *Śaka* 956/1034 CE, making an endowment to the same *mathika*, this time under the auspices of the Silahara dynasty, refers to 'the elders of the *hamyamana*, namely Vallana-*vyavaharaka*, Valkasama-*vyavaharaka*, Alliya, Mahara, Madhumati, and others; the elders of the *paura*, namely the *sreshthi* Kesari, the *suvarnna* Kakkala, the *vanija* Uva, the *suvarnna* Somaiya, and others; the district officer Verthalaiya' (Subbarayalu 2012: 179). D.C. Sircar had already noted that two of these names were clearly Sanskritizations of Arabic Muslim names, namely Alliya for 'Ali and Madhumati for Muhammad (Sircar 1957-58b: 64) and as Subbarayalu concluded, this indicated that at least one member of this *hamyamana* was a Muslim while another went by the Arabic or Persian name Ali. The name Mahara may well be a local rendering of the Persian name Mehr, indicating another West Asian ethnicity.

We are fortunate that a number of grant documents survive for medieval Sanjan, allowing us some insight into the longer term history of the port over the early tenth through eleventh centuries CE. Thus, another mid-tenth century grant document from Sanjan usefully corroborates the importance of links between the port and Bhinmala/Srimala in western Rajasthan as depicted in Ibn Hawqal's text. The grant dates to the reign of Krishna III (r. 939–67), and records benefactions made to another *mathika* or monastery attached to a temple at Sanjan. The name of the temple deity, Bhillamala-deva, an aspect of Vishnu, indicates that it was installed by descendants of merchants from Bhinmala/Srimala (Sircar 1957–8a: 56). The presence of merchants from Bhinmala/Srimala may be part of a more general outward movement of the town's mercantile populations in the mid-tenth century.[24]

The copperplate grants associated with Sanjan offer one of the most detailed insights into the position and workings of a West Asian merchant within the Rastrakutan administration. Thanks to the particular conventions of grant documents, which frequently included biographical elements, the document offers an insight not simply into a particular administrative moment, but into the career and family background of the key individuals involved. The problem nevertheless remains of how far the example of Madhumati Sugatipa can be interpreted as a general model of Rastrakutan administrative practice at major sites of international trade, and even beyond this of administrative practice in other South Asian polities.

Excavations at Sanjan: Archaeological Time and Data Sets

Exceptionally, Ibn Hawqal's account and the Chinchani grant can also be set against archaeological material. Of the four great ports and towns mentioned by Ibn Hawqal as involved in the trade between western India and the Middle East—Srimala/Bhinmala, Cambay, Sanjan and Chaul—two have recently been excavated. Excavations at Sanjan were begun in

2002 under the aegis of the World Zarathusti Cultural Foundation and have led to a substantial number of publications (Gupta et al. 2001–2, 2003, Nanji and Dhalla 2007, Nanji 2011).[25] The site at Chaul was excavated by Deccan College, Pune shortly afterwards and the findings are in course of publication (Tripati 1992, Gogte et al. 2006a). The recent excavations at Sanjan allow us to set the material evidence for their medieval trade alongside these epigraphic sources.

The main trace of historical settlement at Sanjan is a large mound covering some 1 by 1.5 km. on the northern bank of the Varoli River, just at the point where it ceases to be navigable, and which is believed to have constituted Sanjan's main urban core and port area. Traces of a stone fortification wall were located under a coconut grove. The ceramic record, supported by epigraphic evidence, suggest some form of minor settlement in the Early Historic period (RPW found at Sanjan has been dated to the second century CE although it comes from a disturbed context). However, the port appears to have been in its prime between the eighth and fourteenth centuries, at which point silting and the growth of a sandbank made the port impracticable for anything but small craft. Built evidence for trade infrastructure was uncovered in the form of a brick wharf but undoubtedly, the best preserved structure at Sanjan was a large rubble, brick and earth Tower of Silence or *dokhma* which confirmed the importance of the port as a centre of Parsi settlement whilst revealing important data on Parsi mortuary practices. An eleventh century date for the *dokhma* has been suggested.[26] Fragments of Rastrakutan and later Silahara sculpture at the port area and in the surrounding countryside attest in a general fashion to the earlier temples whose endowments we know so much about. Unsurprisingly, the site yielded abundant finds of West Asian ceramics, glass and coins, as well as smaller quantities of Chinese wares, and it is these, coupled with some numismatic and Carbon Dating evidence, that give the site its main chronology. While Sanjan appears to have been settled and in regular contact with the Gulf from the seventh century, it experienced a significant boom in contacts in the eleventh century when 'considerable quantities' of West Asian ceramics appear. Current calculations suggest that 21 per cent of ceramic wares for this level are from the Gulf; alongside TGW storage jars are found all the types typical of the so-called Samarra horizon such as white glaze wares, lustrewares, cobalt wares and splash wares, the majority are tablewares such as bowls and dishes.

Yet in spite of this, the site has not yielded quite the quality of information that might have been hoped for. Excavation was limited to four areas, scattered in a largely haphazard manner due to issues of land ownership, as well as site disturbance after centuries of agricultural activity and brick-making, consequently, there is little spatial information about the contexts in which finds were excavated. In fact, conditions at Sanjan typify the challenges that archaeology faces on India's fertile and crowded west coast and contrast markedly with much of the coast of the Arabian Peninsula and the east African coast where different histories of occupation and different climatic conditions have meant that entire coastal sites can be excavated and mapped back to their first foundation on virgin soil. At present South Asianists can only dream of capturing the kind of picture that emerges at sites such as these. At Sanjan therefore, only four areas were excavated: excavations began in the port area with a large trench measuring 5 by 7.5 m., this yielded the most significant ceramic material and small finds, excavations ended with a small trench on the riverbank of the port area and this trench provided the main stratigraphic sequence for the site. The remaining two areas of excavation were at the Koli Khadi mound, some 500 m. away, which uncovered only a very thin habitational deposit dateable to the fourteenth century, and the eleventh century *dokhma*, which by its very function, yielded little ceramic material although it has contributed considerably to the understanding of Parsi mortuary practices.

Overall then, the excavations reveal little about the specifics of trade or domestic spaces at Sanjan, or about wider urban settlement patterns. Although excavations at the port area and Koli Khadi exposed parts of brick walls, floor surfaces and ringwells, no complete structures were uncovered. It is impossible to judge whether these elements belonged to warehouses, manufacturing areas or perhaps to mixed use residential buildings. Apart from the Tower of Silence, located on the fringe of the mound, no traces of religious architecture or cemeteries of other faith communities have been located to date. As these are likely to have been among the more permanent constructions at the port, this leaves little hope for locating any substantial traces of less permanent domestic and trade spaces which may well have been constructed of perishable materials. We do not even have a clear idea of where the main administrative or residential area was located within the main mound, the very locales where Madhumati Sugatipa would have lived or held office.

The enormous percentage of West Asian ceramics at Sanjan—their lack of spatial context notwithstanding—offers an important opportunity to reflect on the use of West Asian ceramics as material sources for the period. Since ceramics are the single largest category of excavated evidence at most sites, it surely behoves us to be as ambitious as possible in our use of them. Using ceramics to define and date site stratigraphies should really be only the starting point for the discussion of wider, and ultimately much more interesting, questions. The point has already been made in other contexts that ceramics travel for a variety of reasons: as traded goods in their own right, as containers of other commodities, and as personal possessions or as gifts. As such, they offer the chance to ask questions both about trade and traded goods as well as about the material world and culture of medieval Sanjan.

Typically, economic historians bemoan the almost total absence of statistical data on trade in the Indian Ocean before the appearance of European documents in the sixteenth century, yet ceramics offer at least basic quantitative data on such issues, if suitably excavated and analysed. If the percentages of different vessel types are calculated for each period, basic pictures of volumes and directions of exchange, and their change over time, can be established. At Sanjan, analysis of this sort has suggested a significant boom in contacts between the port and West Asia, specifically the head of the Gulf, in the eleventh century when something in the region of 21 per cent of ceramic wares for this level are West Asian ceramics. While Rukshana Nanji has stated that the proportion of West Asian wares at Sanjan contrasts markedly with that at the contemporary Rastrakutan port of Chaul, precise percentages are not currently available for comparison. Shockingly, there is currently little material to compare Sanjan with, only one other site outside the Gulf has looked at percentages of West Asian wares (Kennet forthcoming) although Seth Priestman's work promises to remedy this situation.[27] While we await the publication of this thesis, the only other site we can turn to is the Sri Lankan capital of Anuradhapura where excavators looked at the proportion of Turquoise Glazed Wares—thus a specific sub-set of West Asian wares—to the overall volume of coarse wares in the levels of each period. The analysis suggested that TGW represented only 0.2 per cent of coarse ware rims for the period 600–1100 CE (versus 4 per cent for the period between 200–600 CE). The data suggests a period of particularly intense trade and contact between the Sri Lankan capital and Mesopotamia during the Sasanian period, a period when Iran was indeed a dominant maritime power in the western Indian Ocean, with a substantial fall off after that (Coningham 2006, Tables 5.2 and 6.3; Kennet forthcoming). Of course, the data is still extremely coarse and not directly comparable: the figure of 0.2 per cent over a 500-year timespan at Anuradhapura gives little insight into the finer fluctuations of contact, or perhaps trends in consumption, over this period and the 21 per cent figure given at Sanjan includes all West Asian wares over a period of several centuries. Nevertheless, this is quantitative data and we should be glad to have it, it suggests that Sanjan had a remarkably intense relation to the head of the Gulf but we can only guess as to how much this single port is characteristic of other sites along the western seaboard and of inland sites in South Asia. It is also far from clear how much this 21 per cent figure provides data about trade between the areas, or about cultural contacts and settlement at Sanjan. What proportion of this 21 per cent is constituted by storage jars and is thus directly related to traded items, and what by tableware and thus more directly pertinent to understanding dining cultures?

We also know little about the life of turquoise glazed storage jars. Roberta Tomber's work on torpedo jars has significantly illuminated the trade in wine between Mesopotamia and South Asia in the period before 500 CE (Tomber 2007) but this work rests very heavily on the fact that these jars had a very specific function and a clear relationship to a limited number of commodities. Turquoise Glazed Ware storage jars show a far wider range of sizes and shapes and therefore appear to have carried a far wider range of substances and commodities. Furthermore, while they undoubtedly served to transport traded goods, they may also have served to carry onboard provisions such as water and foodstuffs, and would probably also have had a re-sale value outside the Gulf.[28] This complex life makes the interpretation of their sherds correspondingly complex. TGW tablewares clearly fulfilled quite other functions. Finds of TGW sherds are thus only very basic indicators of 'contact' and it becomes important to look for other clues to their final function at different sites, for example by understanding the spatial contexts in which both types of vessel were found.

Sanjan does appear to have yielded a remarkable range of West Asian glazed tablewares, including all the main types then being produced in the Basra area. One of the most stunning finds was of a set of four lustre bowls all decorated with an identical running hare motif. It has been speculated that the West Asian tablewares found at Sanjan were destined for use by the port's wealthy West Asian mercantile community. As Hindus traditionally avoided eating off ceramics, specifically earthenware, due to their perceived porosity and potential for ritual contamination, the serious question exists of whether glazed ceramics should be read in South Asian contexts as signs of specifically West Asian dining practices and, in fact, presence. Madhumati Sugatipa and other West Asians living at Sanjan may well have eaten off imported glazed ceramics, Chinese and West Asian, preferring these to local earthenwares. Carla Sinopoli observed that imported ceramics such as East Asian celadons and porcelains are relatively rare, though by no means non-existent, in historic sites in areas ruled by Hindu elites, whereas they are more common in contemporaneous sites and regions of South Asia that were dominated by Muslim elites who do not share the same proscriptions on the use of ceramics (Sinopoli 1996).[29] The data Sinopoli presents is fascinating in suggesting that the glazed wares from Sanjan might have been specifically destined for West Asian elites, however, the case is by no means proven. While the concentration of West Asian glazed ceramics in the port area tells us that large quantities of such ceramics were entering Sanjan, it does keep us understand whom they were for. The context in which these glazed ceramics were excavated at Sanjan clarifies nothing since the spatial context of the port area was poorly studied; furthermore, the only two other excavated areas—the *dokhma* and the fourteenth century habitation area—are not directly comparable.

Nor should we exclude the possibility that glazed tablewares might also have been adopted by some Hindus, complementing or perhaps even replacing local traditions of fine tableware production. Were glazed ceramics really seen as equivalent to earthenware vessels and thus unsuitable as tableware? Might attitudes to ceramics and their pollution in fact have changed over time in response to new technological developments? Glaze renders ceramics impermeable: might this have circumvented the problems faced by the porosity of earthenware, making them more like metals? In this scenario, Sanjan's West Asian merchant groups might simply have played a key regional role in the import and distribution of these wares, hence their considerable quantities. One way to answer this question might be to look at the distribution of these imported wares in the wider Sanjan area, beyond the port. However, the absence of archaeological data from the Sanjan hinterland and its associated ports means that we have no idea of the distribution of these glazed ceramics, if any took place at all. Yet it seems hard to believe that all the imported glazed tablewares found around the shores of South Asia were destined only for non-Hindus, such as West Asian or Chinese diasporas.

Obvious as the point may be, it seems important to underline the fact that these imported glazed wares—often shiny and brightly coloured—entered a local culture where ceramics were traditionally unglazed and conformed to a limited earth-coloured palette. They must have made an enormous physical and visual impact and it is difficult to believe that they were never consumed by indigenous South Asian elites. Did glazed wares become high status objects, even exotica, and in so doing how much might they have lost their original functions of storage and containment and instead gained new functions and meanings? If we compare South Asia to the East African coast, another area where unglazed ceramics were also the norm, we see glazed bowls and plates from West Asia and the Far East incorporated into religious buildings and funerary monuments where their colours and patterns and the prestige they embodied clearly enriched these structures both aesthetically and semantically. A lack of archaeological data currently limits our ability to say how South Asian eating and storage practices responded to glazed wares, or not, but it still seems worth asking these questions. Questioning of this sort also highlights the extent to which the study of imported glazed ceramics in South Asia might benefit from the simultaneously examination of both West Asian and Far Eastern wares, as opposed to the largely separate discussions that currently prevail.

Tenth century Sanjan represents one of the densest data sets for West Asian diasporas in South Asia and yet the question for outweigh the answers. While it seems highly probable that the Muslim governor of Sanjan, Madhumati Sugatipa, and later officers of the *anjuman* assembly dined off imported Far and West Asian tablewares, we have little idea of where they did so within the larger urban topography of Sanjan or indeed of how their consumption of these wares fitted into the wider food culture of Sanjan. We do not know whether their non-Muslim peers within the Rastrakuta administration had also taken to using glazed vessels and if so in which contexts. What was eaten in these imported tablewares can only be a matter of even greater speculation as the excavations at Sanjan, as so often in South Asia, did not set out to study archaeo-botanical or archaeo-faunal remains. Archaeology at this scale ultimately yields data not far removed from the kind yielded by contemporary grant documents, a brief bright light in an otherwise dark room.

Beyond Rastrakuta Western India: Glimpses of Kerala, Sri Lanka and the Palk Strait

In Ibn Hawqal's text the Indian coast south of Saymur (Chaul) fades off into the wider Indian Ocean and more southerly ports only begin to appear consistently in Middle Eastern geographies from the twelfth century onwards, for example in al-Idrisi's *Kitab nuzhat al-mushtaq* (AH 548/1154 CE). If the geographers' knowledge of western India and its political structures at this period reflects the proximity and intensity of contact between this area and the Gulf, the South Asian seaboard below Saymur was nevertheless also involved in international maritime trade across the western Indian Ocean to the Arabian Peninsula and the Red Sea, albeit along patterns more heavily subject to monsoon rhythms and the 'open' or 'closed' state of the sea. The central areas of the eastern coast of the Arabian Peninsula, around Shihr and Sharma, benefitted from seasonal winds and currents which facilitated particularly rapid and direct crossings of the western Indian Ocean to southern India, particularly to the northern Malabar coast, and of course back again.

New genres of source come to fill the gaps left in the geographical literature, notably the merchant handbook and the mariner's tale. We have already discussed and used the *Al-Sahihmin akhbar al-bihar*, the second text used here is that written by the merchant Abu Zayd Sirafi sometime in the early tenth century, his account has no formal title and is known variably as Abu Zayd's account or the *Silsila al-tawarikh* (*Chain of Chronicles*). Abu Zayd presents his account as an update to an earlier anonymous manual on trade with India and China written in 851 CE, and known as the *Akhbar al-sin wa-l-hind* (*Akhbar* 1948). Aby Zayd presents his revision as a response necessary and useful due to substantial changes to trade conditions in the eastern Chinese ports in the intervening period.

Sri Lanka and Southern India

The south India that emerges from Abu Zayd's account and the stories compiled in the *Sahih min akhbar al-bihar* (formerly known as Buzurg ibn Shahriyar's *Kitab 'aja'in al-hind*) is almost impossible to compare with contemporary geographical accounts of western India. Neither mentions specific ports along these shores, let alone the distances between them, but perhaps most noticeably the polities governing these regions and their relationship to West Asian trade communities emerge only hazily. At our period, in 910 CE to be precise, Parantaka Cola I (r. 907–55) had ousted the Pandyas from the southern Tamil country while the Sinhala dynasty ruled Sri Lanka from Anuradhapura. Yet Abu Zayd and the *Al-Sahih min akhbar al-bihar* present a fractured geography concerned mainly with anecdotes about Sri Lankan gemstones and cock-fighting, funerary customs, or the role of the Maldives in provisioning ships. The main maritime landscape to emerge from these accounts is the Palk Strait, formed by the northwest coast of Sri Lanka and the facing Tamil coast, a dangerous sailing space known as the gulf (*gubb*) or the gulfs (*aghbab*) of Ceylon, beset by pirate attacks, its shallow waters filled with crocodiles and its shores teeming with snakes and tigers (Buzurg 1981: 66). The evasiveness with which these regions are described in our sources suggests either more intermittent contacts compared to western India or very different patterns of interaction.

The paucity of information about West Asians in South India and Sri Lanka is particularly surprising given the importance of these areas as a producers of pearls and precious stones as well as their strategic location on the sea route to China. Southern Sri Lanka was the main centre of gemstone extraction and an important centre of iron production. New research on the kingdom of Ruhuna and sites such as Tissimaharama have emphasized the region's firm connection to international trade routes well before the seventh century CE. Sri Lanka is currently in the midst of an archaeological fever which will potentially shed much needed light on its Late Antique and medieval maritime trade. Excavations at Anuradhapura (Coningham 1999, 2006) and along the southern coast, notably at the southern site of Tissamaharama (Weisshaar 2001, Walburg 2008), are well-established. The French Mission of Archaeological Co-operation in Sri Lanka is also yielding rich data (Bopearachchi and Wickremesinhe 1999) while the newer Oxford based Sealinks project has been excavating on both the north and south coasts of the island.[30] Abu Zayd specifically mentions Sri Lanka as home to significant Jewish and Manichean populations and the island's sizeable Jewish population is mentioned again in the twelfth century in Benjamin of Tudela's *Book of Travel*. However, recent finds of ninth and tenth century Islamic tombstones along the western coast testify to the contemporary presence of Muslim traders at these ports (Kalus and Guillot 2006). A fine Kufic inscribed tombstone now in the National Museum in Colombo records the death of a certain Khalad ibn Abu Niqaba on the fifth Rajab 337 AH or 317 of the Persian Yazdagirdi era, equivalent to 8 January 949 CE (ibid.: 32–3). While the use of the Persian calendar hints at Iranian connections and ties in with a plethora of Persianate echoes across the contemporary western Indian Ocean, onomastic analysis yields little in this instance and, like the copperplate grants from Sanjan, it is difficult to integrate these micro-historical events into traditional historical narratives of West Asians in South Asian maritime trade.

Another tantalizing source for this region at this early period is the text of a seventeenth century *tabaqat* or biographical dictionary from Tamil Nadu which may well record a now lost ninth century Tamil copperplate grant. The grant's contents are recorded in the context of a discussion of the geneology of a *shaykh* from Kayalpatnam (the Arabic Qa'il) on the southern coast of Tamil Nadu. The original grant was reportedly dated *Sagaptam* 798 or April 875 CE when Kayal was still under Pandya rule (Kokan 1974: 51–2).[31] The *Tabaqat* text mentions the arrival at the port of Kayalpatnam in 232 AH or 846 CE of a group of 224 Muslims, men, women and children, from al-Muqattam, the mountain chain that runs the length of the Red Sea in Egypt. They are stated to have been led by a descendant of the Caliph Abu Bakr. In a pattern familiar from many other South Asian grants, the source states that the group was welcomed by the local ruler and subsequently awarded a grant giving them ownership of the land they had settled. The original grant document reportedly gave them asylum and listed the number of persons involved, including slaves, and the names of the tribes they belonged to. The information provided in this *Tabaqat* is a tantalizing echo of a lost, or perhaps as yet unidentified, copperplate grant. Its details are too specific to be a pure invention, yet it awaits definitive authentication. In spite of the doubts that surround this source it is potentially the ninth century document concerning West Asian diasporas in South Asia, contemporary with the Kollam plates to which I will turn shortly. Kayalpatnam's position on the Palk Strait made it a key transit point in international trade and this group is likely to have arrived via existing shipping and trade connections.

The Port of Kollam

One location stands out from this chronological and geographical haze, the port of Kollam (Quilon) in south Kerala. While we have no information about Kollam's trade in the tenth century, the older *Akhbar al-sin wa-l-hind* offers exceptionally detailed information about this port. The *Akhbar*, upon which Abu Zayd's text rests, is structured according to the main stopping points on the sea route between the Gulf and eastern China and along this route only one Indian port features, that of Kollam. According to the *Akhbar*, Kollam is the principal port of call and taxation before entering the sea of Harkand (the Bay of Bengal) and from here ships sail to Kalah on the Malay Peninsula. We are told that Kollam had a *maslaha* or check point[31] attached to the country of Koullam-Malaya (i.e. the Cera kingdom), and which took taxes on China trade ships to the amount of 1,000 *dirham*s and 10–20 *dinar*s on other ships. Fascinatingly, the *Akhbar* describes Muscat as the last watering and supply stop before the voyage across to Kollam (*Akhbar* 1948: 8). The absence of any updates about Kollam in Abu Zayd's tenth century account suggests that Kollam retained this position at this period, and indeed, it remained the principal port of south Malabar into the fourteenth century CE and beyond.

The coast of Malabar is rich in good port sites, with many rivers providing access to its hinterland, but of all these sites Kollam is the southernmost and largest port. To add to its appeal, it was also easily identifiable to navigators, situated as it was just before a series of steep bluffs, known since Indo-Roman times by the nautical name of the Red Cliffs due to the red coloured tableland that rises above the fringe of palms along the coast. Kollam is believed to have been founded in 825 CE, only some twenty-five years after the establishment of the Cera dynasty, and very possibly in response to the growth of West Asian trade.[32] Ships making for these more southerly sections of India's western seaboard could sail either from the mouth of the Gulf to western India and follow the coast down, or they could make a much more direct open ocean crossing from different points along the eastern coast of the Arabian Peninsula. Similar routes obviously apply for the return journey. With the practice of direct sailing the length of the whole route to China, it made sense to set sail for the southernmost port on the west coast, before rounding the tip of India at Kanyakumari and engaging in the Palk Strait or heading around the southern tip of Sri Lanka into the eastern Indian Ocean.

Coincidentally, we know that at the time of the *Akhbar* the trade of Kollam and the taxes it generated was partly under the control of West Asian mercantile groups headed by an Eastern Christian, Maruvan Sabr'isho who held the formal administrative post of Superintendent of Weights and Measures. A grant document issued in the fifth regnal year of the Cera ruler, Sthanu Ravi, equivalent to 849 CE sets out the donation of land to the church at Kollam as well as the tax privileges awarded to its West Asian chief merchant and two trade groupings, the *Manigramam* and the *Anjuvannam* (Rao 1920). A unique set of group testimonials, witnessing the donations, provide a rare glance into the mix of West Asian mercantile diasporas active at the port: a group of eleven names given in Arabic and written in a monumental if amateurish Kufic, ten names given in Pahlavi and grouping both Iranian Eastern Christians and Iranian Zoroastrians, and finally four names given in Judaeo-Persian, that is Middle Persian written in Hebrew characters. In all probability these merchants belonged to the *anjuman* or assembly, here termed *Anjuvannam* in the Tamil portion of the grant. It is clear from the Tamil text, however, that these West Asian networks collaborated with local trade groupings since a group known as the *Manigramam* were key collaborators in the collection of taxes and the running of the *nagaram* or market. The trade of Kollam remained under substantial Eastern Christian control until the fourteenth century and there is thus every reason to believe that similar systems of control and collaboration persisted at the port throughout the period of our study. Again, it is far from clear how far Kollam represented an exceptional case of West Asian control over international trade, or a standard practice at Cera ports, but it is difficult not to see similarities between Maruvan Sabr'isho's position at Kollam and Muhammad Sugatipa's later governorship of Sanjan.[33]

The Spaces in Between: South Konkan, Kanara and North Kerala

These tenth century reflections of West Asians in South Asian maritime trade are as interesting for their omissions as their inclusions. Large tracts of the Konkan, Kanara, Malabar and Ma'bar coasts are almost totally absent from our sources in spite of their importance in the major maritime trade networks of the period and hints of the presence of West Asians within these. It is unclear at present whether this pattern is simply a reflection of the patchy nature of medieval sources and the problematical historiography of the medieval in South Asia, or reflects qualitatively and quantitatively different patterns of connection and settlement.

Work by Ranabir Chakravarti has shown that several areas of the southern Konkan and north Malabar coast had active ports at this time. Chakravarti lists a number of southern Konkani ports such as Nagarpura (Nagav in Kolaba district), Balipattana (Kharepatan in Ratnagiri district) and Gopakapattana/Gove (Goa) which do not appear in the West Asian sources (1998: 105). Geneviève Bouchon has also highlighted the neglect of the north Kerala ports around Mount Eli, the region known historically as Kulathunad (1975). Prominent among these was the independent Kingdom of Eli, located around the mouth of the Taliparamba River and easily visible to shipping thanks to the massive 259 m. high headland of Mount Eli. The Ramantali inscription dated *Kali* 4029 or 927 CE mentions the port of Ilangopattanam and the presence of the *Manigramam* trade association there, a grouping already mentioned at Kollam in the mid-ninth century where it leased the local market or *nagaram* with the *Anjuvanam* association of West Asian traders. However, the port is absent from our sources (Bouchon 1975: 2, 8).

All Change: Shifting Networks in the Late Tenth–Early Eleventh Century

Ibn Hawqal's political geography of western India was already outdated in 988 CE when he completed it, changed by the disappearance of the Rastrakutas. This was but one of a number of radical changes along the western and southern seaboards of South Asia in the fifty years between 975 and 1025 CE. There can be no doubt that these changes affected international maritime networks but the task of distinguishing the concrete, practical effects of these changes remains a complex and unfinished task. The decline of the Abbasid tradition of geographical, navigational and *'aja'ib* writing robs us of an important West Asian perspective, leaving us to turn to the short geographical chapters of al-Biruni's *Tahqiq ma lil-hind*, composed around 1030 CE, or the relevant sections of al-Idrisi's later *Kitab nuzhat al-mushtaq* (AH 548/1154 CE). South Asian grant documents and the nascent medieval archaeological research sometimes provide our only data, and take our perspectives down to the micro-level of a single event or port. Only in the later eleventh century does a new genre of micro-source appear on the horizon, the first surviving 'India Book' documents from the Cairo Geniza which open a sudden and unexpected window onto Jewish and other trade networks in the western Indian Ocean.[34] As mentioned, due to the volume of material involved, and the timing of its publication, this essay is forced to exclude this material from its discussion.[35]

New Political Geographies of the Western Seaboard: Silaharas and Kadambas

Following a period of enormous Rastrakutan expansion under Krishna III (r. c. 939–67), involving military campaigns against the Colas in southern India and the Gurjara-Pratiharas, Paramaras and Palas in northern and central India, the Rastrakutan empire fragmented rapidly under Krishna's successors. In 972/73 the ruler of Malwa plundered the Rastrakutan capital, and by the early 980s the Rastrakuta dynasty had ceased to exist (Sastri et al. 1981: 483). André Wink raises the interesting question of how far the fall of the Rastrakutas was causally linked to wider patterns in the economy of the western Indian Ocean observing that their decline 'synchronizes exactly with the collapse of the Persian Gulf trading system, first gradually, then rapidly in the eleventh century, when the India trade shifted to Fatimid Egypt and the Red Sea' (1991: 308). In fact, their decline appears to pre-date two of the principal events currently held to be responsible for a decline in Gulf trade at this period, namely the 977 CE Siraf earthquake that substantially damaged the port and, more importantly as suggested in new research by Richard Bulliet, the end of the Iranian cotton boom occasioned by a series of severe cold winters during the course of the tenth century and a cooling climate in the following eleventh century CE (Bulliet 2009). A more apposite question might therefore be the extent to which these local disruptions were compounded by the earlier collapse and fragmentation of the Rastrakutas, the 'Arab's best friend' in South Asia, in the 970s.

Across the previously Rastrakutan controlled coast, former vassals rose as quasi-independent kingdoms. According to an inscription of 993 CE, the Silahara dynasty ruled the entire Konkan coast, from Lata (the coast of south Gujarat) as far south as Goa, and although nominally the vassals of the Rastrakuta's successors, the Western Calukyas, it is clear that they were quasi-independent of the latter (Mirashi 1978: 17–28, verses 31–2). As we have seen, Silahara inscriptions from Sanjan provide evidence of West Asian diasporas continuing to play a role in local assemblies and trade (Sircar 1957–8b), even if no regional governors appear to have been appointed from among their ranks. Furthermore, as we will see later, the archaeological record indicates continued flourishing trade with West Asia into the thirteenth century. It is worth noting that the Silaharas took the title 'Lords of the Western Ocean', a title some have interpreted to refer to their control over trade with West Asia (Thapar 2002: 369). If anything, the rise of the smaller Silahara kingdom appears to have occasioned a massive expansion of local and inter-regional maritime trade on the southern Konkan coast in the following century. Ranabir Chakravarti's comparison of two grant documents from the port of Balipattana (Kharepatan in the Ratnagiri district of Maharashtra) dated 1008 and 1094 CE respectively suggests evidence for 'a growing coastal voyage and trade network to and from Balipattana' over this period (1998: 108). The first record mentions the recent foundation of Balipattana and the existence of shipping routes linking it both to Chaul to the north and to Chandrapura (Sindapur), south of Goa, to the south. By 1094 CE, networks to the north had expanded to include Thana, Supara and Nagarpura (Nagav in Kolaba district) (ibid.). A number of Goan grant documents of the eleventh century, which we will discuss shortly, possibly corroborate the idea that Chaul's central position in the trade of that region declined following the collapse of the Rastrakutas.

On the very southern edge of the Silahara domains, the Kadamba dynasty rose to power in Goa. Here again, Chakravarti's research has revealed a near contemporary growth in maritime connections between Goa and the Saurashtra coast (also referred to as Kathiawar) in the early eleventh century. Various grant documents mention royal seaborne pilgrimages to Kollapura (modern Kohlapur) and to Thana, routes which must reflect established maritime trade routes. However, most exceptional are references to seaborne pilgrimages to Somnatha in Saurashtra, a practice which appears to have started as early as *Śaka* 960/1038 CE and went on to become something of a Kadamba dynastic tradition since instances are recorded into the later twelfth century.

Moving Skills and Networks: From Saymur to Goa

One document relevant to these pilgrimages also includes data on the role of West Asian mercantile groups in Kadamba trade. A copperplate grant from Goa dated to the mid-eleventh century further supports the idea that South Asian politics readily incorporated West Asian merchants into their administration. A grant document dated *Śaka* 975 or 1053 CE, provides exceptional biographical detail about a certain Saddhan, who was Chief Minister in Charge of Ships to Jayakesi I (r. 1050–80) of the Kadamba dynasty in Goa (Pissurlencar 1938). The grant is exceptionally detailed in narrating how Saddhan came to this post. It seems that his grandfather Madhumad (Muhammad) father of Sri Sameil (Arabic Isma'il) of the *Tajiyavamsa* (Arab community) had been based at Sri Vaimulya or Chaul (the Arab Saymur). During a seaborne pilgrimage to Somnatha, the ship on which Jayakesi's grandfather Guhalladeva II (r. *c.* 980–1005) was travelling encountered difficulties and the vessel and its passengers were saved by Saddhan's grandfather who was then Head of the Shipowners at Chaul (ibid.: 391). Subsequently some members of the family left Chaul for the Kadamba court. While certain biographical details here undoubtedly reflect contemporary Kadamba court poetry with its recurrent subtheme of Goa to Somnath pilgrimage, one may also ask whether the timing of the transfer of this Arab seafaring family from Saymur to Goa corresponds in some way with the Rastrakutan collapse in the early 970s CE, marking a period when newly emerging coastal polities were able to attract former Rastrakutan collaborators to their ports and their own administrations. Again we are faced with the problem of gauging how far this single example may be symptomatic of wider movements and trends.

Even more interestingly perhaps, the grant was made in support of a mosque founded by Saddhan at Gopakapura (Goa) and allocated the building substantial revenues from taxes on international shipping visiting the port. While the inscription presents a certain number of problems since it is only known through a 1727 CE Portuguese transcription and translation of the original Sanskrit, made when the grant document was sent back to Lisbon, the general purport of the document is clear. Merchants who agreed to the levy to support the mosque at Goa came from Simhala (Sri Lanka), Zangavar, Kalah, Pandya (south India), Kerala (Malabar), Chouda (south India), Gauda (Bengal), Gurjara (Gujarat), Lat (south Gujarat), Puxta (Madras area), Sri Sthanak (Thana) and Chandrapura (Sindapur, south of present day Goa). In the detailed list of taxes and conditions that follows, further ports and regions find mention, in the south: Malaya-desa (Kerala), Duluka-desa (unidentified) and Gokarna-tirtha (Gokarna), and in the north: Saurashtra, Gurjara, Lata, Sthanak (Thana), Konkan, Veimulya (Chaul), Chippalona (Chiplun), Sangameshvar (a port north-east of Ratnagiri), Valapattan (Balipattana or Kharepatan, in the Ratnagiri district of Maharashtra, and already mentioned as part of the Silahara sponsored boom in south Kanara trade), Chandrapura, Pindayana and Shivapur (both the latter unidentified). The extensive lists of trade partners and contacts given here deserve to be taken seriously. As Daud Ali has pointed out the term 'copperplate grant' used in Western scholarship focuses on the materiality of the object and obscures the degree to which these texts should be understood as orders, in Sanskrit and Tamil they are orders, *sasanam* and *tirumukam* respectively, they are 'texts [which] encode an entire political procedure' (2000: 173). While we should rightly take a light view of the lists of territories conquered or feudatories subdued which are given in the royal eulogies that precede many grant documents, there are no reasons to doubt the data given here since its regulates tax dues and exemptions at the port.

Another grant document dated six years later—the so-called Panjim plates of *Śaka* 981 or 1059 CE—provide another extraordinary biography of a West Asian shipowner at the Kadamba court (Dikshit 1953). The document here concerns a certain Chhadam, the son of Madhumada (Muhammad), himself the son of a certain Aliyama ('Arabic 'Ali), a *nauvittaka* or ship owner from Chaul. The document records the grant in perpetuity of a tract of deserted land in the village of Laghu Morambika to Chhadam and his descendants in perpetuity. In most studies to date, the Chhadam of this grant and the Saddhan of the previous grant have generally been held to be one and the same individual, indeed, both individuals had grandfathers who were shipowners at Chaul and both subsequently moved to Goa. Furthermore, since the Sanskritization of Arabic names was not standardized at this period, Chhadam and Saddhan might well be variant spellings of the same (as yet unidentified) Arabic name. However, the two individuals have entirely different *nasab*s or lines of descent, Chhadam is the son of Madhumada who was the son of Aliyama, while Saddhan is the son of Sri Sameil who was the son of Madhumad. In effect we have a Chhadam ibn Muhammad ibn 'Ali and a Saddhan ibn Isma'il ibn Muhammad. Unless we wish to consider Kadamba scribes particularly lax in their records of genealogies, we might consider the real possibility that these two documents describe two separate individuals and two separate West Asian careers in Kadamba Goa. If so, the common arrival of grandfathers from Chaul would reinforce the idea of a significant southward expansion of mercantile expertise from Chaul, perhaps even a loss of position, following the collapse of the Rastrakutas, and the development of the south Konkan coast.

The situation after the fall of the Rastrakutan kingdom raises the interesting question of the extent to which more fractured political contexts actively hindered or, on the contrary, aided trade. As seen, the fragmentation of the Rastrakutas into smaller kingdoms is followed by a rise in ports involved in maritime trade and an intensification of activity. However, it is difficult to assess the links, if any, between these two events or to understand whether this is also connected to the wider Asian sea trade boom then being experienced in the Indian Ocean. The mention in the Goan copperplate grants of the mid-eleventh century of ships from regions as far afield as Sri Lanka, Bengal, and Kalah certainly illustrates the vastly expanded networks in this area. The most problematical identification, but also that which would evidence the scale of international maritime networks at this period is, of course Zangavar, mentioned in the 1053 CE Goan grant document. Chakravarti suggests that this might be a rendering of Zanzibar and Sung sources certainly mention the arrival of tribute missions from a certain Zanguebar in 1071 and 1081 CE, and comment upon the exceptional distance they had travelled. Hartwell identified this polity as Zanzibar (1983: 209) and East Africanists have generally accepted this identification but, it might also be a rendering of the name of the small coastal town of Zinjibar, often pronounced Zingibar, in the Abyan region north of Aden where extensive finds of Chinese ceramic sherds attest to its role in international trade.

Cola Expansion

Another part of the puzzle to consider here is the contemporary expansion of Cola power in south India. Almost parallel to the Rastrakuta's demise, equally momentous changes were taking place in south India as a phase of massive Colan expansion expanded their domains to southern Tamil Nadu, into northern Kerala, across the Palk Strait to Sri Lanka and even beyond to South-East Asia. Having already pushed into southern Tamil Nadu in the early tenth century, in the later tenth century, the Cola ruler Rajaraja I (r. 985–1014) carried out extensive campaigns against the Ceras in Kerala, as against Sri Lanka and even the Maldives, while his son and successor Rajendra (r. 1014–40) pushed further south against the Pandyas in southernmost Tamil Nadu (c. 1018) and was eventually to lead Cola naval campaigns in South-East Asia. Recently, Romila Thapar has argued that these campaigns were essentially trade-driven, aimed at breaking existing Cera-Pandya monopolies on trade with West Asia, as existed at Kollam, as well as to consolidate Cola trade networks in South-East Asia (2002: 365). However proving this thesis is exceptionally difficult given the data available at present. If this was the case, the task of gauging the effects of these campaigns on local, regional, and international trade is exceptionally difficult not least because the finer chronology of these events is poorly known. Both Kollam and Kodungallur appear to have been plundered, possibly by sea, in 1005 CE but Narayanan suggests that the events were of little political importance. Certainly at Kollam, this appears to have had no effect on the long-term organization of international trade since Eastern Christians continued to control the port's trade into the fourteenth century.

One copperplate grant from Kodungallur also appears to have some connection to this political climate. The Jewish community of Kodungallur preserves a famous grant of privileges issued to Issuppu Irappan in 1000 CE and granting him the headship of the *Anjuvannam* merchant association (Narayanan 1972: 23-30 and 79-82).[36] As earlier at Kollam, the various rights and privileges which he, and indeed his descendants, received in perpetuity make the mercantile activities of the association abundantly clear: he is granted revenue from 'tolls by the boat and by carts, *Anjuvannam* dues' and was 'remitted [the] duty and weighing fee as well as being exempted from [the] payments made by other settlers in the town to the king' (Narayanan 1972: 81). In addition to this he received the right to a range of symbolic privileges, known in a number of Keralan grants as the 72 privileges, among these were 'the right to employ day lamp, decorative cloth, palanquin, umbrella, kettledrum, trumpet, gateway, arch, arched roof' (ibid.: 81). Narayanan has observed that the award was made two years after the launch of the Cola campaigns in Kerala and that the privileges were awarded in the presence of six of the district governors and the head of the army, in effect a council of war. Narayanan therefore suggests that the grant was made in return for the loyalty of West Asian merchant groups and perhaps even in return for their financial support of the Cera campaign against the Colas (Narayanan 1996: 55). We do not know if West Asians remained in control of trade at Kodungallur after the Cola conquests but the Jewish community there certainly continued to be prominent in trade in the long-term. If control of trade networks and their revenues were the main motivating factor behind the Cola campaigns, then in any case West Asian and other trade networks would have been best left undisturbed.

The Cola campaigns also extended into northern Kerala and in 1046 CE Rajaraja Cola defeated the Musaka rulers of Eli (Madayi) (Bouchon 1975: 4). Here, several sources suggest that a period of important changes followed around the Taliparamba River and Mount Eli. An eleventh century source, the *Musakavamsa*, records the existence of a new port of Acalapattana or Kachilpattanam, and the recent foundation of a new royal city at Matayi (ibid.: 8); a contemporary poem, the *Payyanur Patti*, also informs us that trade around Mount Eli was in the hands of the *Manigramam*, *Anjuvannam* and two *Chetti* guilds (Bouchon 1975: 8-9). Since an earlier inscription mentioned only the *Manigramam* association, the possibility exists that this indicates a substantial expansion of trade networks at Madayi both westwards and eastwards into south India after the Cola campaigns? Another sparse piece of evidence for this period is an Islamic tombstone dated AH 471/1078–79 CE and recording the death of a certain 'Ali ibn Kasnuri, which was found at the port of Baliapatnam, close to Madayi (Quddusi 1999).[37] It is difficult at present to judge how far these new port and city foundations, and apparently extended trade networks, occurred as a positive consequence of the Cola campaign in Kerala, or took place in spite of the disruptions these caused, as a natural consequence of the wider expansion of ports and Indian coastal trade then going on in Peninsular India. The Cola campaigns against the Ceras initiated an extended power struggle which lasted until 1122 CE. Sporadic wars between 988 and 1018 CE finally lead to a fifty-year period of Cola control (1018–66) and then a period of renewed Cera ascendancy for a similar period (1066–1122), before the final extinction of the Cera dynasty (Narayanan 1996: 51–2). One might normally expect such intermittent conflict to hinder trade rather than help it, but it is impossible to judge this from the data available at present.

A more promising approach may be to think in terms of the Colas taking over and reconfiguring trade networks at this period. Noboru Karashima's epigraphic studies have suggested changes to the structure of mercantile associations under the Colas, with an overarching mercantile association known as the *Ainurruvar* playing a key role in both local and international early Cola trade. The grouping's rise appears to coincide with the rise of the Colas in south India since the earliest epigraphic reference to the *Ainurruvar* comes from a mid-tenth century Tamil eulogy, and many of the earliest inscriptions mentioning this group come from sites in northern Tamil Nadu. Karashima's studies suggest that this group later came to encompass smaller associations such as the *Manigramam*, the *Nanadesi* and the *Anjuvannam*. Since groups such as the *Manigramam* and the *Anjuvannam*, or at least associations bearing the same names, are known to have existed at Kollam and in the kingdom of Eli before the Cola campaigns, it seems interesting to ask whether the Cola conquests of these locations simply integrated existing, non-Tamil mercantile associations such as these into a larger Tamil-centred and Cola-linked grouping, the *Ainurruvar*. Network specializations no doubt continued, West Asians were probably most involved in trade with West Asia, while Tamil groups continued to dominate the trade of the Bay of Bengal and the eastern Indian Ocean. Indeed, all the inscriptional evidence points to specifically Tamil networks working in the eastern Indian Ocean (Christie 1998). As Chakravarti notes 'many of these inscriptions of Tamil merchants are found in regions outside India, leaving little room for doubt on their regular presence in Sri Lanka, Myanmar, Thailand, Sumatra and China' (2004: 311). Nevertheless, West Asians appear to have integrated Cola trade networks in the east since the Chinese diplomatic records indicate the involvement of individuals with what appear to be Arabic names in the Cola tribute missions to the Sung court. It seems significant that the first ever Cola embassy to China in 1015 CE had an individual with a West Asian name, one Pu Jiaxin (Abu Qasim?), as second in command. The embassy consisted of 52 people who travelled by sea via Srivijaya in South-East Asia (Bielenstein 2005: 77). The Chinese sources sometimes combine to offer us a glimpse of individual lives and trade routes, on a par with the *'aja'ib* literature and the copperplate grants. Thus we know that Pu Jiaxin (Abu Qasim) first appears in Chinese records in 1004 CE simply as a foreign guest. In 1011 CE he was listed as the envoy from Muscat (Wuxun), in 1015 CE, as we have seen, he came with the first ever Cola embassy to China and finally in 1019 CE he was listed as the envoy from the Arab kingdom (Ta-shi) (Hartwell 1983, pp. 188, 198, 200, 206). Pu Jiaxin's shifting routes and allegiances suggest that he was not necessarily permanently settled in the Cola domains but offered his international trade 'address book' to the Cola court.

The 1019 CE Arab embassy to China was to be the last for the next 36 years and brings us back to the question of the Cola's role in reconfiguring trade networks at this period. Recent work on Chinese-South-East Asian trade has suggested that, if we look at trade patterns from a wider perspective, some possible effects of the Cola campaigns may be seen. Geof Wade has observed that 'missions to China from Da-shi (the 'Arab lands') saw a hiatus from 1019 until the 1050s and surmises that Islamic trading links with the Straits [of Malacca] were affected by the attacks on, and possible capture of, the major ports in the region by Cōla forces, even though Arabs appear to have been the suppliers of horses to the Cōlas to support their cavalry' (2009: 233). It is worth noting that the interruption of these Arab tribute missions follows the period of enormous changes to trade routes in the western Indian Ocean around the mid-tenth century. While it may not all be 'the fault of the Colas', it might be useful—as well as more true to the interconnected character of Indian Ocean trade—to think in terms of a combination of causes across Asia: from the rise of the Sung in China, via the Cola campaigns across South and South-East Asia and the collapse of the Rastrakutas, to the Siraf earthquake and the end of the Iranian cotton boom at the other end of the route.

South Asia between the Gulf and Red Sea Routes

The central position of the Arabian coast in international trade routes in the western Indian Ocean raises the obvious question of the balance between Gulf and Red Sea trade. Ships heading across the open ocean between south India and ports such as Shihr, Raysut or Sharma, could sail up the Arabian coast and into the Gulf or south towards Aden and the Red Sea. What then was the balance between these two routes, can we identify any clear trends in the volumes of trade and settlement relating to these two routes and markets? The Gulf is traditionally said to have entered a period of decline in the late tenth century, due to single catastrophic events such as the Siraf earthquake of 977 CE, and wider climatic events which brought about the end of the Iranian cotton boom. Simultaneously, the rise of the Fatimid Empire in north Africa and its eastwards expansion into Egypt (Cairo was conquered in 969 CE) appears to have facilitated the operation of long distance international trade networks via the Red Sea. The later allegiance of the Sulayhids of Yemen (r. 1047–1138) to the Fatimids extended and consolidated this connection to the Red Sea. However, as David Bramoullé has suggested, the Fatimids did not develop an explicit trade policy in the western Indian Ocean until the vizierate of Badr al-Jamali (1074–94) (Bramoullé forthcoming). The nature of our sources in South Asia currently makes it extremely difficult to pick up, let alone quantify, any such changes, but it is clear that there was no simple correlation between Red Sea routes and south Indian trade activity.

Clues to the pull between Egyptian and Red Sea routes in the western Indian Ocean perhaps emerge most clearly of course through the so-called 'India letters' of the Cairo Geniza (Goitein and Friedman 2008). Mainly dating to the late eleventh and twelfth centuries CE they provide a unique insight into the commercial transactions and daily life of Arabic-speaking Jews all along the western Indian seaboard. If traders such as Abraham Ben Yiju settled on the Kanara coast at Mangalore exported to Aden and the Red Sea ports, and thence to Cairo, thanks to their rich networks they collected goods along the entire South Asian seaboard from Kutch to Sri Lanka, and indeed beyond that to South-East Asia and China. Ranabir Chakravarti has explored the importation of indigo from Sanjan over a forty-year period in the first half of the eleventh century as it can be studied through the records of the Cairene Jewish merchant Ibn Awkal (Chakravarti 1991–2). However, it is in the long twelfth century, from the 1080s onwards that 'the geographic range of individual [Jewish] merchants' activities took a breathtaking leap in extent' (Goldberg 2012: 305) entering the western Indian Ocean in a significant way but also reaching as far as the western Mediterranean. We cannot dwell here on the hugely important resource that the some 500 documents and letters of S.D. Goitein's so-called 'India Book' constitute for medieval Indian Ocean history beyond signalling that this is the case. It is worth underlining, however, that the 'India Book' documents are in many ways also micro-histories and their incorporation into the history of South Asian maritime trade faces challenges similar to those already discussed here.

Another example of the complexity of the relationship between these two routes is the pattern of the Isma'ili *da'wa* in South Asia. In AH 460/1067–78 CE, the first Yemeni *da'i* named 'Abd Allah was sent to South Asia but to Cambay in western India, not to the coast of south India as one might have expected (Daftary 1999: 29–43). Little concrete detail is known about the Isma'ili presence in western India at this time although the main nodes of their later activity—at Cambay, Anhilawad Patan, Siddhpur and Bhadresvar (al-Qass/Budlasar)—suggest a deep involvement in the trade networks leading from the coast of western India into the Gangetic plain. It has been suggested that the timing and location of this mission may reflect an attempt to compensate for, or counterbalance, the recent reverses in Sind where Mahmud of Ghazni had annihilated the Isma'ili state based at Multan. Indeed, Isma'ilism continued to thrive in this part of India and we know that the Sumras of Thatta, in the Indus Delta, converted to this branch of Islam and ruled there from *c.* AH 443/1051 CE until the 1350s (Daftary 2007: 443). The current lack of evidence for any Isma'ili proselytization in southern India, in spite of its close connections to Yemen is perplexing and should probably not be read as evidence for an Isma'ili absence.

The history of the Maldives certainly confirms the strength of Red Sea connections even through to the Mediterranean. An African Muslim is credited with the conversion of the ruler of the Maldives to Islam while the islands adopted a school of Islamic law associated with North Africa and Spain. Maldivian sources traditionally ascribe the conversion of the Maldives to Islam in 1143 CE to the intervention of one al-Barbari, a *nisba* indicating links to the Berbera region of the Horn of Africa, and thus to transoceanic routes connecting southern India, via the Maldives, to the Red Sea (Kalus and Guillot 2005). Significantly the Maldives also followed the Maliki school of Sunni law, a school heavily associated with North Africa and al-Andalus and thus with trade routes and cultural influences reaching into to the Mediterranean. The Maliki school prevailed in the Maldives until the sixteenth century when they switched to the Shafi'i school.

Gujarat and Western India after the Rastrakutas

If a key West Asian trade partner was lost with the fall of the Rastrakutas, almost contemporaneously, the Arab's equally noted enemies, the Jurz or Gurjara-Pratiharas, were on the decline too and the power vacuum they left eventually opened the way for the unification of western India and with it new trade routes and settlement patterns. The idea of Gujarat as a naturally unified geographical space is something we take almost for granted today but this was not always so historically. The area we now term Gujarat State was only unified at the very end of the period under discussion here in the mid-twelfth century under Kumarapala (r. 1143–73) of the Calukya or Solanki dynasty and this after a long and slow process of expansion and consolidation. The Calukyas (Solankis) emerged on the very western edge of the Gurjara-Pratihara sphere of influence with their first capital established at Anhilawad Patan (the Nahrwala of the Arabic geographers) by Mularaja I (r. 942–96 CE) around 943 CE. Although the Calukyas did not yet control a great coastal area, Patan was a key intersection point for trade routes running from the Gulf of Cambay and the Little Rann of Kutch to the south and west, from Rajasthan and northern India via the Palanpur Gap in the north-east, and from Malwa via the Godra-Dohad route in the east.

It seems clear that the West Asian trade diaspora of the Rastrakuta period continued to flourish and even expand under the Calukyas. Material evidence is currently sparse because of the lack of survey work and archaeological exploration; however, by the far the most plentiful evidence can be inferred from the biographies of early Muslim *shaykh*s who settled in western India during this period. 'Ali Muhammad Khan, the author of the mid-eighteenth century *Mir'at-i Ahmadi,* basing himself on a lost text called the *Manazil al-Awliya',* provides brief biographical details of five such holy men who settled in the Calukya capital of Anhilawad Patan before the Muslim conquest and were subsequently buried there (1928: 91–3 and 107). The earliest individual mentioned is Hajji Hud ibn Abu 'Ali 'Abdallah who arrived in AH 485/1092-93 CE, during the reign of Karnadeva, and died in AH 536/1141-42 CE. Other individuals mentioned arrived during the succeeding 150 years from Delhi, Ta'if in the Hijaz, and Turkey. Another pre-conquest Muslim settler at Patan is Shaykh Ahmad who died in AH 555/1160 CE and is known through the inscriptions on his tomb (Desai 1974). Muslim communities also clearly existed outside the Calukya capital as evidenced by a mosque foundation inscription from Asawal (the later site of Ahmedabad) which records an earlier foundation inscription reportedly dated AH 445/1035 CE (Lambourn 2008: 85). Unfortunately, no other evidence exists at present for mapping West Asian presences in western India until the late thirteenth century when new Rasulid documents (Lambourn 2008) and a number of thirteenth century CE inscriptions fill in the picture. Here again, survey work and archaeological excavations might bring fresh data to expand the very patchy textual record.

The Calukyas clearly valued and even courted trade communities, including West Asians, and none more so that Siddharaja Jayasimha (r. 1094–1143) who is surrounded by anecdotes about his protection of different communities and even his conversion to different faiths. Isma'ili texts record the conversion of Siddharaja Jayasmiha and two of his ministers to the Isma'ili branch of Islam (Lokhandwala 1955: 117–35), Jain sources often refer to his conversion to Jainism. While these conversion narratives can be taken with a pinch of salt, collectively they are indicative of Jayasimha's promotion and protection of such groups. The fact that many of these faith groups were also active mercantile communities with extensive networks can only have supported Calukya commercial policy.

The Calukyas did not begin as a primarily maritime or coast focused polity and Saurastra and Kutch, together with their important ports, were only incorporated into the Calukya state in the later twelfth century CE. Thus, for the initial period of our study the political geography of this part of the coastline is complex and hard to pin down. In spite of V.K. Jain's masterful *Trade and Traders in Western India (AD 1000–1300)*, it is often difficult to establish detailed 'biographies' of even major port sites in western India. As a whole, his book gives very little sense of the chronological and geographical development of coastal and international maritime trade in western India over this three hundred-year period. Thus, although archaeological excavations back in the 1950s indicated that Somnath was the site of a major temple as early as the ninth or tenth century CE (Nanavati et al. 1971),[40] the port only appears to have become a focus of direct Calukya governance and patronage during the reign of Kumarapala (r. c.1143–72 CE) when inscriptions record his appointment of a governor to protect the port against piracy and looting by local *raja*s, and a chief priest at the famous temple. More than anything it is the raid of Mahmud of Ghazni against Somnatha in 1026 CE which provides the best evidence for the port's importance and prosperity before Kumarapala's time. As the grants of the Kadamba kings have indicated, as early as Śaka 960/1038 CE, Somnath was an important pilgrimage and trade destination from Goa, while Chakravarti observed that 'the description of this voyage from Goa or its neighbouring areas to the Kathiawad coast seems to have been a regular facet of the court poetry in the Kadamba records' (1998: 109–11). We also have al-Biruni's (973–1048) mention of Somnath as 'a harbour for seafaring people, and a station for those who went to and fro between Sufala in the country of the Zanj and China' (1992, vol. 2: 104). While ships from Somnath may not have literally sailed all the way to China and east Africa, the mention of the two furthest ends of the Indian Ocean networks of the period serves to illustrate the port's importance in these.

Other ports in the area were flourishing at this period and provide evidence of closer links with West Asia. Bhadresvar was a small port-polity located on the southern coast of Kutch, and appears to have come to prominence in the early twelfth century CE (Shokoohy 1988).[41] Thanks to Jain sources we know that the port was governed by a Jain merchant council under the leadership of one Jagadu, and we also find some of the strongest material and epigraphic evidence for a thriving West Asian mercantile community, very possibly of Isma'ili persuasion, during the second half of the twelfth century (ibid.). Jain texts inform us that Jagadu had ships which sailed to the Gulf and that he kept factors in the Gulf ports; stylistic and epigraphic analysis of the inscriptions from a structure known as the Shrine of Ibrahim at Bhadresvar (founded AH 554/1159–60 CE) also point to Gulf connections.[42] We do not know whether this community had older links in the subcontinent, for example to the Isma'ili Sumras of Thatta, or whether connections to other Isma'ili areas in the Gulf, notably Bahrayn, help explain this presence. Little concrete information survives for our period about the other ports of Kutch and Saurastra, however, in spite of being remembered for its piracy—a problem that went back to before the Arab conquest of the eighth century and persisted into the nineteenth century—this does not appear to have been a fundamental impediment to trade. Here again very little coastal archaeology has looked beyond the Early Historic period.

Conclusions: Histories of West Asian Mercantile Networks in South Asian Maritime Trade

I opened this analysis with a reference to micro-history and the problems it raises about the relationship of the micro to the macro. As I review the material gathered and the many unanswered questions I have left scattered across this essay, the conclusion seems to be that there is as yet no firm answer as to whether these many individual examples can be read as paradigms for West Asian involvement in medieval maritime trade in South Asia at particular periods and places, let alone for gauging larger trade patterns. Yes, West Asian merchants certainly appear to have occupied a prominent place as intermediaries and facilitators in international trade across the period of our study, and indeed beyond it. West Asians were appointed into local administrations at key ports as regional governors or Superintendents of Weights and Measures, they participated in administrative councils and even headed tribute missions to China. There is perhaps even evidence of competition for their presence and the networks and access to markets that they brought. Nor should we forget that this was not a one-way flow, as the substantial finds of Indian ceramics at Sharma suggest South Asians were also present in West Asia. Faint clues survive in references to how to entertain and dine Indian guests at Siraf, to Indian communities at Sohar or to Jain merchants such as Jagadu of Bhadresvar trading with Hormuz. But these are not exactly new or original conclusions. What our written sources do not give us in any significant amount is quantitative data from which to extrapolate the balances between West Asian and South Asian networks and changes in the flows between regions and ports. Without this level of detail it remains almost impossible to understand how changing networks and flows of goods in South Asia affected, or were affected by, a range of factors from the political or the consumerist, to the geological or the climatic. While limited, there is certainly more data to be extracted from both South Asian and West Asian sources. Ranabir Chakravarti's work on the development of south Konkan ports and the expansion of shipping networks has demonstrated the potential of epigraphic sources and his model might be profitably applied to western India where, V.K. Jain's work not withstanding, a substantial body of medieval grants and inscriptions still awaits better study. However, the entire exercise of writing a 'histoire événementielle' of South Asian maritime trade at this period brings us face to face with the particular nature of the historical record in South Asia.

If I have any firm conclusion to draw at the end of this marathon study it is that we have to seriously consider whether the nature of the historical record in South Asia for the premodern period allows for the writing of 'histoires événementielles' as developed in West Asia and Europe at the same period. With such different data sets, any attempt at correlation between regions faces enormous problems and risks descending into nothing more than speculation. What does seem more feasible is the study of much broader trends over larger timespans, particularly if South Asian maritime trade is incorporated into its pan-Asian setting. At this level, it becomes possible to see more general correlations between regional booms and busts or the rises and falls of particularly large polities. There are clearly many chronological frameworks in Indian Ocean history. Adopting the dynastic or even yearly frameworks seen in West Asian and Chinese history writing as the standard framework across the whole of Asia clearly works against South and South-East Asian historiographical traditions. Dynastic and yearly chronological frameworks risk reducing the histories of South and South-East Asia to footnotes in our narratives and we need to think of better ways to reconcile and work with both.

The particular nature of South Asian historical sources for the premodern period offers unusual micro-histories which have yet to find their full place not only in regional, local histories but also in wider Indian Ocean histories. As my case study of Sanjan illustrates, extracted from grant documents, the extended biographies of individual merchants have the potential to work as part of pluri-disciplinary data sets and towards a form of port biography. Such biographical data is, however, more commonly far sparser and it is by no means clear how a single tombstone and its epitaph might participate in the writing of larger histories. The nature of the South Asian historical record also seems to place an even greater onus on material evidence as a source for history, and economic history in particular. While the first half of this essay has been dedicated to explaining why archaeological evidence currently plays such a minor role in the writing of South Asian maritime history, the field is clearly rich with potential. As Shinu Abraham pointed out, we need fewer site surveys and general data collection and instead more problem-centred research. Learning to ask better questions of material culture and how it can contribute to the study of maritime trade is our next challenge. It will be interesting to see how this new archaeological data will map onto the many different chronological frameworks that characterize the Indian Ocean.

Notes

1. Project participants met in Paris in June 2008 for a one-day workshop (see http://www.islam-medieval.cnrs.fr/pdf/2009_06_05_Sharma_resumes.pdf) and the proceedings are due to be published as *L'horizon Sharma. L'essor du commerce islamique dans l'Océan Indien occidental (v. 980-1150)*, ed. Axelle Rougeulle and Eric Vallet for the Publications de la Sorbonne's Bibliothèque historique des pays d'Islam series. I am grateful to the editors of the Calcutta conference volume for allowing me to rework this material here. As always, I have many people to thank for discussions, suggestions, and feedback in the preparation of this essay as well as for sharing their own unpublished or 'in press' research. Thanks go to Monique Kervran, Roberta Tomber, Carla Sinopoli, Derek Kennet, Alison Gascoigne, Ken Hall, and Annabelle Collinet. This essay was submitted in September 2010 and seeks to include a substantial bibliography up to that date.
2. See S.D. Goitein and Mordechai A. Friedman, *India Traders of the Middle Ages: Documents from the Cairo Geniza ('India Book')*. Études sur le Judaïsme Médiéval. Leiden, Boston: E.J. Brill, 2008. The contribution of these Geniza documents to the history of northern Malabar is discussed in my forthcoming book *Abraham's Luggage* and in an article on 'Geniza Sources and New Perspectives on the Geo-politics of Twelfth Century Malabar (Alupas, Hoysalas and the last of the Ceras).'
3. At the other end of the scale we find the super-macro narratives of Chaudhuri and others which, I have to confess, I intrinsically distrust because of the paucity of primary research into the premodern period.

4. This strand of research was particularly developed in the 1980s and 1990s, for an excellent recent overview of this trend as it has contributed to maritime research see Chakravarti 2004.

5. By contrast, a number of Sultanate capitals have been subject to extensive and long-term archaeological investigation, notably Champaner in Gujarat and Daulatabad in the Deccan.

6. The Harappan port and dock at Lothal in Gujarat are especially famous, see Rao 1979–85. For other Harappan sites along the Saurashtra coast see Gaur, Sundaresh and Odedra 2004; Gaur and Sundaresh 2005. The excavations of Bet Dwarka island, off the very western tip of Saurashtra, focused overwhelmingly on the Harappan to early historic periods see Gaur, Sundaresh, Vora 2005.

7. The site of Arikamedu in Tamil Nadu was first excavated by Mortimer Wheeler, see Wheeler, Ghosh and Krishna Deva 1946, more recently the site has been re-opened, see Begley, ed., 1996–2004. For other sites in the region, see also Sridhar 2005. Indo-Roman trade was a particular focus in R.N. Mehta's excavations at the site of Nagar, a few kilometres north of Cambay, see Mehta 1968. Substantial survey work on Elephanta Island since the 1980s is revealing its critical role in maritime trade, including that of the Early Historic period, for one of the most recent publications see Tripathi 2004. Linked to this interest in Indo-Roman trade see the coastal surveys begun by Sunil Gupta and others from the early 1990s expressly 'for locating Early Historic ports mentioned in the Periplus and Geographia', see Shinde, Gupta and Rajgor 2002, and later Gupta and Aruni 2005. For a later article which usefully summarizes these earlier prospections see Gupta 2007. In the course of these prospections, the site of Kamrej was identified and excavated (see several articles in the *Journal of Indian Ocean Archaeology*, vol. 1, 2004). Good overall coverage of the Pre- and Early Historic periods can be found in two edited volumes: Ray and Salles 1996, and Ray 1999. For Indo-Roman trade see in particular Tomber 2008.

8. For example, the promisingly entitled article 'A preliminary exploration of Prabhasa-Somnatha', terminates at Period IV, Indo-Roman amphorae, leaving no insights into the lively mediaeval trade of the port, see Rao, Tripati and Gaur 1992. At another well-explored port site on the Kathiawar coast, the island of Bet Dwarka, the medieval ceramic chronology is similarly neglected see Gaur and Vora cited earlier. Many similar examples could be cited.

9. For an excellent analysis of the problems of basic archaeological method that have led to the 'disappearance' of medieval archaeological layers see Kennet 2004: 11–17.

10. Data on India from a presentation by Alok Tripathi to UNESCO, available from: http://www.unescobkk.org/fileadmin/user_upload/culture/Underwater/HK_presentations/Day%20One%20-%20Alok%20Tripathi.pdf. Two Indian universities now teach marine archaeology, at Thanjavur the Tamil University has its Centre for Underwater Archaeology while at Visakhapattnam, Andhra University has a Centre for Marine Archaeology. Data on Sri Lanka from the 2007 *UNESCO Experts Meeting on the Protection of the Underwater Cultural Heritage* available from http://www.unescobkk.

org/fileadmin/user_upload/culture/Underwater/SL_presentations/Country_ Reports/Sri_Lanka.pdf, see also the pages on maritime archaeology of the Sri Lankan Navy which actively supports most surveys and excavations, available from http://www.navy.lk/index.php?id=1212.

11. There is no space here to mention the many relevant articles and books emerging in this field, however, the website of the National Institute of Oceanography (see http://www.nio.org/) offers an excellent searchable database of publications by its researchers as well as offering an institutional repository for relevant material. In 2010, a simple search under 'archaeology' yielded 214 hits and many articles connect to a downloadable PDF. A new Archaeological Survey of India webpage now lists ongoing and past offshore and onshore archaeology (see http://asi.nic.in/asi_underw.asp); the dates of excavations at inland sites, and associated publications, can now also be tracked through their excavations pages which are organized by state. If Indian maritime archaeology has never been busier, it has also never been easier to access.

12. To date except for one case (see O. Bopearachchi et al. in this volume), no shipwreck earlier than the sixteenth century CE has been identified, although optimists claim it is just a matter of time. For a Portuguese period wreck excavated off the Goan coast see S. Tripati et al., 'Exploration for Shipwrecks off Sunchi Reef, Goa, West Coast of India', *World Archaeology*, vol. 32, no.3, 2001, pp. 355–67. A considerable number of stone anchors of various types have now been documented along the entire western seaboard.

13. The disparities between excavation methodologies and ceramic typologies was particularly apparent in discussions at a recent collaborative workshop on 'Global Geographies: The Indian Ocean in Historical Perspective', jointly organized by the British Institute in Eastern Africa and the British Association for South Asian Studies, and held at the Royal Asiatic Society in London on 31 October 2009.

14. A sherd reference collection incorporating material from around the western Indian Ocean rim has been built up as part of the CNRS's UMR 8167 Orient et Méditerranée in Paris.

15. While the final publication of Sehwan Sharif is awaited, one can refer to the recently submitted Ph.D. by Annabelle Collinet (2010).

16. One of the most useful summaries of the main South Asian ceramic types involved in Indo-Roman trade is given in Tomber 2008: 44–50.

17. The glazed ceramics from Vijayanagara have never been studied but I am grateful to Dr. Sinopoli for the information that 'the imports are almost all Chinese (I think I saw two sherds of either north Indian or Persian ceramics there)—and are mostly late 15th-early 16th century blue and white bowls, there were a relatively small number of celadon sherds—but fewer than 2 per cent—3 per cent I would imagine. Relatively few imported ceramics seems to have made it [to] Vijayanagara' (personal communication, 19 July 2010). It would be fascinating to know how Vijayanagara's ceramic assemblage compares to that of earlier capitals such as those of the Rastrakutas, the Colas, or the Ceras.

18. See also Stern et al. 2008.

19. I am grateful to Derek Kennet for sharing his unpublished report which contains a useful summary of the problems surrounding the use of TGW.

20. Author's translation from the French edition, 'tout ce qu'il convient de connaître sur chaque région, c'est-à-dire les diverses sources de richesses, les impositions, les dîmes, les impôts fonciers, les distances dans les itinéraires, les exportations et les articles de commerce.'

21. For Rastrakutan dynastic and political history, see the excellent overview in Thapar 2002 which gives a clear bibliography for further reading.

22. For a detailed discussion of the complex relationship between various surviving compilations and the text formerly known as Buzurg in Shahriyar's *Kitab 'Aja'ib al-hind* see Jean-Charles Ducène's review of the new Arabic language edition of this text in the Comptes Rendus of the *Journal Asiatique*, Ducène, 2010.

23. The site of Chinchani itself, located around 27 km. south of Sanjan, shows evidence of maritime activity and connections, see Gogte et al. 2006b.

24. Although Srimala remained an important and prosperous trade hub well into the early thirteenth century, see Jain 1990: 116 and 120.

25. The Sanjan excavations have been amply published by comparison to other sites of similar periods, besides the references given in the main text see volume one of the *Journal of Indian Ocean Archaeology* for 2004 which contains the following: Gupta, Dalal, Dandekar, Nanji, Aravazhi and Bomble 2004; Gokhale 2004. Volume two of the same journal (2005) was dedicated to Sanjan and contains articles by the following: Gupta, Dalal, Nanji et al. 2005, Mitra and Dalal 2005; Mushrif and Walimbe 2005; Rajaguru and Deo 2005.

26. R. Nanji, talk on 'The Zoroastrian Migration to India and the Archaeological Evidence', Ancient India and Iran Trust, Cambridge, 1 May 2009.

27. S. Priestman (2013), *Late Sasanian/Early Islamic Maritime Economy in the Persian Gulf and Western Indian Ocean: Ceramic Trade*, Ph.D. University of Southampton.

28. To my knowledge no TGW storage jars have been excavated from shipwreck contexts, however, for comparison, when the mid-ninth century Belitung wreck, the wreck of an Indian sewn vessel laden with Chinese ceramics, was excavated off the Indonesian coast one large Chinese storage jar was found to have been used to pack smaller ceramic bowls while another small jar contained star anise.

29. The only detailed comparative evidence available to us comes from the late medieval Deccani capital of Vijayanagara where glazed ceramics were particularly prominent in the so-called Islamic Quarter, as compared to the elite royal and nobleman's areas, with a distinct preference for small bowls which accounted for around 20 per cent of ceramic forms in these areas, as opposed to around 10 per cent of forms in the 'Hindu' areas. See Sinopoli 2003: 241.

30. The recent discovery of what may be the most ancient shipwreck in the Indian Ocean (second century BCE) off the south coast of Sri Lanka is being excavated as part of a joint project between the Sri Lanka-French Archaeological Mission,

the Department of Archaeology, Sri Lanka, INA, Texas A & M University, U.C. Berkeley, and CNRS. Numerous online articles have appeared about this site see for example http://www.mausrilanka.lk/sub%20pages/Godawaya. html. For the Sealinks project see http://www.sealinksproject.com/.

31. A paraphrase of the account is published in Kokan 1974 and repeated by later researchers but the fact that the original source has never been properly edited and translated demands that we treat this data with a healthy degree of circumspection.

32. The use of the term in such a meaning is mainly recorded in the Syrian and Jaziran marches during the early Arab conquests.

33. The main English language source on the Cera polity and Kollam is still Narayanan 1996, on the foundation of Kollam and the Kollam era in Kerala, see pp. 34–5. However, in spite of its importance Kollam does not appear to have been the object of consistent archaeological investigation, at least as far as Narayanan was able to state in 1996, see p. 17 and note 64.

34. In 2011–13 the Kollam Plates were the focus of an International Research Network funded by the UK's Art and Humanities Research Council and led by Elizabeth Lambourn and Roberta Tomber. Entitled 'A Persian Church in the Land of Pepper: Routes, Networks and Communities in the Medieval Indian Ocean', this multi-disciplinary project aims to produce a substantially revised edition and translation of the grant together with a series of essays placing the document, and the church and trade associations it describes, within their wider Indian Ocean context. The project's public website is http://www.849CE.org.uk, the collected papers will be published in 2015 (forthcoming) with Primus Books (Delhi).

35. For Books I to II of the 'India Book' see Goitein and Friedman 2008.

36. The contribution of these Geniza documents to the history of northern Malabar is discussed in my forthcoming book, *Abraham's Luggage*.

37. As Ranabir Chakravarti observes, 'the description of this voyage from Goa or its neighbouring areas to the Kathiawad coast seems to have been a regular facet of the court poetry in the Kadamba records', (1998: 109–11).

38. Once again we face the problem of interpreting this Tamil rendering of a Hebrew or Arabic name. Given the evidence from only slightly later Cairo Geniza documents for the strong presence of Yemeni Jews in Kerala, and the fact that they spoke Arabic and used Arabicized names and titles, I would suggest that the name is most likely to be a Tamil rendering of the Arabic Yusuf al-Rubban or Joseph the Sailor or more specifically 'pilot'.

39. I am grateful to Johanna Blayac for bringing my attention to this inscription through her Ph.D. Although substantial archaeological remains in the area point to its prosperity and importance, as well as the diversity of its populations—Madayi is recorded as having a Jewish tank and nineteenth century reports suggested that its mosque contained a foundation inscription dated 1124 CE—none of this material has been scientifically studied.

40. On a recent revival of archaeology at the site, see Gaur, Vora and Sundaresh 2008.

41. At least an inscription at the main Jain temple records the patronage of a number of Jain temples in 1139 CE.
42. Blair 1999: 390–1, where Blair reads the *nisba* al-Sirafi and point to possible Gulf connections in the epigraphic style of the port's Islamic grave markers.

References

Abraham, S. (2009), 'Strategies for Surface Documentation at the Early Historic Site of Pattanam, Kerala: the Malabar Region Archaeological Survey', in *Migration, Trade and Peoples, Part 1: Indian Ocean Commerce and the Archaeology of Western India*, R. Tomber, L. Blue and S. Abraham, eds., London: The British Association for South Asian Studies, The British Academy (2009), pp. 14–28. Available online at www.royalasiaticsociety. org/site/files/Part%201-%20Indian%20Ocean.pdf.

Akhbar (1948), *Akhbar al-Sin wa-al-Hind, Relation de la Chine et de l'Inde*, J. Sauvaget (Arabic ed. and French trans.), Paris: Belles Lettres.

Ali, D. (2000), 'Royal Eulogy as World History: Rethinking Copper-Plate Inscriptions in Cola India', in *Querying the Medieval: The History of Practice in South Asia*, R. Inden, J. Walters and D. Ali, eds., New York: Oxford University press, pp. 165–229.

Begley, V. ed., (1996–2004), *The ancient port of Arikamedu: new excavations and researches 1989-1992*, 2 vols., Pondichéry: École Française d'Extrême Orient.

Bhan, K.K. (2006), 'Towards an Understanding of Medieval Glazed Pottery Manufacture from Lashkarshah, Khambhat, Gujarat', *Man and Environment*, vol. XXXI, no. 2, pp. 90–5.

Bielenstein, H. (2005), *Diplomacy and Trade in the Chinese World 589–1276*, Leiden and Boston: Brill.

Al-Biruni, (1992), *Alberuni's India*, E.C. Sachau (Eng. trans. and ed.), 2 vols., New Delhi.

Blair, S. (1989), '*Bhadresvar: The Oldest Islamic Monuments in India* by Mehrdad Shokoohy; Manijeh Bayani-Wolpert; Natalie H. Shokoohy, *Hisar-i Furuza: Sultanate and Early Mughal Architecture in the District of Hisar, India* by Mehrdad Shokoohy; Natalie H. Shokoohy', *The Journal of the Society of Architectural Historians*, vol. 48, no. 4, pp. 390–1.

Blayac, J. (2009), 'Formation et histoire des premières sociétés indo-musulmanes et indo-islamiques à travers les inscriptions arabes et persanes (VIIe–XIVe siècles)', unpublished Ph.D. thesis, Paris.

Bopearachchi, O. (2002), 'Archaeological Evidence of Shipping Communities of Sri Lanka', in x*Ships and the Development of Maritime Technology in the Indian Ocean*, R. Inden, J. Walters and D. Ali, eds., London: Routledge & Curzon, pp. 92–127.

Bopearachchi, O. and Wickremesinhe R.M. (1999), *Ruhuna, an Ancient Civilisation Re-Visited. Numismatic and Archaeological evidence in Inland and Maritime Trade*, Colombo.

Bouchon, G. (1975), *Mamale de Cananor. Un adversaire de l'Inde portugaise (1507–1528)*, Hautes Études Islamiques et Orientales, EPHE, IVe section. Genève–Paris: Droz.

Bramoullé D. (forthcoming), 'La politique fatimide en mer Rouge (969–1171): entre idéologie et stratégie de survie', in *L'horizon Sharma. L'essor du commerce islamique dans l'océan Indien occidental (v. 980–1150)*, A. Rougeulle and É. Vallet, eds., Paris.

Bulliet, R. (2009), *Cotton, Climate and Camels in Early Islamic Iran: A Moment in World History*, New York: Columbia University Press.

Buzurg ibn Shariyar (1981), *The Book of the Wonders of India*, G.S.P. Grenville, ed., London: East–West Publications (U.K.) Ltd.

Buzurg ibn Shariyar (1990), '*Aja'ib al-hind*, Y. Al-Sharouni (Arabic ed.), London: Riad El-Rayyes Books.

Carswell, J. (1976–7), 'China and Islam in the Maldive Islands', *Transactions of the Oriental Ceramic Society*, pp. 120–98.

—— (1977–8), 'China and Islam: A Survey of the Coast of India and Ceylon', *Transactions of the Oriental Ceramic Society*, pp. 24–68.

——(1989), 'China and the West: recent archaeological research in South Asia', *Asian Affairs*, vol. 20, no. 1, pp. 37–44.

Carswell, J. and Prickett M. (1984). 'Mantai 1980: A preliminary investigation', *Ancient Ceylon*, vol. 5, pp. 3–80.

Chaffee, J. (2006), 'Diasporic identities in the historical development of the maritime Muslim communities of Song-Yuan China', *Journal of the Economic and Social History of the Orient*, vol. 49, no. 4, pp. 395–420.

Chakravarti, R. (1991–2), 'The Export of Sindani Indigo from India to the "west" in the Eleventh Century', *Indian Historical Review*, vol. 18, pp. 12–28.

—— (1998), 'Coastal trade and voyages in Konkan: The early medieval scenario', *Indian Economic Social History Review*, vol. 35, pp. 97–123.

—— (2004), 'An Enchanting Seascape: through epigraphic lens', *Studies in History*, vol. 20, no. 2, pp. 305–15.

Chattopadhyaya, B. (1994), *The making of early medieval India*, New Delhi: Oxford University Press.

—— (1998), *Representing the other? Sanskrit sources and the Muslims (eighth to fourteenth century)*, New Delhi: Manohar.

—— (2003), *Studying early India: archaeology, texts and historical issues*, Delhi: Permanent Black.

Collinet A. (2010), 'Au prisme de la céramique: le Sind et l'Islam. Culture matérielle du sud du Pakistan, IIᵉ–XIIᵉ/VIIIᵉ–XVIIIᵉ siècles', unpublished Ph.D. thesis, Université de Paris I Panthéon-Sorbonne.

Coningham, R. (1999), *Anuradhapura: The British-Sri Lankan Excavations at Anuradhapura Salgaha Watta: Volume 1 The Site*, Oxford: Archaeopress for the Society for South Asian Studies Monograph Series.

——(2006), *Anuradhapura: The British-Sri Lankan Excavations at Anuradhapura Salgaha Watta: Volume 2 The Artefacts*, Oxford: Archaeopress.

Christie, J.W. (1998), 'The medieval Tamil-language inscriptions in South-East Asia and China', *Journal of Southeast Asian Studies*, vol. 29, no. 2, pp. 239–68.

Daftary, F. (2007), *The Isma'ilis. Their History and Doctrines*, Cambridge: Cambridge University Press.

——— (1999), 'The Ismaili da'wa outside the Fatimid dawla', in *L'Égypte Fatimide. Son art et son histoire*, M. Barrucand, ed., Paris: Presses de l'Université de Paris-Sorbonne, pp. 29–43.

Desai, Z.A. (1974), 'An Inscription Dated A.H. 969 from Patan (Gujarat)', *Epigraphia Indica Arabic and Persian Supplement*, pp. 58–61.

Dikshit, M.G. (1953), 'Panjim Plates of Jayakesi (I); Saka 981', *Indica. The Indian Historical Research Institute Silver Jubilee Commemoration Volume*, Bombay: Heras Institute of Indian History and Culture, pp. 89–99.

Ducène, J.C. (2010), 'Compte rendu d'Abu Imran Musa ibn Rabah al. Awsi al-Sirafi, Al-sahih min akhbar al-bihar wa-aga'ibiha, edite per yusu/AL-HADI, Damas: Dar Iqra'li-l-tiba'awa-l-nasr wa-l-tawzi, 1326(L)/2006, 304 pages', *Journal Asiatique*, vol. 298, no. 2, pp. 579–84.

Ferrand, G. (1913), *Relations de voyages et textes géographiques arabes, persans et turks relatifs à l'Extrême-Orient du VIIIe au XVIIIe siècles*, 2 vols., Paris: E. Leroux.

Gaur, A.S., Sundaresh and Odedra Ashok D. (2004), 'New Light on the Maritime Archaeology of Porbandar, Saurashtra Coast, Gujarat', *Man and Environment,* vol. 29, no. 1, pp. 103–7.

Gaur, A.S., Sundaresh (2005), 'A Late Harappan Port at Kindar Kheda on the Saurashtra Coast', *Man and Environment,* vol. 30, no. 2, pp. 44–8.

Gaur A.S., Vora, K.H. and Sundaresh, (2005), *Archaeology of Bet Dwarka Island: An excavation Report.* New Delhi: Aryan Books International.

——— (2008a), *Underwater Archaeology of Dwarka and Somnath*, New Delhi: Aryan Books International.

Gaur A.S., Khedekar V., Ramalingeswara Rao B. (2008b), 'Elemental oxides analysis of the medieval period glazed ware from Gogha, Gulf of Khambhat, Gujarat, India', *Current Science*, vol. 95, no. 5, pp. 670–4.

Ginzburg, C. (1992), 'Clues: roots of an evidential paradigm', in J. and A.C. Tedeschi (Eng. trans.) *Clues, Myths and the Historical Method*, Baltimore: Johns Hopkins University Press, pp. 96–125.

Gogte, V., Pradhan S., Dandekar A., Joshi S., Nanji R., Kadgaonkar S., Marathe V. (2006a), 'The Ancient Port at Chaul', *Journal of Indian Ocean Archaeology*, vol. 4, pp. 62–80.

Gogte, V., Pradhan S., Dandekar A., Joshi S., Kadgaonkar S., Bomble S. (2006b), 'Explorations at Dahanu-Chinchani Ancient Ports on the Western Coast of India', *Journal of Indian Ocean Archaeology*, vol. 3, pp. 137–45.

Goitein, S.D. and Friedman, M.A. (2008), *India Traders of the Middle Ages: Documents from the Cairo Geniza ('India Book')*, Études sur le Judaïsme Médiéval, vol. XXXI, Leiden and Boston: Brill.

Gokhale, S. (2004), 'Coins Found in the Excavations at Sanjan', *Journal of Indian Ocean Archaeology*, vol. 1, pp. 107–12.

Goldberg, J. (2012), *Trade and Institutions in the Medieval Mediterranean: the Geniza Merchants and their Business World*, Cambridge: Cambridge University Press.

Gupta, S. (2007), 'Piracy and trade on the western coast of India (AD 1-250)', *Azania: Archaeological Research in Africa*, vol. 42, pp. 37–51.

Gupta, S.P., Dalal K., Dandekar A., Mitra R., Nanji R., Pandey R. (2001–2), 'A Preliminary Report on the Excavations at Sanjan (2002)', *Puratattva*, vol. 32, pp. 182–98.

———(2003), 'Early Medieval Indian Ocean Trade: Excavations at Sanjan, India', *Circle of Inner Asian Art Newsletter*, vol. 17, pp. 26–34.

Gupta, S.P., Dalal K., Dandekar A., Nanji R., Aravazhi P. and Bomble S. (2004), 'On the Footsteps of the Zoroastrian Parsis in India: Excavations at Sanjan on the West Coast-2003', *Journal of Indian Ocean Archaeology*, vol. 1, pp. 93-106.

Gupta, S. and Aruni S.K. (2005), 'Early Historic Kanara: was it really Ptolemy's Pirate Coast?', *Journal of Indian Ocean Archaeology*, vol. 2, pp. 42–54.

Gupta, S.P., Dalal K., Nanji R., Dandekar A., Bomble S., Mushrif-Tripathi V., Kadgaonkar S., Chaudhuri G., Sharma P. and Abbas R. (2005), 'Preliminary Report on the Third Season of Excavations at Sanjan—2004', *Journal of Indian Ocean Archaeology*, vol. 2, pp. 55-61.

Hall, K. (1980), *Trade and Statecraft in the Age of the Colas*, New Delhi: Abhinav Publications.

Hartwell, R. (1983), *Tribute Missions to China, 960-1126*. Philadelphia: n.p.

Ibn Hawqal (1938), *Kitab surat al-ard*, J.H. Kramers (Arabic ed.), Leiden: Brill.

———(2001) *Configuration de la Terre*, J.H. Kramers and G. Wiet (French trans.), 2 vols., Paris: Maisonneuve et Larose.

Ibn Khurradadhbih (1889), *Kitab al-masalik wa al-mamalik*, M.J. de Goeje, ed., Leiden: Brill.

Ibn Majid (1971), *Arab Navigation in the Indian Ocean before the coming of the Portuguese*, G.R. Tibbetts (Eng. trans. and ed.), London: Royal Asiatic Society of Great Britain and Ireland.

Jain, V.K. (1990), *Trade and Traders in Western India (AD 1000–1300)*, New Delhi: South Asia Books.

Kalus, L. (2003), 'Réinterpretation des plus anciennes stèles funéraires islamiques nousantariennes: I. Les deux inscriptions du "Champa"', *Archipel*, vol. 66, pp. 63–90.

Kalus, L. and Guillot C. (2004), 'Réinterprétation des plus anciennes stèles funéraires islamiques nousantariennes: II. La stèle de Leran (Java) datée de 475/1082 et les stèles associées', *Archipel*, vol. 67, pp. 17–36.

——— (2005), 'Inscriptions islamiques en arabe de l'archipel des Maldives', *Archipel*, vol. 70, pp. 15–52.

——— (2006), 'Réinterprétation des plus anciennes stèles funéraires islamiques nousantariennes: III. Sri Lanka', *Archipel*, vol. 72, pp. 15–68.

Karashima, N. ed., (2004), *In Search of Chinese Ceramic-sherds in South India and Sri Lanka*, Tokyo: Taisho University Press.

———(ed.) (2002), *Ancient and Medieval Commercial Activities in the Indian Ocean: Testimony of Inscriptions and Ceramic-sherds*, Tokyo: Taisho University.

Kennet, D. (forthcoming), 'Report on the Turquoise Glazed wares from the 2007 season at Pattanam (Kerala)', unpublished paper.

Kennet, D. (2004a), *Sasanian and Islamic pottery from Ras al-Khaimah: classification, chronology and analysis of trade in the western Indian Ocean*, Oxford: Archaeopress.

—— (2004b), 'The transition from Early Historic to Early Medieval in the Vakataka realm', in *The Vakataka Heritage: Indian Culture at the Crossroads*, H. Bakker, ed., Groningen: Egbert Forsten, pp. 11–17.

Kervran, M. (1992), 'The fortress of Ratto Kot at the mouth of the Bandhore River (Indus Delta, Sindh, Pakistan)', *Pakistan Archaeology*, vol. 27, pp. 143–70.

—— (1996), 'Indian ceramics in Southern Iran and Eastern Arabia: Repertory, classification and chronology', in *Tradition and Archaeology. Early maritime contacts in the Indian Ocean*, H.P. Ray and J.-F. Salles (eds.), New Delhi: Manohar, pp. 37–58.

—— (1993), 'Vanishing medieval cities of the northwest Indus delta', *Pakistan Archaeology*, vol. 28, pp. 3–54.

—— (2004), 'Archaeological Research at Suhar 1980–1986', *The Journal of Oman Studies*, vol. 13, pp. 263–381.

Khan, A.M. (1928), *Mirat-i-Ahmadi Supplement*, S. Nawab Ali and C.N. Seddon (Eng. trans. and eds.), Gaekwad's oriental series, no. 50. Baroda: Oriental Institute.

Khan, A.N. (1990), *Al-Mansurah, a Forgotten Arab Metropolis in Pakistan*, Karachi: Department of Archaeology & Museums, Government of Pakistan.

Khan, F.A. (1960), *A preliminary report on the recent archaeological excavations at Banbhore*, Karachi: Department of Archaeology and Museums, Ministry of Education & Scientific Research, Govt. of Pakistan.

Kokan, M.Y. (1974), *Arabic and Persian in Carnatic, 1710–1960*, Madras: Hafiza Press.

Lambourn, E. (2003), 'Of jewels and horses—the career and patronage of an Iranian merchant under Shah Jahan', *Iranian Studies*, vol. 36, no. 2, pp. 213–58.

—— (2008) 'India from Aden—Khutba and Muslim Urban Networks in Late Thirteenth-Century India', in K. Hall, ed., *Secondary Cities and Urban Networking in the Indian Ocean Realm, c.1400–1800*, Lanham, MD: Lexington Books, pp. 55–97.

—— (2014), 'Borrowed Words in an Ocean of Objects: Geniza sources and new cultural histories of the Indian Ocean', in *Irreverent History: Essays for M.G.S. Narayanan*, K. Veluthat and D. Davis, Jr., eds., New Delhi.

Lokhandwala, S.T. (1955), 'The Bohras a Muslim Community of Gujarat', *Studia Islamica*, vol. 3, pp. 117–35.

Majumdar, R.C. and Dasgupta, K.K. eds., (1981–82), *A Comprehensive History of India, A.D. 300–985*, vol. 3, pts. 1-2, 2 vols., New Delhi: People's Publishing House.

Manguin, P.-Y. (1991), 'The Merchant and the King: political myths of Southeast Asian coastal polities', *Indonesia*, vol. 52, pp. 41–54.

Maniku, H.A. and Wijayawardhana, G.D. (1986), *Isdho Loamaafaanu*, Colombo.

al-Mas'udi (1962–79), *Les Prairies d'Or*, B. de Meynard and A. Pavet de Courteille (French trans.), C. Pellat (rev.) 5 vols., Paris: P. Geuthner.

Mate, M.S. (2005) *Archaeology of Medieval India*, New Delhi: B.R. Publishing Corporation.

Mehta, R.N. (1978), *Excavations at Nagara*, Department of Archaeology and Ancient History, Faculty of Arts, Baroda: M.S. University of Baroda.

Mirashi, V.V. ed., (1978), *Corpus Inscriptionum Indicarum* VI, Delhi: Archaeological Survey of India.

Mitra, R. and Dalal, K. (2005), 'A Report on the Glass Vessels from Sanjan, 2002', *Journal of Indian Ocean Archaeology*, vol. 2, pp. 62–8.

Mushrif, V. and Walimbe, S.R. (2005), 'Human skeletal remains from Sanjan excavations', *Journal of Indian Ocean Archaeology*, vol. 2, pp. 73-92.

Nanavati, J.M., R.N. Mehta, S.N. Chowdhary (1971), *Somnath, 1956; being a report of excavations*. Ahmedabad, Department of Archaeology, Gujarat State: University Publications Sales Unit, Baroda.

Nanji, R. (2011), *Mariners and Merchants: a study of the ceramics from Sanjan (Gujarat)* (Sanjan Reports Volume 1/BAR International Series 2231), Oxford: Archaeopress.

Nanji, R. and Dandekar A. (2005), 'Excavations at Sanjan Dakhma—2004', *Journal of Indian Ocean Archaeology*, vol. 2, pp. 69-72.

Nanji, R. and Dhalla, H. (2007), 'The Landings of the Zoroastrians at Sanjan', in *Parsis in India and the Diaspora*, J.R. Hinnells and A. Williams, eds., London and New York: Routledge.

Narayanan, M.G.S. (1972), 'The Jewish Copperplates of Cochin', *Cultural Symbiosis in Kerala*. Trivandrum: Kerala Historical Society, pp. 23–30, 51–3, 79–85.

—— (1996), *Perumals of Kerala. Political and Social Conditions of Kerala Under the Cera Perumals of Makotai (c. 800 AD–1124 AD)*, Calicut: Xavier Press.

—— (2002), 'Further Studies in the Jewish Copper Plates of Cochin', *Indian Historical Review*, vol. 29, pp. 66–76.

Pearson, M. (2003), *The Indian Ocean*, London and New York: Routledge.

Pissurlencar, P. (1938), 'Inscrições Pre-Portuguesas de Goa (Breves notas)', *O Oriente Portugês*, vol. 22, pp. 381–460.

Prickett-Fernando, M. (1990), 'Mantai-Mahatittha: the great port and entrepot in the Indian trade', in *Sri Lanka and the Silk Road of the Sea*, S. Bandaranayake et al., eds., Colombo: The Sri Lanka National Commission for UNESCO, pp. 115–22.

Quddusi, M.I. (1999), 'Kerala inscriptions with special reference to an epitaph from Baliapatam', *Journal of the Epigraphic Society of India*, vol. 25, pp. 29–36.

Rajaguru, S.N. and Deo, S.G. (2005), 'Coastal Geomorphology of Sanjan', *Journal of Indian Ocean Archaeology*, vol. 2, pp. 93–8.

Rao, S.R. (1979–85), *Lothal and the Indus civilization,* Bombay: Asia Publishing House, 1973, and S.R. Rao, *Lothal, a Harappan port town (1955–62),* Memoirs of the Archaeological Survey of India, no. 78, New Delhi: Archaeological Survey of India.

—— (1988), 'The future of Marine Archaeology in Indian Ocean Countries', *Proceedings of the first Indian Conference on Marine Archaeology of Indian Ocean Countries, October 1987*, Goa: National Institute of Oceanography, pp. 21–5.

Rao, S.R., Tripati, S. and Gaur, A.S. (1992), 'A preliminary exploration of Prabhasa-Somnatha', *Journal of Marine Archaeology*, vol. 3, pp. 13–16.

Rao, T.A. Gopinatha (1920), 'Three inscriptions of Sthanu Ravi', in *Tamil and Vetteluttu Inscriptions on Stone and Copper-plates Parts I to III*, T.A. Gopinatha Rao and K.V. Subrahmanya Aiyer, Travancore Archaeological Series, vol. II, Trivandrum: Government Press, pp. 60–86.

Ray, H.P. and Salles J.-F. eds., (1996), *Tradition and Archaeology: Early Maritime Contacts in the Indian Ocean*, New Delhi: Manohar.

Ray, H.P. ed., (1999), *Archaeology of Seafaring: The Indian Ocean in the Ancient Period*, New Delhi: Manohar.

Sedov, A.V. (1996), 'Qana' (Yemen) and the Indian Ocean, the Archaeological Evidence', in *Tradition and Archaeology. Early maritime contacts in the Indian Ocean*, H.P. Ray and J.-F. Salles, eds., New Delhi: Manohar, pp. 11–35.

Selvakumar, V., Gopi P.K., Shajan K.P. (2005), 'Trial excavations at Pattanam: a preliminary report', *Journal of the Centre for Heritage Studies*, vol. 2, pp. 57–66.

Shajan, K.P., Cherian, P.J., Tomber, R., Selvakumar, V. (2008), 'The external connections of Early Historic Pattanam, India: the ceramic evidence', *Antiquity* 82, available from http://antiquity.ac.uk/projgall/tomber/index. html#author

—— (2004), 'Locating the ancient port of Muziris: fresh findings from Pattanam', *Journal of Roman Archaeology*, vol. 17, pp. 351–9.

Sharma, R.S. and Shrimali, K.M., eds. (1992–2008), *A Comprehensive History of India. A.D. 985–1206*, vol. 4, pts. 1-2, 2vols. Delhi: People's Publishing House.

Sheriff, A. (2010), *Dhow Cultures of the Indian Ocean: Cosmopolitanism, Commerce and Islam*. New York: Columbia University Press.

Shinde, V., Gupta, S. and Rajgor, D. (2002), 'An Archaeological Reconnaissance of the Konkan Coast from Bharuch to Janjira', *Man and Environment*, vol. 27, no. 1, pp. 73–81.

Shokoohy, M. (1988), *Bhadresvar: The Oldest Islamic Monuments in India*, Leiden: Brill.

—— (2003), *Muslim Architecture of South India. The Sultanate of Ma'bar and the Traditions of the Maritime Settlers on the Malabar and Coromandel Coasts (Tamil Nadu, Kerala and Goa)*, London and New York: Routledge Curzon.

Sinopoli, C. (1996), 'Ceramic Use and Ritual Practices in Hindu India', *ACRO, Asian Ceramics Research Conference, 24–26 May 1996, Chicago, The Field Museum*, published online at http://www.acrochicago.org/Sonopoli.html.

—— (2003), *The Political Economy of Craft Production. Crafting Empire in South India, c. 1350–1650*. Cambridge and New York: Cambridge University Press.

Sirafi, Abu Zayd (1845), *Silsila al-tawarikh* in M. Reinaud (Arabic ed. and French trans.), *Relation des Voyages faits par les arabes et les persans dans l'Inde et à la Chine*, 2 vols., Paris: Imprimerie royale, vol. 1, pp. 61–154.

Sircar, D.C. (1957–8a), 'Rashtrakuta Charters from Chinchani', *Epigraphia Indica*, vol. 32, pp. 45–60.

——— (1957–8b), 'Three Grants from Chinchani', *Epigraphia Indica*, vol. 32, pp. 61–76.

Sridhar, T.S. (2005), *Alagankulam: Ancient Roman Port City of Tamil Nadu,* Chennai: Department of Archaeology, Government of Tamilnadu.

Stern B., Connan J., Blakelock E., Jackman R., Coningham R.A.E., Heron C. (2008), 'From Susa to Anuradhapura reconstructing aspects of trade and exchange in bitumen-coated ceramic vessels between Iran and Sri Lanka from the third to the ninth centuries AD', *Archaeometry*, vol. 50, no. 3, pp. 409–28.

Subbarayalu, Y. (2012), 'Anjuvannam. A Maritime Trade Guild of Medieval Times', in *South India Under the Cholas*, Y. Subbarayalu, Delhi: OUP India, pp. 176–87.

Thapar, R. (2002), *Early India from the Origins to AD 1300*, London: Allen Lane.

Tomber, R. (2008), *Indo-Roman Trade. From pots to pepper*, London: Duckworth.

——— (2007), 'Rome and Mesopotamia—importers into India in the first millennium AD', *Antiquity*, vol. 81, pp. 972–88.

Tripati, S. (1992), 'Chaul: A declining port of Konkan', *Journal of Marine Archaeology*, vol. 3, pp. 54–6.

Tripathi, A. (2004), 'Onshore and offshore exploration in Elephanta Island: evidence of Indo-Mediterranean trade', *Journal of Indian Ocean Archaeology*, vol. 1, pp. 116–23.

Wade, G. (2009), 'An Early Age of Commerce in Southeast Asia, 900–1300 CE', *Journal of Southeast Asian Studies*, vol. 40, no. 2, pp. 221–65.

Wagoner, P. (1999), 'Fortuitous convergences and essential ambiguities: transcultural political elites in the medieval Deccan', *International Journal of Hindu Studies*, vol. 3, no. 3, pp. 241–64.

Walburg, R. (2008), *Coins and Tokens from Ancient Ceylon: Ancient Ruhuna. Sri Lanka-German Archaeological Project in the Southern Province*, vol. 2, Wiesbaden: Dr. Ludwig Reichert.

Weisshaar, H.-J., Roth, H., Wijeyapala, W. eds., (2001), *Ancient Ruhuna. Sri Lanka-German Archaeological Project in the Southern Province*, vol. 1, Mainz: Verlag Philipp von Zabern.

Wheeler, R.E.M., Ghosh A. and Krishna Deva, (1946), 'Arikamedu: an Indo-Roman trading station on the east coast of India', *Ancient India*, vol. 2, pp. 17–124.

Wilkinson, J.C. (1981), 'Oman and East Africa: New Light on Early Kilwan History from the Omani Sources', *The International Journal of African History Studies*, vol. 14, no. 2, pp. 277–81.

Wink, A. (1991), *Al-Hind. The making of the Indo-Islamic World. Early Medieval India and the Expansion of Islam 7th–11th Centuries*, Leiden–New York: Brill.

RELATED AREAS:
SRI LANKA, SOUTH-EAST ASIA

CHAPTER 19

The Oldest Shipwreck in the Indian Ocean

Osmund Bopearachchi, Senarath Disanayaka
and *Nimal Perera*

The discovery of a shipwreck near the southern coast of Sri Lanka, three miles from the ancient port-site of Godavaya may revolutionize our knowledge of the history of maritime trade in South Asia, particularly between India and Sri Lanka. The wreck was first reported in 1998 to Oliver Kessler who was excavating the Godavaya port site.[1] In 2005, Kessler located its exact position through information provided by local fishermen, when the site was photographed and the divers had brought up a few specimens of the cargo. Kessler informed Siran Deraniyagala in 2005, the then Director General of Archaeology about these finds. Two local fishermen[2] brought to the surface a stone object with Hindu symbols (*Nandipada*, *Śrīvatsa* and fish engraved on it) and it aroused the curiosity of the Department of Archaeology. In 2008, a surface excavation was carried out by divers from the Department of Archaeology and the Central Cultural Fund (Maritime Archaeological Unit) with the assistance of the Sri Lanka Navy to assess the archaeological potential of the site. They raised to the surface samples of Black and Red Ware (BRW), as well as two purified glass ingots (Plate 19.1).

Following the first dive in late 2008, we put together an international team of nautical archaeologists to undertake further research. At the time, Dr Sanjyot Mehendale (Department of Near-Eastern Studies, University of California at Berkeley) who was taking part in a collaborative programme with the Department of Archaeology and the French Archaeological Mission in Sri Lanka, accepted to explore the possibilities of launching a collaborative project. It was hoped that a joint collaboration with major European and US institutions would bring in additional expertise, financial

Plate 19.1: Purified glass ingots from the Godavaya shipwreck.

support and equipment to augment the underfunded and inadequately equipped Maritime Research Unit of the Sri Lanka Department of Archaeology. In 2009, Dr Mehendale contacted Professor Deborah Carlson at the Institute of Nautical Archaeology (INA) at the University of Texas A&M to discuss and develop a plan to excavate the shipwreck. The first step was taken in December 2010 by Deborah Carlson and Sheila Matthews, in order to attain a clear picture of the overall dimensions and physical characteristics of the wreck (Plates 19.2 and 19.3). After securing a collaborative research grant from the National Endowment for the Humanities, Sheila Matthews and Ken Trethewey visited Sri Lanka in December 2011 to make further inquiries to determine the plans for the next long-term campaigns. Sri Lankan divers of the newly-founded Maritime Archaeological Unit of the Department of Archaeology (Sri Lanka) were headed by Palitha Weerasinghe and Sanath Karunaratane.[3]

Needless to say, we are still in the early stages of research and our analyses of the wreck so far are preliminary. Further research will be conducted under the direction of Deborah Carlson and other INA scholars. At the end of this essay, we will outline how the Department of Archaeology and the team headed by Professor Carlson have planned to further develop the project. Our first observations are based on the

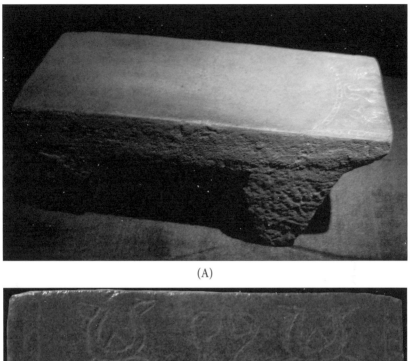

(A)

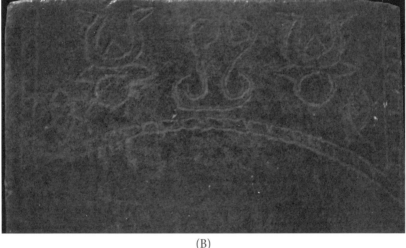

(B)

Plate 19.2 (A & B): 'Stone 'bench', or grinding stone or 'scared seat' from the Godavaya shipwreck.

initial operations conducted so far, and we alone are responsible for any conclusions drawn. The organization of East-West trade is well attested following the conquest of Egypt in 30 BC by Octavian, the future Roman emperor Augustus. The political control of Egypt by Augustus gave rise to a very profitable sea trade utilizing the Red Sea to provide passage to India to acquire luxury goods that had become fashionable within the Empire. Roman ships left Egypt in July to reach the Gulf of Aden and, from there, utilizing the south-west monsoon, sailed to the ports of Barygaza (Broach

(A)

(B)

Plates 19.3 (A & B): Stone object carrying an inscription found buried under the Yatala
stūpa terrace (Tissamaharama).

in Gujarat) or Muziris (in Kerala), on the west coast of India. Pliny the
Elder's *Natural History* provides information on the prices of foreign
goods in first century AD Rome: 'Long pepper . . . is fifteen *denarii* per
pound, while that of white pepper is seven, and of black, four.' Regarding
the cost of foreign commodities, Pliny (*NH*, 12, 101) complains: '. . . in
no year does India absorb less than fifty million *sesterces* of our empire's
wealth, sending back merchandise to be sold with us at a hundred times its
prime cost.' Romans came to India mainly in search of pepper. An Indian

storage jar discovered in a courtyard north of the Serapis Temple at the Red Sea port site of Berenike dated to the first century AD contained 7.5 kg. of black pepper, a vital piece of evidence demonstrating the dynamics of Roman trade with India.[4] It is this trade that is echoed in the Sangam text *Akaṉāṉūṟu*:

Musiri the prosperous city
To which the vessels of the Yavanas
Built with care by skilled ship-builders,
Come laden with gold and return laden with pepper,
Agitating the foaming waters
Of great Suḷḷi river of the Cēra kings.[5]

All the *emporia* and stages where goods could be sold are mentioned in an exceptional trading manual known as the *Periplus of the Erythraean Sea,* probably written *c.* AD 50, which indicates the existence of organized East-West trade at least since the beginning of this period.[6]

Another important piece of evidence for direct Roman trade with India at the close of the first century AD was the discovery of thousands of Roman *aurei* and *denarii* on Indian soil, the majority attributed to the Julio-Claudian Period.[7] Compared to the thousands of early Imperial coins found in India, it is very interesting to note that very few of the early Roman types were discovered in Sri Lanka.[8] Why did the Romans, who had commercial relations with India, not enter into direct trading partnerships with Sri Lanka? Strabo (II.1.14) notes that from Taprobane, ivory, tortoise-shell and other merchandise were brought in abundance to the markets of India. Perhaps, there was no need for Romans to go all the way to Sri Lanka as long as its products could be obtained easily and abundantly at Indian ports. On the contrary, the great abundance of the later (fifth-sixth centuries AD) Roman 'third brass' in Sri Lanka may be a result of the revival of Western powers through Axumite, Himyarite and Persian middlemen, which coincides with the foundation of Constantinople as the seat of the Roman empire on the one hand, and on the other, the gradual shift of the focus of trade from the south Indian coasts to Sri Lanka. Likewise, by the fifth century Sri Lanka became the main centre of trade in the Indian Ocean. From this period onwards, the ports situated on the southern coast of Arabia, connected with the Axumite, Himyarite and Persian traders, played a vital role. The shifting of the starting points, from the Red Sea to the Arabian Sea of the sea voyage and the evolution in the speed of ships made the journey to Sri Lanka and beyond easy. A good image regarding the trade activities during this period emerges from the account of Cosmas Indicopleustes, the Egyptian Greek of the sixth century AD. According to a description in his *Christian Topography* (XI, 13) Sri Lanka was playing an important role in transmitting merchandise between East and West, a role once played by western India.[9] However, south Indian and Sri Lankan regional maritime network had a long history and went back to the early historic periods. Interestingly, the Godavaya shipwreck, which will be discussed later, dates to the second or first century BC, and belongs to a period when Romans were still not engaged in Indian Ocean trade.

The location of the Godavaya shipwreck close the estuary of the Walawe Ganga (river) is very significant for our understanding of the cargo it was carrying. The Walawe Ganga was one of five navigable rivers on the island listed by the Classical author Palladius (i, 6). A series of excavations and explorations carried out by the Department of Archaeology and the French Archaeological Mission at the estuaries and along the rivers brought to light enough evidence to indicate that in ancient times, large ships were anchored in the sea close to the river mouths and trade commodities were taken to inland markets using the rivers and waterfronts.[10] Sri Lanka has an extensive network of 103 rivers flowing in a radial pattern towards the sea. Some permanent rivers arising in the high mountains of the central part of the island facilitated inland trade activities. Their role was essential, because the circumnavigation was practised since the early historic periods as sailing through the Gulf of Mannar because its sandbanks at Adam's bridge would have been too great of a risk for big ships.

Knowledge of the physical and climatic conditions of the island is necessary to understand the role played by these rivers in the development of both international and inland trade. Sri Lanka, located 6 to 10 degrees north of the Equator, has a tropical climate dominated by monsoon winds. Rising above 2,000 m., the central massif in the south/central part of the island stands in the path of monsoonal winds, and irrigates the headwaters of all Sri Lanka's major rivers (Map 19.1). The unequal rainfall determined by the strong south-west monsoon (May-August) and the weak north-west monsoon (November-February) divides the island into Wet and Dry Zones. The river basins originating in the wet zone of the central massif are perennial, but the ones, other than the Mahaveli Ganga, in the dry zone are only occasional. However, prior to the colonial period and the destruction of the tropical forests in the central mountains to make way for coffee and tea plantations, the Dry Zone was certainly abundant with smoothly functioning hydraulic conveyances.

Since the late 1990s, the Department of Archaeology and the French Archaeological Mission explored the following river estuaries: Salavattota (Chilaw) at the Deduru-oya, Wattala at the Kelani Ganga, Kalalittha (Kalutara) at the Kalu Ganga, Bhimatittha (Bentota) at the Bentota Ganga,

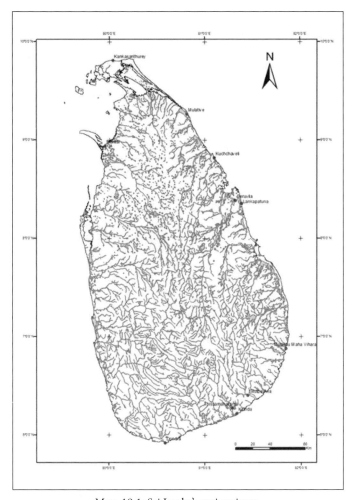

Map. 19.1: Sri Lanka's major rivers.

Gimhatittha (Gintota) at the Gin-Ganga, Mahavalukagama (Weligama) at the Polwatta Ganga and Nilwalatittha (Matara) at the Nilwala Ganga. The team obtained positive results from the excavations and explorations conducted at Giribawa on the left bank of the Kala Oya, which flows to the sea at Uruvelapattna; at Panirendava, on the left bank of Daduru Oya, which flows to the sea at the ancient port of Salavattota; and at the village of Pilapitiya, on the right bank of the Kelani Ganga, about 7 km. from the ancient sea port of Wattala and Ridiyagama on the right bank of the Walawe Ganga which flows to the sea at Godavaya (Map 19.2).[11] This project was further extended to the east coast in the Summer 2011 with the excavations at Kuchchaveli.[12]

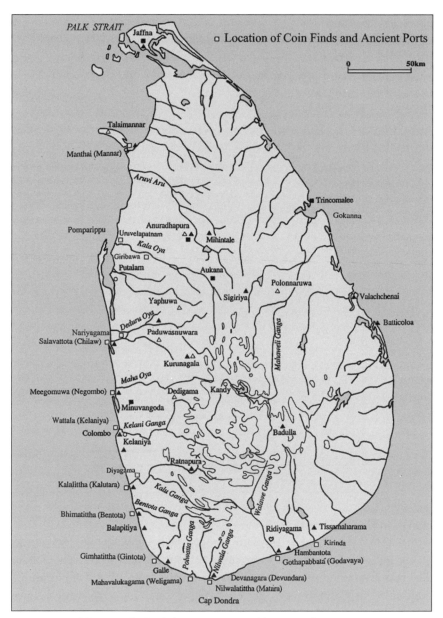

Map 19.2: Sri Lanka's major rivers and location of sea ports.

In spite of the ecological disasters which badly affected the island's water resources, the Kelani Ganga, which flows to the sea at Wattala, is still navigable up to Sitawaka, about 40 km. from the river mouth, where one of the short-lived capitals of the sixteenth century was situated. In Summer 1997, the Department of Archaeology and the French Archaeological

Mission in Sri Lanka jointly carried out three test trenches, at the village of Pilapitiya, on the right bank of the Kelani Ganga, about 7 km. from the estuary of the river Kelani, in order to clarify the stratigraphy and to determine the different chronological phases of the early historic settlements of the site. These sondages yielded layers dating back to the sixth century BC as revealed by the calibrated dating of C14 containing early BRW, followed by Rouletted Ware dating to the first century BC.[13]

From 1994 to 1996, further systematic explorations and excavations were carried out at Ridiyagama, about 12 km. upstream from the mouth of the river Walawe by the Department of Archaeology and the French Archaeological Mission in Sri Lanka jointly. The ancient settlements, clustered around the two ancient reservoirs, are today completely under water as a result of an extension built by the British at the beginning of the twentieth century. In 1995, the excavation brought to light six stratigraphic layers, subdivided into 45 different contexts determined by significant distinct features. Different phases of occupation that go down to occupation levels reached a depth of 1.35 m. Fragments of BRW were numerous in the third layer. The fourth layer yielded copper slags, mica, burnt charcoal, early BRW, terracotta objects and beads. This layer thus was characterized by extensive, different and significant shifts in human activities. The most ancient layer brought to light a small number of potsherds and copper slag, thus pointing to the beginning of human settlement. The approximate dating of the different phases of settlement from the fourth century BC to seventh century AD is supported by BRW, Roman coins and other additional pottery types, copper slags followed by iron slags, and beads. In 1996, more than twenty furnaces structures were excavated. Some of these furnaces may have been used for forging iron or for cementation.[14] The German Archaeological Institute (DAI) and the University of Bonn also explored the land site of ancient Godavaya, where excavations were initiated in 1994. The excavations there have revealed the remains of a quarry, temple, and monastery dating from to the second century AD. Smaller diagnostic finds such as imported Persian and Chinese pottery, Roman coins, beads, bangles and stamped bricks, attest to the scope and vitality of Godavaya's commercial network.[15] It is important to highlight that the Walawe Ganga falls into the sea at Godavaya, where an inscription on a boulder next to the ancient stūpa refers to the presence of an ancient emporium. It states that regular and minor duties in the port or emporium of Goḍapavvata were given to the (Buddhist) Monastery (by) king Gāmini Ahhaya (Gajabahu) 114–136 AD.[16]

The study of the Godavaya wreck's cargo within an archaeological context will provide significant data on the close cultural, social, religious

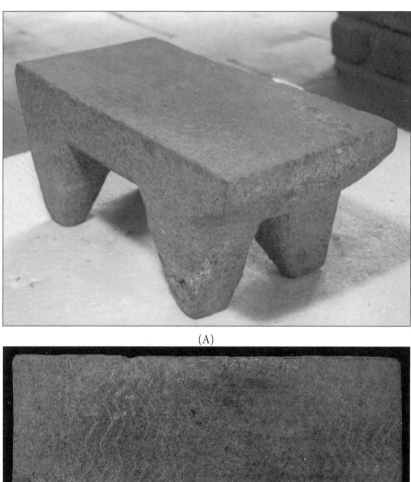

(A)

(B)

Plates 19.4 (A & B): Stone object with *Śrīvatsa* symbol buried under the Yatala stūpa terrace (Tissamaharama).

and commercial interactions between Sri Lanka and Tamil Nadu in south India during the early historical period. According to surface exploration, the ship, wrecked three miles from the estuary of the Walawe Ganga, was carrying stone objects (grinding stones or ceremonial benches), BRW vessels, iron and copper bars, and, very significantly, purified glass ingots. Metal samples taken from the shipwreck were positively identified as copper and iron by Maryse Blet-Lemarquand by MEB-EDX (*SEM-EDX*

*Scanning Electron Microscopy Energy Dispersive X-Ray Analysi*s). The discovery of furnaces, which may have been used for forging iron or for cementation at Ridiyagama and wind-blown furnaces at Samanalawewa in the upper Walawe river valley, are absolute proof for the existence of iron smelting technology as early as the beginning of the Common Era.[17] It is still too early to hypothesize on the relationship between the furnaces and the Godavaya cargo, but further analyses of the iron and copper bars might enable us to determine their origin.

Let us turn to the other objects uncovered from the Godavaya wreckage site. The first object uncovered, and the first piece of evidence regarding the chronology, is a kind of stone 'bench', or grinding stone or 'scared seat' [Plate 19.2 (A & B)][18] analogous to one carrying an inscription found buried under the Yatala stūpa[19] terrace located in Tissamaharama, the ancient capital of Ruhuna. The inscription of the latter is in Prakrit, written in early Brāhmī script, and can be palaeographically dated to the third or second century BC [Plate 19.3 (A & B)]. The stone 'bench' found in the Godavaya shipwreck, though deprived of an inscription written in early Brāhmī, has two Brahmanical symbols carved on the surface of the stone: the *nandipada* (footprint of the bull Nandi, Śiva's vehicle), and the *Śrīvatsa* (Sanskrit for 'endless knot'), the mark on Viṣṇu's chest where his consort Sri Lakṣmī resides. Another stone 'bench' similar in profile also found buried under the present terrace of the Yatala stūpa carries a similar *Śrīvatsa* symbol [Plate 19.4 (A & B)]. As attested by the carvings on a *stambha* (column) at the northern *ayaka* (frontispiece) of the Jetavanarama Dagoba (Plate 19.5) built by King Mahasen (AD 274–301), these two symbols: *Śrīvatsa* and *nandipada* appear in a Buddhist context.[20] In addition to the above-mentioned symbols, there are two carvings of a fish symbol on the Godavaya stone object which can be seen on Sangam age coins of the third and second centuries BC.[21] The same symbol can also be observed on coins depicting a temple on the obverse and the fish symbol on the reverse. The earliest coins in Sri Lanka bear designs derived from the second series of Pandyan multi-type coins, struck during the period *c.* 210–175 BC. It is interesting to note that a similar type of coin was found in the structural period G, which dates to the second century BC from Sri Lankan and British excavations conducted in the ancient citadel of Anuradhapura.[22] This object thus provides strong evidence for the close cultural links between Sri Lanka and India, and confirms further the hypothesis according to which boats leaving India were sailing around the east coast of Sri Lanka, so as to reach the dynamic port sites of the south.

According to their typology, the BRW sherds collected from the surface of the Godavaya shipwreck can be dated by the typology approximately to

Plate 19.5: Carvings on a *stambha* at the northern *ayaka* of the Jetavanarama Dagoba (Anuradhapura).

Plate 19.6: Underwater exploration in progress at the Shipwreck site of Godavaya
by the divers of the Department of Archaeology (Sri Lanka) and INA,
University of Texas A&M.

Plate 19.7: Underwater exploration in progress at the Shipwreck site of Godavaya.

the second century BC. As mentioned earlier, at Ridiyagama and at many sites on the Walawe Ganga, large quantities of early megalithic BRW, some of which were engraved with early historic symbols, have been collected. A comparative study on these post-firing graffiti marks, usually found on the shoulder portion of the BRW, uncovered in excavations at Kodumanal in Tamil Nadu and at Ridiyagama and Kelaniya in Sri Lanka directed by K. Rajan and O. Bopearachchi respectively show that these ceramic objects may have a common origin.[23] The moon symbol, which takes the form of the Brāhmī akṣara 'ma', occurs individually or in composite form on the potsherds collected from both sites. The symbol, as a basic element composed of one vertical line at the centre and two oblique lines on its side meeting at a point on the top, also appears in more elaborate forms with additional strokes. The ladder-like symbol, in simple or composite form, is attested in Kodumanal and Ridiyagama. The *swastika* symbol is found in all sites individually or in various composite forms with arms branched out. It is also interesting to note as we have seen earlier, that the most ancient layers of the excavations at Kelaniya, conducted by the Department of Archaeology and the French Archaeological Mission, brought to light fragments of BRW which can be dated with certainty back to the sixth century BC, as confirmed by the calibrated dating obtained on the basis of C14 analyses. Various scholars have classified these symbols as potter's marks, owner's marks or as clan marks. The limited excavations and lack of proper documentation still prevent a clear understanding of the true meaning that stands behind these signs. However, the occurrence of the same individual or composite graffiti marks in both Sri Lankan and Tamil Nadu sites enables us to suppose without much of a risk that there was a continuous cultural and trade contact between these two regions. Furthermore, the petrographic analysis done on thin-sectioning of BRW samples collected from our excavations at Ridiyagama and Kelaniya, carried out by Jean-Louis Reille, Département des Sciences de la Terre de l'Eau et de l'Espace de l'Université Montpellier II Sciences, shows very clearly, that despite the distance of more than 200 km. which separate the two sites, there remains a homogeneity of the pottery, as far as the characteristic mineral inclusions are concerned.[24] It would be important to carry out similar analyses on the Godavaya BRW fragments in relation to south Indian prototypes.

The C14 analyses carried out on two wood samples date the shipwreck between the second century BC and the first century AD.[25] The C14 analyses further confirm the chronology obtained by the pottery typology and glass testing. Therefore, this Godavaya shipwreck should clearly be considered as the oldest so far attested in the Indian Ocean. The preliminary

Plate 19.8: Ancient *stūpa* and the Godavaya Bay seen from the sea.

investigations on glass ingots from the Godavaya shipwreck carried out by James Lankton and Bernard Gratuze open the door to the study of the glass exchange in South and South-East Asia. These samples are exactly the type of archaeological material essential for a more complete understanding (see the Appendix by Langton and Gratuze at the end of this essay). The results of their analyses strongly suggest a south Indian origin for the Godavaya glass, with a particular focus on such unexplored sites as Manikollai and Appur.

The epigraphic and literary evidence for the active role played by the Tamil merchants in the early phase of Sri Lanka's history is numerous. A study undertaken by I. Mahadevan has revealed the existence of numerous inscribed potsherds in the Prakrit (old Sinhalese) language written in the Brāhmī script, found at or near ancient sea ports along the east coast of India.[26] The 10 inscribed potsherds published by Mahadevan, bearing Prakrit-Brāhmī script were reported from ancient trade centres like Kodumanal, Arikamedu and Alagankulam. According to palaeographic and linguistic features, these inscriptions can be dated from the second century BC to the first century AD. One of them comes from Arikamedu: it reads '*Ku bi ra ha*'. It is a complete inscription written on a Grey Ware in Sinhala-Prakrit and in Sinhala-Brāhmī. '*Kubira*' in Prakrit or '*Kubera*' in Sanskrit is the god of fortune and wealth.

It goes without saying that any research on the maritime trade in the Indian Ocean connected with south India and Sri Lanka has to be based on a scientific survey of the shipwreck at Godavaya. The site in itself is challenging as the ship lies at the depth of a 110 ft. in an area with strong currents during half of the year. Even at such a depth, the water is incredibly clear, which greatly facilitates archaeological work in comparison to sites in the Mediterranean. During the winter monsoon, especially between December and January, the soft currents, make the site conductive to diving. A scientific underwater excavation will help to understand the network of trade and communication between the inland capitals or political centres and the port-towns in river estuaries, opened to long-distance exchanges. In this way, the joint project might lead to a rewriting of the economic, social, religious and cultural history of the area.

Although textual sources and archaeological evidence account for the existence of a significant network of trade connecting Sri Lanka to India and the West, despite many surveys and excavations, no shipwreck has ever been found near the coasts of India or Sri Lanka: the Godavaya shipwreck is the first one to reveal a vast array of well-preserved material. Since the ship remained untouched, there is still a possibility of discovering some wooden structure beneath the cargo. So far, unlike Roman boats of which the architecture is known by the study of many shipwrecks, south Indian boats are only studied through iconography or ethno-archaeology. Whereas Roman boats are strongly built by a system of pegs and mortises, the South Asian ones are likely to have been constructed with sewn planks, as the traditional boats still in use.

In the following seasons, we hope to map, excavate and conserve the artefacts from the Godavaya wreck using methods developed and refined by the Institute for Nautical Archaeology (University of Texas A&M) since the 1960s. First, a string grid will be established to orient divers to the seabed and clarify the relative provenience of visible artefacts. The primary excavation tool under water is the hand, especially in loose overburden such as sand. By hand fanning, sediment can be removed in virtually any quantity, and once the loose overburden has been lifted off the artefacts, it is sucked out of the water column with an air lift. Concretions encountered on the site, if loose and of manageable size, will be mapped and raised for further analysis, by radiography, in the conservation laboratory of the Department of Archaeology. The provenience of all artefacts will be recorded by means of a digital photogrammetry system designed in large part by archaeologists Jeremy Green and Sheila Matthews. The mapping process begins with the installation of fixed datum points (usually metal spikes driven into the rock or weighted steel towers) around the wreck.

Numbered mapping flags of high-contrast vinyl are secured to the seabed atop, next to, or sometimes in place of an artefact, and photographed from a variety of angles using a digital camera with calibrated lens. Using several software programs (notably Site Recorder and Photo-Modeler Pro), it is possible to measure the distances between an individual flag and three or more fixed datum points, thus calculating the precise three-dimensional location of the artefact under the flag. These are the future aims of our collaborative program and the results of these operations will be made available to the scientific community through our websites and by the final reports.

Notes

1. R.P. Sunil and B.G. Preminda informed Oliver Kessler, who was excavating the land around Godavaya at that time, about this discovery.
2. See S.U. Deraniyagala, *Administration Report of the Director-General of Archaeology for the Year 1998. Sri Lanka*, Government Press, Colombo. Dr. Deraniyagala who sensed the importance of this discovery took every possible step to save it from illicit diggings.
3. R.P. Sunil and B.G. Preminda, the two village fishermen who discovered the shipwreck, actively participated in both dives.
4. Cappers 2006: 114.
5. Poem 149, by the poet Erukkāṭṭūr Tāyakaṇṇaṉār. Lines 7–11 in Tamil transliteration by A. Dhakshanalurthy, Bharathidasan University, 1999.
   . . . Cēralar
   culḷiyam pēriyāṟṟu veṇṇurai kalaṅka
   yavaṉar tanta viṉai māṉaṉ kalam
   poṉṉoṭu vantu kariyoṭu peyarum
   vaḷaṅkeḷu muciṟi . . .
6. For a recent study on the Roman trade with India see Tomber 2008.
7. For a critical analysis of these trade activities, see Champakalakshmi 1996: 109, 111, 119 and on the distribution pattern of Roman coins, see Suresh 2004.
8. See Bopearachchi 2006a.
9. See Bopearachchi 2006c: 38–49; also see Weerakkody 1997: 247.
10. Regarding the question of inland trade along the rivers, see Bopearachchi 1999 and 2008.
11. For an overall picture of these excavations, see Bopearachchi 1999.
12. The excavations conducted by the Department of Archaeology (under the supervision of Dr Nimal Perera, Deputy Director, Department of Archaeology) and the French Archaeological Mission (under the directorship of Professor Osmund Bopearachchi) at Kuchchaveli in Summer 2011 have clearly shown that, apart from being a monastic complex, the site was also an ancient sea port. The discovery of BRW, Grey Ware, Rouletted Ware,

Chinese porcelain and Roman coins found in the test-pits denote active trade activities. The earliest stratification dates back to the first century AD as attested by the calibrated dating. Reports of this excavation will be published in the forthcoming *Ancient Ceylon*.

13. Bopearachchi 1999: 10–2.

14. Ibid., pp. 12–16.

15. Kessler, Roth, Recker and Wijeypala 2001.

16. S. Paranavitana (1983: 101, no. 104) translates the term *paṭana* as 'port', while H. Falk (2001: 328) who proposed a revised translation uses the term '*emporium*' where commodities arrive by land or sea.

17. See Bopearachchi 1999: 13–6 and Juleff 1998.

18. The proper use of this object is still unknown. This kind of objects may have been used first as grinding stones and then were offered to the stūpa later. The discovery of another bench-shaped stone and a cylindrical land held grinding stone in 2013 from the shipwreck proves that these stones were used as querns.

19. It is believed that Yatala Dageba (stūpa) was built by a regional king Mahanaga, in the third century BC on the location where his queen bore him a son. Mahanaga was a brother of King Devanampiyathissa (250–210 BC), the first Sri Lankan king to accept the Buddhist doctrine.

20. This ayaka pillar is carved with the following auspicious symbols (from the top to the bottom): *Śrīvatsa, Swastika, Śaṅkha* (conch), *Chauri* (whisk), *Dhvaja* (victory banner) and *Purnagata*.

21. Krishnamurthy and Wickramasinghe 2005: 25–37.

22. Krishnamurthy and Wickramasinghe 2005: 27, coin no. 7. This chronology is based on the excavations conducted by the Department of Archaeology and British Archaeological Mission headed by Robin Coningham, see Bopearachchi 2006b.

23. Bopearachchi and Rajan 2002.

24. Bopearachchi 2008: 8.

25. The first sample analysed by the Centre de Datation par le Radiocarbone, Lyon (France) is dated between 177 BC and AD 23 (we are most grateful to Dr Philippe Galet for communicating these results). The other sample was analysed with the initiation of the INA (Texas A&M) and the results are consistent with the ones from Lyon: 200 BC to 40 BC and 40 BC to AD 80 (these results were communicated to us by Professor Deborah Carlson, INA, and we are very thankful to her).

26. Mahadevan 1996.

Appendix

JAMES LANKTON and BERNARD GRATUZE

Introduction

The glass ingots from the Godavaya shipwreck provide the best physical evidence for the early exchange of raw glass in South Asia. The bowl-shaped form of the ingots, with a thin layer of ceramic attached on the lower surface, suggests that the glass was melted in open ceramic containers, perhaps using a parting agent to prevent more adhesion of ceramic to the glass. However, up to now, very little is known about glass ingot preparation in ancient Asia, and it is thus difficult to draw direct comparisons for the Godavaya ingots. However, scientific analysis of the glass itself may help to answer the following questions:

- Where were the ingots made?
- Does the chemical composition of the glass help to date the shipwreck?

Materials studied

Two samples were selected for analysis. The first of these, GVA 1, has roughly the shape of a triangular prism with longest dimension 25mm. It is a massive fragment from one of the glass ingots. The second, GVA 2, comes from the outside part of an ingot and is composed of a thin slip of ceramic with attached glass, ca 1.2 mm. thick (Plate A.1).

While the glass surface of GVA 2 was freshly broken, and thus recently removed from an ingot, only two of the surfaces of GVA 1 were fresh.

Both samples were translucent to transparent glass that appears to have been coloured greenish blue by the addition of copper. The light microscopic appearance of the two samples was quite different, possibly related to their origins from different parts of the parent ingot. While the glass attached to ceramic in GVA 2 was mostly transparent, with rare bubbles and a few granular inclusions, the glass of GVA 1 contained many irregularly rounded inclusions with projecting crystalline rays, similar in appearance to a sea urchin. These crystalline growths could be seen on all surfaces of the sample, whether freshly broken or weathered (Plate A.2). While the chemical composition of these inclusions will be best studied by electron

Plate A.1: GVA 1 (left) and GVA 2 (right)

Plate A.2: Irregularly rounded inclusions with projecting crystalline
rays observed in GVA 1.

microscopy, their well-formed crystalline structures suggest that they were
formed from the glass melt itself, perhaps as partial devitrification during
slow cooling.

Method of Analysis

In addition to the microscopic examination described above, we performed
chemical compositional analysis of the two glass samples using LA-ICP-
MS (laser ablation-inductively coupled plasma-mass spectrometry) at
IRAMAT (Institut de Recherches sur les Archéomatériaux, Centre Ernest-
Babelon, CNRS/Université d'Orléans). For the study of archaeological
glasses, the LA-ICP-MS technique has the two great advantages of excellent
analytical results for a broad range of elements, coupled with virtually non-
destructive sampling. In general, both precision and accuracy are about

five to ten relative per cent for most elements when the method is applied to standard glasses. For archaeological samples, the results will depend as well on any heterogeneity of the glass, along with possible affects from surface corrosion or weathering. In the case of GVA 1 and GVA 2, the glasses appeared to be relatively homogeneous, and weathering was not a problem. However, the difference in composition observed between GVA1 and GVA2 is probably due to clay pot contamination of the glass during melting: GVA2 contains more silica, alumina, potash and titanium which are the main constituents of the clay.

Results

Chemical compositional results are shown in Table A.1. Both samples are soda glass, with soda (Na_2O) (16 to 21 wt per cent) as the primary flux, and low magnesia (MgO) indicating a mineral source for the soda. Both samples have the high alumina (Al_2O_3) associated with glass produced in Asia. GVA 1 and GVA 2 are relatively higher in lime (CaO) and lower in potash (K_2O) than most Asian glasses, although at least the lime content shows a significant difference between the two samples. Both samples contain moderate iron oxide (Fe_2O_3), as might be expected from the use of

Table A.1: Chemical composition as wt % oxides for major, minor and selected trace elements

Oxide wt %	GVA 1 (in %)	GVA 2 (in %)
Na_2O	21.0	15.9
MgO	0.82	0.62
Al_2O_3	10.3	11.2
SiO_2	57.9	63.8
P_2O_5	0.14	0.08
Cl	0.35	0.58
K_2O	1.39	1.60
CaO	5.42	3.35
TiO_2	0.30	0.34
Fe_2O_3	1.68	1.63
CuO	0.41	0.59
V_2O_5	0.066	0.025
MnO	0.056	0.058
Rb_2O	0.0032	0.0038
SrO	0.046	0.047
ZrO_2	0.049	0.046
BaO	0.061	0.060
UO_2	0.0010	0.0012

a rather impure sand as the silica (SiO_2) source. Chemical analysis confirms the presence of copper as a coloring agent.

Among the trace elements measured, the most striking is vanadium (V). Its content is elevated in both samples, although considerably higher in GVA 1, the ingot block fragment. Up to now, these high vanadium concentrations are characteristic for glass found in southern India at Tamil coast sites such as Alagankulam, Arikamedu, Karur Amaravati and Manikollai, although glass from none of these had the same very high V/Fe_2O_3 ratios as the Godavaya glasses. On the other hand, glass most likely produced at such contemporaneous Sri Lankan site as Giribawa is much lower in vanadium and V/Fe_2O_3 ratios, making Sri Lanka an unlikely source for the Godavaya ingots.

In summary, the glass from both GVA 1 and GVA 2 falls into the broad category m-Na-Al, as defined by Dussubieux (2010). Although the closest subtype would be m-Na-Al 1 (high barium-low uranium), the GVA glass is not a perfect fit for this category since it contains less barium and potash, and more lime, than the typical m-Na-Al 1 glasses. Using the trace element contents, it appears that the Godavaya glass samples shared many chemical features with glasses found or produced on the Tamil coast of south India.

Conclusion

This preliminary investigation of the Godavaya ingot samples helps open the door to the study of glass exchange in South and South-East Asia. These samples are exactly the type of archaeological material essential for a more complete understanding.

In answer to our first question, whether we looked at particular trace element ratios or whole compositions, the results strongly suggest a south Indian origin for the Godavaya glass, with a particular focus on such unexplored sites as Manikollai and Appur. For the second question, based on the compositional evidence, we suggest a possible date range from the first century BCE onward, and probably not before the second century BCE. However, the dating of most South Asian glasses is tenuous, and a firm date for the shipwreck based on other criteria would be an important contribution to our understanding of early glass production and distribution in South Asia.

References

Akanānūru, V., ed., (1990), *Sivasuppiramaniyan*, Chennai: U.V. Saminatha Iyar Library.

Bopearachchi, O. (1999), 'Sites portuaires et emporia de l'ancien Sri Lanka: nouvelles données archéologiques', *Arts Asiatiques*, vol. 54, pp. 5–22.

—— (2006a), 'Circulation of Roman and Byzantine gold coins in Sri Lanka: fact or fiction', in *Dal Denarius al Dinar l'Oriente e la Moneta Romana*, F. De Romanis & S. Sorda, eds., Rome: Ist. Italiano Numismatica, pp. 181–200.

—— (2006b), 'Coins', in *Anuradhapura: The British-Sri Lankan Excavations at Anuradhapura Salgaha Watta 2*, R. Coningham, ed., Oxford: Archaeopress (British Academy Monograph no. 4), pp. 7–26.

—— (2006c), *The Pleasure Gardens of Sigiriya. A New Approach*, Colombo: Godage Book Emporium.

—— (2008), *Tamil Traders in Sri Lanka and Sinhalese Traders in Tamil Nadu*, Colombo: International Centre for Ethnic Studies.

Bopearachchi, O. and K. Rajan (2002), 'Graffiti Marks of Kodumanal (India) and Ridiyagama (Sri Lanka): A Comparative Study', *Man and Environment*, vol. XXVII, no. 2, pp. 97–105.

Cappers, R.T.J. (2006), *Roman Foodprints at Berenike: Archaeobotanical Evidence of Subsistence and Trade in the Eastern Desert of Egypt*, Los Angeles: Cotsen Institute of Archaeology, University of California.

Champakalakshmi, R. (2004), *Trade, Ideology and Urbanization. South India 300 BC to AD 1300*, New Delhi: Oxford University Press.

Deloche, J. (1985), 'Études sur la circulation en Inde. IV. Notes sur les sites de quelques ports anciens du pays tamoul', *Bulletin de l'École française d'Extrême-Orient*, vol. LXXIV, pp. 141–66.

Dussubieux, L., Gratuze, B., and Blet-Lemarquand M. (2010), 'Mineral soda alumina glass: occurrence and meaning', *Journal of Archaeological Science*, vol. 37, issue 7, July, pp. 1646–55.

Falk, H. (2001), 'Three Epigraphs from Goḍavāya, Sri Lanka', in *Ancient Ruhuna. Sri Lanka-German Archaeological Project in the Southern Province*, H.-J. Weisshaar, H. Roth and W. Wijeyapala, eds., Mainz am Rhein: Verlag Philipp von Zabern, vol. 1, pp. 327–34.

Juleff, G. (1998), *Early Iron and Steel in Sri Lanka* (KAVA), Mainz: Verlag Philipp von Zabern.

Kessler, O., H. Roth, U. Recker, and W. Wijeypala (2001), 'The Godavaya Harbour Site. Report on the Excavations 1994-1997', in *Ancient Ruhuna. Sri Lankan-German Archaeological Project in the Southern Province*, H.-J. Weisshaar, H. Roth, and W. Wijeypala, eds., vol. 1, pp. 291–326.

Krishnamurthy, R. and S. Wickramasinghe (2005), *A Catalogue of the Sangam Age Pandya and Chola Coins*, Colombo: Department of the National Museums.

Mahadevan, I. (1996), 'Old Sinhalese inscriptions from Indian ports: New evidence from ancient India-Sri Lanka contacts', *Journal of the Institute of Asian Studies,*vol. 14, pp. 35–65.

Nagaswamy, R. (1991), 'Alagankulam: An Indo-Roman trading port', in *Indian Archaeological Heritage, K.V. Soundara Rajan Felicitation Volume*, C. Margabandhu, K.S. Ramachandran, A.P. Sagar, D.K. Sinha, eds., New Delhi: Agam Kala Prakashan, pp. 247–54.

Paranavitana, S. (1983), *Inscriptions of Ceylon*, vol. II, pt. I, Colombo: Department of Archaeology.

Suresh, S. (2004), *Symbols of Trade: Roman and Pseudo-Roman Objects in India*, New Delhi: Manohar.

Tomber, R. (2008), *Indo-Roman Trade: From Pots to Pepper*, London: Duckworth.

Weerakkody, D.P.M. (1997), *Taprobanê: Ancient Sri Lanka as known to Greeks and Romans*, Turnhout: Brepols.

CHAPTER 20

Environment, Infrastructure and Nature of Ports in Ancient Sri Lanka

Archaeological Evidence from the Port, Monastery, Town and Shipwreck of Godavaya (*Godapavata Pattana*)

Oliver Kessler

This essay will present some considerations concerning the change of trade routes from the Mediterranean to South-East Asia between the fourth and fifth centuries AD. The question to be raised includes: how did the change of trade patterns influence specific views of the world. In addition, issues concerning the specific nature and infrastructure of ports in ancient Sri Lanka and the way they were influenced by the change of trade routes will be addressed. Their links to the hinterland and other Indian Ocean ports will also be discussed.

From an European perspective, the second century Ptolemaic model of Asia was predominant at least until the fourth century, and again from the medieval period to the end of the fifteenth century [Plates 20.1 (A) and (B)] when the journeys of Vasco da Gama and his followers lead to a subsequent replacement of the Ptolemaic tradition in cartography by compiling it with the new contradicting information which has since been gathered.[1]

Taprobane and the History of Cartography

The geographer Brian Harley stated: 'Maps are graphic representations that facilitate a spatial understanding of things, concepts, conditions, processes, or events in the human world.'[2] In this essay, the term 'map' will therefore

(A)

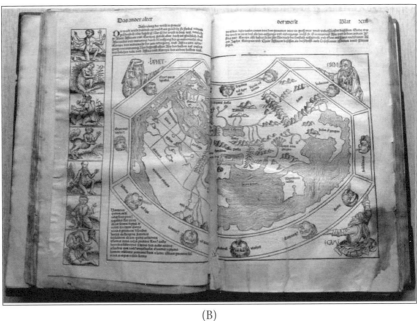

(B)

Plate 20.1 (A) Hartmann Schedel, *Buch der Chroniken*, German edition of the *Historia Mundi* (Nürnberg, 23 Decembre 1493). Exemplar of abbot Candidus [Pfiffer] (1684–1718) of Baumgartenberg, Austria (*Photo*: Oliver Kessler), (B) World Map based on Claudius Ptolemaeus (second century AD) depicting *Taprobane* with its main harbour facing south, op. cit. above, fol. XII-XIII (*Photo*: Oliver Kessler).

be used in its most inclusive form, to redefine the way maps should be studied by scholars in a number of disciplines. Maps are a repository of culturally-embedded and graphically portrayed understandings about space that broadens our knowledge of how people, at different times and places, have experienced their environments.

Cartographic research should include an emphasis on the spatial-cognitive abilities of pre- and early historic societies and their transmission of cartographic concepts through media. Rock art, land surveys, and architectural plans mark the beginning of cartography in ancient societies. The emergence of both theoretical and practical cartographic knowledge at the same time resulted in the existence of diverse mapping traditions.

Western cartographers' interest in Taprobane, in former times also called Lankâ Dvîpa, Îlamantalam, Palaesimundum, Serendib, Zeylan, Ceylon to mention a few and present-day Sri Lanka dates back to the pre-Christian era. It was Onesicritus, companion of Alexander the Great in India and Megasthenes, who introduced the name 'Trapobane' for an island situated in a central position of the Indian Ocean called the Southern Sea by ancient authors from East and West. The term 'Taprobane' probably derived from the word 'Tambapamni' or 'Tambapani', being used in the edicts of King Ashoka.[3]

Determining its size, shape, and exact position was a vexed question from the earliest ages of classical geography. And, there has been speculated among the ancient Greeks and Romans if *Taprobane* was an additional continent or a very great island. The geographer and historian Strabo oriented it wrongly in the direction to Ethiopia, overestimating its length. And yet, he compared Sri Lanka with the African cinnamon land where the port Daphnus is situated. Thus, probably meaning Somalia, he is obviously correct in placing Taprobane on the same latitude.[4] It has also been pointed out by D.P.M. Weerakoddy, that from the times of Strabo, the islands of Britain and Taprobane were seen as counterparts marking both ends of the world.[5]

Repeating a misconception similar to Strabo, the writer of the *Periplus Maris Erythraei* stated, that Taprobane extended from the east to the west and that it was large enough almost to reach the coast of Africa. Pomponius Mela was uncertain whether he should consider Taprobane a large island or the commencement of another world.[6] Due to certain mistakes, Claudius Ptolemaeus depicted Taprobane in his *Geography* as an Indian Ocean island of nearly continental size and located it south of the equator [Plates 20.2 (A) and (B)].[7] Later on it was believed he took Sri Lanka and Sumatra as being one and the same island or even mixed them up. But most probably the mistake was based on an arithmetic error.[8] In fact, the ancient Western

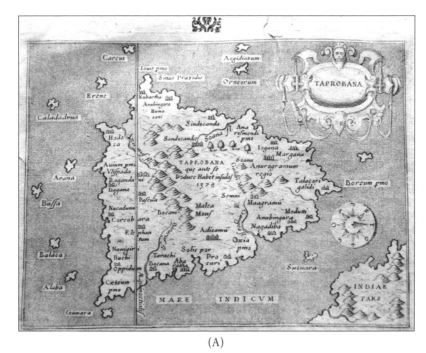

(A)

(B)

Plate 20.2: (A) Sixteenth-century map of *Taprobana* based on Claudius Ptolomaeus (second century AD) (Photograph courtesy: the author); (B) Sixteenth-century map of *India vetus* depicting a modified Ptolomaic model of Asia, *Taprobane* forming a barrier (*Photograph courtesy*: the author).

sources are geographically detailed only up to ancient Taprobane, while the reports of South-East Asia are less precise and more fabulous, except those based on information given by traders from the desert route of the Silk Road.

Long Distance Trade in the Indian Ocean

Despite the fact that the term 'Silk Road' had been overstressed in academic discourse, trade is a global activity of early historic societies, which has received less attention than it deserves. According to Colin Renfrew its 'crucial importance lies in a dual status', as an indicator for scholars that intercultural contact was taking place, and as a prime motive, among pre- and early-historic societies to socialize with each other.[9]

This essay attempts to highlight the unique opportunities which a study of trade holds for the understanding of culture change. The archaeological evidence might reveal the principles of trade, exchange and change as general ones, bearing upon the pre- and early-history of any region. Apart from trade relations, circulations of goods could have been caused by marriage, migration, gifts or losses. Furthermore, the distribution of finds depends on the specific intensity of research and on the quality of documentation.

Godavaya (*Godapavata Pattana*): A Port at the Coastline of the 'Southern Sea'

The history of the late ancient and early medieval long-distance trade can be demonstrated with the help of archaeological finds and findings from southern Asia. In particular, the excavations in the south of Sri Lanka at the port and monastery of Godavaya (*Godapavata Pattana*) (Plate 20.3) will give an idea of the general structure of sea trade from the first century BC to the eighth century AD.

Sri Lanka is located at a crossroad of navigational routes between Arabia and South-East Asia.[10] In the first half of the sixth century, Kosmas Indicopleustes illuminates the role of Sri Lanka, the ancient Taprobane in his *Topographia Christiana*, stating: 'The Island being as it is, in a central position, is much frequented by ships from all parts of India and from Persia and Ethiopia and it likewise sends out many of its own.'[11]

Despite that fact there appeared to be hardly any archaeological interest in the islands coastlines for a long time. Although *Mantai/Mahatitha* in the north was an important ancient port of the Island, the narrow passage between India and Sri Lanka was a dangerous barrier for seafaring ships.

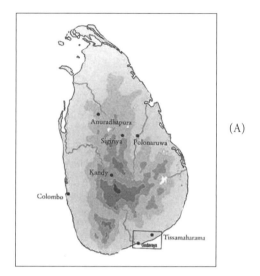

(A)

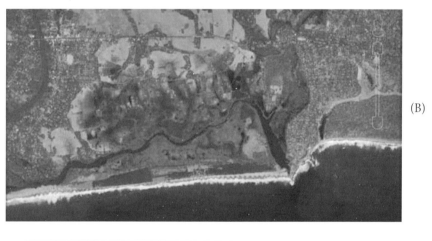

(B)

(C) 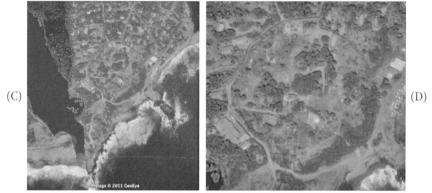 (D)

Plate 20.3: (A–D) Promontorium of Godavaya (*Godapavata Pattana*) at the estuary of the Walawe Ganga, Hambantota District, Sri Lanka

Therefore, an alternative route must have existed along the southern shores.[12]

This conclusion is supported by numerous hoards and settlement finds of late Roman coins and their Sri Lankan imitations after one of its find spots also called 'Naimanas'. They are numbering tenth of thousands from archaeological sites along the coastlines of the ancient Kingdom of Ruhuna in the southernmost part of the island [Plate 20.4(C)].[13]

Godavaya: Monastery and Town
(*Godapavata Vihara* and *Pattana*)

The ancient site of Godavaya consists of a monastic complex, a residential area, several landing places at the riverbanks of the Walawe Ganga connecting the seaport with anchorage to the hinterland.[14] In addition to its outstanding topographical situation, a significant second century Brahmi inscription illuminating the role of *Godapavata Pattana* as a port town and trading centre was found chiselled onto a rock.[15] The reading given by Senarath Paranavitana is:

Siddham | Raja Gamani Abhaya su[ka] su[ri]yi
Godapavata Pattana viharata dini.[16]

Harry Falk reads *su[ka]-sukiye*[17] while I, personally inspecting it during excavation read *suka suriye*. The translation given by Senarat Paranavitana is:

Success! The customs duties of the port of Godapavata,
King Gamani Abhaya granted to the *vihara*.[18]

The occasional discoveries of several late Roman coin–hoards at Godavaya, Beragama, Lunama and Rekava also underline the importance of the site [Plate 20.4(B)].[19] Buddhist monasteries along the Walawe River had been founded and vested with privileges by Sri Lankan kings. These monasteries provided additional landing places to guarantee the transport of goods to the sea and vice versa. A Roman *follis*, reverse type GLORIA EXERCITUS, with mint mark SMAN, struck in 335 AD in Antiochia during the reign of Delmatius Caesar has been found at Girihandu Vihara in Ambalantota and Chinese ceramics from a later period at Rambha Vihara, 10 km. upstream.

On the riverbanks of the Walawe Ganga where the village Ridiyagama is situated 12 km. north of the mouth of the Walawe Ganga, excavations undertaken by a Sri Lankan–French team under the guidance of Osmund Bopearachchi revealed numerous Roman and Naimana coins.[20] A number

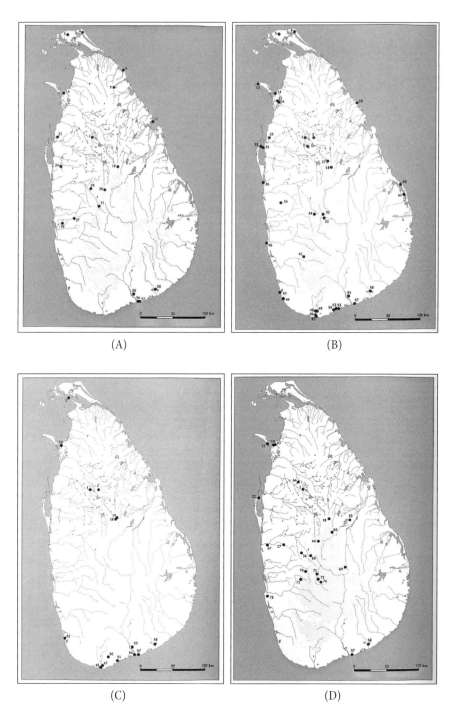

(A)

(B)

(C)

(D)

Plate 20.4 (A–D): Distribution of coin finds in Sri Lanka (after WALBURG 2008),
(A) Indian punch marked coins, (B) Late Roman aes coins, (C) Nâimana coins,
(D) Medieval coins

of efficient ovens fulfilled not only the local demand for steel- or glassware but seemed to have served as a semi-industrial production for export via the deep-water port of *Godapavata Pattana*.[21] A bronze seal found by a cultivator from Ambagahawatte in a field at Ridiyagama was attributed to the Nanadesis, but probably had been used by a trade guild being involved in the commercial activities at *Godapavata Pattana* and its hinterland as their predecessors.[22]

The bay east of the monastery and town of Godavaya meets the conditions for a natural deep-water port. Besides the striking rock formation, the stupa was an important landmark for navigation in coastal waters.

The *buduge* or image house showed at least two building phases dating from the second and fifth centuries AD. The collapsed walls of the entrance hall consisted of 52 layers of brick forming a height of at least 3.5 m. After the fifth century, the building probably had been repaired and enlarged to the north. Although being abandoned in the eighth century, the image house remained a place of worship, testified by a hoard of 2,000 cowries being placed there together with coins struck around AD 1200 under the reign of Queen Lilavati (1197–200, 1209–10, 1211–2).[23]

Godavaya (*Godapavata Vihara*): Small Stupas

In south-west direction of the image house and outside the monastic enclosure, a group of three small stupas had been found (Plate 20.5). Each

Plate 20.5: Godavaya (*Godapavata Pattana*), Goda 7'2003, Trench 2, pl. 2, feat. 1-2. 'Small stupas' situated outside the monastic complex (*Photograph courtesy*: the author).

of them measures only 1.8 m. in diameter. Once being of approximately the same height, they can be compared to those from Kantarodai in northern Sri Lanka, even though the stupas of Godavaya are constructed of burnt bricks.

Godavaya (*Godapavata Pattana*): Graveyard

Close to the sea port some objects belonging to toilet sets made of bronze,[24] as well as several types of collar beads comparable to those found in Tissamaharama[25] and elsewhere in the island and bangles have been found as stray finds (Plate 20.6). Concerning their character as they are made of shell or coral, they are unique, so far. As they were obviously once deposited in a pit and are contextualized with textiles, they can be interpreted as a hint to single burials or an early historic burial ground.

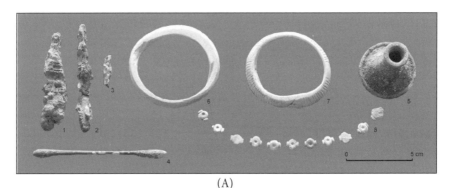

(A)

(B)

Plate 20.6: Godavaya (*Godapavata Pattana*), grave yard, jewellery and (A) toilet set, (B) of a lady (*Photograph courtesy*: the author).

Godavaya (*Godapavata Pattana*): Habitation
Area and Craftsmen Quarter

The earliest layers of the habitation area and craftsmen sector date back to the first century BC, while the latest belong to the eighth century AD.[26] Near Eastern ceramics were discovered in the layers of the fifth up to the eighth century. Along with local pottery of the second/third centuries, Chinese proto-celadon ware, dating from the period of the 'Three Kingdoms' (Wei/Shu/Wu, AD 220–80) has been found, testifying early Chinese-Sri Lankan contacts.[27]

Godavaya (*Godapavata Pattana*): Coins and Sealings

The sequence of coins ranges from early silver punch marked coins, fourth/fifth century Roman coins, *Naimana* imitations and *lakshmi* plaques to coins struck under Queen Lilavati in the early thirteenth century [Plate 20.4 (A–D)].[28]

Economic activities are also illustrated by a clay sealing (3.8 cm.) showing the profile view of a lion standing to the right.[29] This early representation of the Sri Lankan heraldic animal appears identically on tokens of the so-called 'maneless lion type' struck by King Mahasena who reigned from 325 to 352 AD. Because of the slightly carbonized strings on its reverse, the clay seal can be identified as a royal customs seal for goods. This sealing has strongest parallels in a clay sealing found at Kantarodai.[30]

Godavaya (*Godapavata Pattana*): Seaport

Pliny gives the following description of the island reported by a royal diplomatic delegation in the reign of emperor Claudius (AD 41–54). He states: 'Taprobane . . . contains 500 towns, and a harbour facing south (!), adjacent to the town of Palaesimundus . . . a royal residence. . . . Inland there is a lake . . . and out of this lake flow two rivers, (one) running . . . into the harbour, . . . and the other . . ., flowing north in the direction of India' (Pliny *Nat. Hist.* VI. XXIV.).[31]

The localization of the main port in the south connected with a river mouth in accordance with Ptolemaeus (Plate 20.7) is noteworthy and highlights the ancient Sri Lankan Kingdom of Ruhuna, as being in control over the coastline and ports facing the Southern Sea.[32] Christian Lassen already identified Ptolemy's *Azanus Fluvius* with the Walawe Ganga, thus Ptolemaeus' Hodaka/Godaka [Plate 20.7(B)] consequently being the Godapavata of the two second century Brahmi inscriptions.[33]

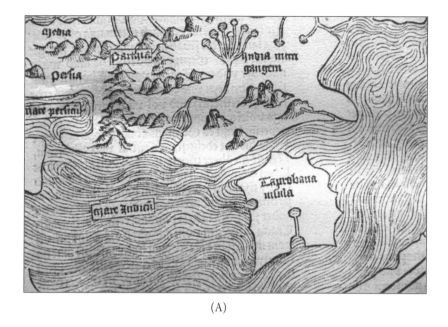

(A)

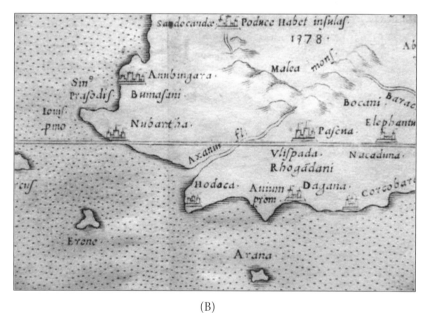

(B)

Plate 20.7: (A) Hartmann Schedel, *Buch der Chroniken*, German edition of the *Historia Mundi* (Nürnberg, 23 Decembre 1493), world map (cutout): *Taprobane insula*. Exemplar of abbot Candidus [Pfiffer] (1684–1718) of Baumgartenberg, Austria (*Photograph courtesy*: the author); (B) Sixteenth-century map of *Taprobane* according to Ptolemaeus. *Azanus/Axanus fl.* can be identified with the Walawe Ganga and *Hodaca/Godaka* with *Godapavata Pattana* (Godavaya) (*Photograph courtesy*: the author).

In 1997, a test pit was opened between the fishing village and the sea. Some of the uncovered structural elements probably once belonged to a footbridge or jetty to assist loading and unloading.[34]

Godavaya (*Godapavata Pattana*): The 'Customs-Gate'

The ancient monastery was originally surrounded by a wall (Plate 20.3). The features which were discovered to the south-east of the stupa belonged to a gate that led to the seaport. Furthermore, a brick building with an almost squarish ground plan measuring 10.5 m. × 11 m. was discovered, attached to the outside of the monastic wall [Plate 20.8 (A–C)].

Due to the numerous late Roman coins, some debris of a goldsmith workshop, the iconography of architectural ornaments and the topic of the

(A)

(B)

Plate 20.8 (A and B)

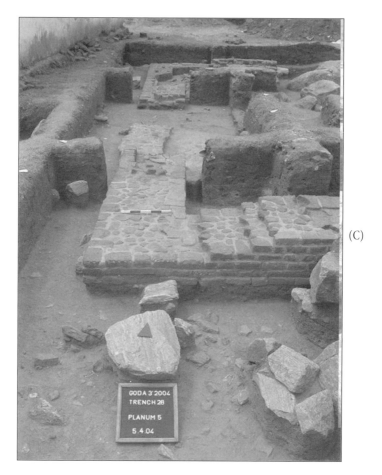

(C)

(D)

Plate 20.8 (A–C): Godavaya (*Godapavata Pattana*), Goda 3, 'Customs Gate' or 'Tax office', find spot of late roman coins (*Photograph courtesy*: the author), (D) Godavaya (*Godapavata Pattana*), Goda 3, 'Customs Gate' or 'Tax office', brick from a frieze, depicting Elephant and Lotus (*Photograph courtesy*: the author).

close by rock inscriptions, this complex was identified as the place from where the royal taxes probably had been collected. The brick-walls were decorated with a frieze depicting the elephant and the lotus-flower [Plate 20.8(D)] and it had a tiled roof fixed with irons nails. In use from the fifth to the eighth century, it was probably erected under the reign of Kassapa I (473–95) from Sigiriya, in line with his politics to increase the country's monetary income by developing its seaports.

Godavaya (*Godapavata Pattana*): Shipwreck

It was back in 1994 when excavations in Godavaya started to locate the ancient seaport. Some small-scale underwater surveys in the bay of Godavaya brought to light interesting sites, leading to the recovery of additional architectural elements and two stone anchors.

One of these stone anchors recovered from the sea in 1998 shows parallels to those found in the Mediterranean as well as in the Arabian Sea and in Indian waters [Plate 20.9(A)]. It is a simple pierced anchor of Arab-

Fig. 20.9: (A) Stone anchor of granitic gneiss, Arab–Indian type, recovered from Godavaya bay. Measurements: 60 × 50 × 25 cm, squarish hole: 17 × 17 cm, weight: 97 kg (*Photograph courtesy*: the author), (b) The Godavaya (*Godapavatta Pattana*) shipwreck, probably first century BC (*Photograph courtesy*: Rasika Muthucumara), (c) Godavaya. Pottery (first century BC/first century AD) at the wreck site (*Photograph courtesy*: Rasika Muthucumara), (d) Glass ingots from the cargo of the Godavaya (*Godapavatta Pattana*) shipwreck (*Photograph courtesy*: Rasika Muthucumara).

Indian type common at least from the fifth to the sixteenth century. The anchor is worked of probably local granitic gneiss and measures 60 × 50 × 25 cm. with a total weight of 97 kg. There is a squared off hole through the centre measuring 17 × 17 cm. Similar stone anchors have been found in Galle and several Indian coastal towns as well. Some authors believe they could also be part of jetty-like building structures.[35]

It was in 1999 when fishermen told me that while diving for shells and lobsters they had found a site where lots of pottery was to be seen, similar to items from the Godavaya excavations.

The first samples from the identified wreck [Plate 20.9(A)] could have been dated to the first century BC and had obviously been part of the ship's cargo. As a result, the discovery of the shipwreck was brought to the notice of the Archaeological Department. Thus, the Godavaya shipwreck is probably the oldest ever found in Sri Lankan and even Indian waters so far. During the excavations of 2003 and 2004 additional finds from the site had been investigated, now being dated to the second half of the first century BC [Plate 20.9(C)]. Since these parts of the cargo had not been used, the sinking of that important ship can probably be dated to the latter decades of the first century BC.

Godavaya (*Godapavata Pattana*):
Shipwreck, The cargo: A 'stool quern'

In 2003, one of at least five 'stool querns' once part of the Godavaya shipwreck cargo had been recovered from the sea [Plate 20.10 (A-B)]. This object made of granitic gneiss hardly showed any signs of abrasion or usage. Therefore, it probably formed part of the cargo dating to the second half of the first century BC and did not belong to the items used on board the ship.

According to its style and typology, it shows some similarities to Egyptian stool querns.[36] Nevertheless, it has closest parallels to the pieces found in Strata I and II of Bhir Mound at Taxila [Plate 20.10(C)][37] and to those from other Indian sites. Stool querns found being re-used in the floor of the Stupa of Yatala Vihara near Tissamaharama in the ancient southern Kingdom of Ruhuna in Sri Lanka also show some iconographic similarities.

On the upper surface of the stone there are several symbols depicted within a frame [Plate 20.10(A-B)], the figure in the middle representing *srivatsa*, the babe of goddess *Sri* in its very early form, having four upwardly curved 'limbs' symmetrically paired. Some terracotta figures from the Indus Valley representing abstractly formed babies suggest, that the emblem *srivatsa* actually derived from a human figure. *Srivatsa* appears

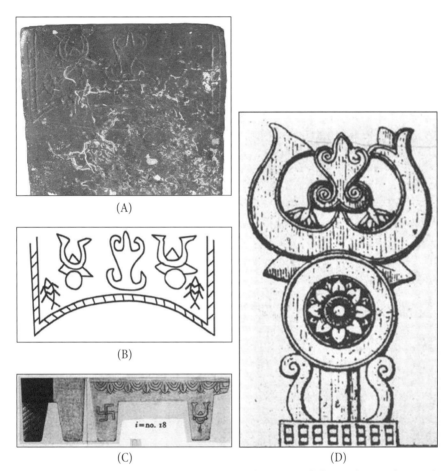

Plate 20.10: (A) A 'stool quern' (detail) from the cargo of the Godavaya shipwreck (second half of first century BC) (Photograph courtesy: the author), (B) 'Stool quern' from Godavaya shipwreck. Line drawing of the image field depicting *srivatsa* and *triratna* in connection with the fish symbol (after Kessler in print), (C) 'Stool quern' from Taxila, Bhir Mound, Strata I and II (Marshall 1951). Likewise the example from the Godavaya shipwreck *triratna* is depicted, (D) Sanchi Stupa I, detail of the eastern gateway depicting *srivatsa* and *triratna* (Marshall et al. 1940).

throughout the history of Indian art even as amulett or token and on coins and clay sealings. It seems to be connected with the Yaksa cult as well as to Hinduism, Buddhism, and Jainism. Nevertheless, *srivatsa* seems to be an iconic representation of the goddess of fortune and fertility throughout the centuries.[38]

On the stool quern from the Godavaya shipwreck *srivatsa* is depicted in a certain dual trinity, consisting of the *triratna*, which has its parallel in a representation on a 'leg' of a stool quern from Taxila[39] [Plate 20.10(C)] and the fish symbol. The iconography of *srivatsa* and *triratna* refers to the eastern Gate of Sanchi Stupa I [Plate 20.10(D)].

Despite being a symbol in Indian religions and Christianity from earliest times, the fish also forms part of the Babylonian zodiac. For example, one may point to the zodiac of the Hathor-temple of Dendara (Tantarer, Egypt, probably erected under Ptolemaios XII, 51 BC, now in Louvre Museum, Paris). The Babylonian astronomy had been adopted in Egypt during the first century BC, the zodiac of the temple of Esne being a famous example.

The iconography of the stool quern from the Godavaya wreck might show similar influences, thus still being reflected in recent Singhalese and Tamil auspices ceremonies connected to the celebrations of New Year. The turn of the year Sinhala *alud avurudhu* is focusing on the steady renewal and occurs in the zodiac sign of the fish.

Godavaya (*Godapavata Pattana*): Shipwreck, the cargo: Lens-shaped Ingots of Raw Glass

A major part of the cargo seemed to consist of lens-shaped raw glass ingots [Plate 20.9(D)]. From the ancient sources we learn that raw glass from the West was one of the important goods in barter trade with South-East Asia. Glass was produced in north India approximately from the end of the second millennium BC onwards. During the centuries when Godapavata Pattana was a port of call, glass beads and bangles seem to be traded from its Indian and Sri Lankan origins to an area from East Africa to South-East Asia.

Detailed compositional data recently summarized has revealed finds of natron-based Mediterranean glass and plant-ash Mesopotamian glass throughout the Indian Ocean.[40] Trade in raw glass from Egypt to India was described in the first century text of the *Periplus of the Erythraean Sea*. Trading of Mesopotamian glass seems to increase with influence on the Indian Ocean from the fourth to sixth centuries AD.

Regardless of whether glass played an insignificant role in the socio-cultural life of India, Sri Lanka, China, and South-East Asia or not, it has always been admired as a valuable trade item. The historical literature of the Han dynasty records that Emperor Wu (140–87 BC) sent delegates to the Southern Sea to buy glass. In the *Mahavamsa*, the Great Chronicle of Sri Lanka, the waters of Ruhuna bear the same name. At Ridiyagama and the region north of Godavaya there was probably a centre of glass beads manufacture during the early Anuradhapura period. It is very likely that the glass found in the South of China was traded from India and Sri Lanka.

However, this is only a conjecture before the Indo-Pacific glass artefacts are chemically analysed.

There is strong archaeological evidence that Roman glasses were imported into China mainly through the maritime route during the Han Dynasty. The author of the *Periplus of the Erythraean Sea* points in the same direction, reporting that glass and crude glass is shipped from the Red Sea to the East in the first century AD.

Precious Stones as Trading Goods

Spices, valuable textiles, precious metal and gemstones are also mentioned as articles of exchange in barter trade. Along with the improvement of methods for the analysis of minerals, it became possible to give further details about the origin and trade of semi-precious stones, especially garnets.

In early medieval times, garnet or almandin was a frequently used stone in the wardrobes of women and men. Many pieces of the gemstone were lost when used as grave goods in Europe. These circumstances might offer an explanation for the huge demand of Indian and Sri Lankan garnets in the West.[41]

In the fourth century BC, Theophrastus mentions that the most precious kind of garnet can be found in Ethiopia, Egypt, Karthago or Marseille, probably referring to the Mediterranean markets where the goods from India and Sri Lanka were traded.

According to Kosmas Indikopleustes, the main place of manufacture and trade was in Caber (Kaveripattanam) in India and in Alabanda (southwest Turkey) from which the name Almandin derived. This reliable source even mentions the suffix 'pattana' for the names of various ports in India, which also occurs in Godapavata Pattana.

Mineral analysis revealed that the demand for garnets in the late ancient world was accomplished with raw material from Indian or Sri Lankan sources, confirming the statement of Indicopleustes.[42] The already preconceived and polished plates were traded to Europe. Garnets of Indian or Sri Lankan origin were used for Merovingian pieces only in the fifth and the sixth century,[43] as the supply ended suddenly in the last two decades of the sixth century.[44] Whether the conquest of the Arabian Peninsula by the Sasanians in 570 had any impact on the trade remains uncertain.

Mineral analysis of beads made of garnet and carnelian from Godavaya revealed that in addition to the local raw material, precious and semi-precious stones from north India too could have been traded via Sri Lanka to the West.

Conclusion

Sri Lanka gained its characteristic function as a centre of sea born trade from its central position in the Indian Ocean. Archaeological finds and findings from Sri Lanka are illuminating the history of ancient overseas trade. The excavations at the port, shipwreck and monastery of Godavaya (*Godapavata Pattana*) may give an idea of the structure of sea trade and the nature of river mouth ports from the first century BC to the eighth century AD.

Historical sources and recent archaeological discoveries are pinpointing the role of southern Sri Lanka as a centre point and as well as a border between the Eastern and the Western world.

The change of trade patterns influenced specific views of the world or even mapping traditions if the term 'map' means a repository of culturally embedded and graphically portrayed understandings about space and environments experienced by different people at different times.

Based on the opinion that long distance trade demanded a powerful central authority, scholars supposed a simultaneous decline of the ancient Asian trade with the Mediterranean and the Roman Empire. In contrast, the archaeological finds represent a diverse view on early medieval trade relations between the Mediterranean and Asia. The Indian Ocean trade never depended on the Mediterranean but closely linked South Asia with Eastern Africa, the Arabian Sea and South-East Asia. For quite a long time Europe did not even play a major part in the Indian Ocean trade. Pertaining to Sri Lanka trade with the West rather increased than declined after the so-called 'fall of the Roman Empire'. Mediterranean seafarers first surrounded Sri Lanka most probably during the fourth or fifth centuries, thus opening the sea route to South-East Asia for early medieval European trade. In the mind of traders from ancient Europe, Sri Lanka had been an unknown continent and barrier before. But while crossing these borders communication produced space and space produced communication.

Throughout the history of cartography, there have been two different types of sources: First there are maps based on scientific cartography trying to describe the world like that conceived by Ptolemy in the second century AD. Second, there are itineraries, portolan charts, and handbooks for traders and sailors giving details on how to travel from one place to another. Even so, map-making, map-minding, mind-mapping and mind-making are closely linked in the human brain. While there are no signs that Sri Lanka ever functioned as an obstacle for seafarers sailing from Arabia or East- and South-East Asia, its assumed dimensions had been a serious barrier for European traders during certain times of its history.

Notes

1. Kessler 2012: 319, 328.
2. Harley and Woodward 1987: xvi.
3. Faller 2000: 16–17.
4. Faller 2000: 43.
5. Weerakoddy 1997: 45–7.
6. Faller 2000: 49.
7. Faller 2000: 115–29.
8. Faller 2000: 118–19.
9. Renfrew 1969: 151.
10. Gollwitzer 1998: 39.
11. Roth 1998: 1.
12. Kessler 2008: 271.
13. Walburg 2008.
14. Kessler 1997: 39.
15. Kessler 1997: 14, 19.
16. Paranavitana 1983: 101.
17. Falk 2001: 328–9.
18. Paranavitana 1983: 101.
19. Roth et al. 2001: 291–2
20. Walburg 2008: 177–8.
21. Bopearachchi 1998: 143.
22. Pathmanathan 1990: 139–50.
23. Kessler 2008: 275.
24. Remains of comparable toilet sets have been found in ancient cities of Sri Lanka like Anuradhapura and Tissamaharama as well as in Taxila and other archaeological sites of the Indian subcontinent.
25. Hannibal-Deraniyagala 2001: 209, 212.
26. Kessler 1996: 43.
27. Kessler 1998: 33.
28. Kessler 2008: 275–6.
29. Kessler 1998: 32; Roth 1998: 9–10.
30. Walburg 2008: 181.
31. Rackham 1947.
32. Kessler 1998: 17–18.
33. Lassen 1858: 211–13.
34. Kessler 1998: 28–31.
35. Tripati et al. 2004: 29–38.
36. Petrie 1917, pl. LV, no. 105.
37. Marshall 1951, pl. 140, nos. 15–18.
38. Radcliffe Bolon 1983: 330–2.
39. Marshall 1951, pl. 140, no. 18.
40. Lankton and Dussubieux 2006: 121–44.
41. Kessler 2001: 113–28.
42. Quast and Schüssler 2000: 75–96.

43. Roth 1980, Figs. 5 A-B.
44. Quast and Schüssler 2000: 75–96.

References

Bopearachchi, O. (1998), 'Archaeological evidence on changing patterns of international trade relations of ancient Sri Lanka', in *Origin, Evolution and Circulation of Foreign Coins in the Indian Ocean*, Bopearachchi, O., Weerakoddy, D.P.M., eds., New Delhi: Manohar, pp. 133–78.

Casson, L. (1989), *The* Periplus Maris Erythraei: *text with introduction, translation, and commentary*, Princeton: Princeton University Press.

Dussubieux, L., Gratuze, B., Blet-Lemarquand, M. (2010), 'Mineral soda alumina glass: occurrence and meaning', *Journal of Archaeological Science*, vol. 37, no. 7, pp. 1646–55.

Falk, II. (2001), 'Three Epigraphs from Godavaya, Sri Lanka', in *Ancient Ruhuna. Sri Lankan-German Archaeological Project in the Southern Province 1*, Weisshaar, H.J., Roth H. and Wijeypala W., eds., Mainz: Philipp von Zabern, pp. 327–34.

Faller, S. (2000), *Taprobane im Wandel der Zeiten. Das Śrî-Lankâ-Bild in griechischen und lateinischen Quellen zwischen Alexanderzug und Spätantike*, Stuttgart: Franz Steiner.

Gerini, G.E. (1909), *Researches on Ptolemy's Geography of Eastern Asia (Further India and Indo-Malay Archipelago)*, London: Royal Asiatic Society, Royal Geographical Society.

Gollwitzer, M. (1998), 'Sri Lanka. Drehscheibe des Handels im Indischen Ozean von den Anfängen bis zur Kolonisierung', in *Der Indische Ozean in historischer Perspektive*, Conermann, S., ed., Beiträge des Zentrums für Asiatische und Afrikanische Studien der Christian-Albrechts-Universität zu Kiel, Hamburg: E.B.-Verlag, pp. 37–56.

Gupta, S. (2001), 'Studies in Indo-Roman Trade to Indian Ocean Archaeology: Brief Review of Research', *Puratattva*, vol. 31, 2000–1, pp. 133–4.

Hannibal-Deraniyagala, A. (2001), 'Beads from Tissamaharama: A Typology of Sri Lankan Glass and Semi-Precious Stone Beads', in *Ancient Ruhuna. Sri Lankan-German Archaeological Project in the Southern Province 1*, Weisshaar, H.J., Roth, H. and Wijeypala, W., eds, Mainz: Philipp von Zabern, pp. 203–26.

Harley, J.B., Woodward, D. (1987), 'Preface', in *The History of Cartography 1*, Harley, J.B., Woodward, D., eds., Chicago: University of Chicago Press, pp. xv–xxi.

Kessler, O. (1996), 'Excavations at Godavaya (*Godapavata Patana*)', in *Administration Report of the Director: General of Archaeology for the year 1996*, Deraniyagala, S.U, ed., Colombo: Department of Government Printing, pp. 40–3.

——— (1997), 'Godavaya', in *Administration Report of the Director: General of Archaeology for the year 1997*, Deraniyagala, S.U. ed., Colombo: Department of Government Printing, pp. 39–41.

———— (1998), 'The Discovery of an Ancient Sea Port at the Silk Road of the Sea. Archaeological Relics of the Godavaya Harbour', in *Sri Lanka, Past and Present*, Domroes, M., Roth, H. eds., Weikersheim: Margraf, pp. 12–37.

———— (2001), 'Der spätantik-frühmittelalterliche Handel zwischen Europa und Asien und die Bedeutung des Almandins als Fernhandelsgut', in Pohl, E., Recker, U., Theune, C., eds., *Archäologisches Zellwerk, Beiträge zur Kulturgeschichte in Europa und Asien. Festschrift für Helmut Roth zum 60. Geburtstag*. Internationale Archäologie: Studia honoraria 16. Rahden/Westfalen: Marie Leidorf, pp. 113–28.

———— (2008), 'Excavations at Godavaya and a Recently Unearthed, Hitherto Unknown 2nd Century Inscription of King Gajabahu I', in *South Asian Archaeology 1999: Proceedings of the Fifteenth International Conference of the European Association of Southeast Asian Archaeologists, held at the Universiteit Leiden, 5–9 July 1999* (Gonda indological studies 15), Raven, E.M., ed., Groningen: Egbert Forsten, pp. 271–82.

———— (2012), 'The Taprobanian Revolution and the Paradigm Shift away from the Ptolemaic Model of Asia: Archaeology and History of Ancient Seafaring in the Indian Ocean', in Tjoa-Bonatz, M.L., Reinecke, A., Bonatz, D. eds., Connecting Empires and States: Selected Papers from the 13th International Conference of the European Association of Southeast Asian Archaeologists, vol. 2.

Lankton, J.W., Dussubieux, L. (2006), 'Early glass in Asian maritime trade: a review and an interpretation of compositional analyses', *Journal of Glass Studies*, vol. 48, pp. 121–44.

Marshall, J.H. (1951), *Taxila, an illustrated account of archaeological excavations carried out at Taxila under the orders of the Government of India between the years 1913 and 1934, 3, plates*, Cambridge: Cambridge University Press.

Marshall, J.H., Foucher, A., Majumdar, N.G., eds., (1940), *Monuments of Sāñchī 2*, London: Probsthain.

Paranavitana, S. (1983), *Inscriptions of Ceylon II (I), Late Brahmi Inscriptions*, Moratuwa.

Pinder-Wilson, R. (1991), 'The Islamic lands and China', in *Five thousand years of glass*, Tait, H., ed., University of Pennsylvania Press, pp. 112–43.

Quast, D., Schüssler, U. (2000), 'Mineralogische Untersuchungen zur Herkunft der Granate merowingerzeitlicher Cloisonnéarbeiten', *Germania*, vol. 78, pp. 75–96.

Rackham, H., ed. (1947), *Pliny Natural History with an English Translation in Ten Volumes, 2, Libri III–VII;* London/Cambridge/Massachusetts: W. Heinemann/Harvard University Press.

Radcliffe Bolon, C. (1983), 'Review of: Agrawala, Prithvi Kumar. Śrivatsa, the Babe of Goddess Śrī', *Artibus Asiae*, vol. 44, no. 4, pp. 330–2.

Renfrew, C. (1969), 'Trade and Culture in European Prehistory', *Current Anthropology*, vol. 10, nos. 2–3, pp. 151–69.

Roth, H. (1980), 'Almandinhandel und verarbeitung im Bereich des Mittelmeeres. Zum archäologischen Befund und der schriftlichen Überlieferung in der Spätantike und im frühen Mittelalter', *Beiträge zur Allgemeinen und Vergleichenden Archäologie*, vol. 2, pp. 309–35.

——— (1997), 'Ausgrabungen am Seehafenplatz Godavaya–Sri Lanka', in *Hundert Jahre Historische Kommission für Hessen 1897–1997. Veröffentlichungen der Historischen Kommission für Hessen 61*, Heinemeyer, W. ed., Marburg: N.G. Elwert, pp. 21–33.

——— (1998), 'Excavations at the Port of Godavaya, Hambantota District, Sri Lanka', in *Sri Lanka, Past and Present*, Domroes, M., Roth, H., eds., Weikersheim: Margraf, pp. 1–11.

Roth, H., Kessler, O., Recker, U., Wijeypala, W. (2001), 'The Godavaya Harbour Site. Report on the Excavations 1994–1997', in *Ancient Ruhuna. Sri Lankan-German Archaeological Project in the Southern Province 1*, Weisshaar, H.J., Roth, H., Wijeypala, W. eds., Mainz: Philipp von Zabern, pp. 291–326.

Schenk, H. (2001a), 'The Development of Pottery at Tissamaharama', in *Ancient Ruhuna. Sri Lankan-German Archaeological Project in the Southern Province 1*, Weisshaar, H.J., Roth, H., Wijeypala, W., eds., Mainz: Philipp von Zabern, pp. 59–195.

——— (2001b), 'Remarks on the pottery from Godavaya', in *Ancient Ruhuna. Sri Lankan-German Archaeological Project in the Southern Province 1*, Weisshaar, H.J., Roth, H., Wijeypala, W. eds., Mainz: Philipp von Zabern, pp. 335–48.

Tripati, S., Gaur, A.S., Sundaresh (2004), 'Marine Archaeology in India', *Man and Environment. Journal of the Indian Society for Prehistoric and Quarternary Studies*, vol. 29, no. 1, pp. 28–41.

Walburg, R. (2008), *Coins and Tokens from Ancient Ceylon. Ancient Ruhuna. Sri Lankan-German Archaeological Project in the Southern Province 2. Forschungen zur Archäologie außereuropäischer Kulturen 5*, Wiesbaden: Reichert.

Weerakoddy, D.P. M. (1997), *Taprobanê. Ancient Sri Lanka as known to Greeks and Romans*, Turnhout: Brepols.

Zorn, B., ed. (2010), *Glass along the Silk Road from 200 BC to AD 1000. International conference within the scope of the 'Sino-German Project on Cultural Heritage Preservation' of the RGZM and the Shaanxi Provincial Institute of Archaeology, 11–12 December 2008*. Mainz: Verlag des Römisch-Germanischen Zentralmuseums.

CHAPTER 21

The Citadel of Tissamaharama: Urban Habitat and Commercial Interrelations

Heidrun Schenk and *Hans-Joachim Weisshaar*

The Sri Lankan-German cooperation at Tissamaharama looks back to two decades of archaeological fieldwork in Mahagama (Tissamaharama), the residence of the old kingdom of Ruhuna in the south of the island. The Archaeological Department of Sri Lanka and the Commission for Archaeology of Non-European Cultures (KAAK) of the German Institute of Archaeology began excavations in 1992.[1] Three sites of the citadel measuring an area of 1.515 m² had been explored.[2]

The ideal plan of the early Singhalese cities is square or rectangular. The citadel of ancient Tissamaharama is probably the nearest to this ideal among all the ancient cities on the island. It lies in a flat open landscape that is covered by paddy fields or banana plantations. From this plain rises a shallow and rectangular hillock, the citadel. It is 600 × 200 m. and 5–8 m. above the water level of the reservoir tank nearby. The tank was built west of the citadel in the second century BC. The ancient reservoir is probably only the northern part of modern Tissawewa that was designed by British engineer Henry Parker (1884), who took great interest in the archaeology of the site. The nearest harbour is Kirinda, about 12 km. off at the coast of the Indian Ocean.

According to the chronicle *Mahavamsa*, King Mahanaga built the citadel around 270 BC. The excavation, however, revealed that the first urban structures date to around 400 BC,[3] built atop a rural settlement with houses of wattle and daub.

New settlers arrived from north India in the fifth century BC. This is in line with the results of the fieldwork. The excavation·showed that they had iron tools and brought horses that are unfamiliar in a tropical South Asian environment. They built a well-organized citadel, surrounded by a rampart that was made up of different layers of soil and pebbles. Noble families lived in the western part, bordering an artificial lake and the south of the Citadel was a Workmen's Quarter.

Most of the oldest buildings were made of brick foundations, the attached terraces were paved with fired bricks and the roofs were thatched with tiles (Plate 21.1). Behind the rampart was an open space of 5–8 m., that served as a public area. A house that faced the lake stood nearby. It was destroyed by fire twice in the third and second centuries BC. The inhabitants left behind bronze items of a cosmetic set and necklaces of flat red beads (Weisshaar & Dissanayake 2010; here Plates 21.1–3).

In the second century BC, two narrow streets joined each other in the centre of the excavation area. Their grey and muddy soils were easy to distinguish from the red-brown areas of the dwellings. Long brick walls bordered both lanes and enclosed square or rectangular-shaped properties. Most of the houses had brick foundations and wooden posts held up the roofs.

Contemporary workmen's quarters were in the south of the citadel. Several long battery furnaces for bronze production are proof of a busy craft area of the citadel with pre-industrial mass production (Weisshaar et

Plate 21.1: Tissamaharama: the earliest brick architecture of the Citadel,
fourth century BC (Photo: H. Wittersheim).

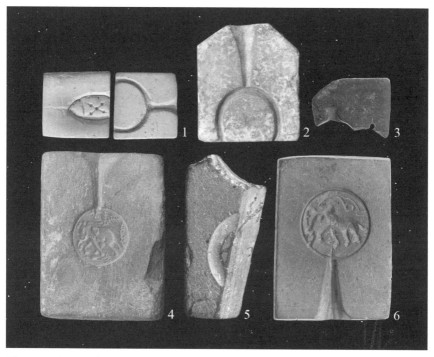

Plate 21.2: Tissamaharama: moulds from the Citadel. No scale (Photos: H. Wittersheim).

al. 2001b: 17–25). The longest furnace was preserved over 11 m. with 18 working places. The furnaces—so far unique in South Asia—demonstrate a high level of handicraft in Ruhuna. The size of crucibles is an argument for small items that have been manufactured. Moulds were absent in the Workmen's Quarter but several for rings or pendants (Plate 21.2, 1–3) were found in different layers of the western citadel.[4] Two moulds for medals from the second century BC depict an elephant spraying water (Plate 21.2, 4–6). Both medals reproduce a motif from the railing of Stupa 2 at Sanchi.[5]

The narrow streets in the settlement of the noble families were not only meant as pathways but also for funnelling rainwater down the slope. They were the main sewers of the community. The streets were on a lower level than the living areas on either side. And, they must have been very muddy (even nowadays one notices a foul and unpleasant smell at the junction on a wet day). The settlers had placed several bricks as stepping stones in the mud to improve passage. The walled areas remained unchanged and were looked after over a long period. They are an indication of private property that was passed on for several generations.

A small pit underneath a house of the first century BC contained a hoard of about 820 tiny *lakshmi* plaques and fragments (Walburg 2010). The plaques are all of the same size, some are poor but others are of a superb quality. Numismatics still argue whether these objects are truly coins and Walburg pleads for a votive character.

On occasion, a house was destroyed by fire in the citadel, but the main obstacle faced by the settlement was the torrential monsoon rains (Weisshaar & Dissanayake 2010).

Many shafts filled with pebbles and bricks were scattered across the excavation area. The shafts were meant as drainage to allow the water to trickle away more easily. Small covered channels directed surplus water from the private areas to the streets. The flow of rainwater in the streets must have been considerable during the rainy season and the settlers had to take care of their terrace walls. Eventually, all precautions were in vain. The subsoil of the streets was too muddy due to heavy rain, foundations dislocated and the walls leaned towards each other, gave way and fell into the streets. As a last resource, the families decided to leave the dwellings and they moved to other places of the citadel.

The site was abandoned, though not for a long time. The character of the area changed after levelling. Several small structures of the first and second centuries AD belonged to the oldest hospital of South Asia excavated so far (Plates 21.3 and 21.1). In fact, the *Mahavamsa* provides details about hospitals even in BC times. The one from the citadel is about six to seven hundred years older than the well known hospitals of Polonnaruwa and Mihintale. Excavations revealed the foundation for a medical basin and large urinals. An enormous number of grinding stones, saddle querns and mullers were used to produce herbal medicines (Weisshaar & Wijeyapala 2005).

The main building of the hospital had a clay floor that was preserved at several places. It covered a shallow pit with a foundation deposit [Plates 21.3 (A) and (B)]. Three saddle querns and four mullers were arranged on top of a small vessel. The grinders and mullers were manufactured of different stone material in pairs.

The seasonal heavy rainfall did not affect the hospital as much as it affected the dwellings a hundred years before. The hospital was built on a higher level due to backfill and levelling and a number of new sewers and covered water channels were built. These facilities of Tissamaharama are an early archaeological proof of the long medical tradition on the island.

Further structural changes with minor architecture of wattle and daub were observed in the third and fourth centuries AD. A small hoard of punch-marked coins that was deposited in a textile bag was published by Reinhold Walburg (2008: 28–9, 192–4, 241).

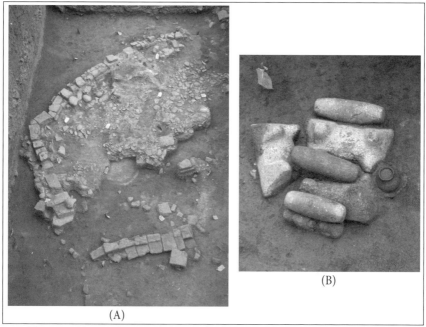

Plate 21.3: Tissamaharama: (A) main building of the hospital, first century AD;
(B) foundation deposit of the hospital with saddle querns and mullers
(*Photos*: H. Wittersheim).

A large brick mansion with several rooms was set up around AD 400. It was rebuilt once but finally collapsed around AD 500 (Weisshaar & Wijeyapala 2005: 355, Fig. 8). Many pits were dug to retrieve bricks that were reused shortly after. In the last layer of the building and especially in these pits, were found innumerable Roman coins from the end of the fourth to the close of the fifth century AD, the latest being two coins of Leo I (457–74).

The recycled bricks had been used for a small monastic building of poor quality that was raised most probably by a monastery south of the Tissawewa (Weisshaar & Wijeyapala 2005: 355). It was erected on top of the last brick mansion after many settlers had left the area. However, it did not last long. Stone pillars collapsed and the clergy gave up the place.

The evidence from excavation sites of Tissamaharama suggests a decline of settlement after AD 500. Royal power collapsed. The citadel, however, was never completely abandoned. We do have finds up to the ninth century AD, and the monasteries south of the Tissawewa still flourished. Yet, many people left the area.

Tissamaharama with its citadel is the southernmost city of a development in South Asia that is called 'Second Urbanization'. To plan and build these early cities needed authority. Peter Eltsov (2005: 322) lists indicators for authority or, in other words, indicators for a structured society. Seals and sealings are one of such indicator. However, seals and sealings are also an indicator for commerce. Therefore, along with the development of authority and cities followed the development of organized trade. Sealed trading goods give an allusion for a marketplace and commercial centre. Sealing a parcel prevented access by unauthorized persons and enabled taxation. Jain literature gives hints in this regard. The *Silappadikaram* reports (Chandra 1977: 159): '*Putabhedana* was that market where the bales of the goods coming from all over the country had their seals broken.'

Much of early society in Sri Lanka was agricultural. They had a developed system of agriculture and made use of irrigation works. However, from the southern province of Sri Lanka, in the kingdom of Ruhuna, emerged traders and trading houses, and therefore a well-to-do commercial establishment. This is illustrated by numerous seals and clay sealings that were found during the excavations (Plate 21.4). The reverse of sealings with string marks and other impressions demonstrate that a considerable variety of goods or containers needed to be sealed: large flasks or *amphorae*, parcels, boxes or doors and letters or documents.[6]

Today many scholars argue that Taprobane was not directly linked to the long distance commerce before around AD 300. One obstacle was the

Plate 21.4: Tissamaharama: clay sealings from the Citadel. No scale
(*Photos*: H. Wittersheim).

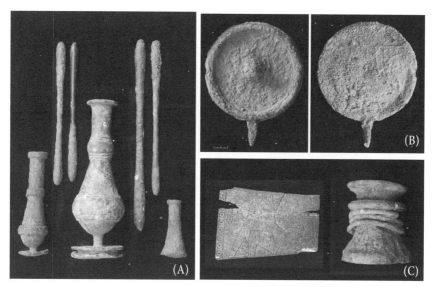

Plate 21.5: Tissamaharama: luxury goods from the Citadel, first century BC—first century AD. (A) cosmetic items; (B) bronze mirror; (C) small ivory panel depicting leopards (left), ivory stand for a mirror (right). No scale (*Photos*: H. Wittersheim).

difficult sea route. When the ships set sail from the south Arabian ports or the Red Sea, they had to catch the suitable wind to carry them across the Indian Ocean. After they passed Bab-el-Mandeb they had to turn southwards towards the Somali coast or the island of Socotra. The Monsoon from the south-west took them to the Malabar Coast. But it would have been very time consuming to head for the region south of Muziris, let alone for Sri Lanka if they wanted to take in time the reversed wind for their voyage home. And, the vessels had to meet their destination on the spot as it was dangerous to ship along the Malabar Coast. In particular, the waters around Muziris held a good chance to meet pirates (Groom 1995: 182), and Pliny (nat. 6: 101, 104) reports that big cargo vessels had a group of archers on board to combat the buccaneers (Bianchetti 2002: 283).

There is a sharp contrast between the Workmen's Quarter of the southern citadel and the noble families that lived at the western border. The small dwellings of the workers were of wattle and daub, and besides some fragments of Indian Rouletted Ware, there are no imports.

In contrast, the community in the western citadel was a prosperous one that lived in brick architecture. It does not matter, whether the families were provided with luxury goods by direct or indirect trade (Plate 21.5). The majority of imports came via ports at the Malabar Coast like Muziris (Pattanam). But single merchants may have found their way to Taprobane.

Two main pottery groups at Tissamaharama testify to long-distance trade at Tissamaharama. The first group has its origins on the Subcontinent and the best known are 'Rouletted Ware' (RW) and 'Red Polished Ware' (RPW). The second group, where Roman *amphorae* belong to, comes from the West.

Out of the first group at Tissamaharama, the earliest is denominated as 'Fine Grey Pottery of North Indian Origin' (Schenk 2006). The various members, among them the significant dish of RW (Plate 21.6, 1-3), are of different dating, for which new results will be presented later in this essay.

The group originates from a definable source region in the Ganges river valley (Gogte 2001)—an origin that is still under discussion (Schenk 2006: 134–6). Gogte's analysis, however, is based on samples of this distinct and significant clay, which is the main characteristic of the above group (Schenk 2006: 128; Fig. 2). And, it is this uniformity that should be fundamental for a commonly agreed definition, but which was not considered in the most recent analysis on RW (Magee 2010). He pointed out a production of RW at Anuradhapura. This is certainly true for local imitations of RW. Apparently samples of genuine RW of fine grey paste were analysed together with those of local fabric. In fact, such local imitations are not confined to Anuradhapura. The characteristic shape belongs to the regional pottery production all over southern India and Sri Lanka. This is exemplified in the local pottery sequence of Tissamaharama and at Arikamedu (Schenk 2006; Pavan/Schenk 2012). The latest results in Tissamaharama show that the local version emerges almost simultaneous to the genuine RW (Plate 21.6 b.d.e.)

The distribution of genuine RW shows a dense pattern in India along the east coast and inland routes via natural transportation routes of river courses. This, in turn, also connects the island of Sri Lanka (Schenk 2006: Figs. 3–4). It represents early relations across the subcontinent. Their discovery in South-East Asia and in Arabia proves an early stage of Indian Ocean long-distance exchange. More detailed evaluation since the close of fieldwork at Tissamaharama has confirmed a previously suggested limited production period for 'Fine Grey Pottery'. According to this, all finds of RW and Wheeler Type 10 and 18 must have arrived during the third–second centuries BC regardless of their later dated context (to be clarified later in the essay).

So-called 'Indian Red Polished Ware' (RPW) also belongs to the first group of pottery that originates in South Asia. This too reveals long-distance connections. This pottery, of a distinct fine fabric, represents the regional pottery manufacture of Gujarat and Maharashtra. A catalogue of RPW (Orton 1992) displays two functional groups with opposing significance

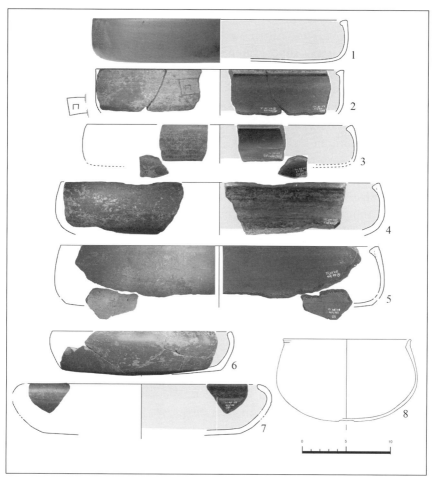

Plate 21.6: Tissamaharama: 1-2. early group of RW and imitation; 3-4. late group of RW and imitation (phase c1); 5. RW-imitation (phase c2); 6-7. Tissa Form G, rim type 11 (phase c2); 8. bowl of 'Fine Grey Pottery' with funnel-shaped oblique rim (phase b). (Scale 1:3).

and distribution. The first group contains the very characteristic Sprinkler jar[7] and a narrow-necked spouted jar with highly bulging shoulders and with a ledged shape of the rim.[8] Together with a monk's begging bowl with an internally thickened rim (Orton 1992; Figs. 4.1.2; 4.22.6), they form a set of ritual function at Tissamaharama. This set appeared not before AD 600. In a kaolin-like fabric,[9] the spouted jar emerges already in the late fifth century AD (Schenk 2005). A kiln from a site in Thailand produced spouted jars and sprinklers in a similar fabric (Srisuchat 2003: 253; Fig. 17.2). At Tissamaharama, the complete set is recorded with different fabrics and paste, covered only by the highly polished and usually red slip (Schenk 2001: 133, Fig. 9). Such vessels are used in ritual Buddhist and Hindu ceremonies. All this points to different regional workshops distributed across the subcontinent and in South-East Asia, reflecting a common religious bond. The second functional group displayed in the catalogue of 'Red Polished Ware in Gujarat', including common utilitarian pottery like cooking pots, is more frequent. They certainly are part of a regional pottery development. It is this pottery that is usually identified at Western sites bordering the Indian Ocean (to be discussed later).

The second group evidencing long-distance contact belongs to container jars originating from the West. They brought luxury goods like wine most probably also to local South Asian elite (Ray 1994: 69; Tomber 2008: 148–50). Type Dressel 2-4 produced in Egypt (Tomber 2007; 2008: 144) and Parthian Green Glazed Pottery from Mesopotamia (Schenk 2007) are the earliest that arrived in Tissamaharama. They were produced almost a century before in the first century AD and their broken remains were deposited in the area of the citadel in the second century AD. This gap might have been caused by repeated use or carefully handling of jars that arrived via intermediate trade, as goods from far countries. This distinctiveness is also underlined by re-use and re-work of fragmented pieces—a frequently recorded feature not only at Tissamaharama (Tomber 2008: 150–1). This applies to most of the amphora sherds and to the above 'Fine Grey pottery'. Very different from the local coarse ware, people fancied the fragments as polishers or skin scrapers in later times too. Late Roman *amphorae* and torpedo jars from Mesopotamia prove a continuous access to long-distance trade, as do Islamic glazed ware and Chinese potteries of later time. However, at Tissamaharama, just like at further sites, such imported finds are rare in terms of statistics.

The bulk of potteries from Tissamaharama were locally produced for common household purposes. This also applies to many finds of South Asian pottery reported from excavations around the Indian Ocean: in the West (Arabia, Egypt) as well as in the East (Indonesia). They were no luxury goods and not traded in them by merchants. They were only used for cooking and storage purchased by sailors or merchants at the ports of embarkation. We do not have much written information as maritime commerce was of no great interest for South Asian authors, contrary to their Greek and Roman counterparts. However, among the active players were also Indians, because some of the Indian jars found in Arabia bear graffiti with Indian script (Tomber 2008: 73–5). Similarly, the many names of sailors written in Brahmi on the walls of Cave Hoq in Socotra have shown (Strauch & Bukharin 2004, Strauch 2006, Strauch in this volume), that South Asians were much more numerous as sailors than previously thought. It might have been their pottery of daily use that they took along on their voyage. Establishing the origin of such domestic pottery might give us information about ports of destination over the centuries.

For this, better chronological differentiation of this common pottery and of imported wares too is needed. Evaluation of the stratigraphic situation at Tissamaharama provides some indications in this regard. A preliminary pottery sequence based on defined contexts is published (Schenk 2001). An update is in preparation. The sequence ranges by now from the fifth/fourth centuries BC to the eighth/ninth centuries AD, supported by radiocarbon dating. The beginning of the sequence, in the late fifth century BC is also confirmed by similar pottery found at a Megalithic burial site at Ibbankatuwa near Sigiryia. Material from two small excavations in the neighbourhood meanwhile allows an extension of the sequence to around the twelfth century AD. Their earliest pottery forms an overlap with the last phases of g (sixth/seventh centuries AD) and h (eighth/ninth centuries AD) of Tissamaharama (Plate 21.7).

Let us turn to the chronological differentiation of 'Fine Grey Pottery of North Indian Origin', for which RW and Wheeler Types 10 and 18 are especially relevant for Indian Ocean research. Fragments of these have been discovered at various sites all over the Indian Ocean region (Schenk 2006: 131, Fig. 4). 'Plain Grey Ware' was the first to arrive at Tissamaharama along with the first settlers. The first fragments of NBP appear in layers of the fourth/third century BC. Already prior to RW emerges a small bowl with bent rim and obliquely smoothened on top (Plates 21.6 and 21.8). Parallels are known from Arikamedu (Begley 1996: 370; Fig. 8/1–3); Amreli (Rao 1966, Fig. 12) and from Pakhanna, West Bengal (IAR 1997–8: pl. 145). Interestingly, this applies also to Wheeler Type 18. The first fragments of RW were discovered in strata directly below Tissa phase c1. Wheeler Type 10, the small cup with the significant stamps on the interior, is the latest of the group of 'Fine Grey pottery' that reached Tissamaharama. It is recorded in the upper layers of phase c1 at the earliest.

The layers of the second century BC are peak time for 'Fine Grey Pottery' to be buried as broken pieces in the soil. At that time this group is largely represented by RW and Wheeler Types 18 and 10. Within this stratum, they are found in high proportion and in the highest quality of preservation. This includes almost complete large fragmented pieces that can be fixed together. From the first century BC onwards, the fragments are found randomly scattered as singled-out pieces, worn and often re-worked. The same observation applies to NBP and Plain Grey Ware. From the first century AD onwards, their numbers are almost completely reduced. This could be observed at Tissa 3, which is characterized by a high level of

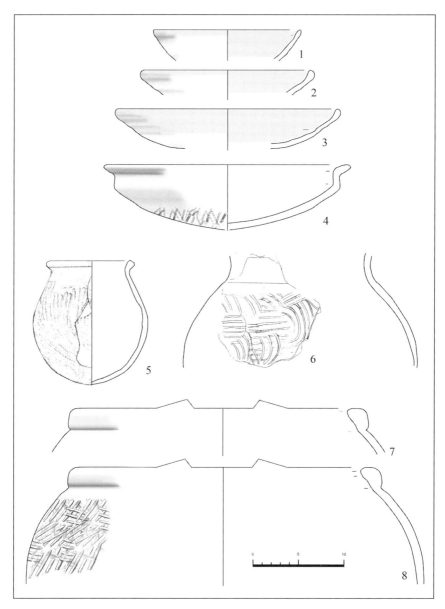

Plate 21.7: Tissamaharama: selection of types from a context of phase g2 (late sixth/ seventh centuries AD). 1-8. Coarse Red Ware; 1-3. with additional red slip. (Scale 1:3).

preserved in situ walking levels and undisturbed deposits. This is in stark contrast to Tissa 1, where these finds appeared in a relative high frequency also in the uppermost layers, displaying the state of high disturbances by later intrusions of this site.

The characteristic dishes of RW were held in high esteem, as evidenced by several examples of broken dishes that were mended by way of riveting (Schenk 2006: 124 Fig. 1c). The production of 'Fine Grey Pottery' seems to have ceased by the end of phase c1 (around 100 BC). If this is true, the discovery of RW and all related types evidence the existence of sites at least in the second century BC. Fragments found in later contexts would then be residual only.

Recent observations demonstrate that this is not just a peculiar situation at Tissamaharama based on a cessation of supply alone. Now that the fieldwork is complete, the study of pottery at Tissamaharama continues with more detailed stratigraphic evaluation. This has revealed the differentiation of genuine RW into three chronologically successive groups. The local imitation follows this modification as well. In the first century BC, these chronologically relevant modifications were terminated. Change of outline is the prominent difference of these groups. RW and the imitation from earlier contexts of Tissamaharama phase c1 (second century BC) have straight wall shapes (Subtype A: Plate 21.6, 1–2). In later contexts of this phase, exemplars of both, RW and the imitation, appear with an inverted shape (Subtype B: Plate 21.6, 3–4). All RW-imitations of this phase are made in the Black and Red firing technique. In the subsequent phase c2 (first century BC), the main bulk of pottery is red-fired, which includes newly emerging types. This new preference of firing applies also to the RW-imitation, now as red-fired a key type of phase c2 (Plate 21.6, 5). Additionally, the earliest layer of phase c2 contained also a few fragments of a simplified shape of genuine RW (Subtype C). All three subtypes can be as well identified in the pottery catalogues of Arikamedu.

With regard to BRW, the RW-imitation of phase c2 is one of the last appearances of this formerly abundant firing technique. From the fifth to third century BC, pottery production was mainly made of BRW and Fine Red Ware. However, in the second century BC, BRW started to decrease. Besides the RW-imitation, Tissa Form G with significantly bent-out shape is the last development of BRW. This is a key type of phase c2 as well (Plate 21.6, 6–7). Thereafter, BRW is almost non-existent and the phase witnesses a total cessation. These results stand for Tissamaharama, though the chronological sequence needs to be cross-checked at other sites.

Fortunately, such a cross-check was possible due to a combined pottery study from Sumhuram (Khor Rori), Oman and Tissamaharama (Pavan/ Schenk 2012). The earliest settlement layers of Sumhuram contained RW and RW-imitation and further potteries related to South Asia. These sherds showed stylistic parallels to shapes of the Tissamaharama sequence. Besides subtype B of RW and its imitations, it includes further exemplars

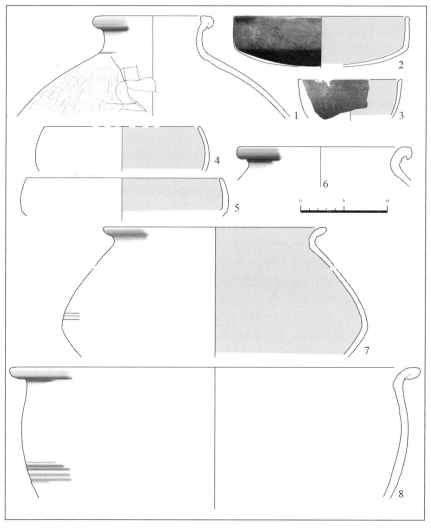

Plate 21.8: Tissamaharama: selection of types from a context of phase b
(third century BC). 2–5.7 BRW; 1.6.8 Fine Red Ware (Scale 1:3).

of BRW and typical shapes of common household pottery. They matched
the pottery forms of later contexts of phase c1 (second century BC) in
Tissamaharama. They are made, however, of slightly different fabrics
pointing to various regional workshops on the southern subcontinent yet
to be located.

In particular, domestic potteries should be regarded as the best witnesses
of time. Frequent use in a daily routine certainly leads to more breakage and
litter and to a frequent replacement over more valuable pots. Accordingly,

they reflect a more immediate and contemporaneous pattern. A better chronological differentiation of common local potteries would contribute to a more genuine reconstruction of the changing interactive structure of Indian Ocean trade in the course of time.

From comparison of such utilitarian pottery from Tissamaharama with material from other sites on the subcontinent indicates a widespread correspondent idea of vessel forms in pottery production.

As an example, pottery from Kodumanal, Tamil Nadu (Rajan 1998) dated to the third century BC could well match an assemblage of the same phase (Phase b or even Phase a) at Tissamaharama (Plate 21.8). From there, a storage jar in situ in the subsequent second century BC (Plate 21.9, 3) corresponds well to a jar from Kondapur, Andhra Pradesh (Ahmad 1950 pl.VI–VII). This is the peak time of RW finds at Tissamaharama, and such fragments also accompany jars from Kondapur (Ahmad 1950 pl.VIII.a). Likewise, similar shapes also occur among the South Asian potteries from Sumhuram from the earliest settlement layer that matched contexts of the later phase c1.

In this early period, the widespread occurrence of Black-and-Red firing technique in south India and Sri Lanka reflects popular methods of pottery making. However, details in fabric point to regional workshops. The spread of such common ideas certainly attests an intensive intercontinental network.

Storage jars with pointed base are known in situ from the third century BC until the second century AD in Tissamaharama (Plate 21.9). With regard to the form, variations in the neck and rim area have been found course of time. Already in the first century AD, they start to have a narrow mouth opening with an increasingly band-shaped outer rim (Plate 21.9, 1–2). Rim fragments from Ras Hafun, Somalia and assigned as Indian (Smith/Wright 1988: 132 Fig.6b.e; 136 Fig. 9a.d.g), correspond to this first century ad appearance. A fragment with a ridge inside the rim could fit well to a storage jar with rounded bottom of the same period at Tissamaharama (Smith/Wright 1988: 136, Fig. 9b).

With regard to 'Indian Red Polished Ware' illustrated in Orton's catalogue, many forms are reminiscent of the medieval period, according to the reappraisal of Arikamedu by Vimala Begley (1996; 2004; Schenk 2006). This refers to a certain lid with internal flange (Begley Form 17) and a pot with a carinated body.[10] At Arikamedu, the latter has a grooved outer rim, a feature that is also typical for rather medieval forms and is existent at Ras Hafun (Smith/Wright 1988, 134 Fig. 8c-f). This applies also to a water jar (Smith/Wright 1988, 134 Fig. 8a) and its parallels at Arikamedu (Begley 2004: Fig. 3.253–6). The grooved rim and the sharply carinated body are

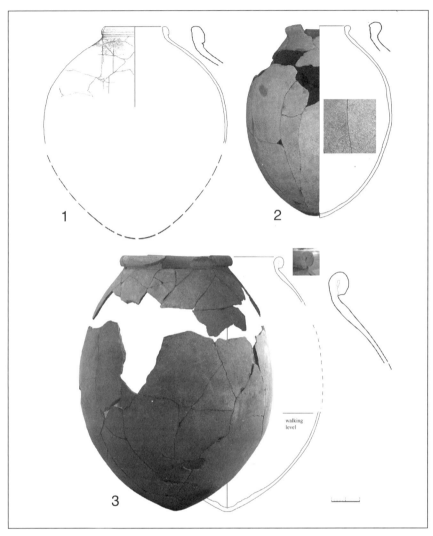

Plate 21.9: Tissamaharama: storage jars with pointed base found in situ. 1-2. phase d1
(first century AD); 3. phase c1 (second century BC) (Scale 1:12).

also typical among pottery compiled by Orton (Schenk 2007: 66–7; Orton
1992: Fig. 4.6.2). This also applies to Sanjan, Gujarat (Gupta et al. 2001–2).
The site also contains Chinese and Islamic pottery and dates to the eighth-
eleventh centuries AD. The flanged lid Begley form 17 also belongs thereto
(Gupta et al. 2001–2: 197 Fig. 7, 17).

Interestingly, such late forms are not among the finds of Sravasti, a site
in Uttar Pradesh. Numerous finds remind one of key types for Tissa phase
g2 (Plate 21.7), assigned to the late sixth/seventh centuries AD.[11] Types later
than Tissa phase h (eighth/ninth centuries AD) like the grooved rim and the

distinctly carinated bowl do not exist in Sravasti. However, Sravasti seems to have a long history and the earliest types correspond to Tissamaharama of BC periods, among them the earlier mentioned storage jar of second century BC (Plate 21.9c, 3) and Tissa form G made of BRW.[12]

The carinated-shaped wide bowl serves as a concluding example for the spread of a common form in south India and Sri Lanka (Plate 21.7d, 4). It has parallels in Nevasa, Arikamedu (Begley 1996; 2004) and in the catalogue for 'Red Polished Ware' (Orton 1992; Fig. 4.6.2). It emerges for the first time in the fourth/fifth century AD at Tissamaharama.

So far, correlations of common form tradition were mostly discovered in the early periods of third to first centuries BC and again in the later periods from the seventh century AD onwards. It indicates varying intensities of contact during the time.

Different fabrics, clay textures and surface treatment, however, pinpoint regional potter workshops. They certainly have their own product development in addition to the shown cross-cultural commonalities of vessel shapes.

'Indian Red Polished Ware' (RPW) is one of those many fabrics that exist on the subcontinent and represents such a regional workshop tradition. The compilation by Orton shows many types that are not similar to the Tissamaharama sequence. This regional manufacture is defined by the fine paste that was mistaken for *terra sigillata*, and derives from clay sources genuine to Gujarat and Maharashtra only. Across the subcontinent, there certainly are many more of these regional workshops. Roberta Tomber has recently recognized another fabric from Gujarat region among the South Asian-related pottery at Berenike, Egypt. In addition, she has found a match to the pottery from Pattanam, Kerala as well (Tomber 2008: 46–9; Tomber et al. 2011). This demonstrates the dynamic of relations. Further studies of common potteries with independent site-by-site research and based on context evaluation will enhance the reconstruction of changing interrelations. The Tissamaharama sequence demonstrates that chronological differentiations of common wares are possible for RPW and other regional potter traditions in South Asia.

Notes

1. For preliminary reports see: Weisshaar & Wijeyapala 1994; 2000; 2005; 2008; Weisshaar et al. 2001a; Weisshaar et al. 2001b; Weisshaar & Dissanayake 2010.
2. Tissa 1 ('Workmen's Quarter') is an industrial area; Tissa 2 ('Court's Garden') a large house of wattle and daub (first and second centuries AD) and Tissa 3 ('Sarvodaya Area') a quarter of noble families.

3. The phases of the settlement are as follows: phase a (fifth/fourth century BC), phase b (third century BC), phase c1 (second century BC), phase c2 (first century BC), phase d1 (first century AD), phase d2 (second century AD), phase e (third century AD), phase f1 (fourth century AD), phase f2 (fifth century AD), phase g1 (late fifth/sixth century AD), phase g2 (late sixth/seventh century AD), phase h (eighth/ninth century AD). As we expect more radiocarbon dates, the preliminary chronology might be subject to minor changes.

4. The moulds are from phase a/fourth century BC (Figs. 21.2 and 21.5), phase c1/second century BC (Figs. 21.2 and 4.6), phase c2/first century BC (Figs. 21.2 and 21.1), phase d2/second century AD (Fig. 21.2) and phase f2/fifth century AD (Figs. 21.2 and 21.3).

5. Marshall & Foucher 1913–14: Pl. 74, 4a; 75, 8b; 77, 15b. We are grateful to Harry Falk who drew our attention to the railings of Sanchi.

6. The reverse of a clay sealing with a swastika-motive (Fig. 21.4, no. 1) shows a fastening of twine that wrapped a thin board (Müller 2001: 246, Fig. 184). The board could well be the cover of a palm leaf manuscript.

7. Orton 1992: Fig. 4.1.6; 4.29.4; for a more complete shape see Rao 1966: Fig. 11.

8. Orton 1992: Fig. 4.15.1; 4.21.3; 4.29.2-3; for a more complete shape see Schenk 2001: 133, Fig. 9; Schenk 2007: 81 Fig. 7.

9. Further examples for this Kaolin-like fabric see Begley 2004: 109–10.

10. Begley 1996: 32 Fig. 1.18-19, 128, Fig. 4.13; later in 2004: 259 the flanged lid (Form 17) is dated from the first century AD to medieval times and is considered as continuing form. Ras Hafun: Smith/Wright 1988: 128 Fig. 5, l; 136 Fig. 9.i.k.

11. Sravasti: Takahashi et al. 1999–2000: Fig. 3 RP 1011-1022 (Tissa form C); Fig. 6 RP 1166 (Tissa Form D3); Fig. 7 RP 2011 (Tissa Form H rim type 16). Tissamaharama: Schenk 2001: 82 Fig. 76; 117 Fig. 99; 121 Fig. 103.

12. Sravasti: Takahashi et al. 1999–2000: Fig. 3 RP 1031 (Tissa Form I); Fig. 3 RP 1001-10; Fig. 5 1089-94 (Tissa Form G); Fig. 7: RP 2032-6 (storage jar); RP 2026 (lid).

References

Ahmad, K.M. (1950), *Inscribed and Riveted Pottery from Kondapur*, Kondapur series 1, Hyderabad: Archaeological Department, Hyderabad Government.

Begley, V. (1996), *The Ancient Port of Arikamedu, Vol. 1. New Excavations and Researches 1989–1992*. Pondicherry: École Française d'Extrême-Orient (Mémoires Archéologiques 22).

Begley, V., Francis Jr., P., Karashima, N., Raman, K.V., Sidebotham, S. and Will E.L., eds. (2004), *The Ancient Port of Arikamedu. New Excavations and Researches 1989–1992*, Vol. 2. Paris: École Française d'Extrême Orient (Mémoires Archéologiques 22.2).

Bianchetti, S. (2002), 'Die Seerouten nach Indien in hellenistischer und in römischer Zeit', in *Stuttgarter Kolloquium zur historischen Geographie des Altertums 7, 1999: Zu Wasser und zu Land. Verkehrswege in der antiken*

Welt, Olshausen, E. and Sonnabend, H., eds., Stuttgart: Franz SteinerVerlag (Geographica Historica 17) , pp. 280–92.

Chandra, M. (1977), *Trade and Trade Routes in Ancient India*, New Delhi: Abhinav Publications.

Eltsov, P.A. (2005), 'The Ancient Indian City and the Thought Expressed in it', in *South Asian Archaeology 2003. Proceedings of the Seventeenth International Conference of the European Association of South Asian Archaeologists, 7-11 July 2003, Bonn*, Franke-Vogt, U. and Weisshaar, H.-J., eds., pp. 319–28. Aachen: Linden Soft (Deutsches Archäologisches Institut; Kommission für Archäologie Außereuropäischer Kulturen und Eurasien-Abteilung; Forschungen zur Archäologie Außereuropäischen Kulturen 1).

Gogte, V.D. (2001), 'XRD Analysis of the Rouletted Ware and Other Fine Grey Ware from Tissamaharama', in *Ancient Ruhuna. Sri Lankan: German Archaeological Project in the Southern Province,* vol. 1, Weisshaar, H.-J., Roth, H. and Wijeyapala, W., eds., Mainz: Philip von Zabern (Materialien zur Allgemeinen und Vergleichenden Archäologie 58) , pp. 197–202.

Groom, N. (1995), 'The *Periplus*, Pliny and Arabia', *Arabian Archaeology and Epigraphy*, vol. 6, no. 3, pp. 180–95.

Gupta, S.P., Dalal, K.F., Dandekar, A., Mitra, R., Nanji R. & Pandey, R. (2001–2), 'A Preliminary Report on the Excavations at Sanjan (2002)', *Puratattva*, vol. 32, pp. 182–98, 240–4 (Plates).

IAR = *Indian Archaeology – A Review.*

Magee, P. (2010), 'Revisiting Indian Rouletted Ware and the impact of Indian Ocean trade in Early Historic south Asia', *Antiquity*, vol. 84, pp. 1043–54.

Marshall, Sir J. and Foucher, A. (1913–14), *The Monuments of Sanchi*, vols. 1-3. Delhi: Archaeological Survey of India: annual report 1913–14 (repr., Delhi, 1982).

Müller, W. (2001) 'The Sealings of Tissamaharama: Function and Typology', in *Ancient Ruhuna. Sri Lankan: German Archaeological Project in the Southern Province,* vol. 1, Weisshaar, H.-J., Roth H. and Wijeyapala, W., eds., pp. 243–52.

Orton, N.P. (1992), 'Red Polished Ware in Gujarat: A Catalogue of Twelve Sites', in *Rome and India. The Ancient Sea Trade*, Begley V. and De Puma, D., eds., Madison, WI: University of Wisconsin Press, pp. 46–81.

Parker, H. (1884), 'Report on Archaeological Discoveries at Tissamaharama', *Journal of the Ceylon Branch of the Royal Asiatic Society*, Reprint as *separatum* 1998, Mattegodagama, vol. VIII, pp. 1–97.

Pavan, A. and Schenk, H. (2012), 'Crossing the Indian Ocean before the *Periplus*: pottery assemblages in comparision. The sites of Sumhuram (Oman) and Tissamaharama (Sri Lanka)', *Arabian Archaeology and Epigraphy,* vol. 23, pp. 191-202.

Rajan, K.V. (1998), 'Further Excavations at Kodumanal, Tamil Nadu', *Man and Environment*, vol. 23, no. 2, pp. 65–76.

Rao, S.R. (1966), *Excavations at Amreli, A Kshatrapa-Gupta Town*, Baroda: Museum and Picture Gallery Baroda (Bulletin 18).

Ray, H.P. (1994), *The Winds of Change. Buddhism and the Maritime Links of Early South Asia*, Delhi: Oxford University Press.

Schenk, H. (2001), 'The Development of Pottery at Tissamaharama', in *Ancient Ruhuna. Sri Lankan–German Archaeological Project in the Southern Province*, vol. 1, Weisshaar, H.-J., Roth H. and Wijeyapala, W., eds., pp. 59–195.

—— (2005), 'Pottery of so-called "Kaolin Fabric" at Tissamaharama-Citadel (Sri Lanka) in the 4th and 5th century AD', in Franke-Vogt, U. and Weisshaar, H.-J., eds., *South Asian Archaeology 2003. Proceedings of the Seventeenth International Conference of the European Association of South Asian Archaeologists, 7-11 July 2003, Bonn*, Aachen: Linden Soft (Deutsches Archäologisches Institut; Kommission für Archäologie Außereuropäischer Kulturen und Eurasien-Abteilung; Forschungen zur Archäologie Außereuropäischen Kulturen 1), pp. 357–64.

—— (2006), 'The Dating and Historical Value of Rouletted Ware', *Zeitschrift für Archäologie Außereuropäischer Kulturen*, vol. 1, pp. 123–52.

—— (2007), 'Parthian Glazed Pottery from Sri Lanka and the Indian Ocean Trade', *Zeitschrift für Archäologie Außereuropäischer Kulturen*, vol. 2, pp. 57–90.

Smith, M.C. and Wright, H.T. (1988), 'The ceramics from Ras Hafun in Somalia: notes on a classical maritime site', *Azania*, vol. 23, pp. 115–41.

Srisuchat, A. (2003), 'Earthenware from Archaeological Sites in Southern Thailand: The First Century BC to the Twelfth Century AD', in *Earthenware in Southeast Asia. Proceedings of the Singapore Symposium on Premodern Southeast Asian Earthenwares*, Miksic, J., ed., Singapore: NUS Press, pp. 249–60.

Strauch, I. (2006), 'Socotra: the western-most outpost of ancient Indian scripts', in *Socotra. A Natural History of the Islands and their People*, Cheung, C. and DeVantier, L., eds., Hong Kong: Odyssey Books and Guides, p. 231.

Strauch, I. and Bukharin, M. (2004), 'Indian Inscriptions from the Cave Hoq on Sukutrā (Yemen)', *Annali dell'Istituto Orientale di Napoli*, vol. 64, pp. 121–38.

Takahashi, T., Yamaoka, T., Yoneda, F. & Uesugi, A. (1999–2000), 'The Ancient City of Sravasti: its Significance on the Urbanisation of North India', *Puratattva*, vol. 30, pp. 74–92.

Tomber, R. (2007), 'Rome and Mesopotamia: importers into India in the first millennium AD', *Antiquity*, vol. 81, pp. 972–88.

—— (2008), *Indo-Roman Trade. From Pots to Pepper*. London: Duckworth.

Tomber, R., Cartwright, C. and Gupta, S. (2011), 'Rice temper: technological solutions and source identification in the Indian Ocean', *Journal of Archaeological Science*, vol. 38, pp. 360–6.

Walburg, R. (2008), *Coins and Tokens from Ancient Ceylon. Being a critical survey of the coins and coin-like objects unearthed in the Island, based on a thoroughly annotated catalogue of finds, and supplemented by an analytical appendix*. Ancient Ruhuna. Sri Lankan–German Archaeological Project in the Southern Province, vol. 2, ed. H.-J. Weisshaar, S. Dissanayake and W. Wijeyapala, Wiesbaden: Reichert (Forschungen zur Archäologie Außereuropäischer Kulturen, Band 5).

———— (2010), 'A deposit of goddess plaques at Tissamahārāma – some preliminary considerations', *Zeitschrift für Archäologie Außereuropäischer Kulturen*, vol. 3, pp. 31–65.

Weisshaar, H.-J. and Dissanayake, S. (2010), 'The Citadel of Tissamaharama and the Torrents of Spring', in *South Asian Archaeology 2007. Proceedings of the 19th Meeting of the European Association of South Asian Archaeology in Ravenna, Italy, July 2007*, volume II, Callieri, P. and Colliva, L., eds., Oxford: Archaeopress (BAR International Series 2133), pp. 361–8.

Weisshaar, H.-J., Roth, H. and Wijeyapala, W., eds (2001a), *Ancient Ruhuna. Sri Lankan–German Archaeological Project in the Southern Province*, vol. 1. Mainz: Philip von Zabern (Materialien zur Allgemeinen und Vergleichenden Archäologie 58).

Weisshaar, H.-J., Schenk, H. and Wijeyapala, W. (2001b), 'Excavations in the Citadel at Akurugoda: The Workmen's Quarter (Tissa 1) and the Court's Garden (Tissa 2)', in *Ancient Ruhuna. Sri Lankan–German Archaeological Project in the Southern Province*, vol. 1, Weisshaar, H.-J., Roth, H. and Wijeyapala, W., eds., pp. 5–39.

Weisshaar, H.-J. and Wijeyapala, W. (1994), 'The Tissamaharama Project 1992-1993 (Sri Lanka): metallurgical remains of the Akurugoda Hill', in *South Asian Archaeology 1993, Proceedings of the Twelfth International Conference of the European Association of South Asian Archaeologists held in Helsinki University, 5-9 July 1993*, vol. II, Parpola, A. & Koskikallio, P., eds., Helsinki: Suomalainen Tiedeakatemia (Annales Academiae Scientiarum Fennicae B271), pp. 803–14.

———— (2000), 'The Tissamaharama Project (Sri Lanka): Excavations in the Citadel Area', in *South Asian Archaeology 1997. Proceedings of the Fourteenth International Conference of the European Association of South Asian Archaeologists, held in the Istituto Italiano per l'Africa e l'Oriente, Palazzo Brancaccio, Rome, 7-14 July 1997*, Taddei, M. and De Marco, G., eds., Rome: Istituto Italiano per l'Africa e l'Oriente (Serie Orientale Roma 90), pp. 633–45.

———— (2005) 'Excavations in the Citadel of Ancient Mahagama (Tissamaharama/ Sri Lanka)', in *South Asian Archaeology 2003. Proceedings of the Seventeenth International Conference of the European Association of South Asian Archaeologists, 7-11 July, 2003, Bonn*, Franke-Vogt, U. and Weisshaar, H.-J., eds., Aachen: Linden Soft (Deutsches Archäologisches Institut; Kommission für Archäologie Außereuropäischer Kulturen und Eurasien-Abteilung; Forschungen zur Archäologie Außereuropäischen Kulturen 1), pp. 351–6.

———— (2008), 'Excavations within the Citadel of Tissamaharama (Sri Lanka)', in *South Asian Archaeology 1999. Proceedings of the Fifteenth International Conference of the European Association of South Asian Archaeologists, held at the Universiteit Leiden, 5-9-July 1999*, Raven, E.M., ed., Groningen: Egbert Forsten, 2008 (Gonda Indological Studies 15), pp. 265–9.

CHAPTER 22

The Inception of the Transnational Processes between the Indian Ocean and the South China Sea from an Early City-State on the Thai-Malay Peninsula (Fourth-Second Centuries BCE)

Bérénice Bellina

Introduction

The fourth–third centuries BCE witnessed the political unifications of Mauryan India and Han China and the establishment of connections between the different regional networks linking the Classical World and Asia. The opening of the overland and maritime so-called 'Silk Roads' led to the emergence of the Eurasian and African world-system, which lasted until the Modern Period in the sixteenth century (Beaujard 2005). This chain of intertwined networks inaugurated a trading boom that some historians qualify as a pre-Modern 'Age of Commerce' (Manguin 2000), and major trans-national cultural processes (Beaujard 2005). For South-East Asia, producer of several products looked for by her two major economic and political neighbours China and South Asia, this interconnection opened the avenue to an economic and cultural integration that historiography has termed the 'Indianization', 'localization' or 'Sanskritization' of South-East Asia. This is a transnational process that is now seen as one of the preceding pre-Modern globalization processes (Assayag 1998). Until the mid-first twentieth century, the notion of 'Indianization' dominated; born in a colonial context, it encapsulated the vision of an unilateral process and the passivity of South-East Asian populations (Cœdès 1968, Majumdar 1941). The term 'localization' was born of an internalist reaction and insisted on the dynamism and the capacity of South-East Asian populations to control these cultural exchanges (Wolters 1999). Even if I recognize the importance of the political and religious aspect of the exchange between the two regions, I do not use the term 'Sanskritization'. Though considering the bilateralism of the process, it only qualifies this transnational activity with political and literary criteria (Pollock 1996). In any of these conceptions, it is only the emergence of politico-religious features in the form of inscriptions in Sanskrit and Hindu-Buddhist statuary and temples by the mid-first millennium CE that are granted authority. Furthermore, if most researchers nowadays commonly accept that the process had to be two-sided, the impact on the Indian populations remains to be investigated and no term translates this idea. Hence, the continuance of the initial term 'Indianization'. Distinct from the orthodox position, I hold that this transnational bilateral process must include a wider range of cultural features than those expressed by the elitist politico-religious texts and monumental culture. To me, the process should also integrate mundane features expressed by commoners in their everyday life, such as technological changes belonging to the industrial, agricultural, domestic spheres. It is not the place here to expand on the long-demonstrated importance of the adoption of technologies by societies and about their significance in the realm of ideational representations and of the organization of economic and social life (Costin and Wright 1998; Leroi-Gourhan 1943, 1945, 1964; Lemonnier 1991). I insist on this aspect as for the period I am dealing with here, those 'mundane' cultural features are those best apprehended thanks to the new methodologies and archaeological sciences as opposed to symbolic representations, especially in a period when the expression of Brahmano-Buddhist features are still tenuous in India itself (an-iconic period).

Indianization and other transnational exchange processes were facilitated by trading nodes concentrating local, regional and long-distance exchange networks, cosmopolitan port-cities and more specifically certain types of City-States,[1] which structured this long chain of intertwined networks (Cartier 1999, Bentley 1999, Curtin 1984, Beaujard 2005, Hansen 2000). They bred mixed socio-cultural configurations of the diverse societies interconnecting there.

It has been acknowledged that for two millennia several city-states developed along the shores of the South China Sea (Hansen 2000)[2] but that their ancestry probably had to be sought in the early port-harbours of the late prehistoric period that developed along the coast of the western façade of South-East Asia (Lombard 1970, 1988; Reid 2000; Manguin 2000; Jacq-Hergoualc'h 2002). Found in comparable geographical contexts and interacting with traders from the Indian subcontinent and China, they were also characterized by a similar socio-political organization and developed a range of shared cultural features, the city-state cultures.

This essay presents data from the excavation of Khao Sam Kaeo[3] in which I identify some of the defining criteria of city-states and city-state cultures, suggesting that the emergence of this form of political system can be traced back to the early days of the maritime roads in the South China Sea. Khao Sam Kaeo was an enclosed early urban settlement, port and craft centre of cosmopolitan configuration. Situated at the junction of both transpeninsular routes connecting the Bay of Bengal to the South China Sea[4] and of the river Tha Taphao that connects the centre of upper regions of the Thai-Malay Peninsula to the South China Sea,[5] the polity was active from the fourth to the second century BC[6] (Map 22.1). There communities from Mainland and Insular South-East Asia, China, and the Indian subcontinent resided and interacted within defined quarters and catalysed the creation of mixed sociocultural configurations reflected in the anthropogenic landscape and in the various craft industries. Because city-states emerged in similar environmental contexts, I will begin introducing briefly some of the geographic peculiarities that characterize the western façade of the South China Sea where emerged Khao Sam Kaeo and several city-states over two millennia. To contextualize the significance of the discovery of Khao Sam Kaeo in South-East Asia, I will quickly review some of traditional urban, political and economic defining traits of main city-states. I will show how the site is at the moment unique in South-East Asia in displaying several of these traits, hence supporting the idea of continuity. But I will also emphasize how some discoveries serve to nuance the economic definition, especially on the significance of agricultural and industrial activities in their development. Industrial activities and the site's configuration also lead me argue for the culturally mixed nature of this prototype of a city-state. I will conclude by discussing the implication of these pieces of evidence in terms of cultural sequence and suggest characterizing some identity strategies developed as early as the inception of this transnational cultural exchange process.

Geographic Peninsular Peculiarities

The western part of the South China Sea comprising the Malayan Peninsula, eastern Sumatra, and the western part of Borneo is characterized by year-round rains that heavily erode and impoverish soils. Historical documents show that fertile soils allowing good agricultural returns were more often found in upland regions distant from the frequently flooded malarial lowland areas where entrepôts emerged. Thus, the latter imported their

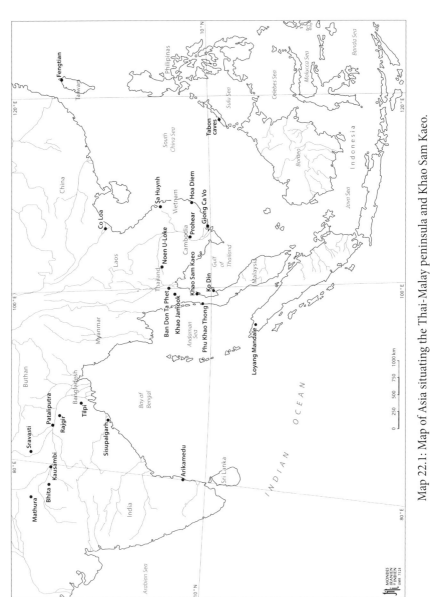

Map 22.1: Map of Asia situating the Thai-Malay peninsula and Khao Sam Kaeo.

food via rivers from the hinterland or via the sea from further away (Reid 2000; Thomaz 1988). The anthropologically-based model of a hierarchic upstream-downstream control of a river basin, whereby the entrepôt located at the mouth of the river or not far from it controlled goods and people moving in and out is commonly called upon (Bronson 1977). City-states were the nodal point of a system of secondary and tertiary polities located further upstream, providing goods for long-distance export and receiving products from the downstream entrepôt, whether produced there or imported from further (Morrison and Junker 2002). Trading polities constituted a necessary step-over for mariners and merchants of the trans-Asiatic network whose stay could extend over several months. Whilst waiting for a change of wind direction, boat repairs, etc., these relay stations allowed ships to offload their cargoes and to pick up other goods. On the Thai-Malay Peninsula, exploiting and deriving advantages from various physical landscapes and ecosystems, social groups took different developmental paths. The western part possesses hill slope fields but lacks even a narrow coastal plain; there populations took advantage of navigational constraints that made this region a practical stopover. Populations on the eastern coast managed to develop attractive and favourable feeder points, not only furnishing staple goods, but also participating in long-distance exchange of goods of local, regional and interregional origins. Those goods stemmed from various ecosystems: agricultural and mineral resources from inland and upland areas, faunal and floral products from the interior tropical forest, and the series of long-distance exchanged goods listed by Wheatley from both local and foreign areas.

Khao Sam Kaeo and the Inception of South-East Asian Urbanism

In South-East Asia, a historiographical tradition has long associated urban and State formation with the external impetus of long-distance exchange, in particular with South Asia. This is specifically the case for coastal trading-cities, as opposed to the agrarian-based royal cities of the interior (Lombard 1970, 1988). In Lombard's dual typology of South-East Asia, cities are systematically opposed: their inception, organization and evolution differ. Long-distance trade-cities developed out of the maritime silk roads, their plan was 'anarchic', in contrast to the geometric cosmic-based plan of the agrarian cities. The city, most often walled, is not structured by a holy centre but by ports and markets. At the heart was the often fortified royal compound built with wood and set on poles like all buildings except the religious ones. Besides the palace, the centre included a religious place with its associated public space and a central market. Malay city-states were monarchies leaning on an urban cosmopolitan ruling elite, some merchants-aristocrats, living in juxtaposed ethnic 'compounds' (Lombard 1988; Reid 2000). Like other cities in South-East Asia, buildings were surrounded by fruit trees, giving the impression of a series of villages. City-states were taken to maintain a poor relationship with their hinterland and to lack agricultural base, entailing the import of most food by sea.

As will be shown, Khao Sam Kaeo conforms to several of those features: an enclosed settlement characterized by ethnically-defined quarters with structures built on piles with omnipresent vegetation. However, maybe due to the intensive destruction of the site by looting, no remains of what could be attributed to a royal residence were recovered. Excavations at Khao Sam Kaeo and comparison with other later trading polities also nuance some of the defining elements, in particular those concerning the agricultural base and the role played by industries, the latter point having been left untouched by previous researchers. At present, Khao Sam Kaeo is the only site presenting such features for this period and until the mid-second millennium CE. Though since the 1990s, excavations of late prehistoric settlements have increased and showed the development of small trade-related sites by the early centuries CE in coastal areas,[7] none has yet provided a comprehensive and extensive vision of their occupation and of their internal organization. Moreover, none has produced evidence of any enclosed early urban cosmopolitan-type of settlement and ethnically-defined quarters found in historical city-states such as the thirteenth century Pasai (North Sumatra) or the fifteenth century Malaka (Nik Hassan Shuhaimi and Kamarrudin 1994; Shuhaimi 1991; Bronson 1990; Veraprasert 1992). Looking at contemporaneous settlements in Mainland South-East Asia, one is left with limited research yet, an emphasis on burial accounting for this situation, and no exact comparative features. Situated in very different environments, the concentric moated sites from eastern Thailand (Higham et al. 2007; Moore 1988; McNeill and Welch 1991) and the so-called Mimotian moated sites in eastern Cambodia (Albrecht et al., 1999) and Vietnam and the Co Loa citadel in Vietnam do not provide satisfactory comparisons (Kim et al. 2010). They nonetheless evidence the existence of an Iron Age moated-settlement tradition in South-East Asia characterized by monumental constructions of earthworks and hydraulic systems. In this context and more especially in the case of Co Loa, Nam Kim argues that the late centuries already attest to the emergence of urbanized and state-level societies (2013). Khao Sam Kaeo can thus be situated in a regional larger context of very little if nothing is known of the emergence of urbanism on Maritime South-East Asia. We are left with no elements to compare Khao Sam Kaeo with. However, Khao Sam Kaeo's general configuration and fortification system may owe more to the early Indian cities that emerge from the mid-first millennium BC than to any contemporary South-East Asian moated settlement from Mainland South-East Asia (Bellina-Pryce and Silapanth 2008).

I believe that Khao Sam Kaeo's features at the same time bear an urban Indian imprint and announce some of the historical city-states of the South China Sea. Khao Sam Kaeo thus provides data on the inception of a particular type of socio-political system centred on a city[8] that thrived in maritime South-East Asia as well as on the significance of agricultural and industrial activities in their development.

Khao Sam Kaeo's Morphology and Dimensions

The site consists of four hills whose summit heights average 30 m. above sea level (Map 22.2). They are separated by ravines oriented North-South (20°) and East-West (110°). The tops of the hills are relatively flat, forming plateaux; summit plateau size ranges are between 150 m. × 150 m. and 200 m. × 200 m. The resulting landscape is an area divided into five subrectangular units. Hills constituted a safe area for settlement since the surrounding lowlands were subjected to flooding in antiquity. Even if it was closer to the sea and its environment was more of a coastal type and mangrove was covering it during the early stage of its occupation, the settlement has never been a coastal site.

On the western side, the river Tha Taphao, whose channel has changed several times, forms both a natural boundary and a protective border whilst to the east, 19 earth embankments (called 'walls' for simplicity) delimited the compound. Two types of earthworks were distinguished: those crossing on hills, enclosing plateaux and flanked with ditches limited areas of the site were interpreted as ramparts. In some areas, instead of embankments, wooden palisades were placed uphill and sharp slopes seemed to have been used. The remains of those wooden structures have not been found, not surprisingly in this climate, but they were likely posted before a step cut into the hill. Different stages of the excavated ramparts have been evidenced: some were relocated; others were renovated by the successive addition of excavated bedrock.

The second type of embankment is shorter and found in the middle of Valleys 1 and 3. At the very eastern part of Valley 1 are parts of a hydraulic system. Seven walls of this type were recorded: Wall 3 in Valley 1; and Walls 6, 9, and 17 in Valley 3 (as well as part of what we currently call Wall

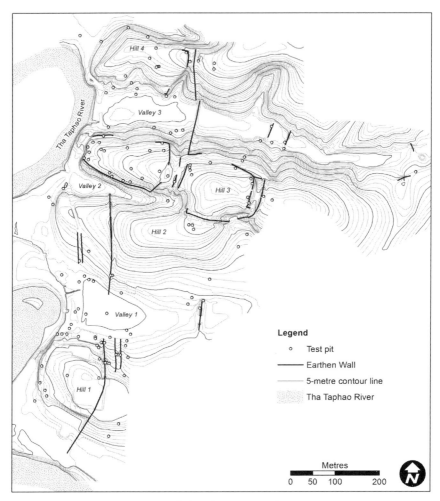

Map 22.2: Map of Khao Sam Kaeo with its ramparts.

7). Those walls were likely used to retain monsoon waters flowing out of the hills from ravines and ditches, to create a water tank upstream (to the east). Meanwhile, they also trapped sediments, preventing the silting-in of the western part of the valley. Their excavation evidenced accumulation of alluvial deposits since the antique period. The creation of water reservoirs could have had several purposes: first domestic, for fresh water; second agricultural; third defensive, water constituting an obstacle on the eastern part of the site and; finally as a mooring place for embarkations.

As for agriculture, comparative data is still scarce in South-East Asia since very few archaeobotanical studies have been conducted yet. This situation makes synchronic or diachronic restitution perilous. However, research in progress seems to indicate that dry land cultivation, rice and millets, was practiced on hills (Castillo 2009, 2011). Dryland rice cultivation seem also to have preceded wetland rice cultivation further south in the peninsula, as Allen suggested for the historical city-state of Kedah located on the south-western coast of the peninsula and that thrived from the early centuries AD to the middle of the second millennium (Allen 1991). Allen had already shown that the late sedimentation of the river mouth, and that only, recently created large areas for wet-rice/lowland cultivation. It is possible that Khao Sam Kaeo, as well as Kedah, and maybe other trading-polities of the peninsula had developed a significant dry-land cereal culture as part of their economic base. At Khao Sam Kaeo, part of the hills was thus inhabited but also hosted cultures and gardens.

Inhabited zones are characterized by a horizontally and vertically dense network of domestic and communal structures. Domestic structures correspond to small-scale constructions on piles driven into individual terraces made from a mixture of gravel, pebbles and lateritic soil used to level the slope and which hosted domestic or small-scale craft activities. Communal structures correspond to large terraces. One was set up at the base of Hill 1, on a gentle slope bordering Valley 1, a terrace that had been cut to drain waters flowing from Hill 1 and from Wall 1's ditch. Above this large terrace, a series of footpaths were observable.

Successive floors, some of them built with gravel, and remains of postholes and hearths reveal a sequence of occupation that seems to have been largely restricted to areas within the walls.

A conservative approach to the sites dimension taking exclusively into account clearly defined zones enclosed by walls (e.g. the eastern plateau of Hill 3) and where artefacts were unearthed provides an estimate of 26 ha. It clearly appeared that the western part of the settlement has been eroded by the river. Different restitution allows defining a working range of 30-40 ha. (Malakie LaClair and Bevan forthcoming).

As for the morphology of the settlement, excavations demonstrated that it resulted from natural, landscaped and human-constructed boundaries. The encircling walls do not trace a distinguishable shape but follow the natural topography, enhancing it. Their morphology and the configuration of the site are not comparable to the contemporary irregular concentric moated sites of Eastern Thailand or to the Mimotian sites in Cambodia. Nor can it be compared to the northern Vietnamese citadel of Co Loa (17 km. north of Hanoi), nowadays located in a lowland and highly productive agricultural zone and which has been interpreted as a manifestation of the coercive and warfare climate that characterized State-level societies of this region (Kim et al. 2010).

The fortified pattern of Khao Sam Kaeo finds pertinent comparisons in early Indian cities that emerge in the north from the mid-first millennium BC (Smith 2003: 274–5). Data concerning the morphology, size, structure, and network integration of early historical cities is still sparse and the changes made during long-term occupations (and thus *tell* formation) of settlements greatly limit the understanding of their earliest phases. Nonetheless, it appears that cities were situated, for the greater part, on flat lands of low or average height but were taking advantage from hills, hillsides or elevations punctuating the landscapes. Most sites are settled on terraces, at the edge of rivers, small or big, because of the defensive qualities that offers this natural obstacle on one of its sides. This is the case for Mathura and Kausambi in the Gangetic plain, Sravasti along an ancient bed of the river Rapti in the Yamuna plain, Sisupalgarh along the Mahanadi in Orissa, etc. (Deloche 1992). Indian cities displayed a wide range of geometrical shapes[9] and uneven morphologies like at Bhita, Rajgir and Rajagrha. Most cities in the north were not uniform in plan and seemed to have adapted to local topography and more especially when integrating the river. They were delimited with ramparts consisting of earthen structures constructed of fill excavated from an adjacent ditch; and which shape followed the natural topography (Smith 2003). Authors agree that their construction answers multiple purposes besides warfare, controlling water disorders, restricting the access of outsiders to markets, materializing the civic identity and, generating cohesion, in particular, through its maintenance. In any case, it embodied a level of political control able to mobilize and organize the labour to produce and maintain them (ibid.). As for their size, they ranged from beyond 241 ha. like Pataliputra the capital of the Maurya Empire to Bhita a city founded during the Maurya period whose modest dimensions was estimated between 16 ha. and 14 ha. (Allchin 1995).

It appears that, Khao Sam Kaeo's morphology, location and type of fortifications find more pertinent comparisons amongst Indian cities than with contemporary South-East Asian settlements.

Khao Sam Kaeo
Internal Organization

Habitation, craft centres, port and burials were evidenced by structures and material found both on the hills and at their base. Data from technological analysis of the materials were integrated in a GIS which revealed a site spatially divided by boundaries that separate areas characterized by different structures and assemblages, spatial differentiations of production and consumption and that have been demonstrated to be statistically significant (Malakie LaClair, 2008, Malakie LaClair and Bevan, forthcoming).

Two clearly defined zones emerged from the spatial analysis: a southern area corresponding to Hills 1 and 2, most likely corresponded to Indigenous occupation and, a northern area, including Hills 3 and 4, occupied by Asian groups of various horizons, South Asian, South-East Asian and East Asian.

The Southern Part of the Settlement: The Indigenous Compound

The southern part of the site provides objects whose style is South China Sea-related, and locally produced using:

- techniques from the South China Sea, as for instance certain types of decorated ceramics with shell incisions and related to the Sa Huynh-Kalanay complex elaborated by W. Solheim (Bellina et al. 2012) (Plate 22.1);
- Indian raw materials probably worked upon under the aegis of a few experienced Indian craftspersons. These productions comprise ornaments in hard stone (Bellina 2003, 2007; Bellina and Silapanth 2006) and facetted lapidary worked glass ornaments and bracelets made with a transparent soda glass especially abundant on the site but restricted to its southern part (KSK m-Na-Al) and on other contemporary sites of the South China Sea (Dussubieux and Bellina, forthcoming). Both ornaments implemented Indian lapidary techniques (Bellina and Silapanth 2006) characterized by a high level of know-how, necessitating an apprenticeship of several years (Roux 2000). For this glass production, the presence of a well-developed glass industry at the earliest occupation levels makes it very unlikely that this glass tradition evolved from a local tradition (Plate 22.2).

The hard stone ornament production I called the 'South China Sea siliceous production' found in the southern part of the settlement consists of finished and unfinished products (Plate 22.3). This type of production combining Indian raw material and highly skilled Indian technologies with South China Sea-related style, is the earliest type I have identified in South-East Asia from the fourth century BCE. It is found in Central Thailand (Ban Don Ta Phet), Sa Huynh South Vietnam sites and in the Tabon Caves in the Palawan Island (Bellina 2001, 2003, 2007).

This type of production took place in the same workshop as those working the facetted glass beads and bracelet at the base of Hills 1 and 2.

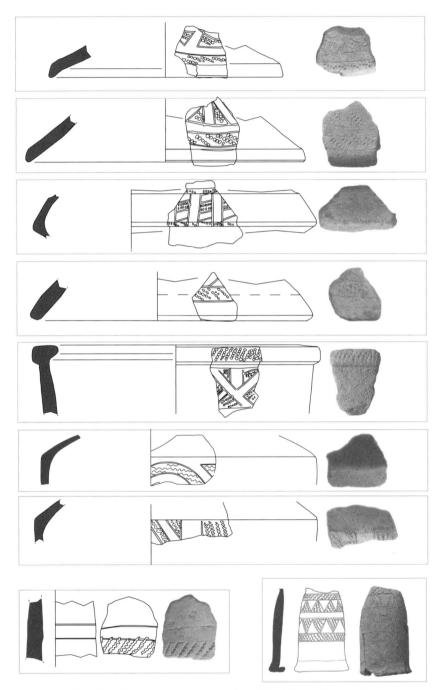

Plate 22.1: Decorated ceramics with shell incisions related to the
Sa Huynh-Kalanay complex.

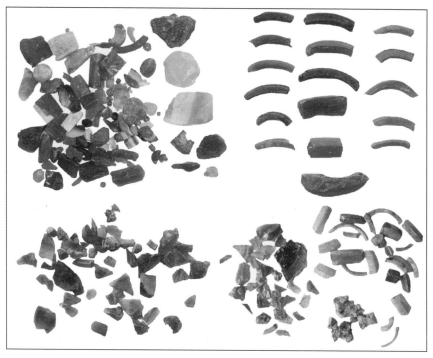

Plate 22.2: Lapidary glass beads, glass bracelets and working evidence.

Due to the multiple and severe disturbances on the site, it is difficult to determine whether this restricted distribution of craft areas in lowlands results from a specific organization of production or from different periods. Two specific findings appear all the more striking. The first is that the glass industry is apparently restricted to flat zones at the base of Hill 2 close to the river. The fire risk related to high-temperature glass-working does not alone explain the necessity to work outside habitation areas. Evidence for metallurgical activities, which also use high-temperature furnaces, was found on hills associated with habitation contexts. A need for proximity to water as a manufacturing requirement or as a means for the transport of raw materials and finished products does not seem an adequate argument, as both hard stone and possibly metal industries also use water, but were not always located near the river. Although the combination stone- and glass-working workshop is located near the river, other stone-working workshops (to be discussed later) occupy the summits of Hills 3 and 4, and both iron workshops are located on Hill 3's western and eastern plateaux. A second peculiarity is the discovery of both glass and hard stone ornament craft remains in the same context. In addition to the fact that the two manufacturing processes are very different, ethnography shows that the

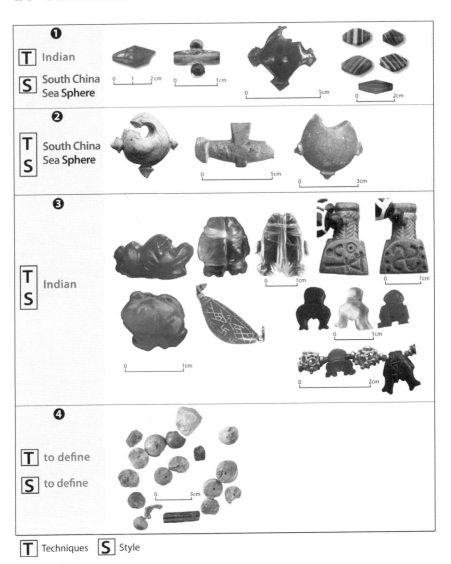

Plate 22.3: The four groups of hard-stone production made at Khao Sam Kaeo.

two industries are also traditionally very distinct in terms of social groups (Francis 2002). A possible explanation may lie in the type of ornament produced: bracelets and lapidary glass beads. Lapidary glass and hard stone beads share some manufacturing stages (Bellina and Silapanth 2006: 386–9).

Located in the vicinity of the glass and stone production at the base of Hill 2 was a cemetery area. Unfortunately, we were not granted permission to excavate in this very severely looted zone. Nonetheless, the fragments of big jars and the very rich material unearthed, consisting of gold and semi-precious highly skilled ornaments, support the assertion that this zone was used as a cemetery. The material found there also belongs to the South China Sea interaction sphere (Pryce et al. 2008). Gold ornaments coming from this zone that we were shown had similarities with ornaments found in Insular South-East Asia. Such is the case of central knobbed beads which finds comparison in Giong Ca Vo (Nguyen et al. 1995) and a five-lobed rosette plate, similar to artefacts recovered by R. Fox from the Tadyaw and Guri Caves (chamber B), part of the Tabon complex on Palawan Island in the Philippines (Fox 1970).

The Northern Part of the Settlement: The Foreign Compounds

The northern part of the settlement (Hills 3 and 4) yielded evidence for habitations and different types of craft production associated with various Asian groups from South, South-East Asia and the East. Some were imported, others were locally produced with exogenous techniques.

Materials associated with South Asia were concentrated on both plateaux of Hill 3 and consisted of goods that were (Plate 22.4):

- imported, like Indian rouletted and knobbed ware (Bouvet 2008);
- locally produced, including some Indian-inspired fine ware ('KSK black polished ware') and hard stone ornaments whose skilled manufacturing techniques, good quality material and part of their stylistic repertoire (auspicious symbols, 'minayugala', 'swastika', 'Hamsa', 'Triratna') were South Asian and South Asian-inspired, as well as seals bearing names of their owners in Prakrit written with Brahmi characters, certain of which were unfinished.

This part of the settlement also yielded evidence for the transfer of Indian metallurgical technologies, more especially of high-tin bronze (Plate 22.5), an intractable alloy, probably chosen because of its resemblance to yellow gold when freshly polished. Even if, so far, more high-tin bronze bowls have been found in Thailand than in India, Srinivasan and Glover showed (1997) that comparable compositional types and forms of high-tin bowls were found more widely in India at an earlier date.

Fragments of high-tin bronze bowls decorated with Indian motives comparable to those found in Central Thailand (Ban Don Ta Phet and Khao Jamook), have been recovered on the site by looters (Glover and Bellina, forthcoming). This type of production is found amongst numerous South-

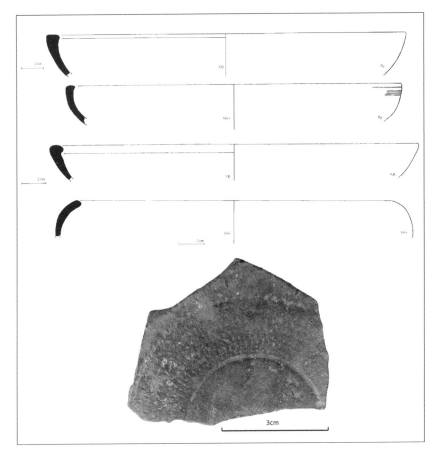

Plate 22.4: Rouletted ware from Khao Sam Kaeo.

East Asian communities during the late prehistoric period and constitutes one of the evidence of early contacts with the Indian subcontinent (Bellina and Glover 2004).

The occurrence of peculiar nippled moulds has been demonstrated to indicate the production of high-tin bronze ingots at Khao Sam Kaeo. The analysis of the remains found in those technical ceramics led to the suggestion that they were used to produce high-tin bronze ingot by cassiterite cementation. Similar material was found associated to high-tin bronze ingots on the broadly contemporary site of Tilpi in West Bengal. It appears most likely that Khao Sam Khaeo imported the copper ores that are lacking in the Thai-Malay Peninsula and exploited rich tin ores of the Peninsula to produce high-tin bronze ingots for bowl manufacture or exchange (Pryce et al. 2008; Murillo-Barroso et al. 2010). Furthermore, KSK's high-tin bronze production represents the most ancient evidence for

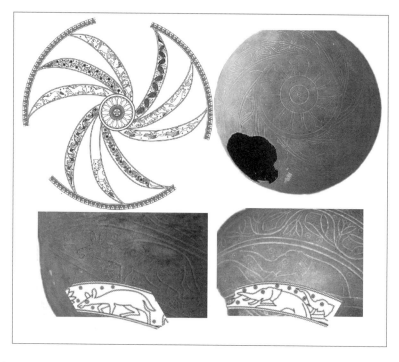

Plate 22.5: Fragment of decorated high-tin bronze bowl.

the exploitation of the Thai-Malay Peninsula's formerly vast tin resources, an industry whose importance to Arabic trade during the Historical period is well known (Murillo-Barroso et al. 2010; Bellina et al. 2010; Pryce et al. 2008).

The earliest iron-working evidence for the Peninsula comes from a workshop on the eastern plateau of Hill 3, a workshop later covered by a embankments and active during the fourth-second century BCE (Bellina-Pryce and Silapanth 2008). At Khao Sam Kaeo, smithing was practiced but, as opposed to other technologies, involved rudimentary skills. The bloomery iron smelting tradition in India is well attested in India (Dikshit 1986). Even if recent work has started to reveal the long suspected co-existence of bloomery smelting alongside cast iron making in China (Yasuyuki 2009), in the well-dated context of Khao Sam Kaeo, South Asia appears a more solid candidate for the export of iron smelting knowledge to Thailand (Biggs et al. 2013).

The materials attesting to the links with the insular world on the site include imported ceramics (which represent a minority on the site) (Bouvet 2009; Bellina et al. 2012), and ornaments such as bicephalous ornaments and lingling'o produced in the workshops of Hill 3 implementing techniques and imported materials, in particular nephrites. An analysis of the last indicated that some of them probably originated from the East Taiwanese source of Fengtian. The green nephrite from the Fengtian source has been used to make these two very specific forms of ear-pendants that were distributed on a network that extended from the Philippines, East Malaysia, South Vietnam, Eastern Cambodia and stretched until Peninsular Thailand (Hung et al. 2007; Hung and Bellwood 2010).

Hills 3 and 4 also yielded what is currently the most important Western Han Chinese corpus beyond North Vietnam. Metallic artefacts include bronze: used in a complete mirror of the type called 'Xing yun jing (mirror with stars and clouds) dated from the Middle Western Han Dynasty, beginning in the reign of Emperor Wudi (156–87 BCE) and a fragment fairly similar to Western Han mirrors from Central and South Vietnam (Pryce et al. 2008) and dated from the middle of the first century BCE to the very beginning of the first century CE. The Han-style metallic assemblage also included a prismatic arrow-head comparable to examples found in quantity at Co Loa Citadel near Hanoi in Northern Vietnam, an axe and two bronze seals. One of these seals (Plate 22.6) has a turtle shape and bears an inscription read as: 'Lü Yougong yin (The seal of Lü Yougong), Lü being a common family name during the Han dynasty, and has been dated to the first century BCE (Peronnet et al. forthcoming). In addition, 84 sherds of Han-style ceramic were recovered on Hills 3 and 4. Those consisted of

Plate 22.6: Chinese inscribed seal from Khao Sam Kaeo.

storage jars. Most were decorated with seal-on-net design. This net pattern was very popular throughout the Han dynasty, especially in South China around Canton; 20 sherds were stamped with checkered design, a type of motif (Plate 22.7). This pattern was very popular in East China during the Han period and jars with this design are numerous in tombs in Zhejiang, Jiangsu or Anhui. Also related to Eastern China are two handles decorated with animal masks (Peronnet et al. forthcoming).

Finally, Hill 4 hosted another stone production characterized by lower quality mass production techniques and mainly ubiquitous morphologies. The extensive and rapid looting that took place on Hill 4 did not afford much opportunity to observe many ornaments and to define the style. It seems to include ubiquitous morphologies such as large spherical and ellipsoid beads besides some flat agate pendants such as those found on prehistoric sites in Central (Bellina 2007) and Eastern Thailand such as in Noen U-Loke (Theunissen 2007). It is likely that this hill was used at the very late stage of the site's activity.

Discussion and Conclusion

Khao Sam Kaeo was settled from the early fourth century BCE in a coastal environment with a mangrove that has been cleared in the course of its occupation, which extended towards the north, leading to the renovation and modification of its enclosure system. Some dryland/upland agriculture seemed to have been practiced, but when it started, where exactly on the site and its vicinity is not yet determined. The lack of excavation and archaeobotanical research in the region of Chumphon leaves us at present

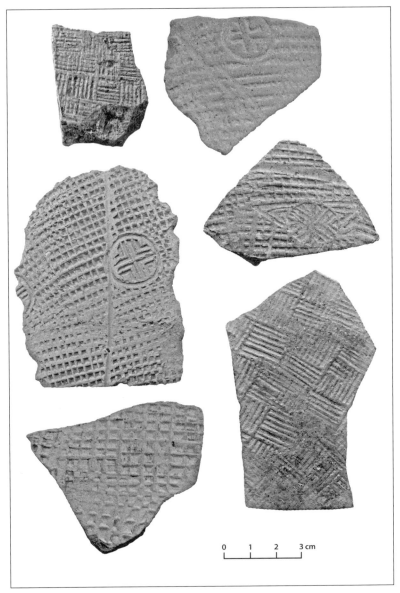

Plate 22.7: Han ceramic decorated with seal-on-net design from Khao Sam Kaeo.

without data to hypothesize whether some of the rice/millet was also imported from further inland or not.

Khao Sam Kaeo seemed to have an agricultural base whose intensity is still under study. Its economy was based on exchange, probably of raw materials and forest products, but also in highly specialized crafts products distributed along different networks.

In the southern part of the settlement thrived local populations who had been participating in a South China Sea sphere of interaction. Autonomous polities were engaged in exchange of commodities such as tin and 'prestige goods' like Dong Son drums (Plate 22.8) and developed a shared symbolic and material culture.

When the Bay of Bengal and the South China Sea networks inter-connected, in nodes such as Khao Sam Kaeo, merchants but also craftsmen could access products and demands from different South-East Asian networks. At Khao Sam Kaeo, the earliest industries involved South Asian craftsmen who implemented highly skilled traditional Indian techniques to produce very fine quality goods, referring to a South China Sea cultural repertoire. Quite plausibly, South Asian craftsmen producing those mixed products contributed to the magnificence of the polities hosting them (Bellina 2007). By doing so, they probably served the strategies of Khao Sam Kaeo's elite engaged in emulating and competitive exchanges with other socio-political systems of the South China Sea, a type of relationship hypothesized to be of the 'peer polity interaction' type (Renfrew and Cherry 1986). This role I credit artisans with probably remained the same during the later occupation of the site where I believe that some crafts were still being produced by South Asian artisans, possibly organized in guilds. Foreign merchants, artisans and possibly other specialists settled in

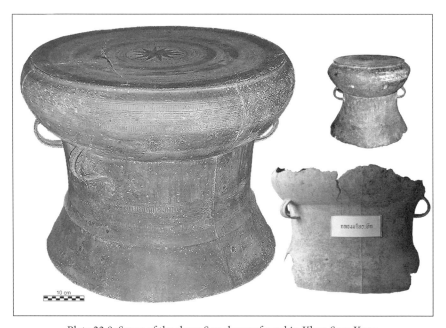

Plate 22.8: Some of the dong Son drums found in Khao Sam Kaeo.

the northern part of Khao Sam Kaeo continued to bring and/or produce goods looked for by other South China Sea polities. They contributed to the making of a South China Sea cultural sphere.

At a later stage, this cultural sphere integrated more ostentatious 'Indianized' elements. It is exemplified by products such as the 'Indianized' hard stone production integrating symbols belonging to the Indian world (at that time undefined Brahmano/Buddhist/Jain) made on the eastern plateau of Hill 3 that I suppose were still made by South Asian craftsmen using South Asian raw materials and high skilled technologies. This Indianized South China Sea repertoire differs in many respects to what would be found in contemporary South Asia in terms of morphologies and their diversity as well as the high quality of the production. Perhaps, the widely distributed high-tin bronze bowls too belonged to this Indianized South China Sea repertoire; besides the remelting possibility, this explanation could account for the absence of exact *comparanda* in South Asia. All these later 'Indianized' productions, whose distribution quickly expanded within South-East Asian sites of the late prehistoric period, would have mainly been aimed at South-East Asian populations in process of Indianization in Khao Sam Kaeo and/or elsewhere, as for instance at the contemporary site of Ban Don Ta Phet (Glover and Bellina 2011). What seems to be one of the characteristics of these Indianized productions are the exaggeration of some of the Indian traits, may this exaggeration be materialized in the technologies, the quality or the style.

But some of the mixed products might have been exported to South Asia. Here, I am referring to the high-tin bronze ingots, made with South Asian techniques, perhaps by South Asian artisans with imported copper and local tin.

These different products implementing Indian cultural, human or material elements co-existed with goods made for Mainland or Insular South-East Asian populations. They cohabited with Chinese imports. Some of the gold and hard stone ornaments found in Chinese tombs show striking similarities with those from Khao Sam Kaeo (Peronnet et al., forthcoming) thus suggesting that industrial sites like Khao Sam Kaeo could also have produced for China. However, to what extent is a question that requires further investigation. So far, no Chinese techniques have been identified on the site.

To sum up, Khao Sam Kaeo attests to the presence of South Asian groups as early as the fourth century BCE in the Upper part of the Thai-Malay peninsula, thus 13 centuries before the earliest attestation of the presence of Indian merchant guilds *Manikkiraman* on the peninsula, the Takua Pa inscription. This inscription relates the digging of a tank placed under the protection of the members of this guild staying in the fortified camp (Wisseman Christie 1998). At Khao Sam Kaeo, South Asian specialists set up industries playing a role in the economic and political strategies of the South China Sea early trading polities. But they also played a role in the acculturation process serving the cultural identity strategies of the elites. Their industries produced elements which became part of this proto-city-state culture. As early as this period, some South Asian representations and technologies began to be transferred to South-East Asia.

The cultural interactions and mixed configurations that formed the cosmopolitan city-port of Khao Sam Kaeo and that it catalysed has shed new light on the early stage of the long-lasting interplay that built the social, cultural and material network binding together the Bay of Bengal and the South China Sea. Some of the cultural productions were perennial and came to characterize later South-East Asian socio-political configurations like the pre-modern city-states. At Khao Sam Kaeo, different foreign cultural, technical and human forces combined to elaborate the earliest form of city-state of the South China Sea and the earliest City-State culture. Furthermore, Khao Sam Kaeo highlighted an important aspect of the acculturation mode: 'Indianized' traits are indeed South China Sea over-emphasized Indian cultural features which, as such, cannot be found in the Indian subcontinent. From a technological perspective, I believed that Indian specialists had implemented the most sophisticated technologies, sometimes being pushed to the limits of their skills, to create a symbolic vocabulary whose diversity and complexity of shapes cannot find comparison in India. The South China Sea culture does not simply adopt Indian cultural features but pushes Indian tradition beyond their envelope. Here is maybe one element to answer to the question of the bilateralism of the cultural exchange process. The first city-state culture exigency necessitated Indian specialists to adapt to go beyond their traditional boundaries. More broadly, South China Sea trading elite's identity strategy over-emphasized the otherness, some of Indian features that were felt emblematic.

Notes

1. The definition given by Hansen is:
   A city-state is a highly institutionalized and highly centralized micro-state consisting of one town (often walled) with its immediate hinterland and settled with a stratified population, of whom some are citizens, some foreigners and sometimes, slaves. . . . The population is ethnically affiliated with the population of neighbouring city-states, but political identity is focused on the city-state itself and based on the differentiation from other

city-states. A significant large fraction of the population is settled in the town, the others are settled in the hinterland. . . . The urban economy implies specialization of function and division of labour to such an extent that the population has to satisfy a significant part of their daily needs by purchase in the city's markets. The city-state is a self-governing but not necessarily an independent political unit. . . . A city-state is a micro-state composed of one town with its immediate hinterland, and a city-state culture is a civilisation which, politically, is organized as a system of city-states (Hansen 2000: 19).

2. The earliest historical city-state emerges from the seventh century CE, the Srivijayan thalassocracy held as the ancestor of the Pre-Modern Malay city-states.

3. The Thai-French archaeological mission is directed by B. Bellina (CNRS, France) and P. Silapanth (Ph.D. student at the EPHE and lecturer at Silpakorn University). The project was supported by the French Ministry of Foreign Affairs (sous-commission consultative des fouilles), the Direction des Relations Européennes et Internationales of the CNRS, the UMR 'Mondes iranien et indien' (CNRS), the École Française d'Extrême-Orient and the French Embassy in Bangkok. It granted permission from the National Research Council of Thailand, the Fine Arts Department and the National Museum of Chumphon. It is composed of: J. Allen (IARI, Hawaii, geoarchaeology), V. Bernard (topograph, archaeologist), P. Bouvet (Ph.D. student, Paris X, ceramicist), C. Castillo (Ph.D. student, Institute of Archaeology, London, archaeobotany), L. Dussubieux (Field Museum of Natural History, Chicago, glass specialist), G. Kozminski (BRGM, geology and remote-sensing), J. Malakie (GIS), S. Peronnet (post-doc, specialist in Chinese ceramics), T.O. Pryce (University of Oxford, archaeometallurgist). I wish to acknowledge the students who joined us and collaborators for one or several seasons: Nattha Chuenwattana, J.-P. Gaston-Aubert (Silpakorn University), R. Bernardes Carvalho (EPHE, Paris), M. Murillo (CSIC, España), Hsiao-chun Hung (Ph.D.), Yoshiyuki Iizuka (Academia Sinica, Taipei), D. Fuller, A. Bevan (University College London), J. Connan (Univ. Louis Pasteur-Strasbourg).

4. It has been suggested that the use of this part of the Peninsula was mainly restricted to the earliest period, an explanation in accordance with Wheatley's suggestion that sea routes superseded the trans-peninsular ones in the first century BC (Wheatley 1961).

5. KSK is situated in the Chumphon Province (district Muang Chumphon). 99° 11′–12″ East and 10° 31′–32″ North.

6. Based on the result of 30 samples consisting of charcoal, wood and organic material found in pottery using conventional (23) and AMS (17) 14C, the site has been securely dated from the very early fourth to second century BCE.

7. See for instance Kuala Selinsing in Peninsula Malaysia, Khlong Thom in Peninsular Thailand, Giong Ca Vo in the Mekong delta in Vietnam: Nik Hassan Shuhaimi & Kamarrudin 1994; Shuhaimi 1991; Bronson 1990 in Glover ed. 1990; Veraprasert 1992; Vu, Dang, Nguyen & Nguyen 1995.

8. The criteria to qualify a city can vary a lot from one author to another. I accept those listed by Hansen, five over the six cited I recognized at Khao

Sam Kaeo. Criteria are as follows: (1) A population of some size, (2) densely settled-in permanent dwellings, (3) and practising a specialization of function and division of labour, (4) so that they acquire an essential part of their necessities of life by trade and not by production, (5) The nucleated form of settlement entails a more institutionalized form of organization than required by dispersed settlement, and (6) the settlement becomes the social, economic, religious and military centre of its immediate hinterland (Hansen 2000: 12).

9. Shapes ranging from an irregular polygon (Ujjain, IAR 1956–7), a quadrilateral shape (Rajagrha, ASI-AR, 1905–6), a kind of trapeze (Kausambi: Sharma 1960), a rectangle (Mahasthan: Salles 2007; Vaisali: Kumar 1986), a square (Sisupalgarh: Lal 1948), and many others.

References

Albrecht, G., Haidle, M., Chhor Sivleng, Heang Leang Hong, Heng Sophady, Heng Than, Mao Someaphivath, Sirik Kada, Som Sophal, Thuy Chanthourn and Laychour, V. (1999), 'Circular Earthworks Krek 62/52: Recent Research on the Prehistory of Cambodia', *Asian Perspectives*, vol. 39, nos. 1-2, 2000, pp. 20–46.

Circular Earthworks in Cambodia (1999), Phnom Penh, Cambodia, 14–19 November, RUFA.

Allchin, F.R. (1995), *Archaeology of Early Historic South Asia*, Cambridge: Cambridge University Press.

Allen, J. (1991), 'Trade and site distribution in early historic period Kedah: geoarchaeological, historic and locational evidence', *Indo-Pacific Prehistory Association Bulletin (BIPPA)*, vol. 10, pp. 307–19.

Assayag, J. (1998), 'La culture comme fait social global? Anthropologie et (post) modernité', *L'Homme*, vol. 38, pp. 201–23.

Beaujard, P. (2005), 'The Indian Ocean in Eurasian and African World-Systems before the Sixteenth Century', *Journal of World History*, vol. 16, pp. 411–65.

Bellina, B. (2001), *Témoignages archéologiques d'échanges entre l'Inde et l'Asie du Sud-Est: morphologie, morphométrie et techniques de fabrication des perles en agate et en cornaline*, PHD, Paris, Université Paris III.

———— (2003), 'Beads, social change and interaction between India and South-East Asia', *Antiquity*, vol. 77, pp. 285–97.

———— (2007), *Cultural exchange between India and South-East Asia: Production and distribution of hard stone ornaments, VI c. BC–VI c. AD*, Paris: Éditions de la Maison des Sciences de l'Homme.

Bellina, B., Bacus, E., Pryce, T.O., J. Wisseman Christie, J., eds. (2010), *50 years of Archaeology in Southeast Asia: Essays in honour of Ian Glover*, Bangkok and London, River Books.

Bellina, B., Epinal G., Favereau, A. (2012), 'Caractérisation préliminaire des poteries marqueurs d'échanges en Mer de Chine Méridionale à la fin de la préhistoire', *Archipel* 84, pp. 7–33.

Bellina, B., Glover, I.C. (2004), 'The archaeology of early contacts with India and the Mediterranean World from the fourth century BC to the fourth century AD', in *Southeast Asia, from the Prehistory to History*, I.C. Glover, P. Bellwood, eds., London: Routledge/Curzon Press, pp. 68–89.

Bellina, B. and Silapanth, P. (2006), 'Khao Sam Kaeo and the Upper Thai Peninsula: understanding the mechanism of early trans-asiatic trade and cultural exchange', in *Uncovering Southeast Asia's Past*, Bacus, E.A., Glover, I.C. and Pigott, V.C., eds., Singapore: National University Press , pp. 379–92.

Bellina-Pryce, B. and Silapanth, P. (2008), 'Weaving cultural identities on trans-Asiatic networks: Upper Thai-Malay peninsula: an early socio-political landscape', *Bulletin de l'École Française d'Extrême-Orient*, vol. 93, pp. 257–93.

Bentley, J.H. (1999), 'Sea and Ocean basins as frameworks of historical analysis', *The Geographical Review*, vol. 89, pp. 215–24.

Biggs, L., Bellina, B., Martinon-Torres, M. and T.O. Pryce (2013), 'Prehistoric iron production technologies in the Upper Thai-Malay Peninsula: metallography and slag inclusion analyses of iron artefacts from Khao Sam Kaco and Phu Khao Thong', *Archaeological and Anthropological Science*, vol. 5, no. 4, pp. 311-29.

Bouvet, P. (2008), 'Étude préliminaire de céramiques 'indiennes' et indianisantes du site de Khao Sam Kaeo', *Bulletin de l'École Française d'Extrême-Orient*, vol. 93, 2006, pp. 353–90.

——— (2009), 'Rapport sur la céramique à Khao Sam Kaeo, saison 2009', in *Mission archéologique franco-thaï à Khao Sam Kheo, campagne 2009*, Bellina, B. *et al.* ed., Unpublished Report for the French Ministry of Foreign and European Affairs. Paris: CNRS

Bronson, B. (1977), 'Exchange at the upstream and downstream ends: notes towards a functional model of the coastal state in Southeast Asia', in *Economic Exchange and Social Interaction in Southeast Asia: perspectives from Prehistory, History and Ethnography*, Hutterer, K.E., ed., Ann Arbor: University of Michigan.

——— (1990), 'Glass and beads at Khuan Lukpad, Southern Thailand', in *Southeast Asian Archaeology 1986*, Glover, I.C. and Glover, E., ed., pp. 213–29. Oxford: BAR [BAR International Series 561].

Cartier, C. (1999), 'Cosmopolitics and the maritime world city', *The Geographical Review*, vol. 89, pp. 278–89.

Castillo, C. (2009), 'The archaeobotany of Khao Sam Kaeo: 2009 season', in Bellina, B., ed. Unpublished Report of the Franco-Thai Archaeological Expedition in Thai-Malay Peninsula. Submitted to the commission consultative des fouilles of the French Ministry of Foreign and European Affairs, Paris: CNRS

——— (2011), 'Rice in Thailand: The Archaeobotanical Contribution', *Rice*, vol. 4, pp. 114–20.

Cœdès, G. (1968), *The Indianised States of South-East Asia*, Canberra: ANU Press.

Costin, C.L. and Wright, R.P. (1998), *Craft and Social Identity*, Arlington, VA: American Anthropological Association.

Curtin, P.D. (1984), *Cross-Cultural Trade in World History*, Cambridge, England: Cambridge University Press.

Deloche, J. (1992), 'Étude sur les fortifications de l'Inde. I. Les fortifications de l'Inde ancienne', *Bulletin de l'École française d'Extrême-Orient*, vol. 79, pp. 89–131.

Dikshit, K.N. (1986), 'The Antiquity of Iron in India', in *Dimensions of Indian Art: Pupul Jayakar seventy, Volume 1*, Lokesh Chandra, Jyotindra Jain, Agam Prasad, Pupul Jayakar, eds., Delhi: Agam Kala Prakashan, pp.109–19.

Dussubieux, L. and Bellina, B. (forthcoming), 'Glass from and early Southeast Asian producing and trading centre', in *Khao Sam Kaeo: an early industrial port-city between the Indian Ocean and the South China Sea*, Bellina, B., ed., Paris.

Fox, R.B. (1970), *The Tabon Caves: Archaeological explorations and excavations on Palawan Island, Philippines*, Manila: National Museum Monograph No. 1.

Francis, P. (2002), *Asia's Maritime Bead Trade 300 B.C. to the Present Honolulu*, Honolulu: University of Hawaii Press.

Glover, I.C. and Bellina, B. (2011) 'Ban Don Ta Phet and Khao Sam Kaeo: The Earliest Indian Contacts Re-assessed', in *Early Interactions between South and Southeast Asia: Reflections on Cross-Cultural Exchange*, Manguin, P.-Y., Mani, A. & Wade, G., eds., Singapore and New Delhi: Institute of Southeast Asian Studies and Manohar, pp. 17–45.

Hansen, M.H. (2000), 'The concepts of City-State and City-State Culture', in *A Comparative Study of Thirty City-State Cultures. An investigation conducted by the Copenhagen Polis Centre*, Hansen, M.H., ed., Copenhagen: Kongelige Danske Videnskabernes Selskab, pp.11–34.

Higham, C.F.W., Kijingam, A. and Talbot, S., eds. (2007), *The excavation of Noen U-Loke and Non Muang Kao*, Bangkok: Thai Fine Arts Department.

Hung, H.-C. and Bellwood, P. (2010) 'Movement of raw materials and manufactured goods across the South China sea after 500 BCE: From Taiwan to Thailand, and back', in *50 Years of Archaeology in Southeast Asia. Essays in Honour of Ian Glover*, Bellina, B., Bacus, E.A., Pryce, T.O. & Wisseman Christie, J., eds., Bangkok: River Books, pp. 234–43.

Hung, H.-C., Iizuka, Y., Bellwood, P., Nguyen, K.D., Bellina, B., Silapanth, P., Dizon, E., Santiago, R., Datani, I. and Manton, J.H. (2007), 'Ancient jades map 3,000 years of prehistoric exchange in Southeast Asia', *Proceedings of the National Academy of Sciences*, vol. 104, pp. 19745–50.

Jacq-Hergoualc'h, M. (2002), *The Malay Peninsula. Cross-roads of the Maritime Silk-Road (100 BC–1300 AD)*, Leiden: Brill.

Kim, N.C. (2013), 'Lasting Monuments and Durable Institutions: Labour, Urbanism and Statehood in Northern Vietnam and Beyond', *Journal of Archaeological Research*, vol. 21, pp. 217-67.

Kim, N.C., Toi, L.V. and Hiep, T.H. (2010), 'Walls, Warfare, and Political Centralization: Recent Excavations at Vietnam's Ancient Capital of Co Loa', *Antiquity*, vol. 84, pp. 1011–27.

Kumar, D. (1986), *Archaeology of Vaishali*, New Delhi: Ramanand Vidya Bhawan.

Lal, B.B. (1948), 'Sisulpalgargh, an early historical fort in eastern India', *AI*, vol. 5, pp. 62–105.

Lemonnier, P. (1991), *Technological Choices: Transformation in Material Cultures since the Neolithic,* London: Routledge.

Leroi-Gourhan, A. (1943), *Évolution et Techniques. L'homme et la Matière,* Paris: Albin Michel (repr., 1971).

——— (1945), *Évolution et Techniques. Milieu et Techniques,* Paris: Albin Michel (repr., 1973).

——— (1964), *Le geste et la parole,* Paris: Éditions de la Maison des Sciences de l'Homme.

Lombard, D. (1970), 'Pour une histoire des villes du Sud-Est asiatique', *Annales, Économies, Sociétés, Civilisations,* vol. 24, pp. 842–56.

———(1988), 'Le sultanat malais comme modèle socio-économique', in *Marchands et hommes d'affaires asiatiques dans l'Océan Indien et la Mer de Chine 13ᵉ-20ᵉ siècles,* Lombard, D. and Aubin, J., eds., Paris: Éditions de l'EHESS, pp. 117–24.

Majumdar, R.C. (1941), *Greater India,* Lahore: Dayanand College Book Depot.

Malakie Laclair, J. (2008), 'Identifying Patterns between the Looting Pits: Spatial Analysis at Khao Sam Kaeo', London: UCL Institute of Archaeology.

Malakie Laclair, J. and Bevan, A. (forthcoming), 'Spatial Analysis of an Early Port City', in *Khao Sam Kaeo. An early industrial port city between the Indian Ocean and the South China Sea,* Bellina, B., ed.

Manguin, P.-Y. (2000), 'City-States and City-State cultures in pre-15th Century Southeast Asia', in *A Comparative Study of Thirty City-State Cultures. An investigation conducted by the Copenhagen Polis Centre,* Hansen, M.H., ed., Copenhagen: C. A. Reitzels Forlag, pp. 409–16.

McNeill, J. and Welch, D. (1991), 'Regional and interregional exchange on the Khorat Plateau', *BIPPA,* vol. 10, pp. 327–41.

Moore, E. (1988), *Moated Sites in Early North East Thailand,* Oxford: British Archaeological Reports (International Series 400).

Morrison, K.D. and Junker, L.L., eds. (2002), *Forager-Traders in South and Southeast Asia–Long Term Histories,* Cambridge: Cambridge University Press.

Murillo-Barroso, M., Pryce, T.O., Bellina, B. and Martinon-Torres, M. (2010), 'Khao Sam Kaeo: an archaeometallurgical crossroads for trans-asiatic technological traditions', *Journal of Archaeological Science,* pp. 1761–72.

Nguyen, K.D., Trinh, C., Thang, D.V., Hien, V.Q. and Hau, N.T. (1995), 'Ornaments from jar burial sites in Can Gio District, Ho Chi Minh City', *Khao Co Hoc,* pp. 27–46.

Nik Hassan Shuhaimi, B.N.A.R. and Kamarrudin, B.Z. (1994), 'Recent archaeological discoveries in Sungei Mas, Kuala Muda, Kedah', *Journal of the Malaysian Branch of the Royal Asiatic Society,* vol. 66, pp. 73–80.

Peronnet, S., Srikanlaya, S. and Bellina, B. (forthcoming), 'The Chinese-related ceramic at Khao Sam Kaeo', in *Khao Sam Kaeo: an early industrial port-city between the Indian Ocean and the South China Sea,* Bellina, B., ed., Paris.

Pollock, S. (1996), 'The Sanskrit Cosmopolis, 300–1300: Transculturation, Vernacularisation, and the Question of ideology', in *Ideology and Status of Sanskrit. Contributions to the History of the Sanskrit Language,* Houben, J.E.M., ed. Leiden: E.J. Brill (Brill's Indological Library 13), pp. 197–247.

Pryce, T.O., Bellina-Pryce, B. and Bennett, A. (2008), 'The development of metal technologies in the Upper Thai-Malay Peninsula: Initial interpretation of the archaeometallurgical evidence from Khao Sam Kaeo', *Bulletin de l'École Française d'Extrême-Orient* 2006, vol. 93, pp. 295–316.

Pryce, T.O. and Natapintu, S. (2009), 'Smelting Iron from Laterite: Technical possibility or Ethnographic Aberration?', *Asian Perspectives: Journal of Archeology for Asia & the Pacific*, vol. 48, pp. 249–64.

Reid, A. (2000), 'Negeri. The culture of Malay-speaking City-States of the Fifteenth and Sixteenth Centuries', in *A Comparative Study of Thirty City-State Cultures. An investigation conducted by the Copenhagen Polis Centre*, Hansen, M.H., ed., Copenhagen: C.A. Reitzels Forlag, pp. 417–29.

Renfrew, C. and Cherry, J.F., eds. (1986), *Peer polity interaction and socio-political change,* Cambridge: Cambridge University Press.

Roux, V., ed. (2000), *Cornaline de l'Inde: Des pratiques techniques de Cambay aux techno-systèmes de l'Indus,* Paris: Éditions de la Maison des Sciences de l'Homme.

Salles, J.-F., Ed. (2007), *Mahasthan I, Pundranagara, cité antique du Bengale : rapport préliminaire 1993-1999,* Turnhout: Brepols.

Sharma, G.R. (1960), *The excavation of Kausambi (1949–50): The defences and the Śyenaciti of the Purusamedha,* Allahabad: Department of Ancient History, Culture & Archaeology, University of Allahabad.

Shuhaimi, N.H. (1991), 'Recent research at Kuala Selinsing, Perak', *Bulletin of the Indo-Pacific Prehistory Association*, vol. 11, pp. 141–52.

Smith, M.L. (2003), 'Early Walled Cities of the Indian Subcontinent as "Small Worlds"', in *The Social Construction of Ancient Cities*, Smith, M.L., ed., Washington DC: Smithsonian Institution Press, pp.269–89.

Srinivasan, S. and Glover, I.C. (1997), 'The archaeological implications of new findings of traditional crafts of making high-tin "delta" bronze mirrors and 'beta' bronze vessels in Kerala State of South India', in *Material Issues in Art and Archaeology*, Vandiver, P.B., Druzik, J.R., Merkel, J.F. and J., S., eds., V. Warrendale, PA: Materials Research Society.

Theunissen, R. (2007), 'The agate and carnelian ornaments', in *The excavations of Noen U-Loke and Non Muang Kao*, Higham, C., Kijngam, A. & Talbot, S., eds., Bangkok: The Thai Fine Arts Department pp. 359–78.

Thomaz, L.F.F.R. (1988), 'Malaka et ses communautés marchandes au tournant du 16e siècle', in *Marchands et hommes d'affaires asiatiques dans l'Océan Indien et la Mer de Chine 13e-20e siècles*, Lombard, D. and Aubin, J., eds., Paris: Éditions de l'EHESS, pp. 31–48.

Veraprasert, M. (1992), 'Khlong Thom: an ancient bead manufacturing locations and an ancient entrepôt', in *Early metallurgy, Trade and Urban Centres in Thailand and Southeast Asia*, Glover, I.C., Suchitta, P. & Villiers, J., eds., Bangkok: White Lotus, pp. 149–61.

Vu, Q.H., Dang, V.T., Nguyen, K.D. and Nguyen, T.H. (1995), *The Giong Phet site (Ho Chi Minh City) (in Vietnamese)*, Report from the Vietnamese Museum of History, pp. 53–75.

Wheatley, P. (1959), 'Geographical Notes on some Commodities involved in Sung Maritime Trade', *Journal of the Malayan Branch of the Royal Asiatic Society*, vol. XXVIII, pp. 1–23.

—— (1961), *The Golden Khersonese,* Kuala Lumpur: Oxford University Press and Kuala Lumpur Univ. Press.

Wisseman Christie, J. (1998), 'The medieval Tamil language inscriptions in Southeast Asia and China', *Journal of Southeast Asian Studies*, vol. 29, no. 2, pp. 239–68.

Wolters, O.W. (1999), *History, Culture, and Region in Southeast Asian Perspectives.* New York and Singapore, South-East Asia Programme: Cornell University, Ithaca, New York. In cooperation with the Institute for South-East Asian Studies, Singapore.

Yasuyuki, M. (2009), 'Iron production in Han and Pre-Han periods in Sichuan Cheng Du Plain China', *World of Iron Conference 16-20 February 2009 London,* London (forthcoming).

FRENCH ARCHIVES

CHAPTER 23

The French *Dépôt des Fortifications des Colonies* Records of the Colonies Fortifications: India Files (Seventeenth–Nineteenth Centuries AD)

Marie-Paule Blasini

Among the Cartographic Collections deposited in the National Centre of Overseas Archives, one stands out for its quality and historical interest: the records called Repository of the Archives of the Colonies Fortifications by a decree issued on Nivôse 15, year VIII (5 January 1800). This collection comprises records of the entire map production and architectural works of the King's engineers, geographers and military engineers, reflecting the most productive period, especially that of the eighteenth century.

The Fortifications of the Colonies Records: History and Origin of the Collection

Ancestor of the French Records Repository of the colonies fortifications, the General collection of maps and plans of the colonies was established in 1778, out of two separate documentary resources. It was initially composed of graphic documents and reports referring to the French overseas possessions kept in the archives of the French Navy Department. In July 1776, when the Collection of public records of colonies was established to keep parish registers and notarial minutes and remedy the significant loss of records written in each colony, Sartine, the then Secretary of State for the Navy, sent a letter to the General Governors, administrators and commanders in the West Indies and Saint Pierre and Miquelon, to 'collect all the maps and plans drawn in the colony by the topographical engineers'. It was specified that the decision concerned the plans 'of the areas surrounding all the cities, towns, batteries, forts, king's and public buildings' and that they should be accompanied by explanatory reports. Thereafter, the same rule was applied to the colonies as the one followed in France by the Engineer officers, an organized body, that is the obligation of sending complete sets of plans/maps drawn in the colonies, duplicates or originals, in a systematic way. In 1792, the Minister of the French Navy, Bertrand Molleville, ordered the Colonial Office records and the navy Collection to be reunited.

But the revolutionary wars demonstrated that it was necessary to establish in Paris a comprehensive archives of the Colonies defence under the control of a Committee for fortifications (set up by two Acts in 1791 and 1795) and to create a Government department to oversee fortifications in the Colonies, along the lines of the War Department. Therefore, the archives dealing with military work in the colonies were again distinguished from the rest of the archives of the Navy. On 15 Nivose, Year VIII (5 January 1800), along with the reorganization of the Engineers body was created the Records Repository of the Colonies Fortifications as well as the relief-plans Collection.

However, in 1880 the War Department closed it down as it could no longer effectively manage military buildings and fortifications in the colonies. Everything was then transferred to the department of the Navy Archives until 1914. It is only thereafter that the archives were handed over to the Archives of the Ministry of Colonies, then in 1959 to the overseas section of the National Archives. In 1986, the whole was transferred to Aix-en-Provence at the Centre for Overseas Archives established in 1966 for housing all the archives of the former French colonies. This centre is now called National Overseas Archives (ANOM).

Description and Composition of the Archives

This collection is much richer than its name suggests. Its 25,000 maps consist of general maps, river routes and land paths, land registers, plans of cities, civil and military buildings. Among the memos kept are travelogues, reports on the economy and local customs, plans for field campaigns as well as accounts of historical or military events, trade projects, instructions to post commanders. But there are also many technical documents, various estimations, land surveys and drafts with the addition of sketches and drawings. All are of an indisputable historic, archaeological and architectural interest.

The archives go beyond plain military history and study of relations with foreign powers. The geographical and historical contexts of the colonies, people, slaves, missionaries, fauna and flora, health situations, land ownership by land grants, urban development and colonial architecture are all themes that the Archives can address.

The maps are of an outstanding cartographic quality and the whole has a great diversity: ink or graphite manuscripts, watercoloured or not, sometimes enhanced with touches of ink wash and colour on paper or tracing paper, prints, charts and drawings of any kind. The accuracy of the pen stroke or the wealth of iconography and the freshness of colours provide an overview of the talents, sometimes tinged with fantasy, shown by the draftsmen, surveyors and military engineers.

Continents and countries drawn are: islands and coasts of Europe, the Americas, Africa and the Indian Ocean, as well as Asia and Oceania.

The Archives are classified according to the French possessions or geographic areas. Maps and memories are classified and listed in a methodical order, reflected by manuscript inventories of the nineteenth century. Maps and plans are kept separate, in portfolios and appropriate plan filing cabinets, depending on their format—they are labelled A, B, or C (from the largest to the smallest).

Another collection should be added: the French Records Repository of the Colonies Fortifications-supplement, corresponding to certain other territories. It was given by the archives of the General Inspectorate of naval artillery (1880–1910 and until 1940) to the overseas section of the National Archives. Later the full set was moved to the CAOM at Aix-en-Provence in 1986.

The India files of the French Records Repository of the Colonies Fortifications

As described earlier, the collection is classified according to the subjects grouped geographically: East India, Pondicherry, Chandernagore, Karaikal, Mahe and Yanam. It consists of separate sets of memoranda or written data and of many cartographic documents kept in different portfolios according to their size.

Memoirs

Far from being exclusively apostillized memoirs, only devoted to aspects of the fortifications of the colonies, to poliorcetics, civil or military architecture, the records also give information about the geographical situation, and supply statistical data about the trade or history, of east India. For example, they detail which routes to follow to reach the coast of Coromandel and Malabar; discuss Dutch companies in the Moluccas, or English ones in the Gulf of Persia; document the first contacts of the French with native princes; the efforts made by religious missions to adapt to climates and customs of south India; and of course deal with the east India trade with Europe.

All these memories, instructions, letters, opinions, accounts, comments, plans and projects accompanied by technical notes (measures, specifications, drawings), are written by different personalities and actors within colonies. They are signed by governors, managers or commanders of the Army such as: Bussy, Charles Joseph (de Patissier), commanding the French troops in India, 1753–84; Dupleix, Joseph Francois, Chief Director of the French settlements in India, 1742–54; Godeheu, Charles, director of the East India Company, Governor of Pondicherry, 1754; de Lauriston Law, John, governor of the French establishments in India, 1764–77, etc. But they are also written by engineers, geographers, surveyors or artists involved in various projects. Some of the names that feature here include: Laffitte de Brassier, Louis Francois Grégoire, engineer, 1777–80; John Bourcet, Chief Engineer at Puducherry, 1759–76; Antoine Nicolas Desclaisons (Sieur), Chief Engineer at Pondicherry, 1769–71); Nyon (or Nyons, Knight), engineer, 1700–9; Jean-Baptiste Solminihac (son), Deputy Engineer at Pondicherry, officer in the India battalion, geographer and engineer, 1767–85; Alexander Sornay, engineer, 1750–67. Each left moving testimonies or tantalizing accounts, accurate descriptions of remote areas or the first trading posts established along the coast, or descriptions of forthright political decisions taken during conflicts or sieges, trade reports. These are genuine historical and military accounts on the political situation in India and relations between India, France and other countries, mostly Holland and England, and even treaties. There are numerous letters exchanged between the engineers of the fortifications in Pondicherry and the Supreme Council of the city, the East India Company in Paris and the Minister of the Navy Antoine de Sartine in Versailles, on the building of fortifications in the late eighteenth century.

Many of these documents are copies sent to Versailles for information to the Minister of Marine or part of information packages, but they are sometimes anonymous. Regretfully, as a consequence of the wanderings and transfers of these archives, some lacks can be detected even if there was no true classification of the records from the start. We are fortunate to find and then to trace the facts through other funds of the Centre (ANOM): older Archives of the Colonies, series of acts issued by the ruling power (A), letters being sent abroad (B) and letters upon arrival at French Establishments in India (C2); territorial records repatriated from India, older series (A of records, B of fliers, C from lodges), and modern records: concerning Karikal (D), Pondicherry (E and F), political affairs (G and H) and finally public series: The Registry of the Superior Council of Pondicherry, criminal trials (M), notarial archives (N), notarial archives of Chandernagore (O), notarial archives of Pondicherry (P), notarial archives of Mahé (Q), criminal trials of Chandernagore (R). In the National Archives in Paris, one can also find in the Navy Collection hydrographers papers (2JJ), geographical and scientific observations (3JJ) and (from JJ 6JJ to 10) maps and hydrographic documents that are targeted at experienced experts in geodesy and overseas navigation.

Maps and Plans

The maps and plans of the DFC Indies are genuine jewels among all the maps and plans preserved in the National Overseas Archives in Aix-en-Provence, and they are as rich and varied as the memoirs which are apostillized to them. They are of course testimonies, sorted and inventoried individually, as graphic or technical documents. They are nonetheless true works of art and quite delightful. Their quality, freshness, their (sometimes and by chance) perfect state of conservation give us a glimpse of the work done by the French builders in the East Indies, during a flourishing period which lasted much of the eighteenth century.

Among them are French maps such as: *Battlefront on the Coromandel Coast, 1770*, a map engraved by C. Croisey, which lists the various forts established (reference: FR ANOM 25DFC154A); Dutch maps: Stadt Negepatnam op Kust van Coromandel, ca. 1756 (reference: FR ANOM 25DFC239B); as well as English ones: *A map of Vellour, Fort* etc. . . . from the accounts of Harcars, by J. Hume (reference: FR ANOM 25DFC338B).

There are also charcoal drawings, watercolour plans (most of them): *Plan of the citadel of Suratte in 1777, belonging to the English,* by Lafitte de Brassier (reference: FR ANOM 25DFC164C), *Plan of Fort William and the City of Calcutta, English Settlement in Bengal,* 1770 by Delamare (reference: FR ANOM 25DFC357A); engraved maps; views of ports and plans of quays and docks: *Plan and view of the city of Cochain on the Malabar Coast,* 1778 by Lafitte de Brassier (reference: FR ANOM 25DFC198B); some not-quite-fascinating projects of fortifications: *Map of the comptoir of Mahe and its surroundings, following the new plan of fortification which was to be built in 1778 . . .* by Lafitte de Brassier (reference: FR ANOM 29DFC51B); sections, and elevations of governors palaces and public buildings: section

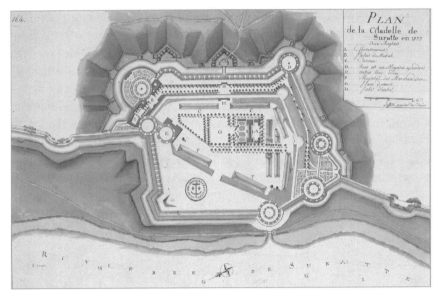

Plate 23.1: *Plan de la citadelle de Suratte en 1777, aux Anglais* [*Plan of the citadel of Surat in 1777, belonging to the English*], by Laffite de Brassier (Archives nationales d'outre-mer, Aix-en-Provence, France. Cote 25DFC164C)

and rear of the Government Palace in Pondicherry, by Dumont (reference: FR ANOM 26DFC85A). However, a few pagodas or local monuments too are represented. These plans have an essentially practical purpose: to describe and forecast the progress of the French Settlements in India. All are attractively illustrated and coloured (watercolour technique or wash), according to the fantasy of the draftsman concerning the subject represented or the drawing reproduced. Coloured cartouches are used for the titles, local scenes are designed to enrich the text or make the project credible. From what we know about short strokes drawing or Indian miniatures, we can deduce that they were influenced by local techniques or prepared with the aid of assistants commissioned to enhance the aesthetics. Obviously, the models for military constructions which were to be built in the colonies as the ones developed in France according to Vauban methods, were somehow adapted according to the fashion of the day in India.

Fortunately, maps and plans of the OFC India are well preserved and worth a wide circulation. After restoration they were publicized through several exhibitions: '*Flower Cities': Adventures and Maps of the French in India in the seventeenth and eighteenth centuries* (CAOM museum in 1996 and the East India Company Museum in 1998), *Chitra: towns and monuments of the eighteenth century in French archives* (Embassy of France in New Delhi, 2000–1); and a CD-Rom—*Bellicose Indies: Adventures and*

Maps of the French in India (CAOM 1999). Besides a database of archival sources about India was launched and developed within an EURINDIA project, by the Centre for Book Conservation in Arles and the National Overseas Archives in Aix-en-Provence (2004–6), with Indian and European partners. Nevertheless, publications devoted to the history of India or the former French trading posts in India widely use illustrations sourced from the collections of the DFC Indies. With the digitalizing of the entire maps collection (558 maps) undertaken since several years as consulting and online research is done instantly through the ANOM site and the database ULYSSES: http://anom. archivesnationales.culture. gouv.fr/sdx/ulysses/index For India or Indies, the various documentary collections are: CFL *East Indies* (25DFC); DFC *Pondicherry* (26DFC); DFC *Chandernagore* (27DFC); DFC *Karaikal* (28DFC); DFC *Mahe* (29DFC); DFC *Yanam* (30DFC).

Plans and Documents Accessible on the Website

Plans of ports in the Indian Ocean and the Bay of Bengal in the East Indies DFC (25DFC).

Théâtre de la guerre sur la côte de Coromandel, 1770 [*Battlefront on the Coromandel coast, 1770*], map engraved by C. Croisey (FR ANOM 25DFC154A FR).

Plans on the Malabar Coast

Plan de la citadelle de Suratte en 1777, aux Anglais [*Map of Suratte Citadel in 1777, belonging to the English*], by Laffite de Brassier (FR ANOM 25DFC164C).

Plan de l'Isle de Bombay en 1777 [*Map of the Island of Bombay in 1777*], by Laffite de Brassier (FR ANOM 25DFC170A).

Plan de Mangalore, à la côte de Malabar, à Hyder Ali Kan [*Map of Mangalore, on the Malabar coast, under the governorship of Hyder Ali Khan*] 1778, by Laffite de Brassier (FR ANOM 25DFC175B).

Plan et vue de la ville de Cochain, à la côte Malabar [*Plan and view of the City of Cochain, on the Malabar Coast*] 1778, by Lafitte de Brassier (FR ANOM 25DFC198B FR).

Plan de la ville et port de Iz-druk, à la côte de Malabar [*Plan of the city and port of Iz-Druk, on the Malabar Coast*] 1778, Anonymous (FR ANOM 25DFC205C).

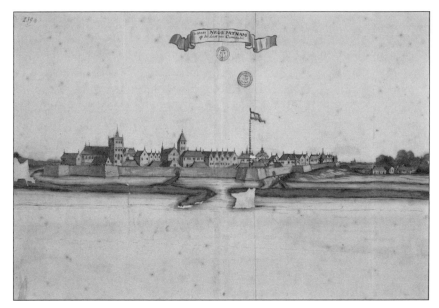

Plate 23.2: *De stadt Negepatnam, op de kust van Cormandel* [*The town of Negapatnam on the Coromandel coast*], ca 1756, Anonymous (Archives nationales d'outre-mer, Aix-en-Provence, France. Cote 25DFC239B).

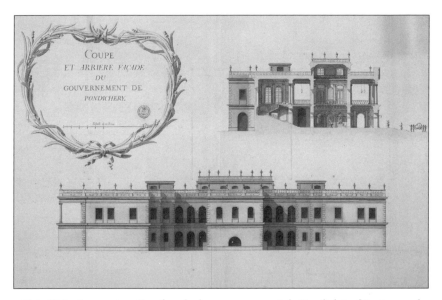

Plate 23.3: *Coupe et arrière-façade du gouvernement de Pondichéry* [*Section and rear facade of the Government of Pondichéry*] 1755, by Dumont (Archives nationales d'outre-mer, Aix-en-Provence, France. Cote 26DFC85A).

De stadt Colombe [*The town of Colombe*], ca 1756, Anonymous (FR ANOM 25DFC213B).

Plan au fort de Trinquemalay [*Map of Trincomale Fort*], 1782, by Benoît, Chevalier des Roys £ Rambaud (FR ANOM 25DFC215A).

Plan au fort d'Ostembourg [*Map of Ostembourg Fort*], September 25, 1782, by B. Rambaud (FR ANOM 25DFC217B).

De stadt Negepatnam, op de kust van Cormandel [*The town of Negapatnam on the Coromandel coast*], ca 1756, Anonymous (FR ANOM 25DFC239B).

Trivatour, Tanjaor, côte de Coromandel [*Trivatour, Tanjaor, Coromandel coast*] (FR ANOM 25DFC247C).

Plan de la ville de Trinquebar aux Danois en 1778 [*Map of the City of Tranquebar to the Danish in 1778*], by Laffite de Brassier (FR ANOM 25DFC251A).

Plan des ville et forteresse de Gengy, dans le Carnate, côte de Coromandel [*Map of the city and fortress of Gengy in Karnataka, Coromandel Coast*], Anonymous (FR ANOM 25DFC268C).

Plan du fort Saint-David et de la ville de Goudelour [tel qu'il étoit en 1754] [*Plan of Fort St. David and the city of Cuddalore*], ca 1754 (FR ANOM 25DFC276A).

Plan du fort Saint-George de Madras et la ville noir (sic), avec ses environs, en 1780 [*Plan of Fort St. George in Madras and the black city, with its surroundings in 1780*], by Laffite de Brassier (FR ANOM 25DFC303A).

Porte-novo, cote de Coromandel, Carnate [Porte-Novo coast of Coromandel, Karnataka], (FR ANOM 25 DFC31OC) Anonymous.

(FR ANOM 25DFC310C) *Plan du fort de Schinglepet, aux Anglais* [*Plan of Shinglepet Fort, to the English*], 1780, by Laffite de Brassier (FR ANOM 25DFC319A);

Plan de Doltabad, tiré par ordre de Monsieur de Bussy, commandant général de l'armée auxiliaire auprès de Salabet-Jingue, souba du Dekan [*Map of Doltabat, drawn by order of Mr. de Bussy, chief commandant of the auxiliary army for Salabet-Jingue, Soubeidar of Deccan*], 2 May 1758, by Frederick Tiintzch (FR ANOM 25DFC341A).

Mazulipatam, aux Anglois, avec les nouvelles fortifications, à la côte d'Orixa [*Masulipatam, to the English, with the new fortifications on the coast of Orissa*], 1777–8, by the Marquis de Valory d'Estilly (FR ANOM 25DFC346B).

Visigapatam, aux Anglois, à la côte d'Orixa [*Visigapatam, to the English, on the coast of Orissa*] 1777–8, by the Marquis de Valory d'Estilly (FR ANOM 25DFC347B).

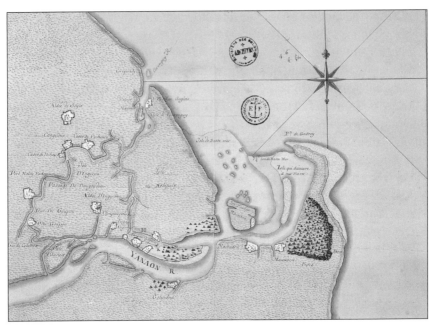

Plate 23.4: *Entrée de la rivière Yanaon* [*Mouth of the Yanaon River*], by Lemoyne (Archives nationales d'outre-mer, Aix-en-Provence, France. Cote 30DFC3C).

Marche de milord Clive à la bataille de Bokcer, royaume de Bengale [*March of mylord Clive at the battle of Bocker, kingdom of Bengal*], by Delamare (FR ANOM 25DFC350B).

Plan du fort Wiliam (sic) et de la ville de Calcutta, colonie angloise a (sic) Bengale, 1770 [*Plan of Fort William and of Calcutta, English colony in Bengal, 1770*], ca 1770 by Delamare (FR ANOM 25DFC357A).

Plan de la loge de Cassimbazard à la Compagnie de France [*Plan of the Lodge of the French Company at Kasimbazar*], ca 1729 (FR ANOM 25DFC369B).

Isle de Java [*Isle of Java*] by Soleille (FR ANOM 25DFC386B rating).

Plans in French Schools

Carte particulière de la ville de Pondichéry et de ses environs, ou est marqués [sic] *les attaques des Anglais du mois d'aoust de 1778 et l'état où était la ville lorsqu'elle* [sic] *a été assiégée* [*Specific map of the city of Pondicherry and its surroundings with mentions of the attacks of the English in the month of August 1778 and the state of the city when it was besieged*], by Lafitte de Brassier (FR ANOM 26DFC557A).

Coupe et arrière-façade du gouvernement de Pondichéry [*Section and rear facade of the Government of Pondicherry*], 1755, by Dumont (FR ANOM 26DFC85A).

Plan de Chandernagor et du fort d'Orleans, établissement français sur le bord occidental du Gange [*Plan of Chandernagore and the Fort of Orleans, French settlement on the western bank of the Ganges*], 1762, by Jean Bourcet (FR ANOM 27DFC7C).

Plan de la rivière de Karikal [*Plan of the Karaikal River*], March 1788, by Mamudde (FR ANOM 28DFC30B).

Plan du comptoir de Mahé et de ses environs, suivant le nouveau plan de fortification qui devoit être mis en exécution en 1778, qui n'a pas eut [sic] *lieu, rapport aux hostilités commencé* [sic] *en ce tems* [sic] [*Map of the comptoir of Mahe and its surroundings, following the new plan of fortification which was to be built in 1778*] . . . By Lafitte de Brassier (FR ANOM 29DFC51B).

Entrée de la rivière Yanaon [*Mouth of the Yanaon River*], by Lemoyne (FR ANOM 30DFC3C).

Written Material from the CD-ROM

Memoir attached to the plan (25DFC319A) detailing the fort Schinglepet by Lafitte de Brassier (FR ANOM 25DFC mem.317, cart.97).

Memoir attached to the map of Madras (25DFC303A) detailing the fort St Georges, by Lafitte de Brassier (FR ANOM 25DFC mem.300, cart 97).

Bourcet, Letter to the Superior Council of Pondicherry, on the fortifications, 10 October 1766 (FR ANOM 26DFC mem.142, cart 99).

Memoir on Trade and businesses to the Indies, by Martin, February 1691 (FR ANOM 25DFC mem.109, cart 95).

Memoir on the situation of the colony of Chandernagore and French institutions that depend on: Balasore, Dhaka, Jougdia, Kassimbazar and Patna, for Helies, 15 September 1778 (FR ANOM 27DFC mem.14, cart 103).

CHAPTER 24

Portraits of Louis XV and Marie Leszczinzka by Carle Van Loo (Presidential Gallery, Rashtrapati Bhavan, New Delhi)

Jean-Marie Lafont

Some state symbols once held positions that are difficult to comprehend today. Among these symbols, the portrait of a sovereign was one of the most powerful. The sovereigns had a large, full-length painting done of themselves that then became the official portrait of their reign. They offered copies of that portrait to other sovereigns as a symbol of high diplomatic gesture, or to a city of their kingdom, or to any person they

*I express my thanks to the President of the Republic of India for granting us permission to photograph the portraits of Louis XV and Queen Marie Leszczinzka in the Rashtrapati Bhavan Gallery, on 4 November 2010. Dr Christy Fernandez, Secretary to the President, and Rasika Chaube, of the President's Secretariat, have kindly provided the necessary authorization. K.K. Sharma, Director of the Gallery, helped us in taking the pictures, and I am grateful to him for giving me a complete copy of the rare book, *Descriptive List of the Pictures in the Viceroy's Residences at New Delhi, Calcutta & Simla, Prepared by order of His Excellency Lord Irwin, now Viscount . . . Halifax,* Calcutta, Government Press, 1936, pp. XIV–117. H.E. Jérôme Bonnafont, Ambassador of France in India, kindly helped me, in this case as in so many others. I also express my gratitude to Caroline Schuh-Senlis, a friend and artist photographer who agreed to shoot portraits of Louis XV and Marie Leszczinzka despite the difficulties of lighting in the picture gallery. In France, my thanks go to Louis Mézin, Chief Curator and Director of the Massena Museum in Nice, Jérémie Benoît, Chief Curator at the Versailles Museum, and Stéphane Loire, Chief Curator at the Department of Painting and Head of the Research and Documentation wing of the Louvre Museum.

wished to distinguish with a mark of special consideration. We know that the sovereign's permission was necessary for an individual desiring to have a copy of the royal portrait made for himself.

This protocol was not confined to Europe. The kings of France sometimes offered their portrait to sovereigns in Asia, but very few seem to have survived.[1] We quote from our latest book, *Mémoire sur l'Inde (1786)* of Piveron de Morlat,[2] the description of the presentation near Cuddalore of a portrait of King Louis XVI by de Launay to Hyder Ali, Regent of Mysore:

He [Hayder Ali] agreed to send M. de Launay an escort of 100 cavalrymen, and a 21-gun salute was to be fired when the picture was presented. Accordingly, on 31th [July 1782] M. de Launay went from Cuddalore to Comte d'Hoffelize's camp at Mangi[coupan].[3] I [Piveron] went to meet him with 100 horsemen of the Nabob. When he left Cuddalore, the place fired a 21-gun salute, and the artillery of the army saluted with an equal number of guns the King's portrait when Mr. de Launay started for the camp of the Nawab, where he was accompanied by Mr. Hoffelize, Mr. Espinassy and Mr. Cossigny[4] with an escort of 100 European soldiers. When they reached my camp,[5] I went to inform the Prince and I returned to bring the delegation into the *Dorbar*. The Nawab hugged Mr. de Launay and received him with great honors. He sat down, and we also, and Mr. de Launay presented his credentials from Mr. de Bussy. I read them and had them translated. He replied in the most graceful manner, announcing his constant intentions to perpetuate forever the alliance that existed for so long between him and the [French] nation. M. de Launay then presented him the King's portrait on a gold plate covered with a rich brocade. The Nawab rose to receive this token of friendship of his Majesty which was instantly honored by a 21-gun salute.

This portrait of Louis XVI was not a full-length portrait. We do not know from which original it was copied, but Hyder Ali received it with protocol honours. It does not seem to have survived the looting of Srirangapatnam by the English in 1799.

The picture gallery of the Palace of the President of the Republic (Rashtrapati Bhavan) in New Delhi has two remarkable full-size portraits splendidly mounted in their gilded frames, one of King Louis XV and the other of Queen Marie Leszczinzka. These portraits were mentioned in 1936 in a limited publication.[6] Practically unknown by specialists of French painting of the eighteenth century, they were both done by Carle Van Loo. In 1936, both of them were still in the drawing room of the Viceroy's House in Calcutta, and we do not know at what date they were moved to New Delhi to be installed in the Ball Room of the palace of the Viceroy.[7] The royal portrait is a copy of *Portrait du roi Louis XV en armure sous sa tente,* painted by Carle Van Loo in 1750 on order of Marigny, brother of the Marquise de Pompadour (Plate 24.1). As Catherine Scheck said, it

Plate 24.1: Copy of *Portrait du roi Louis XV en armure sous sa tente.*

was 'exhibited in Versailles in January 1751, *in the throne room opposite the portrait of Louis XIV* (Luynes), and also exhibited at the Salon of 1751, under a canopy. It served as the official portrait until 1760'.[8] Many copies of this official portrait were executed, and though several paintings survive, the original has disappeared.

The painting now in New Delhi is an excellent copy and in a good state of preservation.[9] The *Descriptive Catalogue* of 1936 describes it as follows:

A full-length figure, the size of life in armour, standing bare-headed towards the left. The right hand rests on a plumed helmet, placed on a red covered table. He wears a blue mantle, powdered with gold *fleurs de lis* and lined with ermine. A red-backed chair appears to the right, behind a curule-shaped stool, and a curtain is suspended behind the figure. The face is seen in three-quarters to the left, and the eyes, fixed on the spectator, are very dark. He appears to have attained middle age. Painted by Carlo Van Loo.[10]

The portrait of Queen Marie Leszczinzka (Plate 24.2), also brought after 1936 from the Viceroy's House of Calcutta to the Rashtrapati Bhavan in New Delhi,[11] is an excellent copy of the painting by Carle Van Loo, whose original is in the Museum of Versailles.[12] Also commissioned for the King's Buildings, it was executed in 1747 and exhibited that year in the Château de Versailles. All travel guides of the eighteenth century mention it, and it is our pleasure to emphasize the fact that the diamond the Queen wears in a pendant at her neck is the famous *Sancy*,[13] the oldest Indian diamond preserved in Europe, taking its name from Nicolas Herblay de Sancey who was said to have bought it in Constantinople in the 1570s. It entered the collection of the jewels of the French Crown in 1589, under Henry III, and after many vicissitudes it is now exhibited in the Louvre Museum, in the salon d'Apollon.[14] Connections between Louis XV, Marie Leszczinzka and the *Sancy* are thus analysed by Balfour in his excellent book, illustrated with another portrait of the Queen of France wearing once again the *Sancy*:[15]

Undoubtedly its most splendid setting was in the great crown made by the Crown Jewellers for the Coronation of Louis XV in 1722. This also contained the 'Regent' diamond, which henceforth was considered the principal gem in the Crown collection.[16] Louis XV also wore the *Sancy* in a large agraffe (loop and hook fastening) in his hat with the Regent set in a knot of pearls and diamonds on a shoulder ornament. His Queen Marie Leszczinzka also wore the *Sancy*, set in a pendant to a necklace at many of the great state occasions at which she was obliged to appear.[17]

The painting at Rashtrapati Bhavan is:

a full-length figure, the size of life, standing, in a richly embroidered dress, turned towards the left. The face is seen in three-quarters to the left, and the dark brown eyes look towards the spectator. A fan hangs from her left hand, and she raises the right

Plate 24.2: Copy of *Portrait of Queen Marie Leszczinzka.*

holding a sprig of jasmine towards a crystal vase of flowers placed on a handsome gilt table beside the royal crown on a cushion, above which, turned in profile, is a bust of her Royal Consort. Over her splendidly decorated and amply spread robe she wears a blue velvet mantle embroidered with *fleurs de lis* and trimmed with ermine. On the pavement at her feet is placed a small spaniel, with a rose-coloured ribbon round its neck. The background to the right is composed of trees under a dark sky and a chair of State. Painted by Carlo Van Loo.[18]

These two paintings, the oldest in the collection of the Indian Presidential Palace,[19] were hanging in 1885 in the Governor's House in Calcutta. Lord

Dufferin decided to send them to London to restore them. They were cleaned, and then presented to the public in the salons of the India House, Westminster, in 1886. V.J. Vaillant, taking cognizance of this exhibition in the British journal *Athenaeum*,[20] published twenty-four lines about them in a review of French art in which he assured that 'they were destined for Mauritius and were placed on board a French ship which was taken by an English vessel: hence their deportation to Calcutta.'[21] Vaillant did not know that the Dutch admiral Stavorinus, visiting the Court House in Calcutta in 1769, had not failed to observe that he saw there 'hung up the portraits of the King of France and of the late Queen [Marie Leszczinzka died in 1768] which were brought up by the English from Chandernagore when they took the place' [in 1757]. This information, revealed by Lord Curzon in 1925[22] and endorsed by Mark Bence-Jones in his *Clive of India*[23] apparently leaves no doubt about the 'Chandernagorian' origin of these two splendid paintings[24] now hanging in the Gallery of the Presidential Palace of the Indian Union, in New Delhi.

There was at least one more official full-length portrait exhibited probably in Chandernagore: the portrait of Philip II, Duke of Orléans and Regent of France during the minority of Louis XV (1715–23), a portrait of which only the head has survived and is kept in the small museum of the former Asiatic Society of Bengal, now the Asiatic Society of Calcutta. I had seen it when it was under restoration, and it obviously came from the portrait of the Duke by Carle Van Loo.[25] Such a large painting could not find a better venue in India than the Fort d'Orléans of Chandernagore, whose Lodge, we must remember, was completed in 1722 under the Regency.[26]

So finally we can be almost certain of the original location in India of these three French paintings, and how they were moved first to Calcutta and then to the collection of the President of the Republic in India (as far as the paintings of the King and Queen of France are concerned), and in the collection of the former Asiatic Society of Bengal (concerning the painting of the Regent). But we also found in Alfred Martineau's papers kept in Aix-en-Provence amazing information from a forgotten English document describing the looting of Pondicherry in 1761. This information comes from a letter whose author's name does not seem to have been preserved, and it is addressed to Lord Pigot, Governor of Madras, victor of Lally and destroyer of Pondicherry through his Commissioner Dupré: 'The three Royal pictures of France which we now have the honour to tender to you in the name of the Squadron and the army . . . .'[27]

It remains to establish when, why, by whom and by what means (which ships) these three beautiful paintings, excellent copies of famous original ones, travelled from Paris to Lorient and transited most probably through

Plate 24.3: Copy of the Portrait of The King of Denmark Frederik V

Pondicherry, if they did not stop there, to end up in Chandernagore. Their place in the new Governor's house in Pondicherry, completed by Dupleix, would not require any comments here.[28] If they ended up in Chandernagore, they remind us of the importance of this 'Comptoir' in the economic exchanges—goods for bullion—between Bengal in France c.1720–57 intensely developed by Dupleix.[29] They would also remind us of the rich but forgotten intellectual and cultural exchanges, starting with the quest for Indian manuscripts conducted in Bengal by Father Pons (Sanskritist) and his Jesuit colleagues for the Bibliothèque du Roi from 1727 onwards,[30] or of the scientific mission of the same Father Pons and Father Boudier—a Jesuit mathematician and astronomer—who was trained in the fields of Indian mathematics and astronomy with Indian scientists on the Hooglee before leaving Chandernagor to visit the *Jantar Mantar* observatories just completed by Raja Jai Singh of Jaipur.[31] Joseph Dupleix, when he was director at Chandernagore (1731–41), had outstanding works done by weavers and craftsmen under his personal supervision for the highest nobility at the court of Versailles, including the Marquise de Pompadour, as his private correspondence shows.[32] When he became Governor General in 1741 and returned to Pondicherry to make that city the most splendid European capital in India, he continued to take care of Chandernagore until his return to France in 1755.

These paintings, those of Louis XV and Queen Marie by Carle Van Loo certainly, and maybe the painting of the Regent also by the same artist, date from the time of the governorship-general of Dupleix in Pondicherry (1742–55). The British most probably took them in Chandernagore in 1757, unless they took them in Pondicherry in 1761. In any case, it is surprising that any relevant information seems to have disappeared from the French as well as the British archives. Fortunately the timeline for the research is restricted to the years 1750–7 for these paintings, the oldest preserved in the gallery of the President of the Republic of India. The research field is now open for younger historians, French as well as Indian.[33]

Addendum

In December 2012 Professor M.K. Chakraborty, General Secretary, Asiatic Society of Calcutta, was kind enough to send me a photograph of the 'Portrait of the Duke of Orleans' kept in the Museum of the Society. The photograph did not correspond to the memory I had of the painting I saw in the Asiatic Society in the 1990's. It does not correspond either to any of the portraits we have of the Regent of France. I sent it to French specialists for identifications, and on 15 January 2014, Xavier Salmon, Conservateur general and Directeur du département des Arts graphiques in the Louvre Museum, identified it as 'The King of Denmark Frederik V by Carl Gustav Pilo 1711-1793'. The portrait most probably was in the Dane settlement of Serampore, called Frederiknagar by the Danes, or less probably in Tranquebar, the headquarters of the settlements of the Danish East India Company in India till they were sold to the English East India Company in 1839-45. We reproduce the painting for further research (Plate 24.3). We thank once again Professor Chakraborty and the

Asiatic Society for providing this photograph, and Xavier Salmon for his identification of the painting.

Notes

1. The Mughal rulers loved to possess portraits of European kings they knew or had heard of. Cf. the interesting miniature representing Emperor Jahangir with the Shah of Persia and James I of England. In his *Memoirs*, Ambassador Thomas Roe relates his surprise when he discovered in the private apartments of the Emperor Jahangir in Ajmer, which the emperor himself was showing him personally in 1613, 'in some panels portraits of the French kings and other Christian princes'. On another register, Dupleix, from Chandernagore, asked Forestier, a French resident at the Mughal court, to purchase paintings of emperors and nobles of the court of Delhi: 'For my personal use, I beg you to let me have these miniatures done on paper in Delhy and Agra, which represent the Mughal kings, princes, lords, ladies, and many other things of that nature in their common as well as in their official dress ['tant à nud qu'habillés']. As I am very curious of these paintings, I will be much obliged for the trouble you take in this regard' (BnF, FR 8979, fol. 6v, letter dated 11 November 1731). These are cases slightly different from those we are discussing today, but are indicative of the French administrators' interest in portraits of Indian rulers.
2. Published by Riveneuve Editions, with the help of the Foundation Del Duca, Institut de France, Académie des Inscriptions et Belles-Lettres, Paris, 2013, pp. 162–3.
3. Comte d'Hoffelize, Colonel of the Régiment d'Austrasie, commanded the first echelon of the French forces sent to India under the command of Marquis de Bussy. Mangicoupan, near Cuddalore, was the headquarters of these forces.
4. Colonel commanding the regiment of Ile de France, which Hoffelize will soon place under Tipu Sultan to help him recover the cities of Bednore and Mangalore recently captured by the English.
5. Piveron, Agent of France to Hyder Ali, Regent of Mysore, has his own encampment in the camp of Hyder Ali. This is where de Launay and his entourage stayed.
6. The *Descriptive List* . . . quoted *supra*, p. 507 note 1.
7. In this *Descriptive List* . . ., paintings numbers 1 to 76 are mentioned as transferred to the Viceroy's House in New Delhi. Numbers 77–107 are those transferred to the Viceregal Lodge in Simla. And finally numbers 108–31 are the paintings remaining in the Viceroy's House in Calcutta. Numbers 110, *Louis XV,* and 111 *Marie Leczinska,* are mentioned to be in the section 'Drawing Room' of the Palace in Calcutta. An inscription in pencil in front of each painting reads: 'Delhi Ball Room'.
8. Scheck 1995: 122. Accession number 265. h. 2.23 m, w. 1.51 m.
9. *A Descriptive List* . . ., pp. 102–3. Ref. no. 110. Size 9′ 1″ × 6′ 2″.
10. Ibid., p. 102.

11. Ibid., pp. 103–4. Ref. No. 111. Size 9′ 1 ¾″ × 6′ 4 ¾″.

12. MV. 8492. H. 2.74 m, W. 1.93 m. Notice in Sahut 1977, No. 109. This painting, whose notice is published in the catalog, was not exhibited in any of these three museums.

13. Mentioned by Constans 1995, No. 5057.

14. My information comes from Balfour 1987: 30–5.

15. Balfour 1987: 34, 'with no indication of provenance (copyright), name of artist and date of painting. It looks like a portrait of the Queen by Jean-Baptiste Van Loo'.

16. The 'Regent', a diamond purchased in India in 1710 by Thomas Pitt who offered it for sale to Louis XIV in 1714. The king could not purchase it, given the financial distress of the Kingdom. The Duke of Orléans, when he was Regent of France, decided in 1720 to purchase it for the Crown at the exorbitant price of 2.5 million pounds, equivalent to two ships of the line of 78 guns. Louis XV wore it for the first time during the reception of the Turkish ambassadors in Versailles on 21 March 1721. He then had it mounted on his crown for his coronation ceremony. Balfour 1987: 61–7. The Regent is also kept today in the Louvre Museum.

17. Balfour 1987: 33.

18. *A Descriptive List . . .*, p. 103.

19. *A Descriptive List . . .*, p. XI: 'The oldest paintings are undoubtedly the portraits of Louis XV and his wife. . . . Next in order of age come the portraits of George III and Queen Charlotte, which are copies of the well-known portraits painted by Allan Ramsay at the time of their Coronation in 1761.'

20. 9 October 1886.

21. 'Deux portraits de Carle Van Loo à Calcutta', in *Revue de l'Art ancien et moderne,* Paris, 12 December 1886, p. 362. This information, erroneous as we shall see, was noticed by Sahut 1977: 66, no. 109, as follows 'Portrait en pied destiné à l'Île Maurice et déporté par un vaisseau anglais à Calcutta où il se trouve encore au xixe siècle' (Vaillant 1886: 362).

22. *British Government in India* (London 1925), vol. I, p. 107.

23. Bence-Jones 1974, chapter IX, 'The Rose and the Lily', pp. 100–18: 'The spoils from Fort Orleans included full-length portraits of Louis XV and Queen Marie Leszcinzka, which were to adorn Government House, Calcutta, down to the present century. It was fitting that the French King and Queen should thus become prisoners of the English for the capture of Chandernagore broke the French power in Bengal and was, as Clive put it, 'an unexpressable blow to the French Company', p. 118.

24. Probably in the director's office in the Lodge of Fort d'Orléans, destroyed by the British in 1757.

25. If Carle is the artist of that portrait as it is generally believed, the picture is certainly posthumous, since the Duke of Orléans died in 1723. But it may have been painted by Louis-Baptiste, and have been installed at Chandernagore much earlier than the other two. I could not find the date proposed for the painting of this portrait of the Regent.

26. In the wake of the resurrection of the East India Company by Law de Lauriston. On Chandernagore, Lafont 2001: 112–17, ill. nos. 41, 42 and 43.

27. ANCOM, APC 3, Alfred Martineau's Papers, 7 boxes, box no. 2. I mention once again here what I have many times pointed out: Baron de Lally, comte de Tollendal, Commander in Chief of the French forces East of the Cape of Good Hope, was an Irish Catholic in the service of France, while his great opponent Lord Pigot, Governor of Madras, was a descendant of French Huguenots who sought refuge in England. Dupré was also a Huguenot of French origin and a trusted assistant of Pigot who sent him to Pondicherry to oversee the destruction of the city and fortress (Fort Louis) in 1761–2.

28. Lafont 2001: 80–3 and ill. 26–7, 'Le Gouvernement de Pondichéry'.

29. Lafont 2001. Also Lafont 2008, pp. 113–16.

30. Lafont 1991: 1–35, reprinted in Lafont 2000: 91-118. Let us mention here that these 287 manuscripts, many of which are in several volumes (one of them, a copy of the *Mahabharata* purchased in Bengal, is in 17 volumes and cost the King of France 177 rupees) had their entries in the *Catalogus Codicum Manuscriptorum Bibliothecae Regiae, Tomus Primus, Codices Orientales,* Paris, 1739. The Indian manuscripts, *Codices Indici,* are pp. 434-48, Nos. 1 to 287. Let us also mention, as a further evidence of the rapid diffusion of knowledge in France and Europe, that a synthesis of these research was written by Father Pons in his letter written from Karikal to Father du Halde, letter dated 23 November 1740, and published in Volume XIV of *Lettres édifiantes et curieuses,* pp. 55–76 (in the reprint of 1810).

31. See now Lafont & Lafont 2010: 36–9 and Figs. 51–5. Briefly: Raja Jai Singh requested a French resident in Delhi, Volton, a former military surgeon, to inquire whether the French authorities in India could send some astronomers to visit his newly established *Jantar Mantar.* Dupleix received this request in Chandernagore, where he had at hand the Jesuit sanskritist Father Pons, but not an astronomer-mathematician. By chance a Jesuit astronomer, Father Boudier, had just arrived in Pondicherry. He joined Fr. Pons in Chandernagore, spent six months with him studying the methods of Indian astronomical calculations with Brahmin scientists who worked in specialized institutions in the Hooghly. Boudier then wrote a synthesis on how the Indians calculated eclipses and the movements of the stars. Father Bonfils, s.j., has at our request kindly looked for this synthesis, and he found it in the Jesuit archives at Vanves. Then Fathers Pons and Boudier embarked upon a long journey starting from Chandernagore on 6 January 1734. They visited Patna, Benares, Delhi, Jaipur and Ujjain (place of meridian zero for the Indians). They returned to Chandernagore 'sick, both having thought to die before their return from diseases caused by fatigue and poor water one is obliged to drink on the way. . .'. The astronomical observations made during this trip were partly published in *Lettres édifiantes et curieuses,* vol. XV, pp. 269–90 of the reprint of 1810.

32. Bibliothèque nationale de France, Fonds français nouveau no 8979 à 8982. I had planned the publication of Dupleix's private correspondence from Chandernagore when I was assigned the scientific direction of the Institute of

Chandernagore in 1995. I still hope to take up this project again with Professor Rila Mukherjee, appointed Director of the Institute by the Government of West Bengal.

33. For the sake of information, this quotation from the French translation of a letter written in Persian in 1757 by Mirziavad to the Nawab Naziafkan Bahadur (Najaf Khan Bahadur): '. . . I have been to Mecca and Medina; and from there I went to the city of Zidda [Jeddah]. There I met Mr. Chevalier, General in Bengal, who took me with him to Europe, where he made me a lot of favor and showered me with goodness. . . . After arriving in Europe, Mr. Chevalier introduced me to the ministers and noblemen who treated me and received me well. *He made me get from the King of France his portrait* [emphasis mine]. Now I plan to go to India. I have a great desire to see you and serve you . . .,' in *Archives de l'Inde française. Lettres et conventions des Gouverneurs de Pondichéry avec différents Princes hindous, 1666 à 1793,* Pondicherry, 1911–1914, pp. 280–2.

Bibliography

Balfour, I. (1987), *Famous Diamonds,* London: Collins.

Bence-Jones, M. (1974), *Clive of India*, London: Constable & Company.

Constans, C. (1995), *Les peintures. Musée national du Château de Versailles*, Paris: Réunion des musées nationaux.

——(1936), Descriptive List of the Pictures in the Viceroy's Residences at New Delhi, Calcutta and Simla, Prepared by order of His Excellency Lord Irwin, now Viscount . . . Halifax, Calcutta: Government Press.

Lafont, J.-M. (1991), 'The Quest of Indian Manuscripts by the French in Eighteenth Century', in *Indo-French relations. History and Perspectives. Seminar Proceedings*, pp. 1–35, Embassy of France, New Delhi [repr. Lafont 2000: 91–118].

—— (2000), *INDIKA. Essays in Indo-French relations. 1630-1976*, New Delhi: Manohar-CSH.

—— (2001), *CHITRA. Cities and Monuments of Eighteenth-Century India from French Archives*, New Delhi: Oxford University Press.

—— (2008), 'The French Factories of Bengal', in *Art of the Ganges Delta. Masterpieces from Bangladeshi Museums*, V. Lefèvre and M.-Fr. Boussac, eds., Paris: Musée Guimet, pp. 113–16.

Lafont, J.-M. and Lafont R. (2010), *The French & Delhi, Agra, Aligarh and Sardhana*, New Delhi: Indian Research Press.

Sahut, M.-C. (1977), *Exposition Carle Vanloo Premier peintre du roi (Nice, 1705 – Paris, 1765),* Nice: Musée Cheret.

Scheck, C. (1995), *XVIIe et XVIIIe siècles : peintures françaises. Catalogue du Musée des Beaux-Arts de Dole*, Châtenois-les-forges: Imprimerie du Lion.

Vaillant, V.J. (1886), 'Deux portraits de Carle Van Loo à Calcutta', *Revue de l'art ancien et moderne*, Paris, 12 décembre, p. 362.

Editors and Contributors

CLAUDE ALLIBERT is Professor of Indian Ocean Civilization at the Institut National des Langues et Civilisations Orientales (INALCO, Paris). He has directed several excavations in the Comoro Archipelago and edited *Etudes Océan Indien*. He is the author of some sixty articles and the books *Mayotte, plaque tournante et microcosme de l'océan Indien occidental* (1984), *Textes anciens sur l'océan Indien occidental* (1990) and *Histoire de la Grande Isle Madagascar d'Etienne de Flacourt* (2007).

ALESSANDRA AVANZINI is full Professor of Semitic Philology at the University of Pisa. She has worked in Yemen since 1981 with an archaeological mission of the University of Florence and since 1989 with an Italian-French-Yemenite mission. Since 1996, she has been the Director of the 'Italian mission to Oman' (IMTO), for excavation and restoration of the two ancient Omani cities of Sumhuram and Salut. Since 2001, she is the director of the project 'Corpus of South Arabian Inscriptions' for a complete edition of the corpus of Ancient South Arabian both on the web and in print.

SATHYABHAMA BADHREENATH has been with the Archaeological Survey of India for the last three decades and is presently working as Director at New Delhi. She has directed the excavations at a Megalithic site called Siruthavur, the temple site at Saluvankuppam and the medieval site at Tranquebar, all in Tamilnadu, India. The report of the first mentioned excavation has been published by the ASI. She has been associated with the conservation of ancient buildings, especially temples.

BÉRÉNICE BELLINA is Senior Researcher at the National Centre for Scientific Research in France. Her research focuses on exchange and cultural processes around the Indian Ocean and more especially between South and South-East Asia. Since 2005, she is the director of the Thai-French Archaeological Mission in Upper Thai-Malay Peninsula that investigates the co-evolution of the different populations and ecosystems in relation to long-distance exchange from the early/mid first millennium BC to the late first millennium AD.

MARIE-PAULE BLASINI is head of Map Library and India Archives at the National Centre of Overseas Archives in Aix-en-Provence (France). She has written and edited inventories of archives of the Department Bouches-du-Rhône (1989–98), of colonial archives since 1998 and an edited volume *Les Dépôt des fortifications et ses archives, Vincennes 2011: Introduction.*

OSMUND BOPEARACHCHI is a Director of research at the French National Centre for Scientific Research (CNRS-ENS Paris) and also member of the Doctoral School VI of the Sorbonne University at Paris. He has published nine books, edited six books and published 150 articles in international journals. He now serves as the director of the Sri Lanka-French Archaeological Mission.

MARIE-FRANÇOISE BOUSSAC is formerly from the French Archaeological School in Athens, is currently Professor of Greek History at Nanterre-La Défense University, Paris. She has worked on Greece, Cyprus, Egypt and Bangladesh. She is the director of the French expedition to Taposiris Magna, a Graeco-Roman site near Alexandria in Egypt. Since 1991 she has edited the journal *Topoi*, issued from Lyon.

DEJANIRAH COUTO is Professor of Early Modern Portuguese Overseas History at École Pratique des Hautes Études, Section des sciences historiques et philologiques (EPHE), Sorbonne, Paris. She has published widely on cross-cultural history, diplomacy, cartography, maritime warfare, port-cities and merchant networks in the Indian Ocean. Her publications include *Harp ve Sulh. Avrupa ve Osmanlilar*, Dejanirah Couto, ed., Sirin Tekeli (çev.), Istanbul: Kitapyayinevi, 2010, and *Revisiting Ormuz. Portuguese Interactions in the Persian Gulf Region in the Early Modern Period (Série Maritime Asia* 19), Dejanirah Couto and Rui M. Loureiro, eds., Wiesbaden: Otto Harrassowitz Verlag, 2008.

SENARATH DISANAYAKA is Director General of Archaeology, Sri Lanka.

JEAN-CHARLES DUCÉNE is Director of Studies at the *Ecole Pratique des Hautes Etudes*, Paris. He has written extensively on the history of the medieval Islamic geography and cartography. His publications include *L'Afrique dans le* Uns al-muhağ wa-rawḍ al-furağ *d'al-Idrīsī* (2010) and *Les tables géographiques du manuscrit du sultan rasūlide al-Malik al-Afḍal* (2013).

JEAN-MARIE LAFONT has a Ph.D. in Greek Archaeology and a Doctorat d'Etat in Modern History. His publications include *La présence française dans le royaume sikh du Penjab 1822–1849* (1992); *Indika. Essays in Indo-French Relations 1630-1976* (2000); *Chitra: Cities and Monuments of Eighteenth-Century India from French Archives* (2001); *Maharaja Ranjit Singh Lord of the Five Rivers* (2002); *Fauj-i-khas. Maharaja Ranjit Singh and his French Officers* (2002); *La Fontaine. The Dream of an Inhabitant of the Mogol* (2005 and 2006); *Lost Palaces of Delhi* (2006); *The French & Lahore* (2007); *The French & Delhi, Agra, Aligarh and Sardhana* (with Rehana Lafont, 2010); *Piveron de Morlat. Mémoire sur l'Inde (1786). Les opérations diplomatiques et militaires françaises aux Indes pendant la guerre d'Indépendance américaine* (2013).

A.S. GAUR is working in the National Institute of Oceanography, Goa. He is currently concentrating his research along the Saurashtra coast and Rann of Kachchh. He has authored *Harappan Maritime Legacies of Gujarat* (2000) and co-authored three books, *Archaeology of Bet Dwarka* (2005), *Underwater Archaeology of Dwarka and Somnath* (2008) and *Maritime Archaeology around Porbandar* (2013). He has also co-edited two books, *Krishnayan: A Peep into the Past* (2004) and *Glimpses of Marine Archaeology in India* (2006).

CLAIRE HARDY-GUILBERT is a researcher since 1981 in Islamic History of Art and Archaeology in CNRS (France) and member of UMR 8167. She is a founder, with Dr Monik Kervran and Dr Axelle Rougeulle, of the APIM project, *Atlas of Ports and Itineraries of the Islamic Maritime Trade*. She is a member of the Direction Committee of the *Bulletin Critique des Annales Islamologiques* published by IFAO (French Institute of Oriental Archaeology of Cairo).

SARA KELLER is a Building Archaeologist and specializes in Urban History of Medieval India. She coordinates multiple research projects on pre-modern architecture and the tangible heritage of Gujarat. Since 2010, she has been conducting surveys and studies on the architectural remains of western Indian ports for the French research unit 'Orient and Mediterranean' and the Department of History, The Maharaja Sayajirao University of Baroda.

OLIVER KESSLER is archaeologist, historian and librarian, Department of Asian and Islamic Art History, Institute of Oriental and Asian Studies, University of Bonn. He was former field director of the excavations at the ancient seaport of Godavaya, Sri Lanka and carried out extensive archaeological fieldwork throughout the southern coastlines of that island. He has also authored numerous articles on ancient Indian Ocean Trade, the excavations at Godavaya and the archaeology of Sri Lanka in general.

ELIZABETH LAMBOURN is Reader in South Asian and Indian Ocean Studies at De Montfort University in the UK. Her research is situated at the intersection of history and material culture and focuses on South Asia and the Middle East (*c*.600 to 1600 CE) within the broader Indian Ocean world. Between 2011 and 2013 she held a Leverhulme Major Research Fellowship for her project *West Asia in the Indian Ocean 500–1500 CE*.

RILA MUKHERJEE is Professor of History at the University of Hyderabad and currently Director, Institut de Chandernagor, India. She has edited *Vanguards of Globalization: Port-Cities from the Classical to the Modern* (2014), *Oceans Connect: Reflections on Waterworlds Across Time and Space*, (2013), *Pelagic Passageways: The Northern Bay of Bengal Before Colonialism* (2011), and *Networks in the First Global Age: 1400–1800* (2011). She is currently editing a series of volumes on sources for Asian history, water history, world history and on connectivities.

NIMAL PERERA is Deputy Director General, Department of Archaeology, Sri Lanka. His latest book *Prehistoric Sri Lanka: Late Pleistocene Rockshelters and the Open-Air Site* is published by the British Archaeology Reports.

JEAN-FRANÇOIS SALLES was Directeur de Recherche in the French National Council for Scientific Research (CNRS). From 1993 to 2013 he was in charge of a research project at Mahasthan (Bogra) in Bangladesh (*Mahasthan I, 2007; Mahasthan II,* forthcoming), and has contributed to many publications in India.

HEIDRUN SCHENK is a research fellow funded by German Research Foundation (DFG) since 2013 at the Commission for Archaeology of Non-

European Cultures (Kommission für Archaeologie Aussereuropäischer Kulturen) of the German Archaeological Institute. Her main articles on South Asian Archaeology are *The Development of Pottery at Tissamaharama* (2001), *The Dating and Historical Value of Rouletted Ware* (2006), *Parthian Glazed Pottery from Sri Lanka and the Indian Ocean Trade* (2007), and together with A. Pavan, *Crossing the Indian Ocean before the Periplus: pottery assemblages in comparision. The sites of Sumhuram (Oman) and Tissamaharama (Sri Lanka)* (2012).

V. SELVAKUMAR is a faculty member in the Department of Epigraphy and Archaeology, Tamil University, Thanjavur. He completed his Ph.D. and post-Doctoral Research from Deccan College, Pune. He has worked at the Centre for Heritage Studies, Tripunithura, Kerala. His areas of interest include archaeological theory, heritage management, history of India, Prehistory and Indian Ocean Cultural Exchanges.

INGO STRAUCH is Professor for Sanskrit and Buddhist Studies at the Université de Lausanne. His publications include *The Lekhapaddhati-Lekhapañcāśikā: Briefe und Urkunden im mittelalterlichen Gujarat* (2002) and *Foreign Sailors on Socotra: The Inscriptions and Drawings from the Cave Hoq* (ed., 2012). He is currently working on Buddhist Kharoṣṭhī manuscripts from north-west Pakistan.

SUNDARESH is a marine archaeologist working in the National Institute of Oceanography, Goa. He has carried out extensive underwater archaeological investigations at Dwarka, Bet Dwarka, Somnath, Mahabalipuram, Poompuhar, Goa and Lakshadweep waters for the study of submerged ports and shipwrecks. He has also co-authored three books *Archaeology of Bet Dwarka* (2005), *Underwater Archaeology of Dwarka and Somnath* (2008) and *Maritime Archaeology around Porbandar* (2012). He is presently working on coastal archaeology and shipwrecks on the south Indian coast.

PIERRE TALLET is Associate Professor in Egyptology at the Sorbonne University in Paris. He is directing or co-directing several archaeological projects in the Sinai peninsula and the Red Sea Shore. His publications include historical essays and monographs. He has also co-edited with El-Sayed Mahfouz (Assiut University) the proceedings of a colloquium held in Cairo and Ayn Soukhna in 2009 (P. Tallet, E. Mahfouz *The Red Sea in Pharaonic Times*, Le Caire, 2012).

ROBERTA TOMBER has been a visiting Researcher in the Department of Conservation and Scientific Research since 2002 (British Museum). Specializing in ceramics, she has worked extensively at sites in the Mediterranean, the Red Sea of Egypt and India. She focuses on ancient economy and technology. She is the author of *Indo-Roman Trade: From Pots to Pepper* (2008).

EMMANUELLE VAGNON is currently Researcher for the Centre National de la Recherche Scientifique in Paris. She specializes in medieval and early modern cartography. Her Ph.D. has been published under the title *Cartographie et représentations de l'Orient méditerranéen en Occident* (*du milieu du XIIIe siècle à la fin du XVe siècle*), Turnhout, Brepols, 2013.

CHERYL WARD is a retired Professor of maritime archaeology who has studied ancient Egyptian boats for more than three decades. Her previous publications include *Sacred and Secular: Ancient Egyptian Ships and Boats* and many peer-reviewed journal articles on the topic.

HANS-JOACHIM WEISSHAAR was referent for South Asian Archaeology at the Commission for Archaeology of Non-European Cultures (Kommission für Archaeology Aussereuropäischer Kulturen) of the German Archaeological Institute. He was co-director of the excavations at Tissamaharama and is retired now.

JEAN-BAPTISTE YON is currently researcher for the Centre National de la Recherche Scientifique in Lyon (France). His research focuses on languages and populations of the Ancient Near East (modern Syria, Lebanon and Jordan), from the Hellenistic to the Byzantine times. His publications include epigraphical corpus (*Inscriptions grecques et latines de la Syrie* 17, *Palmyre*, Beirut [2012]), historical monographs (*Les Notables de Palmyre*, Beirut [2002]), and many peer-reviewed journal articles.

CHIARA ZAZZARO is a lecturer of maritime archaeology at the University of Naples 'L'Orientale'. Her previous publications include *The Ancient Red Sea Port of Adulis and the Eritrean Coastal Region: Previous Investigations and Museum Collections* and many peer-reviewed journal articles on ancient Egyptian boats and on traditional crafts of the southern Red Sea.

Index